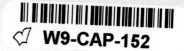

THE SHAPE OF THIS CENTURY

*R*EADINGS FROM THE *D*ISCIPLINES

◆

DIANA WYLLIE RIGDEN
Council for Aid to Education

SUSAN S. WAUGH
St. Louis Community College

Harcourt Brace Jovanovich, Publishers
San Diego New York Chicago Austin Washington, D.C.
London Sydney Tokyo Toronto

To my parents, Albert and Gwendolene Wyllie, for teaching me early to love books and the joy of reading. And special thanks to John S. Rigden for his advice and support.

D.W.R.

To my parents, Jeanette Sias Waugh and Richey L. Waugh, Jr., who taught me to love words and ideas and started my education, and for Mary L. Ramsey, M.D., who saved my life.

S.W.

Cover photograph by Grant Peterson

ISBN: 0-15-580840-0

Library of Congress Catalog Card Number: 89-81177

Acknowledgments and copyrights are continued on pages 724–727, which constitute an extension of the copyright page.

PREFACE

The Shape of This Century: Readings from the Disciplines is a collection of essays and articles that set forth provocative information and ideas. By reading these selections, students will discover some of the ways writers present their ideas, the purposes they have for writing, and their effectiveness at achieving those purposes.

The essays are arranged by six academic disciplines—social sciences, humanities, science and mathematics, journalism, education, and business—and by topics in order to present different points of view and/or different approaches writers take toward a subject. The headnotes which precede each essay provide information about the author as well as the context and occasion for the writing. Questions for Critical Analysis and Questions for Structural Analysis follow each essay; writing suggestions end each major division.

The authors, all professional writers, include journalists, philosophers, scientists, artists, economists, novelists, educators, engineers, poets, and business executives. The work of some of these writers may be familiar to students, while other writers may introduce them to new fields of study.

Our "hidden agenda" is to help students learn to examine not only the issues that inform our lives but also how they respond to those issues. Certainly the selection of the essays and the wording of the questions and writing suggestions reveal our concerns. We hope students are challenged to think about the ideas presented in these essays and to respond—first in their thinking and second in their writing.

The key features of this book include:

1. *The essays* We have selected essays by a variety of authors and from sources as diverse as the *Bulletin of the Museum of Modern Art* and *Business Month*, *Fortune* magazine and *The Progressive*. Our goal was to provide a collection of essays that will challenge students and stimulate critical thinking and creative responses.
2. *"Active reading" suggestions* The Introduction gives practical advice and suggestions on how to prepare for reading the essays and on techniques such as annotating, underlining, and keeping a reading notebook to help students think about what they read. A brief assignment for the reading notebook

appears before each essay to help them prepare for the essay, and questions to direct their responses are provided at the conclusion of the essay.

3. *"Active response" suggestions* The writing suggestions, which conclude each topical section, encourage students to talk with others about the issues they encounter, to examine their ideas in comparison with others', and to consider the implications of these ideas. In this way, the essays serve as a starting point from which students develop their responses and discover effective strategies for presenting those responses to others. Each writing suggestion provides a context that can help direct and focus the assigned papers.
4. *Research activities* Along with general writing suggestions, two or three topics that require additional research are listed along with possible research techniques to follow (such as conducting library research, interviewing experts, conducting surveys, and so forth).
5. *Special sections* Two sections follow the essays and provide specific information on how to use sources (both written and human) when writing essays and on how to write papers that effectively argue a point of view and persuade a reader.

A list of essays appears at the end of this textbook. After the course is completed, we encourage instructors and students to rate the essays and let us know how well they worked. Feel free to send along suggestions for selections to be added to future editions of the text.

Writing and preparing a textbook involves many people other than the authors, and we would like to thank those who have helped us. First of all, we thank the students we've encountered in our writing classes whose experiences with reading textbooks led us to the decision to write our own, and especially Nancy Azerolo, who wrote the reading notes, summary, and analysis to illustrate our points in the Introduction.

For their guidance and suggestions on revising the manuscript, we would like to thank the following reviewers: Lois Cucullur, George Mason University; Nancy Grimm, Michigan Technological University; Richard Larson, Lehman College of the City University of New York; Susan McLeod, Washington State University; Donna Nelson, Bowling Green State University; Marjorie Roemer, University of Cincinnati; Richard Zbaracki, Iowa State University; and Peter Zoller, Wichita State University.

We appreciate the hard work and attention our editor, Marlane A. Miriello, has given to this project. We thank her and the others at Harcourt Brace Jovanovich who helped transform the idea of this book into reality: Margie Rogers, manuscript editor; Karen Denhams, production editor; Linda Wooton Miller, designer; Chris Cohn, production manager; and Eleanor Garner, permissions editor.

Diana Wyllie Rigden
Susan S. Waugh

CONTENTS

Learning Our Responsibilities

Living with Uncertainty

Topics for Writing Essays 121
Research Possibilities 121

Demanding Civil Rights

Langston Hughes, "My America" 123

Hughes' America of 1943 presents difficult contradictions to its black citizens: the restrictions and discrimination blacks encounter daily do not easily coexist with the freedoms of democracy.

Questions for Critical Analysis 124
Questions for Structural Analysis 125

James Baldwin, "Fifth Avenue, Uptown: A Letter from Harlem" 126

Baldwin asserts that white Americans need to understand what living in Harlem means, because only when both white and black America face the problems can we find a solution.

Questions for Critical Analysis 133
Questions for Structural Analysis 134

Martin Luther King, Jr., "Why We Can't Wait" 135

In 1864 President Abraham Lincoln signed the Emancipation Proclamation freeing everyone held as slaves in America; in 1954 the Supreme Court desegregated America's public schools; in the 1960 presidential election both candidates (Richard Nixon and John Kennedy) included sweeping civil rights pronouncements in their party's platforms. According to King, American blacks are not willing to wait any longer to claim their rights as citizens.

Questions for Critical Analysis 144
Questions for Structural Analysis 145

Alice Walker, "The Civil Rights Movement: What Good Was It?" 146

To those who claim the civil rights movement failed because they see no concrete results, Walker counters with examples of important intangible gains: freedom, knowledge, history, hope, and heroes.

Questions for Critical Analysis 152
Questions for Structural Analysis 153
Topics for Writing Essays 154
Research Possibilities 154

Understanding Relationships Between the Sexes

James Thurber, "Courtship Through the Ages" 156

The male's attempts to attract and even interest the female are doomed to failure at every level of the evolutionary ladder, from flies to humans.

Questions for Critical Analysis 159
Questions for Structural Analysis 160

Kim Chernin, "The Flesh and the Devil" 161
Women struggle in an impossible battle to mold themselves into some ideal shape dictated by society.
Questions for Critical Analysis 167
Questions for Structural Analysis 168

Judy Syfers, "I Want a Wife" 169
Having a wife around the house means having someone else responsible for taking care of all the daily details and managing the household.
Questions for Critical Analysis 171
Questions for Structural Analysis 171

Michael Norman, "Standing His Ground" 172
In spite of an attitude shift favoring men as nurturers, most modern men long to reassert their masculinity aggressively.
Questions for Critical Analysis 174
Questions for Structural Analysis 175

Catherine Drinker Bowen, ". . . We've Never Asked a Woman Before" 176
From her own experiences, Bowen knows that women can succeed professionally but that this success comes at some cost.
Questions for Critical Analysis 184
Questions for Structural Analysis 185
Topics for Writing Essays 186
Research Possibilities 186

*P*art *T*wo ◆ *H*umanities

Look at Nature

Gretel Ehrlich, "Wyoming: The Solace of Open Spaces" 189
The open spaces of Wyoming create a feeling of peace and a climate of integrity that Ehrlich did not find in the city.
Questions for Critical Analysis 197
Questions for Structural Analysis 198

E. B. White, "The Ring of Time" 199
Looking at a bareback rider circling the ring, White turns his thoughts to the nature of time, and from time he moves on to consider the American South and its reluctance to confront racism.
Questions for Critical Analysis 205
Questions for Structural Analysis 206

See the World Through Art

PART THREE ◆ SCIENCE AND MATHEMATICS

KNOW ABOUT OUR WORLD

The Meaning of Science

Is Science Evil?

The Threat of Peace

*P*ART *F*OUR ◆ *J*OURNALISM

THE POWER OF THE NEWS

Reporting War

*P*art *F*ive ◆ *E*ducation

The Problem of Illiteracy

Can We Improve the Schools?

*P*art *S*ix ◆ *B*usiness

The Business of Business

PART EIGHT ◆ HOW TO WRITE ARGUMENT AND PERSUASION

THE SHAPE OF THIS CENTURY

*R*EADINGS FROM THE *D*ISCIPLINES

*I*NTRODUCTION

WHY READ TO WRITE?

You may wonder why you should spend time reading essays in a course that is supposed to teach you how to write. The best answer we can give is that reading influences the way you think, which in turn influences the way you write.

Sometimes you are introduced to new information or new ideas through your reading; at other times, what you read prompts you to question assumptions and beliefs and helps you develop your thoughts. Whether you read a newspaper or a novel, a political publication or a textbook, you experience the pain or pleasure of sharing someone else's experiences and insights, of learning something you didn't know about people and events, of confronting new ideas. When you read Eudora Welty's "A Sweet Devouring," you share her childhood passion for reading; through John Hersey's "A Noiseless Flash," you learn how six Japanese citizens survived the atomic bomb on Hiroshima; and you gain a better understanding of how scientists examine nature by reading Carl Sagan's "Can We Know the Universe? Reflections on a Grain of Salt." Reading the essays in *The Shape of This Century* will connect you with other people's ideas and experiences.

Often reading about a subject triggers a response in you that you can develop into an essay of your own. Through writing you learn effective ways to communicate ideas and information to others. In addition, you also learn to understand yourself better; the physical process of writing forces you to clarify and develop your ideas more fully.

When you learn to read critically, you learn to notice the author's presence, the guiding hand and mind of the writer organizing the material and crafting the sentences and paragraphs. Once you begin to take notice, you will soon begin to apply new techniques to your own writing. You can develop your skills by watching how others write and by imitating what works.

How to Read Critically

In an essay entitled "The Price of Reading Is Eternal Vigilance," Anatole Broyard wrote:

> As soon as I open it, I *occupy* the book, I stomp around in it. I underline passages, scribble in the margins, leave my mark—in effect I write my own book, a counterversion. I've come to understand that there are two dramas in reading: the drama of the book's internal relations and the drama of its relation to me. Sometimes, by default, the second is the better one. . . . I like to be able to *hear* myself responding to a book, answering it, agreeing and disagreeing in a manner I recognize as peculiarly my own. . . . I don't see how you can seriously read a book without saying something to the author.[1]

We hope that you will learn to follow Broyard's advice and participate in reading as you would in a debate: make sure the author is following through with what's promised. React to the ideas you encounter: question the author, analyze the arguments, interpret what is said, review the ideas the author presents in relation to your own ideas and then delve further—questioning, analyzing, and developing your ideas. Learn to respond to what you read emotionally (with pleasure, disgust, anger, sadness, laughter) and intellectually (challenging the author with questions, challenging your own ideas). Learning to read critically teaches you to understand what a reader will expect from your own writing.

When you read the selections in this book, notice your responses. Why do you like some essays better than others? Is it because the writer did a better job explaining a difficult subject? or seemed more credible? Is it because you were reminded of experiences and feelings similar to the writer's? How did the writer capture your attention and involve you in the essay? Once you can begin to answer questions like these, you not only become a better reader, but you're on your way to becoming a better writer.

An added benefit to learning active reading skills is that you can apply these skills to any reading assignment you have, and, although the process may seem slow, you will gain better understanding and better control over what you read. Active or critical reading involves annotating, highlighting, keeping notes, looking up what you don't know, and rereading. With especially difficult passages or essays, you may need to summarize main points or even rewrite in your own words. By learning to read critically, you learn to evaluate writing on intellectual terms and not simply to respond emotionally to the prose or the ideas. In other words, you think while you read.

---

[1]Anatole Broyard, "The Price of Reading Is Eternal Vigilance," *New York Times Book Review* (April 10, 1988), p. 11.

BEFORE YOU READ

Different types of writing demand different types of reading. Compare the way you read an article describing the college basketball playoffs in *Sports Illustrated* and the way you read a chapter on electromagnetic theory in a physics textbook. You would be wasting time and energy if you were to read *Sports Illustrated* with the same concentration you read the physics text. Conversely, if you read physics the way you read *Sports Illustrated*, you probably won't understand the concepts well enough to pass the course. When we compare such diverse reading material it becomes clear that you already unconsciously adjust your expectations and attention to what you're reading.

In *The Shape of This Century* we've included some guideposts to help you prepare for the essay before you begin reading. First, read the headnote carefully to find out something about the author and the subject of the essay: Is the subject one you already know something about? Is the author writing to general readers or to an audience of experts? Is the author's purpose to describe his or her personal experiences? or to explain or define a difficult subject? or to convince you to support a point of view? Knowing the purpose and context of an essay helps you prepare yourself to read it appropriately. For example, it will take you longer to read Walt Rostow's examination of America's economic future, "Danger and Commitment," (written for corporate executives) than it will to read Langston Hughes' "Salvation," an account of his childhood experience in church.

Second, keep a reading notebook or journal, and make entries for each essay you read. Preceding each essay is an exercise, "Before you begin reading," which starts you thinking about the subject by writing about a personal experience, or by making a list of images and words, or by describing your reaction to an idea or issue. Spending five or ten minutes on this exercise will prepare you for the essay that follows.

WHEN YOU READ

Active reading takes more time initially, but less time in the long run. You can adapt the suggestions you read here for most of the reading you'll do while in college and, later, on the job.

1. *Annotate the text:* Write comments in the margin of the text as you read. Give yourself clues to your immediate reactions by placing a question mark or exclamation point in the margin, writing "yes" or "no" in the margin, or supplying a cross-reference to another essay or author's treatment of the subject.

2. *Highlight the main points:* Keep track of the author's argument by underlining the main points. When you can quickly identify the progression of ideas in an essay, you're better equipped to analyze and respond to the essay rather than simply accept or reject the writer's point of view.
3. *Use your reading notebook:* Record your immediate reactions to the essay while you are reading. After you've read a paragraph or a page, jot down associations and ideas that occur to you. Make a note of passages you want to return to. Make a list of questions you would like to ask the author—questions about facts presented in the essay or questions about the author's interpretation of facts. By keeping reading notes, you make yourself pay closer attention not only to the reading but also to how well you understand what you're reading.
4. *Look up words and phrases:* Keep a dictionary with you while you're reading. Although you can sometimes get a sense of what a word or phrase means by its context in the essay, to know exactly what the author means by using that specific word, you need to look it up in a dictionary.
5. *Identify allusions:* Write down references to events, myths, people, and publications that you don't recognize and look them up. Many writers depend on a shared body of knowledge between them and their readers and refer to the shared information as a way of explaining new information. If you miss the author's connection, you may miss a crucial element in the argument or analysis and not fully understand or appreciate the essay.

Following is an example of a student's annotations and underlining for Margaret Sanger's "My Fight for Birth Control." The Reading Notes example is on page 14.

MY FIGHT FOR BIRTH CONTROL
MARGARET SANGER

Early in the year 1912 I came to a sudden realization that my work as a nurse and my activities in social service were entirely palliative and consequently futile and useless to relieve the misery I saw all about me.

child care frees her for work

For several years I had had the good fortune to have the children's paternal grandmother living with us and sharing in their care, thereby releasing more of my time and renewed energy for the many activities and professional work of the nursing field. I had longed for this opportunity, and it now enabled me to share in the financial responsibility of the home, which, owing to the heavy expenditures caused by my illness, I felt was the only self-respecting thing to do. I eventually took special obstetrical and surgical cases assigned to me from time to time, and had glimpses into the lives of rich and poor alike.

When I look back upon that period it seems only a short time ago; yet in the brief interval conditions have changed enormously. At that time it was not the usual thing for a poor woman to go to a hospital to give birth to her baby. She preferred to stay at home. She was afraid of hospitals when any serious ailment was involved. That is not the case today. Women of all classes are more likely to have their babies in lying-in hospitals or in private sanatoriums than at home; but in those days a woman's own bedroom, no matter how inconveniently arranged, was the usual place for confinement. That was the day of home nursing, and it gave a trained nurse splendid opportunities to learn social conditions through actual contact with them.

Were it possible for me to depict the revolting conditions existing in the homes of some of the women I attended in that one year, one would find it hard to believe. There was at that time, and doubtless is still today, a sub-stratum of men and women whose lives are absolutely untouched by social agencies.

The way they live is almost beyond belief. They hate and fear any prying into their homes or into their lives. They resent being talked to. The women slink in and out of their homes on their way to market like rats from their holes. The men beat their wives sometimes black and blue, but no one interferes. The children are cuffed, kicked and chased about, but woe to the child who dares to tell tales out of the home! Crime or drink is often the source of this secret aloofness; usually there is something to hide, a skeleton in the closet somewhere. The men are sullen, unskilled workers, picking up odd jobs now and then, unemployed usually, sauntering in and out of the house at all hours of the day and night.

The women keep apart from other women in the neighborhood. Often they are suspected of picking a pocket or "lifting" an article when occasion arises. Pregnancy is an almost chronic condition amongst them. I knew one woman who had given birth to eight children with no professional care whatever. The last one was born in the kitchen, witnessed by a son of ten years who, under his mother's direction, cleaned the bed, wrapped the placenta and soiled articles in paper, and threw them out of the window into the court below.

They reject help of any kind and want you to "mind your own business." Birth and death they consider their own affairs. They survive as best they can, suspicious of everyone, deathly afraid of police and officials of every kind.

They are the submerged, untouched classes which no labor union, no church nor organization of a highly expensive, organized city ever reaches and rarely tries to reach. They are beyond the scope of organized charity or religion; not even the Salvation Army touches them. It was a sad consolation to hear other women in the stratum just slightly above breathe contented sighs and thank God that they had not sunk so low as that.

It is among the mothers here that the most difficult problems arise—the outcasts of society with theft, filth, perjury, cruelty, brutality oozing from beneath.

Ignorance and neglect go on day by day; children born to breathe but a few hours and pass out of life; pregnant women toiling early and late to give food to four or five children, always hungry; boarders taken into homes where there is not sufficient room for the family; little girls eight and ten years of age sleeping in the same room with dirty, foul smelling, loathsome men; women whose weary, pregnant, shapeless bodies refuse to accommodate themselves to the husbands' desires find husbands looking with lustful eyes upon other women, sometimes upon their own little daughters, six and seven years of age.

In this atmosphere abortions and birth become the main theme of conversation. On Saturday nights I have seen groups of fifty to one hundred women going into questionable offices well known in the community for cheap abortions. I asked several women what took place there, and they all gave the same reply: a quick examination, a probe inserted into the uterus and turned a few times to disturb the fertilized ovum, and then the woman was sent home. Usually the flow began the next day and often continued four or five weeks. Sometimes an ambulance carried the victim to the hospital for a curetage, and if she returned home at all she was looked upon as a lucky woman.

This state of things became a nightmare with me. There seemed no sense to it all, no reason for such waste of mother life, no right to exhaust women's vitality and to throw them on the scrap-heap before the age of thirty-five.

Everywhere I looked, misery and fear stalked—men fearful of losing their jobs, women fearful that even worse conditions might come upon them. The menace of another pregnancy hung like a sword over the head of every poor woman I came in contact with that year. The question which met me was always the same: What can I do to keep from it? or, What can I do to get out of this? Sometimes they talked among themselves bitterly.

"It's the rich that know the tricks," they'd say, "while we have all the kids." Then, if the women were Roman Catholics, they talked about "Yankee tricks," and asked me if I knew what the Protestants did to keep their families down. When I said that I didn't believe that the rich knew much more than they did I was laughed at and suspected of holding back information for money. They would nudge each other and say something about paying me before I left the case if I would reveal the "secret."

It all sickened me. It was heartbreaking to witness the rapt, anxious, eager expression on their pale, worried faces as I told them necessary details concerning cleanliness and hygiene of their sex organs. It was appalling how little they knew of the terms I was using, yet how familiar they were with those organs and their functions and how unafraid to try anything, no matter what the results.

I heard over and over again of their desperate efforts at bringing themselves "around"—drinking various herb-teas, taking drops of turpentine on sugar, steaming over a chamber of boiling coffee or of turpentine water, rolling down stairs, and finally inserting slippery-elm sticks, or knitting needles, or shoe hooks into the uterus. I used to shudder with horror as I heard the details and, worse yet, learned of the conditions *behind the reason* for such desperate actions. Day after day these stories were poured into my ears. I knew hundreds of these women personally, and knew much of their hopeless, barren, dreary lives.

What relief I had came when I shifted my work for a few weeks to the then fashionable Riverside Drive or to the upper western section of New York City, but inevitably I was called back into the lower East or West Side as if magnetically attracted by its misery.

The contrast in conditions seemed only to intensify the horrors of those poverty-stricken homes, and each time I returned it was to hear that Mrs. Cohen had been carried to a hospital but had never come back, that Mrs. Kelly had sent the children to a neighbor's and had put her head into the gas oven to end her misery. Many of the women had consulted midwives, social workers and doctors at the dispensary and asked a way to limit their families, but they were denied this help, sometimes indignantly or gruffly, sometimes jokingly; but always knowledge was denied them. Life for them had but one choice: either to abandon themselves to incessant childbearing, or to terminate their pregnancies through abortions. Is it any wonder they resigned themselves hopelessly, as the Jewish and Italian mothers, or fell into drunkenness, as the Irish and Scotch? The latter were often beaten by husbands, as well as by their sons and daughters. They were driven and cowed, and only as beasts of burden were allowed to exist. Life for them was full of fear.

Words fail to express the impressions these lives made on my sensitive nature. My own happy love life became a reproach. These other lives began to clutch at all I held dear. The intimate knowledge of these misshapen, hapless, desperate women seemed to separate me from the right of happiness.

They claimed my thoughts night and day. One by one these women, with their worried, sad, pensive and ageing faces would marshal themselves before me in my dreams, sometimes appealingly, sometimes accusingly. I could not escape from the facts of their misery, neither was I able to see the way out of their problems and their troubles. Like one walking in a sleep, I kept on.

Finally the thing began to shape itself, to become accumulative during the three weeks I spent in the home of a desperately sick woman living on Grand Street, a lower section of New York's East Side.

Mrs. Sacks was only twenty-eight years old; her husband, an unskilled worker, thirty-two. Three children, aged five, three and one, were none too strong nor sturdy, and it took all the earnings of the father and the ingenuity of the mother to keep them clean, provide them with air and proper food, and give them a chance to grow into decent manhood and womanhood.

Both parents were devoted to these children and to each other. The woman had become pregnant and had taken various drugs and purgatives, as advised by her neighbors. Then, in desperation, she had used some instrument lent to her by a friend. She was found prostrate on the floor amidst the crying children when her husband returned from work. Neighbors advised against the ambulance, and a friendly doctor was called. The husband would not hear of her going to a hospital, and as a little money had been saved in the bank a nurse was called and the battle for that precious life began.

It was in the middle of July. The three-room apartment was turned into a hospital for the dying patient. Never had I worked so fast, never so concentratedly as I did to keep alive that little mother. Neighbor women came and went during the day doing the odds and ends necessary for our comfort. The children were sent to friends and relatives and the doctor and I settled ourselves to outdo the force and power of an outraged nature.

Never had I known such conditions could exist. July's sultry days and nights were melted into a torpid inferno. Day after day, night after night, I slept only in brief snatches, ever too anxious about the condition of that feeble heart bravely carrying on, to stay long from the bedside of the patient. With but one toilet for the building and that on the floor below, everything had to be carried down for disposal, while ice, food and other necessities had to be carried three flights up. It was one of those old airshaft buildings of which there were several thousands then standing in New York City.

At the end of the two weeks recovery was in sight, and at the end of three weeks I was preparing to leave the fragile patient to take up the ordinary duties of her life, including those of wifehood and motherhood. Everyone was congratulating her on her recovery. All the kindness of sympathetic and understanding neighbors poured in upon her in the shape of convalescent dishes, soups, custards, and drinks. Still she appeared to be despondent and worried. She seemed to sit apart in her thoughts as if she had no part in these congratulatory messages and endearing welcomes. I thought at first that she still retained some of her unconscious memories and dwelt upon them in her silences.

But as the hour for my departure came nearer, her anxiety increased, and finally with trembling voice she said: "Another baby will finish me, I suppose."

"It's too early to talk about that," I said, and resolved that I would turn the question over to the doctor for his advice. When he came I said: "Mrs. Sacks is worried about having another baby."

"She well might be," replied the doctor, and then he stood before her and said: "Any more such capers, young woman, and there will be no need to call me."

"Yes, yes—I know, Doctor," said the patient with trembling voice, "but," and she hesitated as if it took all of her courage to say it, "*what* can I do to prevent getting that way again?"

"Oh ho!" laughed the doctor good naturedly, "You want your cake while you eat it too, do you? Well, it can't be done." Then, familiarly slapping her on the back and picking up his hat and bag to depart, he said: "I'll tell you the only sure thing to do. Tell Jake to sleep on the roof!"

With those words he closed the door and went down the stairs, leaving us both petrified and stunned.

Tears sprang to my eyes, and a lump came in my throat as I looked at that face before me. It was stamped with sheer horror. I thought for a moment she might have gone insane, but she conquered her feelings, whatever they may have been, and turning to me in desperation said: "He can't understand, can he?—he's a man after all—but you do, don't you? You're a woman and you'll tell me the secret and I'll never tell it to a soul."

She clasped her hands as if in prayer, she leaned over and looked straight into my eyes and beseechingly implored me to tell her something—something *I really did not know*. It was like being on a rack and tortured for a crime one had not committed. To plead guilty would stop the agony; otherwise the rack kept turning.

I had to turn away from that imploring face. I could not answer her then. I quieted her as best I could. She saw that I was moved by the tears in my eyes. I promised that I would come back in a few days and tell her what she wanted to know. The few simple means of limiting the family like *coitus interruptus* or the condom were laughed at by the neighboring women when told these were the means used by men in the well-to-do families. That was not believed, and I knew such an answer would be swept aside as useless were I to tell her this at such a time.

A little later when she slept I left the house, and made up my mind that I'd keep away from those cases in the future. I felt helpless to do anything at all. I seemed chained hand and foot, and longed for an earthquake or a volcano to shake the world out of its lethargy into facing these monstrous atrocities.

The intelligent reasoning of the young mother—how to *prevent* getting that way again—how sensible, how just she had been—yes, I promised myself I'd go back and have a long talk with her and tell her more, and perhaps she would not laugh but would believe that those methods were all that were really known.

But time flew past, and weeks rolled into months. That wistful, appealing face haunted me day and night. I could not banish from my mind memories of that trembling voice begging so humbly for knowledge she had a right to have. I was about to retire one night three months later when the telephone rang and an agitated man's voice begged me to come at once to help his wife who was sick again. It was the husband of Mrs. Sacks, and I intuitively knew before I left the telephone that it was almost useless to go.

I dreaded to face that woman. I was tempted to send someone else in my place. I longed for an accident on the subway, or on the street—anything to prevent my going into that home. But on I went just the same. I arrived a few minutes after the doctor, the same one who had given her such noble advice. The woman was dying. She was unconscious. She died within ten minutes after my arrival. It was the same result, the same story told a thousand times before—death from abortion. She had become pregnant, had used drugs, had then consulted a five-dollar professional abortionist, and death followed.

The doctor shook his head as he rose from listening for the heart beat. I knew she had already passed on; without a groan, a sigh or recognition of our belated presence she had gone into the Great Beyond as thousands of mothers go every year. I looked at that drawn face now stilled in death. I placed her thin hands across her breast and recalled how hard they had pleaded with me on that last memorable occasion of parting. The gentle woman, the devoted mother, the loving wife had passed on leaving behind her a frantic husband, helpless in his loneliness, bewildered in his helplessness as he paced up and down the room, hands clenching his head, moaning "My God! My God! My God!"

The Revolution came—but not as it has been pictured nor as history relates that revolutions have come. It came in my own life. It began in my very being as I walked home that night after I had closed the eyes and covered with a sheet the body of that little helpless mother whose life had been sacrificed to ignorance.

After I left that desolate house I walked and walked and walked; for hours and hours I kept on, bag in hand, thinking, regretting, dreading to stop; fearful of my conscience, dreading to face my own accusing soul. At three in the morning I arrived home still clutching a heavy load the weight of which I was quite unconscious.

I entered the house quietly, as was my custom, and looked out of the window down upon the dimly lighted, sleeping city. As I stood at the window and looked out, the miseries and problems of that sleeping city arose before me in a clear vision like a panorama: crowded homes, too many children; babies dying in infancy; mothers overworked; baby nurseries; children neglected and hungry—mothers so nervously wrought they could not give the little things the comfort nor care they needed; mothers half sick most of their lives—"always ailing, never failing"; women made into drudges; children working in cellars; children aged six and seven pushed into the labor market to help earn a living; another baby on the way; still another; yet another; a baby born dead—great relief; an older child dies—sorry, but nevertheless relief—insurance helps; a mother's death—children scattered into institutions; the father, desperate, drunken; he slinks away to become an outcast in a society which has trapped him.

Another picture of the young couple full of hope with faith in themselves. They start life fresh. They are brave and courageous. The first baby is welcome; parents and relatives come from near and far to witness this mystery. The next year the second baby arrives; all agree it's a little early, but husband receives congratulations. The third child arrives, and yet a fourth. Within five years four children are born. The mother, racked and worn, decides this can't go on, and attempts to interrupt the next pregnancy. The siren of the ambulance—death of the mother—orphan children—poverty, misery, slums, child labor, unhappiness, ignorance, destitution!

One after another these pictures unreeled themselves before me. For hours I stood, motionless and tense, expecting something to happen. I watched the lights go out, I saw the darkness gradually give way to the first shimmer of dawn, and then a colorful sky heralded the rise of the sun. I knew a new day had come for me and a new world as well.

It was like an illumination. I could now see clearly the various social strata of our life; all its mass problems seemed to be centered around uncontrolled breeding. There was only one thing to be done: call out, start the alarm, set the heather on fire! Awaken the womanhood of America to free the motherhood of the world! I released from my almost paralyzed hand the nursing bag which unconsciously I had clutched, threw it across the room, tore the uniform from my body, flung it into a corner, and renounced all palliative work forever.

I would never go back again to nurse women's ailing bodies while their miseries were as vast as the stars. I was now finished with superficial cures, with doctors and nurses and social workers who were brought face to face with this overwhelming truth of women's needs and yet turned to pass on the other side. They must be made to see these facts. I resolved that women should have knowledge of contraception. They have every right to know about their own bodies. I would strike out—I would scream from the housetops. I would tell the world what was going on in the lives of these poor women. I *would* be heard. No matter what it should cost. *I would be heard.*

I went to bed and slept.

That decision gave me the first undisturbed sleep I had had in over a year. I slept soundly and free from dreams, free from haunting faces.

I announced to my family the following day that I had finished nursing, that I would never go on another case—and I never have.

AFTER YOU READ

After you have read the essay and taken notes on your reading, you will almost always need to read the essay at least a second time to understand its meaning, the implications of its conclusions, and its structure. If possible, take a break after first reading an assignment so that when you reread, you are able to bring a fresh perspective to the essay.

Three questions guide your second reading: Do I understand what the writer says? Am I aware of how I'm responding to what is said? Do I recognize techniques the writer used to evoke a response from me? Before rereading the essay, review the headnote, end-of-essay questions, and your own notes to help focus your attention. Two other activities will help you better understand a selection you've just read and your response to it: summarizing (to make sure you know what the essay is about) and evaluating (to discuss your response and how the writer prompted your response).

SUMMARIZE A summary is a brief restatement of a longer selection. You have probably summarized novel and movie plots in conversations with your friends, or summarized a lecture for a classmate who overslept. In these instances, you reduce something to its essential elements so that your audience knows what you read or heard.

Writing a summary is a more formal process than an oral summary because, although you are also reducing material to its essence, you must be sure to include all the main points in the same order the author originally presented them. Summarizing is especially useful when you read a difficult passage or essay because it helps you focus better on its central ideas and master the information.

The following three steps will help you summarize any reading selection. First, reread the material, annotating and taking notes until you have identified the thesis, main ideas, and key terms and concepts. You may want to organize your reading notes into an outline from which to write the summary. Second, once you know and are familiar with the text, use your own words to write a summary that includes all the main points and is a coherent recapitulation of the original. Third, be sure that your summary follows the author's organization and reflects his or her intentions and does not include your responses to the material.

Below is a student's summary of Sanger's essay:

> Many poor women living in the early 1900s were ignorant of birth control methods and, desperate to limit the size of their families, went to illegal clinics and submitted to dangerous abortions. Margaret Sanger, who worked with the poor as a nurse, felt so helpless against the women's ignorance and so appalled by their conditions that she decided she could not continue supporting these conditions as a nurse but must begin educating the women about contraceptive methods.

EVALUATE After you have read an essay critically, try to evaluate how successfully the author wrote the essay. Were the author's tone and style consistent with the topic? Did the main ideas progress logically? Were the ideas clearly developed and supported with vivid descriptions and evidence such as source notes? Has a convincing argument been made? When you evaluate an essay you discover whether each aspect of the essay—thesis, main ideas, supporting ideas, word choice, organization—works together to fulfill the author's purpose in writing the essay. By identifying the strengths of the essays you read, you learn to write better essays.

Below is the student's evaluation of Sanger's essay:

> Margaret Sanger's "My Fight for Birth Control" was a well written and moving account of a life-changing experience. Sanger provided enough background information for me to be able to empathize with the poor women of this time period. She included excellent illustrations and examples to help me feel and understand her frustrations. It was clear to Sanger, and she convinced me, that the massive problems these women faced were centered on their ignorance about birth control. Therefore, I agreed with Sanger's decision to begin birth control counseling.

ONE WRITER'S EXAMPLE

Before you begin reading the essays in this book, consider the following journal entry by writer Ellen Gilchrist:

> I left [the bookstore] with three books, the New Modern Library edition of *On the Origin of the Species* and *The Descent of Man* by Charles Darwin, a book called *Darwin for Beginners* by Jonathan Howard, and the Abraham Pais biography of Einstein.
>
> I was excited. I kept stopping on corners and reading. I went on up the mountain, ran into my house, stuck a diet dinner in the oven, and settled down on the couch to read.
>
> I opened the Pais book on Einstein and began. "There was always about him a wonderful purity, at once childlike and profoundly stubborn. It is no art to be an idealist if one lives in cloud cuckoo land. He, however, was an idealist even though he lived on earth and knew its smell better than almost anyone else.
>
> "Nothing was more alien to Einstein than to settle any issue by compromise, in his life or in his science. When he spoke on political problems he always steered toward their answer. Were I asked for a one-sentence biography of Einstein I would say he was the freest man I have ever known."
>
> Oh, my God, I said. This will take the wide net. I turned off the diet dinner, picked up the phone, ordered a large combination pizza, and settled down—about nine thirty I could take no more. I went on off to bed. As always when I attempt to read about physics I am filled with wonder, a sense of ecstasy, pattern, texture, design. "Subtle is the Lord," said Einstein, "but he is not malicious." We are allowed to see what is going on.[2]

In her journal, Gilchrist captures feelings of excitement and anticipation that preceded her reading as well as the exhilaration she felt while reading Pais' biography of Albert Einstein. All the essays you read may not evoke such a vivid and personal response, but they will certainly move you or challenge you. By paying attention to your reactions, you begin the process of understanding another person's point of view and developing your responses to the ideas that have shaped our century.

[2]Ellen Gilchrist, "Influences," *Falling Through Space: The Journals of Ellen Gilchrist.* Boston: Little, Brown (1987), pp. 64–65.

Sanger, "My Fight for Birth Control"

palliative: something that excuses or makes seem less serious

Why does Sanger have to "share in the financial responsibility of the home"? She says she's been ill and the cost for her care has been great, but I thought that in 1912 women rarely worked outside the home. What did her husband do? How did he feel about her helping to support the family?

Might be interesting to find out what conditions were like for the poor in the early 20th century and compare them to conditions today. All the reports today make homelessness and poverty seem like they're at their worst state. What's the truth?

One question I have: Sanger says "Pregnancy is an almost chronic condition amongst them"—meaning the poor. Today, even with birth control information and contraceptives available, unwanted pregnancies are still a real problem for the poor. The number of teenage pregnancies is supposed to be higher than ever. If, through Sanger's efforts, education is no longer the real problem, what *is* the problem?

Clearly, Sanger would agree with the Supreme Court ruling allowing women the freedom to choose to have an abortion. What would she think about not only anti-abortion advocates, but those who argue against planned parenthood and birth control more generally?

It's hard to read about the men Sanger describes—the husbands who beat their wives, are drunk all the time and won't practice any birth control methods at all; the doctor who makes fun of the sick woman's pleading—and not get really angry.

PART ONE

Social Sciences

Finding Out Who We Are

Memory plays an essential role in much of the writing that we do. By remembering specific details about early experiences, the writers in this section recreate a time in their lives when they began to discover who they are. The narrative style is enhanced by both sensory details and a type of evaluation that indicates the significance of the event.

An American Childhood

Annie Dillard

In most of her work, Annie Dillard (1945–) describes scenes and events she observes in the physical world in terms of their relation to the world of ideas and religion. When she wrote her autobiography, An American Childhood *(1987), Dillard chose to examine the growth of her mind, exploring how common events influenced the development of her thoughts and examining both the physical and mental changes that define growing up. This essay is a chapter from the autobiography.*

Before you begin reading: *Think about your childhood and remember an event that changed or expanded how you thought about something. In your reading notebook, write a paragraph or two about the incident, using dialogue, specific details, and sensory descriptions.*

◆

A TORNADO HIT OUR NEIGHBORHOOD ONE MORNING. Our neighborhood was not only leafy Richland Lane and its hushed side streets, but also Penn Avenue, from which Richland Lane loftily arose. Old Penn Avenue was a messy, major thoroughfare still cobblestoned in the middle lanes, and full of stoplights and jammed traffic. There were drugstores there, old apartment buildings, and some old mansions. Penn Avenue was the city—tangled and muscular, a broad and snarled fist. The tornado broke all the windows in the envelope factory on Penn Avenue and ripped down mature oaks and maples on Richland Lane and its side streets—trees about which everyone would make, in my view, an unconscionable fuss, not least perhaps because they would lie across the streets for a week.

After the tornado passed I roamed around and found a broken power line. It banged violently by the Penn Avenue curb; it was shooting sparks into the street. I couldn't bring myself to leave the spot.

The power line was loosing a fireball of sparks that melted the asphalt. It was a thick twisted steel cable usually strung overhead along Penn Avenue; it carried power—4,500 kilovolts of it—from Wilkinsburg ("City of Churches") to major sections of Pittsburgh, to Homewood and Brushton, Shadyside, and Squirrel Hill.

It was melting a pit for itself in the street. The live wire's hundred twisted ends spat a thick sheaf of useless yellow sparks that hissed. The sparks were cooking the asphalt gummy; they were burning a hole. I watched the cable relax and sink into its own pit; I watched the yellow sparks pool and crackle around the cable's torn end and splash out of the pit and over the asphalt in a stream toward the curb and my shoes. My bare shins could feel the heat. I smelled tarry melted asphalt and steel so hot it smoked.

"If you touch that," my father said, needlessly, "you're a goner."

I had gone back to the house to get him so he could see this violent sight, this cable all but thrashing like a cobra and shooting a torrent of sparks.

While the tornado itself was on—while the buckeye trees in our yard were coming apart—Mother had gathered Amy and Molly and held them with her sensibly away from the windows; she urged my father and me to join them. Father had recently returned from his river trip and was ensconced tamed in the household again. And here was a pleasant, once-in-a-lifetime tornado, the funnel of which touched down, in an almost delicate point, like a bolt of lightning, on our very street. He and I raced from window to window and watched; we saw the backyard sycamore smash the back-porch roof; we saw the air roaring and blowing full of sideways-flying objects, and saw the leafy buckeye branches out front blow white and upward like skirts.

"With your taste for natural disaster," Mother said to me later, "you should try to arrange a marriage with the head of the International Red Cross."

Now the torn cable lay near the curb, away from traffic. Its loose power dissipated in the air, a random destructiveness. If you touched it, you would turn into Reddy Kilowatt. Your skin would wiggle up in waves like an electrified cat's in a cartoon; your hair would rise stiff from your head; anyone who touched you by mistake would stick to you wavy-skinned and paralyzed. You would be dead but still standing, the power surging through your body in electrical imitation of life. Passersby would have to knock you away from the current with planks.

Father placed a ring of empty Coke bottles around the hissing power line and went back home to call Duquesne Light. I stayed transfixed. Other neighborhood children showed up, looked at the cable shooting sparks, and wandered away to see the great killed trees. I stood and watched the thick billion bolts swarm in the street. The cable was as full as a waterfall, never depleted; it dug itself a pit in which the yellow sparks spilled like water. I stayed at the busy Penn Avenue curb all day staring, until, late in the afternoon, someone somewhere turned off the juice.

Streetcars ran on Penn Avenue. Streetcars were orange, clangy, beloved things—loud, jerky, and old. They were powerless beasts compelled to travel stupidly with their wheels stuck in the tracks below them. Each streetcar had one central headlight, which looked fixedly down its tracks and nowhere else. The single light advertised to drivers at night that something was coming that couldn't move over. When a streetcar's tracks and wires rounded a corner, the witless streetcar had to follow. Its heavy orange body bulged out and blocked two lanes; any car trapped beside it had to cringe stopped against the curb until it passed.

Sometimes a car parked at the curb blocked a streetcar's route. Then the great beast sounded its mournful bell: it emitted a long-suffering, monotonous bong . . . bong . . . bong . . . and men and women on the sidewalk shook their heads sympathetically at the motorman inside, the motorman more inferred than seen through the windshield's bright reflections.

Penn Avenue smelled of gasoline, exhaust fumes, trees' sweetness in the spring, and, year round, burnt grit. On the blocks from Lang to Richland Lane were buildings in wild assortment: two drugstores, Henry Clay Frick's mansion with his old daughter somewhere inside, a dark working-class bar called the Evergreen Café, a corner grocery store, the envelope factory, a Westinghouse plant, some old apartment buildings, and a parklike Presbyterian seminary.

You walked on sidewalks whose topography was as intricate as Pittsburgh's, and as hilly. Frost-heaved peaks of cement arose, broke, and, over years, subsided again like Appalachians beside deep pits in which clean grass grew from what looked like black grease. Every long once in a while, someone repaired the sidewalk, to the tune of four or five squares' worth. The sidewalks were like greater Pittsburgh in this, too—cut into so many parts, so many legal divisions, that no one was responsible for all of it, and it all crumbled.

It was your whole body that knew those sidewalks and streets. Your bones ached with them; you tasted their hot dust in your bleeding lip; their gravel worked into your palms and knees and stayed, blue under the new skin that grew over it.

You rode your bike across Penn Avenue with the light: a lane of asphalt, a sunken streetcar track just the width of a thin bike wheel, a few feet of brown cobblestones, another streetcar track, more cobblestones or some cement, more tracks, and another strip of asphalt. The old cobblestones were pale humpy ovals like loaves. When you rode your bike over them, you vibrated all over. A particularly long humpy cobblestone could knock you down in a twinkling if it caught your bike's front wheel. So could the streetcar's tracks, and they often did; your handlebars twisted in your hands and threw you like a wrestler. So you had to pay attention, alas, and could not simply coast along over cobblestones, blissfully vibrating all over. Now the city was replacing all the cobblestones, block by block. The cobblestones had come from Pittsburgh's riverbeds. In the nineteenth century, children had earned pennies by dragging them up from the water and selling them to paving contractors. They had been a great and late improvement on mud.

The streetcars' overhead network of wires made of Penn Avenue a loose-roofed tunnel. The wires cut the sky into rectangles inside which you could compose various views as you walked. Here were a yellow brick apartment top and some flattened fair-weather clouds; here were green sycamore leaves in the foreground, and a faded orange rooftop advertising sign, and a yellow street-light, and a slab of neutral sky.

Streetcars traveled with their lone trolley sticks pushed up by springs into these overhead wires. A trolley stick carried a trolley wheel; the trolley wheel rolled along the track of hot electric wire overhead as the four wheels rolled along the cold grooved track below. At night, and whenever it rained, the streetcars' trolleys sparked. They shot a radiant fistful of sparks at every crossing of wires. Sometimes a streetcar accidentally "threw the trolley." Bumping over a switch or rounding a bend, the trolley lost the wire and the spring-loaded stick flew up and banged its bare side crazily against the hot wire. Big yellow sparks came crackling into the sky and fell glowing toward the roofs of cars. The motorman had to brake the streetcar, go around to its rear, and haul the wayward, sparking trolley stick down with a rope. This happened so often that there was a coil of rope for that purpose at the streetcar's stern, neat and cleated like a halyard on a mast.

So the big orange streetcars clanged and spat along; they stopped and started, tethered to their wires overhead and trapped in their grooves below. Every day at a hundred intersections they locked horns with cars that blocked their paths—cars driven by insensible, semiconscious people, people who had just moved to town, teenagers learning to drive, the dread Ohio drivers, people sunk in rapturous conversation.

"Bong bong," bleated the stricken streetcar, "bong," and its passengers tried to lean around to see what was holding it up, and its berserk motorman gestured helplessly, furiously, at the dumb dreaming car—a shrug, a wave, a fist:

> I'm a streetcar!
> What can I do?
> What can I do
> but wait for you jerks
> to figure out that I'm a streetcar!

I tried to kill a streetcar by overturning it.

Pin Ford and I were hiding under a purple beech tree on the lawn of the Presbyterian seminary on Penn Avenue.

Through the beech's low dense branches she and I could make out Penn Avenue's streetcar lanes. It was midafternoon. Now a streetcar was coming toward us. We had been waiting. We had just stuck a stone in the streetcar track. This one seemed like a stone big enough to throw it over. Would the streetcar go over? Did we hope it would go over? We spotted its jiggling trolley stick first, high above the roofs of cars. Then we saw its round orange shoulder, humped like a cobblestone, and its lone simple eye. I pressed a thumb and finger between ribs on both sides of my breastbone, to try to calm myself.

It had started with pennies. A streetcar's wheel could slick a penny and enlarge it to a stripe. What would it do to a stone? It would crunch and crumble a stone. How big a stone? We ran between moving cars and placed ever bigger stones in the streetcar track; we ran back under the beech tree to watch.

This last stone was a coarse gray conglomerate, five inches by two by two. Was it reinforced concrete? Through the low-slung beech boughs we saw the streetcar draw nigh; we covered our lower faces with our hands.

The streetcar hit the stone audibly and rose like a beached whale. Its big orange body faltered in the air, heaved toward the lane of cars beside it, trembled, and finally fell down on its track and broke the stone. And went on, bumping again only slightly when the rear wheel went over it. Pin Ford and I lay low.

In that instant while the streetcar stopped upraised over its track like an animal bewildered, while it swayed over the cars' lane and hung on its side and its trolley stick dangled askew, I saw it continue its roll; I saw precisely which cars it would fall on, and which dim people silhouetted inside the cars and the streetcar would be the most surprised. I saw, too, in that clear instant, that if the streetcar did derail, I would have to come forward and give myself up to the police, and do time, and all that, for the alternative was living all the rest of life on the lam.

What can we make of the inexpressible joy of children? It is a kind of gratitude, I think—the gratitude of the ten-year-old who wakes to her own energy and the brisk challenge of the world. You thought you knew the place and all its routines, but you see you hadn't known. Whole stacks at the library held books devoted to things you knew nothing about. The boundary of knowledge receded, as you poked about in books, like Lake Erie's rim as you climbed its cliffs. And each area of knowledge disclosed another, and another. Knowledge wasn't a body, or a tree, but instead air, or space, or being—whatever pervaded, whatever never ended and fitted into the smallest cracks and the widest space between stars.

Any way you cut it, colors and shadows flickered from multiple surfaces. Just enough work had already been done on everything—moths, say, or meteorites—to get you started and interested, but not so much there was nothing left to do. Often I wondered: was it being born just now, in this century, in this country? And I thought: no, any time could have been like this, if you had the time and weren't sick; you could, especially if you were a boy, learn and do. There was joy in concentration, and the world afforded an inexhaustible wealth of projects to concentrate on. There was joy in effort, and the world resisted effort to just the right degree, and yielded to it at last. People cut Mount Rushmore into faces; they chipped here and there for years. People slowed the spread of yellow fever; they sprayed the Isthmus of Panama puddle by puddle. Effort alone I loved. Some days I would have been happy to push a pole around a threshing floor like an ox, for the pleasure of moving the heavy stone and watching my knees rise in turn.

I was running down the Penn Avenue sidewalk, revving up for an act of faith. I was conscious and self-conscious. I knew well that people could not fly—as well as anyone knows it—but I also knew the kicker: that, as the books put it, with faith all things are possible.

Just once I wanted a task that required all the joy I had. Day after day I had noticed that if I waited long enough, my strong unexpressed joy would dwindle and dissipate inside me, over many hours, like a fire subsiding, and I would at last calm down. Just this once I wanted to let it rip. Flying rather famously required the extra energy of belief, and this, too, I had in superabundance.

There were boxy yellow thirties apartment buildings on those Penn Avenue blocks, and the Evergreen Café, and Miss Frick's house set back behind a wrought-iron fence. There were some side yards of big houses, some side yards of little houses, some streetcar stops, and a drugstore from which I had once tried to heist a five-pound box of chocolates, a Whitman sampler, confusing "sampler" with "free sample." It was past all this that I ran that late fall afternoon, up old Penn Avenue on the cracking cement sidewalks—past the drugstore and bar, past the old and new apartment buildings and the long dry lawn behind Miss Frick's fence.

I ran the sidewalk full tilt. I waved my arms ever higher and faster; blood balled in my fingertips. I knew I was foolish. I knew I was too old really to believe in this as a child would, out of ignorance; instead I was experimenting as a scientist would, testing both the thing itself and the limits of my own courage in trying it miserably self-conscious in full view of the whole world. You can't test courage cautiously, so I ran hard and waved my arms hard, happy.

Up ahead I saw a business-suited pedestrian. He was coming stiffly toward me down the walk. Who could ever forget this first test, this stranger, this thin young man appalled? I banished the temptation to straighten up and walk right. He flattened himself against a brick wall as I passed flailing—although I had left him plenty of room. He had refused to meet my exultant eye. He looked away, evidently embarrassed. How surprisingly easy it was to ignore him! What I was letting rip, in fact, was my willingness to look foolish, in his eyes and in my own. Having chosen this foolishness, I was a free being. How could the world ever stop me, how could I betray myself, if I was not afraid?

I was flying. My shoulders loosened, my stride opened, my heart banged the base of my throat. I crossed Carnegie and ran up the block waving my arms. I crossed Lexington and ran up the block waving my arms.

A linen-suited woman in her fifties did meet my exultant eye. She looked exultant herself, seeing me from far up the block. Her face was thin and tanned. We converged. Her warm, intelligent glance said she knew what I was doing—not because she herself had been a child but because she herself took a few loose aerial turns around her apartment every night for the hell of it, and by day played along with the rest of the world and took the streetcar. So Teresa of Avila checked her unseemly joy and hung on to the altar rail to hold herself down. The woman's smiling, deep glance seemed to read my own awareness from my face, so we passed on the sidewalk—a beautifully upright woman walking in her tan linen suit, a kid running and flapping her arms—we passed on the sidewalk with a look of accomplices who share a humor just beyond irony. What's a heart for?

I crossed Homewood and ran up the block. The joy multiplied as I ran—I ran never actually quite leaving the ground—and multiplied still as I felt my stride begin to fumble and my knees begin to quiver and stall. The joy multiplied even as I slowed bumping to a walk. I was all but splitting, all but shooting sparks. Blood coursed free inside my lungs and bones, a light-shot stream like air. I couldn't feel the pavement at all.

I was too aware to do this, and had done it anyway. What could touch me now? For what were the people on Penn Avenue to me, or what was I to myself, really, but a witness to any boldness I could muster, or any cowardice if it came to that, any giving up on heaven for the sake of dignity on earth? I had not seen a great deal accomplished in the name of dignity, ever.

QUESTIONS FOR CRITICAL ANALYSIS

1. Why does Dillard enjoy the tornado? How do her parents react to the disaster? to her reaction to the disaster?
2. Did you recall any childhood memories while you read "An American Childhood"? How did your memories affect your experience of reading the essay?
3. One way Dillard "wakes to her own energy and the brisk challenge of the world" is by thinking about knowledge: what is known and what is unknown. How and why is this an important theme in the essay?
4. What does Dillard's "flight" at the end of the essay mean, both in itself and in relation to the entire essay?
5. How do people she encounters in her flight react? Why is it an important aspect of the essay that their responses are different? What do we learn from each?

QUESTIONS FOR STRUCTURAL ANALYSIS

1. Dillard's essay does not include a clearly stated thesis. Neither the streetcar reminiscences nor the flying episode are predicted at the beginning. How does the lack of a thesis at the beginning affect the essay as a whole? What unifies the selection?
2. This essay falls into three sections. What are they, and what are the relationships among them?
3. "An American Childhood" is full of vivid description. What details does Dillard select to describe the live cables, and what is their significance?
4. How does Dillard present Pittsburgh to the reader? Why is this description central to the essay?
5. Look at the way Dillard uses "you" in the section describing her bike rides: "It was your whole body that knew those sidewalks and streets. Your bones ached with them. . . ." Why do you think she uses "you" instead of "I" when it is clearly her experience? Do you like this effect or not?

A SWEET *D*EVOURING

EUDORA WELTY

Eudora Welty (1909–), a novelist and short story writer from Jackson, Mississippi, has earned the reputation of being one of America's finest writers and essayists. Her stories portray people learning to accommodate to changes in their way of life and are written, as Welty says, "not to point the finger in judgment but to part a curtain, that invisible shadow that falls between people, the veil of indifference to each other's presence, each other's wonder, each other's human plight." "A Sweet Devouring," from The Eye of the Story: Selected Essays and Reviews *(1957), describes Welty's early love for reading—an indiscriminate passion that led her to devour books uncritically, for the sheer joy of reading.*

Before you begin reading: *Make a list, in your notebook, of books that you remember reading when you were a child; if you don't remember titles, jot down a phrase to describe each book. After thinking about your list for a few minutes, write a brief description of the types of books you read as a child.*

◆

WHEN I USED TO ASK MY MOTHER WHICH WE WERE, RICH or poor, she refused to tell me. I was nine years old and of course what I was dying to hear was that we were poor. I was reading a book called *Five Little Peppers* and my heart was set on baking a cake for my mother in a stove with a hole in it. Some version of rich, crusty old Mr. King—up till that time not living on our street—was sure to come down the hill in his wheelchair and rescue me if anything went wrong. But before I could start a cake at all I had to find out if we were poor, and poor *enough*; and my mother wouldn't tell me, she said she was too busy. I couldn't wait too long; I had to go on reading and soon Polly Pepper got into more trouble, some that was a little harder on her and easier on me.

Trouble, the backbone of literature, was still to me the original property of the fairy tale, and as long as there was plenty of trouble for everybody and the rewards for it were falling in the right spots, reading was all smooth sailing. At that age a child reads with higher appetite and gratification, and with those two stars sailing closer together, than ever again in his growing up. The home shelves had been providing me all along with the usual books, and I read them with love—but snap, I finished them. I read everything just alike—snap. I even came to the *Tales from Maria Edgeworth* and went right ahead, without feeling the bump—then. It *was* noticeable that when her characters suffered she punished them for it, instead of rewarding them as a reader had rather been led to hope. In her stories, the children had to make their choice between being unhappy and good about it and being unhappy and bad about it, and then she helped them to choose wrong. In *The Purple Jar,* it will be remembered, there was the little girl being taken through the shops by her mother and her downfall coming when she chooses to buy something beautiful instead of something necessary. The purple jar, when the shop sends it out, proves to have been purple only so long as it was filled with purple water, and her mother knew it all the time. They don't deliver the water. That's only the cue for stones to start coming through the hole in the victim's wornout shoe. She bravely agrees she must keep walking on stones until such time as she is offered another choice between the beautiful and the useful. Her father tells her as far as he is concerned she can stay in the house. If I had been at all easy to disappoint, that story would have disappointed me. Of course, I did feel, what is the good of walking on rocks if they are going to let the water out of the jar too? And it seemed to me that even the illustrator fell down on the characters in that book, not alone Maria Edgeworth, for when a rich, crusty old gentleman gave Simple Susan a guinea for some kind deed she'd done him, there was a picture of the transaction and where was the guinea? I couldn't make out a feather. But I liked *reading* the book all right—except that I finished it.

My mother took me to the Public Library and introduced me: "Let her have any book she wants, except *Elsie Dinsmore.*" I looked for the book I couldn't have and it was a row. That was how I learned about the Series Books. The *Five Little Peppers* belonged, so did *The Wizard of Oz*, so did *The Little Colonel*, so did *The Green Fairy Book.* There were many of everything, generations of everybody, instead of one. I wasn't coming to the end of reading, after all—I was saved.

Our library in those days was a big rotunda lined with shelves. A copy of *V. V.'s Eyes* seemed to follow you wherever you went, even after you'd read it. I didn't know what I liked, I just knew what there was a lot of. After *Randy's Spring* there came *Randy's Summer* and *Randy's Fall* and *Randy's Winter.* True, I didn't care very much myself for her spring, but it didn't occur to me that I might not care for her summer, and then her summer didn't prejudice me against her fall, and I still had hopes as I moved on to her winter. I was disappointed in her whole year, as it turned out, but a thing like that didn't keep me from wanting to read every word of it. The pleasures of reading itself—who doesn't remember?—were like those of a Christmas cake, a sweet devouring. The "Randy Books" failed chiefly in being so soon over. Four seasons doesn't make a series.

All that summer I used to put on a second petticoat (our librarian wouldn't let you past the front door if she could see through you), ride my bicycle up the hill and "through the Capitol" (shortcut) to the library with my two read books in the basket (two was the limit you could take out at one time when you were a child and also as long as you lived), and tiptoe in ("Silence") and exchange them for two more in two minutes. Selection was no object. I coasted the two new books home, jumped out of my petticoat, read (I suppose I ate and bathed and answered questions put to me), then in all hope put my petticoat back on and rode those two books back to the library to get my next two.

The librarian was the lady in town who wanted to be it. She called me by my full name and said, "Does your mother know where you are? You know good and well the fixed rule of this library: *Nobody is going to come running back here with any book on the same day they took it out.* Get those things out of here and don't come back till tomorrow. And I can practically see through you."

My great-aunt in Virginia, who understood better about needing more to read than you *could* read, sent me a book so big it had to be read on the floor—a bound volume of six or eight issues of *St. Nicholas* from a previous year. In the very first pages a serial began: *The Lucky Stone* by Abbie Farwell Brown. The illustrations were right down my alley: a heroine so poor she was ragged, a witch with an extremely pointed hat, a rich, crusty old gentleman in—better than a wheelchair—a runaway carriage; and I set to. I gobbled up installment after installment through the whole luxurious book, through the last one, and then came the words, turning me to *un*lucky stone: "To be concluded." The book had come to an end and *The Lucky Stone* wasn't finished! The witch had it! I couldn't believe this infidelity from my aunt. I still had my secret childhood feeling that if you hunted long enough in a book's pages, you could find what you were looking for, and long after I knew books better than that, I used to hunt again for the end of *The Lucky Stone*. It never occurred to me that the story had an existence anywhere else outside the pages of that single green-bound book. The last chapter was just something I would have to do without. Polly Pepper could do it. And then suddenly I tried something—I read it again, as much as I had of it. I was in love with books at least partly for what they looked like; I loved the printed page.

In my little circle books were almost never given for Christmas, they cost too much. But the year before, I'd been given a book and got a shock. It was from the same classmate who had told me there was no Santa Claus. She gave me a book, all right—*Poems by Another Little Girl*. It looked like a real book, was printed like a real book—but it was *by her. Homemade* poems? Illusion-dispelling was her favorite game. She was in such a hurry, she had such a pile to get rid of—her mother's electric runabout was stacked to the bud vases with copies—that she hadn't even time to say, "Merry Christmas!" With only the same raucous laugh with which she had told me, "Been filling my own stocking for years!" she shot me her book, received my Japanese pencil box with a moonlight scene on the lid and a sharpened pencil inside, jumped back into the car and was sped away by her mother. I stood right where they had left me, on the curb in my Little Nurse's uniform, and read that book, and I had no better way to prove when I got through than I had when I started that this was not a real book. But of course it wasn't. The printed page is not absolutely everything.

Then this Christmas was coming, and my grandfather in Ohio sent along in his box of presents an envelope with money in it for me to buy myself the book I wanted.

I went to Kress's. Not everybody knew Kress's sold books, but children just before Christmas know everything Kress's ever sold or will sell. My father had showed us the mirror he was giving my mother to hang above her desk, and Kress's is where my brother and I went to reproduce that by buying a mirror together to give her ourselves, and where our little brother then made us take him and he bought her one his size for fifteen cents. Kress's had also its version of the Series Books, called, exactly like another series, "The Camp Fire Girls," beginning with *The Camp Fire Girls in the Woods*.

I believe they were ten cents each and I had a dollar. But they weren't all that easy to buy, because the series stuck, and to buy some of it was like breaking into a loaf of French bread. Then after you got home, each single book was as hard to open as a box stuck in its varnish, and when it gave way it popped like a firecracker. The covers once prized apart would never close; those books once opened stayed open and lay on their backs helplessly fluttering their leaves like a turned-over June bug. They were as light as a matchbox. They were printed on yellowed paper with corners that crumbled, if you pinched on them too hard, like old graham crackers, and they smelled like attic trunks, caramelized glue, their own confinement with one another and, over all, the Kress's smell—bandannas, peanuts and sandalwood from the incense counter. Even without reading them I loved them. It was hard, that year, that Christmas is a day you can't read.

What could have happened to those books?—but I can tell you about the leading character. His name was Mr. Holmes. He was not a Camp Fire Girl: he wanted to catch one. Through every book of the series he gave chase. He pursued Bessie and Zara—those were the Camp Fire Girls—and kept scooping them up in his touring car, while they just as regularly got away from him. Once Bessie escaped from the second floor of a strange inn by climbing down a gutter pipe. Once she escaped by driving away from Mr. Holmes in his own automobile, which she had learned to drive by watching him. What Mr. Holmes wanted with them—either Bessie or Zara would do—didn't give me pause; I was too young to be a Camp Fire Girl; I was just keeping up. I wasn't alarmed by Mr. Holmes—when I cared for a chill, I knew to go to Dr. Fu Manchu, who had his own series in the library. I wasn't fascinated either. There was one thing I wanted from those books, and that was for me to have ten to read at one blow.

Who in the world wrote those books? I knew all the time they were the false "Camp Fire Girls" and the ones in the library were the authorized. But book reviewers sometimes say of a book that if anyone else had written it, it might not have been this good, and I found it out as a child—their warning is justified. This was a proven case, although a case of the true not being as good as the false. In the true series the characters were either totally different or missing (Mr. Holmes was missing), and there was too much time given to teamwork. The Kress's Campers, besides getting into a more reliable kind of trouble than the Carnegie Campers, had adventures that even they themselves weren't aware of: the pages were in wrong. There were transposed pages, repeated pages, and whole sections in upside down. There was no way of telling if there was anything missing. But if you knew your way in the woods at all, you could enjoy yourself tracking it down. I read the library "Camp Fire Girls," since that's what they were there for, but though they could be read by poorer light they were not as good.

And yet, in a way, the false Campers were no better either. I wonder whether I felt some flaw at the heart of things or whether I was just tired of not having any taste; but it seemed to me when I had finished that the last nine of those books weren't as good as the first one. And the same went for all Series Books. As long as they are keeping a series going, I was afraid, nothing can really happen. The whole thing is one grand prevention. For my greed, I might have unwittingly dealt with myself in the same way Maria Edgeworth dealt with the one who put her all into the purple jar—I had received word it was just colored water.

And then I went again to the home shelves and my lucky hand reached and found Mark Twain—twenty-four volumes, not a series, and good all the way through.

Questions for Critical Analysis

1. What is "the bump" Welty refers to in reading *Tales from Maria Edgeworth*? Why does she describe it as a "bump"? Name a book you have read that included a "bump," and describe what you mean.
2. Why does Welty use a paragraph to retell the story, "The Purple Jar"? What is the point of the story? Examine the second-to-last sentence of the essay. How does Welty relate the purple jar to her own experiences? In what ways does Welty's word choice—"I might have unwittingly dealt with myself"—affect your reaction to her explanation?
3. Define the types of reading Welty describes. Is there a relationship between what is read and how it is read? Use examples from your own reading experiences to define how you read.

4. Describe the progression of Welty's reading patterns. What events occur that begin to change her reading style? How do they suggest the change? Is it significant that change occurred within Welty and was not imposed by her mother, aunt, or librarian? Why?
5. What is implied by the statement, "my lucky hand reached out and found Mark Twain"? Why does Welty present Twain's books as superior to the Camp Fire series? How do you define "good books"?

QUESTIONS FOR STRUCTURAL ANALYSIS

1. What tone does Welty establish in the first paragraph? Is the tone consistent throughout the essay? Compare the style of the first paragraph with the final two paragraphs.
2. What is the thesis of this essay? How do you know?
3. Welty includes specific details about her summer experiences that don't seem to belong in an essay about reading. What are they? Why are they included?
4. How does Welty's inclusion of plots, characters, and details from her books affect the essay?
5. How does Welty use the five people she includes in this essay: her mother, the librarian, her aunt, her friend, and her grandfather? Does she tell you enough about these people? too much about them?

SALVATION

LANGSTON HUGHES

Langston Hughes (1902–1967), who has been called "the poet laureate of Harlem," decided to become a writer when he was elected class poet (although he had never written a poem) in high school. Ten books of poetry, nine works of fiction, essays, plays, and autobiographical pieces all attest to the wisdom of his decision. Through all his works, Hughes brought the African-American experience to life for his readers. "Salvation," a chapter from his autobiography The Big Sea *(1940), is a humorous story which, through the telling, makes us consider the pressures that influence how we make decisions and at what cost.*

Before you begin reading: *Think about some religious experiences you may have had. Were any of these experiences influenced by the expectations of adults in your life? In your reading notebook write a phrase or two to describe some of the religious principles or behaviors adults expected you to learn. Next to these phrases, write a brief description of how you responded. If your responses now are different than they were when you were a child, you may want to include the changes as well.*

◆

I WAS SAVED FROM SIN WHEN I WAS GOING ON THIRTEEN. But not really saved. It happened like this. There was a big revival at my Auntie Reed's church. Every night for weeks there had been much preaching, singing, praying, and shouting, and some very hardened sinners had been brought to Christ, and the membership of the church had grown by leaps and bounds. Then just before the revival ended, they held a special meeting for children, "to bring the young lambs to the fold." My aunt spoke of it for days ahead. That night I was escorted to the front row and placed on the mourners' bench with all the other young sinners, who had not yet been brought to Jesus.

My aunt told me that when you were saved you saw a light, and something happened to you inside! And Jesus came into your life! And God was with you from then on! She said you could see and hear and feel Jesus in your soul. I believed her. I had heard a great many old people say the same thing and it seemed to me they ought to know. So I sat there calmly in the hot, crowded church, waiting for Jesus to come to me.

The preacher preached a wonderful rhythmical sermon, all moans and shouts and lonely cries and dire pictures of hell, and then he sang a song about the ninety and nine safe in the fold, but one little lamb was left out in the cold. Then he said: "Won't you come? Won't you come to Jesus? Young lambs, won't you come?" And he held out his arms to all us young sinners there on the mourners' bench. And the little girls cried. And some of them jumped up and went to Jesus right away. But most of us just sat there.

A great many old people came and knelt around us and prayed, old women with jet-black faces and braided hair, old men with work-gnarled hands. And the church sang a song about the lower lights are burning, some poor sinners to be saved. And the whole building rocked with prayer and song.

Still I kept waiting to *see* Jesus.

Finally all the young people had gone to the altar and were saved, but one boy and me. He was a rounder's son named Westley. Westley and I were surrounded by sisters and deacons praying. It was very hot in the church, and getting late now. Finally Westley said to me in a whisper: "God damn! I'm tired o' sitting here. Let's get up and be saved." So he got up and was saved.

Then I was left all alone on the mourners' bench. My aunt came and knelt at my knees and cried, while prayers and songs swirled all around me in the little church. The whole congregation prayed for me alone, in a mighty wail of moans and voices. And I kept waiting serenely for Jesus, waiting, waiting—but he didn't come. I wanted to see him, but nothing happened to me. Nothing! I wanted something to happen to me, but nothing happened.

I heard the songs and the minister saying: "Why don't you come? My dear child, why don't you come to Jesus? Jesus is waiting for you. He wants you. Why don't you come? Sister Reed, what is this child's name?"

"Langston," my aunt sobbed.

"Langston, why don't you come? Why don't you come and be saved? Oh, Lamb of God! Why don't you come?"

Now it was really getting late. I began to be ashamed of myself, holding everything up so long. I began to wonder what God thought about Westley, who certainly hadn't seen Jesus either, but who was now sitting proudly on the platform, swinging his knickerbockered legs and grinning down at me, surrounded by deacons and old women on their knees praying. God had not struck Westley dead for taking his name in vain or for lying in the temple. So I decided that maybe to save further trouble, I'd better lie, too, and say that Jesus had come, and get up and be saved.

So I got up.

Suddenly the whole room broke into a sea of shouting, as they saw me rise. Waves of rejoicing swept the place. Women leaped in the air. My aunt threw her arms around me. The minister took me by the hand and led me to the platform.

When things quieted down, in a hushed silence, punctuated by a few ecstatic "Amens," all the new young lambs were blessed in the name of God. Then joyous singing filled the room.

That night, for the last time in my life but one—for I was a big boy twelve years old—I cried. I cried, in bed alone, and couldn't stop. I buried my head under the quilts, but my aunt heard me. She woke up and told my uncle I was crying because the Holy Ghost had come into my life, and because I had seen Jesus. But I was really crying because I couldn't bear to tell her that I had lied, that I had deceived everybody in the church, that I hadn't seen Jesus, and that now I didn't believe there was a Jesus any more, since he didn't come to help me.

QUESTIONS FOR CRITICAL ANALYSIS

1. What role does Westley play in "Salvation"? What sort of child is he? Why does Westley seem unaffected by his lying, while Langston is devastated?
2. What upsets Langston about this event? What has he lost, and how?
3. How do you suppose this event will change young Langston's view of his aunt, the church elders, and—by extension—the adult world?
4. Did anything comparable happen to you as a child? When and how did you first realize that adults don't know everything after all? How does your experience affect your response to "Salvation"?
5. Although this is an account of a shattering childhood disillusionment, the tone is not bitter. Why not? How has Hughes managed to maintain lightness about a serious subject? Compare the tone of this story with Hughes' essay, "My America," in the "Demanding Civil Rights" section of this volume.

QUESTIONS FOR STRUCTURAL ANALYSIS

1. Many of the sentences in "Salvation" are short. Even including those that are longer, most sentences are simple in construction. What is the effect of these short sentences?
2. Whose voice dominates the essay: the twelve-year-old Langston or the adult Langston Hughes? How does the dual perspective influence the reader's response to the essay?
3. What experience is the narrator waiting for to know he's been saved? Why does he have these expectations? Why does the writer describe these events in the second paragraph?
4. List descriptive details Hughes provides to evoke the church, congregation, and service. How does Hughes' description enhance his narration?
5. Although this is a short essay, it is dramatic—action-filled, suspenseful, moving directly toward a crisis point, and ending on a thoughtful note. How does Hughes manage this through plot devices? through paragraph development? Select sentences which show how Hughes' prose style contributes to the dramatic effect of the essay.

*T*O *B*E A *J*EW

ELIE WIESEL

Elie Wiesel (1928–), winner of the Nobel Peace Prize in 1986, has been a spokesman on the Holocaust—Nazi Germany's systematic murder of Jews—examining the themes of human suffering, guilt, and injustice in his writings. Wiesel survived his confinement at Auschwitz and Buchenwald, although his family was killed. "To Be a Jew" focuses on the systematic murder of the Jews by Hitler and his followers and its relationship to the nature of both Christian and Jewish communities. Early in this essay Wiesel describes the rich sense of history that is central to the Jewish experience and writes: "To be a Jew meant to live with memory." Wiesel's commitment to this idea is evident in his determination that we never forget our capability for horror and inhumanity.

Before you begin reading: *Make a list of words and images that occur to you when you think about the Holocaust in the Second World War. (Your ideas may result from family stories, from books or stories you've read, from movies, or television shows.) Use this list as a starting point, and write down your feelings about the Holocaust.*

◆

ONCE UPON A TIME, IN A DISTANT TOWN SURROUNDED by mountains, there lived a small Jewish boy who believed himself capable of seeing good in evil, of discovering dawn within dusk and, in general, of deciphering the symbols, both visible and invisible, lavished upon him by destiny.

To him, all things seemed simple and miraculous: life and death, love and hatred. On one side were the righteous, on the other the wicked. The just were always handsome and generous, the miscreants always ugly and cruel. And God in His heaven kept the accounts in a book only He could consult. In that book each people had its own page, and the Jewish people had the most beautiful page of all.

Naturally, this little boy felt at ease only among his own people, in his own setting. Everything alien frightened me. And alien meant not Moslem or Hindu, but Christian. The priest dressed in black, the woodcutter and his ax, the teacher and his ruler, old peasant women crossing themselves as their husbands uttered oath upon oath, constables looking gruff or merely preoccupied—all of them exuded a hostility I understood and considered normal, and therefore without remedy.

I *understood* that all these people, young and old, rich and poor, powerful and oppressed, exploiters and exploited, should want my undoing, even my death. True, we inhabited the same landscape, but that was yet another reason for them to hate me. Such is man's nature: he hates what disturbs him, what eludes him. We depended on the more or less unselfish tolerance of the "others," yet our life followed its own course independently of theirs, a fact they clearly resented. Our determination to maintain and enrich our separate history, our separate society, confused them as much as did that history itself. A living Jew, a believing Jew, proud of his faith, was for them a contradiction, a denial, an aberration. According to their calculations, this chosen and accursed people should long ago have ceased to haunt a mankind whose salvation was linked to the bloodstained symbol of the cross. They could not accept the idea of a Jew celebrating his Holy Days with song, just as they celebrated their own. That was inadmissible, illogical, even unjust. And the less they understood us, the more I understood them.

I felt no animosity. I did not even hate them at Christmas or Easter time when they imposed a climate of terror upon our frightened community. I told myself: They envy us, they persecute us because they envy us, and rightly so; surely *they* were the ones to be pitied. Their tormenting us was but an admission of weakness, of inner insecurity. If God's truth subsists on earth in the hearts of mortals, it is our doing. It is through us that God has chosen to manifest His will and outline His designs, and it is through us that He has chosen to sanctify His name. Were I in their place I, too, would feel rejected. How could they not be envious? In an odd way, the more they hunted me, the more I rationalized their behavior. Today I recognize my feelings for what they were: a mixture of pride, distrust and pity.

Yet I felt no curiosity. Not of any kind, or at any moment. We seemed to intrigue them, but they left me indifferent. I knew nothing of their catechism, and cared less. I made no attempt to comprehend the rites and canons of their faith. Their rituals held no interest for me; quite the contrary, I turned away from them. Whenever I met a priest I would avert my gaze and think of something else. Rather than walk in front of a church with its pointed and threatening belfry, I would cross the street. To see was as frightening as to be seen; I worried that a visual, physical link might somehow be created between us. So ignorant was I of their world that I had no idea that Judaism and Christianity claimed the same roots. Nor did I know that Christians who believe in the eternity and in the divinity of Christ also believe in those of God, *our* God. Though our universes existed side by side, I avoided penetrating theirs, whereas they sought to dominate ours by force. I had heard enough tales about the Crusades and the pogroms, and I had repeated enough litanies dedicated to their victims, to know where I stood. I had read and reread descriptions of what inquisitors, grand and small, had inflicted on Jews in Catholic kingdoms; how they had preached God's love to them even as they were leading them to the stake. All I knew of Christianity was its hate for my people. Christians were more present in my imagination than in my life. What did a Christian do when he was alone? What were his dreams made of? How did he use his time when he was not engaged in plotting against us? But none of this really troubled me. Beyond our immediate contacts, our public and hereditary confrontations, he simply did not exist.

My knowledge of the Jew, on the other hand, sprang from an inexhaustible source: the more I learned, the more I wanted to know. There was inside me a thirst for knowledge that was all-enveloping, all-pervasive, a veritable obsession.

I knew what it meant to be a Jew in day-to-day life as well as in the absolute. What was required was to obey the Law; thus one needed first to learn it, then to remember it. What was required was to love God and that which in His creation bears His seal. And His will would be done.

Abraham's covenant, Isaac's suspended sacrifice, Jacob's fiery dreams, the revelation at Sinai, the long march through the desert, Moses' blessings, the conquest of Canaan, the pilgrimages to the Temple in Jerusalem, Isaiah's and Habakkuk's beautiful but harsh words, Jeremiah's lamentations, the Talmudic legends: my head was abuzz with ancient memories and debates, with tales teeming with kings and prophets, tragedies and miracles. Every story contained victims, always victims, and survivors, always survivors. To be a Jew meant to live with memory.

Nothing could have been easier. One needed only to follow tradition, to reproduce the gestures and sounds transmitted through generations whose end product I was. On the morning of Shavuoth there I was with Moses receiving the Law. On the eve of Tishah b'Av, seated on the floor, my head covered with ashes, I wept, together with Rabbi Yohanan Ben-Zakkai, over the destruction of the city that had been thought indestructible. During the week of Hanukkah, I rushed to the aid of the Maccabees; and on Purim, I laughed, how I laughed, with Mordecai, celebrating his victory over Haman. And week after week, as we blessed the wine during Shabbat meals, I accompanied the Jews out of Egypt—yes, I was forever leaving Egypt, freeing myself from bondage. To be a Jew meant creating links, a network of continuity.

With the years I learned a more "sophisticated," more modern vocabulary. I was told that to be a Jew means to place the accent simultaneously and equally on verb and noun, on the secular and the eternal, to prevent the one from excluding the other or succeeding at the expense of the other. That it means to serve God by espousing man's cause, to plead for man while recognizing his need of God. And to opt for the Creator *and* His creation, refusing to pit one against the other.

Of course, man must interrogate God, as did Abraham; articulate his anger, as did Moses; and shout his sorrow, as did Job. But only the Jew opts for

Abraham—who questions—*and* for God—who is questioned. He claims every role and assumes every destiny: he is both sum and synthesis.

I shall long, perhaps forever, remember my Master, the one with the yellowish beard, telling me, "Only the Jew knows that he may oppose God as long as he does so in defense of His creation." Another time he told me, "God gave the Law, but it is up to man to interpret it—and his interpretation is binding on God and commits Him."

Surely this is an idealized concept of the Jew. And of man. And yet it is one that is tested every day, at every moment, in every circumstance.

At school I read in the Talmud: Why did God create only one man? The answer: All men have the same ancestor. So that no man, later, could claim superiority over another.

And also: A criminal who sets fire to the Temple, the most sacred, the most revered edifice in the world, is punishable with only thirty-nine lashes of the whip; let a fanatic kill him and *his* punishment would be death. For all the temples and all the sanctuaries are not worth the life of a single human being, be he arsonist, profanator, enemy of God and shame of God.

Painful irony: We were chased from country to country, our Houses of Study were burned, our sages assassinated, our schoolchildren massacred, and still we went on tirelessly, fiercely, praising the inviolate sanctity of life and proclaiming faith in man, any man.

An extraordinary contradiction? Perhaps. But to be a Jew is precisely to reveal oneself within one's contradictions by accepting them. It means safeguarding one's past at a time when mankind aspires only to conquer the future; it means observing Shabbat when the official day of rest is Sunday or Friday; it means fervently exploring the Talmud, with its seemingly antiquated laws and discussions, while outside, not two steps away from the heder or the yeshiva, one's friends and parents are rounded up or beaten in a pogrom; it means asserting the right of spirituality in a world that denies spirituality; it means singing and singing again, louder and louder, when all around everything heralds the end of the world, the end of man.

All this was really so. The small Jewish boy is telling only what he heard and saw, what he lived himself, long ago. He vouches for its truth.

Yes, long ago in distant places it all seemed so simple to me, so real, so throbbing with truth. Like God, I looked at the world and found it good, fertile, full of meaning. Even in exile, every creature was in its place and every encounter was charged with promise. And with the advent of Shabbat, the town changed into a kingdom whose madmen and beggars became the princes of Shabbat.

I shall never forget Shabbat in my town. When I shall have forgotten everything else, my memory will still retain the atmosphere of holiday, of serenity pervading even the poorest houses: the white tablecloth, the candles, the meticulously combed little girls, the men on their way to synagogue. When my town shall fade into the abyss of time, I will continue to remember the light and the warmth it radiated on Shabbat. The exalting prayers, the wordless songs of the Hasidim, the fire and radiance of their Masters.

On that day of days, past and future suffering and anguish faded into the distance. Appeased man called on the divine presence to express his gratitude.

The jealousies and grudges, the petty rancors between neighbors could wait. As could the debts and worries, the dangers. Everything could wait. As it enveloped the universe, the Shabbat conferred on it a dimension of peace, an aura of love.

Those who were hungry came and ate; and those who felt abandoned seized the outstretched hand; and those who were alone, and those who were sad, the strangers, the refugees, the wanderers, as they left the synagogue were invited to share the meal in any home; and the grieving were urged to contain their tears and come draw on the collective joy of Shabbat.

The difference between us and the others? The others, how I pitied them. They did not even know what they were missing; they were unmoved by the beauty, the eternal splendor of Shabbat.

And then came the Holocaust, which shook history and by its dimensions and goals marked the end of a civilization. Concentration-camp man discovered the anti-savior.

We became witnesses to a huge simplification. On the one side there were the executioners and on the other the victims. What about the onlookers, those who remained neutral, those who served the executioner simply by not interfering? To be a Jew then meant to fight both the complacency of the neutral and the hate of the killers. And to resist—in any way, with any means. And not only with weapons. The Jew who refused death, who refused to believe in death, who chose to marry in the ghetto, to circumcise his son, to teach him the sacred language, to bind him to the threatened and weakened lineage of Israel—that Jew was resisting. The professor or shopkeeper who disregarded facts and warnings and clung to illusion, refusing to admit that people could so succumb to degradation—he, too, was resisting. There was no essential difference between the Warsaw ghetto fighters and the old men getting off the train in Treblinka: because they were Jewish, they were all doomed to hate, and death.

In those days, more than ever, to be Jewish signified *refusal.* Above all, it was a refusal to see reality and life through the enemy's eyes—a refusal to resemble him, to grant him that victory, too.

Yet his victory seemed solid and, in the beginning, definitive. All those uprooted communities, ravaged and dissolved in smoke; all those trains that crisscrossed the nocturnal Polish landscapes; all those men, all those women, stripped of their language, their names, their faces, compelled to live and die according to the laws of the enemy, in anonymity and darkness. All those kingdoms of barbed wire where everyone looked alike and all words carried the same weight. Day followed day and hour followed hour, while thoughts, numb and bleak, groped their way among the corpses, through the mire and the blood.

And the adolescent in me, yearning for faith, questioned: Where was God in all this? Was this another test, one more? Or a punishment? And if so, for what sins? What crimes were being punished? Was there a misdeed that deserved so many mass graves? Would it ever again be possible to speak of justice, of truth, of divine charity, after the murder of one million Jewish children?

I did not understand, I was afraid to understand. Was this the end of the Jewish people, or the end perhaps of the human adventure? Surely it was the end of an era, the end of a world. That I knew, that was all I knew.

As for the rest, I accumulated uncertainties. The faith of some, the lack of faith of others added to my perplexity. How could one believe, how could one not believe, in God as one faced those mountains of ashes? Who would symbolize the concentration-camp experience—the killer or the victim? Their confrontation was so striking, so gigantic that it had to include a metaphysical, ontological aspect: would we ever penetrate its mystery?

Questions, doubts. I moved through the fog like a sleepwalker. Why did the God of Israel manifest such hostility toward the descendants of Israel? I did not know. Why did free men, liberals and humanists, remain untouched by Jewish suffering? I did not know.

I remember the midnight arrival at Birkenau. Shouts. Dogs barking. Families together for the last time, families about to be torn asunder. A young Jewish boy walks at his father's side in the convoy of men; they walk and they walk and night walks with them toward a place spewing monstrous flames, flames devouring the sky. Suddenly an inmate crosses the ranks and explains to the men what they are seeing, the truth of the night: the future, the absence of future; the key to the secret, the power of evil. As he speaks, the young boy touches his father's arm as though to reassure him, and whispers, "This is impossible, isn't it? Don't listen to what he is telling us, he only wants to frighten us. What he says is impossible, unthinkable, it is all part of another age, the Middle Ages, not the twentieth century, not modern history. The world, Father, the civilized world would not allow such things to happen."

And yet the civilized world did know, and remained silent. Where was man in all this? And culture, how did it reach this nadir? All those spiritual leaders, those thinkers, those philosophers enamored of truth, those moralists drunk with justice—how was one to reconcile their teachings with Josef Mengele, the great master of selections in Auschwitz? I told myself that a grave, a horrible error had been committed somewhere—only, I knew neither its nature nor its author. When and where had history taken so bad a turn?

I remember the words of a young Talmudist whose face was that of an old man. He and I had worked as a team, carrying boulders weighing more than the two of us.

"Let us suppose," he whispered, "let us suppose that our people had not transmitted the Law to other nations. Let us forget Abraham and his example, Moses and his justice, the prophets and their message. Let us suppose that our contributions to philosophy, to science, to literature are negligible or even nonexistent. Maimonides, Nahmanides, Rashi: nothing. Spinoza, Bergson, Einstein, Freud: nothing. Let us suppose that we have in no way added to progress, to the well-being of mankind. One thing cannot be contested: the great killers, history's great assassins—Pharaoh, Nero, Chmelnitzky, Hitler—not one was formed in our midst."

Which brings us back to where we started: to the relations between Jews and Christians, which, of course, we had been forced to revise. For we had been struck by a harsh truth: in Auschwitz all the Jews were victims, all the killers were Christian.

I mention this here neither to score points nor to embarrass anyone. I believe that no religion, people or nation is inferior or superior to another; I dislike facile triumphalism, for us and for others. I dislike self-righteousness. And I feel closer to certain Christians—as long as they do not try to convert me to their faith—than to certain Jews. I felt closer to John XXIII and to François Mauriac than to self-hating Jews. I have more in common with an authentic and tolerant Christian than with a Jew who is neither authentic nor tolerant. I stress this because what I am about to say will surely hurt my Christian friends. Yet I have no right to hold back.

How is one to explain that neither Hitler nor Himmler was ever excommunicated by the church? That Pius XII never thought it necessary, not to say indispensable, to condemn Auschwitz and Treblinka? That among the S.S. a large proportion were believers who remained faithful to their Christian ties to the end? That there were killers who went to confession between massacres? And that they all came from Christian families and had received a Christian education?

In Poland, a stronghold of Christianity, it often happened that Jews who had escaped from the ghettos returned inside their walls, so hostile did they find the outside world; they feared the Poles as much as the Germans. This was also true in Lithuania, in the Ukraine, in White Russia and in Hungary. How is one to explain the passivity of the population as it watched the persecution of its Jews? How explain the cruelty of the killers? How explain that the Christian in them did not make their arms tremble as they shot at children or their conscience bridle as they shoved their naked, beaten victims into the factories of death? Of course, here and there, brave Christians came to the aid of Jews, but they were few: several dozen bishops and priests, a few hundred men and women in all of Europe.

It is a painful statement to make, but we cannot ignore it: as surely as the victims are a problem for the Jews, the killers are a problem for the Christians.

Yes, the victims remain a serious and troubling problem for us. No use covering it up. What was there about the Jew that he could be reduced so quickly, so easily to the status of victim? I have read all the answers, all the explanations. They are all inadequate. It is difficult to imagine the silent processions marching toward the pits. And the crowds that let themselves be duped. And the condemned who, inside the sealed wagons and sometimes on the very ramp at Birkenau, continued not to see. I do not understand. I understand neither the killers nor the victims.

To be a Jew during the Holocaust may have meant not to understand. Having rejected murder as a means of survival and death as a solution, men and women agreed to live and die without understanding.

For the survivor, the question presented itself differently: to remain or not to remain a Jew. I remember our tumultuous, anguished debates in France after the liberation. Should one leave for Palestine and fight in the name of Jewish nationalism, or should one, on the contrary, join the Communist movement and promulgate the ideal of internationalism? Should one delve deeper into tradition, or turn one's back on it? The options were extreme: total commitment or total alienation, unconditional loyalty or repudiation. There was no returning to the earlier ways and principles. The Jew could say: I have suffered, I have been made to suffer, all I can do is draw closer to my own people. And that was understandable. Or else: I have suffered too much, I have no strength left, I withdraw, I do not wish my children to inherit this suffering. And that, too, was understandable.

And yet, as in the past, the ordeal brought not a decline but a renascence of Jewish consciousness and a flourishing of Jewish history. Rather than break his ties, the Jew strengthened them. Auschwitz made him stronger. Even he among us who espouses so-called universal causes outside his community is motivated by the Jew in him trying to reform man even as he despairs of mankind. Though he may be in a position to become something else, the Jew remains a Jew.

Throughout a world in flux, young Jews, speaking every tongue, products of every social class, join in the adventure that Judaism represents for them, a phenomenon that reached its apex in Israel and Soviet Russia. Following different roads, these pilgrims take part in the same project and express the same defiance: "They want us to founder, but we will let our joy explode; they want to make us hard, closed to solidarity and love, well, we will be obstinate but filled with compassion." This is the challenge that justifies the hopes the Jew places in Judaism and explains the singular marks he leaves on his destiny.

Thus there would seem to be more than one way for the Jew to assume his condition. There is a time to question oneself and a time to act; there is a time to tell stories and a time to pray; there is a time to build and a time to rebuild. Whatever he chooses to do, the Jew becomes a spokesman for all Jews, dead and yet to be born, for all the beings who live through him and inside him.

His mission was never to make the world Jewish but, rather, to make it more human.

Questions for Critical Analysis

1. From what Wiesel says, Jews and Christians in his community had little contact and most were unaware that their religions had common roots and shared the same religious text. What does this mean in terms of the essay's final conclusions?
2. Wiesel relies on certain historical and cultural knowledge that not every reader will have. What difference did this make to your reading of the essay? What information or references were familiar to you and what was not?
3. How is the theme of contradiction woven into the essay, and why is contradiction an important theme in this essay?
4. Do any religious beliefs you may have affect your experience with this essay? If you are a Christian or a Jew, you may identify strongly with your group as you read this essay. Examine your reaction, section by section, according to your religious background.
5. Does Wiesel think Jews are morally superior to Christians? If so, on what basis? Do you agree? Why, or why not?
6. How do you respond to Wiesel's recommended response to the Holocaust: "Jews must 'let our joy explode'"?

Questions for Structural Analysis

1. Although he ends his essay addressing the Holocaust, Wiesel begins with a description of his childhood. Why is this an important introduction?
2. Notice that Wiesel begins the essay in the third person and then, at the beginning of the third paragraph, shifts to first person: "Naturally, this little boy felt at ease only among his own people, in his own setting. Everything alien frightened me." Why did he do this? At what other occasions in the essay does he shift person? Why?
3. Wiesel often uses questions as a rhetorical device. Why? Is it effective? Why, or why not?
4. What role does the Shabbat play in the essay? (What is Shabbat?) How would you characterize Wiesel's description of it?
5. Examine the essay as a whole and note the instances when Wiesel uses close description to advance his narrative. What effect does this have on Wiesel's abstract ideas?

*W*E'RE *P*OOR

FLOYD DELL

Floyd Dell (1887–1969), editor of two socialist papers, Masses *and the* Liberator, *wrote for the Works Progress Administration (WPA) during the Depression. Many of Dell's novels and plays present the postwar disillusion of youth during the 1920s. In his autobiography,* Homecoming *(1933), Dell describes the moment he became aware that he was one of the "poor kids" for whom others collected food and money. This recognition stunned Dell and led him to abandon his dreams for college, law school, and the presidency.*

Before you begin reading: *What images occur to you when you think about poverty in America? In the 1930s a third of the nation lived in poverty and that figure fairly accurately describes America at the end of this century as well. Write a paragraph or more in your notebook describing your experiences with poverty.*

◆

(MEMORIES OF CHILDHOOD ARE STRANGE THINGS. THE obscurity of the past opens upon a little lighted space—a scene, unconnected with anything else. One must figure out when it happened. There may be anomalies in the scene, which need explanation. Sometimes the scenes are tiny fragments only. Again they are long dramas. Having once been remembered, they can be lived through again in every moment, with a detailed experiencing of movement and sensation and thought. One can start the scene in one's mind and see it all through again. Exactly so it was—clearer in memory than something that happened yesterday, though it was forty years ago. And, oddly enough, if there is some detail skipped over, lost out of the memory picture, no repetition of the remembering process will supply it—the gap is always there.)

That fall, before it was discovered that the soles of both my shoes were worn clear through, I still went to Sunday school. And one time the Sunday-school superintendent made a speech to all the classes. He said that these were hard times, and that many poor children weren't getting enough to eat. It was the first that I had heard about it. He asked everybody to bring some food for the poor children next Sunday. I felt very sorry for the poor children.

Also, little envelopes were distributed to all the classes. Each little boy and girl was to bring money for the poor, next Sunday. The pretty Sunday-school teacher explained that we were to write our names, or have our parents write them, up in the left-hand corner of the little envelopes. . . . I told my mother all about it when I came home. And my mother gave me, the next Sunday, a small bag of potatoes to carry to Sunday school. I supposed the poor children's mothers would make potato soup out of them. . . . Potato soup was good. My father, who was quite a joker, would always say, as if he were surprised, "Ah! I see we have some nourishing potato soup today!" It was so good that we had it every day. My father was at home all day long and every day, now; and I liked that, even if he was grumpy as he sat reading Grant's 'Memoirs'. I had my parents all to myself, too; the others were away. My oldest brother was in Quincy, and memory does not reveal where the others were: perhaps with relatives in the country.

Taking my small bag of potatoes to Sunday school, I looked around for the poor children; I was disappointed not to see them. I had heard about poor children in stories. But I was told just to put my contribution with the others on the big table in the side room.

I had brought with me the little yellow envelope, with some money in it for the poor children. My mother had put the money in it and sealed it up. She wouldn't tell me how much money she had put in it, but it felt like several dimes. Only she wouldn't let me write my name on the envelope. I had learned to write my name, and I was proud of being able to do it. But my mother said firmly, *no*, I must *not* write my name on the envelope; she didn't tell me why. On the way to Sunday school I had pressed the envelope against the coins until I could tell what they were; they weren't dimes but pennies.

When I handed in my envelope, my Sunday-school teacher noticed that my name wasn't on it, and she gave me a pencil; I could write my own name, she said. So I did. But I was confused because my mother had said not to; and when I came home, I confessed what I had done. She looked distressed. "I told you not to!" she said. But she didn't explain why. . . .

I didn't go back to school that fall. My mother said it was because I was sick. I did have a cold the week that school opened; I had been playing in the gutters and had got my feet wet, because there were holes in my shoes. My father cut insoles out of cardboard, and I wore those in my shoes. As long as I had to stay in the house anyway, they were all right.

I stayed cooped up in the house, without any companionship. We didn't take a Sunday paper any more, but the Barry Adage came every week in the mails; and though I did not read small print, I could see the Santa Clauses and holly wreaths in the advertisements.

There was a calendar in the kitchen. The red days were Sundays and holidays; and that red 25 was Christmas. (It was on a Monday, and the two red figures would come right together in 1893; but this represents research in the World Almanac, not memory.) I knew when Sunday was, because I could look out of the window and see the neighbor's children, all dressed up, going to Sunday school. I knew just when Christmas was going to be.

But there was something queer! My father and mother didn't say a word about Christmas. And once, when I spoke of it, there was a strange, embarrassed silence; so I didn't say anything more about it. But I wondered, and was troubled. Why didn't they say anything about it? Was what I had said I wanted (memory refuses to supply that detail) too expensive?

I wasn't arrogant and talkative now. I was silent and frightened. What was the matter? Why didn't my father and mother say anything about Christmas? As the day approached, my chest grew tighter with anxiety.

Now it was the day before Christmas. I couldn't be mistaken. But not a word about it from my father and mother. I waited in painful bewilderment all day. I had supper with them, and was allowed to sit up for an hour. I was waiting for them to say something. "It's time for you to go to bed," my mother said gently. I *had* to say something.

"This is Christmas Eve, isn't it?" I asked, as if I didn't know.

My father and mother looked at one another. Then my mother looked away. Her face was pale and stony. My father cleared his throat, and his face took on a joking look. He pretended he hadn't known it was Christmas Eve, because he hadn't been reading the papers. He said he would go downtown and find out.

My mother got up and walked out of the room. I didn't want my father to have to keep on being funny about it, so I got up and went to bed. I went by myself without having a light. I undressed in the dark and crawled into bed.

I was numb. As if I had hit by something. It was hard to breathe. I ached all through. I was stunned—with finding out the truth.

My body knew before my mind quite did. In a minute, when I could think, my mind would know. And as the pain in my body ebbed, the pain in my mind began. I *knew*. I couldn't put it into words yet. But I knew why I had taken only a little bag of potatoes to Sunday school that fall. I knew why there had been only pennies in my little yellow envelope. I knew why I hadn't gone to school that fall—why I hadn't any new shoes—why we had been living on potato soup all winter. All these things, and others, many others, fitted themselves together in my mind, and meant something.

Then the words came into my mind and I whispered them into the darkness:

"We're poor!"

That was it. I was one of those poor children I had been sorry for, when I heard about them in Sunday school. My mother hadn't told me. My father was out of work, and we hadn't any money. That was why there wasn't going to be any Christmas at our house.

Then I remembered something that made me squirm with shame—a boast. (Memory will not yield this up. Had I said to some Nice little boy, "I'm going to be President of the United States"? Or to a Nice little girl: "I'll marry you when I grow up."? It was some boast as horribly shameful to remember.)

"We're poor." There in bed in the dark, I whispered it over and over to myself. I was making myself get used to it. (Or—just torturing myself, as one

presses the tongue against a sore tooth? No, memory says not like that—but to keep myself from ever being such a fool again: suffering now, to keep this awful thing from ever happening again. Memory is clear on that; it was more like pulling the tooth, to get it over with—never mind the pain, this will be the end!)

It wasn't so bad, now that I knew. I just *hadn't known!* I had thought all sorts of foolish things: that I was going to Ann Arbor—going to be a lawyer—going to make speeches in the Square, going to be President. Now I knew better.

I had wanted (something) for Christmas. I didn't want it, now. I didn't want anything.

I lay there in the dark, feeling the cold emotion of renunciation. (The tendrils of desire unfold their clasp on the outer world of objects, withdraw, shrivel up. Wishes shrivel up, turn black, die. It is like that.)

It hurt. But nothing would ever hurt again. I would never let myself want anything again.

I lay there stretched out straight and stiff in the dark, my fists clenched hard upon Nothing. . . .

In the morning it had been like a nightmare that is not clearly remembered—that one wishes to forget. Though I hadn't hung up any stocking, there was one hanging at the foot of my bed. A bag of popcorn, and a lead pencil, for me. They had done the best they could, now they realized that I knew about Christmas. But they needn't have thought they had to. I didn't want anything.

QUESTIONS FOR CRITICAL ANALYSIS

1. Why did Dell's mother tell him not to sign the envelope with his donation to the poor? Do you think the teacher knew why his name wasn't on the envelope? Did Dell know why?
2. What does Dell reveal about himself in the first paragraph of the narration? What is significant about this revelation? Name other ways throughout the essay when he reveals this condition.
3. Can you recall a time when you felt a physical reaction to an emotional change? How would you describe the shift from a bodily response to a mental response? Does your experience affect your response to this essay?
4. Dell's concern for the poor echoes throughout the essay. Find instances when he describes how he feels. When he discovers that he is one of "the poor," does he feel sorry for himself? If so, in what way? If not, how do you know? If he isn't feeling sorry for himself, what does he feel?
5. Compare Langston Hughes' essay, "Salvation," with Dell's "We're Poor." The young boys in each essay make life-altering discoveries about themselves. In what ways are their experiences similar? dissimilar?

Questions for Structural Analysis

1. How does Dell's parenthetical introduction about memory relate to the narration that follows? What does it explain about memory? Why is that explanation important to the rest of the essay?
2. Look carefully at paragraph 15 which begins: "I was numb. . . ." How would you characterize the sentence structure in that paragraph? Why does Dell use a sentence fragment? Is it effective? What is the emotional impact of the paragraph, and how do the sentences help create that effect?
3. Dell makes sure that the reader knows about his family's poverty long before he, as a child in the story, does. Why? How did this foreknowledge shape your response to the essay?
4. In this essay Floyd Dell the adult writes about himself as a child. He uses parenthetical asides to provide additional information and an adult perspective to events of the past. How did you react to these interruptions? Were they useful in telling the story? Why did Dell include them?
5. How does the conclusion of the essay relate to the parenthetical introduction about memory?

Shame

Dick Gregory

Dick Gregory (1932–) is an author, civil rights activist, comedian, diet and exercise enthusiast. "Shame," an excerpt from his autobiography Nigger *(1964), describes how Gregory learned to feel ashamed of himself and his poverty. The teacher's remarks dramatically altered his self-perception, affecting his behavior both in school and in the neighborhood. Dick Gregory has spent much of his life teaching others to know themselves, changing if they want to but accepting what they are in any case. In 1968 he ran for president of the United States on the Peace & Freedom Party platform.*

Before you begin reading: *Recall a life-changing event in your life. In a ten-minute session, write about that experience in your reading notebook: what happened? how did it change your life? did others know about the change? how did they respond to you?*

◆

I NEVER LEARNED HATE AT HOME, OR SHAME. I HAD TO GO to school for that. I was about seven years old when I got my first big lesson. I was in love with a little girl named Helene Tucker, a light-complected little girl with pigtails and nice manners. She was always clean and she was smart in school. I think I went to school then mostly to look at her. I brushed my hair and even got me a little old handkerchief. It was a lady's handkerchief, but I didn't want Helene to see me wipe my nose on my hand. The pipes were frozen again, there was no water in the house, but I washed my socks and shirt every night. I'd get a pot, and go over to Mister Ben's grocery store, and stick my pot down into his soda machine. Scoop out some chopped ice. By evening the ice melted to water for washing. I got sick a lot that winter because the fire would go out at night before the clothes were dry. In the morning I'd put them on, wet or dry, because they were the only clothes I had.

Everybody's got a Helene Tucker, a symbol of everything you want. I loved her for her goodness, her cleanness, her popularity. She'd walk down my street and my brothers and sisters would yell, "Here comes Helene," and I'd rub my tennis sneakers on the back of my pants and wish my hair wasn't so nappy and the white folks' shirt fit me better. I'd run out on the street. If I knew my place and didn't come too close, she'd wink at me and say hello. That was a good feeling. Sometimes I'd follow her all the way home, and shovel the snow off her walk and try to make friends with her Momma and her aunts. I'd drop money on her stoop late at night on my way back from shining shoes in the taverns. And she had a Daddy, and he had a good job. He was a paper hanger.

I guess I would have gotten over Helene by summertime, but something happened in that classroom that made her face hang in front of me for the next twenty-two years. When I played the drums in high school it was for Helene and when I broke track records in college it was for Helene and when I started standing behind microphones and heard applause I wished Helene could hear it, too. It wasn't until I was twenty-nine years old and married and making money that I finally got her out of my system. Helene was sitting in that classroom when I learned to be ashamed of myself.

It was on a Thursday. I was sitting in the back of the room, in a seat with a chalk circle drawn around it. The idiot's seat, the troublemaker's seat.

The teacher thought I was stupid. Couldn't spell, couldn't read, couldn't do arithmetic. Just stupid. Teachers were never interested in finding out that you couldn't concentrate because you were so hungry, because you hadn't had any breakfast. All you could think about was noontime, would it ever come? Maybe you could sneak into the cloakroom and steal a bite of some kid's lunch out of a coat pocket. A bite of something. Paste. You can't really make a meal of paste, or put it on bread for a sandwich, but sometimes I'd scoop a few spoonfuls out of the big paste jar in the back of the room. Pregnant people get strange tastes. I was pregnant with poverty. Pregnant with dirt and pregnant with smells that made people turn away, pregnant with cold and pregnant with shoes that were never bought for me, pregnant with five other people in my bed and no Daddy in the next room, and pregnant with hunger. Paste doesn't taste too bad when you're hungry.

The teacher thought I was a troublemaker. All she saw from the front of the room was a little black boy who squirmed in his idiot's seat and made noises and poked the kids around him. I guess she couldn't see a kid who made noises because he wanted someone to know he was there.

It was on a Thursday, the day before the Negro payday. The eagle always flew on Friday. The teacher was asking each student how much his father would give to the Community Chest. On Friday night, each kid would get the money from his father, and on Monday he would bring it to the school. I decided I was going to buy me a Daddy right then. I had money in my pocket from shining shoes and selling papers, and whatever Helene Tucker pledged for her Daddy I was going to top it. And I'd hand the money right in. I wasn't going to wait until Monday to buy me a Daddy.

I was shaking, scared to death. The teacher opened her book and started calling out names alphabetically.

"Helene Tucker?"

"My Daddy said he'd give two dollars and fifty cents."

"That's very nice, Helene. Very, very nice indeed."

That made me feel pretty good. It wouldn't take too much to top that. I had almost three dollars in dimes and quarters in my pocket. I stuck my hand in my pocket and held onto the money, waiting for her to call my name. But the teacher closed her book after she called everybody else in the class.

I stood up and raised my hand.

"What is it now?"

"You forgot me."

She turned toward the blackboard. "I don't have time to be playing with you, Richard."

"My Daddy said he'd . . ."

"Sit down, Richard, you're disturbing the class."

"My Daddy said he'd give . . . fifteen dollars."

She turned around and looked mad. "We are collecting this money for you and your kind, Richard Gregory. If your Daddy can give fifteen dollars you have no business being on relief."

"I got it right now, I got it right now, my Daddy gave it to me to turn in today, my Daddy said . . ."

"And furthermore," she said, looking right at me, her nostrils getting big and her lips getting thin and her eyes opening wide. "We know you don't have a Daddy."

Helene Tucker turned around, her eyes full of tears. She felt sorry for me. Then I couldn't see her too well because I was crying, too.

"Sit down, Richard."

And I always thought the teacher kind of liked me. She always picked me to wash the blackboard on Friday, after school. That was a big thrill, it made me feel important. If I didn't wash it, come Monday the school might not function right.

"Where are you going, Richard?"

I walked out of school that day, and for a long time I didn't go back very often. There was shame there.

Now there was shame everywhere. It seemed like the whole world had been inside that classroom, everyone had heard what the teacher had said, everyone had turned around and felt sorry for me. There was shame in going to the Worthy Boys Annual Christmas Dinner for you and your kind, because everybody knew what a worthy boy was. Why couldn't they just call it the Boys Annual Dinner, why'd they have to give it a name? There was shame in wearing the brown and orange and white plaid mackinaw the welfare gave to 3,000 boys. Why'd it have to be the same for everybody so when you walked down the street the people could see you were on relief? It was a nice warm mackinaw and it had a hood, and my Momma beat me and called me a little rat when she found out I stuffed it in the bottom of a pail full of garbage way over on Cottage Street. There was shame in running over to Mister Ben's at the end of the day and asking for his rotten peaches, there was shame in asking Mrs. Simmons for a spoonful of sugar, there was shame in running out to meet the relief truck. I hated that truck, full of food for you and your kind. I ran into the house and hid when it came. And then I started to sneak through alleys, to take the long way home so the people going into White's Eat Shop wouldn't see me. Yeah, the whole world heard the teacher that day, we all know you don't have a Daddy.

QUESTIONS FOR CRITICAL ANALYSIS

1. List examples of the teacher's insensitive treatment of Gregory. Do you think she was aware of the consequences of her actions? Can you make a case in her defense?
2. Gregory describes the debilitating effect of poverty on a child's education. In 1988, 40 percent of America's poor were children; one school-age child in four lived in a family whose income was below the poverty line. What role should schools play in facing this social crisis? When you answer, remember Floyd Dell's educational experiences in the previous selection. If you were in a position to make educational institutions responsive to students who live in poverty, what would you do?
3. How did Gregory try to "buy me a Daddy"? Why did he do that? What was the result of his action?
4. What did Helene Tucker mean to Gregory as a boy? How do you know? He says he "finally got her out of my system" twenty-two years later. Do you believe him? Why, or why not?
5. In what ways was Gregory's experience in "Shame" similar to Dell's in "We're Poor"? In what ways was it different?

QUESTIONS FOR STRUCTURAL ANALYSIS

1. Gregory identifies the theme of his essay in the first three sentences, and then he seems to go off on a tangent about Helene Tucker. What did you think he was doing when you read the essay? Was the introduction of Helene Tucker too abrupt?
2. The character Helene Tucker helped Gregory develop his narrative. How is she described? What is Gregory's reaction to her? What did she represent for him? Why is this sort of character necessary to the story?
3. The first paragraph introduces us to the two major ideas of the essay: the unapproachable Helene Tucker and the Gregory family's poverty. What is Gregory's tone in this paragraph? When during the essay does the mood darken? What emotion dominates by the end of the essay?
4. Until the incident in the classroom, Gregory has told the reader about his experiences and what his life was like. When he gets to that Thursday in class, he switches to dialogue to carry the story. Why does he use this technique? Is it more effective? Why, or why not?
5. Examine the descriptive details, word choice, and sentence structure of the final paragraph, and discuss the ways Gregory stresses the theme of shame and his own awareness of personal shame.

*F*INDING *O*UT *W*HO *W*E *A*RE

TOPICS FOR WRITING ESSAYS

Many of the questions following each essay can serve as appropriate writing suggestions. The topics listed below expand the prereading exercises, but they can be used without completing that step first.

1. In writing a personal profile for the college placement office, you are asked to write an autobiographical essay that focuses on an idea that shapes your life. Use the material that surfaced in the Dillard prereading exercise as a basis for the essay.
2. Consider the portrayal of the teachers and students in Dell's essay and in Gregory's essay. Use these portrayals as a starting point to write an essay defending the schools; or one suggesting ways they could improve their sensitivity toward all students; or compare these people with those in your elementary school. Write your essay to the Parent-Teacher Association at your old school.
3. Use the Gregory prereading exercise as the basis for writing a narrative essay describing your life-changing event. Write your essay to an adult you admire and who has influenced your life.
4. How did you feel the first time you really understood what the Holocaust was? How did it change your feelings about the human race and its possibilities for cruelty? for survival? Use ideas that grow out of the Wiesel prereading exercise to develop an essay charting your learning experience. Write this essay to a friend who doesn't know much about the Holocaust and has never really considered its implications.

RESEARCH POSSIBILITIES

1. Think of a major event in everyone's growing up experiences: learning that Santa Claus isn't real, the first unchaperoned date, the first crush on a boy or girl, the worst embarrassment in grade school. Interview five or more people to hear the stories of their experiences. Write a paper that uses these stories as the basis for generalizing about the event. Your paper will appear as a feature in the student newspaper.

2. Why is the number of homeless Americans growing at such a rapid rate? Who works with the homeless in your community, and what do they do? What local policy is there to aid the homeless? Your research will take you to local newspaper files, city government, church and civic organizations, and to those who work with the homeless so that you can gather documents and information and even interview community leaders. Analyze the effort in your community for the homeless in an essay directed to the newspaper.

3. What is being done in your community to help the children living in poverty? Using the same research sources as those described above, find out how children are being served and can be better served. Write a position paper advocating college student participation in helping disadvantaged children in your community. Address your paper to your college president and the dean of student affairs.

*L*EARNING *O*UR *R*ESPONSIBILITIES

Martin Luther King, Jr., defines narration by describing how Jesus "pulls the question from mid-air and places it on a dangerous curve between Jerusalem and Jericho." The writers in this section use the narrative technique to bring home the force of their ideas by involving the reader's emotions as well as thoughts.

MARGARET SANGER, "MY FIGHT FOR BIRTH CONTROL"

MAXINE HONG KINGSTON, "NO NAME WOMAN"

JUTHICA STANGL, "INDIA: A WIDOW'S DEVASTATING CHOICE"

MARTIN LUTHER KING, JR., "ON BEING A GOOD NEIGHBOR"

My Fight for *Birth Control*

Margaret Sanger

Margaret Sanger (1879–1966) was one of eleven children born to a woman who died when Margaret was 17. Sanger referred to her mother, and women like her, as "breeders" and spent her life helping women free themselves from a life of yearly childbearing. Sanger had a difficult time getting public support for her work, although medical professors soon helped her make birth control information widely available, and in 1936 the U. S. District Court upheld the right to disseminate the information. In 1937 the American Medical Association publicly endorsed birth control.

Before you begin reading: *Birth control, planned parenthood, freedom of choice, and abortion are volatile subjects. In your notebook, write a paragraph describing your thoughts about each subject.*

◆

EARLY IN THE YEAR 1912 I CAME TO A SUDDEN REALIZATION that my work as a nurse and my activities in social service were entirely palliative and consequently futile and useless to relieve the misery I saw all about me.

For several years I had had the good fortune to have the children's paternal grandmother living with us and sharing in their care, thereby releasing more of my time and renewed energy for the many activities and professional work of the nursing field. I had longed for this opportunity, and it now enabled me to share in the financial responsibility of the home, which, owing to the heavy expenditures caused by my illness, I felt was the only self-respecting thing to do. I eventually took special obstetrical and surgical cases assigned to me from time to time, and had glimpses into the lives of rich and poor alike.

When I look back upon that period it seems only a short time ago; yet in the brief interval conditions have changed enormously. At that time it was not the usual thing for a poor woman to go to a hospital to give birth to her baby. She preferred to stay at home. She was afraid of hospitals when any serious ailment was involved. That is not the case today. Women of all classes are more likely to have their babies in lying-in hospitals or in private sanatoriums than at home; but in those days a woman's own bedroom, no matter how inconveniently arranged, was the usual place for confinement. That was the day of home nursing, and it gave a trained nurse splendid opportunities to learn social conditions through actual contact with them.

Were it possible for me to depict the revolting conditions existing in the homes of some of the women I attended in that one year, one would find it hard to believe. There was at that time, and doubtless is still today, a sub-stratum of men and women whose lives are absolutely untouched by social agencies.

The way they live is almost beyond belief. They hate and fear any prying into their homes or into their lives. They resent being talked to. The women slink in and out of their homes on their way to market like rats from their holes. The men beat their wives sometimes black and blue, but no one interferes. The children are cuffed, kicked and chased about, but woe to the child who dares to tell tales out of the home! Crime or drink is often the source of this secret aloofness; usually there is something to hide, a skeleton in the closet somewhere. The men are sullen, unskilled workers, picking up odd jobs now and then, unemployed usually, sauntering in and out of the house at all hours of the day and night.

The women keep apart from other women in the neighborhood. Often they are suspected of picking a pocket or "lifting" an article when occasion arises. Pregnancy is an almost chronic condition amongst them. I knew one woman who had given birth to eight children with no professional care whatever. The last one was born in the kitchen, witnessed by a son of ten years who, under his mother's direction, cleaned the bed, wrapped the placenta and soiled articles in paper, and threw them out of the window into the court below.

They reject help of any kind and want you to "mind your own business." Birth and death they consider their own affairs. They survive as best they can, suspicious of everyone, deathly afraid of police and officials of every kind.

They are the submerged, untouched classes which no labor union, no church nor organization of a highly expensive, organized city ever reaches and rarely tries to reach. They are beyond the scope of organized charity or religion; not even the Salvation Army touches them. It was a sad consolation to hear other women in the stratum just slightly above breathe contented sighs and thank God that they had not sunk so low as that.

It is among the mothers here that the most difficult problems arise—the outcasts of society with theft, filth, perjury, cruelty, brutality oozing from beneath.

Ignorance and neglect go on day by day; children born to breathe but a few hours and pass out of life; pregnant women toiling early and late to give food to four or five children, always hungry; boarders taken into homes where there is not sufficient room for the family; little girls eight and ten years of age sleeping in the same room with dirty, foul smelling, loathsome men; women whose weary, pregnant, shapeless bodies refuse to accommodate themselves to the husbands' desires find husbands looking with lustful eyes upon other women, sometimes upon their own little daughters, six and seven years of age.

In this atmosphere abortions and birth become the main theme of conversation. On Saturday nights I have seen groups of fifty to one hundred women going into questionable offices well known in the community for cheap abortions. I asked several women what took place there, and they all gave the same reply: a quick examination, a probe inserted into the uterus and turned a few times to disturb the fertilized ovum, and then the woman was sent home. Usually the flow began the next day and often continued four or five weeks. Sometimes an ambulance carried the victim to the hospital for a curetage, and if she returned home at all she was looked upon as a lucky woman.

This state of things became a nightmare with me. There seemed no sense to it all, no reason for such waste of mother life, no right to exhaust women's vitality and to throw them on the scrap-heap before the age of thirty-five.

Everywhere I looked, misery and fear stalked—men fearful of losing their jobs, women fearful that even worse conditions might come upon them. The menace of another pregnancy hung like a sword over the head of every poor woman I came in contact with that year. The question which met me was always the same: What can I do to keep from it? or, What can I do to get out of this? Sometimes they talked among themselves bitterly.

"It's the rich that know the tricks," they'd say, "while we have all the kids." Then, if the women were Roman Catholics, they talked about "Yankee tricks," and asked me if I knew what the Protestants did to keep their families down. When I said that I didn't believe that the rich knew much more than they did I was laughed at and suspected of holding back information for money. They would nudge each other and say something about paying me before I left the case if I would reveal the "secret."

It all sickened me. It was heartbreaking to witness the rapt, anxious, eager expression on their pale, worried faces as I told them necessary details concerning cleanliness and hygiene of their sex organs. It was appalling how little they knew of the terms I was using, yet how familiar they were with those organs and their functions and how unafraid to try anything, no matter what the results.

I heard over and over again of their desperate efforts at bringing themselves "around"—drinking various herb-teas, taking drops of turpentine on sugar, steaming over a chamber of boiling coffee or of turpentine water, rolling down stairs, and finally inserting slippery-elm sticks, or knitting needles, or shoe hooks into the uterus. I used to shudder with horror as I heard the details and, worse yet, learned of the conditions *behind the reason* for such desperate actions. Day after day these stories were poured into my ears. I knew hundreds of these women personally, and knew much of their hopeless, barren, dreary lives.

What relief I had came when I shifted my work for a few weeks to the then fashionable Riverside Drive or to the upper western section of New York City, but inevitably I was called back into the lower East or West Side as if magnetically attracted by its misery.

The contrast in conditions seemed only to intensify the horrors of those poverty-stricken homes, and each time I returned it was to hear that Mrs. Cohen had been carried to a hospital but had never come back, that Mrs. Kelly had sent the children to a neighbor's and had put her head into the gas oven to end her misery. Many of the women had consulted midwives, social workers and doctors at the dispensary and asked a way to limit their families, but they were denied this help, sometimes indignantly or gruffly, sometimes jokingly; but always knowledge was denied them. Life for them had but one choice: either to abandon themselves to incessant childbearing, or to terminate their pregnancies through abortions. Is it any wonder they resigned themselves hopelessly, as the Jewish and Italian mothers, or fell into drunkenness, as the Irish and Scotch? The latter were often beaten by husbands, as well as by their sons and daughters. They were driven and cowed, and only as beasts of burden were allowed to exist. Life for them was full of fear.

Words fail to express the impressions these lives made on my sensitive nature. My own happy love life became a reproach. These other lives began to clutch at all I held dear. The intimate knowledge of these misshapen, hapless, desperate women seemed to separate me from the right of happiness.

They claimed my thoughts night and day. One by one these women, with their worried, sad, pensive and ageing faces would marshal themselves before me in my dreams, sometimes appealingly, sometimes accusingly. I could not escape from the facts of their misery, neither was I able to see the way out of their problems and their troubles. Like one walking in a sleep, I kept on.

Finally the thing began to shape itself, to become accumulative during the three weeks I spent in the home of a desperately sick woman living on Grand Street, a lower section of New York's East Side.

Mrs. Sacks was only twenty-eight years old; her husband, an unskilled worker, thirty-two. Three children, aged five, three and one, were none too strong nor sturdy, and it took all the earnings of the father and the ingenuity of the mother to keep them clean, provide them with air and proper food, and give them a chance to grow into decent manhood and womanhood.

Both parents were devoted to these children and to each other. The woman had become pregnant and had taken various drugs and purgatives, as advised by her neighbors. Then, in desperation, she had used some instrument lent to her by a friend. She was found prostrate on the floor amidst the crying children when her husband returned from work. Neighbors advised against the ambulance, and a friendly doctor was called. The husband would not hear of her going to a hospital, and as a little money had been saved in the bank a nurse was called and the battle for that precious life began.

It was in the middle of July. The three-room apartment was turned into a hospital for the dying patient. Never had I worked so fast, never so concentratedly as I did to keep alive that little mother. Neighbor women came and went during the day doing the odds and ends necessary for our comfort. The children were sent to friends and relatives and the doctor and I settled ourselves to outdo the force and power of an outraged nature.

Never had I known such conditions could exist. July's sultry days and nights were melted into a torpid inferno. Day after day, night after night, I slept only in brief snatches, ever too anxious about the condition of that feeble heart bravely carrying on, to stay long from the bedside of the patient. With but one toilet for the building and that on the floor below, everything had to be carried down for disposal, while ice, food and other necessities had to be carried three flights up. It was one of those old airshaft buildings of which there were several thousands then standing in New York City.

At the end of two weeks recovery was in sight, and at the end of three weeks I was preparing to leave the fragile patient to take up the ordinary duties of her life, including those of wifehood and motherhood. Everyone was congratulating her on her recovery. All the kindness of sympathetic and understanding neighbors poured in upon her in the shape of convalescent dishes, soups, custards, and drinks. Still she appeared to be despondent and worried. She seemed to sit apart in her thoughts as if she had no part in these congratulatory messages and endearing welcomes. I thought at first that she still retained some of her unconscious memories and dwelt upon them in her silences.

But as the hour for my departure came nearer, her anxiety increased, and finally with trembling voice she said: "Another baby will finish me, I suppose."

"It's too early to talk about that," I said, and resolved that I would turn the question over to the doctor for his advice. When he came I said: "Mrs. Sacks is worried about having another baby."

"She well might be," replied the doctor, and then he stood before her and said: "Any more such capers, young woman, and there will be no need to call me."

"Yes, yes—I know, Doctor," said the patient with trembling voice, "but," and she hesitated as if it took all of her courage to say it, "*what* can I do to prevent getting that way again?"

"Oh ho!" laughed the doctor good naturedly, "You want your cake while you eat it too, do you? Well, it can't be done." Then, familiarly slapping her on the back and picking up his hat and bag to depart, he said: "I'll tell you the only sure thing to do. Tell Jake to sleep on the roof!"

With those words he closed the door and went down the stairs, leaving us both petrified and stunned.

Tears sprang to my eyes, and a lump came in my throat as I looked at that face before me. It was stamped with sheer horror. I thought for a moment she might have gone insane, but she conquered her feelings, whatever they may have been, and turning to me in desperation said: "He can't understand, can he?—he's a man after all—but you do, don't you? You're a woman and you'll tell me the secret and I'll never tell it to a soul."

She clasped her hands as if in prayer, she leaned over and looked straight into my eyes and beseechingly implored me to tell her something—something *I really did not know*. It was like being on a rack and tortured for a crime one had not committed. To plead guilty would stop the agony; otherwise the rack kept turning.

I had to turn away from that imploring face. I could not answer her then. I quieted her as best I could. She saw that I was moved by the tears in my eyes. I promised that I would come back in a few days and tell her what she wanted to know. The few simple means of limiting the family like *coitus interruptus* or the condom were laughed at by the neighboring women when told these were the means used by men in the well-to-do families. That was not believed, and I knew such an answer would be swept aside as useless were I to tell her this at such a time.

A little later when she slept I left the house, and made up my mind that I'd keep away from those cases in the future. I felt helpless to do anything at all. I seemed chained hand and foot, and longed for an earthquake or a volcano to shake the world out of its lethargy into facing these monstrous atrocities.

The intelligent reasoning of the young mother—how to *prevent* getting that way again—how sensible, how just she had been—yes, I promised myself I'd go back and have a long talk with her and tell her more, and perhaps she would not laugh but would believe that those methods were all that were really known.

But time flew past, and weeks rolled into months. That wistful, appealing face haunted me day and night. I could not banish from my mind memories of that trembling voice begging so humbly for knowledge she had a right to have. I was about to retire one night three months later when the telephone rang and an agitated man's voice begged me to come at once to help his wife who was sick again. It was the husband of Mrs. Sacks, and I intuitively knew before I left the telephone that it was almost useless to go.

I dreaded to face that woman. I was tempted to send someone else in my place. I longed for an accident on the subway, or on the street—anything to prevent my going into that home. But on I went just the same. I arrived a few minutes after the doctor, the same one who had given her such noble advice. The woman was dying. She was unconscious. She died within ten minutes after my arrival. It was the same result, the same story told a thousand times before—death from abortion. She had become pregnant, had used drugs, had then consulted a five-dollar professional abortionist, and death followed.

The doctor shook his head as he rose from listening for the heart beat. I knew she had already passed on; without a groan, a sigh or recognition of our belated presence she had gone into the Great Beyond as thousands of mothers go every year. I looked at that drawn face now stilled in death. I placed her thin hands across her breast and recalled how hard they had pleaded with me on that last memorable occasion of parting. The gentle woman, the devoted mother, the loving wife had passed on leaving behind her a frantic husband, helpless in his loneliness, bewildered in his helplessness as he paced up and down the room, hands clenching his head, moaning "My God! My God! My God!"

The Revolution came—but not as it has been pictured nor as history relates that revolutions have come. It came in my own life. It began in my very being as I walked home that night after I had closed the eyes and covered with a sheet the body of that little helpless mother whose life had been sacrificed to ignorance.

After I left that desolate house I walked and walked and walked; for hours and hours I kept on, bag in hand, thinking, regretting, dreading to stop; fearful of my conscience, dreading to face my own accusing soul. At three in the morning I arrived home still clutching a heavy load the weight of which I was quite unconscious.

I entered the house quietly, as was my custom, and looked out of the window down upon the dimly lighted, sleeping city. As I stood at the window and looked out, the miseries and problems of that sleeping city arose before me in a clear vision like a panorama: crowded homes, too many children; babies dying in infancy; mothers overworked; baby nurseries; children neglected and hungry—mothers so nervously wrought they could not give the little things the comfort nor care they needed; mothers half sick most of their lives—"always ailing, never failing"; women made into drudges; children working in cellars; children aged six and seven pushed into the labor market to help earn a living; another baby on the way; still another; yet another; a baby born dead—great relief; an older child dies—sorrow, but nevertheless relief—insurance helps; a mother's death—children scattered into institutions; the father, desperate, drunken; he slinks away to become an outcast in a society which has trapped him.

Another picture of the young couple full of hope with faith in themselves. They start life fresh. They are brave and courageous. The first baby is welcome; parents and relatives come from near and far to witness this mystery. The next year the second baby arrives; all agree it's a little early, but husband receives congratulations. The third child arrives, and yet a fourth. Within five years four children are born. The mother, racked and worn, decides this can't go on, and attempts to interrupt the next pregnancy. The siren of the ambulance—death of the mother—orphan children—poverty, misery, slums, child labor, unhappiness, ignorance, destitution!

One after another these pictures unreeled themselves before me. For hours I stood, motionless and tense, expecting something to happen. I watched the lights go out, I saw the darkness gradually give way to the first shimmer of dawn, and then a colorful sky heralded the rise of the sun. I knew a new day had come for me and a new world as well.

It was like an illumination. I could now see clearly the various social strata of our life; all its mass problems seemed to be centered around uncontrolled breeding. There was only one thing to be done: call out, start the alarm, set the heather on fire! Awaken the womanhood of America to free the motherhood of the world! I released from my almost paralyzed hand the nursing bag which unconsciously I had clutched, threw it across the room, tore the uniform from my body, flung it into a corner, and renounced all palliative work forever.

I would never go back again to nurse women's ailing bodies while their miseries were as vast as the stars. I was now finished with superficial cures, with doctors and nurses and social workers who were brought face to face with this overwhelming truth of women's needs and yet turned to pass on the other side. They must be made to see these facts. I resolved that women should have knowledge of contraception. They have every right to know about their own bodies. I would strike out—I would scream from the housetops. I would tell the world what was going on in the lives of these poor women. I *would* be heard. No matter what it should cost. *I would be heard.*

I went to bed and slept.

That decision gave me the first undisturbed sleep I had had in over a year. I slept soundly and free from dreams, free from haunting faces.

I announced to my family the following day that I had finished nursing, that I would never go on another case—and I never have.

QUESTIONS FOR CRITICAL ANALYSIS

1. How do you characterize the audience for this selection? How do Sanger's images and words reveal Sanger's tone?
2. Turn back to Dick Gregory's essay, "Shame," and reread the fifth paragraph in which he writes, "I was pregnant with poverty." This idea echoes throughout Sanger's essay and is developed with vivid examples and illustrations. What responsibility does the rest of society have toward those who live in poverty? How would Sanger answer that question?
3. Is Sanger's characterization of men positive or negative? How does she describe them? Is she fair? Why, or why not?
4. The poor women Sanger describes want, more than anything, information on how to prevent yearly pregnancies. Why was such information not available? Why did the doctor joke around when they asked him?
5. How did Sanger's life change because of the misery she saw? In what ways does her experience compare to those of Hughes, Dell, and Gregory in the previous section?

QUESTIONS FOR STRUCTURAL ANALYSIS

1. Sanger writes in great detail about the quality of life experienced by poor women. List images (metaphors, similes) and examples of word choice Sanger uses both to describe the poverty and to let you know her responses to it.
2. In what ways does Sanger reveal her own personality and life style? How does she change through the story?
3. Sanger, like Dell and Gregory, undergoes a life-changing experience. However, in her story there is no single, dramatic event. With this in mind, discuss the importance of her use of a time-chronology narration to write the essay.
4. How is the story of the Sacks family pivotal to the essay? How would you describe the family? What was their relationship with their neighbors? What is the significance of the episode with the doctor?
5. Look carefully at the section that follows the asterisk break. Why did Sanger use the asterisks to emphasize a break in the narration? How is the style of this section different from the earlier part of the essay?

No Name Woman

Maxine Hong Kingston

Maxine Hong Kingston (1940–), a second-generation Chinese-American, focused her first book, Woman Warrior: Memoirs of a Girlhood Among Ghosts *(1975), on family stories that help her identify who she is: Is she Chinese? Is she American? What is her responsibility to her heritage? A reviewer described* Woman Warrior *as "short and elliptical. It sounds like a Chinese translation, with simple sentences and flat direct statements. As in poetry, much is left to the reader." "No Name Woman," the story of her aunt's suicide and infanticide, is the first selection in this collection.*

Before you begin reading: *Think about a member of your family (immediate family or ancestor) who is often held up as a model of good or bad behavior, or who made wise or unwise decisions. Write a paragraph or two in your reading notebook about what you know about this relative. Then, write a paragraph about how you feel toward this person.*

◆

"You must not tell anyone," my mother said, "what I am about to tell you. In China your father had a sister who killed herself. She jumped into the family well. We say that your father has all brothers because it is as if she had never been born.

"In 1924 just a few days after our village celebrated seventeen hurry-up weddings—to make sure that every young man who went 'out on the road' would responsibly come home—your father and his brothers and your grandfather and his brothers and your aunt's new husband sailed for America, the Gold Mountain. It was your grandfather's last trip. Those lucky enough to get contracts waved goodbye from the decks. They fed and guarded the stowaways and helped them off in Cuba, New York, Bali, Hawaii. 'We'll meet in California next year,' they said. All of them sent money home.

"I remember looking at your aunt one day when she and I were dressing; I had not noticed before that she had such a protruding melon of a stomach. But I did not think, 'She's pregnant,' until she began to look like other pregnant women, her shirt pulling and the white tops of her black pants showing. She could not have been pregnant, you see, because her husband had been gone for years. No one said anything. We did not discuss it. In early summer she was ready to have the child, long after the time when it could have been possible.

"The village had also been counting. On the night the baby was to be born the villagers raided our house. Some were crying. Like a great saw, teeth strung with lights, files of people walked zigzag across our land, tearing the rice. Their lanterns doubled in the disturbed black water, which drained away through the broken bunds. As the villagers closed in, we could see that some of them, probably men and women we knew well, wore white masks. The people with long hair hung it over their faces. Women with short hair made it stand up on end. Some had tied white bands around their foreheads, arms, and legs.

"At first they threw mud and rocks at the house. Then they threw eggs and began slaughtering our stock. We could hear the animals scream their deaths—the roosters, the pigs, a last great roar from the ox. Familiar wild heads flared in our night windows; the villagers encircled us. Some of the faces stopped to peer at us, their eyes rushing like searchlights. The hands flattened against the panes, framed heads, and left red prints.

"The villagers broke in the front and the back doors at the same time, even though we had not locked the doors against them. Their knives dripped with the blood of our animals. They smeared blood on the doors and walls. One woman swung a chicken, whose throat she had slit, splattering blood in red arcs about her. We stood together in the middle of the house, in the family hall with the pictures and tables of the ancestors around us, and looked straight ahead.

"At that time the house had only two wings. When the men came back, we would build two more to enclose our courtyard and a third one to begin a second courtyard. The villagers pushed through both wings, even your grandparents' rooms, to find your aunt's, which was also mine until the men returned. From this room a new wing for one of the younger families would grow. They ripped up her clothes and shoes and broke her combs, grinding them underfoot. They tore her work from the loom. They scattered the cooking fire and rolled the new weaving in it. We could hear them in the kitchen breaking our bowls and banging the pots. They overturned the great waist-high earthenware jugs; duck eggs, pickled fruits, vegetables burst out and mixed in acrid torrents. The old woman from the next field swept a broom through the air and loosed the spirits-of-the-broom over our heads. 'Pig.' 'Ghost.' 'Pig,' they sobbed and scolded while they ruined our house.

"When they left, they took sugar and oranges to bless themselves. They cut pieces from the dead animals. Some of them took bowls that were not broken and clothes that were not torn. Afterward we swept up the rice and sewed it back up into sacks. But the smells from the spilled preserves lasted. Your aunt gave birth in the pigsty that night. The next morning when I went for the water, I found her and the baby plugging up the family well.

"Don't let your father know that I told you. He denies her. Now that you have started to menstruate, what happened to her could happen to you. Don't humiliate us. You wouldn't like to be forgotten as if you had never been born. The villagers are watchful."

Whenever she had to warn us about life, my mother told stories that ran like this one, a story to grow up on. She tested our strength to establish realities. Those in the emigrant generations who could not reassert brute survival died young and far from home. Those of us in the first American generations have had to figure out how the invisible world the emigrants built around our childhoods fit in solid America.

The emigrants confused the gods by diverting their curses, misleading them with crooked streets and false names. They must try to confuse their offspring as well, who, I suppose, threaten them in similar ways—always trying to get things straight, always trying to name the unspeakable. The Chinese I know hide their names; sojourners take new names when their lives change and guard their real names with silence.

Chinese-Americans, when you try to understand what things in you are Chinese, how do you separate what is peculiar to childhood, to poverty, insanities, one family, your mother who marked your growing with stories, from what is Chinese? What is Chinese tradition and what is the movies?

If I want to learn what clothes my aunt wore, whether flashy or ordinary, I would have to begin, "Remember Father's drowned-in-the-well sister?" I cannot ask that. My mother has told me once and for all the useful parts. She will add nothing unless powered by Necessity, a riverbank that guides her life. She plants vegetable gardens rather than lawns; she carries the odd-shaped tomatoes home from the fields and eats food left for the gods.

Whenever we did frivolous things, we used up energy; we flew high kites. We children came up off the ground over the melting cones our parents brought home from work and the American movie on New Year's Day—*Oh, You Beautiful Doll* with Betty Grable one year, and *She Wore a Yellow Ribbon* with John Wayne another year. After the one carnival ride each, we paid in guilt; our tired father counted his change on the dark walk home.

Adultery is extravagance. Could people who hatch their own chicks and eat the embryos and the heads for delicacies and boil the feet in vinegar for party food, leaving only the gravel, eating even the gizzard lining—could such people engender a prodigal aunt? To be a woman, to have a daughter in starvation time was a waste enough. My aunt could not have been the lone romantic who gave up everything for sex. Women in the old China did not choose. Some man had commanded her to lie with him and be his secret evil. I wonder whether he masked himself when he joined the raid on her family.

Perhaps she encountered him in the fields or on the mountain where the daughters-in-law collected fuel. Or perhaps he first noticed her in the marketplace. He was not a stranger because the village housed no strangers. She had to have dealings with him other than sex. Perhaps he worked an adjoining field, or he sold her the cloth for the dress she sewed and wore. His demand must have surprised, then terrified her. She obeyed him; she always did as she was told.

When the family found a young man in the next village to be her husband, she stood tractably beside the best rooster, his proxy, and promised before they met that she would be his forever. She was lucky that he was her age and she would be the first wife, an advantage secure now. The night she first saw him, he had sex with her. Then he left for America. She had almost forgotten what he looked like. When she tried to envision him, she only saw the black and white face in the group photograph the men had had taken before leaving.

The other man was not, after all, much different from her husband. They both gave orders: she followed. "If you tell your family, I'll beat you. I'll kill you. Be here again next week." No one talked sex, ever. And she might have separated the rapes from the rest of living if only she did not have to buy her oil from him or gather wood in the same forest. I want her fear to have lasted just as long as rape lasted so that the fear could have been contained. No drawn-out fear. But women at sex hazarded birth and hence lifetimes. The fear did not stop but permeated everywhere. She told the man, "I think I'm pregnant." He organized the raid against her.

On nights when my mother and father talked about their life back home, sometimes they mentioned an "outcast table" whose business they still seemed to be settling, their voices tight. In a commensal tradition, where food is precious, the powerful older people made wrongdoers eat alone. Instead of letting them start separate new lives like the Japanese, who could become samurais and geishas, the Chinese family, faces averted but eyes glowering sideways, hung on to the offenders and fed them leftovers. My aunt must have lived in the same house as my parents and eaten at an outcast table. My mother spoke about the raid as if she had seen it, when she and my aunt, a daughter-in-law to a different household, should not have been living together at all. Daughters-in-law lived with their husbands' parents, not their own; a synonym for marriage in Chinese is "taking a daughter-in-law." Her husband's parents could have sold her, mortgaged her, stoned her. But they had sent her back to her own mother and father, a mysterious act hinting at disgraces not told me. Perhaps they had thrown her out to deflect the avengers.

She was the only daughter; her four brothers went with her father, husband, and uncles "out on the road" and for some years became western men. When the goods were divided among the family, three of the brothers took land, and the youngest, my father, chose an education. After my grandparents gave their daughter away to her husband's family, they had dispensed all the adventure and all the property. They expected her to keep the traditional ways, which her brothers, now among the barbarians, could fumble without detection. The heavy, deep-rooted women were to maintain the past against the flood, safe for returning. But the rare urge west had fixed upon our family, and so my aunt crossed boundaries not delineated in space.

The work of preservation demands that the feelings playing about in one's guts not be turned into action. Just watch their passing like cherry blossoms. But perhaps my aunt, my forerunner, caught in a slow life, let dreams grow and fade and after some months or years went toward what persisted. Fear at the enormities of the forbidden kept her desires delicate, wire and bone. She looked at a man because she liked the way the hair was tucked behind his ears, or she liked the question-mark line of a long torso curving at the shoulder and straight at the hip. For warm eyes or a soft voice or a slow walk—that's all—a few hairs, a line, a brightness, a sound, a pace, she gave up family. She offered us up for a charm that vanished with tiredness, a pigtail that didn't toss when the wind died. Why, the wrong lighting could erase the dearest thing about him.

It could very well have been, however, that my aunt did not take subtle enjoyment of her friend, but, a wild woman, kept rollicking company. Imagining her free with sex doesn't fit, though. I don't know any women like that, or men either. Unless I see her life branching into mine, she gives me no ancestral help.

To sustain her being in love, she often worked at herself in the mirror, guessing at the colors and shapes that would interest him, changing them frequently in order to hit on the right combination. She wanted him to look back.

On a farm near the sea, a woman who tended her appearance reaped a reputation for eccentricity. All the married women blunt-cut their hair in flaps about their ears or pulled it back in tight buns. No nonsense. Neither style blew easily into heart-catching tangles. And at their weddings they displayed themselves in their long hair for the last time. "It brushed the backs of my knees," my mother tells me. "It was braided, and even so, it brushed the backs of my knees."

At the mirror my aunt combed individuality into her bob. A bun could have been contrived to escape into black streamers blowing in the wind or in quiet wisps about her face, but only the older women in our picture album wear buns. She brushed her hair back from her forehead, tucking the flaps behind her ears. She looped a piece of thread, knotted into a circle between her index fingers and thumbs, and ran the double strand across her forehead. When she closed her fingers as if she were making a pair of shadow geese bite, the string twisted together catching the little hairs. Then she pulled the thread away from her skin, ripping the hairs out neatly, her eyes watering from the needles of pain. Opening her fingers, she cleaned the thread, then rolled it along her hairline and the tops of her eyebrows. My mother did the same to me and my sisters and herself. I used to believe that the expression "caught by the short hairs" meant a captive held with a depilatory string. It especially hurt at the temples, but my mother said we were lucky we didn't have to have our feet bound when we were seven. Sisters used to sit on their beds and cry together, she said, as their mothers or their slaves removed the bandages for a few minutes each night and let the blood gush back into their veins. I hope that the man my aunt loved appreciated a smooth brow, that he wasn't just a tits-and-ass man.

Once my aunt found a freckle on her chin, at a spot that the almanac said predestined her for unhappiness. She dug it out with a hot needle and washed the wound with peroxide.

More attention to her looks than these pullings of hairs and picking at spots would have caused gossip among the villagers. They owned work clothes and good clothes, and they wore good clothes for feasting the new seasons. But since a woman combing her hair hexes beginnings, my aunt rarely found an occasion to look her best. Women looked like great sea snails—the corded wood, babies, and laundry they carried were the whorls on their backs. The Chinese did not admire a bent back; goddesses and warriors stood straight. Still there must have been a marvelous freeing of beauty when a worker laid down her burden and stretched and arched.

Such commonplace loveliness, however, was not enough for my aunt. She dreamed of a lover for the fifteen days of New Year's, the time for families to exchange visits, money, and food. She plied her secret comb. And sure enough she cursed the year, the family, the village, and herself.

Even as her hair lured her imminent lover, many other men looked at her. Uncles, cousins, nephews, brothers would have looked, too, had they been home between journeys. Perhaps they had already been restraining their curiosity, and they left, fearful that their glances, like a field of nesting birds, might be startled and caught. Poverty hurt, and that was their first reason for leaving. But another, final reason for leaving the crowded house was the never-said.

She may have been unusually beloved, the precious only daughter, spoiled and mirror gazing because of the affection the family lavished on her. When her husband left, they welcomed the chance to take her back from the in-laws; she could live like the little daughter for just a while longer. There are stories that my grandfather was different from other people, "crazy ever since the little Jap bayoneted him in the head." He used to put his naked penis on the dinner table, laughing. And one day he brought home a baby girl, wrapped up inside his brown western-style greatcoat. He had traded one of his sons, probably my father, the youngest, for her. My grandmother made him trade back. When he finally got a daughter of his own, he doted on her. They must have all loved her, except perhaps my father, the only brother who never went back to China, having once been traded for a girl.

Brothers and sisters, newly men and women, had to efface their sexual color and present plain miens. Disturbing hair and eyes, a smile like no other threatened the ideal of five generations living under one roof. To focus blurs, people shouted face to face and yelled from room to room. The immigrants I know have loud voices, unmodulated to American tones even after years away from the village where they called their friendships out across the fields. I have not been able to stop my mother's screams in public libraries or over telephones. Walking erect (knees straight, toes pointed forward, not pigeon-toed, which is Chinese-feminine) and speaking in an inaudible voice, I have tried to turn myself

American-feminine. Chinese communication was loud, public. Only sick people had to whisper. But at the dinner table, where the family members came nearest one another, no one could talk, not the outcasts nor any eaters. Every word that falls from the mouth is a coin lost. Silently they gave and accepted food with both hands. A preoccupied child who took his bowl with one hand got a sideways glare. A complete moment of total attention is due everyone alike. Children and lovers have no singularity here, but my aunt used a secret voice, a separate attentiveness.

She kept the man's name to herself throughout her labor and dying; she did not accuse him that he be punished with her. To save her inseminator's name she gave silent birth.

He may have been somebody in her own household, but intercourse with a man outside the family would have been no less abhorrent. All the village were kinsmen, and the titles shouted in loud country voices never let kinship be forgotten. Any man within visiting distance would have been neutralized as a lover—"brother," "younger brother," "older brother"—one hundred and fifteen relationship titles. Parents researched birth charts probably not so much to assure good fortune as to circumvent incest in a population that has but one hundred surnames. Everybody has eight million relatives. How useless then sexual mannerisms, how dangerous.

As if it came from an atavism deeper than fear, I used to add "brother" silently to boys' names. It hexed the boys, who would or would not ask me to dance, and made them less scary and as familiar and deserving of benevolence as girls.

But, of course, I hexed myself also—no dates. I should have stood up, both arms waving, and shouted out across libraries, "Hey, you! Love me back." I had no idea, though, how to make attraction selective, how to control its direction and magnitude. If I made myself American-pretty so that the five or six Chinese boys in the class fell in love with me—everyone else—the Caucasian, Negro, and Japanese boys—would too. Sisterliness, dignified and honorable, made much more sense.

Attraction eludes control so stubbornly that whole societies designed to organize relationships among people cannot keep order, not even when they bind people to one another from childhood and raise them together. Among the very poor and the wealthy, brothers married their adopted sisters, like doves. Our family allowed some romance, paying adult brides' prices and providing dowries so that their sons and daughters could marry strangers. Marriage promises to turn strangers into friendly relatives—a nation of siblings.

In the village structure, spirits shimmered among the live creatures, balanced and held in equilibrium by time and land. But one human being flaring up into violence could open up a black hole, a maelstrom that pulled in the sky. The frightened villagers, who depended on one another to maintain the real, went to my aunt to show her a personal, physical representation of the break she had made in the "roundness." Misallying couples snapped off the future, which was to be embodied in true offspring. The villagers punished her for acting as if she could have a private life, secret and apart from them.

If my aunt had betrayed the family at a time of large grain yields and peace, when many boys were born, and wings were being built on many houses, perhaps she might have escaped such severe punishment. But the men—hungry, greedy, tired of planting in dry soil, cuckolded—had had to leave the village in order to send food-money home. There were ghost plagues, bandit plagues, wars with the Japanese, floods. My Chinese brother and sister had died of an unknown sickness. Adultery, perhaps only a mistake during good times, became a crime when the village needed food.

The round moon cakes and round doorways, the round tables of graduated size that fit one roundness inside another, round windows and rice bowls—these talismen had lost their power to warn this family of the law: a family must be whole, faithfully keeping the descent line by having sons to feed the old and the dead, who in turn look after the family. The villagers came to show my aunt and her lover-in-hiding a broken house. The villagers were speeding up the circling of events because she was too shortsighted to see that her infidelity had already harmed the village, that waves of consequences would return unpredictably, sometimes in disguise, as now, to hurt her. This roundness had to be made coin-sized so that she would see its circumference: punish her at the birth of her baby. Awaken her to the inexorable. People who refused fatalism because they could invent small resources insisted on culpability. Deny accidents and wrest fault from the stars.

After the villagers left, their lanterns now scattering in various directions toward home, the family broke their silence and cursed her. "Aiaa, we're going to die. Death is coming. Death is coming. Look what you've done. You've killed us. Ghost! Dead ghost! Ghost! You've never been born." She ran out into the fields, far enough from the house so that she could no longer hear their voices, and pressed herself against the earth, her own land no more. When she felt the birth coming, she thought that she had been hurt. Her body seized together. "They've hurt me too much," she thought. "This is gall, and it will kill me." Her forehead and knees against the earth, her body convulsed and then released her onto her back. The black well of sky and stars went out and out and out forever; her body and her complexity seemed to disappear. She was one of the stars, a bright dot in blackness, without home, without a companion, in eternal cold and silence. An agoraphobia rose in her, speeding higher and higher, bigger and bigger; she would not be able to contain it; there would be no end to fear.

Flayed, unprotected against space, she felt pain return, focusing her body. This pain chilled her—a cold, steady kind of surface pain. Inside, spasmodically, the other pain, the pain of the child, heated her. For hours she lay on the ground, alternately body and space. Sometimes a vision of normal comfort obliterated reality: she saw the family in the evening gambling at the dinner table, the young people massaging their elders' backs. She saw them congratulating one another, high joy on the mornings the rice shoots came up. When these pictures burst, the stars drew yet further apart. Black space opened.

She got to her feet to fight better and remembered that old-fashioned women gave birth in their pigsties to fool the jealous, pain-dealing gods, who do not snatch piglets. Before the next spasms could stop her, she ran to the pigsty, each step a rushing out into emptiness. She climbed over the fence and knelt in the dirt. It was good to have a fence enclosing her, a tribal person alone.

Laboring, this woman who had carried her child as a foreign growth that sickened her every day, expelled it at last. She reached down to touch the hot, wet, moving mass, surely smaller than anything human, and could feel that it was human after all—fingers, toes, nails, nose. She pulled it up on to her belly, and it lay curled there, butt in the air, feet precisely tucked one under the other. She opened her loose shirt and buttoned the child inside. After resting, it squirmed and thrashed and she pushed it up to her breast. It turned its head this way and that until it found her nipple. There, it made little snuffling noises. She clenched her teeth at its preciousness, lovely as a young calf, a piglet, a little dog.

She may have gone to the pigsty as a last act of responsibility: she would protect this child as she had protected its father. It would look after her soul, leaving supplies on her grave. But how would this tiny child without family find her grave when there would be no marker for her anywhere, neither in the earth nor the family hall? No one would give her a family hall name. She had taken the child with her into the wastes. At its birth the two of them had felt the same raw pain of separation, a wound that only the family pressing tight could close. A child with no descent line would not soften her life but only trail after her, ghostlike, begging her to give it purpose. At dawn the villagers on their way to the fields would stand around the fence and look.

Full of milk, the little ghost slept. When it awoke, she hardened her breasts against the milk that crying loosens. Toward morning she picked up the baby and walked to the well.

Carrying the baby to the well shows loving. Otherwise abandon it. Turn its face into the mud. Mothers who love their children take them along. It was probably a girl; there is some hope of forgiveness for boys.

"Don't tell anyone you had an aunt. Your father does not want to hear her name. She has never been born." I have believed that sex was unspeakable and words so strong and fathers so frail that "aunt" would do my father mysterious harm. I have thought that my family, having settled among immigrants who had also been their neighbors in the ancestral land, needed to clean their name, and a wrong word would incite the kinspeople even here. But there is more to this silence: they want me to participate in her punishment. And I have.

In the twenty years since I heard this story I have not asked for details nor said my aunt's name; I do not know it. People who can comfort the dead can also chase after them to hurt them further—a reverse ancestor worship. The real punishment was not the raid swiftly inflicted by the villagers, but the family's deliberately forgetting her. Her betrayal so maddened them, they saw to it that she would suffer forever, even after death. Always hungry, always needing, she would have to beg food from other ghosts, snatch and steal it from those whose living descendants give them gifts. She would have to fight the ghosts massed at crossroads for the buns a few thoughtful citizens leave to decoy her away from village and home so that the ancestral spirits could feast unharassed. At peace, they could act like gods, not ghosts, their descent lines providing them with paper suits and dresses, spirit money, paper houses, paper automobiles, chicken, meat, and rice into eternity—essences delivered up in smoke and flames, steam and incense rising from each rice bowl. In an attempt to make the Chinese care for people outside the family, Chairman Mao encourages us now to give our paper replicas to the spirits of outstanding soldiers and workers, no matter whose ancestors they may be. My aunt remains forever hungry. Goods are not distributed evenly among the dead.

My aunt haunts me—her ghost drawn to me because now, after fifty years of neglect, I alone devote pages of paper to her, though not origamied into houses and clothes. I do not think she always means me well. I am telling on her, and she was a spite suicide, drowning herself in the drinking water. The Chinese are always very frightened of the drowned one, whose weeping ghost, wet hair hanging and skin bloated, waits silently by the water to pull down a substitute.

Questions for Critical Analysis

1. Why does Kingston suggest several possible fantasies about how her aunt became pregnant? What role does the story serve in Kingston's developing sense of her own sexuality and her self-image as a woman?
2. Kingston writes that she and other children of immigrants must "figure out how the invisible world the emigrants built around our childhood fit in solid America." How does this essay explain the child's dilemma?
3. What role does Kingston's mother play in this account? Why does she tell her daughter the forbidden story?
4. In what ways has Kingston participated in her aunt's punishment?
5. Has a relative or friend ever told you a "warning" story? If so, how has it affected you? Is immigration part of your family experience? How does either experience affect your response to Kingston's essay?

QUESTIONS FOR STRUCTURAL ANALYSIS

1. Kingston tells us a story told to her by her mother. How does she use her mother as a frame around the story? What is the effect of this frame?
2. This essay contains several digressions from Kingston's story about her aunt. Consider the story of her father counting his change while he walked home from a carnival ride. What role does this account play in the essay?
3. Name other digressions in the essay. Since these digressions break the flow of the narrative, what purpose do they serve in the essay?
4. Kingston describes what happens to her aunt in some detail, with special attention paid to the neighbors' raid on the house and on the birth itself. What details make the description powerful?
5. Kingston ends the essay thinking about the consequences of telling a forbidden story. How does the conclusion tie the essay together? Is the ending effective?

*I*NDIA: *A W*IDOW'S *D*EVASTATING *C*HOICE

JUTHICA STANGL

In telling the story of her friend's suicide, Juthica Stangl writes about an issue that is still viable in India today: sati (or suttee), in which young widows follow their husbands into death by ritualistically killing themselves on their husband's funeral pyre. The September 19, 1987, issue of the New York Times *included an article on a widow's sati. Her father was quoted in that article as saying, "The loss has made me sad. But there is grandeur associated with sati and my family's name will be famous all over. Just as we bathe in water, she bathed in fire. She has taken her husband with her. They both live." Stangl sees no difference between a traditional sati and her friend's death.*

Before you begin reading: *No matter how much we try to shield ourselves from social problems, we cannot avoid learning about them and sometimes even getting involved. Pick one of these topics to think carefully about: environment, safety, suicide, racism, drugs, AIDS, poverty. Make a list of words, images, stories that come into mind while you consider the topic. Write a brief description of what a person could do who wants to become involved in finding a solution.*

◆

ON OCTOBER 26, 1981, WHILE DELHI PREPARED FOR DEEVALI, the festival of lights, Anjali Banerji* and her 14-year-old son Ashok each swallowed a lethal handful of sleeping pills. They had already fed a dose to the family dog, Tepi.

Anjali Banerji died four days later; Ashok and Tepi survived, thanks to police officers who pumped their stomachs after the attempt.

A November issue of *India Today* magazine reported the suicide. Anjali Banerji's husband, Rajib, a doctor at the Hindu Rao Hospital, had been hit by a car and, after a lengthy hospitalization, had died the previous January. In time, the widow began searching for work. She had a degree in social work and 14 years experience in West Bengal, but no job came her way. She received little sympathy from her family and from friends—only the advice to move in with relatives. After 10 frustrating months, she decided to follow her husband in death, and to take the rest of the family with her.

---

*The names have been fictionalized.

The reporter noted her meticulous preparations—notes written to the police and her brother, the refrigerator emptied and defrosted, kitchen stocked with food for relatives or whoever came to take care of the possessions left behind.

Two weeks after her death, friends sent the clipping to me in California.

Anjali had been very special to me. We were both about 16 when we met outside a classroom on the first day of college at the University of Calcutta. I still remember it clearly. I was standing alone in an archway, watching a crow feed her little ones. Suddenly I heard footsteps and there was a tall, slender girl with two short braids, wearing a well-starched white sari. Like me, she wore no jewelry, not even the customary thin gold bracelets every middle-class girl wore like a uniform. I had not met anyone before who also rebelled against the prescribed dress code. What we were wearing would be considered a widow's garb. I felt close to her instantly.

I smiled and asked if she was also waiting for room three. She nodded with a smile and said, "Yes, and am I glad to find someone to talk to. None of my friends got into this college. I was so nervous when my father dropped me off at the gate that I didn't sleep all night."

"I can understand that, since I have no old friends here either. My name is Juthica, but everyone calls me Julie."

She stared at me for a few seconds, then told me her name and that she had attended a large school. She hadn't really expected to get into such a good college. She also asked where I had gone to high school. I was sure she had never heard of my school, so I told her it was a small, British missionary boarding school. My graduating class had only 13 students.

"You must be Christian with a name like Julie," she said.

I found myself apologizing: "It is only my nickname. I do have a real, honest-to-goodness Bengali name, too."

She laughed and said, "Oh, it doesn't bother me a bit that you are Christian. As a matter of fact, many people think I'm one too, because of the way I dress."

I tried to explain that I wasn't wearing white because of my religion, but simply because I liked it. I realized we both had many misconceptions about each other's communities. She came from a Hindu Brahmin family, the highest caste, I from a Christian middle-class one. We spoke the same language, but our cultures were very different.

From then on, for four years, we were inseparable. We took the same classes, joined the National Cadet Corps, helped each other learn to ride bikes, and visited each other after school. I always invited her home for Christmas dinner, and spent Hindu feasts at hers. We covered for each other, telling little white lies when doing something or going somewhere our families wouldn't approve. We comforted each other through difficult times, and teased and poked fun at each other. She was quiet and sensible, with an irresistible sense of humor. I was wild, impulsive, and boisterous—we complemented each other well.

Now she is dead.

All those times when I felt that the world had come to an end, that my great love was over, or that I would surely flunk the final, she would patiently listen to my stories, then put her arm around me and reassure me. Even now, 30 years later, the memory of her strength pulls me through difficult times. What could have happened to her strength, her confidence, her optimism?

As I read through the clipping, I found I couldn't help blaming myself that I wasn't there when she really needed someone. I began to feel angry at her family.

Traditionally, the extended Indian family comes to the rescue in times of trouble. What had happened to them? Her father was a scholarly gentleman who taught high school. She had two older brothers, one an army doctor, the other an engineer, and an older sister, who was already married and out of the house by the time I met her. Anytime I was visiting I was always struck by how quiet and peaceful the household was. They all spoke in gentle voices. It seemed unnatural to me, being used to seven children playing, laughing, fighting, and loving in my family. When I commented once on this, she said it was true, nothing much was ever going on. Her father spent most of the time in his study, her mother kept the house. I had an image of trees in the forest, growing near, but never touching, except in a big storm, when the contact results in a broken limb.

Anjali did produce a storm when she married Rajib. She went against her family's expectations by finding her own future husband, rather than waiting for her match to be arranged. What's more, he was from a lower caste.

Rajib's family was even more resentful. Even though Anjali was higher caste, which on one level meant a social achievement, the family missed out on a potentially major dowry. Had Rajib married within his own caste, the family would have been offered clothes, jewelry, and money, and considering that he was a doctor, perhaps even a car or house. His family counted on this; it would have helped with providing Rajib's sisters' dowries. The loss was significant.

In the wake of the storm, both Anjali and Rajib ended up as limbs broken off family trees. They established themselves on their own. Except for a few sticks of furniture they had nothing, but seemed very happy. By then I was living in California; I visited her each time I was in India, sometimes really going out of my way to do so to catch up with their frequent moves. Each time I saw them I was impressed with the intimacy of their relationship. They were two people who genuinely enjoyed and respected each other, who truly shared their life in the best sense of the word. I kept up with her every way I could.

She was overjoyed when her son was born. Her family, at last, showed some interest in the new grandson. However, Rajib's family did not respond even then.

She was determined, with or without the families' support, to continue providing a happy home. From everything I saw, she succeeded. But underneath it, I could tell that she was hurt by her isolation from her family, a feeling of sadness remained for not being accepted by her in-laws.

The last time I saw her was in a hotel room in Delhi. Rajib, Anjali, and Ashok lived outside of town at that point; they took a long bus drive to come to see me and my family. She brought some fried fish, my favorite kind, which she remembered from our college days. Her son by this time was about 12, very bright and friendly. I fantasized about our children developing the kind of friendship Anjali and I had, knowing full well that with the distance between us that would not be possible. The relationship I had been impressed with over the years between Anjali and Rajib obviously was still there, and now included their son. I was particularly happy to see that our children and Ashok got along well.

We parted with the promise of writing more often. We even talked about her sending Ashok to the United States for a year, when he would stay with us.

Is is possible that the article in my hand was about the same Anjali? Suddenly I was furious with her. How could this wonderful woman, this pillar of strength, this model friend and mother, simply do away with herself? What about the promises? How could she just abandon everything, including me?

When I was still in India with my family, I got a letter from her about her husband's car accident. I left India knowing only that he was seriously injured and in the hospital. For months I had had no news, despite my many letters to Anjali. I would have called, but they could never afford a telephone. I felt helpless, but not knowing anyone in the area where they were living at the time, there was nothing I could do.

The next news came in the form of an invitation to a memorial service for Rajib. It was signed by Ashok, as is the custom. The eldest son takes matters into his hands on the father's death. At this time he was barely 14. I could not imagine my own son, three years younger—having to—or being able to do this. But knowing Anjali I knew that if Ashok was anything like his mother, he would perform his duty admirably.

All I could do was to write, offering my help and whatever support I could, long distance. I felt I had failed her completely; I was never there when I might have been able to help.

I never heard from her again. I wrote to all our common acquaintances trying to get news. No one seemed to be in touch with her.

But the *India Today* reporter described the last nine months of her life in great detail. The family had had a comfortable existence, but their modest savings were used up quickly during Rajib's hospitalization after the hit-and-run accident.

In India, of course, accident insurance is uncommon. The application for his life insurance benefit was lost by the company. After months, the company had not responded to the duplicate application. The promised assistance from her husband's employer had not come through despite her repeated appeals. Within weeks she was totally without funds.

Given India's unemployment problem, there were few jobs available even to experienced and highly educated men. It is not surprising then that a woman, out of the job market as long as Anjali had been, was not seriously considered by most employers. Further, she did not have the necessary personal connections, or the know-how to pay bribes to secure a job.

The prospect of being destitute, with no source of support for herself, her son, or even the dog, must have been devastating to her. India is, of course, best known for its poverty. But perhaps just because of this, extreme poverty is even more unthinkable for someone like Anjali who had never before had to worry about it.

The article told of her difficulties with the bureaucratic maze and her resulting depression and loneliness. Her family, whom, according to the article, she had abandoned to marry the man she chose, did not come to her. Her parents had died by now, only her brothers and sisters remained. It is less surprising that her in-laws did not respond either. They considered their son dead once he had married against their wishes.

A reporter interviewed Anjali's brother after the tragedy, and he claimed the family never knew what kind of difficulty she was in. Perhaps her pride kept her from turning to them. Rejected once, she did not want to risk it again.

Anjali's whole life had revolved around her husband and son. She simply couldn't imagine leaving Ashok to other people's mercy. Once she decided to end her life she saw no other way but to take her son with her.

I suddenly realized that, as I was reading on, the image the article conjured up was not of Anjali, but of a women's demonstration I had seen in Delhi during my last trip to India. Hundreds of angry women, mostly villagers, marched with banners, demanding the reinstatement of suttee, the ancient custom in which a widow is to throw herself onto her husband's funeral pyre. The British had outlawed suttee in 1829.

The custom is a testimony to the fact that the life of a widow is superfluous. Once the man is dead, there is no further purpose for the woman. Her role is to bear children; with her husband's death that job is done. Religious tradition holds that her sacrifice helps her husband atone for his sins and for this she becomes a saint.

Despite the established tradition, not all widows had always willingly killed themselves in this way. Village elders and family members often had to force a young wife to follow her husband into death. They would do so not just for religious or traditional reasons, but because the burden of supporting the surviving wife was usually too much for the family.

When I saw that demonstration, I could hardly believe my eyes. How could women, in this day and age, especially in a country where the prime minister is a woman, actually campaign for the right to commit suicide just because their husbands had died?

The demonstration dramatized the fact that the ancient custom still has social and economic relevance today. The marching women realized that by outlawing the custom, the British had succeeded only in making it illegal, not in removing its significance. Even today, India's society has no mechanism to help a woman in a traditional role develop her own identity and avoid becoming a burden. The women were making a statement that suicide is the easier alternative to a life of dependency on unwilling families.

Anjali was an educated and sophisticated woman, with a background and social circle totally different from that of the demonstrators. For her, living in 20th-century Delhi, suttee, in its traditional form, was unthinkable. But, in the end, didn't she find herself forced onto her husband's funeral pyre anyway?

QUESTIONS FOR CRITICAL ANALYSIS

1. Describe Anjali's relationship with her family: both her husband and son, and her parents and siblings. What role does her family play in her suicide? Why did she decide to kill her son at the same time she killed herself? How do you feel about this decision?

2. Stangl's responds to her friend's suicide with anger, sadness, and guilt. How does she reveal these feelings in her essay?

3. Stangl writes: "the life of a widow is superfluous." Consider women's role in Indian society (as presented in this essay) and in American society. How are women valued in each society? Are the cultures more similar or dissimilar?

4. What is suttee (or sati, as it is sometimes called)? Reread the quotation in the headnote from a 1987 *New York Times* article. What do you think about the notion that death by suicide is noble and has grandeur? Under what circumstances is such an attitude tolerated in American culture?

5. If you know a widow, or someone who committed suicide, or if you feel that suicide is wrong under any circumstance, your experiences and knowledge may affect how you read this essay. Can you identify ways your response to the essay was triggered by memories or thoughts outside the essay itself?

QUESTIONS FOR STRUCTURAL ANALYSIS

1. How does the stark, matter-of-fact introduction prepare the reader for the subject of the essay? Is this an effective introduction for an essay about suttee? Why, or why not?

2. How does Stangl present Anjali to the reader? What sort of person is Anjali? Do the stories about Anjali provide clues to her suicide? How?
3. Why does Stangl compare her Christianity with Anjali's Bengali faith? Is the comparison developed well enough to work within the essay? Why, or why not?
4. How is the suttee demonstration significant to the essay?
5. Stangl concludes with a rhetorical question. Why? Is it an effective ending? Are there better ways to end this essay?

On Being a Good Neighbor

Martin Luther King, Jr.

Martin Luther King, Jr. (1929–1968) changed 20th-century America by focusing attention on the unequal, disenfranchised day-to-day existence lived by blacks in the land of the American Constitution. A preacher, writer, and civil rights leader, King became the symbol of black dignity. He led both blacks and whites to protest racial inequities in the 1950s and 60s through marches, sit-ins, and peaceful demonstrations. Following the example of Mahatma Gandhi who successfully won freedom from the British for India, King preached a nonviolent overthrow of white supremacist power. His sermon on the Good Samaritan exemplifies his message: we are all brothers and, as such, are responsible for each other.

Before you begin reading: *Consider this question: Am I my brother's keeper? Make two lists and under the headings* NO *and* YES *write your responses.*

◆

And who is my neighbour?
LUKE 10:29

I SHOULD LIKE TO TALK WITH YOU ABOUT A GOOD MAN, whose exemplary life will always be a flashing light to plague the dozing conscience of mankind. His goodness was not found in a passive commitment to a particular creed, but in his active participation in a life-saving deed; not in a moral pilgrimage that reached its destination point, but in the love ethic by which he journeyed life's highway. He was good because he was a good neighbor.

The ethical concern of this man is expressed in a magnificent little story, which begins with a theological discussion on the meaning of eternal life and concludes in a concrete expression of compassion on a dangerous road. Jesus is asked a question by a man who had been trained in the details of Jewish law: "Master, what shall I do to inherit eternal life?" The retort is prompt: "What is written in the law? how readest thou?" After a moment the lawyer recites articulately: "Thou shalt love the Lord thy God with all thy heart, and with all thy soul, and with all thy strength, and with all thy mind; and thy neighbour as thyself." Then comes the decisive word from Jesus: "Thou hast answered right: this do, and thou shalt live."

The lawyer was chagrined. "Why," the people might ask, "would an expert in law raise a question that even the novice can answer?" Desiring to justify himself and to show that Jesus' reply was far from conclusive, the lawyer asks, "And who is my neighbour?" The lawyer was now taking up the cudgels of debate that might have turned the conversation into an abstract theological discussion. But Jesus, determined not to be caught in the "paralysis of analysis," pulls the question from mid-air and places it on a dangerous curve between Jerusalem and Jericho.

He told the story of a "certain man" who went down from Jerusalem to Jericho and fell among robbers who stripped him, beat him, and, departing, left him half dead. By chance a certain priest appeared, but he passed by on the other side, and later a Levite also passed by. Finally, a certain Samaritan, a half-breed from a people with whom the Jews had no dealings, appeared. When he saw the wounded man, he was moved with compassion, administered first aid, placed him on his beast, "and brought him to an inn, and took care of him."

Who is my neighbor? "I do not know his name," says Jesus in essence. "He is anyone toward whom you are neighborly. He is anyone who lies in need at life's roadside. He is neither Jew nor Gentile; he is neither Russian nor American; he is neither Negro nor white. He is 'a certain man'—any needy man—on one of the numerous Jericho roads of life." So Jesus defines a neighbor, not in a theological definition, but in a life situation.

What constituted the goodness of the good Samaritan? Why will he always be an inspiring paragon of neighborly virtue? It seems to me that this man's goodness may be described in one word—altruism. The good Samaritan was altruistic to the core. What is altruism? The dictionary defines altruism as "regard for, and devotion to, the interest of others." The Samaritan was good because he made concern for others the first law of his life.

I

The Samaritan had the capacity for a *universal altruism*. He had a piercing insight into that which is beyond the eternal accidents of race, religion, and nationality. One of the great tragedies of man's long trek along the highway of history has been the limiting of neighborly concern to tribe, race, class, or nation. The God of early Old Testament days was a tribal god and the ethic was tribal. "Thou shalt not kill" meant "Thou shalt not kill a fellow Israelite, but for God's sake, kill a Philistine." Greek democracy embraced a certain aristocracy, but not the hordes of Greek slaves whose labors built the city-states. The universalism at the center of the Declaration of Independence has been shamefully negated by America's appalling tendency to substitute "some" for "all." Numerous people in the North and South still believe that the affirmation, "All men are created equal," means "All white men are created equal." Our unswerving devotion to monopolistic capitalism makes us more concerned about the economic security of the captains of industry than for the laboring men whose sweat and skills keep industry functioning.

What are the devastating consequences of this narrow, group-centered attitude? It means that one does not really mind what happens to the people outside his group. If an American is concerned only about his nation, he will not be concerned about the peoples of Asia, Africa, or South America. Is this not why nations engage in the madness of war without the slightest sense of penitence? Is this not why the murder of a citizen of your own nation is a crime, but the murder of the citizens of another nation in war is an act of heroic virtue? If manufacturers are concerned only in their personal interests, they will pass by on the other side while thousands of working people are stripped of their jobs and left displaced on some Jericho road as a result of automation, and they will judge every move toward a better distribution of wealth and a better life for the working man to be socialistic. If a white man is concerned only about his race, he will casually pass by the Negro who has been robbed of his personhood, stripped of his sense of dignity, and left dying on some wayside road.

A few years ago, when an automobile carrying several members of a Negro college basketball team had an accident on a Southern highway, three of the young men were severely injured. An ambulance was immediately called, but on arriving at the place of the accident, the driver, who was white, said without apology that it was not his policy to service Negroes, and he drove away. The driver of a passing automobile graciously drove the boys to the nearest hospital, but the attending physician belligerently said, "We don't take niggers in this hospital." When the boys finally arrived at a "colored" hospital in a town some fifty miles from the scene of the accident, one was dead and the other two died thirty and fifty minutes later respectively. Probably all three could have been saved if they had been given immediate treatment. This is only one of thousands of inhuman incidents that occur daily in the South, an unbelievable expression of the barbaric consequences of any tribal-centered, national-centered, or racial-centered ethic.

The real tragedy of such narrow provincialism is that we see people as entities or merely as things. Too seldom do we see people in their true *humanness*. A spiritual myopia limits our vision to external accidents. We see men as Jews or Gentiles, Catholics or Protestants, Chinese or American, Negroes or whites. We fail to think of them as fellow human beings made from the same basic stuff as we, molded in the same divine image. The priest and the Levite saw only a bleeding body, not a human being like themselves. But the good Samaritan will always remind us to remove the cataracts of provincialism from our spiritual eyes and see men as men. If the Samaritan had considered the wounded man as a Jew first, he would not have stopped, for the Jews and the Samaritans had no dealings. He saw him as a human being first, who was a Jew only by accident. The good neighbor looks beyond the external accidents and discerns those inner qualities that make all men human and, therefore, brothers.

Questions for Critical Analysis

1. What role does the lawyer play in the parable of the Good Samaritan? Why does he disappear from the story so quickly?
2. How does the Good Samaritan story answer the question of eternal life? How does King answer the implied question of America's future?
3. Paragraph 8 is the crux of King's message. What important applications does King identify? Can he be accused of oversimplification? Why, or why not?
4. This essay was published in 1963 and was preached even earlier. The Civil Rights Bill, guaranteeing that "all men are created equal" really did mean "all men," was signed into law in 1965. Discuss the significance of this sermon historically. How is its message applicable today?
5. King speaks about the provincialism of group-centered thinking: no one matters outside your own narrow group. Apply this idea to life on the campus, to your church or religious group, to other organizations you have joined. Think more broadly: How does this concept apply to industrial America's competition problems?

Questions for Structural Analysis

1. What is King's thesis? How does he use the story or parable of the Good Samaritan to make his point? How does he use the parable to organize and develop this essay?
2. The purpose of a sermon (which this essay is) is to convince the listener of the truth of the message by presenting incontrovertible arguments. Is King successful in convincing you of what it means to be a good neighbor? Why, or why not?
3. King uses the rhythmic, dramatic language of a preacher in his sentence patterns and word choice. List examples of these rhetorical devices.
4. Twice King develops his theme by moving from a specific incident to a general precept. How does the second story reinforce the first? Do you think it is more powerful than the parable, or less so? Why?
5. Is King's appeal emotional or intellectual? What clues do you find to support your answer?

Learning Our Responsibilities

Topics for Writing Essays

Many of the questions following each essay can serve as appropriate writing suggestions. The topics listed below expand the prereading exercises, but they can be used without completing that step first.

1. Use the Kingston prereading exercise to write a narrative essay about how your relative acquired his (her) role as a model and how a particular story or stories about this relative affected your life. Address your essay to someone important to you (you want your reader to know you better by hearing the story) who does not know the relative you're describing.
2. Select one of the topics listed in the Stangl prereading exercise and develop an essay that takes the subject out of the abstract world of issues and statistics and humanizes it for a reader who is not an unsympathetic person but is ignorant of how personal lives are affected.

   Be careful not to try to do too much in your essay. Look at how Stangl writes about suicide and suttee through the story of her friend Anjali, and how King writes about our responsibility to fellow human beings through the Good Samaritan parable and the story of the accident. Focus on an incident that crystallizes your feelings about the topic.
3. Do you know a person deeply committed to a cause? a person whose life has been greatly affected by a catastrophic event or illness? Write an essay about this person. You may want to select an incident that will reveal the person's strengths and character. You may want to show how her (or his) experience has affected you. Write the essay as if you were going to submit it to *Reader's Digest* for their "Most Unforgettable Person" selection.

Research Possibilities

1. Some students at your school are probably first-generation Americans whose experiences in balancing two cultures are difficult and tricky. Find out how the campus administration helps or hinders these students. Are English as a Second Language courses offered? Is special advice and counsel available? What efforts are made to help these students learn about American culture and become a part of the college community? Your research could include interviews with students, administrators, professors, student loan officers; reading catalogues and program guidelines. Write a

description of college life for a foreign-born student to be published in the college alumni magazine.

2. How soon should children be taught about birth control? Should it be the school's responsibility? the church's? the parent's? Go to the library and look up information on this debate, making sure to balance pro-sex education with antisex education advocates. Based on what you learn, develop your own opinion, and write an essay justifying your stand to a hostile reader.
3. Go to the library and find out about suttee (sati). What is its origin? How did its practice affect life in India before it was outlawed by the British? How did the Indians respond to the British mandate? Is it widely practiced in India today? Write a report to American students who do not know very much about the practice or its religious and cultural implications.

LIVING WITH UNCERTAINTY

Some people live near chemical and nuclear plants by choice so that they can benefit from the high wages and job security that these plants often provide. These individuals accept the risks involved. The writers in this section imply that the gain may not be worth the potential dangers.

DENNIS BERNSTEIN AND CONNIE BLITT, "LETHAL DOSE"

PETER APPLEBOME, "WHERE A CHEMICAL LEAK SEEMS AN ACCEPTED RISK"

A. G. MOJTABAI, "AFTER LONG SILENCE"

CHRISTOPHER MARQUIS, "WHEN THE FIRES GO OUT"

*L*ETHAL *D*OSE

DENNIS BERNSTEIN AND CONNIE BLITT

Dennis Bernstein and Connie Blitt, freelance writers based in Middletown, New York, tell the story about the January 4, 1986, incident at the Gore, Oklahoma, plant where one employee died from sudden exposure to uranium hexafluoride and the town and its inhabitants were exposed to possibly lethal chemicals. Rather than just reporting facts and statistics, Bernstein and Blitt describe the problems with chemical pollution by telling the story of the people who live in an affected town. When you read this essay, be aware that it was written for The Progressive, *a magazine that often presents an antibusiness, pro-environment platform.*

Before you begin reading: *Suppose you learned that a friend of yours died in an industrial accident caused by carelessness and mismanagement. In your reading notebook, write a description of how you would respond to the news.*

◆

THE FIRST SATURDAY OF THE NEW YEAR BROUGHT A CRISP, nearly cloudless morning to Gore, Oklahoma, with a twenty-five-mile-an-hour wind moving from the north. The weekend had begun like any other in the tourist town of 600, as visitors and locals stocked up with fresh bait at the Lucky Seven and set out for a big day of trout fishing at nearby Lake Tenkiller or one of the many well-stocked streams fed by the Illinois and Arkansas rivers.

A little more than a mile south of town, the Sequoyah Fuels Corporation, Kerr-McGee's uranium processing plant, seemed to be operating as usual. The facility processes uranium hexafluoride from milled uranium—"yellowcake"—and ships it to U.S. Department of Energy uranium enrichment plants, which manufacture it into fuel for nuclear reactors.

Late in the morning, most of the workers in the facility's thirty-two-person skeleton crew were having lunch. But James Neil ("Chief") Harrison, a favorite of the workers, was not among them.

The twenty-six-year-old Harrison stood on a small three-story structure some twenty feet above and to the side of the steam chest, where a cylinder overfilled with uranium hexafluoride was being heated. Under the domed top of the chest, the cylinder was bulging with the internal pressure of the 29,500 pounds of uranium hexafluoride, now turning to gas. But Harrison didn't know that.

At about 11:30, while lunch was still in progress at the plant, the cylinder burst, spewing the chemo-nuclear compound in Harrison's direction. The highly toxic and caustic "soup," with the capacity to etch glass, was also filtered into the lunchroom through the plant's air conditioning and ventilation system. Harrison was almost instantly engulfed in the flood of uranium hexafluoride. No respirator was within reach. Blinded and barely able to breathe, Harrison stumbled about as hydrofluoric acid—created when the cylinder burst open and the uranium hexafluoride interacted with the moisture in the air—began to eat away at his lungs.

Virginia Callison, a co-worker and friend of Harrison, managed to wade through the lethal smog, found Harrison, and helped him out of the plant. Several other workers assisted her and put Harrison in a car. Oxygen, which would have been essential for Harrison's survival, was not readily available.

The workers drove eight miles away to pick up a canister of oxygen at a nursing home in Vian before taking Harrison to the Sequoyah Memorial Hospital some eleven miles away in Sallisaw. Kerr-McGee had established no prior emergency plans with Memorial. Harrison was sent off to a larger hospital, Sparks Regional Medical Center in Fort Smith, Arkansas, twenty-one miles away, where he was pronounced dead soon after arrival.

Randy Naylor, an emergency medical technician for Ales Ambulance Service, tried to keep Harrison alive during the journey to Fort Smith. "I don't know what went wrong, but they didn't take care of it," Naylor says. "I had an instructor's course with one of these people down at the plant. And I asked him two years ago, what if something happens. He said the general public's got nothing to be worried about. We have our own facilities to take care of anything that goes wrong."

But Kerr-McGee's emergency plans for medical treatment and evacuation were virtually nonexistent.

"It was chaos," recalls Dearl Anderson, a maintenance mechanic who was in the lunchroom when the accident occurred. "And some people were getting a little panicky."

"The people that we talked to, friends that work there, couldn't even find their way out of the building," says Gore pharmacist William Young. "They didn't even know where the front door was, they were so disoriented. They ran to the fence that surrounds the compound, and that's as far as they could go because they had closed it all up. The workers were lined up against the fence trying to breathe, but they couldn't go any further; they couldn't even run away."

Mike Kingsbury was driving by the plant with his mother about twenty minutes after the accident occurred. "They were teary-eyed, gagging, and coughing," he recalls. "They were all hanging on the fence, and there was no way for them to get out because there's barbed wire on top."

Almost seven years after the near-meltdown at Three Mile Island and eleven years after Karen Silkwood died in mysterious circumstances following the disclosures she made about Kerr-McGee, the hazards of nuclear energy have faded from public consciousness. Reactors and processing plants stand like inactive volcanoes amid a population that views them as just part of the landscape.

But no one in Gore, Oklahoma, perceives them that way any more. Every worker at the plant on the day of the toxic release was hospitalized, along with sixty area residents. "We've all got to wake up and smell the coffee," says Patricia Young, the pharmacist's wife.

As yet, the full story of the accident at Kerr-McGee has not come out. The following facts have been unreported or buried by the media:

- Workers were following business-as-usual procedure when they engaged in the extremely hazardous exercise of heating the overfilled cylinder.
- The accident was not just a chemical leak; it involved the release of uranium.
- Chemical and uranium contamination did occur off-site.
- Far from assisting in the evacuation, Kerr-McGee impeded speedy and effective treatment for exposed workers and residents.

Kerr-McGee officials at the plant and in the company's Oklahoma City headquarters have been falling over one another to deny ultimate responsibility for the accident and shift the blame to workers at the Sequoyah plant. Richard Pereles, director of corporate communications for Kerr-McGee, declared at a press briefing that the procedure being used by the workers at the time of the lethal release was contrary to company guidelines.

"The person who could tell us most, unfortunately, is the person that died," said Pereles. The company initially claimed the cylinder was overfilled because a gauge stuck. It later said the overfilled cylinder was improperly weighed.

But according to officials of the company and the U.S. Nuclear Regulatory Commission (NRC), the workers had permission from shift supervisor Bill Bradley to heat the overfilled cylinder. Dearl Anderson, the maintenance mechanic, who has worked at the uranium processing plant for the last eleven years, says the heating procedure to remove an overload of uranium hexafluoride was frequently used at the plant.

"Yes, not every day," says Anderson, "but it's not uncommon, or how else you gonna get it out?" Ed Henshaw, a former employee at Sequoyah Fuels, says "it's standard procedure to overfill the cylinders."

Kerr-McGee had a great deal to gain financially by violating its own and the NRC's guidelines and heating the cylinders to remove excess uranium hexafluoride. The only other way to get rid of the substance is to vacuum it out, says Clyde Wisner of the NRC, but "it's a very, very, very slow process."

The NRC, for its part, has emphasized the chemical aspect of the Gore accident. "No one was particularly responsible for regulating chemical hazards," said Commissioner Frederick J. Bernthal. "To say we are responsible when we don't have the in-house expertise doesn't cut it."

But the NRC was aware of the hazards of such an accident. Last August, an environmental assessment of the plant predicted that a major release of uranium hexafluoride, though highly unlikely, could cause fatalities among nearby residents.

Both the NRC and Kerr-McGee place the blame on a chemical, not a nuclear, component. Hydrofluoric acid, however, was not the only dangerous release from the accident, for the uranium in the uranium hexafluoride formed particles of uranyl fluoride, which was carried with the billowing cloud of gas.

"Because the hydrofluoric acid kills faster than the uranium, they're going to call it a chemical accident," says Richard Phillips, geologist and author of a study on Kerr-McGee's radioactive waste management at the Gore facility. "It's just sleight-of-hand. They don't want to admit that uranium processing is dangerous and that it can kill people."

"It's irrelevant whether the person died because he breathed in toxic gas or acid or received radiological poisoning," says Ken Bossong, director of the Critical Mass Energy Project in Washington, D.C., a branch of Ralph Nader's Public Citizen. "The fact of the matter is, an accident occurred because the Federal agency responsible for supervising nuclear power is not doing its job."

Kerr-McGee claimed that the radioactive uranyl fluoride, a fairly heavy material, fell on the plant and its immediate environs. The company assured residents that there was no reason to fear radioactive contamination. But urine samples of residents in nearby towns showed significant traces of uranium.

"It's not so that all the particles settle out at the plant boundary," says radioecologist Bernd Franke, who recently completed a study of environmental monitoring at Three Mile Island. In fact, adds Franke, the presence of the chemical hydrofluoric acid increases the possible harm of the uranium particles. "The fluoride, once it reaches the lungs, also decreases the ability of the lungs to get rid of pollutants. So that increases the relative uptake of uranium and other pollutants."

Garland Parks, a consulting physician for Kerr-McGee who rushed to the plant after word of the accident got out, says the whole incident has been blown out of proportion. "You have this '6' [uranium hexafluoride] that they're manufacturing out there. It's not plutonium, it's not like a hydrogen bomb." Parks, who has not been trained in chemical or radiological medicine, asserts that even the workers in the plant who were engulfed in the toxic fog and breathed in substantial amounts of uranium have very little to worry about.

"Yeah, some of them got some of that," he acknowledges. "They had some positive urine. But nothing that should cause any health hazard."

William Young, proprietor of Green Country Drug, was at the pharmacy with his wife when the accident occurred. They had left their children with a sitter. When he heard about the accident, he instructed the sitter to bring the children to his store. He then phoned the plant to find out whether there was imminent danger, for no one in the town had been notified yet.

"I called out there and talked to three or four people," Young recalls. "They said, 'We don't know; I don't know; Let me talk to so and so.' They went to search for somebody, and all we got was 'I don't know.'"

Not knowing what to do next, the angry pharmacist waited for his children, gathered the family in the car, and drove to the front gates of the plant. He arrived just in time for the first press briefing by Kerr-McGee officials. Three hours had passed since the accident had happened.

"Kerr-McGee said it was safe and that most all the stuff was contained to the grounds of the plant," he remembers. Kerr-McGee also announced "that the cloud had completely cleared and there was no further danger." Young went home. Several hours later, a company official called him, suggesting that he take his children to the hospital to get them checked. The next morning, cleanup crews in protective coveralls were scrubbing the highway near the plant and ripping up the earth on which the press briefing had been held the day before.

At the hospital in Sallisaw, Young was again informed that his children had not been dangerously exposed because they were a mile away from the accident, and there would probably be no ill effects. But physicians did find that the Youngs' six-year-old daughter Amber had a red throat; the family was not particularly reassured.

"Here they were dealing with radiation, uranium inhalation, hydrofluoric acid inhalation, skin and eye burns, and they had to repeatedly call Kerr-McGee and ask them what they were dealing with," Young says. "They had never been instructed by the company, and they had no emergency plan."

The frustrated parents insisted on further testing for their three children. Several days later, they were notified that urine samples for all three contained uranium. That came as a shock, since Richard Cunningham, director of fuel cycle and material safety for the NRC, had assured the public that the radiation content of the escaped gas was "very minimal, in fact, nonexistent off-site."

Ninety-year-old Charles Roark, who lives just southeast of the plant, was out in the barn feeding his beagles when he got a telephone call from his daughter, Monnie Davis, who asked him if he saw any smoke coming from the direction of the plant. No emergency sirens had been sounded, Roark said, and he had received no warning from officials at the plant.

"I went out there and boy, it was just all over this county," says Roark, who has lived in the area for almost eighty years. "It looked like fog from the ground up to about two or three hundred feet high in the air. I thought maybe they had been burning some hay. They [Kerr-McGee] used to burn hay there when they couldn't sell it. I began to sniff and smell, and I sucked a whole lot of it down in my lungs, and I found out quick it wasn't hay burning."

Roark felt as if he had a sudden fever, and his nose, throat, and lungs started burning. A week after the accident, his temperature was still high and he felt a burning sensation in his right lung. "After I stay in the house all night," says Roark, "I feel a little bit better, until I go outside and it comes right back on me."

"It used to be that people died of old age around here," says Velma Carter, who works a small farm three miles north of the Sequoyah plant with her husband Ralph. "Now they die of cancer."

Carter tells a reporter she "could make me a long list" of people who have died of cancer and "strange" tumors since Kerr-McGee set up shop in Gore sixteen years ago. The fifty-three-year-old Oklahoman, who barely survived an operation for a brain tumor in 1976, charges that local residents have been "bought off" by Kerr-McGee.

"People are worried that if Kerr-McGee leaves, property taxes will go up," she says. "I been living here fifty years, and I didn't see no one starving before Kerr-McGee came."

For Carter and a growing number of area residents, economic considerations are less important than a clean environment and a safe place to live. Pharmacist Young, for one, is no longer persuaded that Gore is the place to raise his three children.

"You wanna buy my house?" he jokes. "It's a really nice place and really pretty country—as long as you have your gas mask on."

Since the opening of the plant in 1969, "numerous spills and leaks of radioactive materials have contaminated the groundwater and surface water, eventually discharging into the Illinois and Arkansas rivers," according to an environmental study submitted to the NRC which was compiled from Kerr-McGee's own records on public file. Sequoyah Fuels routinely discharges 11,000 pounds of uranium per year into a natural drainage ditch emptying into the Illinois River.

"You want me to send you a one-eyed catfish?" quips pharmacist Young. "You don't even have to cook it." Young, himself a fishing buff, says "a lot of times we get fish with cancers and growths all over them."

Young feels "trapped between a rock and a hard place," he says. He knows his property has depreciated because of accidents at the plant. "They're there for the bucks," he says of Kerr-McGee, "and a town of 600 is not a high price to pay."

Kerr-McGee, which boasts the corporate slogan, "People Helping People," takes an interest in the community only when distrust and dissent begin to arise. The day after Dearl Anderson and another worker were badly burned on the job in a previous accident, the company contributed $1,000 to the Gore school system. The contribution made headlines in the *Sequoyah County Times*; news of the accident was curiously missing. The paper got around to covering the accident only after Jessie Deer in Water, a forty-two-year-old member of the Cherokee Nation and founder of Native Americans for a Clean Environment (NACE), confronted the editor, she recalls.

"Just because it's a good location for Kerr-McGee doesn't mean we should lay down and die," says Jessie Deer in Water.

After the recent accident, many parents demanded the shutting down of Carlile School, less than a mile from the plant. Several rancorous school board meetings resulted in a decision to close the school. Kerr-McGee agreed to rent the school building for five years and pay $250,000 up front—the total rent for the period—so that new classrooms could be added to an existing school in town.

But such philanthropy wears thin in Gore. Many, like pharmacist Young, learned about other Kerr-McGee accidents at the Sequoyah plant and other facilities only after the cylinder burst on January 4 and James Harrison was killed.

"When I heard about them, my mouth dropped open because we were told for years that it was safe," says Young. "They had a big write-up in the Sallisaw paper: 'Kerr-McGee gets a special award for safety. No accident reported in the company for five years.'"

"What makes everybody so nervous about this plant," says Gore Police Chief Jerry Fields, "is that they're so secretive. People are scared about what they don't know, and they don't know what's going on out there. Those people just don't tell anybody anything."

Velma Carter seems resigned to the worst. "This used to be a wonderful place," she says on the verge of tears. "I would have liked to die knowing that my children and grandchildren could live out their lives here on this farm and go ahead raising cattle. And it makes me terribly upset when I think there's not much chance of doing it because of Kerr-McGee."

Carter's daughter, Shelia, single mother of three, grew up on Velma's small farm. After the January 4 accident, Shelia decided to hand out leaflets that called for Kerr-McGee to pack up its operations and move it some place else, "preferably to another planet." Carter tacked up one of her leaflets in the local post office, right next to the FBI poster of the ten most wanted criminals.

QUESTIONS FOR CRITICAL ANALYSIS

1. Appealing to a reader's needs or fears is useful when you want to stir the reader to respond actively to an issue or problem. To what needs and fears does "Lethal Dose" appeal? Is it effective? Can you think of other issues that lend themselves to emotional appeals?
2. Think about industries in your town. What would happen to your community if those industries were closed down? What would happen if they were sources of major accidents? Have you supported causes that set themselves against industrial plants?

What do you think of activists who do? How do your attitudes affect your response to this essay?

3. What responsibility does an industry have to the community in which it resides?
4. If you were a friend of "Chief" Harrison, how would you react to the Bernstein-Blitt article? Why?
5. Look up newspaper accounts of this accident at the Sequoyah Fuels Corporation, and compare the presentations with the one in this essay.

QUESTIONS FOR STRUCTURAL ANALYSIS

1. What is Bernstein and Blitt's thesis? On what evidence do you base your response?
2. "Lethal Dose" expresses a definite point of view. How do the authors reveal their biases by their word choice? by the examples and quotations they select to use?
3. Compare the ways the authors characterize the workers and the Kerr-McGee officials. What techniques do they use to present people in a sympathetic or unsympathetic light?
4. Discuss the relationship between the conclusion of "Lethal Dose" and its introductory story. Is the conclusion too subtle, or is it effective? Why, or why not?
5. How do you characterize the audience for this essay? and on what basis? Rewrite the following two paragraphs for publication in the business and industry section of your local newspaper:

> Kerr-McGee officials at the plant and in the company's Oklahoma City headquarters have been falling over one another to deny ultimate responsibility for the accident and shift the blame to workers at the Sequoyah plant. Richard Pereles, director of corporate communications for Kerr-McGee, declared at a press briefing that the procedure being used by the workers at the time of the lethal release was contrary to company guidelines.
>
> "The person who could tell us most, unfortunately, is the person that died," said Pereles. The company initially claimed the cylinder was overfilled because a gauge stuck. It later said the overfilled cylinder was improperly weighed.

*W*HERE A *C*HEMICAL *L*EAK *S*EEMS AN *A*CCEPTED *R*ISK

PETER APPLEBOME

Journalist Peter Applebome published this brief essay in the New York Times, *presenting the people of Texas City, Texas, who are willing to make a trade-off between safety and relatively high wages. Like the citizens of Gore, Oklahoma, these Texans understand the risk of working with hazardous chemicals, but they accept living with that risk so that they do not lose employment.*

Before you begin reading: *Think about the risks you are willing to take. Consider things like smoking cigarettes, running red lights, making love without using condoms, not completing assignments on time, jaywalking, drinking beverages made with saccarine and so forth. Make a list in your notebook of all the risks you take and next to each risk, write your justification for taking it.*

◆

MORRIS GALLOWAY CAME HOME TODAY TO FIND HIS BE-loved grapevines an eerie dead thicket, turned from green to brown by the hydrofluoric acid leak that caused the evacuation of 3,000 residents from their homes last weekend.

Major accidents are not new here. Texas City was the scene of the worst industrial disaster in American history, the 1947 explosion that killed 576 people and injured 5,000. But Mr. Galloway, a shipyard worker in nearby Galveston, was philosophical about the accident over the weekend.

"You can't be mad—it's just Mother Nature," he said. "The way I look at it, if this didn't happen, maybe there would have been an even bigger explosion. Either way, there isn't anything you can do about it. I drive down the causeway every day, and I've seen some hell of wrecks, but there isn't anything you can do about them either."

There are not many places where residents would describe a toxic chemical leak as the work of Mother Nature. But in this Gulf Coast city of 43,000 residents, whose lives are dominated by the steel towers, yellow flares and gentle plumes of smoke from its massive petrochemical complex, a degree of risk is accepted as part of the natural order.

"I've lived here all my life, and I don't think about those things," said Jimmy Hayley, executive vice president of the Texas City-LaMarque Chamber of Commerce. "For all intents and purposes, these plants are safe. If you feel it's unsafe, you don't work here. Wherever you live, you are susceptible to something. You could be a rancher and be in the pen with a bad bull and get hurt. There's always something."

Nearly all the evacuated residents had returned to their homes by today, washing down the houses and cars, gawking at the sudden change in the trees from green to withered brown, and getting back to normal.

The accident at the Marathon Petroleum Company plant occurred about 5:20 P.M. Friday when a crane dropped a heavy piece of equipment, puncturing a pipeline and releasing the toxic hydrofluoric acid, which is used as a catalyst in the refinery. Marathon officials said they were continuing to investigate the accident.

Hospital officials said 33 people were still being treated at two area hospitals this afternoon, two of them in intensive care. Over all, more than 140 people were admitted to area hospitals and more than 900 were treated for respiratory problems and eye irritation because of the chemical exposure. People were still arriving for treatment today, officials said.

Texas City holds a dark niche in American history because of the explosion on April 16, 1947. It occurred when a French ship, the Grandcamp, loaded with ammonia nitrate, exploded and turned the town into an inferno. The event is enough a part of local lore that even the Chamber of Commerce has copies of the book, "Disaster at Texas City" for sale in its office. By comparison, in the world's worst industrial disaster, 2,500 people died in a 1984 chemical accident in Bhopal, India.

Since 1947 there has been nothing remotely comparable here to the explosion. But industrial accidents are a regular fact of life both for the plant workers and those who live in the modest frame houses nearby.

Over the last 12 months one worker was critically burned in a refinery fire, three others were injured when a petroleum storage tank exploded and a dock worker was killed when a railroad tank car exploded. The most serious recent incident came in 1978 when seven people were killed in a series of refinery explosions.

Still, residents say the accident toll is not bad considering the potential hazards involved. Longtime residents say that because of the 1947 accident, Texas City is extraordinarily conscious of safety. In addition, with the slumping local economy—industrial employment was 6,137 in 1986 against 7,376 in 1982—there is little criticism of the area's economic institutions.

In better times, Texas City, with its relatively high wages at the refineries and accomodating bays and inlets for fishing, had the reputation as something of a blue-collar haven. For some, like Jack Carson, a retiree who spent today painting and tinkering in the shadow of the Marathon plant, that view still holds.

For others though, there's a tougher, almost desperate edge, to the tradeoff between work and safety.

"I was brought up here, so I don't worry too much about those things," said Benny Black, who is unemployed and stood beneath a withered mimosa tree down the street from Mr. Carson. "I'd work anyplace; it don't matter how dangerous it is. I've worked around this stuff all my life. It don't bother me."

Questions for Critical Analysis

1. Do you think this article exceeds simple reporting of a news event? How?
2. Consider other industrial accidents: the Union Carbide accident in Bhopal, India; the closing of Times Beach, MO; the Kerr-McGee plant in Gore, OK; Three Mile Island accident in 1979; Chernobyl in 1987 or the oil spill in Valdez, Alaska, in 1989. What ideas and fears do you bring to the problem of hazardous industry?
3. Compare the way "Lethal Dose" was written with Applebome's reporting on the Texas City accident. How does the writing style reveal the authors' purposes?
4. Compare the conclusions of the two essays. Why do the communities respond differently? In what ways is each conclusion a simplification?

Questions for Structural Analysis

1. "Where a Chemical Leak Seems an Accepted Risk" appeared as a feature story in the *New York Times*. What stylistic devices identify the article as a journalistic piece of writing?
2. Applebome divided his essay into three major sections. What is the relationship between each section?
3. Why does Applebome relate the story of the 1947 accident in Texas City and refer to the accident in Bhopal, India? Do they color the way you respond to the citizen's acceptance of the risk?

*A*FTER *L*ONG SILENCE

A. G. MOJTABAI

A. G. Mojtabai (1938–) visited Amarillo, Texas, to write an article about living with the nuclear bomb. It quickly became apparent that her article was turning into a book, and Mojtabai returned to Amarillo, eventually making her home there. As she describes it, "I remain to make my home here, out on the edge—and yet quite in the middle—of things. Often, these days, I find myself staring at the United States through *Amarillo. Indeed, the longer I look at this city, as Flannery O'Connor liked to say about absolutely anything, 'the more of the whole world I see in it'—the good, the bad, the indifferent, the mixed."*

Before you begin reading: *Remember an incident when you had to face your unwillingness to confront an issue. Think about the people involved, the place where the incident took place, and the emotional changes you experienced. Write down your memories.*

◆

STATEMENT ON THE PRODUCTION AND STOCKPILING OF THE NEUTRON BOMB

The announcement of the decision to produce and stockpile neutron warheads is the latest in a series of tragic anti-life positions taken by our government.

This latest decision allegedly comes as a response to the possibility of a Soviet tank attack in central Europe.

The current administration says the production and stockpiling of neutron bombs is a logical step in a process begun in 1978 under the previous administration. Thus both the Democratic and the Republican administrations seem convinced that in accelerating the arms race they are carrying out the wishes of the American people.

The matter is of immediate concern to us who live next door to Pantex, the nation's final assembly point for nuclear weapons, including the neutron bomb.

It is clear now that the military can—perhaps must—think in only one way: Each enemy advance in arms technology and capability must be met with a further advance on our part. No matter that the enemy must then, perforce, respond with a further advance of its own. No matter that we already have the capability of destroying each other many times over and that soon other nations of this imperiled planet will possess the same awesome power.

God's gifts may be used for evil or good, for war or peace. The God of Israel warned the people of ancient times that the military use of the horse is "a vain hope for safety. Despite its power it cannot save" (Psalm 33:17). Is not the military use of nuclear energy likewise a vain hope for safety? Despite its incredible power it cannot save.

Enough of this greater and greater destructive capability. Let us stop this madness. Let us turn our attention and our energies to the peaceful uses of nuclear energy: For the production of food, fiber, clothing, shelter, transportation.

We beg our administration to stop accelerating the arms race.

We beg our military to use common sense and moderation in our defense posture.

We urge individuals involved in the production and stockpiling of nuclear bombs to consider what they are doing, to resign from such activities, and to seek employment in peaceful pursuits.

Let us educate ourselves on nuclear armaments. Let us support those who are calling for an end to the arms race. Let us join men and women everywhere in prayer that peace may reign.

—Bishop L. T. Matthiesen, *West Texas Catholic*, August 23, 1981.

THE PANTEX ARMY ORDNANCE PLANT WAS ESTABLISHED IN 1942 to assemble conventional ammunition shells and bombs. It is generally recalled by Amarilloans as a "shell-loading plant." In 1945, after the end of World War II, the plant was closed, and in 1949 Texas Tech University took over the grounds as an experimental agricultural station.

A year later, the Atomic Energy Commission reclaimed the plant for the assembly of nuclear warheads and the continuing manufacture of conventional high explosives. Many private industries—Dupont, Bendix, General Electric, Monsanto, Rockwell International, and Union Carbide, among them—were becoming involved in managing government-owned, contractor-operated ("Go-Co") plants, and Procter & Gamble was the first operating contractor of Pantex as a nuclear weapons facility. Mason & Hanger–Silas Mason Company, the Kentucky-based engineering firm, known for its work on the building of the Lincoln Tunnel and Grand Coulee Dam, took over operations from Procter & Gamble in 1956.

The current functions of Pantex are—or ought to be—public knowledge by now: fabrication and testing of conventional high explosives, nuclear weapons assembly, disassembly, modification, and repair. Its production rate, according to figures published in the *Bulletin of the Atomic Scientists*, is "almost 1,500 new nuclear warheads per year, significantly higher than the rate of the mid-1970's."[1] (This would mean an average of at least four nuclear warheads assembled at Pantex a day.) Pantex officials decline to comment on these numbers, since workload and production figures are classified.

Despite its apparent isolation, Amarillo is, in fact, the center of a vast web of connections with military-industrial operations throughout the nation.[2] By truck, rail, sometimes by air, the components come in. From the Savannah River plant in Aiken, South Carolina, come plutonium and tritium for nuclear warheads; from the Rocky Flats plant in Golden, Colorado, come plutonium cores; from the Kansas City plant in Missouri, electronic arming, fusing, and firing switches; from the Mound Laboratory in Miamisburg, Ohio, detonators and timers; from the Pinellas plant in Clearwater, Florida, neutron-generators; from the Y-12 plant in Oak Ridge, Tennessee, uranium and testing devices.

And, from Pantex, the assembled weapons go forth, ready for—whatever it is that they are ready for. They go forth to the Sierra Army Depot in Herlong, California, to the King's Bay Naval Submarine Support Base in Georgia, to Wurtsmith Air Force Base in Oscoda, Michigan, to Malmstrom Air Force Base in Great Falls, Montana, to the Lake Meade Nuclear Storage Depot of Nellis Air Force Base in Nevada, to Kirtland Air Force Base in Albuquerque, New Mexico, to Griffiss Air Force Base in Rome, New York, and the Seneca Army Depot in Romulus, New York, to Grand Forks Air Force Base in Emerado, North Dakota, to Charleston Naval Base in South Carolina, to Carswell Air Force Base in Fort Worth, Texas, to the Yorktown Naval Weapons Station in Virginia, to the Bangor Naval Submarine Base and the Silverdale Strategic Weapons Facility in Washington, to bases in New Hampshire, New Jersey, Florida, Maine, Louisiana, Missouri, Arkansas, North and South Dakota, Wyoming, Alaska, Hawaii, and overseas.[3] The white trains move slowly in and out of Pantex under cover of night; the stainless steel, unmarked trucks, bearing smaller but more frequent loads, move in broad day, rumbling down the interstate where the traffic never stops.

The "white train"—now a powerful symbol of the antinuclear movement—remained invisible for over two decades as it traveled slowly back and forth across the nation. Its discovery was roundabout, almost accidental. It happened in Bangor, Washington, not in Amarillo.

In 1981, peace activists Jim and Shelley Douglass purchased a house on a hill overlooking the gate where railroad shipments enter the Trident base in Bangor, Washington. For four years, they had had their eye on the house as an appropriate site for their Ground Zero Center for Nonviolent Action.

Living in this house also enabled the Douglasses to closely observe shipping activities at the base. Their attention was first focused upon the weekly railroad shipments from Salt Lake City, Utah, near the Hercules Corporation, source of the Trident's missile motor shipments.

In December 1982, a newspaper reporter alerted Jim Douglass to an all-white armored train, rumored to be carrying nuclear warheads and on its way to the Trident base. Douglass knew nothing about such shipments but, stepping outside, noticed intense activity at the gate of the Trident base and an unusually heavy concentration of security cars. Then came his first sight of the white train.[4] He thought of the boxcars during World War II, moving invisibly across the landscape of Europe, carrying their doomed human freight. He was stunned by the whiteness of the train.

By the time of the next shipment on March 18–22, 1983, the first trackside vigils were held in thirty-five towns along the route from La Junta, Colorado, to Bangor, Washington. Branching out from Ground Zero, a community of witnesses formed along the Trident tracks in Utah, Idaho, Oregon, and Washington. It was called the Agape Community.[5] Since then, the Agape Community has become an extensive telephone network, and the trackside vigils have multiplied.

Moving at a speed of thirty-five miles an hour, carrying a variable load (estimates range from one hundred to two hundred hydrogen bombs a shipment), the white train has been observed leaving Pantex and arriving at the Trident submarine base in Bangor at intervals of two to four months. Accelerated speeds of fifty to sixty miles an hour were observed by trackside witnesses in 1985. And the train is no longer white: it is multicolored.

The official reason for the whiteness of the train had been to keep the interior temperatures down. Since the colors were changed, rather playfully, to red, green, blue, brown, gray, and even black in 1985, one might question the official reason, and really begin to wonder about that whiteness. Certainly, for those who kept vigil along the tracks, the whiteness of the train had a disturbing symbolic propriety, a symbolism rich with contradiction, and they were apt to invoke "the incantation of this whiteness" in the spirit of Herman Melville's *Moby-Dick*.[6] White for shrouds and bridals, white for purity and mildness ("the most meaning symbol of spiritual things, nay, the very veil of the Christian's Deity"), white for sterility ("not so much a color as the visible absence of color . . . a dumb blankness, full of meaning, in a wide landscape of snows—a colorless, all-color of atheism from which we shrink"), white for the blinding white night of annihilation (for thoughts of annihilation, which "stab us from behind . . . when beholding the white depths of the milky way").

Truck traffic in and out of Pantex is more frequent and accident-prone than the passage of trains, yet, somehow, the dramatic symbolism is absent, so it has long proceeded without protest. The trucks are, of course, harder to spot than the trains; indeed, they move with the ease of Safeway bread trucks. The backs of the trailers used to have diagonal safety stripes of black and white or black and orange—the kind you see at the beginnings and ends of concrete embankments—but the stripes are gradually being removed. Except for the presence of station wagon escorts, and the thicket of boxed antennae on the roofs of the drivers' cabins, they look and move much like any other eighteen-wheelers on the highway. The lack of markings is perhaps their most distinguishing feature. These vehicles are exempt from regulations that require trucks to carry signs indicating the presence of explosives or radioactive cargo.

In August 1984, a group of observers sponsored by Nukewatch, the educational arm of the Wisconsin-based Progressive Foundation, kept a round-the-clock vigil at Pantex. During the course of eight days and nights, they observed the movement of fourteen trucks and eleven escort cars. Allowing for decoys, it seems reasonable to infer that truck shipments move in and out of Pantex several times a week. It is estimated that assembled warheads, components, and fuel—including plutonium—are transported 4.5 million miles a year, by public highway, to depots all over the country.[7] Yet, despite periodic vigils since 1984, in Amarillo, Oak Ridge, and Rocky Flats, their movements are largely unremarked, if not unnoticed, to this day.

More puzzling than the invisibility of trucks and trains is the long invisibility of the Pantex plant itself. An illustrated poster map, produced in 1981, advertises the glories of Amarillo—the civic center, the hospitals, the churches, the looming Southwestern Public Service utility company, the large commercial banks, the massive grain elevators. Then, in the upper right-hand corner, between an "awl and gas" pump and a mechanical bull, is a small yard, fenced by garden wire. A spotlight stands alongside the fence, fanning out its rays like the petals of a flower. The fence surrounds a sunny blank space and the words "Pantex Plant." It might be a deserted playground, a grass patch. But, unlike the grassy stretches elsewhere on the map, there is not the faintest feathering of the surface to suggest vegetation—not a stem, not a speck, of detail. The wire fence encloses nothing at all.[8]

"I know from my own experience that the fact that Pantex plant assembles nuclear weapons has been public knowledge for at least twenty years," claims Claud Gay, a high-ranking administrator at Pantex. People differ widely on that count. Some say ten years; most put it at "a couple of years." Why is there so much variation?

Jerry Huff, executive editor of the Amarillo newspaper, argues that the relaxation of secrecy concerning Pantex was a gradual development that started when the Atomic Energy Commission was disbanded in 1974, continued through the establishment of the Energy Research and Development Administration, and became noticeable with the establishment of the Department of Energy in 1977.

The Atomic Energy Commission had been protected by the Joint Congressional Committee on Atomic Energy, composed of high-ranking senators and representatives who were able to maintain secrecy.

Huff notes that the Department of Energy, like any other government department, is more subject to public scrutiny, to Federal Freedom of Information laws, and open-meeting pressures. In his view, no precise decision to declassify previously classified information need have taken place. The nature of the work at Pantex, for which authorizations and appropriations were being made, was not a protectable secret. People found out according to their need, or desire, to know.

There *is* agreement on one date: until Bishop Matthiesen issued his call to conscience in August 1981, the plant was not much discussed in Amarillo. (It is rarely a spontaneous subject of conversation, even now.) And Matthiesen, himself, admits that for many years he did, and did not, know—he almost guessed, but preferred not to know—what went on at Pantex.

When I ask the bishop what he had been thinking of in all those years of driving past Pantex, his answer is curiously, typically, double:

"The sign said: DEPARTMENT OF ENERGY RESEARCH AND DEVELOPMENT. It might have meant development of peaceful uses of energy . . . I guess I knew about Pantex. I knew about it during World War II, when it manufactured conventional bombs and bullets. I must confess that I suspected but never dared ask."

Bishop Leroy Theodore Matthiesen resembles his photographs—all of them, and there are many. His most frequent expression is one of imperturbable patience, a sort of stolid sweetness, yet his shifts of expression are rapid, abrupt. Slower and more deliberate are the motions of his hands. Liturgical motions: there are no wasted gestures; each signifies.

Catholics who are uncomfortable with the bishop's outspokenness on the nuclear arms race often speak of him as "an outsider," in contrast to his predecessor, Bishop De Falco, who was "one of us" and made no waves. In point of fact, Bishop De Falco was born and raised in Pennsylvania, and Bishop Matthiesen is really a "good ol' boy" from Texas.

He was born in 1921, one of eight children, and grew up on a cotton farm near Olfen, Texas. Olfen is a small rural Catholic community, out on the rolling prairie northeast of San Angelo. With the exception of a sister and an older brother in the church, the bishop's brothers and sisters continue to live and farm around Olfen.

In 1946, he was ordained as a priest. Until 1980, he performed routine parish duties in and around Amarillo, serving also as teacher, principal, and athletic coach at the local Catholic high school. He edited the diocesan newspaper, as well, and, for over thirty years, has written a column called "Wise and Otherwise."[9] In 1980, he was ordained a bishop. "From now on," he wrote, "this column will be more wise than otherwise."

A line from a 1960 column reads oddly in retrospect: "Maybe someone should start an organization of Americans and Others United for the Separation of Ministers and Politics."

Until 1981, Matthiesen led a busy, but enclosed, life. Support for parochial schools was one of the issues in the foreground of his thought. (He voted for Reagan in 1980, in large part on this issue.) Politically, he was alert to the needs of rural families, farmworkers, and migrants, and especially to the problems of Hispanics, who then made up about 75 percent of the ninety thousand Catholics in his diocese.[10] His religious concerns also focused upon the diocese: the problem of making the church present in smaller communities, the need for spiritual support and renewal of geographically isolated priests. These concerns have never left him but, since the spring of 1981, his interests have broadened well beyond the bounds of the diocese. Even as his diocese has contracted (it was halved from 44,500 to 25,800 square miles in 1982), his concerns have continued to expand, until they are now nothing short of global.

Newspaper reporters often speak of Bishop Matthiesen's "conversion," of a dramatically sudden reversal of his old values. A slow incubation and convergence would be more accurate. There are glimmerings and hints of a pacific outlook scattered *passim* throughout his earlier columns, although they are not consistently brought together until 1981. But his advocacy of gun control stands out in retrospect: it was, and continues to be, an especially unpopular stand in Texas.

With Reagan's accession to the presidency in 1981, questions of military spending and the morality of the nuclear arms race were in the air, and some of this drifted into the Panhandle. In March 1981, six demonstrators, including a priest, were arrested for trespassing in a nonviolent, prayerful vigil at Pantex. Visiting the priest in jail, the bishop found certain of his preconceptions shattered: "I found him to be a gentle, well-informed individual—not the flaming radical I had thought he might be."

In April of that year, when Matthiesen attended public hearings in Amarillo on whether to locate the MX missile system in West Texas and New Mexico, he was provoked enough to issue a public declaration: "Like you, we love our country, and more than you, we love this part of it," he said. "I do not ask you to move the MX missile system elsewhere. We do not want it anywhere. I ask you to forget it entirely . . . The present atomic armament race is madness. That we can assure the destruction of the enemy even as we are being destroyed makes it no less mad."

Then a deacon in the diocese asked for a conference with the bishop; he was having a problem of conscience regarding his work at Pantex. His wife was particularly concerned. The deacon's age and health made re-employment difficult. The bishop temporized, advising the deacon to stay on at the job—unless an employment alternative presented itself.

The bishop did not temporize when the go-ahead order for production of the neutron bomb was issued in August. His reiterated plea was for "common sense and moderation in our defense posture," but his final appeal was a radical one: "We urge individuals involved in the production and stockpiling of nuclear bombs to consider what they are doing, to resign from such activities, and to seek employment in peaceful pursuits."

Although no resignations followed, the statement and its ensuing publicity caused a furor in Amarillo. To many, it seemed a betrayal of the hometown. Speaking to Mayor Rick Klein about this, months after the bishop's call to conscience, I find him still bristling: "I don't have anything to say about the bishop. All I can say is that Pantex is good for the business community. It's good for Amarillo. We've never had any trouble with Pantex. I don't understand people coming down here and making a fuss about it. It's been here for forty years."

In the past, some Amarilloans who were in the know used to jest about the product turned out at Pantex. The old joke was: "That's where they make the cups for flying saucers." Or: "whipsocket handles." And they tell me that way back in the days when the plant was operated by Procter & Gamble, people would say: "soap—*lots* of soap." People do not joke all that much about Pantex any more—at least, not to strangers. But they laugh as they remember.

What kind of laughter? All kinds. The kinds of laughter we all know. There is the laughter of safe-and-secure: this can't touch me. Of incongruity: laughter as a form of speech, inchoate, bewildered speech—What can I say? What would you have me say? And social laughter. You laugh because others are laughing—not to be left out.

I have been asking people ever since my arrival in 1982: "Do you know what Pantex does?" Sooner or later, I always come round to this question. There are still people who claim not to know, although there were many more at the time of my first visit. But, even at first, people were not ignorant. As S. B. Whittenburg, former publisher of the *Amarillo Globe-News*, explains: "You can't help having a big old operation like that without people guessing." On the whole, people knew and did not know—a contradiction, by any other name—and the best way I can think of explaining it is to let people explain themselves:

Dave Harter, television sales representative for Channel 7, and a member of the local Mensa chapter:

"I think it's fascinating that Bishop Matthiesen didn't realize what Pantex did. It shows again what he's fighting. He's intelligent and sensitive, and still it took him all that time, and yet he's trying to convert people. I don't think it's so much conscious resistance. His basic confrontation is against momentum—lots of years and lots of money."

Jack P. Thompson, director of classification at Pantex:

"Let me give you a little history and it will be easier. Back when, say, we started like in the fifties, early fifties, all of it was—still is—highly classified. We're just not so covert about it any more. Back then, you'd ask—somebody'd say: 'What do you do at Pantex?'

"'At Pantex, well, we make cups for flying saucers.' You've heard that. But, see, and people laughed, and—and knew, and said: 'Well, we're not going to ask.' They don't even ask today. The old hands won't even talk about it, even though it's not classified any more . . . The old guy—he kinda chokes on saying anything about this."

Tol Ware, chairman of Amarillo National Bank:

"For so many years when the thing was originally out there—now I'm saying 'after the war' because it was just an ordnance storage facility, I believe, during the war—but when it was reactivated out there, it was so hush-hush, and I don't think anybody really knew what was going on out there.

"*We* didn't, initially. Back about—oh, I imagine, it was '51, probably, Korean wartime, I believe—they reactivated it. And at that time, Procter &

Gamble was the prime contractor. And they were customers of our bank. We had two or three, we felt, close contacts out there, but we didn't know what was going on.

"Later, when the Silas Mason bunch went in there, they kept it, I feel, in the same sort of quiet posture. And I think that only recently have the people in Amarillo really realized that nuclear warheads were being manufactured out there, but they were very hush-hush. They were contributing to United Way, and various civic enterprises on sort of a low profile . . . There wasn't a great deal of conversation about it. The local people who worked out there all seem to enjoy their jobs. It was well-paying."

Thomas H. Thompson, retired editor of the *Amarillo Globe-Times:*

"Of course, it kind of slipped up on us that they were actually making nuclear bombs out there. Back in the sixties I was first aware. SAC was carrying nuclear missiles. We were a prime target. We were more worried about that. In Naples, they don't worry about Vesuvius. They're used to it."

Stanley Marsh 3rd, financier:

"It crept up on us, and I never quite knew. I used to think Pantex was building—for a long time, I thought, my friends thought that they made mechanisms at Pantex that went inside the bombs . . . It seemed that we knew and it seeped in, but then there was something. Maybe there was something in one of the congressional budgets.

"I used to think that they made bombs in ten different places. What I don't like about Pantex is the stigma of living in the town which is the only town in the United States where they make death machines. Now I personally believe in the kind of *Time* magazine conventional wisdom that says that we've avoided atomic war for the last thirty years because of the threat of atomic weapons . . . But I don't like living in the town where they make them. I think they should move the plant. And I think they did an awful, stinking, dirty trick to the town, hoodwinked us, to make us into the murder capital without even telling us—'cause I don't like it. And I think they did it intentionally because they knew that if they publicized the fact that this was going to be the one place—you know, America's Buchenwald—then I think that we wouldn't have let them do it . . .

"I'm really irritated about it. And I feel like this is my town, as much as it's anyone else's. And I've been tricked. Like somebody let me drink and said, 'Let's do something fun. Let's get our nose tattooed.' The next morning I woke up and I had a beetle tattooed on my nose!"

T. Boone Pickens, president of Mesa Petroleum Company:

(Distinctly annoyed): "I really don't worry about things like that. And, once, sure, there was a period, I guess, the first time they said 'Pantex,' I said 'What's that?' And then they said, 'Well, that's a big plant out here—it has some—it's a government plant, and all.' And I'm not sure . . . that I didn't say: 'Well, wait a minute, what is the plant doing out there?' I think that over a period of time, it, you know, it evolved that 'Oh, well, you mean it's the final assembly point for the nuclear bomb? . . .'

"I think it's been, you know, it's been generally known. It hasn't been anybody tried to hide anything. They haven't publicized it either, but I don't think there's any doubt that they're assembling the nuclear bomb at Pantex. But that's one of those things that happened a long time ago. And it's—once that's established—it's extremely difficult to do anything about it.

"And it has to be done someplace. I'm convinced that we have to have that protection for our country. So it's gonna be done someplace. It just so happened that we got stuck with it."

John Ward, city manager:

"I don't ever lose any sleep over Pantex, and I'm sure that to an outsider having the nuclear warheads assembly factory a short distance from your city would be terrifying. And I don't really think the people of Amarillo ever really worry about it. It's here. It's been here for a long time. People accept it. It's an important industry for the area. I guess if there ever was a problem, then people will realize what the dangers are.

"I knew it was there when I was ten years old. I can remember going down Highway 66 and seeing the bunkers and asking what they were, asking probably my dad or whoever I was with. And, of course, they knew—and they did not live in Amarillo. So I think at that time it seemed to be common knowledge of what it was. And it never really bothered me. I thought it was strange, or whatever, I guess, when I was a child. And I think people around the city, the ones I've come into contact with, know it's there and know what they do. I don't think any one of them, including myself, knows exactly what they do. I know that they're the final assembly point."

Dr. Winfred Moore, pastor of First Baptist Church:

"I think it's something you don't really think about too much. You don't see Pantex like you do the B-52s when they were out there going over all the time. I don't see how anybody could have lived here and not know what was being done out there. It's kinda like knowing the Santa Fe railroad is here. You know it hauls things. You don't really pay attention to what percentage of cars are coal cars, or whatever."

Buck Ramsey, writer:

"In high school, we shared a certain pride that we were in the top ten targets for the Russians. We thought that was pretty neat.

"For years, I thought of myself as a sort of minor investigative reporter, but, truthfully, I was so accustomed to that plant being out there that I don't remember it occurring to me to ever break a story on the place.

"But the story started breaking itself. I think it surprised everyone in Amarillo—it sure did me. I don't know anyone who knew that Pantex was *the* final assembly point—the only final assembly point—they left here ready to go off. They kept it the best known secret, or the least known secret.

"I became aware of it through this silly thing, the column they run in the evening paper on page two—'Ask So-and-So.'[11] Questions like: What's the best solution for getting out grease? They snuck it in the middle of one of those columns: 'It it true that Pantex is the final assembly point?' That's how they snuck it through."

In point of fact, a fact routinely overlooked by surprising numbers of people, the Amarillo newspaper did not sneak this information through. The story was written with progressively fuller disclosure over the years.

Stories about Pantex during the sixties tended to be small and sporadic—announcements of personnel changes, or concerning a tour of the unclassified sections of the plant for local community leaders. By 1972, the plant's nuclear operations were plainly stated, although buried in a mass of miscellaneous detail. But, in 1977, a series of articles were devoted, solely and specifically, to the plant's nuclear functions.

On Sunday, December 11, 1977, the newspaper gave over the front pages of its new *Impact* (Business, Energy, Farm, and Ranch) section to Pantex. *Pantex* was the lead caption on the index of the first page of the news section, and the capsule summary evaded nothing:

> America's nuclear eggs all go into the same basket at one time or another—at the Pantex Plant a scant 17 miles from Amarillo. It is the only final assembly plant for nuclear weapons presently operating in the United States.[12]

The *Sunday News-Globe* feature on Pantex was a lucid, detailed, two-page spread, with aerial and ground photographs of the plant, and interviews with high-ranking Pantex officials. The lead article by Jerry Huff, "U.S. Nuclear Arsenal Assembled at Pantex," concluded with these words:

> The Pantex Plant is likely to be around for a long time no matter what company operates it. The plant is valued at about $100 million, and another $15 million will be spent there before the end of 1980.
>
> After all, when you put all your nuclear eggs in one basket, the basket tends to become a permanent fixture.

It remains a puzzle—what people have known, and what they have thought about what they have known. So much so that, in 1982, the Los Alamos National Laboratory commissioned a consulting firm, Adcock & Associates, and a team of sociologists to conduct an attitude and opinion survey among local residents. Faced with the need for future expansion and renovation of Pantex, the Department of Energy wanted to know whether to continue putting all their nuclear eggs in the Amarillo basket.

The first response to the survey was "an unusually high refusal rate . . . an incomprehensible [that is, incomprehensibly low] response rate."[13] A change in the contact procedure, along with publicized assurances of the official nature of the project (that is, that it was not sponsored by a peace group) and that the names of the respondents would be held strictly confidential, helped somewhat, although the refusal rate remained high.

Unsurprisingly, community support tended to be highly favorable on all three counts—continued operation, expansion, and renovation of Pantex. When the figures are broken down, though, there are some striking inconsistencies. Almost unanimously, local residents agreed that Amarillo was a good (acceptable, or better than average) place to raise children.[14] This would not be at all puzzling but for the fact that significant numbers (22 percent) of the group also believed that there was a good chance of an accidental nuclear explosion at Pantex. An even greater number (37 percent) thought there was a good chance of an accident during transport of radioactive material. What is more, nearly 84 percent of those polled agreed that the presence of Pantex increased the chance of the area's becoming a military target in time of war, yet the overwhelming majority—83 percent—favored the continued presence and operation of Pantex; 78 percent favored its expansion; 82 percent favored its renovation.

Of course, the realization that *no* community would be safe in the event of nuclear war, and the mixture of patriotism and pride at being a vital part of the defense establishment, might help account for a certain tolerance of risks. But it goes beyond patriotism and pride, beyond the much-prized common sense and pragmatic conservatism of the area to assert that a place that is certainly a prime Soviet target, and commonly believed to be subject to accidental release of radioactive material or accidental explosion, is a good place to raise children.

The low level of stress caused by living under these circumstances might give pause for thought. Then again, a survey of this kind can only register *acknowledged* stress. The fact that over half the people interviewed had friends or relatives working at Pantex might explain a certain degree of reticence about seeming to criticize the plant. But even the authors of the survey saw fit to pause over one particularly mystifying response. They observed: "One somewhat surprising result was that *not one* respondent pointed to a moral position as the cause for stress resulting from Pantex."[15] This is especially surprising in the case of Catholics, for whom the nuclear arms race and the question of working at Pantex had become a definite moral issue.

One has to wait and listen hard to discern the faintest moral qualm. Asking pointblank "How do you feel about Pantex?" of anyone and everyone I meet in the streets of Amarillo, the first response is usually one of astounding blankness. "It's out there—that's all it means to me. I really had never thought about it."—"I don't get too excited about it one way or the other."—"It's all right with me. We need it, I guess, for sure. It would be better if I had a job there."

Again and again: "No feeling. No, not really."

NOTES

1. William M. Arkin, Thomas B. Cochran, and Milton M. Hoenig, "Resource Paper on the U.S. Nuclear Arsenal," *Bulletin of the Atomic Scientists*, August/September 1984, p. 38. The same rate of production of nuclear warheads continues as of January 1986, according to William Arkin, director of nuclear weapons research at the Institute for Policy Studies in Washington, D.C. In addition, Arkin notes that "joint test assemblies" (test warheads) have been moved from Pantex to Rocky Flats, thus freeing up additional capacity that could be applied to new warheads at Pantex.

2. According to the Center for Defense Information, the rationale for having but a single final assembly plant for nuclear weapons, and for the location of that plant to be a matter of public knowledge, is this:

> In our democracy, fortunately, there would be no way to keep the location of an industrial facility the size of Pantex secret from the citizenry. Unlike the Soviet Union, the U.S. cannot close off militarily-important cities to citizens and travelers. Most assuredly, Pantex would be a prime target for the Soviet Union in the initial salvo of World War III, but then it is impossible to conceive of the circumstances in modern warfare in which the U.S. would be able to continue churning out nuclear warheads in the midst of war. During the next war, both sides will have to go with what they have. It promises to be quite a short and devastating conflict. (Gene R. La Rocque, Rear Admiral, USN [Ret.], Director, Center for Defense Information, letter to author, July 9, 1985).

3. This is, of course, only a smattering, a rough indication, of geographical spread in the U.S. For the most complete listing to date of nuclear weapons storage sites across the nation and the world, see: William M. Arkin and Richard W. Fieldhouse, *Nuclear Battlefields: Global Links in the Arms Race* (Cambridge, Mass.: Ballinger Publishing Co., 1985).
4. For an account of the history of the train-monitoring movement, see Jim Douglass, "Tracking the White Train," *Sojourners*, February 1984, p. 13ff.

   Documents from the Washington Utilities and Transportation Commission on hazardous rail shipments revealed that these trains were coming from an unspecified location in Texas. Douglass guessed that Pantex was the point of origin, and the guess was confirmed by Les Breeding of Amarillo on January 5, 1983, when he saw the returning white train enter the grounds of Pantex.
5. It was called the Agape community for the kind of (brotherly/sisterly, all-inclusive) love that animated the early Christian communities. The conviction here is that spiritual transformation—the power of shared concern and nonviolent witnessing—will stop the arms race.
6. Herman Melville, *Moby-Dick* (New York: New American Library, 1961), p. 196.
7. Samuel H. Day, Jr., "H-Bombs on Our Highways: That Truck up Ahead Could Be Hauling 1.2 Megatons," *The Progressive*, November 22, 1984, p. 18ff. Since August 1984, truck movements have been monitored at six-month intervals. The Benedictine Peace House in Oklahoma City has organized regular vigils.
8. Map produced by Tom Knutson Enterprises of Amarillo in 1981.
9. As of December 15, 1985, the title of this column was changed to "Thy Will Be Done."
10. An estimated 60 percent Hispanic in 1984, after the division of the diocese.
11. "Ask Adam" is the name of the column.
12. "Sunday Sampler," *Amarillo Sunday News-Globe*, December 11, 1977, p. 1-A.
13. Adcock and Associates, *Attitude and Opinion Survey Regarding the Pantex Plant*, prepared for Los Alamos National Laboratory under contract #9-Xi2-2920Y-1, Albuquerque, N.Mex., September 1982, p. III-11.

    The survey itself remains puzzling in a number of respects. To start with: Why did so few people respond?

    Only 400 out of the 1070 people randomly selected responded to contact. Were the nonresponses indifferent, or motivated? What differences in attitude might have shown up had the other 670 people answered?

    Conceivably, the endorsement of Pantex might have been still stronger. The consultants suggest that a wider participation might have been had from the first had not the suspicion prevailed that a peace group was behind the questionnaire.

    The first ten days of contacting potential respondents by telephone produced what Adcock called "an unusually high refusal rate . . . an incomprehensible response rate. Over the ten-day period, almost 100 refusals were received compared to fewer than 50 completed interviews."

A change in the initial contact procedure was clearly in order. Thereafter, potential respondents were contacted first by mail. The mailings contained a letter describing the survey and "assurances of the official nature of the project, the anonymity of respondents, and confidentiality of responses, as well as an expression of Adcock and Associates' desire to have all points of view represented. Also included in the mailing was a copy of a local newspaper article that announced and described the survey project" (p. III-12).

The response rate improved after this: viz., "50%, a significant increase over the 33% experienced before the mailings" (p. III-12). Still, the nonresponse rate remained high. A recent article in *Public Opinion Quarterly*, dealing with nonresponse, asserts that a nonresponse rate of 25 percent is typical for good, state-of-the-art surveys (Tom W. Smith, "The Hidden 25 Percent: An Analysis of Nonresponse on the 1980 General Social Survey," Fall 1983, no. 47, pp. 386–402).

Another question: Why wasn't there a demographic breakdown of characteristics among the local population? For there were, by Adcock's own admission, certain nonrepresentative aspects to the group polled. For example: 18–24-year-olds should make up around 20 percent of the population. In this survey, they constituted 7.3 percent of the population. Since younger people tended to be more critical of Pantex (see table IV-24), this underrepresentation of youth was not without significance.

On the other hand, if conservatives, alienated by the rumor that the survey was sponsored by a peace group were also underrepresented, these two possible sources of statistical bias (conservatives, and the more liberal youth) may have canceled each other out.

14. Ibid., p. IV-22.
15. Ibid., p. IV-56.

Questions for Critical Analysis

1. What goes on at Pantex? Why was it kept secret? What point does Mojtabai make about the secrecy? How do you think she feels about the plant? the secrecy? How do you know?
2. What is the "white train"? What symbolic references does Mojtabai make to the color "white"? How do these symbols expand the description of the train? Can you think of other references Mojtabai doesn't use, but could have? Why was the train repainted?
3. What was Bishop Matthiesen's "call to conscience"? What prompted it? How did the townspeople respond? What is your reaction to his statement?
4. Why do you think Amarillo citizens denied knowing what went on at Pantex? Compare their attitude toward this plant with the attitude of the people of Gore, Oklahoma, and Texas City, Texas in previous selections in this section. Where would you rather live? Why?
5. Mojtabai reports that, when the Department of Energy interviewed people about their feelings toward expanding the operation at Pantex, no one mentioned a moral difficulty with the idea. How does Mojtabai feel about this? How do you know? Do you have the same reaction? Why, or why not?

QUESTIONS FOR STRUCTURAL ANALYSIS

1. What effect does Bishop Matthiesen's statement have on your response to the essay that follows? How do you imagine you would have responded if you hadn't read the statement first?
2. Mojtabai went to Amarillo to find out how people felt about living with a nuclear bomb assembly plant. What evidence do you find in this essay about the kinds of research she conducted?
3. Do you like the way Mojtabai incorporates interviews into her text? Why does she "let the people explain themselves"? Is this effective? Why, or why not?
4. Do you think there is a "hidden agenda," an unspecified motive, in Mojtabai's report? If so, how can you identify it?
5. This essay is a chapter from the book, *Blessed Assurance: At Home with the Bomb in Amarillo, Texas*. When you read this essay, are you aware that it is part of a larger story? How do you know that?

*W*HEN THE *F*IRES GO OUT

CHRISTOPHER MARQUIS

Christopher Marquis is an Inter-American Press Association scholar working for La Nación, *a Buenos Aires daily. "When the Fires Go Out," was published by* The Progressive, *a liberal magazine intended for an intellectual audience. In his essay, Marquis describes the decay that settled on Clairton, Pennsylvania, when the steel mills closed. He tells the story of Clairton's slow self-destruction through the eyes and voices of its citizenry.*

Before you begin reading: *What kinds of events or situations make you feel like a failure? Write a list of failure-producing things, and next to that list write a statement of how you could change the failure into something positive.*

◆

LLOYD FUGE DOWNS A MARTINI AMID THE CHEAP SPLENdor of a small restaurant in Clairton, Pennsylvania, eleven miles from Pittsburgh. Fuge, a tall, balding man, is blind. His eyes stray and dampen as he recalls the last time he saw his hometown.

"It was a mill town," he says, singing "mill" with a blend of affection and pity. "A mill town is not a goddam residential neighborhood."

Clairton used to be a community. This immigrant city of 20,000 had a club for every pioneer—Yugoslav, Italian, Irish—and a corner church for every Lutheran, Presbyterian, and Catholic.

People couldn't pronounce their neighbor's name, but they could work together. Running a mill and energy plant in the world's steel-making capital, Clairton covered itself with the grit of prosperity. Mornings, women wiped soot off the window panes; evenings, men scrubbed the black band of grime from their necks.

They played together, too, Fourth of July was Clairton's big holiday, Fuge remembers, when families packed picnics and headed to the park. With the pride of settlers, they celebrated their hard-won security in America's middle-class.

Fuge was fourteen when an accident sealed these images in his mind. While experimenting with his chemistry set, a mixture exploded in his face and blinded him. Today, the only thing Fuge sees in Clairton is decay.

"I can see the deterioration," says Fuge, a former mayor of Clairton. "When I walk on the sidewalk, I know when it's heaving from tree roots."

Clairton's pocked streets are only one sign of recent decline. The city is so strapped financially that it can't even pay its light bill; banks won't renew its line of credit.

Clairton has, unofficially at least, gone bankrupt. Yet unlike New York City, the mill town has no mystique or unused resources to exploit. This is municipal bankruptcy in the 1980s, when little-known industrial cities are suddenly dangerously exposed. Clairton is one of the first towns to tumble, perhaps irretrievably, into the rift as the national economy moves from manufacturing to servicing. No public-relations blitz whips up support for these towns; no government bailout showers them with funds.

"Clairton is just the tip of the iceberg," says Pennsylvania Senate Minority Leader Edward Zemprelli, who hails from Clairton. The Democrat introduced a relief bill for failing cities that calls for early identification and state auditors' intervention. Since similar bills stalled in the House, the lawmaker took out his personal checkbook. Clairton officials politely declined a loan from Zemprelli but marveled at the offer from the ambitious kid who used to sell hot dogs and sodas at the public pool.

Welcome to Clairton, the City of Prayer, reads a soot-smeared sign near the mill road. Rows of tidy, modest homes with painted trim and immaculate lawns rise up the hill carved by the Monongahela River. A downtown of diners, a five-and-dime, and a public library serve the city's 11,000 residents.

On St. Clair Avenue, the main street, a youth huddles with a cluster of gray-haired men sporting the Clairton uniform: windbreakers and brimmed caps. Football ranks with church here and perhaps holds the edge. Weekend afternoons, the Pitt (University of Pittsburgh) and Steelers games hold the town captive. At Somer Lee's diner, the waitress worries about next week's game: There's $200 in the kitty.

So runs Clairton, a modest third-class city that acts like a small town. The janitor at city hall hides office keys behind a bulletin board.

But this is Norman Rockwell with a cruel stroke. "I tell people I live in a quaint little hamlet upriver," says Thomas Meade, education professor at the University of Pittsburgh and Clairton council member. "This is a hell-hole."

When the steel industry went down, it took Clairton and a half-dozen other Monongahela Valley townships down with it. U.S. Steel, the valley's largest employer, owns a vast network of mills stretching for miles up river. Each mill has tremendous capacity: The Clairton works alone produced seventy million tons of steel during World War II.

Fifty thousand workers once labored in the valley mills for U.S. Steel. Today, the company counts only 5,100, and unemployment has flowed from one town to the next. Officially, the jobless rate stands at 8.7 per cent, but that figure reflects only those persons still receiving severance benefits. The underemployed and discouraged workers who have exhausted their benefits nearly double that rate, according to a study sponsored by the Catholic Diocese of Pittsburgh. Bishop John McDowell, who headed the research project, says that in such mill towns as Clairton, fully 35 per cent are unemployed.

Valley residents have been "brutally affected by what has occurred," concedes U.S. Steel spokesman Bill Hoffman. Several thousand have left Clairton since 1980. Others stand packed and waiting. Eight hundred Clairton homes flood the market, most selling for $30,000.

For months, boxes crowded Sharon and Tom Schwab's tiny living room. Tom, a steelworker for seventeen years, had scraped together enough money to go to Florida, where he found a landscaping job. When the time came to move the family, though, the couple couldn't afford it.

"We live from day to day," says Sharon, thirty-one, who sometimes works as a reading tutor. The Schwabs are trapped in their cozy house with its monthly mortgage payment, a refrigerator full of charity groceries, two kids, and each other.

"If he weren't busy every day, I'd have to kill him," Sharon says. Tom hustles to find odd jobs, which keeps him from sinking into self-pity. "I love Tom, and our steelworker friends," she adds, "but they followed their fathers into the mills. They don't have any other skills. Where else in this society do you need somebody who can heat steel?"

Sharon talks about one of Tom's unemployed friends from the mill. For months, the man had insisted his job would reappear. "He just waited," Sharon says. Then his wife left him. She packed up the kids and moved to California. Soon after, the man wrecked his car and shot his dog in the head.

"Now is worse than the Depression," says Wayne Cochran, a retired bus driver. "It seems twenty years ago, people in the steel business saw this coming and didn't alter their outlook of what was going to happen."

Like valley residents, the city of Clairton has depended on earnings from U.S. Steel. In 1980 the company paid $805,000 in taxes to the city; by 1985, payments dropped to $331,000. For a city that has maintained a budget of about $3 million a year, this decline has been disastrous.

"Technically, we're bankrupt," commented Clairton controller John Marflak after a council meeting.

The city has taken shears to its payroll, laying off sixteen employees in various departments as well as its entire fourteen-member police force. Firefighters, afraid of being replaced by volunteers, offered to work without pay.

"The only way to be sure of ambulance service is to buy one yourself," a council member told a horrified elderly resident last fall. The city eventually hired a private contractor after a child who had suffered a seizure went unattended for several hours.

At seventy-three, Wayne Cochran is digging in his heels. A sign on his door still reads MR. & MRS. COCHRAN, though she died ten years ago. He's staying put on Walnut Street.

"I've lived here all my life. I know everyone," he says. "Walk out on the street and there isn't anyone I don't know. If I go to a strange place, I'll miss that."

Clairton's first census counted "10,000 souls." Most were Pennsylvania coalminers and merchants looking for steady work. But the demand for steel sent job notices half a world away—to Yugoslavia, Italy, and Poland.

Blacks from the South were brought in "by the trainload" to work the coke and byproducts, recalls Lloyd Fuge. These operations, which provided gas for mills throughout the valley, were shunned by steelworkers because the work was so difficult.

By the end of World War II, the Clairton coke works was the largest in the world. The byproducts division made components for 200,000 different products, including fertilizer, laughing gas, resin, and dye.

Now, it's all Clairton has left.

"We lost a lot of power in the last couple of years," says Charlie Grese, president of the Steelworkers' local. Outside his office, six laid-off coke workers debate whether the copy machine was built in America. A photograph of Franklin D. Roosevelt hangs on his wall and a picture of Norma Rae is posted on his door.

"We wanted this, we wanted that. And we got it," says Grese. "Now, if we can hold our own, we're very fortunate."

In the valley, unions and industry grew up together. With ever-increasing orders for steel, unions could virtually write their own tickets. Workers bought second cars, television sets, homes. U.S. Steel, in turn, became the largest and richest producer in the world.

"This was a helluva wedding around here," says George Zdrale, whose family came from Yugoslavia in 1915. "There was no competition from anywhere."

But the honeymoon was short-lived. In 1960, U.S. Steel, citing decreased demand, snuffed out the furnaces at Clairton's steel mill. Clairton's boom was over.

Over the next two decades, U.S. Steel named a new demon: foreign competition. Japan and Korea, which paid workers less, undercut American producers. U.S. Steel continued to whittle down its operations rather than modernize them. Since 1978, it has reduced its valley work force by nearly 80 per cent.

"Industry, in my opinion, has raped these towns for many goddam years," says Zdrale, who went from mill work into solid-waste management. Others, like Millie Worrell, blame the union. "People from out of state keep going on about 'poor Pittsburgh.' Well, steelworkers won't take a job for $8 or $10 an hour. Those unions drove the mills to where they are. I was a recipient of it, and I know."

Today, the average coke worker in Clairton earns about $12 in wages and $11 in benefits for an hour's work, says Charlie Grese. But these jobs are vanishing, and those that remain are paying less and less.

U.S. Steel is rapidly diversifying. Though still the nation's largest steel producer, its 1984 sales from steel accounted for 34 per cent of all revenues and only 9 per cent of total operating income.

"Right now, they're anxious about the bottom line," says Lloyd Fuge. "They're selling off facilities. They have no more social conscience than a snake."

On Sunday mornings, the men and women of Clairton worship at the city's churches. Each week, Presbyterian minister Larry Roth sprinkles hopeful words into his sermon. Then he gives out food by the truckload.

The charity began in 1983, when he distributed six cupboards full of food to laid-off workers; now the operation provides free groceries to 140 households a month, 300 at Christmas. Last year, the food bank received $23,000, much of it in nickels and dimes from Clairton residents. "I have never experienced this type of generosity," says volunteer Diane Vangura.

Most people are uneasy about receiving free food. "Some of them put it off to the last minute," says Vangura. "There's one family where a woman waited too long. She really should have come before and asked for help. Now all their savings are gone."

The suicide rate in Clairton hovers at twice the national average. A fifty-three-year-old Clairton man, who was given early retirement from his foreman position last July, went home and put a bullet through his head. "I guess he just wasn't ready to retire," says a coroner's aide.

The divorce rate, too, stands at double the national average. Often the wife, who has always stayed home, finds work more easily than her husband, which can fuel his resentment.

"The first thing he says is she's screwing the boss," notes Valerie Tutokey, who counsels battered women. "He'll go to the office and make accusations and try to drag her out, or he won't give her the car to go to work."

Violence implodes in Clairton, destroying individuals and families singly. Clairton's cohesion once lent something human to the shadow of smokestacks. Now the young are drifting off, and the elderly grow weary. "My life is over," says Wayne Cochran. "It's the young people who are coming up I'm worried about. A town can't survive without young blood."

Lloyd Fuge, blind eyes glistening, sips a third martini. "Have you read Lucretius?" he asks. "'No single thing abides, but all things flow. Fragment by fragment we lift and grow.'"

QUESTIONS FOR CRITICAL ANALYSIS

1. Where does the blame lie for the failure of Clairton, Pennsylvania? What clues in the essay led to your response?
2. What is Marquis' attitude toward industry and big business? How does he reveal his attitude? Is he fair in his treatment of the steel industry? Why, or why not?
3. Marquis describes life in Clairton as "Norman Rockwell with a cruel stroke." What does he mean? Why refer to painter Norman Rockwell? What images do Rockwell's paintings evoke, and what are the implications of the phrase "a cruel stroke"?
4. The mill's failure is reflected in the lives of the townspeople on many levels: economic, social, psychological, personal. What happens to human beings when they must live with failure? Do you think these people can turn things around? How?
5. Compare Gore, Oklahoma, of the Bernstein-Blitt essay to Clairton. How are their experiences similar? How do their citizens respond to the crises? Do the authors of each essay seem to share similar points of view or not?

QUESTIONS FOR STRUCTURAL ANALYSIS

1. Marquis begins his essay in the present tense and throughout the essay switches back and forth between present and past tense. Why does he do this? Is it effective? How do the stories and their implications reinforce the dual verb tenses?
2. What images in the essay portray Clairton as a typical American small town? What is the significance of such a portrayal? What is Marquis' point is stressing this?
3. What role does Lloyd Fuge play in the essay? How does Marquis use this character to develop his ideas? to unify the essay? What is the significance of using a blind man for this role?
4. What is Marquis' thesis? How did you determine the thesis? Is it ever explicitly stated?
5. What is the significance of the quotation from Lucretius at the conclusion of the essay? Is this an effective conclusion? Why, or why not?

Living with Uncertainty

Topics for Writing Essays

Many of the questions following each essay can serve as appropriate writing suggestions. The topics listed below expand the prereading exercises, but they can be used without completing that step first.

1. Take the memories you focused on for the Mojtabai prereading exercise and write an essay about the incident. Would you behave the same way a second time? What did you learn about yourself? about the issue? Using your experience as the focus, write an editorial (for your school paper, if the incident is campus-related; for your local paper, if the issue is broader-based) to encourage other people to face hard issues and be willing to take a stand.
2. Look up a newspaper account of the Sequoyah plant accident in Gore, Oklahoma, and compare and contrast those accounts with Bernstein and Blitt's essay. Develop a clear thesis for your essay.
3. Use the list of risks you wrote in response to the Applebome prereading exercise as the basis for an essay justifying your behavior to someone who is unwilling to take the same risks.

Research Possibilities

1. Tell the other side of the story. Look carefully at a town that is dominated by an industry and write a report on how that community and its people benefit in their relationship with the company. Examine newspaper accounts and industry magazines, interview townspeople who work for the company and those who don't, talk with town and school officials. Write a feature article on the city/industry partnership for a state magazine.
2. What do you know about the recent concerns about the nation's nuclear plants? The fourth paragraph of "After Long Silence" lists six facilities other than Pantex: Savannah River in South Carolina, Rocky Flats in Colorado, Kansas City in Missouri, Mound Laboratory in Ohio, Pinellas in Florida and Oak Ridge in Tennessee. Most of these are old facilities, and reports of mismanagement and safety problems have upset local communities. Select a nuclear facility close to you and find out about it: When was it built? How has it been run and maintained? What is its safety record? and so forth. Do you want to live and work next to this plant in its present condition? Write a report to your state senator making one (or more) of the following recommendations: changes to the plant to make it safer, closing the plant permanently, the need for government attention to the plant, better plant management.
3. Are there citizen-action groups in your community? on the campus? How do they work? Are they effective? Interview leaders of a group that interests you, read their materials, read newspaper accounts of their work, and write a feature story about the group for your city or state magazine.

DEMANDING CIVIL RIGHTS

The four essays in this section were all written before 1968. In order to understand the characteristics of America's relationships among races today, we need to know something about where we've been and how far we've come. Langston Hughes' America was a different one from Alice Walker's, and neither is the America of privileged white citizens then or now.

LANGSTON HUGHES, "MY AMERICA"

JAMES BALDWIN, "FIFTH AVENUE, UPTOWN: A LETTER FROM HARLEM"

MARTIN LUTHER KING, JR., "WHY WE CAN'T WAIT"

ALICE WALKER, "THE CIVIL RIGHTS MOVEMENT: WHAT GOOD WAS IT?"

My *America*

Langston Hughes

Langston Hughes (1902–1967) wrote "My America" in 1943, describing to the academic readers of The Journal of Educational Sociology *the contradictions of being black and disenfranchised in America, the country founded on individual rights and freedoms. His unsettling picture of discriminatory America is set against his comment, "Yet America is . . . where . . . I can write this article."[For further information on Langston Hughes, see the headnote in the first section, "Finding Out Who We Are."]*

Before you begin reading: *Write in your reading notebook about your first encounter with racism.*

◆

THIS IS MY LAND AMERICA. NATURALLY, I LOVE IT—IT IS home—and I am vitally concerned about its mores, its democracy, and its well-being. I try now to look at it with clear, unprejudiced eyes. My ancestry goes back at least four generations on American soil—and, through Indian blood, many centuries more. My background and training is purely American—the schools of Kansas, Ohio, and the East. I am old stock as opposed to recent immigrant blood.

Yet many Americans who cannot speak English—so recent is their arrival on our shores—may travel about the country at will securing food, hotel, and rail accommodations wherever they wish to purchase them. I may not. These Americans, once naturalized, may vote in Mississippi or Texas, if they live there. I may not. They may work at whatever job their skills command. But I may not. They may purchase tickets for concerts, theaters, lectures wherever they are sold throughout the United States. I may not. They may repeat the Oath of Allegiance with its ringing phrase of "liberty and justice for all," with a deep faith in its truth—as compared to the limitations and oppressions they have experienced in the Old World. I repeat the oath, too, but I know that the phrase about "liberty and justice" does not fully apply to me. I am an American—but I am a colored American.

I know that all these things I mention are not *all* true for *all* localities *all* over America. Jim Crowism varies in degree from North to South, from the mixed schools and free franchise of Michigan to the tumbledown colored schools and open terror at the polls of Georgia and Mississippi. All over America, however, against the Negro there has been an economic color line of such severity that since the Civil War we have been kept most effectively, as a racial group, in the lowest economic brackets. Statistics are not needed to prove this. Simply look around you on the Main Street of any American town or city. There are no colored clerks in any of the stores—although colored people spend their money there. There are practically never any colored street-car conductors or bus drivers—although these public carriers run over streets for which we pay taxes. There are no colored girls at the switchboards of the telephone company—but millions of Negroes have phones and pay their bills. Even in Harlem, nine times out of ten, the man who comes to collect your rent is white. Not even that job is given a colored man by the great corporations owning New York real estate. From Boston to San Diego, the Negro suffers from job discrimination.

Yet America is a land where, in spite of its defects, I can write this article. Here the voice of democracy is still heard—Roosevelt, Wallace, Willkie, Agar, Pearl Buck, Paul Robeson. America is a land where the poll tax still holds in the South but opposition to the poll tax grows daily. America is a land where lynchers are not yet caught—but Bundists are put in jail, and majority opinion condemns the Klan. America is a land where the best of all democracies has been achieved for some people—but in Georgia, Roland Hayes, world-famous singer, is beaten for being colored and nobody is jailed—nor can Mr. Hayes vote in the State where he was born. Yet America is a country where Roland Hayes *can* come from a log cabin to wealth and fame—in spite of the segment that still wishes to maltreat him physically and spiritually, famous though he is.

This segment, however, is not all of America. If it were, millions of Negroes would have no heart for this war in which we are now engaged. If it were, we could see no difference between our ideals and Hitler's, in so far as our own dark lives are concerned. But we know, on the other hand, that America is a land in transition. And we know it is within our power to help in its further change toward a finer and better democracy than any citizen has known before. The American Negro believes in democracy. We want to make it real, complete, workable, not only for ourselves—the thirteen million dark ones—but for all Americans all over the land.

QUESTIONS FOR CRITICAL ANALYSIS

1. This essay was published in *The Journal of Educational Sociology* in 1943. Who was Hughes' audience? What was his attitude toward his reader?
2. Describe Hughes' America in 1943. How did he feel toward America? toward its citizens? How do you know?

3. Identify the names and events Hughes mentions in this essay. How does the context of the essay help you identify these?
4. What was Hughes' purpose in writing this essay? Do you think he achieved it? How did you respond to the essay while you read it?
5. Make a list of every act of discrimination Hughes mentions. Next to each item, write your opinion of how the situation has changed.

QUESTIONS FOR STRUCTURAL ANALYSIS

1. What is Hughes' thesis? Where is it stated?
2. Why does Hughes provide his personal history in the first paragraph? How does his biography affect your response to the essay?
3. Look at the transitions between the five paragraphs. How does Hughes build the essay from one paragraph to the next? Draw a diagram of the essay, showing the relationships among the paragraphs.
4. What is Hughes' tone in this essay? How does his language reveal his attitude? Compare his language, tone, attitude toward the subject with "Salvation," the Hughes essay in Section I.
5. In his final paragraph Hughes refers to the Second World War. Why? What are the implications of this reference? How do you think his readers responded to this conclusion?

*F*IFTH *A*VENUE, *U*PTOWN: *A L*ETTER FROM *H*ARLEM

JAMES BALDWIN

James Baldwin (1924–1987), an author and playwright, lecturer, and civil rights activist, uses the backdrop of five blocks of Harlem to describe racism in America in the early 1960s. Fifth Avenue in New York City includes the upper-class world of Tiffany's and Saks Fifth Avenue with its wealth and diamonds as well as the drugs and despair in the slums of Harlem. Baldwin addresses the privileged upperclass when he shows them what life is like for blacks in white America, both in the North and the South.

Before you begin reading: *If you had the power to enact change, what would you do to eliminate racial barriers? Make a list of recommendations you would make. Next to each recommendation, describe how you would begin to implement the change.*

◆

THERE IS A HOUSING PROJECT STANDING NOW WHERE THE house in which we grew up once stood, and one of those stunted city trees is snarling where our doorway used to be. This is on the rehabilitated side of the avenue. The other side of the avenue—for progress takes time—has not been rehabilitated yet and it looks exactly as it looked in the days when we sat with our noses pressed against the windowpane, longing to be allowed to go "across the street." The grocery store which gave us credit is still there, and there can be no doubt that it is still giving credit. The people in the project certainly need it—far more, indeed, than they ever needed the project. The last time I passed by, the Jewish proprietor was still standing among his shelves, looking sadder and heavier but scarcely any older. Farther down the block stands the shoe-repair store in which our shoes were repaired until reparation became impossible and in which, then, we bought all our "new" ones. The Negro proprietor is still in the window, head down, working at the leather.

These two, I imagine, could tell a long tale if they would (perhaps they would be glad to if they could), having watched so many, for so long, struggling in the fishhooks, the barbed wire, of this avenue.

The avenue is elsewhere the renowned and elegant Fifth. The area I am describing, which, in today's gang parlance, would be called "the turf," is bounded by Lenox Avenue on the west, the Harlem River on the east, 135th Street on the north, and 130th Street on the south. We never lived beyond these boundaries; this is where we grew up. Walking along 145th Street—for example—familiar as it is, and similar, does not have the same impact because I do not know any of the people on the block. But when I turn east on 131st Street and Lenox Avenue, there is first a soda-pop joint, then a shoeshine "parlor," then a grocery store, then a dry cleaners', then the houses. All along the street there are people who watched me grow up, people who grew up with me, people I watched grow up along with my brothers and sisters; and, sometimes in my arms, sometimes underfoot, sometimes at my shoulder—or on it—their children, a riot, a forest of children, who include my nieces and nephews.

When we reach the end of this long block, we find ourselves on wide, filthy, hostile Fifth Avenue, facing that project which hangs over the avenue like a monument to the folly, and the cowardice, of good intentions. All along the block, for anyone who knows it, are immense human gaps, like craters. These gaps are not created merely by those who have moved away, inevitably into some other ghetto; or by those who have risen, almost always into a greater capacity for self-loathing and self-delusion; or yet by those who, by whatever means—World War II, the Korean war, a policeman's gun or billy, a gang war, a brawl, madness, an overdose of heroin, or, simply, unnatural exhaustion—are dead. I am talking about those who are left, and I am talking principally about the young. What are they doing? Well, some, a minority, are fanatical churchgoers, members of the more extreme of the Holy Roller sects. Many, many more are "moslems," by affiliation or sympathy, that is to say that they are united by nothing more—and nothing less—than a hatred of the white world and all its works. They are present, for example, at every Buy Black street-corner meeting—meetings in which the speaker urges his hearers to cease trading with white men and establish a separate economy. Neither the speaker nor his hearers can possibly do this, of course, since Negroes do not own General Motors or RCA or the A & P, nor, indeed, do they own more than a wholly insufficient fraction of anything else in Harlem (those who *do* own anything are more interested in their profits than in their fellows). But these meetings nevertheless keep alive in the participators a certain pride of bitterness without which, however futile this bitterness may be, they could scarcely remain alive at all. Many have given up. They stay home and watch the TV screen, living on the earnings of their parents, cousins, brothers, or uncles, and only leave the house to go to the movies or to the nearest bar. "How're you making it?" one may ask, running into them along the block, or in the bar. "Oh, I'm TV-ing it"; with the saddest, sweetest, most shame-faced of smiles, and from a great distance. This distance one is compelled to respect; anyone who has traveled so far will not easily be dragged again into the world. There are further retreats, of course, than the TV screen or the bar. There are those who are simply sitting on their stoops, "stoned," animated for a moment only, and hideously, by the approach of someone who may lend them the money for a "fix." Or by the approach of someone from whom they can purchase it, one of the shrewd ones, on the way to prison or just coming out.

And the others, who have avoided all of these deaths, get up in the morning and go downtown to meet "the man." They work in the white man's world all day and come home in the evening to this fetid block. They struggle to instill in their children some private sense of honor or dignity which will help the child to survive. This means, of course, that they must struggle, stolidly, incessantly, to keep this sense alive in themselves, in spite of the insults, the indifference, and the cruelty they are certain to encounter in their working day. They patiently browbeat the landlord into fixing the heat, the plaster, the plumbing; this demands prodigious patience; nor is patience usually enough. In trying to make their hovels habitable, they are perpetually throwing good money after bad. Such frustration, so long endured, is driving many strong, admirable men and women whose only crime is color to the very gates of paranoia.

One remembers them from another time—playing handball in the playground, going to church, wondering if they were going to be promoted at school. One remembers them going off to war—gladly, to escape this block. One remembers their return. Perhaps one remembers their wedding day. And one sees where the girl is now—vainly looking for salvation from some other embittered, trussed, and struggling boy—and sees the all-but-abandoned children in the streets.

Now I am perfectly aware that there are other slums in which white men are fighting for their lives, and mainly losing. I know that blood is also flowing through those streets and that the human damage there is incalculable. People are continually pointing out to me the wretchedness of white people in order to console me for the wretchedness of blacks. But an itemized account of the American failure does not console me and it should not console anyone else. That hundreds of thousands of white people are living, in effect, no better than the "niggers" is not a fact to be regarded with complacency. The social and moral bankruptcy suggested by this fact is of the bitterest, most terrifying kind.

The people, however, who believe that this democratic anguish has some consoling value are always pointing out that So-and-So, white, and So-and-So, black, rose from the slums into the big time. The existence—the public existence—of, say, Frank Sinatra and Sammy Davis, Jr. proves to them that America is still the land of opportunity and that inequalities vanish before the determined will. It proves nothing of the sort. The determined will is rare—at the moment, in this country, it is unspeakably rare—and the inequalities suffered by the many are in no way justified by the rise of a few. A few have always risen—in every country, every era, and in the teeth of regimes which can by no stretch of the imagination be thought of as free. Not all of these people, it is worth remembering, left the world better than they found it. The determined will is rare, but it is not invariably benevolent. Furthermore, the American equation of success with the big times reveals an awful disrespect for human life and human achievement. This equation has placed our cities among the most dangerous in the world and has placed our youth among the most empty and most bewildered. The situation of our youth is not mysterious. Children have never been very good at listening to their elders, but they have never failed to imitate them. They must, they have no other models. That is exactly what our children are doing. They are imitating our immorality, our disrespect for the pain of others.

All other slum dwellers, when the bank account permits it, can move out of the slum and vanish altogether from the eye of persecution. No Negro in this country has ever made that much money and it will be a long time before any Negro does. The Negroes in Harlem, who have no money, spend what they have on such gimcracks as they are sold. These include "wider" TV screens, more "faithful" hi-fi sets, more "powerful" cars, all of which, of course, are obsolete long before they are paid for. Anyone who has ever struggled with poverty knows how extremely expensive it is to be poor; and if one is a member of a captive population, economically speaking, one's feet have simply been placed on the treadmill forever. One is victimized, economically, in a thousand ways—rent, for example, or car insurance. Go shopping one day in Harlem—for anything—and compare Harlem prices and quality with those downtown.

The people who have managed to get off this block have only got as far as a more respectable ghetto. This respectable ghetto does not even have the advantages of the disreputable one—friends, neighbors, a familiar church, and friendly tradesmen; and it is not, moreover, in the nature of any ghetto to remain respectable long. Every Sunday, people who have left the block take the lonely ride back, dragging their increasingly discontented children with them. They spend the day talking, not always with words, about the trouble they've seen and the trouble—one must watch their eyes as they watch their children—they are only too likely to see. For children do not like ghettos. It takes them nearly no time to discover exactly why they are there.

The projects in Harlem are hated. They are hated almost as much as policemen, and this is saying a great deal. And they are hated for the same reason: both reveal, unbearably, the real attitude of the white world, no matter how many liberal speeches are made, no matter how many lofty editorials are written, no matter how many civil-rights commissions are set up.

The projects are hideous, of course, there being a law, apparently respected throughout the world, that popular housing shall be as cheerless as a prison. They are lumped all over Harlem, colorless, bleak, high, and revolting. The wide windows look out on Harlem's invincible and indescribable squalor: the Park Avenue railroad tracks, around which, about forty years ago, the present dark community began; the unrehabilitated houses, bowed down, it would seem, under the great weight of frustration and bitterness they contain; the dark, the ominous schoolhouses from which the child may emerge maimed, blinded, hooked, or enraged for life; and the churches, churches, block upon block of churches, niched in the walls like cannon in the walls of a fortress. Even if the administration of the projects were not so insanely humiliating (for example: one must report raises in salary to the management, which will then eat up the profit by raising one's rent; the management has the right to know who is staying in your apartment; the management can ask you to leave, at their discretion), the projects would still be hated because they are an insult to the meanest intelligence.

Harlem got its first private project, Riverton*—which is now, naturally, a slum—about twelve years ago because at that time Negroes were not allowed to live in Stuyvesant Town. Harlem watched Riverton go up, therefore, in the most violent bitterness of spirit, and hated it long before the builders arrived. They began hating it at about the time people began moving out of their condemned houses to make room for this additional proof of how thoroughly the white world despised them. And they had scarcely moved in, naturally, before they began smashing windows, defacing walls, urinating in the elevators, and fornicating in the playgrounds. Liberals, both white and black, were appalled at the spectacle. I was appalled by the liberal innocence—or cynicism, which comes out in practice as much the same thing. Other people were delighted to be able to point to proof positive that nothing could be done to better the lot of the colored people. They were, and are, right in one respect: that nothing can be done as long as they are treated like colored people. The people in Harlem know they are living there because white people do not think they are good enough to live anywhere else. No amount of "improvement" can sweeten this fact. Whatever money is now being earmarked to improve this, or any other ghetto, might as well be burnt. A ghetto can be improved in one way only: out of existence.

Similarly, the only way to police a ghetto is to be oppressive. None of the Police Commissioner's men, even with the best will in the world, have any way of understanding the lives led by the people they swagger about in twos and threes controlling. Their very presence is an insult, and it would be, even if they

*The inhabitants of Riverton were much embittered by this description; they have, apparently, forgotten how their project came into being; and have repeatedly informed me that I cannot possibly be referring to Riverton, but to another housing project which is directly across the street. It is quite clear, I think, that I have no interest in accusing any individuals or families of the depredations herein described: but neither can I deny the evidence of my own eyes. Nor do I blame anyone in Harlem for making the best of a dreadful bargain. But anyone who lives in Harlem and imagines that he has *not* struck this bargain, or that what he takes to be his status (in whose eyes?) protects him against the common pain, demoralization, and danger, is simply self deluded.

spent their entire day feeding gumdrops to children. They represent the force of the white world, and that world's real intentions are, simply, for that world's criminal profit and ease, to keep the black man corraled up here, in his place. The badge, the gun in the holster, and the swinging club make vivid what will happen should his rebellion become overt. Rare, indeed, is the Harlem citizen, from the most circumspect church member to the most shiftless adolescent, who does not have a long tale to tell of police incompetence, injustice, or brutality. I myself have witnessed and endured it more than once. The businessmen and racketeers also have a story. And so do the prostitutes. (And this is not, perhaps, the place to discuss Harlem's very complex attitude toward black policemen, nor the reasons, according to Harlem, that they are nearly all downtown.)

It is hard, on the other hand, to blame the policeman, blank, good-natured, thoughtless, and insuperably innocent, for being such a perfect representative of the people he serves. He, too, believes in good intentions and is astounded and offended when they are not taken for the deed. He has never, himself, done anything for which to be hated—which of us has?—and yet he is facing, daily and nightly, people who would gladly see him dead, and he knows it. There is no way for him not to know it: there are few things under heaven more unnerving than the silent, accumulating contempt and hatred of a people. He moves through Harlem, therefore, like an occupying soldier in a bitterly hostile country; which is precisely what, and where, he is, and is the reason he walks in twos and threes. And he is not the only one who knows why he is always in company: the people who are watching him know why, too. Any street meeting, sacred or secular, which he and his colleagues uneasily cover has as its explicit and implicit burden the cruelty and injustice of the white domination. And these days, of course, in terms increasingly vivid and jubilant, it speaks of the end of that domination. The white policeman standing on a Harlem street corner finds himself at the very center of the revolution now occurring in the world. He is not prepared for it—naturally, nobody is—and, what is possibly much more to the point, he is exposed, as few white people are, to the anguish of the black people around him. Even if he is gifted with the merest mustard grain of imagination, something must seep in. He cannot avoid observing that some of the children, in spite of their color, remind him of children he has known and loved, perhaps even of his own children. He knows that he certainly does not want *his* children living this way. He can retreat from his uneasiness in only one direction: into a callousness which very shortly becomes second nature. He becomes more callous, the population becomes more hostile, the situation grows more tense, and the police force is increased. One day, to everyone's astonishment, someone drops a match in the powder keg and everything blows up. Before the dust has settled or the blood congealed, editorials, speeches, and civil-rights commissions are loud in the land, demanding to know what happened. What happened is that Negroes want to be treated like men.

Negroes want to be treated like men: a perfectly straightforward statement, containing only seven words. People who have mastered Kant, Hegel, Shakespeare, Marx, Freud, and the Bible find this statement utterly impenetrable. The idea seems to threaten profound, barely conscious assumptions. A kind of panic paralyzes their features, as though they found themselves trapped on the edge of a steep place. I once tried to describe to a very well-known American intellectual the conditions among Negroes in the South. My recital disturbed him and made him indignant; and he asked me in perfect innocence, "Why don't all the Negroes in the South move North?" I tried to explain what *has* happened, unfailingly, whenever a significant body of Negroes move North. They do not escape Jim Crow: they merely encounter another, not-less-deadly variety. They do not move to Chicago, they move to the South Side; they do not move to New York, they move to Harlem. The pressure within the ghetto causes the ghetto walls to expand, and this expansion is always violent. White people hold the line as long as they can, and in as many ways as they can, from verbal intimidation to physical violence. But inevitably the border which has divided the ghetto from the rest of the world falls into the hands of the ghetto. The white people fall back bitterly before the black horde; the landlords make a tidy profit by raising the rent, chopping up the rooms, and all but dispensing with the upkeep; and what has once been a neighborhood turns into a "turf." This is precisely what happened when the Puerto Ricans arrived in their thousands—and the bitterness thus caused is, as I write, being fought out all up and down those streets.

Northerners indulge in an extremely dangerous luxury. They seem to feel that because they fought on the right side during the Civil War, and won, they have earned the right merely to deplore what is going on in the South, without taking any responsibility for it; and that they can ignore what is happening in Northern cities because what is happening in Little Rock or Birmingham is worse. Well, in the first place, it is not possible for anyone who has not endured both to know which is "worse." I know Negroes who prefer the South and white Southerners, because "At least there, you haven't got to play any guessing games!" The guessing games referred to have driven more than one Negro into the narcotics ward, the madhouse, or the river. I know another Negro, a man very dear to me, who says, with conviction and with truth, "The spirit of the South is the spirit of America." He was born in the North and did his military training in the South. He did not, as far as I can gather, find the South "worse"; he found it, if anything, all too familiar. In the second place, though, even if Birmingham *is* worse, no doubt Johannesburg, South Africa, beats it by several miles, and Buchenwald was one of the worst things that ever happened in the entire history of the world. The world has never lacked for horrifying examples; but I do not believe that these examples are meant to be used as justification for our own crimes. This perpetual justification empties the heart of all human feeling. The emptier our hearts become, the greater will be our crimes. Thirdly, the South is not merely an embarrassingly backward region, but a part of this country, and what happens there concerns every one of us.

As far as the color problem is concerned, there is but one great difference between the Southern white and the Northerner: the Southerner remembers, historically and in his own psyche, a kind of Eden in which he loved black people and they loved him. Historically, the flaming sword laid across this Eden is the Civil War. Personally, it is the Southerner's sexual coming of age, when, without any warning, unbreakable taboos are set up between himself and his past. Everything, thereafter, is permitted him except the love he remembers and has never ceased to need. The resulting, indescribable torment affects every Southern mind and is the basis of the Southern hysteria.

None of this is true for the Northerner. Negroes represent nothing to him personally, except, perhaps, the dangers of carnality. He never sees Negroes. Southerners see them all the time. Northerners never think about them whereas Southerners are never really thinking of anything else. Negroes are, therefore, ignored in the North and are under surveillance in the South, and suffer hideously in both places. Neither the Southerner nor the Northerner is able to look on the Negro simply as a man. It seems to be indispensable to the national self-esteem that the Negro be considered either as a kind of ward (in which case we are told how many Negroes, comparatively, bought Cadillacs last year and how few, comparatively, were lynched), or as a victim (in which case we are promised that he will never vote in our assemblies or go to school with our kids). They are two sides of the same coin and the South will not change—*cannot* change—until the North changes. The country will not change until it re-examines itself and discovers what it really means by freedom. In the meantime, generations keep being born, bitterness is increased by incompetence, pride, and folly, and the world shrinks around us.

It is a terrible, an inexorable, law that one cannot deny the humanity of another without diminishing one's own: in the face of one's victim, one sees oneself. Walk through the streets of Harlem and see what we, this nation, have become.

QUESTIONS FOR CRITICAL ANALYSIS

1. What changes does Baldwin find when he returns to his old neighborhood? What is his attitude toward both the place and the changes?
2. Baldwin describes Harlem by place and people. What images are most effective? What description seemed especially vivid to you? What did you like about it?
3. Baldwin writes, "an itemized account of the American failure does not console me and it should not console anyone else." In his essay, "Mass Culture and the Creative

Artist" (which appears in Part Two), Baldwin also mentions the failure of the American dream. *What* has failed? How? Who is "consoled" by this view?

4. According to Baldwin, what do blacks think of the projects? Why? the police? Why? the whites? Why? This essay was written in 1960; do you think these attitudes have changed since then? Why, or why not?
5. Baldwin alludes to several popular and historical figures and events. Who and/or what are they? How do they serve the purpose of his essay?

QUESTIONS FOR STRUCTURAL ANALYSIS

1. Who is Baldwin's audience? What is his purpose in writing this essay? Does he succeed? Why or why not? Why does he call this essay a "letter"?
2. Describe Baldwin's tone in this essay, providing examples to support your opinion. What is the source of this tone? How does his language reflect it?
3. Baldwin divides the essay into two sections. Why? How do the two sections relate to each other?
4. Examine Baldwin's comparison of whites in the North and South. What distinguishes them? Why does Baldwin include this comparison? How does it relate to the rest of the essay? What is Baldwin's opinion of whites?
5. The final paragraph provides a powerful conclusion to the essay. How you do react to it? How do the conditions Baldwin describes in this 1960 essay reflect the situation today? From what you've read or know, would Baldwin feel more optimistic or less if he returned to his Harlem neighborhood today? Why?

*W*HY *W*E CAN'T *W*AIT

MARTIN LUTHER KING, JR.

Martin Luther King, Jr. (1929–1968), the leader and spokesman for America's Civil Rights Movement, personalizes the future of American black children for his white reading audience at the beginning of "Why We Can't Wait." Published in Saturday Review *in May 1964, this essay clearly presents the facts: (1) it's been 100 years since the Emancipation Proclamation was signed, (2) it's been 10 years since desegregation of the schools, (3) the presidential candidates promised a civil rights platform, and black citizens are still disenfranchised in America. King advocates nonviolent direct action as the most effective weapon available to the blacks in gaining their freedom and realizing their rights. (For more information on Martin Luther King, see the headnote in the earlier section, "Learning Our Responsibilities.")*

Before you begin reading: *Do you know a person deeply committed to a cause? Concentrate on that person for several minutes. Make a list of words to describe the person, and use that list while you describe an incident you remember involving the person.*

◆

IT IS THE BEGINNING OF THE YEAR OF OUR LORD 1963.

I see a young Negro boy. He is sitting on a stoop in front of a vermin-infested apartment house in Harlem. The stench of garbage is in the halls. The drunks, the jobless, the junkies are shadow-figures of his everyday world. The boy goes to a school attended mostly by Negro students, with a scattering of Puerto Ricans. His father is one of the jobless. His mother is a sleep-in domestic, working for a family on Long Island.

I see a young Negro girl. She is sitting on the stoop of a rickety wooden one-family house in Birmingham. Some visitors would call it a shack. It needs paint badly and the patched-up roof appears in danger of caving in. Half a dozen small children, in various stages of undress, are scampering about the house. The girl is forced to play the role of their mother. She can no longer attend the all-Negro school in her neighborhood because her mother died only recently after a car accident. Neighbors say if the ambulance hadn't come so late to take her to the all-Negro hospital, the mother might still be alive. The girl's father is a porter in a downtown department store. He will always be a porter, for there are no promotions for the Negro in this store, where every counter serves him except the one that sells hot dogs and orange juice.

This boy and this girl, separated by stretching miles, are wondering: Why does misery constantly haunt the Negro? In some distant past, had their forebears done some tragic injury to the nation, and was there a curse of punishment upon the black race? Had they shirked their duties as patriots, betrayed their country, denied their national birthright? Had they refused to defend their land against a foreign foe?

Not all of history is recorded in the books supplied to school children in Harlem or Birmingham. Yet this boy and this girl know something of the part of history that has been censored by the white writers and purchasers of board-of-education books. They know that Negroes were with George Washington at Valley Forge. They know that the first American to shed blood in the revolution that freed his country from British oppression was a black seaman named Crispus Attucks. The boy's Sunday-school teacher has told him that one of the team who designed the capital of their nation, Washington, D.C., was a Negro, Benjamin Banneker. Once the girl had heard a speaker, invited to her school during Negro History Week. This speaker told how, for two hundred years, without wages, black people, brought to this land in slave ships and in chains, had drained the swamps, built the homes, made cotton king, and helped, on whip-lashed backs, to lift this nation from colonial obscurity to commanding influence in domestic commerce and world trade.

Wherever there was hard work, duty work, dangerous work—in the mines, on the docks, in the blistering foundries—Negroes had done more than their share.

The pale history books in Harlem and Birmingham told how the nation had fought a war over slavery. Abraham Lincoln had signed a document that would come to be known as the Emancipation Proclamation. The war had been won, but not a just peace. Equality had never arrived. Equality was a hundred years late.

The boy and the girl knew more than history. They knew something about current events. They knew that African nations had burst the bonds of colonialism. They knew that a great-great-grandson of Crispus Attucks might be ruled out of some restricted, all-white restaurant in some restricted, all-white section of a Southern town, his United States Marines uniform notwithstanding. They knew that Negroes living in the capital of their own nation were confined to ghettos and could not always get a job for which they were qualified. They knew that white supremacists had defied the Supreme Court and that Southern governors had attempted to interpose themselves between the people and the highest law of the land. They knew that for years their own lawyers had won great victories in the courts that were not being translated into reality.

They were seeing on television, hearing from the radio, reading in the newspapers that this was the 100th birthday of their freedom.

But freedom had a dull ring, a mocking emptiness when, in their time—in the short life spans of this boy and girl—buses had stopped rolling in Montgomery; sit-inners were jailed and beaten; freedom riders were brutalized and murdered; dogs' fangs were bared in Birmingham; and in Brooklyn, New York, there were certain kinds of construction jobs for whites only.

It was the summer of 1963. Was emancipation a fact? Was freedom a force?

The boy in Harlem stood up. The girl in Birmingham arose. Separated by stretching miles, both of them squared their shoulders and lifted their eyes toward heaven. Across the miles they joined hands and took a firm, forward step. It was a step that rocked the richest, most powerful nation to its foundations.

The bitterly cold winter of 1962 lingered throughout the opening months of 1963, touching the land with chill and frost, and was then replaced by a placid spring. Americans awaited a quiet summer. That it would be pleasant they had no doubt. The worst of it would be the nightmare created by 60,000,000 cars, all apparently trying to reach the same destination at the same time. Fifty million families looked forward to the pleasure of two hundred million vacations in the American tradition of the frenetic hunt for relaxation.

It would be a pleasant summer because, in the mind of the average man, there was little cause for concern. The blithe outlook about the state of the nation was reflected from as high up as the White House. The Administration confidently readied a tax-reduction bill. Business and employment were at comfortable levels. Money was—for many Americans—plentiful.

Summer came, and the weather was beautiful. But the climate, the social climate of American life, erupted into lightning flashes, trembled with thunder, and vibrated to the relentless, growing rain of protest come to life through the land. Explosively, America's third revolution—the Negro revolution—had succeeded the American Revolution and the Civil War.

For the first time in the long and turbulent history of the nation, almost 1,000 cities were engulfed in civil turmoil, with violence trembling just below the surface. As in the French Revolution of 1789, the streets had become a battleground, just as they had become the battleground, in the 1830s, of England's tumultuous Chartist movement. As in these two revolutions, a submerged social group, propelled by a burning need for justice, lifting itself with sudden swiftness, moving with determination and a majestic scorn for risk and danger, created an uprising so powerful that it shook a huge society from its comfortable base.

Never in American history had a group seized the streets, the squares, the sacrosanct business thoroughfares, and the marbled halls of government to protest and proclaim the unendurability of their oppression. Had room-size machines turned human, burst from the plants that housed them, and stalked the land in revolt, the nation could not have been more amazed. Undeniably, the Negro had been an object of sympathy and wore the scars of deep grievances, but the nation had come to count on him as a creature who could quietly endure, silently suffer, and patiently wait. He was well trained in service and, whatever the provocation, he neither pushed back nor spoke back.

Just as lightning makes no sound until it strikes, the Negro Revolution generated quietly. But when it struck, the revealing flash of its power and the impact of its sincerity and fervor bespoke a force of frightening intensity. Three hundred years of humiliation, abuse, and deprivation cannot be expected to find voice in a whisper. The storm clouds did not release a "gentle rain from heaven" but a whirlwind, which has not yet spent its force or attained its full momentum.

Because there is more to come; because American society is bewildered by the spectacle of the Negro in revolt; because the dimensions are vast and the implications deep in a nation with 20,000,000 Negroes, it is important to understand the history that is being made today.

Some years ago I sat in a Harlem department store, surrounded by hundreds of people. I was autographing copies of *Stride Toward Freedom*, my book about the Montgomery bus boycott of 1955-56. As I signed my name to a page, I felt something sharp plunge forcefully into my chest. I had been stabbed with a letter opener, struck home by a woman who would later be judged insane. Rushed by ambulance to Harlem Hospital, I lay in a bed for hours while preparations were made to remove the keen-edged blade from my body. Days later, when I was well enough to talk with Dr. Aubrey Maynard, the chief of the surgeons who performed the delicate, dangerous operation, I learned the reason for the long delay that preceded surgery. He told me that the razor-sharp tip of the instrument had been touching my aorta and that my whole chest had to be opened to extract it.

"If you had sneezed during all those hours of waiting," Dr. Maynard said, "your aorta would have been punctured and you would have drowned in your own blood."

In the summer of 1963 the knife of violence was just that close to the nation's aorta. Hundreds of cities might now be mourning countless dead but for the operation of certain forces that gave political surgeons an opportunity to cut boldly and safely to remove the deadly peril.

What was it that gave us the second chance? To answer this we must answer another question. Why did this Revolution occur in 1963? Negroes had for decades endured evil. In the words of the poet, they had long asked: "Why must the blackness of nighttime collect in our mouth; why must we always taste grief in our blood?" Any time would seem to have been the right time. Why 1963?

Why did a thousand cities shudder almost simultaneously and why did the whole world—in gleaming capitals and mud-hut villages—hold its breath during those months? Why was it in this year that the American Negro, so long ignored, so long written out of the pages of history books, tramped a declaration of freedom with his marching feet across the pages of newspapers, the television screens, and the magazines? Sarah Turner closed the kitchen cupboard and went into the streets; John Wilkins shut down the elevator and enlisted in the nonviolent army; Bill Griggs slammed the brakes of his truck and slid to the sidewalk; the Reverend Arthur Jones led his flock into the streets and held church in jail. The words and actions of parliaments and statesmen, of kings and prime ministers, movie stars and athletes, were shifted from the front pages to make room for the history-making deeds of the servants, the drivers, the elevator operators, and the ministers. Why in 1963, and what has this to do with why the dark threat of violence did not erupt in blood?

The Negro had been deeply disappointed over the slow pace of school desegregation. He knew that in 1954 the highest court in the land had handed down a decree calling for desegregation of schools "with all deliberate speed." He knew that this edict from the Supreme Court had been heeded with all deliberate delay. At the beginning of 1963, nine years after this historic decision, approximately 9 per cent of Southern Negro students were attending integrated schools. If this pace were maintained, it would be the year 2054 before integration in Southern schools would be a reality.

In its wording the Supreme Court decision had revealed an awareness that attempts would be made to evade its intent. The phrase "all deliberate speed" did not mean that another century should be allowed to unfold before we released Negro children from the narrow pigeonhole of the segregated schools; it meant that, giving some courtesy and consideration to the need for softening old attitudes and outdated customs, democracy must press ahead, out of the past of ignorance and intolerance, and into the present of educational opportunity and moral freedom.

Yet the statistics make it abundantly clear that the segregationists of the South remained undefeated by the decision. From every section of Dixie, the announcement of the high court had been met with declarations of defiance. Once recovered from their initial outrage, these defenders of the status quo had seized the offensive to impose their own schedule of change. The progress that was supposed to have been achieved with deliberate speed had created change for less than 2 per cent of Negro children in most areas of the South, and not even one-tenth of 1 per cent in some parts of the deepest South.

There was another factor in the slow pace of progress, a factor of which few are aware and even fewer understand. It is an unadvertised fact that soon after the 1954 decision, the Supreme Court retreated from its own position by giving approval to the Pupil Placement Law. This law permitted the states themselves to determine where school children might be placed by virtue of family background, special ability, and other subjective criteria. The Pupil Placement Law was almost as far-reaching in modifying and limiting the integration of schools as the original decision had been in attempting to eliminate segregation. Without technically reversing itself, the court had granted legal sanction to tokenism and thereby guaranteed that segregation, in substance, would last for an indefinite period, though formally it was illegal.

To understand, then, the deep disillusion of the Negro in 1963, one must examine his contrasting emotions at the time of the decision and during the nine years that followed. One must understand the pendulum swing between the elation that arose when the edict was handed down and the despair that followed the failure to bring it to life.

A second reason for the outburst in 1963 was rooted in disappointment with both political parties. From the city of Los Angeles in 1960, the Democratic party had written an historic and sweeping civil rights pronouncement into its campaign platform. The Democratic standard bearer had repeated eloquently and often that the moral weight of the Presidency must be applied to this burning issue. From Chicago, the Republican party had been generous in its convention vows on civil rights, although its candidate had made no great effort in his campaign to convince the nation that he would redeem his party's promises.

Then 1961 and 1962 arrived, with both parties marking time in the cause of justice. In the Congress, reactionary Republicans were still doing business with the Dixiecrats. And the feeling was growing among Negroes that the Administration had oversimplified and underestimated the civil rights issue. President Kennedy, if not backing down, had backed away from the key pledge of his campaign—to wipe out housing discrimination immediately "with the stroke of a pen." When he had finally signed the housing order, two years after taking office, its terms, though praiseworthy, had revealed a serious weakness in its failure to attack the key problem of discrimination in financing by banks and other lending institutions.

While Negroes were being appointed to some significant jobs, and social hospitality was being extended at the White House to Negro leaders, the dreams of the masses remained in tatters. The Negro felt that he recognized the same old bone that had been tossed to him in the past—only now it was being handed to him on a platter, with courtesy.

The Administration had fashioned its primary approach to discrimination in the South around a series of lawsuits chiefly designed to protect the right to vote. Opposition toward action on other fronts had begun to harden. With each new Negro protest we were advised, sometimes privately and sometimes in public, to call off our efforts and channel all of our energies into registering voters. On each occasion we would agree with the importance of voting rights, but would patiently seek to explain that Negroes did not want to neglect all other rights while one was selected for concentrated attention.

It was necessary to conclude that our argument was not persuading the Administration any more than the government's logic was prevailing with us. Negroes had manifested their faith by giving a substantial majority of their votes to President Kennedy. They had expected more of him than of the previous Administration. In no sense had President Kennedy betrayed his promises. Yet his Administration appeared to believe it was doing as much as was politically possible and had, by its positive deeds, earned enough credit to coast on civil rights. Politically, perhaps, this was not a surprising conclusion. How many people understood, during the first two years of the Kennedy Administration, that the Negroes' "Now" was becoming as militant as the segregationists' "Never"? Eventually, the President would set political considerations aside and rise to the level of his own unswerving moral commitment. But this was still in the future.

No discussion of the influences that bore on the thinking of the Negro in 1963 would be complete without some attention to the relationship of this revolution to international events. Throughout the upheavals of cold war politics, Negroes had seen their government go to the brink of nuclear conflict more than once. The justification for risking the annihilation of the human race was always expressed in terms of America's willingness to go to any lengths to preserve freedom. To the Negro, that readiness for heroic measures in the defense of liberty disappeared or became tragically weak when the threat was within our own borders and was concerned with the Negro's liberty. While the Negro is not so selfish as to stand isolated in concern for his own dilemma, ignoring the ebb and flow of events around the world, there is a certain bitter irony in the picture of his country championing freedom in foreign lands and failing to ensure that freedom to 20,000,000 of its own.

From beyond the borders of his own land, the Negro had been inspired by another powerful force. He had watched the decolonization and liberation of nations in Africa and Asia since World War II. He knew that yellow, black, and brown people had felt for years that the American Negro was too passive, unwilling to take strong measures to gain his freedom. He might have remembered the visit to this country of an African head of state, who was called upon by a delegation of prominent American Negroes. When they began reciting to him their long list of grievances, the visiting statesman had waved a weary hand and said:

"I am aware of current events. I know everything you are telling me about what the white man is doing to the Negro. Now tell me: What is the Negro doing for himself?"

The American Negro saw, in the land from which he had been snatched and thrown into slavery, a great pageant of political progress. He realized that just thirty years ago there were only three independent nations in the whole of Africa. He knew that by 1963 more than thirty-four African nations had risen from colonial bondage. The Negro saw black statesmen voting on vital issues in the United Nations—and knew that in many cities of his own land he was not permitted to take that significant walk to the ballot box. He saw black kings and potentates ruling from palaces—and knew he had been condemned to move from small ghettos to larger ones. Witnessing the drama of Negro progress elsewhere in the world, witnessing a level of conspicuous consumption at home exceeding anything in our history, it was natural that by 1963 Negroes would rise with resolution and demand a share of governing power and living conditions measured by current American standards rather than by the obsolete standards of colonial impoverishment.

An additional and decisive fact confronted the Negro and helped to bring him out of the houses into the streets, out of the trenches and into the front lines. This was his recognition that 100 years had passed since emancipation, with no profound effect on his plight.

With the dawn of 1963, plans were afoot all over the land to celebrate the Emancipation Proclamation, the 100th birthday of the Negro's liberation from bondage. In Washington, a federal commission had been established to mark the event. Governors of states and mayors of cities had utilized the date to enhance their political image by naming commissions, receiving committees, issuing statements, planning state pageants, sponsoring dinners, endorsing social activities. Champagne, this year, would bubble on countless tables. Appropriately attired, over thick cuts of roast beef, legions would listen as luminous phrases were spun to salute the great democratic landmark that 1963 represented.

But alas! All the talk and publicity accompanying the centennial only served to remind the Negro that he still wasn't free, that he still lived a form of slavery disguised by certain niceties of complexity. As the then Vice President, Lyndon B. Johnson, phrased it: "Emancipation was a proclamation but not a fact." The pen of the Great Emancipator had moved the Negro into the sunlight of physical freedom, but actual conditions had left him behind in the shadow of political, psychological, social, economic, and intellectual bondage. In the South, discrimination faced the Negro in its obvious and glaring forms. In the North, it confronted him in hidden and subtle disguise.

The Negro also had to recognize that 100 years after emancipation he lived on a lonely island of economic insecurity in the midst of a vast ocean of material prosperity. Negroes are still at the bottom of the economic ladder. They live within two concentric circles of segregation. One imprisons them on the basis of color; the other confines them within a separate culture of poverty. The average Negro is born into want and deprivation. His struggle to escape his circumstances is hindered by color discrimination. He is deprived of normal education and normal social and economic opportunities. When he seeks opportunity, he is told in effect to lift himself by his own bootstraps—advice that does not take into account the fact that he is barefoot.

By 1963 most of America's working population had forgotten the Great Depression or had never known it. The slow and steady growth of unemployment had touched some of the white working force, but the proportion was still not more than one in twenty. This was not true for the Negro. There were two and one-half times as many jobless Negroes as whites in 1963, and their median income was half that of the white man. Many white Americans of good will have never connected bigotry with economic exploitation. They have deplored prejudice but tolerated or ignored economic injustice. But the Negro knows that these two evils have a malignant kinship. He knows this because he has worked in shops that employ him exclusively because the pay is below a living standard. He knows it is not an accident of geography that wage rates in the South are significantly lower than those in the North. He knows that the growth in the number of women who work is not a phenomenon in Negro life. The average Negro woman has always had to work to help keep her family in food and clothes.

To the Negro, as 1963 approached, the economic structure of society appeared to be so ordered that a precise sifting of jobs took place. The lowest-paid employment and the most tentative jobs were reserved for him. If he sought to change his position, he was walled in by the tall barrier of discrimination. As summer came, more than ever the spread of unemployment had visible and tangible dimensions to the colored American. Equality meant dignity, and dignity demanded a job that was secure and a paycheck that lasted throughout the week.

The Negro's economic problem was compounded by the emergence and growth of automation. Since discrimination and lack of education confined him to unskilled and semi-skilled labor, the Negro was and remains the first to suffer in these days of great technological development. The Negro knew all too well that there was not in existence the kind of vigorous retraining program that could really help him to grapple with the magnitude of his problem.

The symbol of the job beyond the great wall was construction work. The Negro whose slave labor helped build a nation was being told by employers on the one hand and unions on the other that there was no place for him in this industry. Billions were being spent on city, state, and national building for which the Negro paid taxes but could draw no paycheck. No one who saw the spanning bridges, the grand mansions, the sturdy docks and stout factories of the South could question the Negro's ability to build if he were given a chance for apprenticeship training. It was plain, hard, raw discrimination that shut him out of decent employment.

In 1963 the Negro, who had realized for many years that he was not truly free, awoke from a stupor of inaction with the cold dash of realization that 1963 meant 100 years had passed since Lincoln gave his autograph to the cause of freedom.

The milestone of the centennial of emancipation gave the Negro a reason to act—a reason so simple and obvious that he almost had to step back to see it.

Simple logic made it painfully clear that if this centennial was to be meaningful, it must be observed not as a celebration, but rather as a commemoration of the one moment in the country's history when a bold, brave *start* had been made, and as a rededication to the obvious fact that urgent business was at hand—the resumption of that noble journey toward the goals reflected in the Preamble to the Constitution, the Constitution itself, the Bill of Rights and the Thirteenth, Fourteenth, and Fifteenth Amendments.

Yet not all of these forces conjoined could have brought about the massive and largely bloodless revolution of 1963 if there had not been at hand a philosophy and a method worthy of its goals. Nonviolent direct action did not originate in America, but it found its natural home in this land, where refusal to cooperate with injustice was an ancient and honorable tradition and where Christian forgiveness was written into the minds and hearts of good men. Tested in Montgomery during the winter of 1955-56 and toughened throughout the South in the eight ensuing years, nonviolent resistance had become, by 1963, the logical force in the greatest mass-action crusade for freedom that has ever occurred in American history.

Nonviolence is a powerful and just weapon. It is a weapon unique in history, which cuts without wounding and ennobles the man who wields it. It is a sword that heals. Both a practical and a moral answer to the Negro's cry for justice, nonviolent direct action proved that it could win victories without losing wars, and so became the triumphant tactic of the Negro Revolution of 1963.

QUESTIONS FOR CRITICAL ANALYSIS

1. King states that black history was not included in most history books in 1964, and he identifies two black figures often left out: Crispus Attucks and Benjamin Banneker. Who were they? Examine an American history book used today on your campus. Which black Americans are mentioned?
2. What was the Negro Revolution King refers to? What events took place during this revolution? How was history made?
3. "Why We Can't Wait" was published in the *Saturday Review* in May 1964. Who is the audience for this essay? How do you think this audience reacted to an essay describing events and plans in the Negro Revolution? What did King want the audience to do in response to reading this essay? Do you think he was successful?
4. Compare King's argument for the revolution with the main ideas in Baldwin's essay. How are they similar? how different? In what ways does the Hughes essay, written

almost twenty years earlier, predict and supplement the points being made by both King and Baldwin?

5. How did international affairs influence the civil rights movement? What are the international implications of the Negro Revolution?

QUESTIONS FOR STRUCTURAL ANALYSIS

1. Why does King begin his argument with the children in Harlem and Birmingham? How do you respond to this beginning?
2. What reasons does King give for "Why We Can't Wait"? How does he organize his argument?
3. Why does King include the story of being stabbed in a Harlem department store? In his essay "On Being a Good Neighbor" (in Section II), King describes how Jesus "pulls the question from mid-air and places it on a dangerous curve between Jerusalem and Jericho." How does King use this same technique in this essay? Make a list of examples.
4. How does King develop each point of his argument? Which reason that King offers strikes you as the most important one? Why?
5. Why does King examine economic problems at the end of the essay? How does he predict this problem will be addressed? Was his prediction accurate? Relate the conclusion of the essay to your understanding of race relations in the United States today.

*T*HE *C*IVIL *R*IGHTS *M*OVEMENT: *W*HAT *G*OOD *W*AS *I*T?

ALICE WALKER

Alice Walker (1944–), poet, novelist, essayist, and critic, focuses much of her writing on the experiences of black American women dealing with sexual and racial oppression. "The Civil Rights Movement: What Good Was It?" is a personal statement that challenges the conclusion that nothing much was gained for the black community. Walker points to attitude changes not only of whites toward blacks but, more importantly, of blacks toward their own options and possibilities. The Civil Rights Movement, Walker claims, gave her knowledge, and with knowledge she gained freedom, dignity, and hope.

Before you begin reading: *What do you know about your heritage—the type of people your family came from and their history? In your notebook write a brief description of your family heritage.*

◆

I wrote the following essay in the winter of 1966–67 while sharing one room above Washington Square Park in New York with a struggling young Jewish law student who became my husband. It was my first published essay and won the three-hundred-dollar first prize in the annual *American Scholar* essay contest. The money was almost magically reassuring to us in those days of disaffected parents, outraged friends, and one-item meals, and kept us in tulips, peonies, daisies, and lamb chops for several months.

SOMEONE SAID RECENTLY TO AN OLD BLACK LADY FROM Mississippi, whose legs had been badly mangled by local police who arrested her for "disturbing the peace," that the Civil Rights Movement was dead, and asked, since it was dead, what she thought about it. The old lady replied, hobbling out of his presence on her cane, that the Civil Rights Movement was like herself, "if it's dead, it shore ain't ready to lay down!"

This old lady is a legendary freedom fighter in her small town in the Delta. She has been severely mistreated for insisting on her rights as an American citizen. She has been beaten for singing Movement songs, placed in solitary confinement in prisons for talking about freedom, and placed on bread and water for praying aloud to God for her jailers' deliverance. For such a woman the Civil Rights Movement will never be over as long as her skin is black. It also will never be over for twenty million others with the same "affliction," for whom the Movement can never "lay down," no matter how it is killed by the press and made dead and buried by the white American public. As long as one black American survives, the struggle for equality with other Americans must also survive. This is a debt we owe to those blameless hostages we leave to the future, our children.

Still, white liberals and deserting Civil Rights sponsors are quick to justify their disaffection from the Movement by claiming that it is all over. "And since it is over," they will ask, "would someone kindly tell me what has been gained by it?" They then list statistics supposedly showing how much more advanced segregation is now than ten years ago—in schools, housing, jobs. They point to a gain in conservative politicians during the last few years. They speak of ghetto riots and of the survey that shows that most policemen are admittedly too anti-Negro to do their jobs in ghetto areas fairly and effectively. They speak of every area that has been touched by the Civil Rights Movement as somehow or other going to pieces.

They rarely talk, however, about human attitudes among Negroes that have undergone terrific changes just during the past seven to ten years (not to mention all those years when there was a Movement and only the Negroes knew about it). They seldom speak of changes in personal lives because of the influence of people in the Movement. They see general failure and few, if any, individual gains.

They do not understand what it is that keeps the Movement from "laying down" and Negroes from reverting to their former *silent* second-class status. They have apparently never stopped to wonder why it is always the white man—on his radio and in his newspaper and on his television—who says that the Movement is dead. If a Negro were audacious enough to make such a claim, his fellows might hanker to see him shot. The Movement is dead to the white man because it no longer interests him. And it no longer interests him because he can afford to be uninterested: he does not have to live by it, with it, or for it, as Negroes must. He can take a rest from the news of beatings, killings, and arrests that reach him from North and South—if his skin is white. Negroes cannot now and will never be able to take a rest from the injustices that plague them, for they—not the white man—are the target.

Perhaps it is naïve to be thankful that the Movement "saved" a large number of individuals and gave them something to live for, even if it did not provide them with everything they wanted. (Materially, it provided them with precious little that they wanted.) When a movement awakens people to the possibilities of life, it seems unfair to frustrate them by then denying what they had thought was offered. But what was offered? What was promised? What was it all about?

What good did it do? Would it have been better, as some have suggested, to leave the Negro people as they were, unawakened, unallied with one another, unhopeful about what to expect for their children in some future world?

I do not think so. If knowledge of my condition is all the freedom I get from a "freedom movement," it is better than unawareness, forgottenness, and hopelessness, the existence that is like the existence of a beast. Man only truly lives by knowing; otherwise he simply performs, copying the daily habits of others, but conceiving nothing of his creative possibilities as a man, and accepting someone else's superiority and his own misery.

When we are children, growing up in our parents' care, we await the spark from the outside world. Sometimes our parents provide it—if we are lucky—sometimes it comes from another source far from home. We sit, paralyzed, surrounded by our anxiety and dread, hoping we will not have to grow up into the narrow world and ways we see about us. We are hungry for a life that turns us on; we yearn for a knowledge of living that will save us from our innocuous lives that resemble death. We look for signs in every strange event; we search for heroes in every unknown face.

It was just six years ago that I began to be alive. I had, of course, been living before—for I am now twenty-three—but I did not really know it. And I did not know it because nobody told me that I—a pensive, yearning, typical high-school senior, but Negro—existed in the minds of others as I existed in my own. Until that time my mind was locked apart from the outer contours and complexion of my body as if it and the body were strangers. The mind possessed both thought and spirit—I wanted to be an author or a scientist—which the color of the body denied. I had never seen myself and existed as a statistic exists, or as a phantom. In the white world I walked, less real to them than a shadow; and being young and well hidden among the slums, among people who also did not exist—either in books or in films or in the government of their own lives—I waited to be called to life. And, by a miracle, I was called.

There was a commotion in our house that night in 1960. We had managed to buy our first television set. It was battered and overpriced, but my mother had gotten used to watching the afternoon soap operas at the house where she worked as maid, and nothing could satisfy her on days when she did not work but a continuation of her "stories." So she pinched pennies and bought a set.

I remained listless throughout her "stories," tales of pregnancy, abortion, hypocrisy, infidelity, and alcoholism. All these men and women were white and lived in houses with servants, long staircases that they floated down, patios where liquor was served four times a day to "relax" them. But my mother, with her swollen feet eased out of her shoes, her heavy body relaxed in our only comfortable chair, watched each movement of the smartly coiffed women, heard each word, pounced upon each innuendo and inflection, and for the duration of these "stories" she saw herself as one of them. She placed herself in every scene she saw, with her braided hair turned blond, her two hundred pounds compressed into a sleek size-seven dress, her rough dark skin smooth and *white*. Her husband became "dark and handsome," talented, witty, urbane, charming. And when she turned to look at my father sitting near her in his sweat shirt with his smelly feet raised on the bed to "air," there was always a tragic look of surprise on her face. Then she would sigh and go out to the kitchen looking lost and unsure of herself. My mother, a truly great woman who raised eight children of her own and half a dozen of the neighbors' without a single complaint, was convinced that she did not exist compared to "them." She subordinated her soul to theirs and became a faithful and timid supporter of the "Beautiful White People." Once she asked me, in a moment of vicarious pride and despair, if I didn't think that "they" were "jest naturally smarter, prettier, better." My mother asked this: a woman who never got rid of any of her children, never cheated on my father, was never a hypocrite if she could help it, and never even tasted liquor. She could not even bring herself to blame "them" for making her believe what they wanted her to believe: that if she did not look like them, think like them, be sophisticated and corrupt-for-comfort's-sake like them, she was a nobody. Black was not a color on my mother; it was a shield that made her invisible.

Of course, the people who wrote the soap-opera scripts always made the Negro maids in them steadfast, trusty, and wise in a home-remedial sort of way; but my mother, a maid for nearly forty years, never once identified herself with the scarcely glimpsed black servant's face beneath the ruffled cap. Like everyone else, in her daydreams at least, she thought she was free.

Six years ago, after half-heartedly watching my mother's soap operas and wondering whether there wasn't something more to be asked of life, the Civil Rights Movement came into my life. Like a good omen for the future, the face of Dr. Martin Luther King, Jr., was the first black face I saw on our new television screen. And, as in a fairy tale, my soul was stirred by the meaning for me of his mission—at the time he was being rather ignominiously dumped into a police van for having led a protest march in Alabama—and I fell in love with the sober and determined face of the Movement. The singing of "We Shall Overcome"—that song betrayed by nonbelievers in it—rang for the first time in my ears. The influence that my mother's soap operas might have had on me became impossible. The life of Dr. King, seeming bigger and more miraculous than the man himself, because of all he had done and suffered, offered a pattern of strength and sincerity I felt I could trust. He had suffered much because of his simple belief in nonviolence, love, and brotherhood. Perhaps the majority of men could not be reached through these beliefs, but because Dr. King kept trying to reach them in spite of danger to himself and his family, I saw in him the hero for whom I had waited so long.

What Dr. King promised was not a ranch-style house and an acre of manicured lawn for every black man, but jail and finally freedom. He did not promise two cars for every family, but the courage one day for all families everywhere to walk without shame and unafraid on their own feet. He did not say that one day it will be us chasing prospective buyers out of our prosperous well-kept neighborhoods, or in other ways exhibiting our snobbery and ignorance as all other ethnic groups before us have done; what he said was that we had a right to live anywhere in this country we chose, and a right to a meaningful well-paying job to provide us with the upkeep of our homes. He did not say we had to become carbon copies of the white American middle class; but he did say we had the right to become whatever we wanted to become.

Because of the Movement, because of an awakened faith in the newness and imagination of the human spirit, because of "black and white together"—for the first time in our history in some human relationship on and off TV—because of the beatings, the arrests, the hell of battle during the past years, I have fought harder for my life and for a chance to be myself, to be something more than a shadow or a number, than I had ever done before in my life. Before, there had seemed to be no real reason for struggling beyond the effort for daily bread. Now there was a chance at that other that Jesus meant when He said we could not live by bread alone.

I have fought and kicked and fasted and prayed and cursed and cried myself to the point of existing. It has been like being born again, literally. Just "knowing" has meant everything to me. Knowing has pushed me out into the world, into college, into places, into people.

Part of what existence means to me is knowing the difference between what I am now and what I was then. It is being capable of looking after myself intellectually as well as financially. It is being able to tell when I am being wronged and by whom. It means being awake to protect myself and the ones I love. It means being a part of the world community, and being *alert* to which part it is that I have joined, and knowing how to change to another part if that part does not suit me. To know is to exist: to exist is to be involved, to move about, to see the world with my own eyes. This, at least, the Movement has given me.

The hippies and other nihilists would have me believe that it is all the same whether the people in Mississippi have a movement behind them or not. Once they have their rights, they say, they will run all over themselves trying to be just like everybody else. They will be well fed, complacent about things of the spirit, emotionless, and without the marvelous humanity and "soul" that the Movement has seen them practice time and time again. "What has the Movement done," they ask, "with the few people it has supposedly helped?" "Got them white-collar jobs, moved them into standardized ranch houses in white neighborhoods, given them nondescript gray flannel suits?" "What are these people now?" they ask. And then they answer themselves, "Nothings!"

I would find this reasoning—which I have heard many, many times from hippies and nonhippies alike—amusing if I did not also consider it serious. For I think it is a delusion, a cop-out, an excuse to disassociate themselves from a world in which they feel too little has been changed or gained. The real question, however, it appears to me, is not whether poor people will adopt the middle-class mentality once they are well fed; rather, it is whether they will ever be well fed enough to be able to choose whatever mentality they think will suit them. The lack of a movement did not keep my mother from *wishing* herself bourgeois in her daydreams.

There is widespread starvation in Mississippi. In my own state of Georgia there are more hungry families than Lester Maddox would like to admit—or even see fed. I went to school with children who ate red dirt. The Movement has prodded and pushed some liberal senators into pressuring the government for food so that the hungry may eat. Food stamps that were two dollars and out of the reach of many families not long ago have been reduced to fifty cents. The price is still out of the reach of some families, and the government, it seems to a lot of people, could spare enough free food to feed its own people. It angers people in the Movement that it does not; they point to the billions in wheat we send free each year to countries abroad. Their government's slowness while people are hungry, its unwillingness to believe that there are Americans starving, its stingy cutting of the price of food stamps, make many Civil Rights workers throw up their hands in disgust. But they do not give up. They do not withdraw into the world of psychedelia. They apply what pressure they can to make the government give away food to hungry people. They do not plan so far ahead in their disillusionment with society that they can see these starving families buying identical ranch-style houses and sending their snobbish children to Bryn Mawr and Yale. They take first things first and try to get them fed.

They do not consider it their business, in any case, to say what kind of life the people they help must lead. How one lives is, after all, one of the rights left to the individual—when and if he has opportunity to choose. It is not the prerogative of the middle class to determine what is worthy of aspiration. There is also every possibility that the middle-class people of tomorrow will turn out ever so much better than those of today. I even know some middle-class people of today who are not *all* bad.

I think there are so few Negro hippies because middle-class Negroes, although well fed, are not careless. They are required by the treacherous world they live in to be clearly aware of whoever or whatever might be trying to do them in. They are middle class in money and position, but they cannot afford to be middle class in complacency. They distrust the hippie movement because they know that it can do nothing for Negroes as a group but "love" them, which is what all paternalists claim to do. And since the only way Negroes can survive (which they cannot do, unfortunately, on love alone) is with the support of the group, they are wisely wary and stay away.

A white writer tried recently to explain that the reason for the relatively few Negro hippies is that Negroes have built up a "super-cool" that cracks under LSD and makes them have a "bad trip." What this writer doesn't guess at is that

Negroes are needing drugs less than ever these days for any kind of trip. While the hippies are "tripping," Negroes are going after power, which is so much more important to their survival and their children's survival than LSD and pot.

Everyone would be surprised if the Israelis ignored the Arabs and took up "tripping" and pot smoking. In this country we are the Israelis. Everybody who can do so would like to forget this, of course. But for us to forget it for a minute would be fatal. "We Shall Overcome" is just a song to most Americans, *but we must do it.* Or die.

What good was the Civil Rights Movement? If it had just given this country Dr. King, a leader of conscience, for once in our lifetime, it would have been enough. If it had just taken black eyes off white television stories, it would have been enough. If it had fed one starving child, it would have been enough.

If the Civil Rights Movement is "dead," and if it gave us nothing else, it gave us each other forever. It gave some of us bread, some of us shelter, some of us knowledge and pride, all of us comfort. It gave us our children, our husbands, our brothers, our fathers, as men reborn and with a purpose for living. It broke the pattern of black servitude in this country. It shattered the phony "promise" of white soap operas that sucked away so many pitiful lives. It gave us history and men far greater than Presidents. It gave us heroes, selfless men of courage and strength, for our little boys and girls to follow. It gave us hope for tomorrow. It called us to life.

Because we live, it can never die.

Questions for Critical Analysis

1. Why do people claim that the civil rights movement is over? Who are the people making these claims? What does Walker think of them?
2. This essay was published in the *American Scholar* in 1967. Describe Walker's audience. What is her purpose in writing about this subject to them? What response does she want from them? Do you think she'll get it? Why, or why not?
3. Why does Walker believe the civil rights movement is far from over?
4. Walker claims that knowledge is better than ignorance even when knowledge brings pain. In what context does she say this? Do you agree with her? Why, or why not? Can you think of other examples of knowledge bringing pain?
5. How did Martin Luther King, Jr., influence Walker's life? What did he give her?

Questions for Structural Analysis

1. Why does Walker include the preface describing the circumstances under which she wrote this essay? What do you learn about her? How do these elements influence your reading of the essay?

2. Walker begins the essay with an anecdote about an elderly black woman. What does the woman represent? Why does Walker begin with her story? How does she use the woman's experience?
3. What reasons does Walker give for why the civil rights movement is alive? Examine Walker's tone and language. What attitude is evident in her discussion? Compare Walker's essay with Baldwin's. How are their ideas similar? How are their conclusions and ideas different?
4. What is the effect of Walker's personal experience in the movement? What sort of person is the persona, the "I," of the essay? How do you respond to her?
5. Toward the conclusion Walker writes about hippies and their drug culture and the relationships between the hippies and the blacks. What point is she making? How is this section important to the essay? Do the dated language and examples affect your response to the essay as a whole? How?

*D*EMANDING CIVIL *R*IGHTS

TOPICS FOR WRITING ESSAYS

Many of the questions following each essay can serve as appropriate writing suggestions. Some of the topics listed below expand the prereading exercises, but they can be used without completing that step first.

1. Describe the America you find in reading all four essays from this section: Hughes, Baldwin, King, and Walker. How does this America differ from what you think of as "The American Dream"? In what ways does it reflect "The American Dream"? Write your analysis to a skeptical audience.
2. Write an argument asserting that a black child born in urban America enjoys equality and justice. You may want to refer to Dick Gregory's essay, "Shame," or Langston Hughes' essay, "Salvation," and/or to ideas mentioned in the essays about the schools in the Education section, as well as the four essays you read in this section. Write your argument to a hostile audience.
3. Select a race other than your own and examine how people of that race are portrayed by the media: in commercials, television shows, movies, news articles, essays, books, stories, textbooks, and so forth. Write an argument that the portrayal is unfair. Be sure to support your position with specific details as well as with a clear definition of what you mean by "unfair." Your essay will be published in a magazine whose readers are dominated by members of the race you are examining.

RESEARCH POSSIBILITIES

1. Discover what life was like for black members of your town in 1935. What rights did they have? Where did they work? Where did their children go to school? What shops, restaurants, banks, and other places of business did they frequent? What did they do for entertainment? By reading newspaper accounts and editorials, can you develop a sense of the town's attitude toward them? Write a feature article on their experience for your hometown newspaper.
2. Analysts and news commentators are concerned that since the early 1980s there has been an upsurge in racially-motivated incidents. Is this true? Focus on a specific area (a region, state, city, campus) and compare events between 1970–1980 and 1980–today. Investigate newspapers, statistical digests, government reports, specialized documents, editorials, and personal opinions and write a report of your findings to leaders of the region, state, city, or campus.
3. What is the racial climate on your campus? Are students discriminated against because of their race? Interview students, administrators, faculty and staff and "take the temperature." Read accounts of incidents on other campuses and make comparisons. If there are campus organizations formed to help increase minority enrollment and/or minority faculty, talk with the members and leaders. Write an essay for a national college magazine about race relations on your campus.

UNDERSTANDING RELATIONSHIPS BETWEEN THE SEXES

All of the essays in this section examine men and women and, either directly or implicitly, their relationship to each other. Is there an undercurrent of hostility in each essay? Does the humor have an edge? These essays confirm certain differences between the sexes; not only are physical differences not mentioned, but they appear to be minor when considered against great psychological and emotional differences.

JAMES THURBER, "COURTSHIP THROUGH THE AGES"

KIM CHERNIN, "THE FLESH AND THE DEVIL"

JUDY SYFERS, "I WANT A WIFE"

MICHAEL NORMAN, "STANDING HIS GROUND"

CATHERINE DRINKER BOWEN, ". . . WE'VE NEVER ASKED A WOMAN BEFORE"

COURTSHIP THROUGH THE AGES

JAMES THURBER

James Thurber (1894–1961), humorist and cartoonist, amused readers with essays and drawings depicting the continual struggle for understanding between men and women. Two popular depictions of the battle were Is Sex Necessary? *(written with E. B. White in 1929) and "The Secret Life of Walter Mitty," a short story describing Walter Mitty's escape into fantasy each time Mrs. Mitty's presence became too overpowering. "Courtship Through the Ages" sets the case in the first sentence: no matter how hard the male tries he will never please the female. Through examples from many levels in the animal kingdom, it is evident that there are no exceptions.*

Before you begin reading: *Fantasize about the ideal courtship. How would the man behave? How would the woman behave? What are the best conditions for courtship to flourish? In your reading notebook, write a description of ideal courtship.*

◆

SURELY NOTHING IN THE ASTONISHING SCHEME OF LIFE can have nonplussed Nature so much as the fact that none of the females of any of the species she created really cared very much for the male, as such. For the past ten million years Nature has been busily inventing ways to make the male attractive to the female, but the whole business of courtship, from the marine annelids up to man, still lumbers heavily along, like a complicated musical comedy. I have been reading the sad and absorbing story in Volume 6 (Cole to Dama) of the Encyclopaedia Britannica. In this volume you can learn all about cricket, cotton, costume designing, crocodiles, crown jewels, and Coleridge, but none of these subjects is so interesting as the Courtship of Animals, which recounts the sorrowful lengths to which all males must go to arouse the interest of a lady.

We all know, I think, that Nature gave man whiskers and a mustache with the quaint idea in mind that these would prove attractive to the female. We all know that, far from attracting her, whiskers and mustaches only made her nervous and gloomy, so that man had to go in for somersaults, tilting with lances, and performing feats of parlor magic to win her attention; he also had to bring her candy, flowers, and the furs of animals. It is common knowledge that in spite of all these "love displays" the male is constantly being turned down, insulted, or thrown out of the house. It is rather comforting, then, to discover that the peacock, for all his gorgeous plumage, does not have a particularly easy time in courtship; none of the males in the world do. The first peahen, it turned out, was only faintly stirred by her suitor's beautiful train. She would often go quietly to sleep while he was whisking it around. The Britannica tells us that the peacock actually had to learn a certain little trick to wake her up and revive her interest: he had to learn to vibrate his quills so as to make a rustling sound. In ancient times man himself, observing the ways of the peacock, probably tried vibrating his whiskers to make a rustling sound; if so, it didn't get him anywhere. He had to go in for something else; so, among other things, he went in for gifts. It is not unlikely that he got this idea from certain flies and birds who were making no headway at all with rustling sounds.

One of the flies of the family Empidae, who had tried everything, finally hit on something pretty special. He contrived to make a glistening transparent balloon which was even larger than himself. Into this he would put sweetmeats and tidbits and he would carry the whole elaborate envelope through the air to the lady of his choice. This amused her for a time, but she finally got bored with it. She demanded silly little colorful presents, something that you couldn't eat but that would look nice around the house. So the male Empis had to go around gathering flower petals and pieces of bright paper to put into his balloon. On a courtship flight a male Empis cuts quite a figure now, but he can hardly be said to be happy. He never knows how soon the female will demand heavier presents, such as Roman coins and gold collar buttons. It seems probable that one day the courtship of the Empidae will fall down, as man's occasionally does, of its own weight.

The bowerbird is another creature that spends so much time courting the female that he never gets any work done. If all the male bowerbirds became nervous wrecks within the next ten or fifteen years, it would not surprise me. The female bowerbird insists that a playground be built for her with a specially constructed bower at the entrance. This bower is much more elaborate than an ordinary nest and is harder to build; it costs a lot more, too. The female will not come to the playground until the male has filled it up with a great many gifts: silvery leaves, red leaves, rose petals, shells, beads, berries, bones, dice, buttons, cigar bands, Christmas seals, and the Lord knows what else. When the female finally condescends to visit the playground, she is in a coy and silly mood and has to be chased in and out of the bower and up and down the playground before she will quit giggling and stand still long enough even to shake hands. The male bird is, of course, pretty well done in before the chase starts, because he has worn himself out hunting for eyeglass lenses and begonia blossoms. I imagine that many a bowerbird, after chasing a female for two or three hours, says the hell with it and goes home to bed. Next day, of course, he telephones someone else and the same trying ritual is gone through with again. A male bowerbird is as exhausted as a night-club habitué before he is out of his twenties.

The male fiddler crab has a somewhat easier time, but it can hardly be said that he is sitting pretty. He has one enormously large and powerful claw, usually brilliantly colored, and you might suppose that all he had to do was reach out and grab some passing cutie. The very earliest fiddler crabs may have tried this, but, if so, they got slapped for their pains. A female fiddler crab will not tolerate any cave-man stuff; she never has and she doesn't intend to start now. To attract a female, a fiddler crab has to stand on tiptoe and brandish his claw in the air. If any female in the neighborhood is interested—and you'd be surprised how many are not—she comes over and engages him in light badinage, for which he is not in the mood. As many as a hundred females may pass the time of day with him and go on about their business. By nightfall of an average courting day, a fiddler crab who has been standing on tiptoe for eight or ten hours waving a heavy claw in the air is in pretty sad shape. As in the case of the males of all species, however, he gets out of bed next morning, dashes some water on his face, and tries again.

The next time you encounter a male web-spinning spider, stop and reflect that he is too busy worrying about his love life to have any desire to bite you. Male web-spinning spiders have a tougher life than any other males in the animal kingdom. This is because the female web-spinning spiders have very poor eyesight. If a male lands on a female's web, she kills him before he has time to lay down his cane and gloves, mistaking him for a fly or a bumblebee who has stumbled into her trap. Before the species figured out what to do about this, millions of males were murdered by ladies they called on. It is the nature of spiders to perform a little dance in front of the female, but before a male spinner could get near enough for the female to see who he was and what he was up to, she would lash out at him with a flatiron or a pair of garden shears. One night, nobody knows when, a very bright male spinner lay awake worrying about calling on a lady who had been killing suitors right and left. It came to him that this business of dancing as a love display wasn't getting anybody anywhere except the grave. He decided to go in for web-twitching, or strand-vibrating. The next day he tried it on one of the nearsighted girls. Instead of dropping in on her suddenly, he stayed outside the web and began monkeying with one of its strands. He twitched it up and down and in and out with such a lilting rhythm that the female was charmed. The serenade worked beautifully; the female let him live. The Britannica's spider-watchers, however, report that this system is not always successful. Once in a while, even now, a female will fire three bullets into a suitor or run him through with a kitchen knife. She keeps threatening him from the moment he strikes the first low notes on the outside strings, but usually by the time he has got up to the high notes played around the center of the web, he is going to town and she spares his life.

Even the butterfly, as handsome a fellow as he is, can't always win a mate merely by fluttering around and showing off. Many butterflies have to have scent scales on their wings. Hepialus carries a powder puff in a perfumed pouch. He throws perfume at the ladies when they pass. The male tree cricket, Oecanthus, goes Hepialus one better by carrying a tiny bottle of wine with him and giving drinks to such doxies as he has designs on. One of the male snails throws darts to entertain the girls. So it goes, through the long list of animals, from the bristle worm and his rudimentary dance steps to man and his gift of diamonds and sapphires. The golden-eye drake raises a jet of water with his feet as he flies over a lake; Hepialus has his powder puff, Oecanthus his wine bottle, man his etchings. It is a bright and melancholy story, the age-old desire of the male for the female, the age-old desire of the female to be amused and entertained. Of all the creatures on earth, the only males who could be figured as putting any irony into their courtship are the grebes and certain other diving birds. Every now and then a courting grebe slips quietly down to the bottom of a lake and then, with a mighty "Whoosh!," pops out suddenly a few feet from his girl friend, splashing water all over her. She seems to be persuaded that this is a purely loving display, but I like to think that the grebe always has a faint hope of drowning her or scaring her to death.

I will close this investigation into the mournful burdens of the male with the Britannica's story about a certain Argus pheasant. It appears that the Argus displays himself in front of a female who stands perfectly still without moving a feather. (If you saw "June Moon" some years ago and remember the scene in which the songwriter sang "Montana Moon" to his grim and motionless wife, you have some idea what the female Argus probably thinks of her mate's display.) The male Argus the Britannica tells about was confined in a cage with a female of another species, a female who kept moving around, emptying ashtrays and fussing with lampshades all the time the male was showing off his talents. Finally, in disgust, he stalked away and began displaying in front of his water trough. He reminds me of a certain male (Homo sapiens) of my acquaintance who one night after dinner asked his wife to put down her detective magazine so that he could read her a poem of which he was very fond. She sat quietly enough until he was well into the middle of the thing, intoning with great ardor and intensity. Then suddenly there came a sharp, disconcerting *slap!* It turned out that all during the male's display, the female had been intent on a circling mosquito and had finally trapped it between the palms of her hands. The male in this case did not stalk away and display in front of a water trough; he went over to Tim's and had a flock of drinks and recited the poem to the fellas. I am sure they all told bitter stories of their own about how their displays had been interrupted by females. I am also sure that they all ended up singing "Honey, Honey, Bless Your Heart."

QUESTIONS FOR CRITICAL ANALYSIS

1. What lengths has man had to go to in order to attract a woman? Can you attest to any of these activities from experience?
2. How do the males of other species try to attract the females? How are they different from men's attempts? Which of the illustrations do you like the best? Why?
3. In what ways do the females spurn the males?
4. If someone suggested to you that underlying Thurber's essay is his dislike of women, how would you respond? Is it a valid position to take? Why, or why not?
5. Why were the men in the bar singing "Honey, Honey Bless Your Heart"?

QUESTIONS FOR STRUCTURAL ANALYSIS

1. What is Thurber's thesis? What evidence does Thurber marshall to support his thesis?
2. How do you know Thurber wrote this as a humorous essay? What was your first clue? How does Thurber sustain the humor?
3. What is the relationship between Thurber's final animal story, the Argus pheasant, and the story about his friend that concludes the essay? Did you like the way the essay ended? Why, or why not?

*T*HE *F*LESH AND THE *D*EVIL

KIM CHERNIN

Kim Chernin (1940–   ), a freelance writer, editor, and consultant for writing projects, describes her politics as "feminist humanist" and in 1972 legally took her mother's maiden name as her own. Chernin's concern about women's unwillingness to accept themselves is part of the focus of "The Flesh and the Devil," a chapter from The Obsession: Reflections on the Tyranny of Slenderness *(1981). Chernin uses examples, stories, and formal research to expose each woman's struggle to deny her own body while she molds herself into an ideal form.*

Before you begin reading: *Make a list in your notebook of all the characteristics you can think of to describe the ideal woman.*

◆

We know that every woman wants to be thin. Our images of womanhood are almost synonymous with thinness.
SUSIE ORBACH

. . . I must now be able to look at my ideal, this ideal of being thin, of being without a body, and to realize: "it is a fiction."
ELLEN WEST

When the body is hiding the complex, it then becomes our most immediate access to the problem.
MARIAN WOODMAN

THE LOCKER ROOM OF THE TENNIS CLUB. SEVERAL EXERcise benches, two old-fashioned hair dryers, a mechanical bicycle, a treadmill, a reducing machine, a mirror, and a scale.

A tall woman enters, removes her towel; she throws it across a bench, faces herself squarely in the mirror, climbs on the scale, looks down.

A silence.

"I knew it," she mutters, turning to me. "I knew it."

And I think, before I answer, just how much I admire her, for this courage beyond my own, this daring to weigh herself daily in this way. And I sympathize. I know what she must be feeling. Not quite candidly, I say: "Up or down?" I am hoping to suggest that there might be people and cultures where gaining weight might not be considered a disaster. Places where women, stepping on scales, might be horrified to notice that they had reduced themselves. A mythical, almost unimaginable land.

"Two pounds," she says, ignoring my hint. "Two pounds." And then she turns, grabs the towel and swings out at her image in the mirror, smashing it violently, the towel spattering water over the glass. "Fat pig," she shouts at her image in the glass. "You fat, fat pig. . . ."

Later, I go to talk with this woman. Her name is Rachel and she becomes, as my work progresses, one of the choral voices that shape its vision.

Two girls come into the exercise room. They are perhaps ten or eleven years old, at that elongated stage when the skeletal structure seems to be winning its war against flesh. And these two are particularly skinny. They sit beneath the hair dryers for a moment, kicking their legs on the faded green upholstery; they run a few steps on the eternal treadmill, they wrap the rubber belt of the reducing machine around themselves and jiggle for a moment before it falls off. And then they go to the scale.

The taller one steps up, glances at herself in the mirror, looks down at the scale. She sighs, shaking her head. I see at once that this girl is imitating someone. The sigh, the headshake are theatrical, beyond her years. And so, too, is the little drama enacting itself in front of me. The other girl leans forward, eager to see for herself the troubling message imprinted upon the scale. But the older girl throws her hand over the secret. It is not to be revealed. And now the younger one, accepting this, steps up to confront the ultimate judgment. "Oh God," she says, this growing girl. "Oh God," with only a shade of imitation in her voice: "Would you believe it? I've gained five pounds."

These girls, too, become a part of my work. They enter, they perform their little scene again and again; it extends beyond them and in it I am finally able to behold something that would have remained hidden—for it does not express itself directly, although we feel its pressure almost every day of our lives. Something, unnamed as yet, struggling against our emergence into femininity. This is my first glimpse of it, out there. And the vision ripens.

I return to the sauna. Two women I have seen regularly at the club are sitting on the bench above me. One of them is very beautiful, the sort of woman Renoir would have admired. The other, who is probably in her late sixties, looks, in the twilight of this sweltering room, very much an adolescent. I have noticed her before, with her tan face, her white hair, her fashionable clothes, her slender hips and jaunty walk. But the effect has not been soothing. A woman of advancing age who looks like a boy.

I've heard about that illness, anorexia nervosa," the plump one is saying, "and I keep looking around for someone who has it. I want to go sit next to her. I think to myself, maybe I'll catch it. . . ."

"Well," the other woman says to her, "I've felt the same way myself. One of my cousins used to throw food under the table when no one was looking.

Finally, she got so thin they had to take her to the hospital. . . . I always admired her."

What am I to understand from these stories? The woman in the locker room who swings out at her image in the mirror, the little girls who are afraid of the coming of adolescence to their bodies, the woman who admires the slenderness of the anorexic girl. Is it possible to miss the dislike these women feel for their bodies?

And yet, an instant's reflection tells us that this dislike for the body is not a biological fact of our condition as women—we do not come upon it by nature, we are not born to it, it does not arise for us because of anything predetermined in our sex. We know that once we loved the body, delighting in it the way children will, reaching out to touch our toes and count over our fingers, repeating the game endlessly as we come to knowledge of this body in which we will live out our lives. No part of the body exempt from our curiosity, nothing yet forbidden, we know an equal fascination with the feces we eliminate from ourselves, as with the ear we discover one day and the knees that have become bruised and scraped with falling and that warm, moist place between the legs from which feelings of indescribable bliss arise.

From that state to the condition of the woman in the locker room is a journey from innocence to despair, from the infant's naive pleasure in the body, to the woman's anguished confrontation with herself. In this journey we can read our struggle with natural existence—the loss of the body as a source of pleasure. But the most striking thing about this alienation from the body is the fact that we take it for granted. Few of us ask to be redeemed from this struggle against the flesh by overcoming our antagonism toward the body. We do not rush about looking for someone who can tell us how to enjoy the fact that our appetite is large, or how we might delight in the curves and fullness of our own natural shape. We hope instead to be able to reduce the body, to limit the urges and desires it feels, to remove the body from nature. Indeed, the suffering we experience through our obsession with the body arises precisely from the hopeless and impossible nature of this goal.

Cheryl Prewitt, the 1980 winner of the Miss America contest, is a twenty-two-year-old woman, "slender, bright-eyed, and attractive."[1] If there were a single woman alive in America today who might feel comfortable about the size and shape of her body, surely we would expect her to be Ms. Prewitt? And yet, in order to make her body suitable for the swimsuit event of the beauty contest she has just won, Cheryl Prewitt "put herself through a grueling regimen, jogging long distances down back-country roads, pedaling for hours on her stationary bicycle." The bicycle is still kept in the living room of her parents' house so that she can take part in conversation while she works out. This body she has created, after an arduous struggle against nature, in conformity with her culture's ideal standard for a woman, cannot now be left to its own desires. It must be perpetually shaped, monitored, and watched. If you were to visit her at home in Ackerman, Mississippi, you might well find her riding her stationary bicycle in her parents' living room, "working off the calories from a large slice of homemade coconut cake she has just had for a snack."

And so we imagine a woman who will never be Miss America, a next-door neighbor, a woman down the street, waking in the morning and setting out for her regular routine of exercise. The eagerness with which she jumps up at six o'clock and races for her jogging shoes and embarks upon the cold and arduous toiling up the hill road that runs past her house. And yes, she feels certain that her zeal to take off another pound, tighten another inch of softening flesh, places her in the school of those ancient wise men who formulated that vision of harmony between mind and body. "A healthy mind in a healthy body," she repeats to herself and imagines that it is love of the body which inspires her this early morning. But now she lets her mind wander and encounter her obsession. First it had been those hips, and she could feel them jogging along there with their own rhythm as she jogged. It was they that had needed reducing. Then, when the hips came down it was the thighs, hidden when she was clothed but revealing themselves every time she went to the sauna, and threatening great suffering now that summer drew near. Later, it was the flesh under the arms—this proved singularly resistant to tautness even after the rest of the body had become gaunt. And finally it was the ankles. But then, was there no end to it? What had begun as a vision of harmony between mind and body, a sense of well-being, physical fitness, and glowing health, had become now demonic, driving her always to further exploits, running farther, denying herself more food, losing more weight, always goaded on by the idea that the body's perfection lay just beyond her present achievement. And then, when she began to observe this driven quality in herself, she also began to notice what she had been thinking about her body. For she would write down in her notebook, without being aware of the violence in what she wrote: "I don't care how long it takes. One day I'm going to get my body to obey me. I'm going to make it lean and tight and hard. I'll succeed in this, even if it kills me."

But what a vicious attitude this is, she realizes one day, toward a body she professes to love. Was it love or hatred of the flesh that inspired her now to awaken even before it was light, and to go out on the coldest morning, running with bare arms and bare legs, busily fantasizing what she would make of her body? Love or hatred?

"You know perfectly well we hate our bodies," says Rachel, who calls herself the pig. She grabs the flesh of her stomach between her hands. "Who could love this?"

There is an appealing honesty in this despair, an articulation of what is virtually a universal attitude among women in our culture today. Few women who diet realize that they are confessing to a dislike for the body when they weigh and measure their flesh, subject it to rigorous fasts or strenuous regimens of exercise. And yet, over and over again, as I spoke to women about their bodies, this antagonism became apparent. One woman disliked her thighs, another her stomach, a third the loose flesh under her arms. Many would grab their skin and squeeze it as we talked, with that grimace of distaste language cannot translate into itself. One woman said to me: "Little by little I began to be aware that the pounds I was trying to 'melt away' were my own flesh. Would you believe it? It never occurred to me before. These 'ugly pounds' which filled me with so much hatred were my body."

The sound of this dawning consciousness can be heard now and again among the voices I have recorded in my notebook, heralding what may be a growing awareness of how bitterly the women of this culture are alienated from their bodies. Thus, another woman said to me: "It's true, I never used to like my body." We had been looking at pictures of women from the nineteenth century; they were large women, with full hips and thighs. "What do you think of them?" I said. "They're like me," she answered, and then began to laugh. "Soft, sensual, and inviting."

The description is accurate; the women in the pictures, and the woman looking at them, share a quality of voluptuousness that is no longer admired by our culture:

> When I look at myself in the mirror I see that there's nothing wrong with me—now! Sometimes I even think I'm beautiful. I don't know why this began to change. It might have been when I started going to the YWCA. It was the first time I saw so many women naked. I realized it was the fuller bodies that were more beautiful. The thin women, who looked so good in clothes, seemed old and worn out. Their bodies were gaunt. But the bodies of the larger women had a certain natural mystery, very different from the false illusion of clothes. And I thought, I'm like them; I'm a big woman like they are and perhaps my body is beautiful. I had always been trying to make my body have the right shape so that I could fit into clothes. But then I started to look at myself in the mirror. Before that I had always looked at parts of myself. The hips were too flabby, the thighs were too fat. Now I began to see myself as a whole. I stopped hearing my mother's voice, asking me if I was going to go on a diet. I just looked at what was really there instead of what should have been there. What was wrong with it? I asked myself. And little by little I stopped disliking my body.[2]

This is the starting point. It is from this new way of looking at an old problem that liberation will come. The very simple idea that an obsession with weight reflects a dislike and uneasiness for the body can have a profound effect upon a woman's life.

> I always thought I was too fat. I never liked my body. I kept trying to lose weight. I just tortured myself. But if I see pictures of myself from a year or two ago I discover now that I looked just fine.
>
> I remember recently going out to buy Häagen Dazs ice cream. I had decided I

> was going to give myself something I really wanted to eat. I had to walk all the way down to the World Trade Center. But on my way there I began to feel terribly fat. I felt that I was being punished by being fat. I had lost the beautiful self I had made by becoming thinner. I could hear these voices saying to me: "You're fat, you're ugly, who do you think you are, don't you know you'll never be happy?" I had always heard these voices in my mind but now when they would come into consciousness I would tell them to shut up. I saw two men on the street. I was eating the Häagen Dazs ice cream. I thought I heard one of them say "heavy." I thought they were saying: "She's so fat." But I knew that I had to live through these feelings if I was ever to eat what I liked. I just couldn't go on tormenting myself any more about the size of my body.
>
> One day, shortly after this, I walked into my house. I noticed the scales, standing under the sink in the bathroom. Suddenly, I hated them. I was filled with grief for having tortured myself for so many years. They looked like shackles. I didn't want to have anything more to do with them. I called my boyfriend and offered him the scales. Then, I went into the kitchen. I looked at my shelves. I saw diet books there. I was filled with rage and hatred of them. I hurled them all into a box and got rid of them. Then I looked into the ice box. There was a bottle of Weight Watchers dressing. I hurled it into the garbage and watched it shatter and drip down the plastic bag. Little by little, I started to feel better about myself. At first I didn't eat less, I just worried less about my eating. I allowed myself to eat whatever I wanted. I began to give away the clothes I couldn't fit into. It turned out that they weren't right for me anyway. I had bought them with the idea of what my body should look like. Now I buy clothes because I like the way they look on me. If something doesn't fit it doesn't fit. I'm not trying to make myself into something I'm not. I weigh more than I once considered my ideal. But I don't seem fat to myself. Now, I can honestly say that I like my body.[3]

Some weeks ago, at a dinner party, a woman who had recently gained weight began to talk about her body.

"I was once very thin," she said, "but I didn't feel comfortable in my body. I fit into all the right clothes. But somehow I just couldn't find myself any longer."

I looked over at her expectantly; she was a voluptuous woman, who had recently given birth to her first child.

"But now," she said as she got to her feet, "now, if I walk or jog or dance, I feel my flesh jiggling along with me." She began to shake her shoulders and move her hips, her eyes wide as she hopped about in front of the coffee table. "You see what I mean?" she shouted over to me. "I love it."

This image of a woman dancing came with me when I sat down to write. I remembered her expression. There was in it something secretive, I thought, something knowing and pleased—the look of a woman who has made peace with her body. Then I recalled the faces of women who had recently lost weight. The haggard look, the lines of strain around the mouth, the neck too lean, the tendons visible, the head too large for the emaciated body. I began to reason:

There must be, I said, for every woman a correct weight, which cannot be discovered with reference to a weight chart or to any statistical norm. For the size of the body is a matter of highly subjective individual preferences and natural endowments. If we should evolve an aesthetic for women that was appropriate to women it would reflect this diversity, would conceive, indeed celebrate and even love, slenderness in a woman intended by nature to be slim, and love the rounded cheeks of another, the plump arms, broad shoulders, narrow hips, full thighs, rounded ass, straight back, narrow shoulders or slender arms, of a woman made that way according to her nature, walking with head high in pride of her body, however it happened to be shaped. And then Miss America, and the woman jogging in the morning, and the woman swinging out at her image in the mirror might say, with Susan Griffin in *Woman and Nature:*

> And we are various, and amazing in our variety, and our differences multiply, so that edge after edge of the endlessness of possibility is exposed . . . none of us beautiful when separate but all exquisite as we stand, each moment heeded in this cycle, no detail unlovely. . . .[4]

NOTES

1. Sally Hegelson, *TWA Ambassador*, July 1980.
2. Private communication.
3. Private communication.
4. Susan Griffin, *Woman and Nature: The Roaring Inside Her*, New York, 1978.

QUESTIONS FOR CRITICAL ANALYSIS

1. Why does Chernin begin the essay with the stories about Rachel and the young girls? How do Rachel and the girls reveal their attitudes toward themselves? What does Chernin think of their behavior? How do you know? What do you think of them?
2. What is "the sort of woman Renoir would have admired"? Why does Chernin use this image to describe the woman in the sauna?
3. How do women show hatred for their bodies? Why does Chernin portray this dislike as an obsession with the body rather than an obsession with fat?
4. What changed the attitude of some of the women Chernin interviewed? How did they learn to accept themselves? What do you think about this change of behavior? Does it strike you as realistic? Why, or why not?
5. What part of the essay did you think was the most effective? Did you learn anything in this essay you didn't know before reading it? If you're a woman reading this essay, are you convinced by Chernin's thesis? If you're a man reading this essay, what do you think of Chernin's thesis in relation to women you know?

QUESTIONS FOR STRUCTURAL ANALYSIS

1. What is the effect of an opening paragraph made up of sentence fragments? Chernin uses fragments throughout the essay. Why? If you wrote this essay and turned it in for a grade, how would you try to convince your instructor you needed to use the fragments for effect?
2. What is Chernin's thesis? When does it become clear to the reader?
3. Why does Chernin include the story of Cheryl Prewitt, Miss America 1980?
4. Chernin quotes journal entries that record ideas from women she interviewed. How did you respond to these sections? Are they effective illustrations to support Chernin's thesis? Why, or why not?
5. The essay concludes with a passage quoted from Susan Griffin. Why does Chernin use this quote? Is this an effective conclusion to the essay? Would you have ended it this way?

*I W*ANT A *W*IFE

JUDY SYFERS

Judy Syfers' essay, "I Want a Wife," appeared in the first issue of Ms. *magazine, written to an audience of women newly awakened to the need to break out of society's limiting expectations for them and create new options and freedoms for themselves. Syfers' "wife" is the sacrificial servant, a role many women were taught to live and most men came to expect. Written with humor, "I Want a Wife" struck a chord with many readers and is one of* Ms. *magazine's most anthologized essays.*

Before you begin reading: *If you had a wife, what would you want her to do? Write a list of every duty you would expect your wife to perform.*

◆

I BELONG TO THAT CLASSIFICATION OF PEOPLE KNOWN AS wives. I am A Wife. And, not altogether incidentally, I am a mother.

Not too long ago a male friend of mine appeared on the scene fresh from a recent divorce. He had one child, who is, of course, with his ex-wife. He is obviously looking for another wife. As I thought about him while I was ironing one evening, it suddenly occurred to me that I, too, would like to have a wife. Why do I want a wife?

I would like to go back to school so that I can become economically independent, support myself, and, if need be, support those dependent upon me. I want a wife who will work and send me to school. And while I am going to school I want a wife to take care of my children. I want a wife to keep track of the children's doctor and dentist appointments. And to keep track of mine, too. I want a wife to make sure my children eat properly and are kept clean. I want a wife who will wash the children's clothes and keep them mended. I want a wife who is a good nurturant attendant to my children, who arranges for their schooling, makes sure that they have an adequate social life with their peers, takes them to the park, the zoo, etc. I want a wife who takes care of the children when they are sick, a wife who arranges to be around when the children need special care, because, of course, I cannot miss classes at school. My wife must arrange to lose time at work and not lose the job. It may mean a small cut in my wife's income from time to time, but I guess I can tolerate that. Needless to say, my wife will arrange and pay for the care of the children while my wife is working.

I want a wife who will take care of *my* physical needs. I want a wife who will keep my house clean. A wife who will pick up after me. I want a wife who will keep my clothes clean, ironed, mended, replaced when need be, and who will see to it that my personal things are kept in their proper place so that I can find what I need the minute I need it. I want a wife who cooks the meals, a wife who is a *good* cook. I want a wife who will plan the menus, do the necessary grocery shopping, prepare the meals, serve them pleasantly, and then do the cleaning up while I do my studying. I want a wife who will care for me when I am sick and sympathize with my pain and loss of time from school. I want a wife to go along when our family takes a vacation so that someone can continue to care for me and my children when I need a rest and change of scene.

I want a wife who will not bother me with rambling complaints about a wife's duties. But I want a wife who will listen to me when I feel the need to explain a rather difficult point I have come across in my course of studies. And I want a wife who will type my papers for me when I have written them.

I want a wife who will take care of the details of my social life. When my wife and I are invited out by my friends, I want a wife who will take care of the babysitting arrangements. When I meet people at school that I like and want to entertain, I want a wife who will have the house clean, will prepare a special meal, serve it to me and my friends, and not interrupt when I talk about the things that interest me and my friends. I want a wife who will have arranged that the children are fed and ready for bed before my guests arrive so that the children do not bother us.

And I want a wife who knows that sometimes I need a night out by myself.

I want a wife who is sensitive to my sexual needs, a wife who makes love passionately and eagerly when I feel like it, a wife who makes sure that I am satisfied. And, of course, I want a wife who will not demand sexual attention when I am not in the mood for it. I want a wife who assumes the complete responsibility for birth control, because I do not want more children. I want a wife who will remain sexually faithful to me so that I do not have to clutter up my intellectual life with jealousies. And I want a wife who understands that *my* sexual needs may entail more than strict adherence to monogamy. I must, after all, be able to relate to people as fully as possible.

If, by chance, I find another person more suitable as a wife than the wife I already have, I want the liberty to replace my present wife with another one. Naturally, I will expect a fresh, new life; my wife will take the children and be solely responsible for them so that I am left free.

When I am through with school and have a job, I want my wife to quit working and remain at home so that my wife can more fully and completely take care of a wife's duties.

My God, who *wouldn't* want a wife?

Questions for Critical Analysis

1. This essay appeared in the first issue of *Ms.* magazine. How would you describe its intended audience? Does knowing its audience change the way you think about the essay? How?
2. Why did Syfers write "I Want a Wife"? Are you an ideal reader for this essay? Why, or why not?
3. What is the tone of the essay? Is it a humorous essay? Why, or why not?
4. How do you suppose readers reacted to this essay in 1970? Did you respond differently? Are Syfers' points still valid today? In what way(s)?

Questions for Structural Analysis

1. What is Syfers' thesis? How do you know? Does it appear explicitly in the essay?
2. What is the recurring phrase of the essay? How do you respond to this repetition? Is it an effective rhetorical device?
3. How is the essay organized? Is there a development of the ideas? How?
4. Is the one-sentence conclusion effective? How did you respond to the conclusion?

Standing *His* Ground

Michael Norman

Michael Norman, a journalist and newspaper columnist, wrote "Standing His Ground" for the About Men *feature in the* New York Times Sunday Magazine *(1984). Remembering the simplicity of sixth grade boys settling their arguments with fist fights, Norman tries to reconcile these machismo instincts with the new role of reasonable, sensitive "modern man." Norman concludes that even the most nurturing man is ready to "throw a punch."*

Before you begin reading: *Make a list in your notebook of all the characteristics you can think of to describe the ideal man.*

◆

I HAVE BRUISED A KNUCKLE AND BLOODIED ANOTHER man's nose, but I am not, by most measures, a fighter. The last time I broke the peace was more than a decade ago in a small restaurant on the west slope of the Rocky Mountains in Colorado. My stepfather had encountered an old nemesis. Words were exchanged and the distance between the two narrowed. I stepped in to play the peacemaker and ended up throwing the first punch. For the record, my target, a towering 230-pound horseman, easily absorbed the blow and then dispatched the gnat in front of him.

The years since have been filled with discretion—I preach it, embrace it and hide behind it. I am now the careful watchman who keeps his eye on the red line and reroutes pressure before it has a chance to blow. Sometimes, I backslide and turn a domestic misdemeanor into a capital case or toss the cat out of the house without bothering to see where he lands. But I do not punch holes in the plaster or call my antagonists to the woodshed. The Furies may gather, but the storm always stays safely out to sea. And yet, lately, I have been struggling with this forced equanimity. The messenger of reason, the advocate of accord, once again has the urge to throw the first punch—in spirit at least.

All of this began rather quietly, a deep stirring that would come and go and never take form, an old instinct, perhaps, trying to reassert itself. I was angry, restless, combative, but I could not say why. It was a mystery of sorts. I was what I was expected to be, the very model of a modern man, a partner instead of a husband, a proponent of peace over action, thin-skinned rather than thick, a willow instead of a stone. And yet there was something about this posture that did not fit my frame. Then, an acquaintance, a gentle man who spent his Peace Corps days among the villagers of Nepal, suddenly acted out of character. He got into an argument with a local brute in a neighborhood tavern and instead of walking away from trouble, stood his ground. It was, he said, a senseless confrontation, but he had no regrets, and it made me think of Joey.

Joey, the bully of the sixth grade, used to roam the hallways picking victims at random and slugging them on the arm. When he rounded a corner, we scattered or practiced a crude form of mysticism and tried to think ourselves invisible in the face of the beast. Since I was slow and an inept mystic, my mother kept on hand an adequate supply of Ben Gay to ease the bruises and swelling.

One day, a boy named Tony told the marauder that he had had enough and an epic duel was scheduled in the playground after school. Tony had been taking boxing lessons on the sly. He had developed a stinging left jab and when the appointed hour arrived, he delivered it in the name of every bruised shoulder in the school.

The meek pack of which Tony was once a part took courage from his example and several weeks later when a boy at my bus stop sent me sprawling, I returned the favor.

There were only a few challenges after that. On the way up, a Joey would occasionally round the corner. But in the circles I traveled, he was the exception rather than the rule. In the Marine Corps in Vietnam, we were consumed by a much larger kind of warfare. In college, faculty infighting and bullying aside, violence was considered anti-intellectual. And in the newsrooms where I have practiced my trade, reporters generally have been satisfied with pounding a keyboard instead of their editors.

And then came Colorado and the battle of the west slope. For years, I was embarrassed by the affair. I could have walked away and dragged my stepfather with me. As it was, we almost ended up in jail. I had provoked a common brawl, a pointless, self-destructive exercise. The rationalist had committed the most irrational of acts. It was not a matter of family or honor, hollow excuses. I had simply succumbed to instinct, and I deeply regretted it. But not any longer. Now I see virtue in that vulgar display of macho. It disqualifies me from the most popular male club—the brotherhood of nurturers, fraternity sensitivus.

From analyst's couch to tavern booth, their message is the same: The male animus is out of fashion. The man of the hour is supposed to be gentle, thoughtful, endearing and compassionate, a wife to his woman, a mother to his son, an androgynous figure with the self-knowledge of a hermaphrodite. He takes his lumps on the psyche, not the chin, and bleeds with emotion. Yes, in the morning, he still puts on a three-piece suit, but his foulard, the finishing touch, is a crying towel.

He is so ridden with guilt, so pained about the sexist sins of his kind, he bites at his own flanks. Not only does he say that he dislikes being a man, but broadly proclaims that the whole idea of manhood in America is pitiful.

He wants to free himself from the social conditioning of the past, to cast off the yoke of traditional male roles and rise above the banality of rituals learned at boot camp or on the practice field. If science could provide it, he would swallow an antidote of testosterone, something to stop all this antediluvian thumping and bashing.

And he has gone too far. Yes, the male code needs reform. Our rules and our proscriptions have trapped us in a kind of perpetual adolescence. Why else would a full-grown rationalist think he could get even with Joey by taking a poke at another bully 25 years later in a bar in Colorado? No doubt there is something pitiful about that.

But the fashion for reform, the drive to emasculate macho, has produced a kind of numbing androgyny and has so blurred the lines of gender that I often find myself wanting to emulate some of the women I know—bold, aggressive, vigorous role models.

It sometimes seems that the only exclusively male trait left is the impulse to throw a punch, the last male watermark, so to speak, that is clear and readable. Perhaps that is why the former Peace Corps volunteer jumped into a brawl and why I suspect that the new man—the model of sensitivity, the nurturer—goes quietly through the day with a clenched fist behind his back.

QUESTIONS FOR CRITICAL ANALYSIS

1. How does Norman describe his current life of discretion? Are you convinced? What makes Norman feel uncomfortable about his life as a peaceful man?
2. What sort of person is the "I" of the essay? Is he someone you believe? Are you comfortable with his point of view? What do you like/dislike about him?
3. What happened between Joey and Tony in grade school? How did Tony's behavior inspire his friends? Why does this story come to Norman at this time? What does that imply for his behavior in the future?
4. How does Norman define the "male code"? Do you agree with this definition? How would Norman like to redefine the code? Would you redefine the code? How? What do you think of the modern male? How would Norman change the modern male?
5. What is the relationship between Norman's modern male and Syfers' wife? Do you think Syfers would recognize Norman's description of the modern male? What would Norman think of Syfers' wife?

Questions for Structural Analysis

1. Why does Norman tell the story about Colorado and his stepfather at the beginning of this essay? What significance does this story have to the essay?
2. Norman writes: "I was what I was expected to be, the very model of a modern man, a partner instead of a husband, a proponent of peace over action, thin-skinned rather than thick, a willow instead of a stone." How do you respond to that statement? On the surface, what does this statement mean? When you read between the lines, does the statement change meaning? How?
3. Compare the sentence quoted above with paragraphs 9 and 10, where Norman provides a more detailed picture of the modern man. What is his point? What is his tone in these sentences? Do you think he's exaggerating? Do you agree with him?
4. What is the thesis of this essay? How does Norman develop the thesis?
5. How does the essay conclude? Are you sympathetic to Norman's conclusion? Why, or why not?

. . . *W*E'VE *N*EVER *A*SKED A *W*OMAN *B*EFORE

CATHERINE DRINKER BOWEN

Catherine Drinker Bowen (1897–1973) was an historian and biographer, the author of many famous and highly-regarded biographies including Yankee from Olympus *(on Justice Oliver Wendell Holmes),* John Adams and the American Revolution, *and* The Lion and the Throne *(on Sir Edward Coke), which won the National Book award. Bowen's autobiographical essay, ". . . We've Never Asked a Woman Before," was written late in her life and first appeared in the March 1970* Atlantic Monthly. *In this essay she describes many of the difficulties she encountered during her career and wonders how different things might have been had she been a male biographer.*

Before you begin reading: *At which kinds of professions do you think women are successful? List them in your notebook and next to each profession describe why women succeed in that profession.*

◆

FOR THIRTY YEARS I HAVE BEEN WRITING ABOUT LAWYERS and the law. And for almost as many years I have been the recipient of invitations to stand on platforms and address large assemblies of legal experts. I enjoy receiving these invitations; it shows that people are reading my books. Yet I often hesitate; the program means serious preparation. A non-lawyer—and a non-man—cannot stand up and talk drivel for thirty minutes or fifty (as specified) to a hall bristling with five hundred or so hard-minded professional gentlemen. Therefore I hold off, saying into the telephone that I haven't the time; I am writing a new book and must stay home by myself, where writers belong. Perhaps the committee will send a letter, giving details? "Mrs. Bowen!" says an urgent voice from Houston or San Francisco. "This is our law society's big annual celebration. We've had Senator Fulbright as speaker, and Wechsler of Columbia, and the Lord Chief Justice of England [and God and Santa Claus]. But we've never asked a woman before."

At this moment all my latent feminism rises up. Why haven't they asked a woman before—aren't there any women lawyers? Impossible to refuse this challenge! In Washington there exists a prestigious group called the American Law

Institute. The cream of the profession belongs to it; the work they do is significant to the country at large. After I spoke at the Institute's annual dinner, women lawyers crowded to shake my hand. They said they had sat for years watching those men at the head table; they wanted me to know what it meant to see a woman sitting there. It made me very glad that I had come.

The word feminism is outmoded. "The movement," young women call it today. We know of the ferocity with which the goal is pursued. We have heard of the extremists—ten thousand strong—called Women's Liberation, how they crop their hair short, wear baggy trousers and loose sweaters to conceal the more notable evidences of sex. "Abolish sexism!" is their slogan. Brassieres must go, and beauty contests. "Miss America!" say their banners. "Men make money off *your* body too. Pornography, Bunnies, Playboy Magazine are as degrading to women as racism is to blacks."

But of course! And why, one asks oneself, has it taken the sisters so long to find this out, so long to proclaim that for women sex is neither cute nor funny and can result in pain, disgrace, or years of virtual—though respectable—servitude? Sex jokes are a male invention. It is indeed a naïve girl who grows up in our society unaware of what her world considers the primary function of women. To suggest that women don't have to be beautiful is the worst kind of heresy; it means women have more important functions than pleasing men.

How does all this affect women writers? The answer is, profoundly. Nobody writes from a vacuum; writers compose from their life experience. They use what they know and feel in the environment round about, the stuff of life as it has been handed out or as they have been able to grasp it, hold it up and look at it with courage and with truth. For many centuries girls have been told that their business is wifehood, motherhood—and nothing else. "When children cease to be altogether desirable, women cease to be altogether necessary," said John Langdon Davis in *A Short History of Women*. I once had a husband who liked to say that nothing is expected of a wife-and-mother but respectability. Yet writers, male and female, belong in the category artist. (Muriel Rukeyser, the poet, puts women into four classes: whores, saints, wives, and artists.) No artist can operate lacking belief in his mission. *His* mission; the very pronoun confesses an age-old situation. I hope the young activists in the movement wipe out that generalized pronoun, so bland, so denigrating to the woman professional in any field.

Without a clear view of their capabilities, men and women cannot function. Convince a two-legged man that he has but one leg, and he will not be able to walk. A writer must know her horizon, how wide is the circle within which she, as artist, extends. The world still professes to wonder why there has been no female Shakespeare or Dante, no woman Plato or Isaiah. Yet people do what society looks for them to do. The Quaker Meeting House has existed for centuries, but it has produced no Bach and no B Minor Mass. Music was not desired by Quakers, it was frowned on. Poetry, fiction, playwriting have been expected from women only recently, as history counts time. Of the brilliant, erratic Margaret Cavendish, her husband, the Duke of Newcastle, remarked, circa 1660, "A very wise woman is a very foolish thing." As lately as 1922, Christina Rossetti's biographer wrote of her, that "like most poetesses, she was purely subjective, and in no sense creative." What a beautiful triple sneer, and how it encompasses the entire second sex! One recalls the fiery poet*ess*, Lady Winchelsea, born 1661, said to be "lost in melancholy"—and small wonder:

> Debarred from all improvements of the mind [she wrote],
> And to be dull, expected and designed. . . .
> Alas! a woman that attempts the pen,
> Such a presumptuous creature is esteemed,
> The fault can by no virtue be redeemed.
> Good breeding, fashion, dancing, dressing, play,
> Are the accomplishments we should desire;
> To write, or read, or think, or to enquire,
> Would cloud our beauty, and exhaust our time,
> And interrupt the conquests of our prime,
> Whilst the dull manage of a servile house
> Is held by some our utmost art and use.

Because I write about the law and the Constitution I am often asked why I entered "a man's field." Men tell me I write like a man. "Mrs. Bowen," they say with pleased smiles, "you *think* like a man." No, gentlemen, thank you, I do not, I write like a woman. I enjoy being a woman and thinking like a woman, which means using my mind and using it hard. Women have an advantage as writers because they are trained from childhood to notice the relationships between people. Upon such perceptions all their later welfare can depend. Is it not a mother's business, a wife's business to soothe hurt feelings, pacify the male, keep peace within her household? She is vitally concerned therefore with human motivation, what trial lawyers call *intent*. In my own field, intent lies at the base of the entire structure; the motivation of mankind makes up the plot of every biography that is written.

Women writers do not think like men. It is when I am told so that I remember Lady Winchelsea, remember also the ladies who had to use men's names on their books: George Eliot, George Sand, Currer Bell and her sisters, the Brontës.

I have used the word ladies in speaking of artists. I ask their forgiveness. No writer, no artist, is a lady. She can't afford to be. The novelist, biographer, historian, looks bleakly at life, lingers to squint at its sorrier aspects, reaches out to touch the dirty places, and raises the hand to the nostrils to make sure. Charles

Beard once told me, "You have to have a strong stomach to study history." Happily, I was early indoctrinated against being a lady. At sixteen, the family decided to send me to boarding school, in order to correct certain provincialisms of speech and deportment picked up from schoolmates in the Lehigh Valley town where we lived. I didn't want to go, and protested furiously. A brother, Cecil, ten years my senior, protested also. "That place," he told me morosely, "is called a finishing school. They want to make a lady of you, Katz. But you're born for something better, and don't you ever forget it."

I did not forget it. I was the youngest of six; the four brothers were considerably older. They taught me their skills; in fact, they insisted that I learn. "Push out, Katz, with that right skate. *Don't be scared!* Get your whole body into it." I grew up believing that girls were supposed to compete with boys, not just compete *for* boys. Our mother devoted herself wholly to domesticity. Yet she told my sister and me that a girl could be just as independent and well educated as a boy, there was no reason not. My Aunt Cecilia Beaux was earning a living painting portraits by the time she was twenty-five, though Cecilia, my mother said, resented being referred to in the newspapers as a woman painter. "They don't talk about a *man* painter," Cecilia Beaux said. Aunt Beaux made money enough to buy six acres in Gloucester, Massachusetts, and build a house and studio there called Green Alley.

It would be hard to exaggerate the effect this had on a girl of twelve, fourteen, eighteen. I have been told that women feel guilty competing intellectually with men. Anaïs Nin, the writer, so confesses in her diary, and I have seen graphs drawn by psychologists, showing that girls do badly in what the professors call "achievement-oriented situations vis-à-vis boys." Guilt at competing? To me it is a contradiction in terms. I would have thought myself guilty in *not* competing. My parents expected high marks at school examinations, and if I brought home a bad paper, "What's wrong?" my brother Cecil would ask, "lose your nerve this time, Katz, or just lazy?" As for Beaux's Green Alley, it has become the family summer place. I have written four books there, in Aunt Beaux's studio by the bay; her spirit sustained me while I wrote. "We think back through our mothers if we are women." It was Virginia Woolf who said it.

Nevertheless the female brain does not reside in the uterus, though women as well as men try their best so to persuade us. A recent newspaper showed Grace Kelly on a platform receiving an award from the YWCA. Glittering in sequins, she announced complacently that today's women, pushing into a man's world, were sacrificing their femininity. (Nothing was said about the twenty-nine million American women who work for their living.) A day or so later, a woman newspaper columnist eagerly affirmed this by recounting at length the joys of motherhood, ending with the dictum that once the children grow up and depart the scene, mothers never again experience a like happiness and sense of fulfillment. Wives too come forward with proud claims: the self-sacrifice, the best years given. "There is no career more exciting or exacting for a woman than marriage to a great man." So writes a recent biographer of Mrs. Gladstone, and a female biographer at that.

Against this flood of bilge water I am fortified by a line in my great-great-grandmother's diary. Elizabeth Drinker, having given birth to nine and reared five, wrote in the year 1790 that she had often thought a woman's best years came after she left off bearing and rearing. I myself happen to be the mother of two and grandmother of four. I always expected to be married and looked forward to it—but not as sole career; never, never as sole career. It is not the maternal chores that oppress but the looming of that altar which has been erected to motherhood, its sacro-sanctity, the assumption that nothing but motherhood is important. For the woman artist this ideal can prove as bewildering as the onset of a national war. Nothing matters but this patriotism, this motherhood. One is praised and petted for being a mother, all other values put in the discard. When the baby comes: "You have joined the human race!" women cry, bringing gifts, adding gleefully that you won't have time *now* for writing (or sculpting or painting or playing the violin). When my two children, a girl and then a boy, came along, I had already published two small books and twelve magazine articles. A local newspaper, the Easton *Daily Express*, paid me a dollar a day for a three-hundred-word column, handsomely boxed in. I looked on the pay as munificent and was terrified that I wouldn't be worth it. When time came for the first baby to be born I wrote two weeks' columns ahead, told the editor, a red-headed Irishman, that I'd be back in a fortnight, received his blessing, and never wrote another line until both children were in nursery school, five years later, and the mornings were once more my own. It was about this time that I came on Katherine Mansfield's thrice-blessed words: "Mothers of children grow on every bush."

A writer's regimen can reduce certain nagging moralisms to dust—the notion, for instance, that housework is ennobling to women, or at least instinctive to them as scuffing leaves to clean his bed is instinctive to a dog. Love of cooking is thought by many to be a secondary female sex characteristic. So is the exercise of following little children interminably about the yard. If I had not been a writer, these moralistic conceptions would have defeated me before I reached the age of thirty. Writing saved me. The housework still had to be done and done cheerfully. The children still had to be followed around the yard. But these activities, repeated day after day for years, were no longer defeating because they were no longer the be-all and end-all of existence.

"How fortunate, dear, that you have this hobby of writing to occupy you while your husband is away!" Thus my mother-in-law in September of the year 1941. I was two years along with *Yankee from Olympus*. My husband, a surgeon and member of the Naval Reserve, had gone to Honolulu on a hospital ship. By this time I had published six books and become inured to married women's attitudes toward the professional writer, so I merely told my mother-in-law, yes, it *was* lucky, and I had better get upstairs to my typewriter. Back and forth in the family the question raged: Should I take our daughter out of college, our son from school, and migrate to Honolulu, Hawaii was paradise! people said. We'd all love it, and what an opportunity! I could do my Holmes research in the Honolulu University's splendid library. Palm trees and warm sea—a paradise!

The notion of Oliver Wendell Holmes of New England revealing himself at the University of Honolulu belonged, of course, in the realms of fantasy. Also, my daughter loved Radcliffe and my son Haverford School. I listened to women spelling out my duty (what today they call a husband-supportive program), and I developed stomachaches, a pain in the lower back. Then one night I had a dream that settled everything, so vivid I can see it today. I sat in a room filled with people; my father, white-haired, white-whiskered, and long since dead, stood across the carpet. He raised an arm and pointed at me. "Thou shalt not go to Paradise!" he said.

Next morning I announced we were staying home, and went on with *Yankee from Olympus*. Nor did I suffer further qualms, Dr. Freud notwithstanding.

Subject A, young women call it today, bringing me the age-old query: How to manage a career, a husband, and children. Despite "the movement" and the liberation fronts, the problem is still here, sharp and demanding. I am likely to give a twofold answer. "You manage it by doing double work, using twice the energy other wives use: housework *and* writing. Or you do what Mrs. Eleanor Roosevelt told me. I quote her, verbatim: 'If a woman wants to pursue her own interests after marriage, she must choose the right husband. Franklin stood back of me in everything I wanted to do.'"

Competition was bred in my bones. Yet I never wrote to rival men; such a thing would not have occurred to me. Actually it was a man—my first husband—who started me writing, in my twenties. And once I saw my product in print, nothing mattered but to get on with the work, get on with studying history and with learning how to write sentences that said what I wanted to say. Many writers hate writing. I happen to love it. With my hands on the typewriter I feel like the war-horse in the Bible that smells the battle far off and saith among the trumpets, Ha, ha. Writers have in them a vast ambition . . . hunger . . . egotism—call it what you will. A writer wants to be read, wants to be known. If there is talent, it must come out or it will choke its host, be she three times wife-and-mother. Scholarship also is a hungry thing, the urge to know. A great legal historian, Maitland, spoke of "the blessing which awaits all those who have honestly taught themselves anything."

A woman biographer must, like anybody else, earn her place in the sun. When I turned from writing about musical subjects to legal subjects, I entered a man's world with a vengeance, though some time passed before I was fully aware of it. The Holmes' Papers were guarded by two literary executors, John Gorham

Palfrey (father of the tennis champion) and Felix Frankfurter, of the United States Supreme Court. In the six years since Holmes's death, quite evidently the executors had expected hordes of hungry biographers to descend. It came as a shock that the first to approach was a non-Bostonian, a non-lawyer, and a non-man. Nevertheless, Mr. Palfrey handed me five hundred of Holmes's letters, neatly copied in typescript, saying I could take all the notes I wished. I procured four court stenographers—this was before the days of Xerox—who copied profusely. In Washington I saw Felix Frankfurter, who greeted me jovially (he was an old friend), said of course I didn't plan to present the big cases, the Lochner dissent, Rosika Schwimmer, the Gitlow dissent—the great issues of free speech, the ten-hour day, and so on? I said of course I did, why else would I be writing the book?

I went home and back to work. Two months later a letter came from Mr. Palfrey, enclosing what he called "some of the more unfavorable replies" to his queries among Holmes's legal friends and associates. Nothing in Mrs. Bowen's previous experience, these said, qualified her to write about a lawyer, a New Englander, or indeed an American. In short, the executors had decided to deny access to all unpublished material, even for the purpose of establishing chronology or telling me where Holmes had been at a given time. My work and my Boston visits, Mr. Palfrey said, had spurred the executors to appoint the "definitive biographer," Mark Howe of the Harvard Law School, secretary to the Justice the year before he died.

Plainly, the executors hoped to stop me from writing the book. I let the initial shock wear off and laid plans. Scores of men and women existed who had known Holmes. Whatever I needed from those letters I must get by legwork—even when letters had been sent me by recipients, like Rosika Schwimmer and others. I must persuade the writers to tell me what the Justice had said and done on the occasions their letters described. This exercise took perhaps an added year, but was well worth it. Meanwhile, Frankfurter wrote from time to time. He heard I had been at the Supreme Court building and had left some unsolved questions with the Marshal. Was I actually making an effort to attain accuracy, ceasing to be an artist and becoming merely a thinker? The letters were wonderful and awful. They kindled the anger that sends one on ever harder quests; Frankfurter could be a formidable antagonist. I talked with Irving Olds of United States Steel, Attorney General Francis Biddle, and ten other legal secretaries of Holmes's, choosing them not because of their worldly prominence but because their particular secretarial year coincided with an important Supreme Court case. I think my book benefited from the program, rigorous though it was, and by the denial of those hundreds of letters. A biography can smother under too much quoted material.

When finally the Book-of-the-Month chose my manuscript, Frankfurter sent me a long congratulatory telegram: "I always knew you could do it." I did not see him, however, until ten years and several biographies later. After my book on Sir Edward Coke was published, the director of the Folger Shakespeare Library, Louis Wright, invited me to speak in their Washington theater. He said Justice Frankfurter had telephoned, asking to introduce me, and why was this? Frankfurter never made such requests, Louis said.

On the appointed evening, the Justice sat on the platform with me; I had no notion of his intentions. He got up and told the audience that he had done all he could to stop Mrs. Bowen from writing *Yankee from Olympus*, but there were people who worked better under difficulties and I was one of them. He had not read the book, he would never read it, though he had read my other biographies. But he wished to make public apology, public amends. Then he bowed, grinned at me where I sat, and returned to his chair.

It was handsome of Frankfurter. Yet I had wondered how much of the entire feud, and its climax, could be laid to the fact of my sex. I do not know. But as time passed and I proceeded to other legal biographies—John Adams, Sir Edward Coke, Francis Bacon, *Miracle at Philadelphia*—I know that the rigors I underwent with *Yankee* stood me in good stead, toughened me, made me ready for whatever might come. With John Adams I was again refused unpublished material and again went on my quest, though this time it had to be in research libraries and took five years. Sir Edward Coke's college was Trinity, at Cambridge University. And even Bluebeard did not consider women more expendable than does a Cambridge don. All but one of the law and history professors I met there brushed aside my project and did it smiling, with the careless skill of the knowledgeable Englishman. "Are you planning to write a popular book about Coke?" they asked. I smiled in turn, and said by popular they no doubt meant cheap, and that only the finished manuscript could answer their question. "At least," remarked another, "Mrs. Bowen has been shrewd enough to see that a book about Edward Coke will sell. And a person has to begin to learn *somewhere*." After inquiring how many copies my other biographies had sold, one history professor looked glum. "Someday," he said, snapping his fingers, "I'm going to take a year off and write a popular book."

Seven years later the Acting Master of Trinity wrote to me in Philadelphia, saying he had read the English edition of my Coke biography, *The Lion and the Throne*. Did I recall how he had not, initially, been enthusiastic about the project? He went on to say kind things about the book, acknowledging that he had been mistaken. And next time I was in Cambridge, would I permit him to give a small celebration in my honor?

Again, I cannot know how much of the battle—the defeats and the victories—can be laid to my being a woman. I know only that I spent days of anger, of outrage, and that I enjoyed the challenge. How could one not enjoy it? "*We never invited a woman before. . . .*"

One honors those who march in the streets for a cause; one knows that social liberation does not come peacefully. I have not taken part in the movement, though feminine activists greet me as a sister. I think they know that the woman writer who stays outside the movement by no means dodges the issue. She takes a risk too, though of another kind. Instead of the dangers of marching, she assumes the risks of lifelong dedication to her profession—a program that runs counter to many cherished slogans. As a young woman conversing with young men, I learned to caution myself: "Let him win! When a woman wins she loses." Yet even as I said it I knew that such capitulation was merely for the purposes of flirtation, where a woman can afford the delicious indulgence of yielding. Only when men—or women—block and balk her progress in the professions must a woman strike back, and then she must use every weapon in her artillery.

To bear and rear a child is all that it is said to be; it is joy and sorrow, the very heart of living. There is no comparing it with a woman's profession beyond the home. Simply, the two things do not bear comparison. It is false to say the home comes first, the career second. For the woman writer, there can be no first or second about these matters; even to think it is an offense. For myself I enjoy housekeeping, by which I mean I like living in an attractive house and entertaining my friends. I look on house and garden as the most delightful toys, and take pleasure in every facet. But I know also that if house-and-garden should interfere seriously with work, with writing, house-and-garden would go.

Women in the professions must make their choices. That many refuse, sidestepping to easy pursuits, is a reason why American women have not kept pace with their sisters in India and Russia. The United States Senate of 100 has one woman member.

Perhaps the real turn in the road will come—and I predict it is coming soon—when more than two children to a family will seem bad taste, like wearing mink in a starving village. No woman can devote a life to the rearing of two, she cannot even make a pretense of it. When the mother image loses its sanctity, something will take its place on the altar. And any writer knows that when the image of the heroine changes, the plot changes with her. Such an event could alter, for both men and women, the whole picture of American life.

QUESTIONS FOR CRITICAL ANALYSIS

1. What do you think Bowen's purpose is in writing this essay? How does the tone of her remarks affect her purpose? How did you respond to the essay?
2. At one point Bowen writes: "when a woman wins, she loses." What does that phrase mean? What other assumptions about women does Bowen reveal? This essay was written 20 years ago. Do you think these assumptions have changed? How? Why, or why not?
3. Why does Bowen think women writers have a hard time? How have her experiences led her to this attitude? Do you agree with her? Why, or why not?

4. Is it possible for a woman to balance career, marriage, and family successfully? Bowen suggests several answers. Do you agree with them? How do you answer that question? If you are not a working, married woman, talk with some people who are and compare their answers with Bowen's and with yours.
5. Consider the implications of Bowen's final two paragraphs in light of Margaret Sanger's essay. Remember that Bowen writes of privileged women who have the freedom of making choices and Sanger writes of poor women living in desperation. How do the two essays relate to each other?

QUESTIONS FOR STRUCTURAL ANALYSIS

1. What is the point of the opening illustration? Why did Bowen insert "[and God and Santa Claus]" in brackets?
2. Bowen furthers her argument through over 30 quotes from historical sources, professionals, and family members. Are these quotations effective? How?
3. Make a list of the people Bowen refers to in her essay. Write a phrase or two describing the ones whose names you recognize and look up the others. How does knowing who these people are affect your reading of the essay?
4. Describe the progression of ideas in the essay. How do Bowen's anecdotes, illustrations, and allusions expand and support her ideas?
5. What does the conclusion of the essay mean? Did it surprise you? How were you prepared for her statements? Do you agree with Bowen's conclusion?

Understanding Relationships Between the Sexes

Topics for Writing Essays

Many of the questions following each essay can serve as appropriate writing suggestions. The topics listed below expand the prereading exercises, but they can be used without completing that step first.

1. Use the list you wrote for the Norman prereading exercise as a starting point to define "the male code." Write your essay for a student magazine which has both male and female readers.
2. Why is it hard for men to understand women? or women to understand men? Use the items on your lists in the prereading exercises to write an essay directed to the opposite sex. (In other words, explain why men have trouble understanding women to readers of a women's magazine; explain women's trouble understanding men to readers of a men's magazine.)
3. Bowen wrote that "people do what society looks for them to do." Think about that statement in relation to expectations we have for men and women in social behavior, academics, sports, professional careers, and so forth. Describe how "society's expectations" have influenced the sort of person you are today in an essay written to junior high students to help them develop broader options for their futures.
4. Is the ideal male-female relationship impossible? Why? Use the essays from this section as well as ideas from your prereading exercises to write an explanation to curious male and female readers.

Research Possibilities

1. What is the ideal beauty? How has it changed over time? Look at photographs, read books and articles about women in earlier times as well as today, and write a paper defining female beauty.
2. Look at old books on etiquette and social behavior to find out what was once identified as an ideal mate. How does this ideal compare with the men and women you meet everyday? Narrow your focus to one or two considerations and write a comparison/contrast essay describing the ideal of former days with the reality of today.
3. Interview career women who are juggling husbands, children, and careers. Read studies and articles about the feminization of the workplace and its impact on the family and society in general. Write a paper to be delivered at a women's caucus meeting on the choices women in the professions must make.

PART TWO
HUMANITIES

LOOK AT NATURE

These essays focus on the feelings that a place and/or time evokes in the author. But more than just describing feelings, they recreate the feelings through detailed descriptions appealing to the senses: readers see the wide sweep of Wyoming vistas, smell the circus ring, feel sand between their toes, hear the voices of querulous New Yorkers, and recognize the passions of summer.

*W*YOMING: *T*HE *S*OLACE OF *O*PEN *S*PACES

GRETEL EHRLICH

When Gretel Ehrlich (1946–) went to Wyoming from New York City in 1976 to film a documentary for public television, she did not intend to stay. For a variety of reasons, however, Ehrlich moved to Wyoming and was surprised to find that the isolation and spaciousness of the state revitalized and awakened her. This essay, growing out of a personal journal Ehrlich wrote about her new life for a friend who had left Wyoming to move to Hawaii, was first published in the Atlantic Monthly*, a magazine with a predominately eastern audience. Ehrlich describes not only the physical and spiritual characteristics of Wyoming's space, but also how nature itself defines human behavior and values.*

Before you begin reading: *Think about the American West. What images come into your mind? In your reading notebook, list all the sights, sounds, smells, and feelings you think of when you picture the West.*

◆

IT'S MAY, AND I'VE JUST AWAKENED FROM A NAP, CURLED against sagebrush the way my dog taught me to sleep—sheltered from wind. A front is pulling the huge sky over me, and from the dark a hailstone has hit me on the head. I'm trailing a band of 2000 sheep across a stretch of Wyoming badland, a fifty-mile trip that takes five days because sheep shade up in hot sun and won't budge until it cools. Bunched together now, and excited into a run by the storm, they drift across dry land, tumbling into draws like water and surging out again onto the rugged, choppy plateaus that are the building blocks of this state.

The name Wyoming comes from an Indian word meaning "at the great plains," but the plains are really valleys, great arid valleys, 1600 square miles, with the horizon bending up on all sides into mountain ranges. This gives the vastness a sheltering look.

Winter lasts six months here. Prevailing winds spill snowdrifts to the east, and new storms from the northwest replenish them. This white bulk is sometimes dizzying, even nauseating, to look at. At twenty, thirty, and forty degrees below zero, not only does your car not work but neither do your mind and body. The landscape hardens into a dungeon of space. During the winter, while I was riding to find a new calf, my legs froze to the saddle, and in the silence that such cold creates I felt like the first person on earth, or the last.

Today the sun is out—only a few clouds billowing. In the east, where the sheep have started off without me, the benchland tilts up in a series of red-earthed, eroded mesas, planed flat on top by a million years of water; behind them, a bold line of muscular scarps rears up 10,000 feet to become the Big Horn Mountains. A tidal pattern is engraved into the ground, as if left by the sea that once covered this state. Canyons curve down like galaxies to meet the oncoming rush of flat land.

To live and work in this kind of open country, with its hundred-mile views, is to lose the distinction between background and foreground. When I asked an older ranch hand to describe Wyoming's openness, he said, "It's all a bunch of nothing—wind and rattlesnakes—and so much of it you can't tell where you're going or where you've been and it don't make much difference." John, a sheepman I know, is tall and handsome and has an explosive temperament. He has a perfect intuition about people and sheep. They call him "Highpockets," because he's so long-legged; his graceful stride matches the distances he has to cover. He says, "Open space hasn't affected me at all. It's all the people moving in on it." The huge ranch he was born on takes up much of one county and spreads into another state; to put 100,000 miles on his pickup in three years and never leave home is not unusual. A friend of mine has an aunt who ranched on Powder River and didn't go off her place for eleven years. When her husband died, she quickly moved to town, bought a car, and drove around the States to see what she'd been missing.

Most people tell me they've simply driven through Wyoming, as if there were nothing to stop for. Or else they've skied in Jackson Hole, a place Wyomingites acknowledge uncomfortably, because its green beauty and chic affluence are mismatched with the rest of the state. Most of Wyoming has a "lean-to" look. Instead of big, roomy barns and Victorian houses, there are dugouts, low sheds, log cabins, sheep camps, and fence lines that look like driftwood blown haphazardly into place. People here still feel pride because they live in such a harsh place, part of the glamorous cowboy past, and they are determined not to be the victims of a mining-dominated future.

Most characteristic of the state's landscape is what a developer euphemistically describes as "indigenous growth right up to your front door"—a reference to waterless stands of salt sage, snakes, jackrabbits, deerflies, red dust, a brief respite of wildflowers, dry washes, and no trees. In the Great Plains, the vistas look like music, like kyries of grass, but Wyoming seems to be the doing of a mad architect—tumbled and twisted, ribboned with faded, deathbed colors, thrust up and pulled down as if the place had been startled out of a deep sleep and thrown into a pure light.

I came here four years ago. I had not planned to stay, but I couldn't make myself leave. John, the sheepman, put me to work immediately. It was spring, and shearing time. For fourteen days of fourteen hours each, we moved thousands of sheep through sorting corrals to be sheared, branded, and deloused. I suspect that my original motive for coming here was to "lose myself" in new and unpopulated territory. Instead of producing the numbness I thought I wanted, life on the sheep ranch woke me up. The vitality of the people I was working with flushed out what had become a hallucinatory rawness inside me. I threw away my clothes and bought new ones; I cut my hair. The arid country was a clean slate. Its absolute indifference steadied me.

Sagebrush covers 58,000 square miles of Wyoming. The biggest city has a population of 50,000, and there are only five settlements that could be called cities in the whole state. The rest are towns, scattered across the expanse with as much as sixty miles between them, their populations 2000, fifty, or ten. They are fugitive-looking, perched on a barren, windblown bench, or tagged onto a river or a railroad, or laid out straight in a farming valley with implement stores and a block-long Mormon church. In the eastern part of the state, which slides down into the Great Plains, the new mining settlements are boomtowns, trailer cities, metal knots on flat land.

Despite the desolate look, there's a coziness to living in this state. There are so few people (only 470,000) that ranchers who buy and sell cattle know each other statewide; the kids who choose to go to college usually go to the state's one university, in Laramie; hired hands work their way around Wyoming in a lifetime of hirings and firings. And, despite the physical separation, people stay in touch, often driving two or three hours to another ranch for dinner.

Seventy-five years ago, when travel was by buckboard or horseback, cowboys who were temporarily out of work rode the grub line—drifting from ranch to ranch, mending fences or milking cows, and receiving in exchange a bed and meals. Gossip and messages traveled this slow circuit with them, creating an intimacy between ranchers who were three and four weeks' ride apart. One old-time couple I know, whose turn-of-the-century homestead was used by an outlaw gang as a relay station for stolen horses, recall that if you were traveling, desperado or not, any lighted ranch house was a welcome sign. Even now, for someone who lives in a remote spot, arriving at a ranch or coming to town for supplies is cause for celebration. To emerge from isolation can be disorienting. Everything looks bright, new, vivid. After I had been herding sheep for only three days, the sound of the camp-tender's pickup flustered me. Longing for human company, I felt a foolish grin take over my face, yet I had to resist an urgent temptation to run and hide.

Things happen suddenly in Wyoming: the change of seasons and weather; for people, the violent swings in and out of isolation. But goodnaturedness is concomitant with severity. Friendliness is a tradition. Strangers passing on the road wave hello. A common sight is two pickups stopped side by side far out on a range, on a dirt track winding through the sage. The drivers will share a cigarette, uncap their thermos bottles, and pass a battered cup, steaming with coffee, between windows. These meetings summon up the details of several generations, because in Wyoming, private histories are largely public knowledge.

Because ranch work is a physical and, these days, economic strain, being "at home on the range" is a matter of vigor, self-reliance, and common sense. A person's life is not a series of dramatic events for which he or she is applauded or exiled but a slow accumulation of days, seasons, years, fleshed out by the generational weight of one's family and anchored by a land-bound sense of place.

In most parts of Wyoming, the human population is visibly outnumbered by the animal. Not far from my town of fifty, I rode into a narrow valley and startled a herd of 200 elk. Eagles look like small people as they eat car-killed deer by the road. Antelope, moving in small, graceful bands, travel at 60 miles an hour, their mouths open as if drinking in the space.

The solitude in which westerners live makes them quiet. They telegraph thoughts and feelings by the way they tilt their heads and listen; pulling their Stetsons into a steep dive over their eyes, or pigeon-toeing one boot over the other, they lean against a fence with a fat wedge of snoose beneath their lower lips and take the whole scene in. These detached looks of quiet amusement are sometimes cynical, but they can also come from a dry-eyed humility as lucid as the air is clear.

Conversation goes on in what sounds like a private code; a few phrases imply a complex of meanings. Asking directions, you get a curious list of details. While trailing sheep, I was told to "ride up to that kinda upturned rock, follow the pink wash, turn left at the dump, and then you'll see the waterhole." One friend told his wife on roundup to "turn at the salt lick and the dead cow," which turned out to be a scattering of bones and no salt lick at all.

Sentence structure is shortened to the skin and bones of a thought. Descriptive words are dropped, even verbs; a cowboy looking over a corral full of horses will say to a wrangler, "Which one needs rode?" People hold back their thoughts in what seems to be a dumbfounded silence, then erupt with an excoriating, perceptive remark. Language, so compressed, becomes metaphorical. A rancher ended a relationship with one remark: "You're a bad check," meaning bouncing in and out was intolerable, and even coming back would be no good.

What's behind this laconic style is shyness. There is no vocabulary for the subject of feelings. It's not a hangdog shyness, or anything coy—always there's a robust spirit in evidence behind the restraint, as if the earth-dredging wind that pulls across Wyoming had carried its people's voices away but everything else in them had shouldered confidently into the breeze.

I've spent hours riding to sheep camp at dawn in a pickup when nothing was said; eaten meals in the cookhouse when the only words spoken were a mumbled "Thank you, ma'am" at the end of dinner. The silence is profound. Instead of talking, we seem to share one eye. Keenly observed, the world is transformed. The landscape is engorged with detail, every movement on it chillingly sharp. The air between people is charged. Days unfold, bathed in their own music. Nights become hallucinatory; dreams, prescient.

Spring weather is capricious and mean. It snows, then blisters with heat. There have been tornadoes. They lay their elephant trunks out in the sage until they find houses, then slurp everything up and leave. I've noticed that melting snowbanks hiss and rot, viperous, then drip into calm pools where ducklings hatch and livestock, being trailed to summer range, drink. With the ice cover gone, rivers churn a milkshake brown, taking culverts and small bridges with them. Water in such an arid place (the average annual rainfall where I live is less than eight inches) is like blood. It festoons drab land with green veins: a line of cottonwoods following a stream; a strip of alfalfa; and on ditchbanks, wild asparagus growing.

I've moved to a small cattle ranch owned by friends. It's at the foot of the Big Horn Mountains. A few weeks ago, I helped them deliver a calf who was stuck halfway out of his mother's body. By the time he was freed, we could see a heartbeat, but he was straining against a swollen tongue for air. Mary and I held him upside down by his back feet, while Stan, on his hands and knees in the blood, gave the calf mouth-to-mouth resuscitation. I have a vague memory of being pneumonia-choked as a child, my mother giving me her air, which may account for my romance with this windswept state.

If anything is endemic to Wyoming, it is wind. This big room of space is swept out daily, leaving a boneyard of fossils, agates, and carcasses in every stage of decay. Though it was water that initially shaped the state, wind is the meticulous gardener, raising dust and pruning the sage.

I try to imagine a world of uncharted land, in which one could look over an uncompleted map and ride a horse past where all the lines have stopped. There is no wilderness left; wildness, yes, but true wilderness has been gone on this continent since the time of Lewis and Clark's overland journey.

Two hundred years ago, the Crow, Shoshone, Arapaho, Cheyenne, and Sioux roamed the intermountain West, orchestrating their movements according to hunger, season, and warfare. Once they acquired horses, they traversed the spines of all the big Wyoming ranges—the Absarokas, the Wind Rivers, the Tetons, the Big Horns—and wintered on the unprotected plains that fan out from them. Space was life. The world was their home.

What was life-giving to native Americans was often nightmarish to sodbusters who arrived encumbered with families and ethnic pasts to be transplanted in nearly uninhabitable land. The great distances, the shortage of water and trees, and the loneliness created unexpected hardships for them. In her book *O Pioneers!*, Willa Cather gives a settler's version of the bleak landscape:

> The little town behind them had vanished as if it had never been, had fallen behind the swell of the prairie, and the stern frozen country received them into its bosom.

> The homesteads were few and far apart; here and there a windmill gaunt against the sky, a sod house crouching in a hollow.

The emptiness of the West was for others a geography of possibility. Men and women who amassed great chunks of land and struggled to preserve unfenced empires were, despite their self-serving motives, unwitting geographers. They understood the lay of the land. But by the 1850s, the Oregon and Mormon trails sported bumper-to-bumper traffic. Wealthy landowners, many of them aristocratic absentee landlords, known as remittance men because they were paid to come West and get out of their families' hair, overstocked the range with more than a million head of cattle. By 1885, the feed and water were desperately short, and the winter of 1886 laid out the gaunt bodies of dead animals so closely together that when the thaw came, one rancher from Kaycee claimed to have walked on cowhide all the way to Crazy Woman Creek, twenty miles away.

Territorial Wyoming was a boy's world. The land was generous with everything but water. At first there was room enough, food enough, for everyone. And, as with all beginnings, an expansive mood set in. The young cowboys, drifters, shopkeepers, schoolteachers, were heroic, lawless, generous, rowdy, and tenacious. The individualism and optimism generated during those times have endured.

John Tisdale rode north with the trail herds from Texas. He was a college-educated man with enough money to buy a small outfit near the Powder River. While driving home from the town of Buffalo with a buckboard full of Christmas toys for his family and a winter's supply of food, he was shot in the back by an agent of the cattle barons who resented the encroachment of small-time stockmen like him. The wealthy cattlemen tried to control all the public grazing land by restricting membership in the Wyoming Stock Growers Association, as if it were a country club. They ostracized from roundups and brandings cowboys and ranchers who were not members, then denounced them as rustlers. Tisdale's death, the second such cold-blooded murder, kicked off the Johnson County cattle war, which was no simple good-guy-bad-guy shoot-out but a complicated class struggle between landed gentry and less affluent settlers—a shocking reminder that the West was not an egalitarian sanctuary after all.

Fencing ultimately enforced boundaries, but barbed wire abrogated space. It was stretched across the beautiful valleys, into the mountains, over desert badlands, through buffalo grass. The "anything is possible" fever—the lure of any new place—was constricted. The integrity of the land as a geographical body, and the freedom to ride anywhere on it, was lost.

I punched cows with a young man named Martin, who is the great-grandson of John Tisdale. His inheritance is not the open land that Tisdale knew and prematurely lost but a rage against restraint.

Wyoming tips down as you head northeast; the highest ground—the Laramie Plains—is on the Colorado border. Up where I live, the Big Horn River leaks into difficult, arid terrain. In the basin where it's dammed, sandhill cranes gather and, with delicate legwork, slice through the stilled water. I was driving by with a rancher one morning when he commented that cranes are "old-fashioned." When I asked why, he said, "Because they mate for life." Then he looked at me with a twinkle in his eyes, as if to say he really did believe in such things but also understood why we break our own rules.

In all this open space, values crystallize quickly. People are strong on scruples but tenderhearted about quirky behavior. A friend and I found one ranch hand, who's "not quite right in the head," sitting in front of the badly decayed carcass of a cow, shaking his finger and saying, "Now, I don't want you to do this ever again!" When I asked what was wrong with him, I was told, "He's goofier than hell, just like the rest of us." Perhaps because the West is historically new, conventional morality is still felt to be less important than rock-bottom truths. Though there's always a lot of teasing and sparring around, people are blunt with each other, sometimes even cruel, believing honesty is stronger medicine than sympathy, which may console but often conceals.

The formality that goes hand in hand with the rowdiness is known as "the Western Code." It's a list of practical dos and don'ts, faithfully observed. A friend, Cliff, who runs a trapline in the winter, cut off half his foot while axing a hole in the ice. Alone, he dragged himself to his pickup and headed for town, stopping to open the ranch gate as he left, and getting out to close it again, thus losing, in his observance of rules, precious time and blood. Later, he commented, "How would it look, them having to come to the hospital to tell me their cows had gotten out?"

Accustomed to emergencies, my friends doctor each other from the vet's bag with relish. When one old-timer suffered a heart attack in hunting camp, his partner quickly stirred up a brew of red horse liniment and hot water and made the half-conscious victim drink it, then tied him onto a horse and led him twenty miles to town. He regained consciousness and lived.

The roominess of the state has affected political attitudes as well. Ranchers keep up with world politics and convulsions of the economy but are basically isolationists. Being used to running their own small empires of land and livestock, they're suspicious of big government. It's a "don't fence me in" holdover from a century ago. They still want the elbow room their grandfathers had, so they're strongly conservative, but with a populist twist.

Summer is the season when we get our "cowboy tans"—on the lower parts of our faces and on three fourths of our arms. Excessive heat, in the nineties and higher, sends us outside with the mosquitoes. In winter, we're tucked inside our houses, and the white wasteland outside appears to be expanding, but in summer, all the greenery abridges space. Summer is a go-ahead season. Every living thing is off the block and in the race: battalions of bugs in flight and biting; bats swinging around my log cabin as if the bases were loaded and someone had hit a home run. Some of summer's high-speed growth is ominous: larkspur-death camas, and green greasewood can kill sheep—an ironic idea, dying in this desert from eating what is too verdant. With sixteen hours of daylight, farmers and ranchers irrigate feverishly. There are first, second, and third cuttings of hay, some crews averaging only four hours of sleep a night for weeks. And like the cowboys who in summer ride the night rodeo circuit, nighthawks make dare-devil dives at dusk with an eerie whirring that sounds like a plane going down on the shimmering horizon.

In the town where I live, they've had to board up the dance-hall windows because there have been so many fights. There's so little to do except work that people wind up in a state of idle agitation that becomes fatalistic, as if there were nothing to be done about all this untapped energy. So the dark side to the grandeur of these spaces is the small-mindedness that seals people in. Men become hermits; women go mad. Cabin fever explodes into suicides, or into grudges and lifelong family feuds. Two sisters in my area inherited a ranch but found they couldn't get along. They fenced the place in half. When one's cows got out and mixed with the other's, the women went at each other with shovels. They ended up in the same hospital room, but never spoke a word to each other for the rest of their lives.

Eccentricity ritualizes behavior. It's a shortcut through unmanageable emotions and strict social conventions. I knew a sheepherder named Fred who, at seventy-eight, still had a handsome face, which he kept smooth by plastering it each day with bag balm and Vaseline. He was curious, well-read, and had a fact-keeping mind to go along with his penchant for hoarding. His reliquary of gunnysacks, fence wire, wood, canned food, unopened Christmas presents, and magazines matched his odd collages of meals: sardines with maple syrup; vegetable soup garnished with Fig Newtons. His wagon was so overloaded that he had to sleep sitting up because there was no room on the bed. Despite his love of up-to-date information, Fred died from gangrene when an old-timer's remedy of fresh sheep manure, applied as a poultice to a bad cut, failed to save him.

After the brief lushness of summer, the sun moves south. The range grass is brown. Livestock has been trailed back down from the mountains. Waterholes begin to frost over at night. Last fall Martin asked me to accompany him on a pack trip. With five horses, we followed a river into the mountains behind the tiny Wyoming town of Meeteetse. Groves of aspen, red and orange, gave off a light that made us look toasted. Our hunting camp was so high that clouds skidded across our foreheads, then slowed to sail out across the warm valleys. Except for a bull moose who wandered into our camp and mistook our black gelding for a rival, we shot at nothing.

One of our evening entertainments was to watch the night sky. My dog, who also came on the trip, a dingo bred to herd sheep, is so used to the silence and empty skies that when an airplane flies over he always looks up and eyes the distant intruder quizzically. The sky, lately, seems to be much more crowded than it used to be. Satellites make their silent passes in the dark with great regularity. We counted eighteen in one hour's viewing. How odd to think that while they circumnavigated the planet, Martin and I had moved only six miles into our local wilderness, and had seen no other human for the two weeks we stayed there.

At night, by moonlight, the land is whittled to slivers—a ridge, a river, a strip of grassland stretching to the mountains, then the huge sky. One morning a full moon was setting in the west just as the sun was rising. I felt precariously balanced between the two as I loped across a meadow. For a moment, I could believe that the stars, which were still visible, work like cooper's bands, holding everything above Wyoming together.

Space has a spiritual equivalent and can heal what is divided and burdensome in us. My grandchildren will probably use space shuttles for a honeymoon trip or to recover from heart attacks, but closer to home we might also learn how to carry space inside ourselves in the effortless way we carry our skins. Space represents sanity, not a life purified, dull, or "spaced out" but one that might accommodate intelligently any idea or situation.

From the clayey soil of northern Wyoming is mined bentonite, which is used as a filler in candy, gum, and lipstick. We Americans are great on fillers, as if what we have, what we are, is not enough. We have a cultural tendency toward denial, but, being affluent, we strangle ourselves with what we can buy. We have only to look at the houses we build to see how we build *against* space, the way we drink against pain and loneliness. We fill up space as if it were a pie shell, with things whose opacity further obstructs our ability to see what is already there.

QUESTIONS FOR CRITICAL ANALYSIS

1. How did life on the sheep ranch change Ehrlich? What does she mean when she says that Wyoming's "absolute indifference steadied me"? How does she illustrate her point?
2. What jobs did Ehrlich perform in Wyoming? What is your opinion of such jobs and people who perform them? Does it surprise you that a woman does these jobs, and that the woman who does them also wrote this essay? Why, or why not?
3. Describe the relationship between Wyoming and its inhabitants. How does the physical environment determine the sort of person who lives there? How does it change the people? Do you agree with Ehrlich's opinion of the role environment plays in shaping our lives? Why, or why not?
4. What is the "Western Code"? How do the people Ehrlich describes fit your stereotype of a cowboy? In what ways are they different?
5. In the final paragraph of the essay, Ehrlich writes: "Americans are great on fillers."

What does she mean? Do you agree with her? What exanples can you give to support her claim?

QUESTIONS FOR STRUCTURAL ANALYSIS

1. "Wyoming: The Solace of Open Spaces" provides an excellent example of a descriptive essay; Ehrlich includes not only vivid visual details, but opens the Wyoming landscape to all the senses. List some examples that struck you as particularly good. Is description the point of this essay, or is it a vehicle for something else? On what do you base your answer?
2. Ehrlich has divided this essay into nine separate sections. Why did she think this was important to the structure of her essay? What is the topic of each section? How do the sections relate to each other? to the subject as a whole?
3. In order for the reader to get the whole picture of Wyoming, Ehrlich describes its physical appearance, provides facts and statistics, tells its history, and relates stories by old timers. How did you respond to all this information? How would you have used all this information if you had written the essay?
4. The first sentence of the essay introduces you to "I," the persona of the essay. You see Wyoming through her eyes and her experiences. What sort of person is she? Is she a reliable narrator? Do you accept her vision of what she sees? Why, or why not?
5. How do the last two sections work together to conclude the essay? What is their relationship with each other? with the rest of the essay?

*T*HE *R*ING OF *T*IME

E. B. WHITE

E. B. White (1899–1985) made his living as a writer and editor for the New Yorker. *He contributed essays to* Harper's, *wrote the classic children's book* Charlotte's Web, *and revised William Strunk's* Elements of Style, *which remains the best guide to writing clearly and concisely. Among other prizes, White received a Gold Medal from the American Academy of Arts and Letters, the Presidential Medal of Freedom (1963), the National Medal for Literature (1971), and a Pulitzer Special Citation (1978). "The Ring of Time" is an example of how White uses his detailed observation of a young woman standing on a horse riding around the circus ring as a basis for a thoughtful meditation on time which, in turn, leads to a forceful description of racism in the 1950s South. In the American South, he finds it easy to forget time's passing and to continue in an unreal ring of suspended time.*

Before you begin reading: *Think about time. What is "time?" When does it differ from clock- or calendar-time? In your reading notebook, write ideas and phrases that express the meaning of time to you.*

◆

Fiddler Bayou, March 22, 1956

AFTER THE LIONS HAD RETURNED TO THEIR CAGES, creeping angrily through the chutes, a little bunch of us drifted away and into an open doorway nearby, where we stood for a while in semidarkness, watching a big brown circus horse go harumphing around the practice ring. His trainer was a woman of about forty, and the two of them, horse and woman, seemed caught up in one of those desultory treadmills of afternoon from which there is no apparent escape. The day was hot, and we kibitzers were grateful to be briefly out of the sun's glare. The long rein, or tape, by which the woman guided her charge counterclockwise in his dull career formed the radius of their private circle, of which she was the revolving center; and she, too, stepped a tiny circumference of her own, in order to accommodate the horse and allow him his maximum scope. She had on a short-skirted costume and a conical straw hat. Her legs were bare and she wore high heels, which probed deep into the loose tanbark and kept her ankles in a state of constant turmoil. The great size and meekness of the horse, the repetitious exercise, the heat of the afternoon, all exerted a hypnotic charm that invited boredom; we spectators were experiencing a languor—we neither expected relief nor felt entitled to any. We had paid a dollar to get into the grounds, to be sure, but we had got our dollar's worth a few minutes before, when the lion trainer's whiplash had got caught around a toe of one of the lions. What more did we want for a dollar?

Behind me I heard someone say, "Excuse me, please," in a low voice. She was halfway into the building when I turned and saw her—a girl of sixteen or seventeen, politely threading her way through us onlookers who blocked the entrance. As she emerged in front of us, I saw that she was barefoot, her dirty little feet fighting the uneven ground. In most respects she was like any of two or three dozen showgirls you encounter if you wander about the winter quarters of Mr. John Ringling North's circus, in Sarasota—cleverly proportioned, deeply browned by the sun, dusty, eager, and almost naked. But her grave face and the naturalness of her manner gave her a sort of quick distinction and brought a new note into the gloomy octagonal building where we had all cast our lot for a few moments. As soon as she had squeezed through the crowd, she spoke a word or two to the older woman, whom I took to be her mother, stepped to the ring, and waited while the horse coasted to a stop in front of her. She gave the animal a couple of affectionate swipes on his enormous neck and then swung herself aboard. The horse immediately resumed his rocking canter, the woman goading him on, chanting something that sounded like "Hop! Hop!"

In attempting to recapture this mild spectacle, I am merely acting as recording secretary for one of the oldest of societies—the society of those who, at one time or another, have surrendered, without even a show of resistance, to the bedazzlement of a circus rider. As a writing man, or secretary, I have always felt charged with the safekeeping of all unexpected items of worldly or unworldly enchantment, as though I might be held personally responsible if even a small one were to be lost. But it is not easy to communicate anything of this nature. The circus comes as close to being the world in microcosm as anything I know; in a way, it puts all the rest of show business in the shade. Its magic is universal and complex. Out of its wild disorder comes order; from its rank smell rises the good aroma of courage and daring; out of its preliminary shabbiness comes the final splendor. And buried in the familiar boasts of its advance agents lies the modesty of most of its people. For me the circus is at its best before it has been put together. It is at its best at certain moments when it comes to a point, as through a burning glass, in the activity and destiny of a single performer out of so many. One ring is always bigger than three. One rider, one aerialist, is always greater than six. In short, a man has to catch the circus unawares to experience its full impact and share its gaudy dream.

The ten-minute ride the girl took achieved—as far as I was concerned, who wasn't looking for it, and quite unbeknownst to her, who wasn't even striving for it—the thing that is sought by performers everywhere, on whatever stage, whether struggling in the tidal currents of Shakespeare or bucking the difficult motion of a horse. I somehow got the idea she was just cadging a ride, improving a shining ten minutes in the diligent way all serious artists seize free moments to hone the blade of their talent and keep themselves in trim. Her brief tour included only elementary postures and tricks, perhaps because they were all she was capable of, perhaps because her warmup at this hour was unscheduled and the ring was not rigged for a real practice session. She swung herself off and on the horse several times, gripping his mane. She did a few knee-stands—or whatever they are called—dropping to her knees and quickly bouncing back up on her feet again. Most of the time she simply rode in a standing position, well aft on the beast, her hands hanging easily at her sides, her head erect, her straw-colored ponytail lightly brushing her shoulders, the blood of exertion showing faintly through the tan of her skin. Twice she managed a one-foot stance—a sort of ballet pose, with arms outstretched. At one point the neck strap of her bathing suit broke and she went twice around the ring in the classic attitude of a woman making minor repairs to a garment. The fact that she was standing on the back of a moving horse while doing this invested the matter with a clownish significance that perfectly fitted the spirit of the circus—jocund, yet charming. She just rolled the strap into a neat ball and stowed it inside her bodice while the horse rocked and rolled beneath her in dutiful innocence. The bathing suit proved as self-reliant as its owner and stood up well enough without benefit of strap.

The richness of the scene was in its plainness, its natural condition—of horse, of ring, of girl, even to the girl's bare feet that gripped the bare back of her proud and ridiculous mount. The enchantment grew not out of anything that happened or was performed but out of something that seemed to go round and around and around with the girl, attending her, a steady gleam in the shape of a circle—a ring of ambition, of happiness, of youth. (And the positive pleasures of equilibrium under difficulties.) In a week or two, all would be changed, all (or almost all) lost: the girl would wear makeup, the horse would wear gold, the ring would be painted, the bark would be clean for the feet of the horse, the girl's feet would be clean for the slippers that she'd wear. All, all would be lost.

As I watched with the others, our jaws adroop, our eyes alight, I became painfully conscious of the element of time. Everything in the hideous old building seemed to take the shape of a circle, conforming to the course of the horse. The rider's gaze, as she peered straight ahead, seemed to be circular, as though bent by force of circumstance; then time itself began running in circles, and so the beginning was where the end was, and the two were the same, and one thing ran into the next and time went round and around and got nowhere. The girl wasn't so young that she did not know the delicious satisfaction of having a perfectly behaved body and the fun of using it to do a trick most people can't do, but she was too young to know that time does not really move in a circle at all. I thought: "She will never be as beautiful as this again"—a thought that made me acutely unhappy—and in a flash my mind (which is too much of a busybody to suit me) had projected her twenty-five years ahead, and she was now in the center of the ring, on foot, wearing a conical hat and high-heeled shoes, the image of the older woman, holding the long rein, caught in the treadmill of an afternoon long in the future. "She is at that enviable moment in life [I thought] when she believes she can go once around the ring, make one complete circuit, and at the end be exactly the same age as at the start." Everything in her movements, her expression, told you that for her the ring of time was perfectly formed, changeless, predictable, without beginning or end, like the ring in which she was traveling at this moment with the horse that wallowed under her. And then I slipped back into my trance, and time was circular again—time, pausing quietly with the rest of us, so as not to disturb the balance of a performer.

Her ride ended as casually as it had begun. The older woman stopped the horse, and the girl slid to the ground. As she walked toward us to leave, there was a quick, small burst of applause. She smiled broadly, in surprise and pleasure; then her face suddenly regained its gravity and she disappeared through the door.

It had been ambitious and plucky of me to attempt to describe what is indescribable, and I have failed, as I knew I would. But I have discharged my duty to my society; and besides, a writer, like an acrobat, must occasionally try a stunt that is too much for him. At any rate, it is worth reporting that long before the circus comes to town, its most notable performances have already been given. Under the bright lights of the finished show, a performer need only reflect the electric candle power that is directed upon him; but in the dark and dirty old training rings and in the makeshift cages, whatever light is generated, whatever excitement, whatever beauty, must come from original sources—from internal fires of professional hunger and delight, from the exuberance and gravity of youth. It is the difference between planetary light and the combustion of stars.

The South is the land of the sustained sibilant. Everywhere, for the appreciative visitor, the letter "s" insinuates itself in the scene: in the sound of sea and sand, in the singing shell, in the heat of sun and sky, in the sultriness of the gentle hours, in the siesta, in the stir of birds and insects. In contrast to the softness of its music, the South is also cruel and hard and prickly. A little striped lizard, flattened along the sharp green bayonet of a yucca, wears in its tiny face and watchful eye the pure look of death and violence. And all over the place, hidden at the bottom of their small sandy craters, the ant lions lie in wait for the ant that will stumble into their trap. (There are three kinds of lions in this region: the lions of the circus, the ant lions, and the Lions of the Tampa Lions Club, who roared their approval of segregation at a meeting the other day—all except one, a Lion named Monty Gurwit, who declined to roar and thereby got his picture in the paper.)

The day starts on a note of despair: the sorrowing dove, alone on its telephone wire, mourns the loss of night, weeps at the bright perils of the unfolding day. But soon the mockingbird wakes and begins an early rehearsal, setting the dove down by force of character, running through a few slick imitations, and trying a couple of original numbers into the bargain. The redbird takes it from there. Despair gives way to good humor. The Southern dawn is a pale affair, usually, quite different from our northern daybreak. It is a triumph of gradualism; night turns to day imperceptibly, softly, with no theatrics. It is subtle and undisturbing. As the first light seeps in through the blinds I lie in bed half awake, despairing with the dove, sounding the A for the brothers Alsop. All seems lost, all seems sorrowful. Then a mullet jumps in the bayou outside the bedroom window. It falls back into the water with a smart smack. I have asked several people why the mullet incessantly jump and I have received a variety of answers. Some say the mullet jump to shake off a parasite that annoys them. Some say they jump for the love of jumping—as the girl on the horse seemed to ride for the love of riding (although she, too, like all artists, may have been shaking off some parasite that fastens itself to the creative spirit and can be got rid of only by fifty turns around a ring while standing on a horse).

In Florida at this time of year, the sun does not take command of the day until a couple of hours after it has appeared in the east. It seems to carry no authority at first. The sun and the lizard keep the same schedule; they bide their time until the morning has advanced a good long way before they come fully forth and strike. The cold lizard waits astride his warming leaf for the perfect moment; the cold sun waits in his nest of clouds for the crucial time.

On many days, the dampness of the air pervades all life, all living. Matches refuse to strike. The towel, hung to dry, grows wetter by the hour. The newspaper, with its headlines about integration, wilts in your hand and falls limply into the coffee and the egg. Envelopes seal themselves. Postage stamps mate with one another as shamelessly as grasshoppers. But most of the time the days are models of beauty and wonder and comfort, with the kind sea stroking the back of the warm sand. At evening there are great flights of birds over the sea, where the light lingers; the gulls, the pelicans, the terns, the herons stay aloft for half an hour after land birds have gone to roost. They hold their ancient formations, wheel and fish over the Pass, enjoying the last of day like children playing outdoors after suppertime.

To a beachcomber from the North, which is my present status, the race problem has no pertinence, no immediacy. Here in Florida I am a guest in two houses—the house of the sun, the house of the State of Florida. As a guest, I mind my manners and do not criticize the customs of my hosts. It gives me a queer feeling, though, to be at the center of the greatest social crisis of my time and see hardly a sign of it. Yet the very absence of signs seems to increase one's awareness. Colored people do not come to the public beach to bathe, because they would not be made welcome there; and they don't fritter away their time visiting the circus, because they have other things to do. A few of them turn up at the ballpark, where they occupy a separate but equal section of the left-field bleachers and watch Negro players on the visiting Braves team using the same bases as the white players, instead of separate (but equal) bases. I have had only two small encounters with "color." A colored woman named Viola, who had been a friend of my wife's sister years ago, showed up one day with some laundry of ours that she had consented to do for us, and with the bundle she brought a bunch of nasturtiums, as a sort of natural accompaniment to the delivery of clean clothes. The flowers seemed a very acceptable thing and I was touched by them. We asked Viola about her daughter, and she said she was at Kentucky State College, studying voice.

The other encounter was when I was explaining to our cook, who is from Finland, the mysteries of bus travel in the American Southland. I showed her the bus stop, armed her with a timetable, and then, as a matter of duty, mentioned the customs of the Romans. "When you get on the bus," I said, "I think you'd better sit in one of the front seats—the seats in back are for colored people." A look of great weariness came into her face, as it does when we use too many dishes, and she replied, "Oh, I know—isn't it silly!"

Her remark, coming as it did all the way from Finland and landing on this sandbar with a plunk, impressed me. The Supreme Court said nothing about silliness, but I suspect it may play more of a role than one might suppose. People are, if anything, more touchy about being thought silly than they are about being thought unjust. I note that one of the arguments in the recent manifesto of Southern Congressmen in support of the doctrine of "separate but equal" was that it had been founded on "common sense." The sense that is common to one generation is uncommon to the next. Probably the first slave ship, with Negroes lying in chains on its decks, seemed commonsensical to the owners who operated it and to the planters who patronized it. But such a vessel would not be in the realm of common sense today. The only sense that is common, in the long run, is the sense of change—and we all instinctively avoid it, and object to the passage of time, and would rather have none of it.

The Supreme Court decision is like the Southern sun, laggard in its early stages, biding its time. It has been the law in Florida for two years now, and the years have been like the hours of the morning before the sun has gathered its strength. I think the decision is as incontrovertible and warming as the sun, and, like the sun, will eventually take charge.

But there is certainly a great temptation in Florida to duck the passage of time. Lying in warm comfort by the sea, you receive gratefully the gift of the sun, the gift of the South. This is true seduction. The day is a circle—morning, afternoon, and night. After a few days I was clearly enjoying the same delusion as the girl on the horse—that I could ride clear around the ring of day, guarded by wind and sun and sea and sand, and be not a moment older.

P.S. (April 1962). When I first laid eyes on Fiddler Bayou, it was wild land, populated chiefly by the little crabs that gave it its name, visited by wading birds and by an occasional fisherman. Today, houses ring the bayou, and part of the mangrove shore has been bulkheaded with a concrete wall. Green lawns stretch from patio to water's edge, and sprinklers make rainbows in the light. But despite man's encroachment, Nature manages to hold her own and assert her authority: high tides and high winds in the gulf sometimes send the sea crashing across the sand barrier, depositing its wrack on lawns and ringing everyone's front door bell. The birds and the crabs accommodate themselves quite readily to the changes that have taken place; every day brings herons to hunt around among the roots of the mangroves, and I have discovered that I can approach to within about eight feet of a Little Blue Heron simply by entering the water and swimming slowly toward him. Apparently he has decided that when I'm in the water, I am without guile—possibly even desirable, like a fish.

The Ringling circus has quit Sarasota and gone elsewhere for its hibernation. A few circus families still own homes in the town, and every spring the students at the high school put on a circus, to let off steam, work off physical requirements, and provide a promotional spectacle for Sarasota. At the drugstore you can buy a postcard showing the bed John Ringling slept in. Time has not stood still for anybody but the dead, and even the dead must be able to hear the acceleration of little sports cars and know that things have changed.

From the all-wise *New York Times*, which has the animal kingdom ever in mind, I have learned that one of the creatures most acutely aware of the passing of time is the fiddler crab himself. Tiny spots on his body enlarge during daytime hours, giving him the same color as the mudbank he explores and thus protecting him from his enemies. At night the spots shrink, his color fades, and he is almost invisible in the light of the moon. These changes are synchronized with the tides, so that each day they occur at a different hour. A scientist who experimented with the crabs to learn more about the phenomenon discovered that even when they are removed from their natural environment and held in confinement, the rhythm of their bodily change continues uninterrupted, and they mark the passage of time in their laboratory prison, faithful to the tides in their fashion.

QUESTIONS FOR CRITICAL ANALYSIS

1. As the essay opens, what is White doing? Why? How does he describe his role?
2. Why does White think that the circus is the "world in microcosm"? Do you agree with him? Why, or why not? How does this idea relate to his comments on time?
3. When you begin reading the second section, what clues do you have that White is going to do more than merely describe the South? Who do you suppose is his audience?

4. White wrote this essay in 1956. What does White find disheartening about Florida and its treatment of blacks? How do you characterize White's "two small encounters with 'color'"? What Supreme Court decision is he referring to?
5. Why did White add the P.S.? How does it relate with the themes of time and race discussed in the essay?

QUESTIONS FOR STRUCTURAL ANALYSIS

1. The opening paragraph introduces the reader to the circus, White's attitude toward the scene, and his participation in it. How does this paragraph set the stage for the ideas that follow?
2. White describes himself as "merely acting as recording secretary." In what ways is this an accurate description? Do you think he is more than just a recording secretary? Why? If he is, why did he describe himself in that way?
3. How does White shift the focus of his essay from the circus event to a discussion of time? Is the shift natural? How does he keep the rest of the first section on course?
4. The second part of the essay shifts even further into a discussion of the South. How does this section relate to the first one? Did you appreciate what White was doing? Why, or why not?
5. Look specifically at White's technique in the first paragraph of the second section: How does he illustrate the two sides of the South?
6. What effect does the P.S., written six years later, have on the rest of the essay? What is the point of describing the fiddler crab?

Going Barefoot

John Updike

John Updike (1932–   ), author of fiction, poetry, reviews and essays, is best known to the general public for his novels about the tensions and frustrations of suburban life. (Recent novels include The Witches of Eastwick, *1985,* Roger's Version, *1986, and* S, *1988). "Going Barefoot," is Updike's paean to summers in Martha's Vineyard, Massachusetts. Written to accompany a collection of Peter Simon's photographs of the Vineyard, the essay combines Updike's memories with allusions to an Edenic Paradise and the cost of freedom.*

Before you begin reading: *Remember your favorite summer? What did it feel like? In your reading notebook write a description of that summer without stopping—include as many sensory details as possible.*

◆

WHEN I THINK OF THE VINEYARD, MY ANKLES FEEL good—bare, airy, lean. Full of bones. I go barefoot there in recollection, and the island as remembered becomes a medley of pedal sensations: the sandy rough planks of Dutcher Dock; the hot sidewalks of Oak Bluffs, followed by the wall-to-wall carpeting of the liquor store; the pokey feel of an accelerator on a naked sole; the hurtful little pebbles of Menemsha Beach and the also hurtful half-buried rocks of Squibnocket; the prickly weeds, virtual cacti, that grew in a certain lawn near Chilmark Pond; the soft path leading down from this lawn across giving, oozing boards to a bouncy little dock and rowboats that offered another yet friendly texture to the feet; the crystal bite of ocean water; the seethe and suck of a wave tumbling rocks across your toes in its surge back down the sand; sand, the clean wide private sand by Windy Gates and the print-pocked, overused public sand by the boat dock that one kicked around in while waiting for friends to be deferried; the cold steep clay of Gay Head and the flinty littered surface around those souvenir huts that continued to beguile the most jaded child; the startling dew on the grass when one stepped outside with the first cup of coffee to gauge the day's weather; the warmth of the day still lingering in the dunes underfoot as we walked back, Indian-file, through the dark from a beach party and its diminishing bonfire. Going to the post office in bare feet had an infra-legal, anti-totalitarian, comical, gentle feel to it, in the days before the Postal Service moved to the other side of Beetlebung Corner and established itself in a lake of razor-sharp spalls. (When Bill Seward ran the postal annex in his store, it was one of the few spots in the United States that would hand over mail on Sundays.) Shopping at Seward's, one would not so carefreely have shelled out "island prices" for such luxuries as macadamia nuts and candied snails had one been wearing shoes; their absence, like the cashless ease of a charge account, gave a pleasant illusion of unaccountability. The friend of mine who took these photographs used to play golf at Mink Meadows barefoot. My children and I set up a miniature golf course on a turnaround covered with crushed clamshells; after we had been treading this surface for a while, it did not seem too great a transition, even for a middle-aged father of four, to climb a tree barefoot or go walking on a roof. The shingles felt pleasantly peppery, sun-baked.

These are summer memories, mostly August memories; for that's the kind of resident I was. Now it has been some summers since I was even that, and a danger exists of confusing the Vineyard with my children's childhood, which time has swallowed, or with Paradise, from which we have been debarred by well-known angels. Let's not forget the rainy days, the dull days, the cranky-making crowding, and the moldy smell summer furniture gives off when breezes don't blow through the screen door that one keeps meaning to fix, though it's really the landlord's responsibility. Beach pebbles notoriously dry to a disappointing gray on the mantel. The cozy roads and repeated recreations can begin to wear a rut. One wet summer we all, kids and cousins and friends of cousins, kept walking down through poison ivy, *not* barefoot, to look at a heap of large stones that was either a ninth-century Viking cromlech or a nineteenth-century doghouse, nobody was certain which. Still, there was under it all, fair days and foul, a kicky whiff of freedom, a hint, whispered from the phalanges to the metatarsals, from the calcaneus to the astragalus, that one was free from the mainland's paved oppressions.

Going barefoot is increasingly illegal and does have its dangers. One house we rented overlooked Menemsha Bight from a long porch whose spaced boards had the aligned nicety of harp strings or the lines of type in a book. One of my boys, performing some stunt on these boards, rammed splinters into the soles of his feet so deeply a doctor in Edgartown had to cut them out with a surgeon's knife. I wonder if even the most hardened hippies still pad along the tarry streets of Oak Bluffs barefoot as they used to. At Jungle Beach, I remember, nudity spread upward from toes to head and became doctrinaire. But then nudism, interwoven with socialism in the island's history, has always had a doctrinaire side. Being naked approaches being revolutionary; going barefoot is mere populism. "Barefoot boy with cheek of tan" was a rote phrase of my own childhood, quaint even then. But that cliché had once lived and can be seen, not only in illustrations of Mark Twain but also in Winslow Homer's level-eyed etchings and oils of his contemporary America, a place of sandy lanes and soft meadows. There are few places left, even summer places, where one can go barefoot. Too many laws, too much broken glass. On Long Island, the cuffs of one's leisure suit will drag on the ground, and on the Cape, pine needles stick to the feet. Even on Nantucket, those cobblestones are not inviting. But the presiding spirits of Martha's Vineyard, willfully and not without considerable overhead, do preserve this lowly element of our Edenic heritage: treading the earth.

QUESTIONS FOR CRITICAL ANALYSIS

1. Is it useful to know that this essay was originally published to accompany photographs of Martha's Vineyard? Does that information change your response to the essay? Why, or why not?
2. What social ramifications does going barefoot have? How does this affect the author's behavior? Do you like going barefoot? Have you ever thought of it in these terms?
3. What role does memory play in this essay? Does it change your response to the essay to think that all these memories may not be Updike's own?
4. What does Updike mean when he says, "Being naked approaches being revolutionary; going barefoot is mere populism"?
5. How do Updike's references to specific places and events on Martha's Vineyard differ from his references to Mark Twain, Winslow Homer, and "Barefoot boy with cheek of tan"? Did any of these references strike a chord with you?

QUESTIONS FOR STRUCTURAL ANALYSIS

1. What is the point of this essay? Is there a thesis?
2. Updike organized the essay into three paragraphs. Describe what each paragraph contains and the relationship among the paragraphs.
3. Look carefully at the first three sentences of the essay. The first sentence is brief, clean—like its subject. The second sentence is a three-word fragment. The third sentence is 234 words long. How did you respond to this opening? Is Updike's list of images effective? Did you read the third sentence word for word? Why, or why not?
4. How would you describe Updike's tone in this essay? What do you know about the "I," or persona, of the essay? How does he reveal himself? Do you trust his descriptions?
5. What does the final sentence of the essay mean? How does it relate to the rest of the essay?

PONDS

LEWIS THOMAS

Lewis Thomas (1913–), physician, educator, writer, and administrator, directed Sloan Kettering Memorial hospital in New York City and taught at Cornell Medical Hospital and at Rockefeller University. For his many medical and popular books, Thomas has been honored by the American Medical Writers Association (1978) and the American Booksellers Association (1978) and won the National Book Award (1975). "Ponds," which first appeared in the New England Journal of Medicine, *describes the reaction of New Yorkers at finding goldfish-stocked ponds in east Manhattan. The appearance of the ponds, and of the goldfish, can be accounted for; the angry response of the people may be harder to explain.*

Before you begin reading: *Every community has some quirky characteristics. Write about a town you know well, describing an event or place that is unique to that community.*

◆

LARGE AREAS OF MANHATTAN ARE AFLOAT. I REMEMBER when the new Bellevue Hospital was being built, fifteen years ago; the first stage was the most spectacular and satisfying, an enormous square lake. It was there for the two years, named Lake Bellevue, while the disconsolate Budget Bureau went looking for cash to build the next stage. It was fenced about and visible only from the upper windows of the old hospital, but pretty to look at, cool and blue in midsummer, frozen gleaming as Vermont in January. The fence, like all city fences, was always broken, and we could have gone down to the lake and used it, but it was known to be an upwelling of the East River. At Bellevue there were printed rules about the East River: if anyone fell in, it was an emergency for the Infectious-Disease Service, and the first measures, after resuscitation, were massive doses of whatever antibiotics the hospital pharmacy could provide.

But if you cleaned the East River you could have ponds all over town, up and down the East Side of Manhattan anyway. If you lifted out the Empire State Building and the high structures nearby, you would have, instantly, an inland sea. A few holes bored in the right places would let water into the subways, and you'd have lovely underground canals all across to the Hudson, uptown to the Harlem River, downtown to the Battery, a Venice underground, without pigeons.

It wouldn't work, though, unless you could find a way to keep out the fish. New Yorkers cannot put up with live fish out in the open. I cannot explain this, but it is so.

There is a new pond, much smaller than Lake Bellevue, on First Avenue between Seventieth and Seventy-first, on the east side of the street. It emerged sometime last year, soon after a row of old flats had been torn down and the hole dug for a new apartment building. By now it is about average size for Manhattan, a city block long and about forty feet across, maybe eight feet deep at the center, more or less kidney-shaped, rather like an outsized suburban swimming pool except for the things floating, and now the goldfish.

With the goldfish, it is almost detestable. There are, clearly visible from the sidewalk, hundreds of them. The neighborhood people do not walk by and stare into it through the broken fence, as would be normal for any other Manhattan pond. They tend to cross the street, looking away.

Now there are complaints against the pond, really against the goldfish. How could people do such a thing? Bad enough for pet dogs and cats to be abandoned, but who could be so unfeeling as to abandon goldfish? They must have come down late at night, carrying their bowls, and simply dumped them in. How could they?

The ASPCA was called, and came one afternoon with a rowboat. Nets were used, and fish taken away in new custodial bowls, some to Central Park, others to ASPCA headquarters, to the fish pound. But the goldfish have multiplied, or maybe those people with their bowls keep coming down late at night for their furtive, unfeeling dumping. Anyway, there are too many fish for the ASPCA, for which this seems to be a new kind of problem. An official stated for the press that the owners of the property would be asked to drain the pond by pumping, and then the ASPCA would come back with nets to catch them all.

You'd think they were rats or roaches, the way people began to talk. Get those goldfish out of that pond, I don't care how you do it. Dynamite, if necessary. But get rid of them. Winter is coming, someone said, and it is deep enough so that they'll be swimming around underneath the ice. Get them out.

It is this knowledge of the East River, deep in the minds of all Manhattan residents, more than the goldfish themselves, I think. Goldfish in a glass bowl are harmless to the human mind, maybe even helpful to minds casting about for something, anything, to think about. But goldfish let loose, propagating themselves, worst of all *surviving* in what has to be a sessile eddy of the East River, somehow threaten us all. We do not like to think that life is possible under some conditions, especially the conditions of a Manhattan pond. There are four abandoned tires, any number of broken beer bottles, fourteen shoes and a single sneaker, and a visible layer, all over the surface, of that grayish-green film that settles on all New York surfaces. The mud at the banks of the pond is not proper country mud but reconstituted Manhattan landfill, ancient garbage, fossilized coffee grounds and grapefruit rind, the defecation of a city. For goldfish to be swimming in such water, streaking back and forth mysteriously in small schools, feeding, obviously feeding, looking as healthy and well-off as goldfish in the costliest kind of window-box aquarium, means something is wrong with our standards. It is, in some deep sense beyond words, insulting.

I thought I noticed a peculiar sort of fin on the undersurface of two of the fish. Perhaps, it occurs to me now in a rush of exultation, in such a pond as this, with all its chemical possibilities, there are contained some mutagens, and soon there will be schools of mutant goldfish. Give them just a little more time, I thought. And then, with the most typically Manhattan thought I've ever thought, I thought: The ASPCA will come again, next month, with their rowboat and their nets. The proprietor will begin pumping out the pond. The nets will flail, the rowboat will settle, and then the ASPCA officials will give a sudden shout of great dismay. And with a certain amount of splashing and grayish-greenish spray, at all the edges of the pond, up all the banks of ancient New York landfill mud, crawling on their new little feet, out onto the sidewalks, up and down and across the street, into doorways and up the fire escapes, some of them with little suckers on their little feet, up the sides of buildings and into open windows, looking for something, will come the goldfish.

It won't last, of course. Nothing like this ever does. The mayor will come and condemn it in person. The Health Department will come and recommend the purchase of cats from out of town because of the constitutional boredom of city cats. The NIH will send up teams of professionals from Washington with a new kind of antifish spray, which will be recalled four days later because of toxicity to cats.

After a few weeks it will be finished anyway, like a lot of New York events. The goldfish will drive deep and vanish, the pond will fill up with sneakers, workmen will come and pour concrete over everything, and by next year the new building will be up and occupied by people all unaware of their special environmental impact. But what a time it was.

QUESTIONS FOR CRITICAL ANALYSIS

1. Where do these lakes in Manhattan come from, according to Thomas? How does the city respond to their appearance?
2. What are some possible ways fish get into these lakes? Why is it detestable to New Yorkers that fish live in the lakes? What does Thomas say New Yorkers want to do to the fish?
3. According to Thomas, what did the ASPCA try to do? (What is the ASPCA?)
4. How does Thomas figure the fish-in-the-lakes event will end? What does the second to last paragraph reveal about New York City? about Thomas? What is your response to the end of the event?

QUESTIONS FOR STRUCTURAL ANALYSIS

1. What is the point of this essay? Is there a thesis? Who is the intended audience?
2. How would you describe the tone of the essay? Is Thomas serious about all this? Does he really think New Yorkers are as he describes them? Do you know any New Yorkers? Do you think they would respond this way? Why, or why not?
3. What do you think of Thomas's speculations about the mutant goldfish? What prompts these thoughts? Why does he describe this as "most typically Manhattan thought I've ever thought"?
4. What is Thomas's vision of the future of the lake? How does his concluding paragraph relate to the rest of the essay in tone? in substance? in what it reveals about New Yorkers?

*T*HE *H*EART OF THE *S*EASONS

ELIZABETH HARDWICK

Elizabeth Hardwick (1916–   ), founder and present advisory editor of The New York Review of Books, *has written three novels and three volumes of essays. In an autobiographical sketch, Hardwick talked about writing essays: "I have great affection for the form and have given to it everything and more than would be required of fiction, that is, everything I possibly could. Indeed I have always written essays as if they were examples of imaginative writing, as I believe them to be." "The Heart of the Seasons" first appeared in the monthly magazine* House & Garden.

Before you begin reading: *Which is your favorite season? Why? In your reading notebook write about the images, sensory details, and feelings that make the season special to you.*

◆

SUMMER—A HIGH, CANDID, DEFINITE TIME. IT MAY SLITHER out of the ambiguity, hesitance, or too early ripeness of spring and edge toward the soothing peculiarities of autumn, but summer is downright, a true companion of winter. It is an extreme, a returning, a vivid comparative. It does not signify that some are cool and some are dry and sweltering; summer is a kind of entity, poetic, but not a poetic mystery. The sun is at its zenith in the tropic of Cancer, a culmination.

Our frantic, crowded summers are not now as they once were. There was a time when girls did not lie about the beach in pieces of string, offering an intimidating revelation. Think of those yellow afternoons of the last century, lazy moments one can imagine by turning the pages of a collection of paintings in the new Terra Museum of American Art in Chicago. Then, we believe, it was another world—quiet, perhaps not so much reflective as drowsy and wondering. Summer was a luxurious pause, an inattention except for the concentration on pleasure. A caesura to honor the sun, the warm waters, the breezes of the mountains, and the hope of some dreamlike diversion of destiny in the pause.

There is a languorous game of croquet painted by Winslow Homer. It appears that this game may be one too many, too much like yesterday, a routine, and nothing to surprise. And Charles Curran's bursting, voluptuous water lilies.

The sun has ravished the flowers, full force, and how ferocious they are amid the passive, sheltered glances of the young women in the boat.

What a lot of clothes the women are dragging about in these rich-toned landscapes. Hats, sleeves, petticoats, ties at the neck, parasols—a shroud of protection, giving a somewhat fatigued femininity to these lost summer days. Sargent's summer painter must be putting the bush and the field and the reflection of the stream on canvas. He looks much as a man would today: white suit, coquettish red belt, and what appears to be a handkerchief on his head.

But she, the companion, is reading in a hat like a haystack, a dark skirt, and holding the inevitable lacy umbrella, a thing of no apparent utility unless it be a weapon against a change of his mood there in the erotic sleepiness of a full summer afternoon, and the ground dry and not even a dog in sight.

I like to remember the summer season coming to those who just stay at home the year round, that is, most of the world. The plain patterns of simple domestic life meet each year with a routine. Nothing is unexpected. An almanac of memories disputes claims of the hottest day in decades or the level of the rainfall.

The furnace is shut down and the fireplace, if there should be one, is emptied and the tiles relieved of grit and polished to an oily sienna sheen. Windows washed, everything aired; moths seeking the bedroom light bulb; grass and weeds pushing up out of the hard winter soil; leaves on the maples and elms—nothing special; doors latched back and covered by a flapping screen—with a hole in it and rusty hinges; voices calling out of the windows; perennials determined to exhibit their workhorse nature, if most a little disgruntled and with more stem than flower; insects strong as poison; the smell of chlorine in a child's hair—from the community pool across town.

The congratulation of summer is that it can make the homely and the humble if not exactly beautiful, beautifully acceptable. Such brightness at midday and then the benign pastels, blues and pinks and lavenders of the summer sky. Much may wither and exhaust, but so great is the glow and greater the freedom of the season that every extreme will be accommodated. There are great gardens filled with jewels as precious as those dug out of the earth and then the hand that planted the sparse petunias and impatiens in the window box—there's that, too.

I remember days from the summers in the upper South and sights from certain towns in the Middle West, in Ohio and Indiana, places just passed through long ago. There's something touching about the summer streets of middle-size towns: everything a bit worn down in July, all slow and somnolent except for the supersonic hummingbird in the browning hydrangea bush at the edge of the porch. The disaster of the repetitive but solid architecture of the 1920s—once perceived as quite an accomplishment of ownership, and suitable—comfortable according to what was possible.

The front porches. That unalterable, dominating, front-face mistake left over from the time before the absolute, unconditional surrender to the automobile and to traffic. There was a time when not everyone had a car, and to children then the traffic was interesting. The brand names, the out-of-state license plates—a primitive pleasure to take note of them, like stamping your palm at the sight of a white horse. And the family on the front porch, watching the life of the street.

This porch in front and so unsightly and useless and awful in the winter with the gray of the splintered planks and the soggy sag of the furniture often left out to hibernate in public view. The old eyesores, defining the houses, many of them spacious, with gables, and bits of colored glass from a catalogue over the door, in a fan shape. If nothing else, summer redeems the dismal overhang of the porch, for a few months, and even the darkened halls and parlors within might be glad of an escape from the heat.

Somewhere there is water. Not too far away there will be an abandoned quarry, difficult to climb into and cold as a lake in Nova Scotia. There will be a stream or a river, not very deep and muddy at the banks—Middle Western water.

If there are no neighbors to be seen on the streets, they can be seen and heard at the back, there on the patio where tubs standing on tripods and filled with charcoal lumps are ready to receive marinated bits of flesh. There is pleasure in all this, in the smoke, in the luscious brown of the chicken leg—on your own little plot where you fed the chickadee last winter.

These scenes, local as the unearned wildflower, the goldenrod with its harsh cinnamon scent, are not splendid. Little of the charm of the ocean view and the table set with blue linen, and the delectable salmon, so well designed for painterly display, laid out on a platter among scattered stems of watercress. Still the American town streets—those angling off the main drag seen on the way to the airport—are a landscape of the American summer. And why should we groan with pain at the sight of the plastic flamingo on the lawn or the dead whiteness of the large inflated duck coming into its decorative own nowadays? There's not much else to buy downtown, for one thing.

These things remind me of those elders who used to go abroad every summer to the same pension, to dusty interiors and dining rooms where the wine bottle with your name on it returned every night to the table until it was empty. Perhaps in Florence or outside Siena or in the north, to the band concert in the park by a German lake.

In Russian fiction people go off to the Crimea and sigh, how dull it is here. But since there is to be a plot, the scene is not to be so dull after all. In the salon, with the violin whining and the fish overcooked, the same faces take up their posts for the same complaints and posturings. Then someone new appears to the defensive snubs of the old-timers or to the guarded curiosity of the bored. It might be a sulky young girl with a chaperone or her mother; or a woman, not a girl, to be seated on the same side of the room as the tall man from Moscow, away from his family for two weeks and subject to dreaming. And it begins to begin . . .

Summer romance—when the two words are brought together, each takes on a swift linguistic undercurrent. As a phrase, it is something akin to "summer soldier"—the romance carries away and the summer soldier runs away from duty or from the reality of things. Heaven is something with a girl in summer: a line of Robert Lowell's. The summer romance will have the sharpness and sweetness and the indescribable wonder of the native strawberry, raspberry, blueberry, and toward the end the somewhat gritty cling of the late blackberry.

The sun-filled romance is the dramatic background of much fiction. There is the accident of the meeting and the unreasonable heightening of the season. And classically there is often an imbalance in the lovers, an imbalance of class or situation, hard, chilly truths swept away by the soft clouds, the fields and the urgency of the burst-open water lilies.

Edith Wharton wrote a short novel called *Summer*. In it you will find a love affair between a pretty and poor young girl from the New England hills and a clever young man from the city who likes to study the old houses of the region. As always, he is alone, happily solitary, idling about in the sunshine, and she is there, as she has always been. In the way of these sudden romances everything before and ahead seems to fade. Of course, it is not to last, at least not to last for the young man who, as it turns out, is engaged to someone of his own sort . . . and so on.

Tess of the D'Urbervilles: "Rays from the sunrise drew forth the buds and stretched them in long stalks, lifted up sap in noiseless streams, opened petals, and sucked out scents in invisible jets and breathings." This is the summer landscape that engulfs Tess and Angel Clare and finally leads to a despair of such magnitude only the genius of Thomas Hardy could imagine it and embody it in the changing seasons and the changing structure of the English countryside.

In Chekhov's story "The Lady with the Dog," the lady and the man are both married. They meet in Yalta in the summer and the romance flows along on a pitiless tide, without any possible ending except misery. When they believe the love will at last end or the devastation will have a solution, the final line says no, "it was only just beginning."

So in spite of the meadows and the picnic under the shade of the copper beech tree, the days will grow longer and there will again be buying and selling and coming and going elsewhere. The romantic ritual of the season fades, even if it will be staged again next summer with other lovers in other places. The freedom of the summer remains in the memory.

In the mountains, there you feel free . . . Yes. Under Mount Monadnock in New Hampshire—a storm of stars in the heavens, a pattern of gorgeous gleaming dots on the dark blue silk of the sky, all spreading down like a huge soft cloak to the edge of the field.

The mountains are perhaps not quite in such demand as they once were in summer. Too lonely and overwhelming, the pleasures offered no longer quite suitable to the extraordinary energies of those who rush to the long, long expressways on a Friday afternoon—flat roads ahead, and yet they mean getting there. The weekend, commuting distance, breads and cheeses and bottles of wine, Vivaldi on the cassette, and a lot of work to be done and gladly.

Impatience with the division of city and country, or what is more or less "country," has changed the heart of the seasons. Many face a February weekend as if it were July. There is a need for an eternal summer, some mutant need created by the demand for nature, for weekend nature, even as nature disappears along the route.

Eternal summer, kind only as a metaphor. Night is the winter of the tropics, as the saying has it. On the equator the days are twelve hours long. Withering rivers and unrelenting lassitude in the never-ending summertime. In Bombay in January, blissful for the citizens, but to those accustomed to the temperate sections of the United States, the heat of January in India spreads around like an infamous August swelter.

The gardens, the terraces, the flowers in vases. The first peas, the lettuce out of the ground, the always too greatly abundant zucchini—and at last a genuine tomato. No doubt the taste for these has grown sharper from the fact that we have them all year round in an inauthentic condition of preservation. Where the memory is never allowed to subside, according to each thing in its time, the true taste is more astonishing. One of summer's intensifications. Very much like actually swimming or sailing after the presence of the sea or lake known only as a view.

Summer, the season of crops. The concreteness of it. Not as perfumed and delicate and sudden as spring and not as *triste* as autumn. Yet for the enjoyment of summer's pleasures, for the beach, the crowded airplane to Venice, most of us consent to work all year long.

QUESTIONS FOR CRITICAL ANALYSIS

1. Describe the ways you reacted to Hardwick's prose. What is her purpose in this essay? What response does she expect from a reader?
2. Where does Hardwick get her ideas about summers in previous eras? What family stories have you been told about summers your grandparents and others knew? Compare those summers with your own summers.
3. Look carefully at Hardwick's remarks about the architecture and lifestyle in small and mid-sized American towns. How does she describe these places? What is her attitude toward them? How do you know? Do you agree with her comments?
4. How did your recognition of the art and literature Hardwick mentions—or your lack

of recognition—affect your reading of the essay? Describe how summer plays a critical role in other novels, stories, works of art, or movies.

5. According to Hardwick, what has changed about summer? How has it changed? Do you agree with her? Why, or why not?

QUESTIONS FOR STRUCTURAL ANALYSIS

1. Look at the words Hardwick uses to describe summer: "high, candid, definite," "downright;" it "slithers" out of spring and "edges toward" autumn. At one point she talks about "the congratulation of summer." Why does she use these words to describe summer? What feelings do they evoke? Describe Hardwick's feelings about summer.
2. After describing summer as seen in works of art, Hardwick begins the next sections with the words: "I like to remember," "I remember," "These things remind me." How does this device affect her relationship with the reader? How do her memories affect her remarks about summer?
3. Chart the progression of ideas about summer. At what point does the essay shift from purely descriptive to analytical? What other rhetorical devices does she use? What other topics does Hardwick examine along with summer?
4. How does Hardwick relate the visual images of place to the passing years?
5. Describe the ways Hardwick echoes the introduction in her conclusion.

*L*OOK AT *N*ATURE

TOPICS FOR WRITING ESSAYS

Many of the questions following each essay can serve as appropriate writing suggestions. The topics listed below expand the prereading exercises, but they can be used without completing that step first.

1. How would you characterize the people who live in your town (or state, or region)? In what ways does the town itself, the *place*, affect the type of people who live there? If it's appropriate, use your prereading exercises to provide focus to an essay telling someone who has never been to your town what it is like, what the people are like who live there, and how the town and people reflect each other.

2. The classic writing assignment: Describe your favorite summer. Use descriptive details (many will come from the Updike prereading exercise) as well as narrative techniques to make the reader wish she or he had been with you (or not been with you). Write your essay for publication in the pre-summer issue of the campus magazine.

3. The ideas you wrote during the White prereading exercise can serve as a basis for an essay exploring what time means. Like White, use an event to help explain your ideas. (It's often easier, when you're writing about an abstract subject, to hook it into a concrete world.) Address your essay to general readers of a popular magazine.

4. Compare Updike's vision of summer with Hardwick's. Be sure to consider their sense of audience and purpose, their use of descriptive details, their use of illustrations and examples. When you write your comparison, express your opinions about the essays and support your point of view with specific references. Write your essay for a writing instructor.

RESEARCH POSSIBILITY

Follow the model provided by Gretel Ehrlich and conduct research about a place that means a lot to you. Find out about its history, interview people who have lived there for a long time, discover statistics about the place. Then combine these facts and statistics with your own experiences and feelings and write an essay that creates a definite "feel" of the place for a reader who has never been there.

SEE THE WORLD THROUGH ART

The artists who wrote these essays define art and photography in terms of their passion for their work. Because they use words to provide almost a verbal alternative to their art, they require work from their readers. To enjoy Beckmann, Calder, and de Kooning's essays fully, you should try to spend on hour or two at a library or museum looking at their work.

JOHN SZARKOWSKI, "THE PHOTOGRAPHER'S EYE"

MAX BECKMANN, "ON MY PAINTING"

ALEXANDER CALDER, "WHAT ABSTRACT ART MEANS TO ME"

WILLEM DE KOONING, "WHAT ABSTRACT ART MEANS TO ME"

*T*HE *P*HOTOGRAPHER'S *E*YE

JOHN SZARKOWSKI

John Szarkowski (1925–), director of the Department of Photography at the Museum of Modern Art in New York City since 1962, has been instrumental in elevating photography to an accepted art form. This essay, published as the introduction to The Photographer's Eye *(1980), a collection of photographs, examines the history of the public's response to photography and its position now in the art world. According to Szarkowski, photography takes a subject out of context; it focuses on a small image, creating relationships that may not be present outside the photograph itself. Photography has no past or present; it is "now."*

Before you begin reading: *Study a photograph of a familiar object: is it real? is it fact? is it truth? Write a paragraph in your reading notebook about how the photograph both obscures and reveals reality.*

◆

THE INVENTION OF PHOTOGRAPHY PROVIDED A RADICALLY new picture-making process—a process based not on synthesis but on selection. The difference was a basic one. Paintings were *made*—constructed from a storehouse of traditional schemes and skills and attitudes—but photographs, as the man on the street put it, were *taken*.

The difference raised a creative issue of a new order: how could this mechanical and mindless process be made to produce pictures meaningful in human terms—pictures with clarity and coherence and a point of view? It was soon demonstrated that an answer would not be found by those who loved too much the old forms, for in large part the photographer was bereft of the old artistic traditions. Speaking of photography Baudelaire said: "This industry, by invading the territories of art, has become art's most mortal enemy."[1] And in his own terms of reference Baudelaire was half right; certainly the new medium could not satisfy old standards. The photographer must find new ways to make his meaning clear.

These new ways might be found by men who could abandon their allegiance to traditional pictorial standards—or by the artistically ignorant, who had no old allegiances to break. There have been many of the latter sort. Since its earliest days, photography has been practiced by thousands who shared no common tradition or training, who were disciplined and united by no academy or guild, who considered their medium variously as a science, an art, a trade, or an entertainment, and who were often unaware of each other's work. Those who invented photography were scientists and painters, but its professional practitioners were a very different lot. Hawthorne's daguerreotypist hero Holgrave in *The House of the Seven Gables* was perhaps not far from typical:

"Though now but twenty-two years old, he had already been a country schoolmaster; salesman in a country store; and the political editor of a country newspaper. He had subsequently travelled as a peddler of cologne water and other essences. He had studied and practiced dentistry. Still more recently he had been a public lecturer on mesmerism, for which science he had very remarkable endowments. His present phase as a daguerreotypist was of no more importance in his own view, nor likely to be more permanent, than any of the preceding ones."[2]

The enormous popularity of the new medium produced professionals by the thousands—converted silversmiths, tinkers, druggists, blacksmiths and printers. If photography was a new artistic problem, such men had the advantage of having nothing to unlearn. Among them they produced a flood of images. In 1853 the *New York Daily Tribune* estimated that three million daguerreotypes were being produced that year.[3] Some of these pictures were the product of knowledge and skill and sensibility and invention; many were the product of accident, improvisation, misunderstanding, and empirical experiment. But whether produced by art or by luck, each picture was part of a massive assault on our traditional habits of seeing.

By the latter decades of the nineteenth century the professionals and the serious amateurs were joined by an even larger host of casual snapshooters. By the early eighties the dry plate, which could be purchased ready-to-use, had replaced the refractory and messy wet plate process, which demanded that the plate be prepared just before exposure and processed before its emulsion had dried. The dry plate spawned the hand camera and the snapshot. Photography had become easy. In 1893 an English writer complained that the new situation had "created an army of photographers who run rampant over the globe, photographing objects of all sorts, sizes and shapes, under almost every condition, without ever pausing to ask themselves, is this or that artistic? . . . They spy a view, it seems to please, the camera is focused, the shot taken! There is no pause, why should there be? For art may err but nature cannot miss, says the poet, and they listen to the dictum. To them, composition, light, shade, form and texture are so many catch phrases. . . ."[4]

These pictures, taken by the thousands by journeyman worker and Sunday hobbyist, were unlike any pictures before them. The variety of their imagery was prodigious. Each subtle variation in viewpoint or light, each passing moment, each change in the tonality of the print, created a new picture. The trained artist could draw a head or a hand from a dozen perspectives. The photographer discovered that the gestures of a hand were infinitely various, and that the wall of a building in the sun was never twice the same.

Most of this deluge of pictures seemed formless and accidental, but some achieved coherence, even in their strangeness. Some of the new images were memorable, and seemed significant beyond their limited intention. These remembered pictures enlarged one's sense of possibilities as he looked again at the real world. While they were remembered they survived, like organisms, to reproduce and evolve.

But it was not only the way that photography described things that was new; it was also the things it chose to describe. Photographers shot ". . . objects of all sorts, sizes and shapes . . . without ever pausing to ask themselves, is this or that artistic?" Painting was difficult, expensive, and precious, and it recorded what was known to be important. Photography was easy, cheap and ubiquitous, and it recorded anything: shop windows and sod houses and family pets and steam engines and unimportant people. And once made objective and permanent, immortalized in a picture, these trivial things took on importance. By the end of the century, for the first time in history, even the poor man knew what his ancestors had looked like.

The photographer learned in two ways: first, from a worker's intimate understanding of his tools and materials (if his plate would not record the clouds, he could point his camera down and eliminate the sky); and second he learned from other photographs, which presented themselves in an unending stream. Whether his concern was commercial or artistic, his tradition was formed by all the photographs that had impressed themselves upon his consciousness.

The pictures reproduced in this book were made over almost a century and a quarter. They were made for various reasons, by men of different concerns and varying talent. They have in fact little in common except their success, and a shared vocabulary: these pictures are unmistakably photographs. The vision they share belongs to no school or aesthetic theory, but to photography itself. The character of this vision was discovered by photographers at work, as their awareness of photography's potentials grew.

If this is true, it should be possible to consider the history of the medium in terms of photographers' progressive awareness of characteristics and problems that have seemed inherent in the medium. Five such issues are considered below. These issues *do not* define discrete categories of work; on the contrary they should be regarded as interdependent aspects of a single problem—as section views through the body of photographic tradition. As such, it is hoped that they may contribute to the formulation of a vocabulary and a critical perspective more fully responsive to the unique phenomena of photography.

THE THING ITSELF

The first thing that the photographer learned was that photography dealt with the actual; he had not only to accept this fact, but to treasure it; unless he did, photography would defeat him. He learned that the world itself is an artist of incomparable inventiveness, and that to recognize its best works and moments, to anticipate them, to clarify them and make them permanent, requires intelligence both acute and supple.

But he learned also that the factuality of his pictures, no matter how convincing and unarguable, was a different thing than the reality itself. Much of the reality was filtered out in the static little black and white image, and some of it was exhibited with an unnatural clarity, an exaggerated importance. The subject and the picture were not the same thing, although they would afterwards seem so. It was the photographer's problem to see not simply the reality before him but the still invisible picture, and to make his choices in terms of the latter.

This was an artistic problem, not a scientific one, but the public believed that the photograph could not lie, and it was easier for the photographer if he believed it too, or pretended to. Thus he was likely to claim that what our eyes saw was an illusion, and what the camera saw was the truth. Hawthorne's Holgrave, speaking of a difficult portrait subject said: "We give [heaven's broad and simple sunshine] credit only for depicting the merest surface, but it actually brings out the secret character with a truth that no painter would ever venture upon, even could he detect it. . . . the remarkable point is that the original wears, to the world's eye . . . an exceedingly pleasant countenance, indicative of benevolence, openness of heart, sunny good humor, and other praiseworthy qualities of that cast. The sun, as you see, tells quite another story, and will not be coaxed out of it, after half a dozen patient attempts on my part. Here we have a man, sly, subtle, hard, imperious, and withal, cold as ice."[5]

In a sense Holgrave was right in giving more credence to the camera image than to his own eyes, for the image would survive the subject, and become the remembered reality. William M. Ivins, Jr. said "at any given moment the accepted report of an event is of greater importance than the event, for what we think about and act upon is the symbolic report and not the concrete event itself."[6] He also said: "The nineteenth century began by believing that what was reasonable was true and it would end up by believing that what it saw a photograph of was true."[7]

THE DETAIL

The photographer was tied to the facts of things, and it was his problem to force the facts to tell the truth. He could not, outside the studio, pose the truth; he could only record it as he found it, and it was found in nature in a fragmented and unexplained form—not as a story, but as scattered and suggestive clues. The photographer could not assemble these clues into a coherent narrative, he could only isolate the fragment, document it, and by so doing claim for it some special significance, a meaning which went beyond simple description. The compelling clarity with which a photograph recorded the trivial suggested that the subject had never before been properly seen, that it was in fact perhaps *not* trivial, but filled with undiscovered meaning. If photographs could not be read as stories, they could be read as symbols.

The decline of narrative painting in the past century has been ascribed in large part to the rise of photography, which "relieved" the painter of the necessity of story telling. This is curious, since photography has never been successful at narrative. It has in fact seldom attempted it. The elaborate nineteenth century montages of Robinson and Rejlander, laboriously pieced together from several posed negatives, attempted to tell stories, but these works were recognized in their own time as pretentious failures. In the early days of the picture magazines the attempt was made to achieve narrative through photographic sequences, but the superficial coherence of these stories was generally achieved at the expense of photographic discovery. The heroic documentation of the American Civil War by the Brady group, and the incomparably larger photographic record of the Second World War, have this in common: neither explained, without extensive captioning, what was happening. The function of these pictures was not to make the story clear, it was to make it *real*. The great war photographer Robert Capa expressed both the narrative poverty and the symbolic power of photography when he said, "If your pictures aren't good, you're not close enough."

THE FRAME

Since the photographer's picture was not conceived but selected, his subject was never truly discrete, never wholly self-contained. The edges of his film demarcated what he thought most important, but the subject he had shot was something else; it had extended in four directions. If the photographer's frame surrounded two figures, isolating them from the crowd in which they stood, it created a relationship between those two figures that had not existed before.

The central act of photography, the act of choosing and eliminating, forces a concentration on the picture edge—the line that separates in from out—and on the shapes that are created by it.

During the first half-century of photography's lifetime, photographs were printed the same size as the exposed plate. Since enlarging was generally impractical, the photographer could not change his mind in the darkroom, and decide to use only a fragment of his picture, without reducing its size accordingly. If he had purchased an eight by ten inch plate (or worse, prepared it), had carried it as part of his back-bending load, and had processed it, he was not likely to settle for a picture half that size. A sense of simple economy was enough to make the photographer try to fill the picture to its edges.

The edges of the picture were seldom neat. Parts of figures or buildings or features of landscape were truncated, leaving a shape belonging not to the subject, but (if the picture was a good one) to the balance, the propriety, of the image. The photographer looked at the world as though it was a scroll painting, unrolled from hand to hand, exhibiting an infinite number of croppings—of compositions—as the frame moved onwards.

The sense of the picture's edge as a cropping device is one of the qualities of form that most interested the inventive painters of the latter nineteenth century. To what degree this awareness came from photography, and to what degree from oriental art, is still open to study. However, it is possible that the prevalence of the photographic image helped prepare the ground for an appreciation of the Japanese print, and also that the compositional attitudes of these prints owed much to habits of seeing which stemmed from the scroll tradition.

TIME

There is in fact no such thing as an instantaneous photograph. All photographs are time exposures, of shorter or longer duration, and each describes a discrete parcel of time. This time is always the present. Uniquely in the history of pictures, a photograph describes only that period of time in which it was made. Photography alludes to the past and the future only in so far as they exist in the present, the past through its surviving relics, the future through prophecy visible in the present.

In the days of slow films and slow lenses, photographs described a time segment of several seconds or more. If the subject moved, images resulted that had never been seen before: dogs with two heads and a sheaf of tails, faces without features, transparent men, spreading their diluted substance half across the plate. The fact that these pictures were considered (at best) as partial failures is less interesting than the fact that they were produced in quantity; they were familiar to all photographers, and to all customers who had posed with squirming babies for family portraits.

It is surprising that the prevalence of these radical images has not been of interest to art historians. The time-lapse painting of Duchamp and Balla, done before the First World War, has been compared to work done by the photographers such as Edgerton and Mili, who worked consciously with similar ideas a quarter-century later, but the accidental time-lapse photographs of the nineteenth century have been ignored—presumably *because* they were accidental.

As photographic materials were made more sensitive, and lenses and shutters faster, photography turned to the exploration of rapidly moving subjects. Just as the eye is incapable of registering the single frames of a motion picture projected on the screen at the rate of twenty-four per second, so is it incapable of following the positions of a rapidly moving subject in life. The galloping horse is the classic example. As lovingly drawn countless thousands of times by Greeks and Egyptians and Persians and Chinese, and down through all the battle scenes and sporting prints of Christendom, the horse ran with four feet extended, like a fugitive from a carousel. Not till Muybridge successfully photographed a galloping horse in 1878 was the convention broken. It was this way also with the flight of birds, the play of muscles on an athlete's back, the drape of a pedestrian's clothing, and the fugitive expressions of a human face.

Immobilizing these thin slices of time has been a source of continuing fascination for the photographer. And while pursuing this experiment he discovered something else: he discovered that there was a pleasure and a beauty in this fragmenting of time that had little to do with what was happening. It had to do rather with seeing the momentary patterning of lines and shapes that had been previously concealed within the flux of movement. Cartier-Bresson defined his commitment to this new beauty with the phrase *The decisive moment*, but the phrase has been misunderstood; the thing that happens at the decisive moment is not a dramatic climax but a visual one. The result is not a story but a picture.

VANTAGE POINT

Much has been said about the clarity of photography, but little has been said about its obscurity. And yet it is photography that has taught us to see from the unexpected vantage point, and has shown us pictures that give the sense of the scene, while withholding its narrative meaning. Photographers from necessity choose from the options available to them, and often this means pictures from the other side of the proscenium, showing the actors' backs, pictures from the bird's view, or the worm's, or pictures in which the subject is distorted by extreme foreshortening, or by none, or by an unfamiliar pattern of light, or by a seeming ambiguity of action or gesture.

Ivins wrote with rare perception of the effect that such pictures had on nineteenth-century eyes: "At first the public had talked a great deal about what it called photographic distortion. . . . [But] it was not long before men began to think photographically, and thus to see for themselves things that it had previously taken the photograph to reveal to their astonished and protesting eyes. Just as nature had once imitated art, so now it began to imitate the picture made by the camera."[8]

After a century and a quarter, photography's ability to challenge and reject our schematized notions of reality is still fresh. In his monograph on Francis Bacon, Lawrence Alloway speaks of the effect of photography on that painter: "The evasive nature of his imagery, which is shocking but obscure, like accident or atrocity photographs, is arrived at by using photography's huge repertory of visual images. . . . Uncaptioned news photographs, for instance, often appear as momentous and extraordinary. . . . Bacon used this property of photography to subvert the clarity of pose of figures in traditional painting."[9]

The influence of photography on modern painters (and on modern writers) has been great and inestimable. It is, strangely, easier to forget that photography has also influenced photographers. Not only great pictures by great photographers, but *photography*—the great undifferentiated, homogeneous whole of it—has been teacher, library, and laboratory for those who have consciously used the camera as artists. An artist is a man who seeks new structures in which to order and simplify his sense of the reality of life. For the artist photographer, much of his sense of reality (where his picture starts) and much of his sense of craft or structure (where his picture is completed) are anonymous and untraceable gifts from photography itself.

The history of photography has been less a journey than a growth. Its movement has not been linear and consecutive, but centrifugal. Photography, and our understanding of it, has spread from a center; it has, by infusion, penetrated our consciousness. Like an organism, photography was born whole. It is in our progressive discovery of it that its history lies.

NOTES

1. Charles Baudelaire, "Salon de 1859," translated by Jonathan Mayne for *The Mirror of Art, Critical Studies by Charles Baudelaire*. London: Phaidon Press, 1955. (Quoted from *On Photography, A Source Book of Photo History in Facsimile,* edited by Beaumont Newhall. Watkins Glen, N.Y.: Century House, 1956, p. 106.)
2. Nathaniel Hawthorne, *The House of the Seven Gables*. New York: Signet Classics edition, 1961, pp. 156–7.
3. A. C. Willers, "Poet and Photography," in *Picturescope*, Vol. XI, No. 4. New York: Picture Division, Special Libraries Association, 1963, p. 46.
4. E. E. Cohen, "Bad Form in Photography," in *The International Annual of Anthony's Photographic Bulletin*. New York and London: E. and H. T. Anthony, 1893, p. 18.
5. Hawthorne, op. cit., p. 85.
6. William M. Ivins, Jr., *Prints and Visual Communication*. Cambridge, Mass.: Harvard University Press, 1953, p. 180.
7. Ibid., p. 94.
8. Ibid., p. 138.
9. Lawrence Alloway, *Francis Bacon*. New York: Solomon R. Guggenheim Foundation, 1963, p. 22.

QUESTIONS FOR CRITICAL ANALYSIS

1. According to Szarkowski, what is the major difference between painting and photography? Why is it a critical difference?

2. What effect did its enormous popularity have on photography? How did this popularity influence its acceptance as art? Do you think photography is, in fact, art? Why, or why not?

3. What is the relationship between an object and a photograph of an object? What makes an image "unmistakably [a] photograph"? How does a photographer transform an object?

4. What does Szarkowski mean when he says: "The photographer was tied to the facts of things, and it was his problem to force the facts to tell the truth." How could facts *not* tell the truth? What does this mean about the role of the photographer? How is the photograph different from reality? different from truth?
5. According to Szarkowski, the function of great war photographers is not to make the story clear but to make it real. Look at some war photographs: pictures in *Life, Look, Time* or some other magazine on Vietnam, Korea, the Second World War, or in books about a war. Do you agree with Szarkowski after looking at these photographs? In what ways do these photographs serve as symbols rather than stories? What do you bring to the photographs when you look at them?

QUESTIONS FOR STRUCTURAL ANALYSIS

1. How is Szarkowski's theme presented in the first two paragraphs? Can you tell by these paragraphs what his point of view might be? How?
2. Look at the way Szarkowski uses direct quotes in his essay. How does he introduce them into his essay? What function do these quotes serve? Are all of them useful? effective?
3. Compare Szarkowski's use of direct quotes to his paraphrased material. Why did he choose to paraphrase some of his research?
4. How do you react to the way Szarkowski organized his essay? Do the headings seem useful or obtrusive? Why? How would you characterize his approach to this subject?
5. Szarkowski concludes his essay by saying: "The history of photography has been less a journey than a growth." What does he mean? Has he developed his ideas to support this conclusion? Do you agree with him?

On *My Painting*

Max Beckmann

Max Beckmann (1884–1950), a German expressionist painter, describes his work as an attempt to get to "the idea which hides itself behind so-called reality." The events of the First World War changed Beckmann's earlier artistic conservatism, and he began to paint works that revealed "brutally expressive images of physical and psychological mutilation, emphasized by tension between forms and space." Beckmann's "On My Painting," originally given as a lecture in 1938 at the New Burlington Galleries in London, is less an explanation than it is a verbal extension of his artistic vision.

Before you begin reading: *Reread the headnote. What do the quoted phrases mean? What kinds of images do they evoke for you? Write a paragraph describing the types of paintings you suppose Beckmann created, based on this description. Take your notebook with you to the library and look at some reproductions of Beckmann's work. Underneath the first paragraph, write your reactions to Beckmann's paintings.*

◆

BEFORE I BEGIN TO GIVE YOU AN EXPLANATION, AN EXPLAnation which it is nearly impossible to give, I would like to emphasize that I have never been politically active in any way. I have only tried to realize my conception of the world as intensely as possible.

Painting is a very difficult thing. It absorbs the whole man, body and soul—thus I have passed blindly many things which belong to real and political life.

I assume, though, that there are two worlds: the world of spiritual life and the world of political reality. Both are manifestations of life which may sometimes coincide but are very different in principle. I must leave it to you to decide which is the more important.

What I want to show in my work is the idea which hides itself behind so-called reality. I am seeking for the bridge which leads from the visible to the invisible, like the famous cabalist who once said: "If you wish to get hold of the invisible you must penetrate as deeply as possible into the visible."

My aim is always to get hold of the magic of reality and to transfer this reality into painting—to make the invisible visible through reality. It may sound paradoxical, but it is, in fact, reality which forms the mystery of our existence.

What helps me most in this task is the penetration of space. Height, width, and depth are the three phenomena which I must transfer into one plane to form the abstract surface of the picture, and thus to protect myself from the infinity of space. My figures come and go, suggested by fortune or misfortune. I try to fix them divested of their apparent accidental quality.

One of my problems is to find the Self, which has only one form and is immortal—to find it in animals and men, in the heaven and in the hell which together form the world in which we live.

Space, and space again, is the infinite deity which surrounds us and in which we are ourselves contained.

That is what I try to express through painting, a function different from poetry and music but, for me, predestined necessity.

When spiritual, metaphysical, material, or immaterial events come into my life, I can only fix them by way of painting. It is not the subject which matters but the translation of the subject into the abstraction of the surface by means of painting. Therefore I hardly need to abstract things, for each object is unreal enough already, so unreal that I can only make it real by means of painting.

Often, very often, I am alone. My studio in Amsterdam, an enormous old tobacco storeroom, is again filled in my imagination with figures from the old days and from the new, like an ocean moved by storm and sun and always present in my thoughts.

Then shapes become beings and seem comprehensible to me in the great void and uncertainty of the space which I call God.

Sometimes I am helped by the constructive rhythm of the Cabala, when my thoughts wander over Oannes Dagon to the last days of drowned continents. Of the same substance are the streets with their men, women, and children; great ladies and whores; servant girls and duchesses. I seem to meet them, like doubly significant dreams, in Samothrace and Piccadilly and Wall Street. They are Eros and the longing for oblivion.

All these things come to me in black and white like virtue and crime. Yes, black and white are the two elements which concern me. It is my fortune, or misfortune, that I can see neither all in black nor all in white. One vision alone would be much simpler and clearer, but then it would not exist. It is the dream of many to see only the white and truly beautiful, or the black, ugly and destructive. But I cannot help realizing both, for only in the two, only in black and in white, can I see God as a unity creating again and again a great and eternally changing terrestrial drama.

Thus without wanting it, I have advanced from principle to form, to transcendental ideas, a field which is not at all mine, but in spite of this I am not ashamed.

In my opinion all important things in art since Ur of the Chaldees, since Tel Halaf and Crete, have always originated from the deepest feeling about the mystery of Being. Self-realization is the urge of all objective spirits. It is this Self for which I am searching in my life and in my art.

Art is creative for the sake of realization, not for amusement; for transfiguration, not for the sake of play. It is the quest of our Self that drives us along the eternal and never-ending journey we must all make.

My form of expression is painting; there are, of course, other means to this end such as literature, philosophy, or music; but as a painter, cursed or blessed with a terrible and vital sensuousness, I must look for wisdom with my eyes. I repeat, with my eyes, for nothing could be more ridiculous or irrelevant than a "philosophical conception" painted purely intellectually without the terrible fury of the senses grasping each visible form of beauty and ugliness. If from those forms which I have found in the visible, literary subjects result—such as portraits, landscapes, or recognizable compositions—they have all originated from the senses, in this case from the eyes, and each intellectual subject has been transformed again into form, color, and space.

Everything intellectual and transcendent is joined together in painting by the uninterrupted labor of the eyes. Each shade of a flower, a face, a tree, a fruit, a sea, a mountain, is noted eagerly by the intensity of the senses to which is added, in a way of which I am not conscious, the work of my mind, and in the end the strength or weakness of *my soul*. It is this genuine, eternally unchanging center of strength which makes mind and sense capable of expressing personal things. It is the strength of the soul which forces the mind to constant exercise to widen its conception of space.

Something of this is perhaps contained in my pictures.

Life is difficult, as perhaps everyone knows by now. It is to escape from these difficulties that I practice the pleasant profession of a painter. I admit that there are more lucrative ways of escaping the so-called difficulties of life, but I allow myself my own particular luxury, painting.

It is, of course, a luxury to create art and, on top of this, to insist on expressing one's own artistic opinion. Nothing is more luxurious than this. It is a game and a good game, at least for me; one of the few games which make life, difficult and depressing as it is sometimes, a little more interesting.

Love in an animal sense is an illness, but a necessity which one has to overcome. Politics is an odd game, not without danger I have been told, but certainly sometimes amusing. To eat and to drink are habits not to be despised but often connected with unfortunate consequences. To sail around the earth in 91 hours must be very strenuous, like racing in cars or splitting the atoms. But the most exhausting thing of all—is boredom.

So let me take part in your boredom and in your dreams while you take part in mine which may be yours as well.

To begin with, there has been enough talk about art. After all, it must always be unsatisfactory to try to express one's deeds in words. Still we shall go on and on, talking and painting and making music, boring ourselves, exciting ourselves, making war and peace as long as our strength of imagination lasts.

Imagination is perhaps the most decisive characteristic of mankind. My dream is the imagination of space—to change the optical impression of the world of objects by a transcendental arithmetic progression of the inner being. That is the precept. In principle any alteration of the object is allowed which has a sufficiently strong creative power behind it. Whether such alteration causes excitement or boredom in the spectator is for you to decide.

The uniform application of a principle of form is what rules me in the imaginative alteration of an object. One thing is sure—we have to transform the three-dimensional world of objects into the two-dimensional world of the canvas.

If the canvas is only filled with a two-dimensional conception of space, we shall have applied art, or ornament. Certainly this may give us pleasure, though I myself find it boring as it does not give me enough visual sensation. To transform height, width, and depth into two dimensions is for me an experience full of magic in which I glimpse for a moment that fourth dimension which my whole being is seeking.

I have always on principle been against the artist speaking about himself or his work. Today neither vanity nor ambition causes me to talk about matters which generally are not to be expressed even to oneself. But the world is in such a catastrophic state, and art is so bewildered, that I, who have lived the last thirty years almost as a hermit, am forced to leave my snail's shell to express these few ideas which, with much labor, I have come to understand in the course of the years.

The greatest danger which threatens mankind is collectivism. Everywhere attempts are being made to lower the happiness and the way of living of mankind to the level of termites. I am against these attempts with all the strength of my being.

The individual representation of the object, treated sympathetically or antipathetically, is highly necessary and is an enrichment to the world of form. The elimination of the human relationship in artistic representation causes the vacuum which makes all of us suffer in various degrees—an individual alteration of the details of the object represented is necessary in order to display on the canvas the whole physical reality.

Human sympathy and understanding must be reinstated. There are many ways and means to achieve this. Light serves me to a considerable extent on the one hand to divide the surface of the canvas, on the other to penetrate the object deeply.

As we still do not know what this Self really is, this Self in which you and I in our various ways are expressed, we must peer deeper and deeper into its discovery. For the Self is the great veiled mystery of the world. Hume and Herbert Spencer studied its various conceptions but were not able in the end to discover the truth. I believe in it and in its eternal, immutable form. Its path is, in some strange and peculiar manner, our path. And for this reason I am immersed in the phenomenon of the Individual, the so-called whole Individual, and I try in every way to explain and present it. What are you? What am I? Those are the questions that constantly persecute and torment me and perhaps also play some part in my art.

Color, as the strange and magnificent expression of the inscrutable spectrum of Eternity, is beautiful and important to me as a painter; I use it to enrich the canvas and to probe more deeply into the object. Color also decided, to a certain extent, my spiritual outlook, but it is subordinated to light and, above all, to the treatment of form. Too much emphasis on color at the expense of form and space would make a double manifestation of itself on the canvas, and this would verge on craft work. Pure colors and broken tones must be used together, because they are the complements of each other.

These, however, are all theories, and words are too insignificant to define the problems of art. My first unformed impression, and what I would like to achieve, I can perhaps only realize when I am impelled as in a vision.

One of my figures, perhaps one from the "Temptation," sang this strange song to me one night—

> Fill up again your pumpkins with alcohol, and hand up the largest of them to me. . . . Solemn, I will light the giant candles for you. Now in the night. In the deep black night.
>
> We are playing hide-and-seek, we are playing hide-and-seek across a thousand seas. We gods, we gods when the skies are red at dawn, at midday, and in the blackest night.
>
> You cannot see us, no you cannot see us but you are ourselves. . . . Therefore we laugh so gaily when the skies are red at dawn, at midday, and in the blackest night.
>
> Stars are our eyes and the nebulae our beards. . . . We have people's souls for our hearts. We hide ourselves and you cannot see us, which is just what we want when the skies are red at dawn, at midday, and in the blackest night.
>
> Our torches stretch away without end . . . silver, glowing red, purple, violet, green-blue, and black. We bear them in our dance over the seas and the mountains, across the boredom of life.
>
> We sleep and stars circle in the gloomy dream. We wake and the suns assemble for the dance across bankers and fools, whores and duchesses.

Thus the figure from my "Temptation" sang to me for a long time, trying to escape from the square on the hypotenuse in order to achieve a particular constellation of the Hebrides, to the Red Giants and the Central Sun.

And then I awoke and yet continued to dream . . . painting constantly appeared to me as the one and only possible achievement. I thought of my grand old friend Henri Rousseau, that Homer in the porter's lodge whose prehistoric dreams have sometimes brought me near the gods. I saluted him in my dream. Near him I saw William Blake, noble emanation of English genius. He waved friendly greetings to me like a super-terrestrial patriarch. "Have confidence in objects," he said, "do not let yourself be intimidated by the horror of the world. Everything is ordered and correct and must fulfil its destiny in order to attain perfection. Seek this path and you will attain from your own Self ever deeper perception of the eternal beauty of creation; you will attain increasing release from all that which now seems to you sad or terrible."

I awoke and found myself in Holland in the midst of a boundless world turmoil. But my belief in the final release and absolution of all things, whether they please or torment, was newly strengthened. Peacefully I laid my head among the pillows . . . to sleep, and dream, again.

QUESTIONS FOR CRITICAL ANALYSIS

1. Beckmann says his art has so consumed his life that he has no time for politics. How does that statement strike you? He delivered his speech in 1938. Do you think he should have tried to understand what was going on and respond to world events? What is a citizen's responsibility?
2. What is the aim of Beckmann's painting? How does he hope to achieve this? Have you ever seen any of his work? (If not, go look him up in the library or museum.) Do you think he was successful at accomplishing his aim? Why, or why not?
3. What does Beckmann mean when he says that it is "reality which forms the mystery of our existence"? Do you agree? Does he explain what he means? How?
4. How does Beckmann explain the artist's responsibility to paint what he sees? How does he define the relationship between the senses and the mind?
5. What does Beckmann see as the greatest danger to mankind? In the context of 1938, what is he referring to? How does he plan to stand against it? What does he want you to do about it?

QUESTIONS FOR STRUCTURAL ANALYSIS

1. From the first paragraph, it is clear that "On My Painting" is a speech. How can you tell?

2. Does Beckmann provide a clear explanation of why he paints? If you had attended this lecture, how would you feel when you left? Why? Write a paragraph to a friend explaining what Beckmann said.
3. What indication do you have that Beckmann's approach to art is essentially religious? In what way is it religious?
4. Beckmann seems to shift his subject in paragraph 21, beginning with the sentence "Life is difficult, as perhaps everyone knows by now." Why does he include the next three paragraphs in this speech? What is their relationship to the rest of the speech? How do you respond to his statements? Which one do you like/dislike the most?
5. Why did Beckmann include the poem from one of his figures? How does this poem echo the themes of the essay? How does it illuminate the essay?

*W*HAT *A*BSTRACT *A*RT *M*EANS TO *M*E

ALEXANDER CALDER

Alexander Calder (1898–1976) graduated from Stevens Institute of Technology as a mechanical engineer in 1919 and by 1922 had begun taking his art work seriously. In 1930 Calder experimented with manual and motorized mobiles and began using motion as an integral element in his art, as important as color and form. This essay, written especially for the Bulletin of the Museum of Modern Art, *is, like his art, an approximation of a definition. By describing how he puts his mobiles together, how he sees and what he feels about the shapes, he "defines" abstract art—leaving it to the reader to make the necessary connections.*

Before you begin reading: *Have you ever seen a mobile? What is the most striking feature of mobiles? What do you like best about them? In your reading notebook make a list of descriptive words and phrases that evoke the feeling and sight of mobiles.*

◆

MY ENTRANCE INTO THE FIELD OF ABSTRACT ART came about as the result of a visit to the studio of Piet Mondrian in Paris in 1930.

I was particularly impressed by some rectangles of color he had tacked on his wall in a pattern after his nature.

I told him I would like to make them oscillate—he objected. I went home and tried to paint abstractly—but in two weeks I was back again among plastic materials.

I think that at that time and practically ever since, the underlying sense of form in my work has been the system of the Universe, or part thereof. For that is a rather large model to work from.

What I mean is that the idea of detached bodies floating in space, of different sizes and densities, perhaps of different colors and temperatures, and surrounded and interlarded with wisps of gaseous condition, and some at rest, while others move in peculiar manners, seems to me the ideal source of form.

I would have them deployed, some nearer together and some at immense distances.

And great disparity among all the qualities of these bodies, and their motions as well.

A very exciting moment for me was at the planetarium—when the machine was run fast for the purpose of explaining its operation: a planet moved along a straight line, then suddenly made a complete loop of 360° off to one side, and then went off in a straight line in its original direction.

I have chiefly limited myself to the use of black and white as being the most disparate colors. Red is the color most opposed to both of these—and then, finally, the other primaries. The secondary colors and intermediate shades serve only to confuse and muddle the distinctness and clarity.

When I have used spheres and discs, I have intended that they should represent more than what they just are. More or less as the earth is a sphere, but also has some miles of gas about it, volcanoes upon it, and the moon making circles around it, and as the sun is a sphere—but also is a source of intense heat, the effect of which is felt at great distances. A ball of wood or a disc of metal is rather a dull object without this sense of something emanating from it.

When I use two circles of wire intersecting at right angles, this to me is a sphere—and when I use two or more sheets of metal cut into shapes and mounted at angles to each other, I feel that there is a solid form, perhaps concave, perhaps convex, filling in the dihedral angles between them. I do not have a definite idea of what this would be like, I merely sense it and occupy myself with the shapes one actually sees.

Then there is the idea of an object floating—not supported—the use of a very long thread, or a long arm in cantilever as a means of support seems to best approximate this freedom from the earth.

Thus what I produce is not precisely what I have in mind—but a sort of sketch, a man-made approximation.

That others grasp what I have in mind seems unessential, at least as long as they have something else in theirs.*

*Questions for this article appear after the following selection.

*W*hat *A*bstract *A*rt *M*eans to *M*e

Willem de Kooning

Willem de Kooning (1904–) came to New York City from Holland in 1926 and was instrumental in creating what is known as American Abstract Expressionism. De Kooning influenced other artists through his emphasis on the relationship defining the placement of each object on the canvas and the space containing the object. In this essay de Kooning defines abstract art in part by discussing this relationship between word, idea, and object. De Kooning's essay, which appeared in the same issue of the Bulletin of the Museum of Modern Art *as did Calder's essay, presents a more theoretical and historical definition of abstract art.*

Before you begin reading: *Think about what the term "abstract art" means. Write a paragraph or two in your notebook describing what comes to mind when you consider abstract art.*

◆

THE FIRST MAN WHO BEGAN TO SPEAK, WHOEVER HE WAS, must have intended it. For surely it is talking that has put "Art" into painting. Nothing is positive about art except that it is a word. Right from there to here all art became literary. We are not yet living in a world where everything is self-evident. It is very interesting to notice that a lot of people who want to take the talking out of painting, for instance, do nothing else but talk about it. That is no contradiction, however. The art in it is the forever mute part you can talk about forever.

For me, only one point comes into my field of vision. This narrow, biased point gets very clear sometimes. I didn't invent it. It was already here. Everything that passes me I can see only a little of, but I am always looking. And I see an awful lot sometimes.

The word "abstract" comes from the lighttower of the philosophers, and it seems to be one of their spotlights that they have particularly focussed on "Art." So the artist is always lighted up by it. As soon as it—I mean the "abstract"—comes into painting, it ceases to be what it is as it is written. It changes into a feeling which could be explained by some other words, probably. But one day, some painter used "Abstraction" as a title for one of his paintings. It was a still life. And it was a very tricky title. And it wasn't really a very good one. From then on the idea of abstraction became something extra. Immediately it gave some people the idea that they could free art from itself. Until then, Art meant everything that was in it—not what you could take out of it. There was only one thing you could take out of it sometime when you were in the right mood—that abstract and indefinable sensation, the esthetic part—and still leave it where it was. For the painter to come to the "abstract" or the "nothing," he needed many things. Those things were always things in life—a horse, a flower, a milkmaid, the light in a room through a window made of diamond shapes maybe, tables, chairs, and so forth. The painter, it is true, was not always completely free. The things were not always of his own choice, but because of that he often got some new ideas. Some painters liked to paint things already chosen by others, and after being abstract about them, were called Classicists. Others wanted to select the things themselves and, after being abstract about them, were called Romanticists. Of course, they got mixed up with one another a lot too. Anyhow, at that time, they were not abstract about something which was already abstract. They freed the shapes, the light, the color, the space, by putting them into concrete things in a given situation. They *did* think about the possibility that the things—the horse, the chair, the man—were abstractions, but they let that go, because if they kept thinking about it, they would have been led to give up painting altogether, and would probably have ended up in the philosopher's tower. When they got those strange, deep ideas, they got rid of them by painting a particular smile on one of the faces in the picture they were working on.

The esthetics of painting were always in a state of development parallel to the development of painting itself. They influenced each other and vice versa. But all of a sudden, in that famous turn of the century, a few people thought they could take the bull by the horns and invent an esthetic beforehand. After immediately disagreeing with each other, they began to form all kinds of groups, each with the idea of freeing art, and each demanding that you should obey them. Most of these theories have finally dwindled away into politics or strange forms of spiritualism. The question, as they saw it, was not so much what you *could* paint but rather what you could *not* paint. You could *not* paint a house or a tree or a mountain. It was then that subject matter came into existence as something you ought *not* to have.

In the old days, when artists were very much wanted, if they got to thinking about their usefulness in the world, it could only lead them to believe that painting was too worldly an occupation and some of them went to church instead or stood in front of it and begged. So what was considered too worldly from a spiritual point of view then, became later—for those who were inventing the new esthetics—a spiritual smoke-screen and not worldly enough. These latter-day artists were bothered by their apparent uselessness. Nobody really seemed to pay any attention to them. And they did not trust that freedom of indifference.

They knew that they were relatively freer than ever before *because* of that indifference, but in spite of all their talking about freeing art, they really didn't mean it that way. Freedom to them meant to be useful in society. And that is really a wonderful idea. To achieve that, they didn't need *things* like tables and chairs or a horse. They needed ideas instead, social ideas, to make their objects with, their constructions—the "pure plastic phenomena"—which were used to illustrate their convictions. Their point was that until they came along with their theories, Man's own form in space—his body—was a private prison; and that it was because of this imprisoning misery—because he was hungry and overworked and went to a horrid place called home late at night in the rain, and his bones ached and his head was heavy—because of this very consciousness of his own body, this sense of pathos, they suggest, he was overcome by the drama of a crucifixion in a painting or the lyricism of a group of people sitting quietly around a table drinking wine. In other words, these estheticians proposed that people had up to now understood painting in terms of their own private misery. Their own sentiment of form instead was one of comfort. The beauty of comfort. The great curve of a bridge was beautiful because people could go across the river in comfort. To compose with curves like that, and angles, and make works of art with them could only make people happy, they maintained, for the only association was one of comfort. That millions of people have died in war since then, because of that idea of comfort, is something else.

This pure form of comfort became the comfort of "pure form." The "nothing" part in a painting until then—the part that was not painted but that was there because of the things in the picture which were painted—had a lot of descriptive labels attached to it like "beauty," "lyric," "form," "profound," "space," "expression," "classic," "feeling," "epic," "romantic," "pure," "balance," etc. Anyhow that "nothing" which was always recognized as a particular something—and as something particular—they generalized, with their bookkeeping minds, into circles and squares. They had the innocent idea that the "something" existed "in spite of" and not "because of" and that this something was the only thing that truly mattered. They had hold of it, they thought, once and for all. But this idea made them go backward in spite of the fact that they wanted to go forward. That "something" which was not measurable, they lost by trying to make it measurable; and thus all the old words which, according to their ideas, ought to be done away with got into art again: pure, supreme, balance, sensitivity, etc.

Kandinsky understood "Form" as *a* form, like an object in the real world; and an object, he said, was a narrative—and so, of course, he disapproved of it. He wanted his "music without words." He wanted to be "simple as a child." He intended, with his "inner-self," to rid himself of "philosophical barricades" (he sat down and wrote something about all this). But in turn his own writing has become a philosophical barricade, even if it is a barricade full of holes. It offers a kind of Middle-European idea of Buddhism or, anyhow, something too theosophic for me.

The sentiment of the Futurists was simpler. No space. Everything ought to keep on going! That's probably the reason they went themselves. Either a man was a machine or else a sacrifice to make machines with.

The moral attitude of Neo-Plasticism is very much like that of Constructivism, except that the Constructivists wanted to bring things out in the open and the Neo-Plasticists didn't want anything left over.

I have learned a lot from all of them and they have confused me plenty too. One thing is certain, they didn't give me my natural aptitude for drawing. I am completely weary of their ideas now.

The only way I still think of these ideas is in terms of the individual artists who came from them or invented them. I still think that Boccioni was a great artist and a passionate man. I like Lissitzky, Rodchenko, Tatlin and Gabo; and I admire some of Kandinsky's painting very much. But Mondrian, that great merciless artist, is the only one who had nothing left over.

The point they all had in common was to be both inside and outside at the same time. A new kind of likeness! The likeness of the group instinct. All that it has produced is more glass and an hysteria for new materials which you can look through. A symptom of love-sickness, I guess. For me, to be inside and outside is to be in an unheated studio with broken windows in the winter, or taking a nap on somebody's porch in the summer.

Spiritually I am wherever my spirit allows me to be, and that is not necessarily in the future. I have no nostalgia, however. If I am confronted with one of those small Mesopotamian figures, I have no nostalgia for it but, instead, I may get into a state of anxiety. Art never seems to make me peaceful or pure. I always seem to be wrapped in the melodrama of vulgarity. I do not think of inside or outside—or of art in general—as a situation of comfort. I know there is a terrific idea there somewhere, but whenever I want to get into it, I get a feeling of apathy and want to lie down and go to sleep. Some painters, including myself, do not care what chair they are sitting on. It does not even have to be a comfortable one. They are too nervous to find out where they ought to sit. They do not want to "sit in style." Rather, they have found that painting—any kind of painting, any style of painting—to be painting at all, in fact—is a way of living today, a style of living, so to speak. That is where the form of it lies. It is exactly in its uselessness that it is free. Those artists do not want to conform. They only want to be inspired.

The group instinct could be a good idea, but there is always some little dictator who wants to make his instinct the group instinct. There *is* no style of painting now. There are as many naturalists among the abstract painters as there are abstract painters in the so-called subject-matter school.

The argument often used that science is really abstract, and that painting could be like music and, for this reason, that you cannot paint a man leaning against a lamp-post, is utterly ridiculous. That space of science—the space of the physicists—I am truly bored with by now. Their lenses are so thick that seen through them, the space gets more and more melancholy. There seems to be no end to the misery of the scientists' space. All that it contains is billions and billions of hunks of matter, hot or cold, floating around in darkness according to a great design of aimlessness. The stars *I* think about, if I could fly, I could reach in a few old-fashioned days. But physicists' stars I use as buttons, buttoning up curtains of emptiness. If I stretch my arms next to the rest of myself and wonder where my fingers are—that is all the space I need as a painter.

Today, some people think that the light of the atom bomb will change the concept of painting once and for all. The eyes that actually saw the light melted out of sheer ecstasy. For one instant, everybody was the same color. It made angels out of everybody. A truly Christian light, painful but forgiving.

Personally, I do not need a movement. What was given to me, I take for granted. Of all movements, I like Cubism most. It had that wonderful unsure atmosphere of reflection—a poetic frame where something could be possible, where an artist could practice his intuition. It didn't want to get rid of what went before. Instead it added something to it. The parts that I can appreciate in other movements came out of Cubism. Cubism *became* a movement, it didn't set out to be one. It has force in it, but it was no "force-movement." And then there is that one-man movement, Marcel Duchamp—for me a truly modern movement because it implies that each artist can do what he thinks he ought to—a movement for each person and open for everybody.

If I *do* paint abstract art, that's what abstract art means to me. I frankly do not understand the question. About twenty-four years ago, I knew a man in Hoboken, a German who used to visit us in the Dutch Seamen's Home. As far as he could remember, he was always hungry in Europe. He found a place in Hoboken where bread was sold a few days old—all kinds of bread: French bread, German bread, Italian bread, Dutch bread, Greek bread, American bread and particularly Russian black bread. He bought big stacks of it for very little money, and let it get good and hard and then he crumpled it and spread it on the floor in his flat and walked on it as on a soft carpet. I lost sight of him, but found out many years later that one of the other fellows met him again around 86th street. He had become some kind of a Jugend Bund leader and took boys and girls to Bear Mountain on Sundays. He is still alive but quite old and is now a Communist. I could never figure him out, but now when I think of him, all that I can remember is that he had a very abstract look on his face.

QUESTIONS FOR CRITICAL ANALYSIS

1. How does Calder define what abstract art means to him? How does de Kooning respond to the same question? Which answer do you prefer? Why? What are the strengths and weaknesses of each answer?
2. What does de Kooning mean when he says: "it is talking that put 'Art' in painting"? Do you agree with him? Would Calder agree? Beckmann? Why, or why not?

3. What does *abstract* mean? How does the term "abstract art" expand the definition? What do you mean when you say "abstract art"?
4. Calder's final sentence states that he doesn't care whether anyone understands his art or not. Do you believe him? What does his statement reveal about his opinion of art as a form of communication? How does Calder's conclusion relate to de Kooning's discussion in paragraph five about the freedom of art? What's your opinion about this?
5. In paragraph 15 de Kooning takes on the physicists and their concept of space. Do you agree with de Kooning's assessment? Why? How does de Kooning's paragraph compare with the type of physics described by the Sagan and Bush essays in Part 3?

QUESTIONS FOR STRUCTURAL ANALYSIS

1. Most of Calder's paragraphs are one-sentence long; some are even made of sentence fragments. Does his writing remind you of his art? In what ways? Is his writing style effective? How?
2. De Kooning emphasizes the relationship between language and painting, and considers the term "abstract" at some length. What did you learn by this discussion? Do you agree with him?
3. In what ways are de Kooning's ideas similar to Beckmann's? What does each one think of "philosophy of art" or "schools of art"?
4. Is de Kooning's concluding paragraph a surprise? Why? What does the story of the man in Hoboken have to do with the rest of the essay? Why did de Kooning end with this story?
5. Based on the essays in this section, do you think artists write clearly? Do they develop ideas fully? Were these essays easy to read? Why, or why not?

SEE THE *WORLD* *THROUGH* *ART*

TOPICS FOR WRITING ESSAYS

Many of the questions following each essay can serve as appropriate writing suggestions. The topics listed below expand the prereading exercises, but they can be used without completing that step first.

1. Write about Beckmann, de Kooning, or Calder to discuss how the artist's work illustrates points he made in his essay. Look carefully at reproductions or examples of their art to include details about your responses to their work, and expand the exercise to include your responses to their essay as well. Write your essay to a reader who has not seen the art work of the artist and who must rely on your description.
2. How does an artist or photographer make an object or event *real*? How does he or she make it *visible*? Use Beckmann and Szarkowski as sources in your paper about the artist's job of presenting objects to us. Write your paper to a reader who thinks the whole idea of an artist making a physical object real doesn't make any sense.
3. What do you think the artist's responsibility is to political events? Should they record the horrors of war (as Picasso did in "Guernica") or ignore the events in their work? Do your ideas coincide or differ from the essayists? How? Write an essay in which you argue for or against an artist's social responsibility.

RESEARCH POSSIBILITIES

1. Look at photographs about a war or historical event. Read some articles and commentary about the event. Then write an essay examining the photographer's rendition of the event: What reality do they show that words cannot, or how is their record of the event different from the verbal one?
2. What is the purpose of art? Use a single work of art to answer the question. You may want to discuss why the artist created the piece, how the audience responded to it, what your feelings are toward it. Include a vivid description of the piece of art in your essay written to an audience that appreciates art but may not know the single work you selected.

*T*he *R*ole of the *A*rtist

What is art? And what is the artist trying to accomplish by creating works of art? Does the artist and/or the work of art have any responsibility to society? The three writers in this section examine these questions and come up with remarkably similar answers: The artist must look at the world clearly, express its reality uncompromisingly, and help the public experience the same feeling of discovery.

*T*HE *A*RTIST AND THE *W*ORLD

JOYCE CARY

Joyce Cary (1888–1957) is best known as the novelist of colonial Africa and English social history. Cary's early training as an artist served in his depiction of a painter's life in The Horse's Mouth *(1944), his best known work. In "The Artist and the World," Cary describes the moment when an artist, whether visual or verbal, discovers "a truth" about the world and strives to recreate the feeling of that discovery for his audience.*

Before you begin reading: *Look carefully at an object as if you had never seen it before. List words or phrases that make that object real to you. Using your list of words or phrases, write a description of the object that will make your reader experience the same reaction you had toward it.*

◆

THIS IS AN ATTEMPT TO EXAMINE THE RELATION OF THE artist with the world as it seems to him, and to see what he does with it. That is to say, on the one side with what is called the artist's intuition, on the other with his production, or the work of art.

My only title to discuss the matter is some practical knowledge of two arts. I know very little about aesthetic philosophy, so I shall try, as far as possible, to speak from practical experience.

It is quite true that the artist, painter, writer or composer starts always with an experience that is a kind of discovery. He comes upon it with the sense of a discovery; in fact, it is truer to say that it comes upon *him* as a discovery. It surprises him. This is what is usually called an intuition or an inspiration. It carries with it always the feeling of directness. For instance, you go walking in the fields and all at once they strike you in quite a new aspect: you find it extraordinary that they should be like that. This is what happened to Monet as a young man. He suddenly saw the fields, not as solid flat objects covered with grass or useful crops and dotted with trees, but as colour in astonishing variety and subtlety of gradation. And this gave him a delightful and quite new pleasure. It was a most exciting discovery, especially as it was a discovery of something real. I mean, by that, something independent of Monet himself. That, of course, was half the pleasure. Monet had discovered a truth about the actual world.

This delight in discovery of something new in or about the world is a natural and primitive thing. All children have it. And it often continues until the age of twenty or twenty-five, *even* throughout life.

Children's pleasure in exploring the world, long before they can speak, is very obvious. They spend almost all their time at it. We don't speak of their intuition, but it is the same thing as the intuition of the artist. That is to say, it is direct knowledge of the world as it is, direct acquaintance with things, with characters, with appearance, and this is the primary knowledge of the artist and writer. This joy of discovery is his starting point.

Croce, probably the most interesting of the aesthetic philosophers, says that art is simply intuition. But he says, too, that intuition and expression are the same thing. His idea is that we can't know what we have intuited until we have named it, or given it a formal character, and this action is essentially the work of art.

But this is not at all the way it seems to an artist or a writer. To him, the intuition is quite a different thing from the work of art. For the essential thing about the work of art is that it is work, and very hard work too. To go back to the painter. He has had his intuition, he has made his discovery, he is eager to explore it, to reveal it, to fix it down. For, at least in a grown, an educated man, intuitions are highly evanescent. This is what Wordsworth meant when he wrote of their fading into the light of common day.

I said the joy of discovery often dies away after twenty years or so. And this is simply a truth of observation; we know it from our own experience. The magic object that started up before our eyes on a spring day in its own individual shape, is apt, in the same instant, to turn into simply another cherry tree, an ordinary specimen of a common class. We have seen it and named it pretty often already. But Housman, as poet, fixed his vision of the cherry tree before it had changed into just another tree in blossom.

Housman fixed it for himself and us, but not by an immediate act, indistinguishable from the intuition. He had to go to work and find words, images, rhyme, which embodied his feeling about the tree, which fixed down its meaning for him, so that he could have it again when he wanted it, and also give it to us. He made a work of art, but he made it by work.

So for the painter, when he has his new, his magic landscape in front of him; he has to fix it down. And at once he is up against enormous difficulties. He has only his paints and brushes, and a flat piece of canvas with which to convey a sensation, a feeling, about a three-dimensional world. He has somehow to translate an intuition from real objects into a formal and ideal arrangement of colours and shapes, which will still, mysteriously, fix and convey his sense of the unique quality, the magic of these objects in their own private existence. That is to say, he has a job that requires thought, skill, and a lot of experience.

As for the novelist, his case is even worse. He starts also with his intuition, his discovery; as when Conrad, in an Eastern port, saw a young officer come out from a trial, in which he had been found guilty of a cowardly desertion of his ship and its passengers after a collision. The young man had lost his honour and Conrad realised all at once what that meant to him, and he wrote *Lord Jim* to fix and communicate that discovery in its full force.

For that he had to invent characters, descriptions, a plot. All these details, as with the painter, had to enforce the impression, the feeling that he wanted to convey. The reader had to *feel*, at the end of the tale, 'That is important, that is true'. It's no good if he says, 'I suppose that is true, but I've heard it before'. In that case Conrad has failed, at least with that reader. For his object was to give the reader the same discovery, to make him feel what it meant to that young man to lose his honour, and how important honour is to men.

And to get this sharp and strong feeling, the reader must not be confused by side issues. All the scenes and characters, all the events in the book, must contribute to the total effect, the total meaning. The book must give the sense of an actual world with real characters. Otherwise they won't engage the reader's sympathy, his feelings will never be concerned at all.

But actual life is not like that, it doesn't have a total meaning, it is simply a wild confusion of events from which we have to select what we think significant for ourselves. Look at any morning paper. It makes no sense at all—it means nothing but chaos. We read only what we think important; that is to say, we provide our own sense to the news. We have to do so because otherwise it wouldn't be there. To do this, we have to have some standard of valuation, we have to know whether the political event is more important than a murder, or a divorce than the stock market, or the stock market than who won the Derby.

The writer, in short, has to find some meaning in life before he gives it to us in a book. And his subjectmatter is much more confused than that of a painter. Of course, in this respect, everyone is in the same boat. Everyone, not only the writer, is presented with the same chaos, and is obliged to form his own idea of the world, of what matters and what doesn't matter. He has to do it, from earliest childhood, for his own safety. And if he gets it wrong, if his idea does not accord with reality, he will suffer for it. A friend of mine, as a child, thought he could fly, and jumped off the roof. Luckily he came down in a flower-bed and only broke a leg.

This seems to contradict what I said just now about the chaos which stands before us every morning. For the boy who failed to fly did not suffer only from bad luck. He affronted a law of gravity, a permanent part of a reality objective to him. As we know very well, underneath the chaos of events, there are laws, or if you like consistencies, both of fact and feeling. What science calls matter, that is to say, certain fixed characteristics of being, presents us with a whole framework of reality which we defy at our peril. Wrong ideas about gravity or the wholesomeness of prussic acid are always fatal.

So, too, human nature and its social relations present certain constants. Asylums and gaols are full of people who have forgotten or ignored them. On the other hand, we can still comprehend and enjoy palaeolithic art and Homer. Homer's heroes had the same kind of nature as our own.

These human constants are also a part of reality objective to us, that is, a permanent character of the world as we know it. So we have a reality consisting of permanent and highly obstinate facts, and permanent and highly obstinate human nature. And human nature is always in conflict with material facts, although men are themselves most curious combinations of fact and feeling, and actually require the machinery of their organism to realise their emotions, their desires and ambitions. Though the ghost could not exist without the machine which is at once its material form, its servant, its limitation, its perfection and its traitor, it is always trying to get more power over it, to change it.

Men have in fact obtained more power over matter, but to change it is impossible. It may be said that all works of art, all ideas of life, all philosophies are 'As if,' but I am suggesting that they can be checked with an objective reality. They might be called propositions for truth and their truth can be decided by their correspondence with the real. Man can't change the elemental characters. If you could, the world would probably vanish into nothing. But because of their very permanence, you can assemble them into new forms. You can build new houses with the bricks they used for the oldest Rome, because they are still bricks. For bricks that could stop being bricks at will would be no good to the architect. And a heart that stopped beating at its own will would be no good to the artist. The creative soul needs the machine, as the living world needs a fixed character, or it could not exist at all. It would be merely an idea. But by a paradox we have to accept, part of this fixed character is the free mind, the creative imagination, in everlasting conflict with facts, including its own machinery, its own tools.

QUESTIONS FOR CRITICAL ANALYSIS

1. According to Cary, what is the starting point of art? Do you remember experiencing the type of sensation he describes? In what context?
2. How does Croce (as Cary paraphrases him) describe the relationship between intuition and expression? Why does Cary differ with this analysis? (Who is Croce? When did he live? Why is he a reliable reference?)
3. How does the "joy of discovery" disappear? Consider the personal example you thought of in response to Question number 1 above. How do you respond to that object or event now? What makes the experience different?
4. Why does Cary emphasize the work involved in writing and painting? What is the artist's task, and what makes it so difficult?
5. In what ways is everyone faced with the same job as the artist? How does the artist's job differ?

Questions for Structural Analysis

1. How do you respond to Cary's first two paragraphs? What is his purpose in beginning the essay like this?
2. Cary says that he intends to "examine the relation of the artist with the world." Write a list of ways Cary says the artist relates to the world. What evidence does he give to support each of these?
3. What does Cary expect of his reader? Did you feel uncomfortable by his suppositions? by his references to artists and works? Which references did you recognize? Which ones could you figure out by the context of the essay?
4. How is meaning ascribed to objects and events? Is this the sole responsibility of the artist? How do you bring meaning to the world?
5. What does Cary mean by his conclusion? Paraphrase his final paragraph for a person who has not read the essay.

*T*HE *A*RTIST AND *S*OCIETY

WILLIAM GASS

William Gass (1924–   ), a philosopher and author, reveals his love for language and formalism through both his fiction and his essays. For Gass, the relationship between a writer and the work is sensual, like that between a woman and her lover, and the relationship must be based on reality. In "The Artist and Society" Gass examines the public's desire to rob both the artist and the work of reality through denying its existence or by changing its appearance. An artist must use honesty, unity, awareness, and other virtues to bring life to the work.

Before you begin reading: *Think of a story or poem you have read which moved you. Do you think it was "honest"? Write an explanation of why that story or poem touched you.*

◆

THE TAME BEAR'S NO BETTER OFF THAN WE ARE. YOU'VE seen how he sways in his cage. At first you might think him musical, but the staves are metal, and his movements are regular and even like the pulses of a pump. It's his nerves. Even when he claps his paws, rises like a man to his hind feet and full height, he looks awkward, feels strange, unsure (his private parts and underbelly are exposed); he trembles. Smiling (you remember the fawning eyeshine of the bear), he focuses his nose and waits for the marshmallow we're about to toss, alert to snap up the sweet cotton in his jaws. There's something terrible about the tame caged bear . . . all that wildness become marshmallow, terrible for his heart, his liver, his teeth (a diet so sugary and soft and unsubstantial, the bowels seek some new employment), and terrible for us—for what we've lost. His eyes, too, are filled with a movement that's not in the things he sees, but in himself. It is the movement of his own despair, his ineffectual rage.

My subject is the artist and society, not the tamed, trained bear, but in many ways the subjects are the same. Artists are as different as men are. It would be wrong to romanticize about them. In our society, indeed, they may live in narrower and more frightened corners than most of us do. We should not imitate their ways; they're not exemplary, and set no worthy fashions. Nor does the artist bear truth dead and drooping in his arms like a lovelorn maiden or a plump goose. His mouth hasn't the proper shape for prophecies. Pot or bottle ends or words or other mouths—whole catalogs of kissing—noisy singing, the folds of funny faces he's created and erased, an excess of bugling have spoiled it for philosophy. In the ancient quarrel between the poets and philosophers, Plato was surely right to think the poets liars. They lie quite roundly, unashamedly, with glee and gusto, since lies and fancies, figments and inventions, outrageous falsehoods are frequently more real, more emotionally pure, more continuously satisfying to them than the truth, which is likely to wear a vest, fancy bucket pudding, technicolor movies, and long snoozes through Sunday.

W. H. Auden remarked quite recently, when pestered, I think it was, about Vietnam:

> Why writers should be canvassed for their opinion on controversal political issues I cannot imagine. Their views have no more authority than those of any reasonably well-educated citizen. Indeed, when read in bulk, the statements made by writers, including the greatest, would seem to indicate that literary talent and political common sense are rarely found together. . . .

Israel makes war, and there are no symposia published by prizefighters, no pronouncements from hairdressers, not a ding from the bellhops, from the dentists not even a drill's buzz, from the cabbies nary a horn beep, and from the bankers only the muffled chink of money. Composers, sculptors, painters, architects: they have no rolled-up magazine to megaphone themselves, and are, in consequence, ignored. But critics, poets, novelists, professors, journalists—those used to shooting off their mouths—they shoot (no danger, it's only their own mouth's wash they've wallowed their words in); and those used to print, they print; but neither wisdom nor goodwill nor magnanimity are the qualities which will win you your way to the rostrum . . . just plentiful friends in pushy places and a little verbal skill.

If it is pleasant to be thought an expert on croquet, imagine what bliss it is to be thought an authority on crime, on the clockwork of the human heart, the life of the city, peace and war. How hard to relinquish the certainty, which most of us have anyway, of *knowing*. How sweet it is always to be asked one's opinion. What a shame it is, when asked, not to have one.

Actually Auden's observation can be spread two ways: to include all artists, not writers merely, and to cover every topic not immediately related to their specialized and sometimes arcane talents. It's only the failed artist and his foolish public who would like to believe otherwise, for if they can honestly imagine that the purpose of art is to teach and to delight, to double the face of the world as though with a mirror, to penetrate those truths which nature is said to hold folded beneath her skirts and keeps modestly hidden from the eyes and paws of science, then they will be able to avoid art's actual impact altogether, and the artist's way of life can continue to seem outrageous, bohemian, quaint, a little sinful, irresponsible, hip, and charming, something to visit like the Breton peasants on a holiday, and not a challenge *to* and denial *of* their own manner of existence, an accusation concerning their own lack of reality.

Yet the social claims for art, and the interest normal people take in the lives of their artists, the examinations of the psychologists, the endless studies by endlessly energetic students of nearly everything, the theories of the philosophers, the deadly moral danger in which art is periodically presumed to place the young, unhappily married women, sacred institutions, tipsy souls, and unsteady parliaments, and all those nice persons in positions of power: these claims and interests are so regularly, so inevitably, so perfectly and purely irrelevant that one must begin to suspect that the tight-eyed, squeeze-eared, loin-lacking enemies of art are right; that in spite of everything that's reasonable, in spite of all the evidence, for example, that connoisseurs of yellowing marble statuary and greenish Roman coins are no more moral than the rest of us; that artists are a murky-headed, scurvy-living lot; that if art told the truth, truth must be polkadot; in spite, in short, of insuperable philosophical obstacles (and what obstacles, I ask you, could be more insuperable than those), art does tell us, in its manner, how to live, and artists are quite remarkable, even exemplary, men. We are right to keep them caged.

Thus I begin again, but this time on the other side.

Ronald Laing begins his extraordinary little book *The Politics of Experience*[1] by saying:

> Few books today are forgivable. Black on the canvas, silence on the screen, an empty white sheet of paper, are perhaps feasible. There is little conjunction of truth and social "reality." Around us are pseudo-events, to which we adjust with a false consciousness adapted to see these events as true and real, and even as beautiful. In the society of men the truth resides now less in what things are than in what they are not. Our social realities are so ugly if seen in the light of exiled truth, and beauty is almost no longer possible if it is not a lie.

You can measure the reality of an act, a man, an institution, custom, work of art in many ways: by the constancy and quality of its effects, the depth of the response which it demands, the kinds and range of values it possesses, the actuality of its presence in space and time, the multiplicity and reliability of the sensations it provides, its particularity and uniqueness on the one hand, its abstract generality on the other—I have no desire to legislate concerning these conditions, insist on them all.

We can rob these men, these acts and objects, of their reality by refusing to acknowledge them. We pass them on the street but do not see or speak. We have no Negro problem in our small Midwestern towns. If someone has the experience of such a problem, he is mistaken. What happened to him did not happen;

[1](New York: Pantheon, 1967).

what he felt he did not feel; the urges he has are not the urges he has; what he wants he does not want. Automatically I reply to my son, who has expressed his desire for bubble gum: Oh, Peppy, you don't want that. Number one, then: we deny. We nullify the consciousness of others. We make their experiences unreal.

Put yourself in a public place, at a banquet—one perhaps at which awards are made. Your fork is pushing crumbs about upon your plate while someone is receiving silver in a bowler's shape amid the social warmth of clapping hands. How would you feel if at this moment a beautiful lady in a soft pink nightie should lead among the tables a handsome poodle who puddled under them, and there was a conspiracy among the rest of us not to notice? Suppose we sat quietly; our expressions did not change; we looked straight through her, herself as well as nightie, toward the fascinating figure of the speaker; suppose, leaving, we stepped heedlessly in the pools, and afterward we did not even shake our shoes. And if you gave a cry, if you warned, explained, cajoled, implored; and we regarded you then with amazement, rejected with amusement, contempt, or scorn every one of your efforts, I think you would begin to doubt your senses and your very sanity. Well, that's the idea: with the weight of our numbers, our percentile normality, we create insanities: yours, as you progressively doubt more and more of your experience, hide it from others to avoid the shame, saying "There's that woman and her damn dog again," but now saying it silently, for your experience, you think, is private; and ours, as we begin to believe our own lies, and the lady and her nightie, the lady and her poodle, the lady and the poodle's puddles, all *do* disappear, expunged from consciousness like a stenographer's mistake.

If we don't deny, we mutilate, taking a part for the whole; or we rearrange things, exaggerating some, minimizing others. There was a lady, yes, but she was wearing a cocktail dress, and there was a dog, too, very small, and very quiet, who sat primly in her lap and made no awkward demonstrations. Or we invert values, and assume strange obligations, altogether neglecting the ones which are obvious and demanding: we rob the poor to give to the rich rich gifts, to kings their kingdoms, to congressmen bribes, to companies the inexpensive purchase of our lives. We rush to buy poodles with liquid nerves—it has become, like so much else, *the rage*. Teas are fun, we say, but necking's not nice. Imagine. We still *do* say that. Or we permit events to occur for some people but not for others. Women and children have no sexual drives; men don't either, thank god, after fifty—sixty? seventy-five? We discredit events by inserting in otherwise accurate accounts outrageous lies. It was the lady who made the mess, not the poodle. In short, we do what we can to destroy experience—our own and others'. But since we can only act according to the way we see things, "*if our experience is destroyed, our behavior will be destructive*." We live in ruins, in bombed-out shells, in the basements of our buildings. In important ways, we are all mad. You don't believe it? This company, community, this state, our land, is normal? Healthy, is it? Laing has observed that normal healthy men have killed perhaps one hundred million of their fellow normal healthy men in the last fifty years.

Nudists get used to nakedness. We get used to murder.

Why are works of art so socially important? Not for the messages they may contain, not because they expose slavery or cry hurrah for the worker, although such messages in their place and time might be important, but because they insist more than most on their own reality; because of the absolute way in which they exist. Certainly, images exist, shadows and reflections, fakes exist and hypocrites, there are counterfeits (quite real) and grand illusions—but it is simply not true that the copies are as real as their originals, that they meet all of the tests which I suggested earlier. Soybean steak, by god, is soybean steak, and a pious fraud is a fraud. Reality is not a matter of fact, it is an achievement; and it is rare—rarer, let me say—than an undefeated football season. We live, most of us, amidst lies, deceits, and confusions. A work of art may not utter the truth, but it must be honest. It may champion a cause we deplore, but like Milton's Satan, it must in itself be noble; it must be *all there*. Works of art confront us the way few people dare to: completely, openly, at once. They construct, they comprise, our experience; they do not deny or destroy it; and they shame us, we fall so short of the quality of their Being. We live in Lafayette or Rutland—true. We take our breaths. We fornicate and feed. But Hamlet has his history in the heart, and none of us will ever be as real, as vital, as complex and living as he is—a total creature of the stage.

This is a difficult point to make if the reality or unreality of things has not been felt. Have you met a typical nonperson lately? Then say hello, now, to your neighbor. He may be male, but his facial expressions have been put on like lipstick and eyelashes. His greeting is inevitable; so is his interest in the weather. He always smiles; he speaks only in clichés; and his opinions (as bland as Cream of Wheat, as undefined, and—when sugared—just as sweet) are drearily predictable. He has nothing but good to say of people; he collects his wisdom like dung from a Digest; he likes to share his experiences with "folks," and recite the plots of movies. He is working up this saccharine soulside manner as part of his preparation for the ministry.

These are the "good" people. "Bad" people are unreal in the same way.

Nonpersons unperson persons. They kill. For them no one is human. Like cash registers, everyone's the same, should be addressed, approached, the same: all will go ding and their cash drawers slide out when you strike the right key.

So I don't think that it's the message of a work of art that gives it any lasting social value. On the contrary, insisting on this replaces the work with its interpretation, another way of robbing it of its reality. How would you like to be replaced by your medical dossier, your analyst's notes? They take much less space in the file. The analogy, I think, is precise. The aim of the artist ought to be to bring into the world objects which do not already exist there, and objects which are especially worthy of love. We meet people, grow to know them slowly, settle on some to companion our life. Do we value our friends for their social status, because they are burning in the public blaze? do we ask of our mistress her meaning? calculate the usefulness of our husband or wife? Only too often.

Works of art are meant to be lived with and loved, and if we try to understand them, we should try to understand them as we try to understand anyone—in order to know *them* better, not in order to know something else.

Why do public officials, like those in the Soviet Union, object so strenuously to an art which has no images in it—which is wholly abstract, and says nothing? Because originals are dangerous to reproductions. For the same reason that a group of cosmetically constructed, teetotal lady-maidens is made uneasy by the addition of a boozy uncorseted madam. Because it is humiliating to be less interesting, less present, less moving, than an arrangement of enameled bedpans. Because, in a system of social relations based primarily on humbug, no real roaches must be permitted to wander. Because, though this may be simply my helpless optimism, your honest whore will outdraw, in the end, any sheaf you choose of dirty pictures.

Pornography is poor stuff, not because it promotes lascivious feelings, but because these feelings are released by and directed toward unreal things. The artist, in this sense, does not deal in dreams.

Of course there are many objects labeled works of art, I know, which are fakes—the paint, for instance, toupeed to the canvas—but I am thinking of the artist, now, as one who produces the honest article, and obviously, *he* is valuable to society if what he *produces* is valuable to it. He is presently valuable because in his shop or study he concocts amusements for our minds, foods for our souls—foods so purely spiritual and momentary they leave scarcely any stools. However, I wanted to say that despite the good reasons for wondering otherwise, the artist could be regarded an exemplary man—one whose ways are worthy of imitation. How can this be? The fellow sleeps with his models and paint jams the zipper on his trousers.

I think we can regard him as exemplary in this way: we judge it likely that a man's character will show up somewhere in his work; that if he is hot-tempered and impetuous, or reckless and gay . . . well, find somebody else to be your surgeon. And we regularly expect to see the imprint of the person in the deed, the body in the bedclothes. I think it is not unreasonable to suppose, too, that the work a man does works on him, that the brush he holds has his hand for its canvas, that the movements a man makes move the man who makes them just as much, and that the kind of ideals, dreams, perceptions, wishes his labor loves must, in him, love at least that labor.

Often enough we lead split lives, the artist as often as anybody; yet it isn't Dylan Thomas or D. H. Lawrence, the drunkard or sadist, I'm suggesting we admire, but the poets they were, and the men they had to be to be such poets. It would have been better if they had been able to assume in the world the virtues they possessed when they faced the page. They were unable. It's hard. And for that the world is partly to blame. It does not *want* its artists, after all. It especially does not want the virtues which artists must employ in the act of their work lifted out of prose and paint and plaster into life.

What are some of these virtues?

Honesty is one . . . the ability to see precisely what's been done . . . the ability to face up . . . because the artist wants his every line to be lovely—that's quite natural—he wants to think well of himself, and cover himself with his own praise like the sundae with its syrup. We all know that artists are vain. But they're not vain while working. We know, too, that they're defensive, insecure. But they dare not be defensive about a bad job, explain their mistakes away, substitute shouting for skill. If a runty tailor dresses himself in his dreams, he may measure for himself the suit of a wrestler. You can fill yourself with air, but will your skin hold it? They don't make balloons with the toughness and resiliency of genius.

Presence is one. The artist cannot create when out of focus. His is not another theatrical performance. There's no one to impress, no audience. He's lived with his work, doubtless, longer than he's had a wife, and it knows all about him in the thorough, hard-boiled way a wife knows. No poseur wrote "The Ballad of Reading Goal." Presence is a state of concentration on another so complete it leaves you quite without defenses, altogether open; for walls face both ways, as do the bars of a cage. Inquire of the bears how it is. To erect bars is to be behind them. Withholding is not a requirement of poetry.

Unity is another. The artist does not create with something special called imagination which he has and you haven't. He can create with his body because that body has become a mind; he can create with his feelings because they've turned into sensations. He thinks in roughness, loudness, and in color. A painter's hands are magnified eyes. He *is* those fingers—he becomes his medium—and as many fingers close simply in a single fist, so all our faculties can close, and hold everything in one clasp as the petals close in a rose or metal edges crimp.

Awareness is another. Honesty, concentration, unity of being: these allow, in the artist, the world to be *seen*—an unimaginable thing to most of us—to fully take in a tree, a tower, a hill, a graceful arm. If you've ever had an artist's eyes fall on you, you'll know what I mean. Only through such openings may the world pass to existence.

Sensuality is another. Painting and poetry (to name just two) are sexual acts. The artist is a lover, and he must woo his medium till she opens to him; until the richness in her rises to the surface like a blush. Could we adore one another the way the poet adores his words or the painter his colors—what would be the astonishing result?

Totality is still another. I mean that the artist dare not fail to see the whole when he sees with the whole of him. He sees the ant in the jam, yet the jam remains sweet. He must fall evenly on all sides, like a cloak. If he stops to sing a single feeling, he can do so well because he knows how feelings move; he knows the fish is offset from its shadow; knows the peck of the crow does not disturb the beauty of its beak or the dent it makes in the carrion. There is, it seems to me, in the works of the great, an inner measure, wound to beat, a balance which extends through the limbs like bones, an accurate and profound assessment of the proportion and value of things.

Naturally the artist is an enemy of the state. He cannot play politics, succumb to slogans and other simplifications, worship heroes, ally himself with any party, suck on some politician's program like a sweet. He is also an enemy of every ordinary revolution. As a man he may long for action; he may feel injustice like a burn; and certainly he may speak out. But the torn-up street is too simple for him when he sculpts or paints. He undermines everything. Even when, convinced of the rightness of a cause, he dedicates his skills to a movement, he cannot simplify, he cannot overlook, he cannot forget, omit, or falsify. In the end the movement must reject or even destroy him. The evidence of history is nearly unanimous on this point.

The artist's revolutionary activity is of a different kind. He is concerned with consciousness, and he makes his changes there. His inaction is only a blind, for his books and buildings go off under everything—not once but a thousand times. How often has Homer remade men's minds?

An uncorrupted consciousness . . . what a dangerous thing it is.

One could compile, I do not doubt, another list. These are examples, although central ones. I could so easily be wrong that no one's going to pay me any mind, and so I shall suggest most irresponsibly that we and our world might use more virtues of this kind—the artist's kind—for they are bound to the possibility of Being itself; and occasionally it strikes me as even almost tragic that there should be artists who were able, from concrete, speech, or metal, to release a brilliant life, who nevertheless could not release themselves, either from their own cage, or from ours . . . there is no difference. After all, we are—artists and society—both swaying bears *and* rigid bars. Again, it may be that the *bars* are moving, and the bears, in terror—stricken—are standing behind them . . . no, in front of them—among them—quite, quite still.

QUESTIONS FOR CRITICAL ANALYSIS

1. How does Gass compare the artist and the bear? What qualities of an artist does he describe? What do you think is Gass's attitude toward artists? Why do you give that answer?
2. Analyze the following sentence:

   It's only the failed artist and his foolish public who would like to believe otherwise, for if they can honestly imagine that the purpose of art is to teach and to delight, to double the face of the world as though with a mirror, to penetrate those truths which nature is said to hold folded beneath her skirts and keeps modestly hidden from the eyes and paws of science, then they will be able to avoid art's actual impact altogether, and the artist's way of life can continue to seem outrageous, bohemian,

> quaint, a little sinful, irresponsible, hip, and charming, something to visit like the Breton peasants on a holiday, and not a challenge *to* and denial *of* their own manner of existence, an accusation concerning their own lack of reality.

What did Auden say that the "failed artist and foolish public" want to believe? Why, according to Auden (and Gass), is this at odds with the purpose of art? What is the purpose of art?

3. In what two ways do we deny reality? Give some examples of how we "destroy experience" and live in madness today.
4. According to Gass, why is art socially important? What does he mean? Do you agree with him? Why, or why not?
5. Gass lists six virtues the artist must use in his or her work. What are these virtues? How are they discovered in a work of art?

QUESTIONS FOR STRUCTURAL ANALYSIS

1. What does the first sentence of the essay mean? What feelings does it evoke? How does the rest of the paragraph build on that feeling? How did you respond to the first paragraph?
2. Gass uses words gracefully and playfully. In the second paragraph, for example, when he speaks about artists and bears, he includes the sentence: "Nor does the artist bear truth dead and drooping in his arms. . . ." The juxtaposition of "artist" and "bear"—in the context of the discussion—makes the reader stop and look carefully at the sentence. Find other examples of Gass's attention to language.
3. Describe Gass's sentence structure to someone who has not read anything he wrote. What literary devices does Gass use? List some examples from this selection.
4. Who is the "I" of this essay? What do you think of him? Do you trust him? agree with him? Why? What do you base your response on? How does he compare with the "I" in Baldwin's essay? the "I" of Cary's essay?
5. Look carefully at the final paragraph. What is Gass's tone? What is his conclusion? How does he relate the conclusion to his introduction? Is this an effective conclusion for the essay?

*M*ASS CULTURE AND THE CREATIVE *A*RTIST

JAMES BALDWIN

James Baldwin (1924–1987), a major figure in contemporary American literature, wrote profound stories and essays of the Black experience in America. A high school graduate, Baldwin supported his writing with a variety of odd jobs. Among his best-known works are Go Tell It on the Mountain *(1953),* Notes of a Native Son *(1955),* Nobody Knows My Name *(1961), and* Another Country *(1962). Disappointed by the limited options available to blacks in America, Baldwin maintained a permanent residence in France. In "Mass Culture and the Creative Artist," first published in* Daedalus, *an intellectual journal, Baldwin describes the attitudes of an American public satisfied with the fantasies of mass culture and unresponsive to truth as it is revealed by a creative artist. [For further information on James Baldwin, see the headnote in Part I, "Demanding Civil Rights."]*

Before you begin reading: *What is the meaning of art? Does an artist have a responsibility to society? What is it? Jot down some responses to these questions in your reading notebook.*

◆

SOMEONE ONCE SAID TO ME THAT THE PEOPLE IN GENERAL cannot bear very much reality. He meant by this that they prefer fantasy to a truthful re-creation of their experience. The Italians, for example, during the time that De Sica and Rossellini were revitalizing the Italian cinema industry, showed a marked preference for Rita Hayworth vehicles; the world in which she moved across the screen was like a fairy tale, whereas the world De Sica was describing was one with which they were only too familiar. (And it can be suggested perhaps that the Americans who stood in line for *Shoe Shine* and *Open City* were also responding to images which they found exotic, to a reality by which they were not threatened. What passes for the appreciation of serious effort in this country is very often nothing more than an inability to take anything very seriously.)

Now, of course the people cannot bear very much reality, if by this one means their ability to respond to high intellectual or artistic endeavor. I have never in the least understood why they should be expected to. There is a division of labor in the world—as I see it—and the people have quite enough reality to bear, simply getting through their lives, raising their children, dealing with the eternal conundrums of birth, taxes, and death. They do not do this with all the wisdom, foresight, or charity one might wish; nevertheless, this is what they are always doing and it is what the writer is always describing. There is literally nothing else to describe. This effort at description is itself extraordinarily arduous, and those who are driven to make this effort are by virtue of this fact somewhat removed from the people. It happens, by no means infrequently, that the people hound or stone them to death. They then build statues to them, which does not mean that the next artist will have it any easier.

I am not sure that the cultural level of the people is subject to a steady rise: in fact, quite unpredictable things happen when the bulk of the population attains what we think of as a high cultural level, i.e., pre-World War II Germany, or present-day Sweden. And this, I think, is because the effort of a Schönberg or a Picasso (or a William Faulkner or an Albert Camus) has nothing to do, at bottom, with physical comfort, or indeed with comfort of any other kind. But the aim of the people who rise to this high cultural level—who rise, that is, into the middle class—is precisely comfort for the body and the mind. The artistic objects by which they are surrounded cannot possibly fulfill their original function of disturbing the peace—which is still the only method by which the mind can be improved—they bear witness instead to the attainment of a certain level of economic stability and a certain thin measure of sophistication. But art and ideas come out of the passion and torment of experience; it is impossible to have a real relationship to the first if one's aim is to be protected from the second.

We cannot possibly expect, and should not desire, that the great bulk of the populace embark on a mental and spiritual voyage for which very few people are equipped and which even fewer have survived. They have, after all, their indispensable work to do, even as you and I. What we are distressed about, and should be, when we speak of the state of mass culture in this country, is the overwhelming torpor and bewilderment of the people. The people who run the mass media are not all villains and they are not all cowards—though I agree, I must say, with Dwight Macdonald's forceful suggestion that many of them are not very bright. (Why should they be? They, too, have risen from the streets to a high level of cultural attainment. They, too, are positively afflicted by the world's highest standard of living and what is probably the world's most bewilderingly empty way of life.) But even those who are bright are handicapped by their audience: I am less appalled by the fact that *Gunsmoke* is produced than I am by the fact that so many people want to see it. In the same way, I must add, that a thrill of terror runs through me when I hear that the favorite author of our President is Zane Grey.

But one must make a living. The people who run the mass media and those who consume it are really in the same boat. They must continue to produce things they do not really admire, still less, love, in order to continue buying things they do not really want, still less, need. If we were dealing only with fintails, two-tone cars, or programs like *Gunsmoke*, the situation would not be so grave. The trouble is that serious things are handled (and received) with the same essential lack of seriousness.

For example: neither *The Bridge On the River Kwai* nor *The Defiant Ones*, two definitely superior movies, can really be called serious. They are extraordinarily interesting and deft: but their principal effort is to keep the audience at a safe remove from the experience which these films are not therefore really prepared to convey. The kind of madness sketched in *Kwai* is far more dangerous and widespread than the movie would have us believe. As for *The Defiant Ones*, its suggestion that Negroes and whites can learn to love each other if they are only chained together long enough runs so madly counter to the facts that it must be dismissed as one of the latest, and sickest, of the liberal fantasies, even if one does not quarrel with the notion that love on such terms is desirable. These movies are designed not to trouble, but to reassure; they do not reflect reality, they merely rearrange its elements into something we can bear. They also weaken our ability to deal with the world as it is, ourselves as we are.

What the mass culture really reflects (as is the case with a "serious" play like *J.B.*) is the American bewilderment in the face of the world we live in. We do not seem to want to know that we are *in* the world, that we are subject to the same catastrophes, vices, joys, and follies which have baffled and afflicted mankind for ages. And this has everything to do, of course, with what was expected of America: which expectation, so generally disappointed, reveals something we do not want to know about sad human nature, reveals something we do not want to know about the intricacies and inequities of any social structure, reveals, in sum, something we do not want to know about ourselves. The American way of life has failed—to make people happier or to make them better. We do not want to admit this, and we do not admit it. We persist in believing that the empty and criminal among our children are the result of some miscalculation in the formula (which can be corrected), that the bottomless and aimless hostility which makes our cities among the most dangerous in the world is created, and felt, by a handful of aberrants, that the lack, yawning everywhere in this country, of passionate conviction, of personal authority, proves only our rather appealing tendency to be gregarious and democratic. We are very cruelly trapped between what we would like to be, and what we actually are. And we cannot possibly become what we would like to be until we are willing to ask ourselves just why the lives we lead on this continent are mainly so empty, so tame and so ugly.

This is a job for the creative artist—who does not really have much to do with mass culture, no matter how many of us may be interviewed on TV. Perhaps life is not the black, unutterably beautiful, mysterious, and lonely thing the creative artist tends to think of it as being; but it is certainly not the sunlit playpen in which so many Americans lose first their identities and then their minds.

I feel very strongly, though, that this amorphous people are in desperate search for something which will help them to re-establish their connection with themselves, and with one another. This can only begin to happen as the truth begins to be told. We are in the middle of an immense metamorphosis here, a metamorphosis which will, it is devoutly to be hoped, rob us of our myths and give us our history, which will destroy our attitudes and give us back our personalities. The mass culture, in the meantime, can only reflect our chaos: and perhaps we had better remember that this chaos contains life—and a great transforming energy.

Questions for Critical Analysis

1. Why do people prefer unrealistic books and movies, according to Baldwin? Do you agree with him?
2. What does Baldwin think the function of art is? Why is this an important function? How does art lose this function as a society reaches a "high cultural level"? Baldwin refers to pre-war Germany and post-war Sweden as examples of what he means. Why?
3. What is the most disturbing thing about popular art in the United States? Why does Baldwin find this disturbing? Do you agree with him? Why, or why not?
4. How do the publications and productions of popular culture "weaken our ability to deal with the world as it is, ourselves as we are"? What is your opinion of this assertion? What evidence would you give to support it? to refute it?
5. What is the job of the creative artist? Do you think that a creative artist so defined can be successful? Name creative artists you know about who fit Baldwin's definition.

Questions for Structural Analysis

1. What is Baldwin's thesis? Where is it stated? How does he support his thesis?
2. What kind of person is the persona, the "I," of this essay? Do you trust him? like him? What does he think of the general public? Do you share his opinions?
3. Baldwin refers to movies, TV shows, plays and books popular in 1960 when this essay was written. What do you know about these works? What does the context of the essay tell you about them? Substitute names of current movies, TV shows, plays, and books that Baldwin would use if he wrote this essay today.
4. How does Baldwin relate the public's response to art and popular culture with an examination of the American way of life? What is the connection between them as Baldwin sees it? Have you thought of it this way before? Write a brief summary of his analysis for someone who has not read this essay.
5. What about the conclusion reveals its historical (1960) context? Would Baldwin's conclusion be different if he wrote the essay today? How?

THE ROLE OF THE ARTIST

TOPICS FOR WRITING ESSAYS

Many of the questions following each essay can serve as appropriate writing suggestions. Some of the topics listed below expand the prereading exercises, but they can be used without completing that step first.

1. What does William Gass mean when he writes, "A work of art may not utter the truth, but it must be honest"? Select a work of art (poem, novel, play, painting, sculpture) and explain Gass's statement in light of the work of art. Write your essay for a special issue of a student magazine on "Art and Society."
2. You will lose a $2 million trust fund unless you reject your plans to become an artist and agree to join your family's business. You feel that you have a deep responsibility to your art and cannot justify (even for the money) turning your back on your talent. Write a letter to the lawyers who handle the trust fund, explaining what you think your duty is and why you have decided to remain an artist. Use specific examples as you describe your role as an artist.
3. In the previous section, three visual artists examined the role of the artist in society. In this section, three verbal artists examine the same role. Compare the attitudes and conclusions of Baldwin, Cary, and Gass with Beckmann, de Kooning, and Calder. Define the creative artist and his or her function in society, using these six artists as sources. Write your definition to an audience familiar with the works of these artists.

RESEARCH POSSIBILITIES

1. The essays in this section suggest that life is chaotic and writers can establish order and beauty by facing and presenting reality. Select an event or object and write a paper in which you analyze how a writer presents the reality of the subject. For example, you may want to read one of James Baldwin's novels and analyze how his fiction relates to his essay; or you may want to use a book like Philip Caputo's *Indian County* or Larry Heineman's *Paco's Story* to discuss their success or failure in revealing the Vietnam War; or Joyce Cary's *The Horse's Mouth* to compare with the points he makes in his essay.
2. Select an object about which several authors have written and compare the way they present the object. For example, many modern poets have written about Queen Anne's Lace. How do their poems relate to the weed and extend its meaning? Are they successful in making the reader see what they saw, experience what they experienced? Write an analysis of the artist's role by using a concrete example such as this. Your reader, though educated, should not be expected to know the specific poems or stories you're referring to.

*L*EARNING *T*HROUGH *B*OOKS

The first three authors in this section, Simic, Himmelfarb, and Raine, exemplify the tradition of academic education. Their essays reveal that they have studied ideas and literature from the past, have questioned and thought about what they've read, and have assimilated these ideas into their lives. Bird argues that such education is effete and worthless, that it teaches little, and that it perpetuates myths held dear by the upper class.

CHARLES SIMIC, "READING PHILOSOPHY AT NIGHT"

GERTRUDE HIMMELFARB, "MANNERS INTO MORALS: WHAT THE VICTORIANS KNEW"

KATHLEEN RAINE, "PREMISES AND POETRY"

CAROLINE BIRD, "THE LIBERAL ARTS RELIGION"

*R*EADING *P*HILOSOPHY AT *N*IGHT

CHARLES SIMIC

Charles Simic (1938–), an American poet, writes many poems in a matter-of-fact style while revealing the dark terrors which fuel human fears. This approach is echoed in the first paragraph of the following essay: "I could have been sitting on the edge of a cliff with my back to the abyss trying to look normal." Born in Yugoslavia, Simic has published many translations of Yugoslav, French, and Russian poetry as well as twelve books of poetry and one book of essays. "Reading Philosophy at Night" appeared in Anteaus, *a journal devoted to publishing contemporary poetry and fiction.*

Before you begin reading: *Remember a time when you read something that made you stretch your mind, that caused you to understand, if briefly, an idea or concept that had puzzled you before. In your reading notebook, describe that moment of understanding.*

◆

It is night again around me; I feel as though there had been lightning—for a brief span of time I was *entirely* in my element and in my light.

Nietzsche

The mind loves the unknown. It loves images whose meaning is unknown, since the meaning of the mind itself is unknown.

Magritte

I WORE BUSTER KEATON'S EXPRESSION OF EXAGGERATED calm. I could have been sitting on the edge of a cliff with my back to the abyss trying to look normal.

Now I read philosophy in the morning. When I was younger and lived in the city it was always at night. "That's how you ruined your eyes," my mother keeps saying. I sat and read late into the night. The quieter it got, the more clearheaded I became—or so it seemed to me. In the sparsely furnished room above the Italian grocery, I would be struggling with some intricate epistemological argument which promised a magnificent insight at its conclusion. I could smell it, so to speak. I couldn't put the book away, and it was getting very late. I had to be at work in the morning. Even had I tried to sleep my head would have been full of Immanuel Kant. So, I wouldn't sleep. I remember well such moments of decision: the great city that had suddenly turned quiet, the open book, and my face reflected dimly in the darkened windowpane.

At such hours I thought I understood everything. The first time it happened I was twenty. It was six o'clock in the morning. It was winter. It was dark and very cold. I was in Chicago riding the El to work seated between two heavily bundled-up old women. The train was overheated, but each time the door opened at one of the elevated platforms, a blast of cold air would send shivers through us. The lights, too, kept flickering. As the train changed tracks, the lights would go out and I would stop reading the history of philosophy I had borrowed the previous day from the library. "Why is there something rather than nothing?" the book asked, quoting Parmenides. It was as if my eyes were opened. I could not stop looking at my fellow passengers. How incredible, I thought, being here, existing.

I have a recurring dream about the street where I was born. It is always night. I'm walking past vaguely familiar buildings trying to find our house, but somehow it is not there. I retrace my steps on that short block of only a few buildings, all of which are there except the one I want. The effort leaves me exhausted and saddened.

In another version of this same dream, I catch a glimpse of our house. There it is, at last, but for some reason I'm unable to get any closer to it. No lights are on. I look for our window, but it is even darker there on the third floor. The whole building seems abandoned. "It's not possible," I tell myself.

Once in one of these dreams, many years ago, I saw someone at my window, hunched over, watching the street intently. That's how my grandmother would wait late into the night for us to come home, except this was a stranger. Even without being able to make out his face, I was sure of that.

Most of the time, however, there's no one in sight during the dream. The façades of buildings still retain the pockmarks and other signs of the war. The streetlights are out and there's no moon in the sky so it's not clear to me how I am able to see all that in complete darkness.

Whoever reads philosophy reads himself as much as he reads the philosopher. I am in a dialogue with certain decisive events in my life as much as I am with the ideas on the page. Meaning is the matter of my existence. My effort to understand is a perpetual circling around a few obsessive images.

Like everyone else, I have my hunches. All my experiences make a kind of untaught ontology which precedes all my readings. What I am trying to conceptualize with the help of the philosopher is that which I have already intuited.

That's one way of looking at it.

> The Meditation of yesterday filled my mind with so many doubts that it is no longer in my power to forget them. And yet, I do not see in what manner I can resolve them; and, just as if I had all of a sudden fallen into very deep water, I am so disconcerted that I can neither make certain of setting my feet on the bottom, nor can I swim and so support myself on the surface. I shall nevertheless make an effort and follow anew the same path as that on which I yesterday entered, i.e., I shall proceed by setting aside all that in which the least doubt could be supposed to exist, just as if I had discovered that it was absolutely false; and I shall ever follow in this road until I have met with something which is certain, or at least, if I can do nothing else, until I have learned for certain that there's nothing in the world that is certain. Archimedes, in order that he might draw the terrestrial globe out of its place, and transport it elsewhere, demanded only that one point should be fixed and immovable; in the same way I shall have the right to conceive high hopes if I am happy enough to discover one thing only which is certain and indubitable.

I love this passage of Descartes; his beginning again, his not wanting to be fooled. It describes the ambition of philosophy in all its nobility and desperation. I prefer this doubting Descartes to his famous later conclusions. Here everything is still unsettled. The poetry of the moment still casts its spell. Of course, he's greedy for the absolute, but so is his reader.

There's an Eastern European folk song which tells of a girl who tossed an apple higher and higher in the air until she tossed it as high as the clouds. To her surprise the apple didn't come down. The cloud got it. She waited with arms outstretched, but the apple stayed up there. All she could do is plead with the cloud to return her apple, but that's another story. I like the first part when the impossible happens.

I remember lying in a ditch and looking at some pebbles while German bombers were flying over our heads. That was long ago. I don't remember the face of my mother nor the faces of the people who were there with us, but I still see those perfectly ordinary pebbles.

"It is not *how* things are in the world that is mystical, but that it exists," says Wittgenstein. I had a feeling of great clarity. Time had stopped. I was watching myself watching the pebbles and trembling with fear. Then time moved on.

The pebbles stayed in their otherness, stayed forever as far as I am concerned. I'm talking about the experience of heightened consciousness. Can language do it justice? Speech is always less. When it comes to consciousness, one approximates, one speaks poorly. Competing phenomenologies are impoverishments, splendid poverties.

Wittgenstein puts it this way: "What finds its reflection in language, language cannot represent. What expresses *itself* in language, we cannot express by means of language." We are not, most certainly, thinking about the same thing, nor were he and his followers subsequently very happy with this early statement of his, but this has been my experience on a number of occasions.

I knew someone who once tried to persuade me otherwise. He considered himself a logical positivist. There are people who tell you, for example, that you can speak of a pencil's dimension, location, appearance, state of motion or rest but not of its intelligence and love of music. The moment I hear that the poet in me rebels and I want to write a poem about an intelligent pencil in love with music. In other words, what they regard as nonsense, I suspect to be full of unknown imaginative possibilities.

There's a wonderful story told about Wittgenstein and his Cambridge colleague, the Italian economist Piero Sraffa. Apparently they often discussed philosophy. "One day," as Justus Hartnack has it, "when Wittgenstein was defending his view that a proposition has the same logical form as the fact it depicts, Sraffa made a gesture used by Neapolitans to express contempt and asked Wittgenstein what the logical form of that was. According to Wittgenstein's own recollection, it was this question which made him realize that his belief that a fact could have a logical form was untenable."

As for my logical friend, we argued all night: "What cannot be said, cannot be thought." And then again, after I blurted out something about silence being the language of consciousness, "you're silent because you have nothing to say." It got to the point where we were calling each other "you dumb shit." We were drinking large quantities of red wine, misunderstanding each other liberally, and only stopped bickering when his disheveled wife came to the bedroom door and told us to shut up.

Then I told him a story.

One day in Yugoslavia, just after the war, we made a class trip to the town War Museum. At the entrance we found a battered German tank which delighted us. Inside the museum one could look at a few rifles, hand grenades and uniforms, but not much else. Most of the space was taken up by photographs. These we were urged to examine. One saw people hanged and people about to be hanged; people on tips of their toes. The executioners stood around smoking. There were piles of corpses everywhere. Some were naked. Men and women with their genitals showing. That made some kid laugh.

Then we saw a man having his throat cut. The killer sat on the man's chest with a knife in his hand. He seemed pleased to be photographed. The victim's eyes I don't remember. A few men stood around gawking. There were clouds in the sky.

There were always clouds, as well as blades of grass, tree stumps, bushes and rocks no one was paying any attention to. At times the earth was covered with snow. A miserable, teeth-chattering January morning and someone making someone's life even more miserable. Or the rain would be falling. A small hard rain that would wash the blood off the hands immediately, that would make one of the killers catch a bad cold. I imagined him sitting that same night with his feet in a bucket of hot water and sipping tea.

That occurred to me much later. Now that we had seen all there was to see, we were made to sit on the lawn outside the museum and eat our lunch. It was poor fare. Most of us had plum jam spread on slices of bread. A few had lard sprinkled with paprika. One kid had nothing but bread and scallions. Everybody thought that was funny. Someone threw his thick slice of black bread in the air and got it caught in a tree. The poor fellow tried to get it down by throwing pebbles at it. He kept missing. Then, he wanted to climb the tree. He kept sliding back. Even our teacher who came over to look thought it was hilarious.

As for the grass, there was plenty of it, each blade distinct and carefully sharpened, as it were. There were also clouds in the sky and many large flies of the kind one encounters at slaughterhouses that kept interrupting our thoughts and our laughter.

And here's what went through my head just the other night as I lay awake in the dark:

The story had nothing to do with what you were talking about.

The story had everything to do with what we were talking about.

I can think of a hundred objections.

Only idiots want something neat, something categorical . . . and I never talk unless I know!

Aha! You're mixing poetry and philosophy. Bertrand Russell wouldn't give you the time of day . . .

"Everything looks very busy to me," says Jasper Johns, and that's the problem. I remember a strange cat, exceedingly emaciated, that scratched on my door the day I was scratching my head over Hegel's phenomenology.

Who said, "Whatever can be thought must be fictitious"?

You got me there! Error is my first love. I'm shouting her name from the rooftops.

Still and all! And nevertheless! And above all! Let's not forget "above all."

"The Only Humane Way to Catch a Metaphysical Mouse" is the name of the book I work on between three and four in the morning.

Here's what Nietzsche said to the ceiling: "The rank of the philosopher is determined by the rank of his laughter." But he couldn't really laugh. No matter how hard he tried he couldn't laugh.

I know because I'm a connoisseur of chaos. All the good-looking oxymorons come to visit me in my bed . . .

Wallace Stevens has several beautiful poems about solitary readers. "The House Was Quiet and the World Was Calm" is one. It speaks of a "truth in a calm world." It happens! The world and the mind being so calm that truth becomes visible.

It must be late night—"where shines the light that lets be the things that are"—which might be a good description of insomnia. The solitude of the reader and the solitude of the philosopher drawing together. The impression that one is on the verge of anticipating another man's next turn of thought. My own solitude doubled, tripled, as if I were the only one awake on the earth.

Understanding depends upon the relation of what I am to what I have been. The being of the moment, in other words. Consciousness waking up conscience—waking up history. Consciousness as clarity and history as the dark night of the soul.

The pleasures of philosophy are the pleasures of reduction—the epiphanies of saying in a few words what seems to be the gist of the matter. It pleases me, for instance, to think of both philosophy and poetry as concerned with Being. What is a lyric poem, one might say, but an acknowledgment of the Being of beings. The philosopher thinks Being; the poet in the lyric poem re-creates the experience of Being.

History, on the other hand, is antireductive. Nothing tidy about it. Chaos! Bedlam! Hopeless tangle! My history and the History of this century like a child and his blind mother on the street—and the blind mother leading the way! You'd think the sole purpose of history is to stand truth happily upon its head.

Poor poetry! For some reason I can't get Buster Keaton out of my mind. Poetry as imperturbable Keaton alone with the woman he loves on an ocean liner set adrift on the stormy sea. Or, poetry as that kid throwing stones at a tree to bring down his lunch. Wise enough to play the fool, perhaps?

And always the dialectic: I have Don Quixote and his windmills in my head and Sancho Panza and his mule in my heart.

That's a figure of speech—one figure among many other figures of speech. Who could live without them? Do they tell the truth? Do they conceal it? I don't know. That's why I keep going back to philosophy.

It is morning. It is night. The book is open. The text is difficult, the text is momentarily opaque. My mind is wandering. My mind is struggling to grasp the always elusive . . . the always hinting . . . What do you call it?

It, it, I keep calling it. An infinity of *it* without a single antecedent—like a hum in my ear.

Just then, about to give up, I find the following on a page of Heidegger:

> No thinker has ever entered into another thinker's solitude. Yet it is only from its solitude that all thinking, in a hidden mode, speaks to the thinking that comes after or that went before.

And it all comes together: poetry, philosophy, history. I see—in the sense of being able to picture and feel the human weight of another's solitude. So many of them. Seated with a book. Day breaking. Thought becoming image. Image becoming thought.

QUESTIONS FOR CRITICAL ANALYSIS

1. When does Simic feel as if he understood everything? Reread the second and final sections of the essay and discuss ways Simic says he responds to philosophical ideas. How does the Heidegger quote in the conclusion relate to Simic's earlier description of reading philosophy?
2. Simic relates three stories or dreams. Why does he include them in the essay? What do they add to his discussion? Or, do they detract from the ideas? How?
3. Reread Simic's long quote from Descartes. Do you agree with Simic's response to the quote? Why, or why not? Is Simic looking for "the absolute" himself?
4. Why does Simic tell the story of a class trip to the War Museum? In the next section, he says: "The story had nothing to do with what you were talking about. The story had everything to do with what you were talking about." Think of reasons why each statement is accurate. How do the ideas Simic expresses in section nine relate to the story in section eight?
5. Consider Simic's essay in relation to those you read in "The Role of the Artist." How do the ideas Simic expresses agree or disagree with the ideas you encountered in the essays by Cary and Gass?

QUESTIONS FOR STRUCTURAL ANALYSIS

1. Reread the two opening quotations. What does each one mean? How do they relate to each other? Why did Simic use them to preface his essay?
2. What does the opening paragraph mean? What relation does it have to the rest of the essay? What tone does it set?
3. The essay is divided by extra spacing into ten sections. Write a brief one- or two-sentence summary of each section. How do these sections relate to one another? Describe the progression of ideas in the essay.
4. Describe Simic's tone, style, and language. Provide examples of his vivid images and use of descriptive techniques. How do they affect the way you feel about him? Why?
5. How do Simic's language and sentences change in the final section? What do they reveal about the meaning of this section?

*M*ANNERS INTO *M*ORALS: *W*HAT THE *V*ICTORIANS *K*NEW

GERTRUDE HIMMELFARB

Gertrude Himmelfarb (1922–) is a distinguished university professor at the City University of New York, an historian of ideas who studies and writes on the political and cultural values of Victorian England. Himmelfarb is actively concerned about the purpose of history and worries that current historical methodology may "subvert clear thinking about past and present." "Manners into Morals" first appeared in American Scholar, *the Phi Beta Kappa journal published for education readers interested in current affairs, literature, arts, culture, and philosophy.*

Before you begin reading: *When you hear the word "Victorian," what images come into your mind? Make a list in your notebook of words, phrases, and images that define Victorians for you.*

◆

"MANNERS AND MORALS"—THE EXPRESSION IS PECULIARLY, unmistakably Victorian. Not "manners" alone: Lord Chesterfield in the eighteenth century was fond of discoursing to his son on the supreme importance of manners (manners as distinct from—if necessary, in opposition to—morals). And not "morals" alone: philosophers had always taken this as their special province—indeed, had made it so elevated a subject that it had little to do with anything so mundane as manners.

It was the Victorians who combined those words so that they came trippingly off the tongue, as if they were one word. Manners were sanctified and moralized, so to speak, while morals were secularized and domesticated. When Thackeray earlier in the century, or Trollope later, protested that manners were taking precedence over morals, that "the way we live now" (in the memorable title of one of Trollope's last novels) encouraged the cultivation of manners at the expense of morals, it was because they themselves attached so much importance not only to morals but to the continuum of manners and morals.

Margaret Thatcher has been reported as saying that she would be pleased to restore all of the Victorian virtues with the exception of hypocrisy. If she did say that, she betrayed a serious misunderstanding of Victorian virtues. Hypocrisy, as La Rochefoucauld memorably put it, is "the homage that vice pays to virtue." It is also the homage that manners pay to morals. The Victorians thought it no small virtue to maintain the appearance, the manner, of good conduct even while violating some basic precept of morality.

This was, in fact, what the eminent Victorians did when they felt obliged to commit some transgression. They did not flout conventional morality; on the contrary, they tried to observe at least the manner of it. George Eliot, living with a man whom she could not marry because he could not legally be divorced from his wife, reproduced in their relationship all the forms of propriety. They lived together in a perfectly domestic, monogamous arrangement, quite as if they had been married. Indeed she called herself, and insisted that others call her, "Mrs. Lewes," and had the great satisfaction of hearing the real Mrs. Lewes voluntarily call her that. And when George Lewes died, after twenty-four years of this pseudo-marriage (one can hardly call it an affair), she almost immediately took the occasion to enter a real, a legal marriage with John Cross—with all the appurtenances thereof: a proper trousseau, a formal wedding in a church, a honeymoon. All of this shocked her friends more than her earlier pseudo-marriage because this seemed to them to be a real misalliance; her new husband was twenty years her junior and much her intellectual inferior.

And so too with other notorious "irregularities," as the Victorians delicately put it: extra-marital relationships (like that of John Stuart Mill and Harriet Taylor), or marital relationships that were unconsummated (the Carlyles and Ruskins), or homosexual relationships (such as were presumed to exist in the Oxford Movement). Those Victorians caught up in an irregular situation of this kind tried, as far as was humanly possible, to "regularize" it, to contain it within conventional forms, to domesticate and normalize it. When they could not do so (or even when they did), they agonized over it in diaries and letters—which they carefully preserved, and which is why we now know so much about these scandals. Like the "fastidious assassin" in Camus's *The Rebel*, who deliberately gave up his own life when he took the tyrant's life, so the Victorians insisted upon paying for their indiscretions. In the process they tormented themselves, one has the impression, more than they enjoyed themselves.

So, at least, it was until the end of the century, when the moral certitudes began to falter. "For the Englishman," Nietzsche wrote in 1889, "morality is not yet a problem." Not yet a problem, he thought, because the English still had the illusion that they could sustain a morality in the absence of religion; they did not realize how firmly rooted in Christianity their morality was. When Christianity lost its ascendancy, as it inevitably would, Nietzsche predicted, the English would discover how tenuous, how problematic, their morality was.

Nietzsche's words were prophetic—not, to be sure, for the English as a whole. But then Nietzsche was not talking about the English as a whole—the masses, or "slave class," as he called them, who mindlessly observed the manners and morals imposed upon them by the "priestly class." He was talking about the priestly class itself, the intellectual aristocracy, many of whom were atheists and some of whom came to think of themselves as "free souls," liberated from both religion and morality.

Nietzsche had no sooner made that pronouncement than public confirmation of it began to appear in the *fin de siècle* movement celebrated by such "esthetes" and "decadents," as they proudly described themselves, as Oscar Wilde and Aubrey Beardsley. It is interesting that from the beginning the movement was known under that French label, as if to suggest how alien it was to England—rather like the "French flu" or the "French pox." A character in a novel of the period remarks, in an execrable accent, "It's *fang-de-seeaycle* that does it, my dear, and education, and reading French."

The movement was well-named; it did not survive the *siècle*. The *Yellow Book* expired in 1897, Beardsley died the following year, and Wilde died in exile (appropriately in France) in 1900. In his last, and perhaps best, play, *The Importance of Being Earnest*, Wilde delivered himself of one of those witticisms that was possibly truer than the author himself knew. "I hope," a young woman says, "you have not been leading a double life, pretending to be wicked and being really good all the time. That would be hypocrisy."

It was a nice accident of history that had Queen Victoria die in January 1901, so that the end of the reign coincided with the start of the new century. The end of the reign and, for an influential group of intellectuals—the new priestly class—the end of Victorianism. The high priests of Bloomsbury were not hypocritical in pretending to be more wicked than they were. Their only hypocrisy, recent scholarship has shown, was in concealing from the public the wickedness they flaunted in private. After the death of Leslie Stephen (the Victorian paterfamilias of Bloomsbury), his children moved from respectable Kensington to what was to become the new bohemia, Bloomsbury. "Everything was going to be new," his daughter announced. "Everything was going to be different. Everything was on trial." Later Virginia Stephen (Virginia Woolf, as we now know her) assigned a different date to that new era. "In or about December 1910," she pronounced with remarkable assurance, "human character changed." December 1910 was the date of the Post-Impressionist exhibition (organized by another member of the clan, Roger Fry) that so dramatically altered the artistic sensibilities of her generation. It was also, as Virginia Woolf saw it, the time when a new ethic was beginning to emerge to complement the new esthetic. Just as art now appeared to be autonomous, dependent on no external reality but only on the vision and imagination of the artist, so the character of the artist (or of the writer, or any other person of superior sensibility) was seen as autonomous, self-contained, not subject to the judgment of others nor bound by any sense of "obligation to others." The conventional idea, Virginia Woolf declared, of "living for others, not for ourselves," was intended for "timid natures who dare not allow their souls free play." Bloomsbury was made of sterner stuff. Later one of its founding fathers described its basic tenet. "We repudiated entirely," Maynard Keynes wrote, "customary morals, conventions and traditional wisdom. We were, that is to say, in the strict sense of the term, immoralists."

"Everything was on trial," Virginia Woolf had said. What was mainly on trial was Victorian morals and manners. Another member of Bloomsbury, Lytton Strachey, its most flamboyant member, had the audacious idea of putting on trial some of the most eminent Victorians—and by implication Victorianism as such. Strachey's *Eminent Victorians* was published in 1918. A half century earlier that title could have been used and understood in all sincerity. When Strachey used it, no one could mistake its satiric intent. Strachey made no secret of his purpose or his method. Ordinary history, he explained in his preface, proceeded by "the direct method of a scrupulous narration." The historian of the Victorian age had to adopt a "subtler strategy."

> He will attack his subject in unexpected places; he will fall upon the flank, or the rear; he will shoot a sudden, revealing searchlight into obscure recesses, hitherto undivined. He will row out over that great ocean of material, and lower down into it, here and there, a little bucket, which will bring up to the light of day some characteristic specimen, from those far depths, to be examined with a careful curiosity.

Strachey concluded his preface with the familiar adage: "Je n'impose rien; je ne propose rien; j'expose."

The eminent Victorians Strachey chose to expose were eminent in different fields. Cardinal Manning was an eminent ecclesiastic; Florence Nightingale an eminent social reformer; Dr. Arnold an eminent educator; General Gordon an eminent soldier and patriot. They were all eminences and, more to the point, heroes. Strachey's intention was to belittle and disparage them—"demystify" them, we say today, but "de-hero-ize" them would be more accurate. In each case what Victorians knew as heroism Strachey interpreted as megalomania, a ruthless drive for self-aggrandizement. It is interesting that in seeking out the defects that would belie their heroism—in dipping his bucket into the depths of that murky sea—Strachey never came up with the two "dirty secrets" that a muckraking biographer would look for today: money and sex. Drunkenness, yes, and vanity, and willfulness, and irrationality, and physical flaws, but not financial gain and not sexual misconduct. If there was anything sexually scandalous about them, Strachey intimated, it was either their celibacy, as in the cases of Manning and Nightingale, or their conspicuous normality, as in the case of Dr. Arnold, who fulfilled his marital duties all too faithfully, as the existence of his ten children testified. (It is not surprising that there is no mention of Gordon's reputed homosexuality; that might have required Strachey to present him in a more sympathetic light.)

Apart from their megalomania, the one flaw they had in common, in Strachey's view, was their weakness for religion. They were all religious to a fault. Cardinal Manning might be forgiven for this; it was, after all, his job to be religious, although he went beyond the call of duty by believing what he preached. The others not only professed to believe when they had no obligation to do so; they actually did believe. Strachey's wicked comment about Florence Nightingale is often quoted: "She felt towards Him [God] as she might have felt towards a glorified sanitary engineer; . . . she seems hardly to distinguish between the Deity and the Drains." But Strachey was even more distressed by her truly religious feelings, her "mysterious moods of mysticism," her "morbid longings" to find peace in God. So, too, he was contemptuous of Dr. Arnold not merely because of his vulgar conception of education (the public school as a nursery for English gentlemen) but also because of his habit of communing with the "invisible world" and his resolve to do battle with the "wicked one." Some of Strachey's readers protested that he maligned General Gordon in the famous scene where the General is found seated at a table "upon which were an open Bible and an open bottle of brandy"; it was the open bottle of brandy that offended them. But Strachey himself made far more of the open Bible: the first paragraph of that essay has Gordon wandering in Jerusalem with a Bible under his arm, and the last paragraph has him "in some remote Nirvana" fluttering the pages of a "phantasmal Bible."

To "expose" the religious proclivities of these eminent Victorians, as Strachey saw it, was to expose, and undermine, the very foundations of their morality. It was also to expose them as frauds—not in the sense that they were hypocritical; they were true believers. What was fraudulent, Strachey suggested, was their claim (or the claim made on their behalf) that they were heroes. Heroes could not be religious, any more than heroines could be seen—as Strachey depicted Florence Nightingale—putting a dog's wounded paw in a splint.

There were, in fact, no heroes in Strachey's scheme of things, because the heroic virtues were as suspect as all other virtues. And not only heroic virtues but heroic attitudes—the manners and morals, as it were, of heroism. For Strachey, religion, public service, civic education, and patriotism were absurd in themselves. But they were even more absurd in the manner of their pursuit—in the passionate, extravagant way heroes were wont to pursue them. And they were more absurd still in the manner of their reception, in the respect accorded them by a credulous and deferential public.

Early in Victoria's reign, another eminent Victorian (not satirized by Strachey, but he could well have been) wrote the classic defense of heroism. "Society," Carlyle wrote, "is founded on Hero-worship, . . . [the] reverence and obedience due to men really great and wise." Like Nietzsche anticipating the time when morality would have become "a problem" in England, so Carlyle anticipated the time when the heroic virtues would become problematic. Indeed he thought that time had already come. "Show our critics," he wrote in 1840, "a great man, a Luther for example, they begin to what they call 'account' for him; not to worship him, but take the dimensions of him,—and bring him out to be a little kind of man!" It is not clear which critics Carlyle had in mind when he wrote that—perhaps Mill or Bentham, those pettifogging, "dry-as-dust" rationalists. But his words apply even more aptly to Strachey.

> We will always take the liberty [Carlyle wrote] to deny altogether that [mot] of the witty Frenchman, that no man is a Hero to his valet-de-chambre. Or if so, it is not the Hero's blame, but the Valet's: that his soul, namely, is a mean *valet*-soul! . . . The Valet does not know a Hero when he sees him! Alas, no: it requires a kind of *Hero* to do that.

This is not to say that Carlyle saw no flaws in his heroes; on the contrary, he expected a hero's flaws, his vices, to be as large, as heroic, as his virtues. When the biographer of Sir Walter Scott was criticized by some reviewers for being indiscreet, for recounting episodes that made Scott appear (so the critics said) unheroic, Carlyle came to the biographer's defense. He took the occasion to mock the conventional pious biography. "How delicate, decent, is English biography, bless its mealy mouth."

In deriding the mealy-mouthed biography, Carlyle did not mean to condone the Strachey kind of biography that poor-mouths or bad-mouths its subject, reducing the hero to a "little kind of man." Still less would he have condoned the currently fashionable genre of history that disdains any kind of heroism or eminence, that reads history "from below," as is said, celebrating not individual heroes, not great men (or even great women), but rather *le petit peuple*, the "common men," the "anonymous masses."

One of the paradoxes of this new mode of history is that it professes to celebrate the common man while demeaning the virtues commonly associated with the common man. If Strachey's *Eminent Victorians* is in disfavor today, it is not so much because it is unscholarly history as because it is "elitist" history. It disparages the manners and morals of eminent Victorians but says nothing about the manners and morals of ordinary Victorians. It is, a Marxist would say, insufficiently "critical"; it "de-mystifies" the heroic virtues but not the bourgeois virtues. Like Marx exhorting philosophers to turn their attention from the "holy forms" of alienation to the "unholy forms"—from the illusory world of religion to the real world of exploitation—so the new historian is more interested in exposing the unholy, bourgeois virtues than the more exalted holy, heroic ones.

These bourgeois virtues are what Margaret Thatcher is presumably trying to restore—or rather bourgeois "values," as she is commonly misquoted, *virtues* being too moralistic, indeed too Victorian, a word for our enlightened age. These virtues—thrift, prudence, diligence, temperance, self-reliance—were indeed bourgeois virtues. But they were also classical virtues; they were hardly unfamiliar to the Greeks. They were also religious virtues; it was, after all, from the Jews and Christians that the Puritans derived them. And they were also working class virtues. At least they were the virtues aspired to (not always successfully, but then all of us fall short of our aspirations) by the respectable Victorian working class.

"Respectable"—there's another Victorian word that makes us uncomfortable, that we can hardly utter without audible quotation marks around it. An influential school of historians today interprets the idea of respectability, and all the virtues connected with it, as instruments of "social control," the means by which the middle class sought to dominate the working class—a subtle and covert way of conducting the class struggle.

Some early applications of the social-control thesis were plausible, such as the idea that the modern clock made possible habits—promptness, regularity, conformity, rationality—that were useful for the "work-discipline" or "time-discipline" of an industrial, capitalist economy. Even here, however, the thesis has been extended to the point where it sometimes seems as if the clock had been invented for that very purpose (this a couple of centuries before the emergence of industrialism and capitalism), and as if the rural economy knew no form of "work-discipline," no imperatives of time—as if nature did not have its own rhythms that could be no less compelling and oppressive.

But there is a more serious flaw at the heart of this thesis. This is the assumption that the "Puritan ethic"—all those values invoked by Margaret Thatcher—was little more than a "work ethic" designed to "moralize" and "socialize" the new industrial proletariat, to imbue them with "middle-class values" that would make them more productive members of the labor force and more docile members of society. These "alien" values, the argument goes, were imposed upon the workers by a middle class that enjoyed a cultural as well as economic and political "hegemony," and were accepted by a working class beguiled by "false consciousness" and unable to perceive its own "indigenous" values and interests.

It is not clear what those indigenous values are supposed to have been—communal, presumably, rather than individualistic, and cooperative rather than competitive. One historian has said that it is only through the "distorting lens of middle-class aspirations to gentility" that the idea of "self-help," for example, can be understood. But does this mean that this idea—the value of self-reliance and independence—was alien to Victorian workers? Are we then to understand that dependency was more congenial to them? And what of the other alien, middle-class values supposedly imposed on them? Is it to be assumed that workers were naturally indolent rather than industrious, or profligate rather than frugal, or drunk rather than sober? And if these middle-class values reflected the interests of a capitalist society, does it mean that a socialist society would embrace a proletarian set of values—indolence, perhaps, or profligacy, or intemperance?

It must be remembered that the social-control thesis is advanced not by reactionary historians but by radical historians who are avowedly sympathetic to the working class, who, as E. P. Thompson put it in an often-quoted passage, want to rescue the poor and the oppressed from "the enormous condescension of posterity." One wonders, however, which is more condescending: to attribute to the Victorian working class a radically different set of values from those professed by the rest of society, or to assume that most workers essentially shared these so-called middle-class values and that, if they sometimes failed to abide by them, it was because of the difficult circumstances of life or the natural weaknesses of the human condition. Is it more condescending to describe these workers as the victims of "false consciousness" or to credit them with a true consciousness of their values and interests? False consciousness is a crucial part of the social-control thesis, because the radical historian has to account for the inconvenient fact that a great many workers seemed to view their own lives through that "distorting lens" of middle-class values. It was not only the so-called "labor aristocracy," as is sometimes claimed, that suffered from this myopia; lesser-skilled and unskilled workers did so as well, perhaps because they had most to lose if they lost their respectability.

These values, moreover, were shared—and consciously so—by the most radical workers. The memoirs of the Chartists provide poignant testimony of their efforts to remain hard-working, sober, frugal, clean—in short, respectable—in spite of all the temptations to the contrary. There were groups among the Chartists who made this their main concern—the Temperance Chartists and Education Chartists, as they were called. Indeed the central tenet of Chartism, universal suffrage, was based on just this claim to respectability. The argument for political equality depended on the argument for natural equality, a common human nature—common values, aspirations, and capacities.

As for those middle-class reformers, educators, political economists, and politicians who encouraged these values among the working classes—how condescending were they? Was it condescending on their part to credit the poor with the values that they prized so highly for themselves—and not only the values but the ability and the will to fulfill those values? Were they patronizing the poor when they applied to them a single standard of values rather than the double standard that had prevailed for so long—a double standard, incidentally, implicit in the social-control thesis? So far from keeping the working classes in a condition of inferiority and subservience, that single standard was an invitation to economic betterment, social advance, and, ultimately, political equality. It was also an attempt to bridge the "two nations" barrier dramatized by Disraeli. A single standard of values was conducive to a single culture, a single society, a single polity—and a single nation.

To the degree to which the Victorians succeeded in "bourgeoisifying" the ethos, they also democratized it. That ethos was not, to be sure, an exalted or heroic one. Hard work, sobriety, frugality, foresight—these were modest, mundane virtues, even lowly virtues. But they were virtues within the capacity of everyone; they did not assume any special breeding, or status, or talent, or valor, or grace—or even money. They were common virtues within the reach of common people. They were, so to speak, democratic virtues.

They were also liberal virtues. By putting a premium on ordinary virtues attainable by ordinary people, this Victorian ethos located responsibility and authority within each individual. It was no longer only the exceptional, heroic individual who was the master of his fate; all individuals could be their own masters. So far from promoting social control, the ethos had the effect of promoting self-control. This was, in fact, at the heart of Victorian morality: self-control, self-help, self-reliance, self-discipline. A liberal society, the Victorians believed, depended upon a moral citizenry. The stronger the voluntary exercise of morality on the part of each individual—the more internalized that morality—the weaker need be the external, coercive instruments of the state. For the Victorians, morality served as a substitute for law, just as law was a substitute for force.

And so too, in a sense, manners were a substitute for morals. Or perhaps not quite a substitute; that puts it too strongly. The Victorians were no utopians. They were acutely aware of the frailties of human nature, and thus of the need for whatever inducements or sanctions—social, religious, legal, ultimately physical—might be required to encourage virtue and discourage vice. A better image is that of the continuum. Manners were placed in a continuum with morals, as morals were with laws, and laws, as a last resort, with force. It was that great realist, and moralist, Machiavelli who said: "For as laws are necessary that good manners may be preserved, so there is need of good manners that laws may be maintained." And it was another great realist and moralist, the mentor of so many eminent Victorians, Edmund Burke, who wrote:

> Manners are of more importance than laws. Upon them, in a great measure, the laws depend. The law touches us but here and there, and now and then. Manners are what vex or soothe, corrupt or purify, exalt or debase, barbarize or refine us, by a constant, steady, uniform, insensible operation, like that of the air we breathe in. They give their whole form and colour to our lives. According to their quality, they aid morals, they supply them, or they totally destroy them.

QUESTIONS FOR CRITICAL ANALYSIS

1. What are "manners"? Describe the relationship between manners and morals in Victorian times. Why does Himmelfarb imply that hypocrisy was a critical element in the equation? What is different about the relationship today?
2. Himmelfarb makes the statement: "The English still had the illusion that they could sustain a morality in the absence of religion; they did not realize how firmly rooted in Christianity their morality was." What virtues reflected Victorian morality? How are they "rooted in Christianity"?
3. How did everything become "new," as Virginia Woolf put it, at the turn of the century? Why does Strachey's *Eminent Victorians* exemplify this newness?
4. How does the way history is taught today reflect post-Victorian changes? Think about history classes you took in high school and college. Did they celebrate the common

people, as Himmelfarb suggests? Why does she criticize this approach to history? What prompted historians to adopt this approach?

5. At several instances, Himmelfarb refers to Margaret Thatcher's misunderstandings of Victorian England. What does Thatcher say, and how is she inaccurate? Why does Himmelfarb bring Thatcher into the essay?
6. How were Victorians democratic? Compare Victorian virtues with those we associate with our founding fathers. How are they similar? How are they dissimilar?

Questions for Structural Analysis

1. What is the point of this essay? Can you identify the thesis? What does Himmelfarb hope to accomplish through the essay?
2. Himmelfarb refers to many people, ideas, and events from history to support her analysis. How did these references affect your reading of the essay? How many of them can you identify? (Look up those you can't.)
3. Two themes are central to Himmelfarb's discussion of Victorians: religion and economics. Describe how she treats each of these in the essay. How does she reveal her attitudes to the reader?
4. What kind of person is Himmelfarb? Do you trust her? Why, or why not? Point out techniques she uses to connect with the reader.
5. Himmelfarb pulls together the themes of morals, manners, and the law in her conclusion. Why does she end with a quote from Edmund Burke? How do his comments reflect on her ideas? Is this an effective conclusion?

*P*REMISES AND *P*OETRY

KATHLEEN RAINE

Kathleen Raine (1908–) studied botany and zoology at Girton College, Cambridge, but soon began writing and publishing poetry. Although she rejected orthodox religion, her poetry is marked by religious interests. She published her first collection of poems in 1943 and has published over a dozen volumes of poetry since then. Raine earned an international reputation as a Blake scholar, literary critic, and essayist. "Premises and Poetry," a scholarly paper delivered to the Institute of Christian Studies in London, was later published in The Inner Journey of the Poet *(1982), a collection of Raine's essays and occasional papers.*

Before you begin reading: *What makes poetry different from other types of writing? Think beyond the obvious short lines and occasional rhymes and consider the world poets present to their readers. In your reading notebook, write a paragraph describing the underlying differences between poetry and other types of writing.*

◆

ALTHOUGH IN THIS PAPER SCHOLARSHIP WOULD BE INAPpropriate the conclusions I shall suggest have been reached through much reading, though of books not generally considered necessary to the understanding of 'English Literature' as taught in the universities. But I claim poetic licence—and poetic precedent—for the unorthodoxy of my studies. The poets do not read the same books as the academics, or even the same kind of books; or if the same books, read them in a different way. Thomas Taylor the Platonist, whom Emerson called the best 'feeder of poets since Shakespeare', for example, was veritably persecuted by the reviewers of the end of the eighteenth century and the early nineteenth century because he read Plato, Plotinus and Proclus for the truths they taught and not for the sake of mere erudition (which Taylor himself castigated in no uncertain terms). 'Feeder of poets' is true of 'the modern Plethon', as Taylor called himself; for it was through his translations and commentaries of the neo-Platonists and Plato himself that the Romantic poets learned their Plotinian aesthetics and their symbolic language of mythology, their doctrine of imagination and the soul. Blake and Flaxman were among his friends, Shelley's intimate friend Thomas Love Peacock (who put Taylor in his novel *Melincourt*) his admiring follower. Coleridge had read his works while still at school, and we may trace Wordsworth's mind and Keats's also, I believe, travelling over the pages of his paraphrase translation of Plotinus's *Concerning the Beautiful* (*Ennead* I, book VI), which went into a second edition and was most obviously a source book among the Romantics. Samuel Palmer in Italy planned to read Plato on his return to London; presumably in Taylor's translation, since there was no other at the time. Emerson and Bronson Alcott made of Taylor's works (scorned by the dons of Oxford) the foundation of the American Transcendentalist movement. His translation of Porphyry's *De Antro Nympharum* was early known to Yeats, doubtless through the Theosophical Society and John M. Watkins, the theosophical publisher and bookseller who reissued Porphyry's *Cave of the Nymphs*. AE called him 'the uncrowned king'. And for all this, his very name, until recently, was not to be found in academic works on the Romantic poets. His books, even the few reprinted by the Theosophical Society and by John M. Watkins (and one or two in America), are extremely rare and to be found on no university syllabus, so far as I know. But I name Taylor as an example—though a central one—to illustrate my argument that there is a great field of excluded knowledge which the schools, dominated by the materialist climate of the time, do not recognize.

I was fortunate in not reading English Literature at the university (I read Natural Sciences). I did not do so because I saw no reason why educated people cannot read for themselves the literature of our own language. But from my own point of vantage (or disadvantage) I saw something of the revolution in the reading of poetry, whose beginnings lie outside the universities, in larger social changes; and whose consequences likewise go far beyond the English schools. I was spectator, but never participator in this cultural revolution; which may conceivably mark the beginning of a new civilization but assuredly marks the end of what C. S. Lewis has called 'old western' culture; of which (so he told Cambridge in his inaugural lecture as Regius Professor in the mid-1950s) he was among the last examples. But, as a student of natural sciences, I did come under the influence of the materialist ideology, and have, over the intervening years, piece by piece and with much toil and some pain re-structured my thought. I do not know how many of my own generation have shared my experience; when I meet old Cambridge contemporaries I find most of them still of the party I deserted. It is in a younger generation that I see a questioning of the materialist premises of the kind which led me to discover the excluded knowledge; which indeed is not far to seek when once we know what we are looking for.

What I saw happening (and indeed I attended several of Dr. I. A. Richards's open lectures on Practical Criticism, delivered in—I think—1925 or '26) was, as I now see it, a brilliant exercise in the reading of a whole body of English poetry—almost, though not quite, of *the* whole body of English poetry—in the context of a culture not only unlike, but in its fundamental premises opposed to, that which had produced the literature of 'old western' culture. The method is now well known to all who have taught English in the universities; a poem is taken, preferably one unknown to the students. The exercise of dating and ascription is a secondary one, and the real purpose of Richards's now famous method is to see the poem in itself and precisely 'out of context'. This way of reading a poem works best (works only, perhaps) when the culture of the student is, in general, the same as that of the poet. Only then does the answer to the question 'What does the poem mean to me?' approximate to what the poem meant to its author.

It was never Richards's intention that his 'scientific' criticism should replace the reading of poems in the context of the poet's whole work and thought, or poets in the context of their culture. But what he had designed as a teaching method, a way of focusing vague minds upon the text before them, happened to coincide with that social change which was sending for the first time to the universities students from classes hitherto uneducated. In this cultural revolution it was Leavis who made of Richards's teaching method a weapon. For it was an excellent way of encouraging such students, burdened with the sense of their own ignorance, to say 'Never mind the past, or the poet, read the poem word by word and register your own responses'. The poem was, as it presently became fashionable to say, 'the words on the page'. Add to this Leavis's performances in the art of demolishing some trifling poem by an obscure poet (with an occasional hit-and-run on the great Milton, or Shelley) and his popularity in the decades of the 'inferiority complex' is understandable. But again, Leavis, and his magazine *Scrutiny* (how well the word expresses the attitude, carried over from that phase of the natural sciences that murdered to dissect), rose on the tide of a world revolution with a new religion—scientific materialism. In this situation it could be said that the new 'scientific' criticism was an attempt to save for the new age the literature of the older culture by demonstrating how much remains to be admired and understood even when the system of thought of which it is an expression is discarded and replaced by another, whose answer to the question 'What is Man?' is so radically different. Recently, to the English television audience (popular culture in the early 1970s having overtaken Cambridge undergraduate culture of the mid-1920s) Dr Bronowski, another Cambridge contemporary, interpreted the cathedral of Rheims in terms of its construction. The vision of God and his Mother, the theology of Aquinas, the aspiration of worshipping multitudes, might never have existed. Of course Gothic architecture is, as Bronowski demonstrated, a marvel of engineering; but can it be explained in terms of the curiosity of the mastermasons about the stresses and strains in stone? Is Michelangelo's statue in the marble to be understood in so literal a way? Bronowski too was clearly concerned to save the bare ruined choirs for the post-revolutionary world in which it is supposed that materialism must prevail even in those countries where Marxism as yet does not. Why the same passion for engineering has in our own time produced not Rheims or Chartres but Megalopolis Dr. Bronowski did not say; or did he see no significant difference in meaning between a Gothic cathedral and one of New York's temples of commerce?

Plotinus in *Concerning the Beautiful* takes architecture as his example in illustrating a very different thesis. For him the building is not a 'construction in space' (to use a phrase popular among modern sculptors) but an idea in the artist's mind. Architectural harmony is a matter not of engineering but of intellect. (I quote Taylor's paraphrase translation of 1787.)

> But how can that which is inherent in body accord with that which is above body? Let us reply by asking how the architect pronounces the building beautiful, by accommodating the external structure to the fabric in his soul? Perhaps, because the outward building, when entirely deprived of the stones, is no other than the intrinsic form, divided by the external mass of matter, but indivisibly existing, though appearing in the many. When, therefore, sense beholds the form in bodies, at strife with matter binding and vanquishing its contrary nature, and sees form gracefully shining forth in other forms, it collects together the scattered whole, and introduces it to itself, and to the indivisible form within; and renders it consonant, congruous and friendly to its own intimate form.

For Plotinus, a building is beautiful insofar as it expresses a triumph of mind over matter's innate formlessness. Matter 'is base, and separate from the divine reason, the great fountain of forms; and whatever is entirely remote from this immortal source, is perfectly base, and deformed. And such is matter, which by its nature is ever averse from the supervening irradiations of form.' The principle of form, which Bronowski (speaking for this time and place) found in matter, Plotinus finds in mind. The 'construction in space' is redeemed from being that conglomerate heap of stones that works so named very often appear to be, by the organizing form of the idea. A circle is a circle whether it be drawn in ink or chalk or inscribed on the stone of New Grange or the turf of Stonehenge; and is neither 'the ink on the page' nor the 'construction in space'.

The poem as the 'words on the page' is the literary equivalent of Bronowski's view of architecture. The student of literature begins with the words on the page; the poet with an idea which does not yet exist in words but which does exist as an idea, a mood, an intuition; even as a wordless form, somewhat like music. My own experience as a poet is that, like Plotinus's builder, one attempts to match words to an idea, the poem in the mind; or, rather, hovering just beyond the reach of the conscious mind. But our success in communication (in this the poet is less fortunate than architect or musician) is dependent upon the reader's knowledge of words, his range of literary associations. For words mean nothing in themselves; they are only a currency supported by meanings; the gold is in the bank, as it were, and the paper currency has more or less value against the reader's own equivalence in the realms of gold. The poet's too, of course; which in the present literary situation is very often more meagre than his reader's.

When the reader's field of association, which alone gives meaning to words, is very different from that of the poet, he will not be reading, through 'the words on the page', the same poem as the poet wrote. He 'speaks a different language', though the words he uses may be the same on the page. But they do not carry the same meaning.

In my own lifetime I have seen—indeed experienced—the sleight of hand by which the central canon of English poetry has come to be read in a context of thought, and according to premises alien to the poets themselves. Poets of the imagination write of the soul, of intellectual beauty, of the living spirit of the world. What does such work communicate to readers who do not believe in the soul, in the spirit of life, or in anything that can be (unless the physically desirable) called 'the beautiful'? For in René Guénon's 'reign of quantity' such terms of quality become, as the linguistic philosophers would say, 'meaningless', because there is nothing for which they stand.

This is only in part a matter of period; far more it is a matter of culture; for not all who are contemporary share the same culture. Take Hopkins, who can be said to have been I. A. Richards's great discovery. Two of his pupils—William Empson and E. E. Phare—wrote on poems by Hopkins using the method of Richards's 'scientific' criticism. William Empson in his book *Seven Types of Ambiguity* wrote on *The Windhover*; as brilliant a misreading of 'the words on the page' as could be found. I remember he made much play with the key word, 'buckle':

> Brute beauty and valour and act, oh, air, pride, plume, here
> Buckle! AND the fire that breaks from thee then. . . .

'Buckle', William Empson argues, could mean that the priest will 'buckle' these virtues on (like St Paul's 'whole armour of God') in the life he has chosen; or that these virtues 'buckle like a bicycle wheel'; and he draws from that crumpling of the wheel those conclusions about the Jesuit's life which we should expect from the Cambridge of Russell and Wittgenstein in the heyday of Freud; who so conveniently permits the critic to argue that the poet knew not what he wrote; the dire ambiguity is there on the page. Father Arthur Thomas, S. J., has surely settled the matter once and for all by his discovery that 'buckle' is a term of falconry, and that Hopkins knew the term.

I remember secretly and rather sadly contrasting with the brilliant game my Cambridge friends were playing my own first acquaintance with Hopkins; in another world altogether, as it then seemed, in which I had, as a child, imagined I loved poetry for quite other reasons than for the barbed pleasure of picking the prickles from a hedgehog. I first heard poems by Hopkins recited by a young musician, then hovering on the brink of a monastic vocation, who had recited to me (as though in the words of the poem his own tormented aspiration found expression) those early poems Hopkins wrote in a mood of religion (or religiosity) which to many of his own generation and a few even of mine (though not in Cambridge) was a living reality. Which had read the poems more truly? Hopkins indeed was interested, as Empson was, in what could be done with words. In some ways their minds are alike, highly literate products of the classical education of the English public schools. They might have greatly enjoyed an exchange of letters; just as the freemasons of Rheims would have found much in common with Mies van der Rohe. The 'how' of construction—the quantifiable part of knowledge—they would have shared; but as to the 'what'—the qualitative—they would have spoken different languages. The materialist scientific mentality supposes the 'how' to be the 'what', the meaning of a building to be no other than its engineering.

Yeats, whose thought and whose poetry are related to a world-order totally other than the atheist humanism of his time, has suffered from radical misreading by the critics. John Wain, in an essay, 'Among Schoolchildren', dismissed Yeats's own allusion to Porphyry as of no account, and, for the 'drug' Lethe that brings forgetfulness to the generating soul, substituted the chloroform of a modern maternity ward. Clearly he had no thought of injuring Yeats's reputation—on the contrary, his misreading of the poem is an attempt to save Yeats from himself and reshape his image in a way more congenial to his own society. And Mr Wain is by no means alone in his attempt to cover up the great poet's supposedly ridiculous beliefs and discreditable studies. We are not so much concerned with 'period' (though of course the premises of societies do change) but with the changes, the losses of meaning that come about when the reader's premises are not those of the poet, when they are in the most literal sense living in different worlds.

What can be saved from a culture whose premises are of a spiritual order in an iron age peopled by Plato's 'men of clay' (the human primate of the scientist) is the quantifiable; the mechanics of construction, in whatever art. And the engineering element in the making of a poem is negligible in comparison with that of that most impressive and typical work of the reign of quantity, the space-ship. What meaning is there, in materialist terms, to the word 'poet'; or the essence—the 'poetry'—and the quality—the 'poetic'—of works of art? The adjective 'poetic' carries a certain contempt as the critics use it, and the 'poetic' element (as we use the word of the music of Schubert or Chopin, the painting of Claude or Palmer) is avoided by those typical of the 'modern movement'. Proust and even Balzac called themselves 'poets', indicating by the word at least the intention of giving expression to precisely this intangible quality that used to be called the 'poetry' of life. The preferred word in the modern movement is 'the artist'—placing the emphasis on the execution rather than the informing idea. A sculpture is a 'construction in space', a musical work a 'construction in time'. The 'work of art' is no longer an embodiment, but a body.

Beyond the question of how much a materialist present can understand, in its own terms, of the art and poetry of a spiritual past, there is the question of the kind of art—the kind of poetry—the reign of quantity can produce. The modern megalopolis, for all our understanding of the stresses and strains (in ferroconcrete if not in the soul of man), is not encouraging. It has yet to be demonstrated that, once a materialist society has exhausted the excitement of sacking the treasuries of the past in such 'revolutionary' anti-art movements as surrealism and 'pop' art, spent its nostalgia for tastes and manners inherited from a rejected culture (whose values these manners reflect), it can, or will even wish to, include poetry or 'the poetic' in its way of life.

A new culture, a new civilization, is born of a change of premises. At the height of Roman power the seed of Christianity began to germinate among slaves and social outcasts. In the age of apparent triumph of materialism, is there a comparable process already at work among a younger generation who reject the materialist Utopia?

Knowledge, in any culture, is only an agreed area of the known and the knowable; 'Let X equal knowledge' is premised and the proofs follow. Every X can of course yield its results. But there is always an excluded knowledge; and as the crude beginnings of science were the excluded knowledge of pre-Renaissance Christendom, so theology and all the wisdom of the spirit is the excluded knowledge of a materialist society. As R. P. Blackmur (apropos Eliot and Yeats) wrote in 1957, 'the supernatural is simply not part of our mental furniture'. But reality does not change its nature because we are unaware of it; a fact which the scientists themselves would not deny.

Just as science has its *gnosis* within its own terms (the quantifiable) so there is a *gnosis* of mind, which has been known and formulated in every civilization. Coomaraswamy wrote of a universal language of which the several theologies, mythologies and arts are dialectical variations. If mind is premised—is the 'X' of knowledge—the same truths will always be rediscovered. Plotinus, who wrote that 'there is nothing higher than the truth', was not a scientist; though only from scientists, in our society, is that appeal recognized. This gnosis (implicitly or explicitly) is the ground of all works of imagination. A work of art is precisely an expression in words of some intuition of imaginative reality. Poets may or may not have been religious men (who knows if Shakespeare was?) but all poetry of the imagination is the language of spiritual intuition and spiritual knowledge.

This is not the place to give chapter and verse in support of what is not after all a particularly original view, that our European variation of 'the universal and unanimous tradition' has been, with variations and accretions, neo-Platonism. Christian theology has itself its roots in Greek philosophy, and differs in no essential first principles from Platonic (or Aristotelean) metaphysics. From the point of view of religion neo-Platonism might seem a dead language; the Mysteries of Hellenic civilization no longer exist as religious cults with places of worship, rituals, a priesthood and so on. From the standpoint of the poets this very freedom has perhaps made the Platonic theology more amenable to poetic purposes than the Christian religion with its involvement in history and its other worldly ramifications. Cult belongs to time and place; and this aspect of the Christian Church itself is now assailed by inevitable change. But the first principles themselves, from which have sprung many cults and their various rituals, are defined in the Platonic theology, which is itself an embodiment of tradition. Religion is, after all, a collective art embodying a vision shared by a nation or an age. The essence of reality cannot be captured or held in any of the forms, however wonderful, which may at some time embody it. Involvement with a cult may be as dangerous to the poet as involvement in politics; however sincere, such involvement is, for the imagination, at best a symbol and at worst an irrelevance. But, as a symbolic description of the nature of things, all myths whose origin is in the imagination are unageing and may live again in poetry (as Hyperion in Keats, Prometheus in Shelley or the Greek gods in Hölderlin) after centuries. 'Religious' poetry is only a small category (unless we beg the question by calling all profoundly imaginative poetry 'religious') and often a somewhat uneasy one, since the self-searchings or conflicts of the poet as a personality often obscure and impede the imaginative vision, which comes from a deeper and impersonal source; from the Collective Unconscious, the Muse, the *anima mundi*, the Holy Spirit, the God. The name varies, the experience is constant. It is not the religion (if any) of the poet, in the personal and moral sense, that is in question. Even among poets professing the Christian religion (in forms so various to include Dante and Spenser, Milton and Vaughan, Blake and Edwin Muir) their metaphysics—their spiritual geometry—commonly proves to be neo-Platonic in essence. Coleridge, a Christian in his prose, is a neo-Platonist in his poems.

Obviously every poet's field of culture is different; but in my own detailed study of Blake's sources I have been astonished to discover how many of these he shared with the poets named, and with Yeats, Shelley, Wordsworth and others not professing the Christian faith. The canon of the learning of the imagination is constant. Such knowledge does not, like the discarded hypotheses of science, become obsolete; for it is not cumulative but a priori; or as poets and metaphysicians alike would say, not amassed by experiment but 'revealed' by inspiration; or as Plato says, by 'recollection'—*anamnesis*. To our European canon the present century has added many texts from the spiritual literature of the world without changing the essence of the knowledge or the intelligibility of its language. Such additions are no confusion, but an enrichment which in no way alters or weakens the structure. Yeats, typical of the eclectic modern situation, through theosophy, and later through his teacher Shri Purohit Swami, learned from Hindu philosophy. Early in his intellectual life he had read Swedenborg; studied Christian Cabala; the Buddhism of the Japanese *No* plays, besides Spiritualism, the folklore of Ireland and the primitive beliefs of the whole world, formed, for him, together with Plato and Plotinus, the Gnostic texts and the Hermetica, a body of imaginative learning as self-consistent as (within its own terms, as an account of the phenomenal world) modern science. This structure, within which human consciousness finds its ultimate orientation, stands the test not only of intellectual analysis but of experience; opening ways that materialism can but close. I believe that this knowledge (whether intuitive or learned, or, as is usually the case, more or less of both), is no less essential to the production of works of imagination than is knowledge of, and respect for, the 'laws of nature' essential to those who launch space-missiles. Certain experiences are not otherwise attainable than by exploring regions of experience whose very existence is destroyed by the materialist philosophy which denies access to them. For if the supernatural be 'no part of our mental furniture' how can we discover those modes of being, experience our own nature, or know

What Worlds, or what vast Regions hold
The immortal mind that hath forsook
Her mansion in this fleshly nook:
And of those *Daemons* that are found
In fire, air, flood, or under ground?

The imagination opens, now as always, into heavens and hells of the mind, beyond which lies boundless mystery.

The scientists seek in vain to quantify such knowledge; whereas, conversely, nature itself, for the imagination, becomes a living image, reflection, expression, incarnation, and language of spiritual realities, 'higher' in that they are causes of the phenomena of nature; which is 'lower' only insofar as it is the world of the effects of these causes. To the scientists themselves the Berkeleyan argument—that mind, or spirit is the only substantial reality—must, in terms of modern physics, seem unanswerable as an account of all that we actually see, hear and touch, and call a world; *maya*, as the Eastern philosophies have always understood. To the imagination everything in nature speaks of the mind which it reflects; of qualities; of 'the beautiful', that highest concept of Greek philosophy. *Nihil vacuum neque sine signum apud deum.* Without this implicit doctrine of the *signatura rerum*, the 'signatures' and 'correspondences' of things earthly to things heavenly, poetry cannot operate, being precisely the language of such correspondences. Such discourse, whether the poem be the *Divina Commedia* or Yeats's 'little song about a rose' is, I would say, what poetry simply is, if it is anything at all. It is a sacred language because it speaks of qualities; and behind qualities, and sustaining them, mysteries, meanings; the holy ground of the soul's country.

Poetry, God knows, does not deal in certainties so much as in the glimpses of that country seen at certain moments by that eternal exile Psyche. The Russian Metropolitan Archbishop Anthony Bloom reproved me when I said to him that atheism could probably have no poetry. No, he said, 'poetry is the language of longing'; only when the soul is dead can there no longer be poetry. But what can the atheist (the materialist, that is, not the a-theist of Buddhism, who in no way denies the spirit) long for, unless that things should be otherwise than he believes?

What if all traditional sources were to be lost and the learning of the spirit forgotten? This of course cannot happen; since virtually the whole human inheritance of the arts, all the literature of wisdom, proclaims the 'universal and unanimous tradition' which forms the structure of all possible experience. But if—unimaginably—this were to be so; or—and this is the actual situation of innumerable people in the modern world—a generation were to grow up in ignorance of traditional spiritual teaching, yet the nature of the soul must reaffirm itself. Jung has described the 'individuation process' by which, through our own dreams and intuitions, the ego discovers its hidden and holy 'ground'. Or truth may come, as Yeats heard it spoken, 'out of a medium's mouth'. Reality being always such as it is, it must be discovered and re-experienced countless times and in various ways. And those who discover the matter will soon discover the books of knowledge and works of art which bear witness to such experience; for our own enlightenment makes accessible all that tells of what we have ourselves perceived. As Plato says, we can learn only what we already know, but do not yet know we know. The learning of the imagination can remain an excluded knowledge only so long as the premises of material science remain unquestioned and their exclusions undetected.

QUESTIONS FOR CRITICAL ANALYSIS

1. What is the "materialist climate" or "materialist ideology" Raine keeps mentioning? Does she define it or explain it? What is her attitude towards it?
2. Raine discusses I. A. Richards' method of studying poetry that came to be called the "new criticism." Describe the process. Did you ever study poetry this way? What are the advantages of this method? What are the disadvantages? What is Raine's opinion of this approach? Why?
3. Raine takes on Jacob Bronowski and rejects his discussion of Rheims Cathedral. Why? What does Raine object to? Can you argue with her on this point? What seems to be Raine's attitude toward science and engineering more generally? How does she reveal it?
4. Raine claims that losses of meaning come about "when the reader's premises are not those of the poet." How can we know whether this is true or not? What does this mean for twentieth century American readers of Milton, Homer, Dostoyevski, Lady Murasaki? Does Raine mean that we should only read literature of our own time and place? On what do you base your answer?
5. Raine implies that poetry (and, by extension, the humanities) are exclusively driven by quality, imagination, and mystery, while science and engineering are in the domain

of quantity, finite knowledge, and the "what" of life. Do you agree with her? Name ways that imagination is crucial to scientific understanding and accomplishment.

QUESTIONS FOR STRUCTURAL ANALYSIS

1. State in one or two sentences the theme of Raine's essay. What attitudes and assumptions underlie her essay?
2. Raine mentions nearly 60 different writers and thinkers in this paper. Why does she bring their names into the essay? Did this enhance her ideas for you? How many of these people did you recognize?
3. Raine argues by making bald claims and statements that challenge the reader to come up with an alternative idea. Find some of these statements and examine the supporting evidence Raine provides. Do you agree with her statements? Why, or why not?
4. This paper was delivered at the Institute of Christian Studies in London. What indicators do you have about the nature of its intended audience?
5. What is Raine's conclusion? What action does she anticipate from her readers? Do you agree with her conclusion? Why, or why not?

*T*HE *L*IBERAL *A*RTS *R*ELIGION

CAROLINE BIRD

Caroline Bird (1915–   ), writer, political activist, and feminist, conducted research for Newsweek *and* Fortune *magazines before moving into public relations as a writer and researcher. Her work on* The Invisible Scar *(1966), a socioeconomic study of the Great Depression, led Bird to a feminist perspective as she discovered the discrimination women and other minorities encountered in employment. After she wrote* Born Female: The High Cost of Keeping Women Down *(1968), she began actively working for women's rights. "The Liberal Arts Religion" is from* The Case Against College *(1975), an argument against higher education which suggests alternative, and better, routes to learning.*

Before you begin reading: *Think carefully about why you enrolled in college. What good is a college education? Write at least a paragraph in your reading notebook explaining to someone who didn't go to college why you decided college was important for you.*

◆

THE ACADEMIC DEAN OF A FAMOUS OLD COLLEGE LOWERED her voice, glanced apprehensively around her office, and confessed: "I just wish I had the guts to tell parents that when you get out of this place you aren't prepared to *do anything*."

Actually, it did not take much guts. The "best" colleges are the liberal arts schools which are the most "academic"—they don't teach students anything useful in particular. Even after they have to face the world, alumni expect no more. In a study intended to probe what graduates seven years out of college thought their colleges should have given them, the Carnegie Commission found overwhelming preference for "liberal" over "vocational" goals.[1]

What does anyone mean by "a liberal education"? People shift their ground when they try to explain what it is and why it is so important. It's hard to tell whether they're talking about *subjects* that can be studied in school, such as philosophy and literature; a *process* of learning or thinking; or a *personal transformation* ("college opened my eyes"); or a *value system* to which the wise and honest can repair.

The *subject matter* of the liberal arts used to be the classics. If not the ancients, then newer books on history, sociology, economics, science, and other products of the minds of men. As we near the twenty-first century, however, most educators have given up the attempt to pass on the "great tradition of Western man" in a four-year core curriculum. It's not *what* you study, they say, it's *how* you study it.

"A liberal education is an experience that is philosophical in the broadest sense," David Truman, dean of Columbia and later president of Mount Holyoke, has said. "The particular subjects do not so much contain this quality as provide jointly a possible means of approaching it. The liberal arts, then, include those subjects that can most readily be taught so as to produce an understanding of the modes of thought, the grounds of knowledge, and their interrelations, established and to be discovered."

In plainer language alumni say, "College taught me how to think for myself." If you ask people what they mean by thinking and how college teaches it, they recoil from the implication that the kind of thinking they mean is a specific skill, such as the art of rhetoric, but start talking about a "whole new way of looking at the world"—a personal transformation.

Personal transformation, not only in how one's mind works but in how one views the world and oneself, is the most cherished expectation—and sometimes it is achieved. "College changed me inside," one alumnus told us. Some wax poetic. "The liberal arts education aspires to expand the imaginative space and time in which a person lives." Others talk about the "broadening" that occurs when a young woman from a Midwest farming town encounters adults who don't regret the fact that MacArthur was not elected President, or when the son of a city plumber learns that the police are not always right and that some people on welfare aren't cheating. Discoveries like this are valuable, alumni say, because they force students to "formulate the values and goals of my life," as the Carnegie Commission puts it.

And this turns out to be the hidden agenda of a liberal arts education. A value system, a standard, a set of ideals to keep you pointed in the right direction, even if you can't get there. "Like Christianity, the liberal arts are seldom practiced and would probably be hated by the majority of the populace if they were," said one defender.

The analogy is apt. The fact is, of course, that the liberal arts are a religion in every sense of that term. When people talk about them, their language becomes elevated, metaphorical, extravagant, theoretical, and reverent.

In answering a black student who charged the Kirkland College curriculum with "irrelevance," President Samuel F. Babbitt remonstrated that her liberal arts education aimed to expose her "to the values, the successes, the failures of great minds, great men and women engaged in every conceivable endeavor through the study of history and literature and art and the other disciplines that man has formed in order to understand where he has been and how to order his world."

"The purpose of the liberal arts is not to teach businessmen business," Alfred Whitney Griswold, former president of Yale, told an alumni gathering. Rather, he went on, it is to "awaken and develop the intellectual and spiritual powers in the individual before he enters upon his chosen career, so that he may bring to that career the greatest possible assets of intelligence, resourcefulness, judgment, and character."

These thickets of verbal foliage are embarrassing to the more sensitive spokesmen for higher education. John T. Retalliata, president of the Illinois Institute of Technology, told an audience of parents in 1973, "I suppose a generalized goal is to have your sons and daughters, somehow, become 'educated' and, with that education, become well-employed and happy." Clark Kerr, notable as the embattled president of the University of California during the 1960s, told a 1972 television audience that "generally, the studies show that people who've been to college, oh, enjoy life more, they have more varied interests, they participate more in community activities." On another occasion, he told Alan Pifer, president of the Carnegie Corporation, that "with all that has happened in the world of knowledge in recent years, it is really impossible for people in higher education to come to agreement on what constitutes a liberal education."

Intellectuals have trouble describing the benefits of a liberal education because the liberal arts are a religion, the established religion of the ruling class. The exalted language, the universal setting, the ultimate value, the inability to define, the appeal to personal witness, the indirectness, the aphorisms—these are all the familiar modes of religious discourse.

As with religion, no proof is required, only faith. You don't have to prove the existence of God. You don't have to understand the Virgin Birth. You don't have to prove that Camus is better than Jacqueline Susann. Camus is sacred, so Camus is better and so are the people who dig him. If you don't dig Camus, the trouble is not with Camus, but with you.

Faith in personal salvation by the liberal arts is professed in a creed intoned on ceremonial occasions such as commencements. It is blasphemy to take the promises literally, and if you don't understand what the words mean, you are only admitting your lack of grace.

Take, for instance, the goal of college most fervently sought by the alumni queried by the Carnegie Commission, "development of my abilities to think and express myself." Only the captious dare to ask, "What do you mean by your ability to think?" If you inquire, it very quickly develops that those who value this objective aren't talking about what the Swiss educator Jean Piaget, the semanticist Noam Chomsky, or the Harvard psychologist Jerome Bruner mean when they talk about "thinking."[2] The kind of "thinking" the cognitive psychologists are talking about has to be acquired long before you are old enough to go to college, and if Piaget is right, most of it has to be learned before a child is old enough to go to school. What the alumni and employers expect college to teach is the habit of logical analysis and the conventions of rhetoric that make it possible to resolve differences of view on human affairs by debate and discussion. Colleges with very small classes try to give their students practice in the art of dialogue, but the students who speak up in class are usually the ones who have already learned how at the dinner table at home and in bull sessions with friends.

If the liberal arts are a religious faith, the professors are its priests. Professors are not accountable to the laity they serve. They themselves define the boundaries of their authority and choose their own successors. Their authority is unassailable, because by definition they know best. As such, they are invulnerable to lay criticism. One of the educators with whom I talked dismissed the doubts of students out of hand. "I am not convinced that eighteen-year-olds can or should be expected to know what college will ultimately do for them."

The professors disclaim arbitrary personal power. They go by rules. They contend that right is not what they think but what the sacred scriptures or the ecclesiastical courts decree. Professors say that truth is what comes out when you subject data to a process called the scientific method, and it is this process, rather than its product, that is written in the stars. But the process itself, this very scientific method, is also a product of the mind of man, and it may not be the only process the mind of man can devise. Other processes may produce other kinds of truth. No one, for instance, would suggest that the visions of William Blake could be "disproved" by the scientific method.

Colleges govern themselves by their own rules and sometimes confront civil authority. Only during the 1960s, when the students were out of control, did college administrators admit the right of the local police to "invade" the campus. And, like the church, American colleges have used their credibility to exercise political, economic, and social power in an irresponsible way. Along with access to heaven, they don't mind controlling access to the good things of this world. So long as the diploma is a credential for good jobs, giving or withholding it determines the fate of students here on earth. The colleges do not claim that they are preparing candidates for executive work, for instance, but they do not renounce their role as gatekeeper of the best jobs. As one professor told us, "We can't help it that the big companies like to hire our graduates."

To be blunt, the colleges have been as willing as the church to grab the power the faithful thrust upon them. Through their power to issue the diploma, they decide the fate of individuals. Through their power to determine who shall be admitted to college, they select as "naturally better" those who manipulate abstract symbols and unwittingly consign to the damnation of dead-end, second-class role, those whose intelligence is manual, visual, or artistic. The power we allow them to have makes our society more vulnerable to words and abstractions than it would otherwise be, and it is not necessary to have a settled opinion on whether this is good or bad to recognize the danger of subjecting young people during their formative years to control by authorities who are pursing objectives that leave most of the population cold. We think they are benign, therefore we accept their rule over our young. Imagine the outcry at the very idea of turning our surplus young people over to the military for safekeeping!

Americans have always been sensitive to the attempts of their armed forces to use military competence as a basis for exercising political power. But we do not distrust the same kind of bid when it comes from the professoriate. Through their control of research, they decide what frontiers of knowledge shall be pushed back. Through their interpretation of the scientific method, if not the sacred writings of "the great Western tradition," they decide what shall be accepted as good, or true, or even beautiful.

But just as technical progress threatened the various monopolies of the church at the end of the Middle Ages, so the information explosion today threatens the monopoly of college over knowledge.

Of all the forms in which ideas are disseminated, the college professor lecturing his class is the slowest and the most expensive. The culturally deprived for whom college is supposedly so broadening are in the best position to see this. "I can read a book just as good as the man can talk," a black woman student told us. "Nine chances out of ten that's all you get—a professor who's just reading out of a book."

A better college experience would, no doubt, have provided more stimulation than students encountered in the overloaded colleges of the 1960s. But this begs the issue.

Today you don't have to go to college to read the great books. You don't have to go to college to learn about the great ideas of Western man. If you want to learn about Milton, or Camus, or even Margaret Mead, you can find them. In paperbacks. In the public library. In museum talks. In the public lectures most colleges offer for free. In adult education courses given by local high schools. People don't storm these sources because they aren't interested, and there's no particular reason why they should be. Forcing people to "learn" about them by all sorts of social and economic carrots and sticks implies that those who have had contact with "high culture" are somehow better than other people.

And if you do want to learn, it isn't always necessary to go to the original source. I say this knowing that I am stamping myself as an academic heretic. But the culture consumer should be able to decide for himself exactly why, when, how much, and in what form he would like to partake of Daniel Defoe's *Robinson Crusoe*, or Milton's *Areopagitica*, or Simone de Beauvoir's *The Second Sex*. When I was in high school during the 1920s, the whole English class took a month to read *Ivanhoe*, Sir Walter Scott's novel about the crusades. In 1969 my eight-year-old son zipped through a Classic Comic version in fifteen minutes, and I don't think the original warranted the extra time it would have taken him. If you are not interested in the development of the English novel, *Robinson Crusoe* can be an exasperating, slow-moving yarn, significant only because the name has become a symbol of lone adventure and one of the passwords recognized by all men who consider themselves educated. Milton's *Areopagitica* is another password, important for what it says and when it was said. There's a benefit in knowing about these works, but the benefit to any particular person at a particular time may not justify the cost of taking them raw. For many people, and many purposes, it makes more sense to read a summary, an abstract, or even listen to a television critic.

The problem is no longer how to provide access to the broadening ideas of the great cultural tradition, nor even how to liberate young people so that they can adopt a different life-style than the one in which they were reared. The problem is the other way around: how to choose among the many courses of action proposed to us, how to edit the stimulations that pour into our eyes and ears every waking hour. A college experience that piles option on option and stimulation on stimulation merely adds to the contemporary nightmare. Increasingly, overloaded undergraduates give up the attempt to reason and flirt, half seriously, with the occult, which leaves vexing decisions to fate.

In order to deal with options, you need values. When Morris Keeton and Conrad Hilberry attempted to define a liberal education in their book *Struggle and Promise: A Future for Colleges*, they found that one of the recurrent themes was that it provides "an integrated view of the world which can serve as an inner guide,"[3] and more than four-fifths of the alumni queried by the Carnegie Commission said they expected that their college should have "helped me to formulate values and goals of my life." The formation of values may not be the first goal mentioned in discussions of a liberal education, but it tends to be the final ground on which hard-pressed defenders take their stand.

How does a student acquire a standard of values? The liberally educated are forbidden, by their own creed, from any procedure so simple as telling students what is right and good. In theory a student is taught how to decide for himself, but in practice it doesn't work quite that way. All but the wayward and the saints take their values of the good, the true, and the beautiful from the people around them. When we speak of students acquiring "values" in college, we often mean that they will acquire the values—and sometimes we mean only the tastes—of their professors.

The values of professors may well be "higher" than many students can expect to encounter elsewhere, but often those values aren't relevant to the situations in which students find themselves in college or later. Too many academics systematically overvalue symbols and abstractions. Historians will recall that it was a professor of history, President Woodrow Wilson, who sent American soldiers abroad to "make the world safe for democracy."

In addition to a distressing confusion of symbol and thing, professors are sometimes painfully ignorant of many essential facts of life. A lot of them know very little about the economic structure of the United States, and their notions of what goes on inside major corporations are based on books written forty years ago about conditions prevailing fifty years ago. And they may also be partially responsible for some of the "alienation" of the young because they have encouraged the belief that transactions of power and money are to be avoided as a dirty business.

In so doing, of course, they are intuitively defending the legitimacy of their own power. A poor boy who wanted to make good in the Middle Ages had to become a priest and at least profess to see the world in spiritual terms. A poor boy who wants to make good in twentieth-century America has to get a liberal education and at least profess to see the world in intellectual terms.

The academic elite are the self-proclaimed guardians of what's right. Who's to tell them when they are wrong? Academics pride themselves on introducing students to a free marketplace of ideas, but they are the ones who make the rules, and the rules themselves can perpetuate dangerous distortions of reality. Not so long ago, for instance, no painter who drew pubic hair on a nude figure could expect to be taken seriously as an artist. It would have been vulgar to see it. The oversight is amusing now, but it was not trivial. Victorian prudery was hard to combat because it was a convention of the "best people." It's easy to laugh, but harder to be sure that we are not overlooking some other facts of life today.

A liberal arts education does, of course, transmit standards of value, and those in charge assume, almost as self-confidently as that great Victorian, Matthew Arnold, that "the best that has been known and thought in the world" is what they say it is. Intellectual leaders today worry about sounding snobbish, but they are just as sure as the great eighteenth-century English essayist Richard Steele that "it is the great aim of education to raise ourselves above the vulgar." And those who have been so educated are happy to accept the distinction. At Harvard commencements there is an audible sigh of emotion when the president, as he has done for 300 years, welcomes the new graduates into "the fellowship of educated men." (Since 1970, it has been "the fellowship of educated men and women.")

NOTES

1. "When alumni were forced to choose between a general education and a career-oriented education, they overwhelmingly endorsed the idea of a general education," Joe L. Spaeth and Andrew M. Greeley reported in *Recent Alumni and Higher Education*, a Carnegie Commission study published by McGraw-Hill, New York, in 1970. The study queried 40,000 graduates of the class of 1961 in 135 colleges in 1961, 1962, 1963, 1964, and 1968.
2. For a quick introduction to the slippery concepts involved in thinking about thinking, see the section "The Elements and Vehicles of Thought," pp. 188–237, in Berelson & Steiner, *Human Behavior, An Inventory of Scientific Findings*, Harcourt Brace, New York, 1964.
3. A dogged attempt to cope with the verbal foliage surrounding definitions of a liberal education appears in Morris Keeton and Conrad Hilberry's *Struggle and Promise: A Future for Colleges*, McGraw-Hill, New York, 1969, p. 260. They identify several common elements including cultivation of the intellect; encouragement of "independent judgment" or "critical thought"; liberating the individual so that he can see the world in perspectives other than his own; evoking an integrated view of the world which can serve as an inner guide; equipping the individual to serve his society.

Questions for Critical Analysis

1. Bird criticizes academic colleges that "don't teach students anything useful in particular." What is her assumption about higher education? Do you agree with her? Why, or why not?
2. Bird claims that the "liberal arts are a religion in every sense of that term." How does she support this claim? Compare liberal arts and religion either to show that Bird is correct or to show that her claim is false. Does her argument by analogy work? Why, or why not?
3. Colleges exercise political, economic and social power irresponsibly, according to Bird. What does she mean? What evidence does she offer for this statement? From your own experiences in college, either support or differ with her statement.
4. What is Bird's opinion of professors? What role do they play in "the liberal arts religion"? Describe the way Bird argues her case against professors. Does she convince you by her argument? Why, or why not?
5. What is your definition of a liberal arts education? Why are you enrolled in college, taking academic courses, rather than attending a vocational or trade school? How do you defend your decision to friends who decided not to attend college?

Questions for Structural Analysis

1. What tone does Bird establish by her title and first paragraph? How does she reveal her attitude toward a liberal arts education so quickly? Does she come across as someone you could discuss the subject with reasonably? What affect does her tone have on your response to the essay?
2. This essay comes from a book, *The Case Against College*, which readers describe as a controversial argument, or polemic. Point out phrases, words, images, and sentences that contribute to the emotional appeal of Bird's argument.
3. How many times does Bird quote an authority? Why does she rely on this device to further her argument? Do you think she presents her authorities fairly? Give examples of Bird's misuse of quotations and/or speakers.
4. Review the comments on pages 717–723 on writing argument and then study the form of Bird's argument. (It may be helpful to outline her argument, stating the main points and the evidence she gives to support them.) Discuss any logical fallacies you encounter in Bird's essay.
5. How does Bird conclude her essay? What response does she expect from her reader?
6. Bird's essay opposes the premises of the other three essays in this section. How would Bird respond to their ideas and values? What might their response be toward her?

*L*EARNING *T*HROUGH *B*OOKS

TOPICS FOR WRITING ESSAYS

Many of the questions following each essay can serve as appropriate writing suggestions. Some of the topics listed below expand the prereading exercises, but they can be used without completing that step first.

1. Raine discusses scientific materialism in terms of religion, and Bird describes the liberal arts as the religion of the upper class. Why do these writers draw the analogy between an idea they dislike and religion? What makes religion a good comparison for them? What assumptions do they seem to have about religion? Write a paper that explains the nature of religion *as these writers seem to understand it.* Use both Raine and Bird to support your analysis. Write your paper to an educated nonreligious reader. (NOTE: If you have strongly held religious beliefs that will turn your paper into a testimonial for your beliefs, it would be better for you to select a different topic.)
2. Remember a time when you have been deeply moved by reading the ideas of a major writer. Write an essay that explains how those ideas affected your life by changing your attitudes, beliefs and/or behavior. Write your paper in response to a college application form that requests such an essay.
3. Your younger brother (or sister) has just read Caroline Bird's essay (possibly the entire book from which the essay was taken) and has written to tell you that not only is he or she not going to attend college but he or she thinks you are wasting your time and should drop out and get a decent job. Write a paper to him or her and explain—using Bird's arguments as a starting point—why you think your college education is important now and will be important to you in the future.

RESEARCH POSSIBILITIES

1. Take a major—though manageable—historical event (the Battle of Gettysburg, for example, not the Civil War; or the bombing of Pearl Harbor, not the Second World War) and read descriptions of that event from as many sources as possible. Make sure that you read accounts written years apart from each other. Notice how the event is described: what is different in all these accounts? Are the people, events, dialogue, ideas, motivations treated exactly the same? When you take your notes, be careful to indicate the date for each source. Write a paper describing how the historical record describing the event has changed over the years. Plan to publish the paper in a popular

magazine for readers who enjoy reading history and may be surprised to find out that the "facts" are often changed through interpretation.

2. How do you think people on your campus would respond to Bird's argument against a liberal arts education? Use some of the points Bird raises as a basis to interview students and faculty to find out why they think a liberal arts education is important. Write a report for the student newspaper that uses Bird's essay as a vehicle from which to launch an argument on the virtues of a liberal arts education—or to reveal that most students and faculty support her anti-intellectualism.

PART THREE

SCIENCE AND MATHEMATICS

KNOW ABOUT OUR WORLD

The authors in this section use several different methods as they attempt to define science to the nonscientist: Sagan offers the most straightforward definition; Wilson looks at scientists—who they are and why they love science; Bush provides a philosophical context for developing a definition of how science affects our thoughts and lives; Morowitz describes the tools of science: why science depends on mathematics for its expression; Kraus describes how physicists study nature, and Calandra portrays a student "doing" science.

*C*AN *W*E *K*NOW THE *U*NIVERSE? *R*EFLECTIONS ON A *G*RAIN OF *S*ALT

CARL SAGAN

Carl Sagan (1934–), an astronomer at Cornell University, conducts research on the physics and chemistry of planetary atmospheres and surfaces, explores the origins of life, and has been closely involved in the Mariner, Viking, and Voyager space explorations. Sagan, the creator of the Cosmos *television series (1980), is a popular author uniquely able to explain complex scientific ideas in terms a layman can understand. "Can We Know the Universe?," a chapter from* Broca's Brain *(1979) defines science not as a body of knowledge but as a way of questioning the universe. Sagan uses an investigation into a grain of salt to illustrate how we must examine below the surface if we want to practice science and discover the meaning of nature.*

Before you begin reading: *For at least five minutes look carefully at a simple object, such as a leaf, paper clip, twig, piece of paper, or stone and think about what it is you're looking at. Then, in your reading notebook, write down as many questions as you can about the object.*

◆

Nothing is rich but the inexhaustible wealth
of nature. She shows us only surfaces,
but she is a million fathoms deep.
RALPH WALDO EMERSON

SCIENCE IS A WAY OF THINKING MUCH MORE THAN IT IS A body of knowledge. Its goal is to find out how the world works, to seek what regularities there may be, to penetrate to the connections of things—from subnuclear particles, which may be the constituents of all matter, to living organisms, the human social community, and thence to the cosmos as a whole. Our intuition is by no means an infallible guide. Our perceptions may be distorted by training and prejudice or merely because of the limitations of our sense organs, which, of course, perceive directly but a small fraction of the phenomena of the world. Even so straightforward a question as whether in the absence of friction a pound of lead falls faster than a gram of fluff was answered incorrectly by Aristotle and almost everyone else before the time of Galileo. Science is based on experiment, on a willingness to challenge old dogma, on an openness to see the universe as it really is. Accordingly, science sometimes requires courage—at the very least the courage to question the conventional wisdom.

Beyond this the main trick of science is to *really* think of something: the shape of clouds and their occasional sharp bottom edges at the same altitude everywhere in the sky; the formation of a dewdrop on a leaf; the origin of a name or a word—Shakespeare, say, or "philanthropic"; the reason for human social customs—the incest taboo, for example; how it is that a lens in sunlight can make paper burn; how a "walking stick" got to look so much like a twig; why the Moon seems to follow us as we walk; what prevents us from digging a hole down to the center of the Earth; what the definition is of "down" on a spherical Earth; how it is possible for the body to convert yesterday's lunch into today's muscle and sinew; or how far is up—does the universe go on forever, or if it does not, is there any meaning to the question of what lies on the other side? Some of these questions are pretty easy. Others, especially the last, are mysteries to which no one even today knows the answer. They are natural questions to ask. Every culture has posed such questions in one way or another. Almost always the proposed answers are in the nature of "Just So Stories," attempted explanations divorced from experiment, or even from careful comparative observations.

But the scientific cast of mind examines the world critically as if many alternative worlds might exist, as if other things might be here which are not. Then we are forced to ask why what we see is present and not something else. Why are the Sun and the Moon and the planets spheres? Why not pyramids, or cubes, or dodecahedra? Why not irregular, jumbly shapes? Why so symmetrical, worlds? If you spend any time spinning hypotheses, checking to see whether they make sense, whether they conform to what else we know, thinking of tests you can pose to substantiate or deflate your hypotheses, you will find yourself doing science. And as you come to practice this habit of thought more and more you will get better and better at it. To penetrate into the heart of the thing—even a little thing, a blade of grass, as Walt Whitman said—is to experience a kind of exhilaration that, it may be, only human beings of all the beings on this planet can feel. We are an intelligent species and the use of our intelligence quite properly gives us pleasure. In this respect the brain is like a muscle. When we think well, we feel good. Understanding is a kind of ecstasy.

But to what extent can we *really* know the universe around us? Sometimes this question is posed by people who hope the answer will be in the negative, who are fearful of a universe in which everything might one day be known. And sometimes we hear pronouncements from scientists who confidently state that everything worth knowing will soon be known—or even is already known—and who paint pictures of a Dionysian or Polynesian age in which the zest for intellectual discovery has withered, to be replaced by a kind of subdued languor, the lotus eaters drinking fermented coconut milk or some other mild hallucinogen. In addition to maligning both the Polynesians, who were intrepid explorers (and whose brief respite in paradise is now sadly ending), as well as the inducements to intellectual discovery provided by some hallucinogens, this contention turns out to be trivially mistaken.

Let us approach a much more modest question: not whether we can know the universe or the Milky Way Galaxy or a star or a world. Can we know, ultimately and in detail, a grain of salt? Consider one microgram of table salt, a speck just barely large enough for someone with keen eyesight to make out without a microscope. In that grain of salt there are about 10^{16} sodium and chlorine atoms. This is a 1 followed by 16 zeros, 10 million billion atoms. If we wish to know a grain of salt, we must know at least the three-dimensional positions of each of these atoms. (In fact, there is much more to be known—for example, the nature of the forces between the atoms—but we are making only a modest calculation.) Now, is this number more or less than the number of things which the brain can know?

How much *can* the brain know? There are perhaps 10^{11} neurons in the brain, the circuit elements and switches that are responsible in their electrical and chemical activity for the functioning of our minds. A typical brain neuron has perhaps a thousand little wires, called dendrites, which connect it with its fellows. If, as seems likely, every bit of information in the brain corresponds to one of these connections, the total number of things knowable by the brain is no more than 10^{14}, one hundred trillion. But this number is only one percent of the number of atoms in our speck of salt.

So in this sense the universe is intractable, astonishingly immune to any human attempt at full knowledge. We cannot on this level understand a grain of salt, much less the universe.

But let us look a little more deeply at our microgram of salt. Salt happens to be a crystal in which, except for defects in the structure of the crystal lattice, the position of every sodium and chlorine atom is predetermined. If we could shrink ourselves into this crystalline world, we would see rank upon rank of atoms in an ordered array, a regularly alternating structure—sodium, chlorine, sodium, chlorine, specifying the sheet of atoms we are standing on and all the sheets above us and below us. An absolutely pure crystal of salt could have the position of every atom specified by something like 10 bits of information.* This would not strain the information-carrying capacity of the brain.

If the universe had natural laws that governed its behavior to the same degree of regularity that determines a crystal of salt, then, of course, the universe would

*Chlorine is a deadly poison gas employed on European battlefields in World War I. Sodium is a corrosive metal which burns upon contact with water. Together thay make a placid and unpoisonous material, table salt. Why each of these substances has the properties it does is a subject called chemistry, which requires more than 10 bits of information to understand.

be knowable. Even if there were many such laws, each of considerable complexity, human beings might have the capability to understand them all. Even if such knowledge exceeded the information-carrying capacity of the brain, we might store the additional information outside our bodies—in books, for example, or in computer memories—and still, in some sense, know the universe.

Human beings are, understandably, highly motivated to find regularities, natural laws. The search for rules, the only possible way to understand such a vast and complex universe, is called science. The universe forces those who live in it to understand it. Those creatures who find everyday experience a muddled jumble of events with no predictability, no regularity, are in grave peril. The universe belongs to those who, at least to some degree, have figured it out.

It is an astonishing fact that there *are* laws of nature, rules that summarize conveniently—not just qualitatively but quantitatively—how the world works. We might imagine a universe in which there are no such laws, in which the 10^{80} elementary particles that make up a universe like our own behave with utter and uncompromising abandon. To understand such a universe we would need a brain at least as massive as the universe. It seems unlikely that such a universe could have life and intelligence, because beings and brains require some degree of internal stability and order. But even if in a much more random universe there were such beings with an intelligence much greater than our own, there could not be much knowledge, passion or joy.

Fortunately for us, we live in a universe that has at least important parts that are knowable. Our common-sense experience and our evolutionary history have prepared us to understand something of the workaday world. When we go into other realms, however, common sense and ordinary intuition turn out to be highly unreliable guides. It is stunning that as we go close to the speed of light our mass increases indefinitely, we shrink toward zero thickness in the direction of motion, and time for us comes as near to stopping as we would like. Many people think that this is silly, and every week or two I get a letter from someone who complains to me about it. But it is a virtually certain consequence not just of experiment but also of Albert Einstein's brilliant analysis of space and time called the Special Theory of Relativity. It does not matter that these effects seem unreasonable to us. We are not in the habit of traveling close to the speed of light. The testimony of our common sense is suspect at high velocities.

Or consider an isolated molecule composed of two atoms shaped something like a dumbbell—a molecule of salt, it might be. Such a molecule rotates about an axis through the line connecting the two atoms. But in the world of quantum mechanics, the realm of the very small, not all orientations of our dumbbell molecule are possible. It might be that the molecule could be oriented in a horizontal position, say, or in a vertical position, but not at many angles in between. Some rotational positions are forbidden. Forbidden by what? By the laws of nature. The universe is built in such a way as to limit, or quantize, rotation. We do not experience this directly in everyday life; we would find it startling as well as awkward in sitting-up exercises, to find arms outstretched from the sides or pointed up to the skies permitted but many intermediate positions forbidden. We do not live in the world of the small, on the scale of 10^{-13} centimeters, in the realm where there are twelve zeros between the decimal place and the one. Our common-sense intuitions do not count. What does count is experiment—in this case observations from the far infrared spectra of molecules. They show molecular rotation to be quantized.

The idea that the world placed restrictions on what humans might do is frustrating. Why *shouldn't* we be able to have intermediate rotational positions? Why *can't* we travel faster than the speed of light? But so far as we can tell, this is the way the universe is constructed. Such prohibitions not only press us toward a little humility; they also make the world more knowable. Every restriction corresponds to a law of nature, a regularization of the universe. The more restrictions there are on what matter and energy can do, the more knowledge human beings can attain. Whether in some sense the universe is ultimately knowable depends not only on how many natural laws there are that encompass widely divergent phenomena, but also on whether we have the openness and the intellectual capacity to understand such laws. Our formulations of the regularities of nature are surely dependent on how the brain is built, but also, and to a significant degree, on how the universe is built.

For myself, I like a universe that includes much that is unknown and, at the same time, much that is knowable. A universe in which everything is known would be static and dull, as boring as the heaven of some weak-minded theologians. A universe that is unknowable is no fit place for a thinking being. The ideal universe for us is one very much like the universe we inhabit. And I would guess that this is not really much of a coincidence.

Questions for Critical Analysis

1. How does Sagan define science? What is your definition of science? How close is Sagan's definition to yours? Do you think scientists approach their work differently than other people? In what ways?
2. What does Sagan mean when he says that the universe "forces those who live in it to understand it"? What attitude is implicit in his statement: "The universe belongs to those who, at least to some degree, have figured it out"? Do you agree with these statements?
3. What characteristic of a grain of salt makes it possible for the human mind to understand it? By extension, does Sagan imply that we can understand the universe? How?
4. Under what conditions does our understanding of natural laws not apply to understanding the universe? When is common sense and experience not enough in predicting behavior? How can scientists know what goes on under these conditions?

5. How do restrictions make the world more knowable? What is the advantage of not knowing all the answers? Does this attitude apply to areas of life other than science?

QUESTIONS FOR STRUCTURAL ANALYSIS

1. How does the epigram by Ralph Waldo Emerson relate to the essay? Why did Sagan choose to preface his essay by it?
2. Why does Sagan attempt to answer the question of whether we can know the universe through considerations of a grain of salt? Why select a grain of salt as his subject instead of something else?
3. Sagan writes: "Understanding is a kind of ecstasy." What does he mean? How does the essay reflect his attitude?
4. Sagan answers the question of his title in at least three ways. What are his answers? Do they contradict each other?
5. In the concluding paragraph of the essay, Sagan's tone changes to become more direct and personal. Why did he do that? What does he mean by the sentences: "The ideal universe for us is one very much like the universe we inhabit. And I would guess that this is not really much of a coincidence"? What clues does this paragraph offer about Sagan's philosophy towards life?

On Being a Scientist

Mitchell Wilson

Mitchell Wilson (1913–1973) conducted physics research at Columbian Carbon Company for five years during the Second World War, leaving to become a freelance writer in 1945 until his death in 1973. Wilson's later novels dealt with the conflict many scientists experience between their passion for knowledge and the applications made of that knowledge. In "On Being a Scientist," Wilson presents the human side of science by looking at the people who practice science: how do they describe their work? how do scientists differ from other scientists, and from the rest of us? By discussing the problems between the "two cultures" of science and the humanities, Wilson wonders about society's distrust of technology and science. He focuses on the creative aspect of science, showing how it affects us in a way the arts can never do.

Before you begin reading: *Think about your favorite branch of science: astronomy, biology, chemistry, geology, physics. Make a list of images, experiences, and words that evoke the subject for you.*

◆

TO THE OUTSIDE WORLD, THE WORD *SCIENTIST* REFERS TO a jumble of strange bedfellows—physicists, chemists, biologists, and at least thirty other clans—who spend their lives among the riddles and realities of nature. Each man is convinced that his particular science is more important than the others—and totally different in the intellectual and temperamental qualities it requires. Physicists speak of organic chemistry as being as boring as bookkeeping. Biologists retort that the intellectual austerity of physics is as airless and soul-numbing as the inside of an ether cone. Lord Todd, white-haired Nobel laureate in organic chemistry, once while telling how he had taken over a problem from biochemistry, assured me that the two chemistries were totally different disciplines, even though to a nonscientist they seem to be concerned with almost identical material.

With preferences so passionately defended, and distinctions so finely drawn, one would assume that a man ought to be able to tell you why he made his particular choice. I. I. Rabi at Columbia said flatly: "Because physics is the only basic science there is. Everything else is to the right of it and depends on it. Nothing is to the left of it."

Max Perutz in Cambridge said just as flatly: "Molecular biology is the basic science of life; it is now the only way one knows what one is talking about."

Allan Sandage at Mount Palomar says: "Astronomy and cosmogony—that's where the great questions still have to be answered."

Jacques Monod of the Pasteur Institute says: "Why biology? Well, because I felt that was where the most work was to be done."

Picasso, when asked why he chose to be an artist, lost his temper and retorted that when a man finds himself asking why he is doing what he is doing, it is time for him to give it up. The men of science whom I questioned kept their tempers; still, what they gave me were not reasons at all but only statements of preference. These highly analytical men were no more able to describe precisely what had captured their minds than is any young lover to explain why he is deeply in love with a particular girl and not her sister. They knew there would never be wealth as the world measures it, nor even success in the popular sense. Why, then, do they do what they do? They don't know.

I had assumed, too, that the scientist's objectivity would enable him to discern not only new ideas but the men who generate new ideas. Among physicists, the saying goes that "there are really only two categories of men who become theoreticians; the geniuses, and the men who are merely brilliant. Those less than brilliant needn't bother to come around." Scientists themselves, of course, know their ranks include a great many who are far from brilliant, and some who are incompetent. They know, too, that among them are science snobs and climbers who want to be—and be seen—in the presence of famous and accomplished scientists. There are also the science politicians and influence brokers. But no matter how contemptible, foolish, fatuous, or venal a man may be, the work he does and has done weighs more with his fellow scientists than the ugliness which is all the outside world may see.

In the end, among themselves, scientists respect only one quality—excellence. No scientist cares that Newton could be meanly vindictive, that Michelson compulsively chased girls, that Pauli's wit could be malevolent and destructive. The scientist reveres talent when it exists, but the men whose careers are dedicated to increasing man's perception of the universe are not always able to perceive among themselves those who will emerge and tower over everyone else.

Albert Einstein was thought to have so little promise at graduation that no school or university bothered to offer him a job. Five years later, in 1905, at the age of twenty-six, the still supposedly untalented man working as an obscure patent clerk in Bern published three original papers in a single year, each of which was destined to become a classic of scientific thought. The response from the world of science to this unprecedented performance was total indifference. That silence persisted for another five years.

When Niels Bohr in 1913—also in his twenties—worked out the bizarre conditions under which an atom could have the planetary structure which experiment seemed to call for, it was only one of dozens of alternative atomic theories that had been appearing in the journals month after month for decades. No one paid very much attention even though, a few months after publication, Einstein confided to a friend that Bohr's ideas, however radical, were of the greatest importance. "I once had similar ideas but I didn't dare publish them!" was his amazing confession. Albert Szent-Gyorgyi, who has ranged over half a dozen fields in the life sciences with brilliance and Hungarian wit, admits that he once so despaired of any recognition in the early years in biochemistry that he actually determined on suicide.

These are instances of overlooked talent far worse than these—cases where true ability went unacknowledged until ten, twenty, thirty years after the man's death. The monk Mendel, for example, founded the science of genetics in a monastery garden; the physician Semmelweis was hounded out of Vienna for pioneering prophylaxis; and even Sadi Carnot's membership in one of France's more eminent families did not keep his work on thermodynamics from being totally ignored during his lifetime and for twenty years after his death.

Currently an attempt is being made to soften the latent but growing hostility to technology and science by insisting that the scientist *is* really quite human. Just like everyone else, he likes tennis, sports cars, cookouts, his family. The DuPont Corporation assures you that their scientists are just as active in local and community affairs as their neighbors—if not more so. A recent book stated that its "main aim is to present to the reader the American scientist just as he is—a person who happens to enjoy science as much as a lawyer enjoys law, or a doctor enjoys the practice of medicine, or a businessman enjoys the daily hassle of business."

Well, "enjoy" is a pretty pale word for what goes on. The scientist is like everyone else *only* if "everyone else" is restricted to that infinitely small number of fortunate men who manage to find in life precisely that one pursuit that engages their best abilities, their minds and passions, with more felicity than most wives ever do.

There is pleasure—profound pleasure, both of touch and mind—to the experimentalist in the manipulation of apparatus. If he has designed it himself, there is the added pleasure of seeing it perform its delicate intricacies exactly as he conceived it, under his direct control. The theorist, in addition, has the overwhelming satisfaction of feeling that he has been intuitively attuned to the subtlest nuances of nature when one of his hypotheses turns out to be true.

Richard Feynman at fifty wears his Nobel Prize like an open-collared shirt. Twenty-five years ago at Los Alamos, he was an *enfant terrible*, bubbling with quick brilliance on the theoretical problems of bomb-building that came his way. "It was a succession of successes—but easy successes. After the war, I moved over to the kind of problems [like the self-energy of the electron] that men spend years thinking about. On that level there are no easy successes; and the satisfaction you get when you're proved right is so great that even if it occurs only twice in a lifetime, everything else is worth it!"

Recently, Jack Peter Green, who does pharmacology in terms of quantum chemistry, was polishing a research paper during a country weekend. He had spent more than a year working over the molecular structure of a number of chemically diverse hallucinogens—LSD, mescaline, and others—and was finally able to prove that one specific atomic configuration can be discerned somewhere in the molecular structure of each. I was amazed to hear sounds of private satisfaction come from his room; but later when he was discussing his results, it was clear that his delight had nothing to do with pride in his own performance or with the prestige that would be coming to him for his discovery. It was purely aesthetic pleasure in the exquisite way nature ordered things. "How elegant it is!" he kept saying. "And so simple!"

A young Italian scientist's English was slow and meticulous. "I feel guilty about coming back to the lab after hours to get a little more done, and still I always come back," he said to me. "I know very well that whether I come in or not on Sunday, there will be no great change in science. I neglect my wife and my little daughter for those few extra hours—yet I keep coming. Why? Is it really only curiosity? Because if that's all that's driving me, then it's wrong for me to come for that additional time." "Then why *do* you come in?" I persisted. "Because it is my happiness," he said simply. "This is where I want most in the world to be—this is what I want most in the world to be doing."

Only young artists, actors, musicians, and writers know the same immersion, because what is involved is the deep engagement of a talent; and only a talent at work allows the hours, days, and years of a life to roll by without being counted. That is why, in such lives, there is a far more dangerous risk than failure—there is the terrifying possibility that some day the love affair may stop. Then, tragically, all that is left is the pain of disillusion and the stunned sense of all those wasted years. A scientist, like the artist, is not only different from other men; he had better go on being different!

Whatever is different about the scientist must begin with the particular kind of intelligence such a man possesses. It is said that the scientist must have an inquiring mind—which is true; and that he must also be one of those people who take deep pleasure in learning—which is also true, and also superficial; because both these qualities are demanded also by any number of other disciplines. The particular kind of sensibilities required by a scientist are more complicated.

Begin with his intense awareness of words and their meanings. While the poet's affinity for words makes him sensitive to their sound, emotion, and rhythm, the scientist uses them as instruments of precision. He must be capable of inventing the words to express new physical concepts. He must be able to reason verbally by analogy—to explain "that this thing is like that thing," and to be able to put the many resemblances into one single generation that covers them all.

The scientist must think graphically, in terms of dynamical models, three-dimensional arrangements in space. The dynamical model of a bacterial cell, for example, is a hollow rigid capsule that may be either spherical or tubular, containing an otherwise shapeless living cell enclosed within a soft sac, the plasma membrane. Niels Bohr's dynamical model of an atom is a miniature solar system with relatively enormous electrons orbiting about an almost inconceivably small sun—the atomic nucleus—a tremendous distance away. Scientists keep these three-dimensional pictures in mind as vividly as if they were actually seeing them. Formulas and equations printed on a two-dimensional page have three-dimensional meanings, and the scientist must be able to read in three dimensions to "see the picture" at once. There is nothing "abstract" about a scientist's thinking.

This visualization is so vivid that a scientist examining a theoretical problem is really like a jeweler peering through his loupe at a gem which he holds close to his eye, turning it over and over in his fingers. To Einstein, there was nothing abstract about his theory of relativity. Even the slightest apparent deviation from the hard world of physical reality made him intellectually uncomfortable. For more than a decade, meeting at international science conferences, he and Bohr, by then both in middle age, had monumental arguments over the meaning of the uncertainty principle, with Einstein the one who stuck stolidly to the basic mechanistic principle of cause and effect. "I cannot believe that God throws dice," he said.

The split between the so-called "Two Cultures" is much more than a matter of humanists learning more about science, and the scientists spending more time on aesthetics. Unless a man has some kind of spatial imagination along with his verbal sensibility he will always be—as far as understanding science goes—in the role of the tone-deaf struggling with a course in music appreciation. On the other hand, the possessor of both verbal and spatial sensibility will rather quickly be bored if asked to limit his imagination to only the verbal domain, in the case of the humanities; or to only the spatial domain, in the case of the graphic arts.

A man accustomed to working at the peak of his powers has no patience with anything that calls on him to work at only half-load. With this dual sensibility then, the true scientist would find it difficult "to be like everyone else" even if he wanted to.

Not only is there a split between scientists and other people, there is also a sharp split among scientists themselves. Within specializations, a division runs across every field—a sort of trans-science geological fault, which results from the fact that there are two kinds of scientific knowledge. Claude Bernard, the founder of experimental medicine, pointed out that there is the knowledge we already possess, and there is the knowledge we still have to discover. One type of scientist—the man with encyclopedic knowledge of past and current thought in science—can make an inspiring teacher or a brilliant research administrator, but he is not necessarily the man who is most creative. The other type of scientist—a beachcomber on the edge of the sea of the unknown—may be so haphazardly versed in the literature of his own field that he sometimes invents and discovers things that have been invented and discovered before.

Szent-Gyorgyi says he feels embarrassed, isolated, and ignorant at meetings in the presence of these highly articulate scientists who seem to have all knowledge at their fingertips, even though he is the one with the Nobel Prize and they are not. The Polaroid inventor, Edwin Land, feels that discoveries are made by those scientists who have freed themselves "from a way of thinking that is held by friends and associates who may be more intelligent, better educated, better disciplined, but who have not mastered the art of the fresh clean look at the old, old knowledge."

In the main it is these intellectual ragamuffins who are responsible for the great advances; just as the great novels and poems are not written by men of the widest erudition and critical ability. History is a cruel bookkeeper and carries on its ledgers only the names of those who create what is enduring; it drops forever the men who appear to scintillate in their own times with the knowledge only of their own time. J. Robert Oppenheimer was a brilliant administrator of other men's work; he was a brilliant interpreter of other men's work, and a judge who could make piercing evaluations of other men's work. But when it came time—figuratively speaking—to write his own poetry in science, his work was sparse, angular, and limited, particularly when judged by the standards he himself set for everyone else. He knew the major problems of his time; he attacked them with style; but he apparently lacked that intuition—that faculty beyond logic which logic needs—in order to make great advances. If one were speaking not of science but of religion, one could say that Oppenheimer's religiosity was the kind that could make him a bishop but never a saint.

This particular quality which is so essential to the scientist is almost indefinable. Years ago, as a graduate student, I was present at a three-way argument between Rabi, Szilard, and Fermi. Szilard took a position and mathematically stated it on the blackboard. Rabi disagreed and rearranged the equations to the form he would accept. All the while Fermi was shaking his head. "You're both wrong," he said. They demanded proof. Smiling a little, he shrugged his shoulders as if proof weren't needed. "My intuition tells me so," he said.

I had never heard a scientist refer to his intuition, and I expected Rabi and Szilard to laugh. They didn't. The man of science, I soon found works with the procedures of logic so much more than anyone else that he, more than anyone else, is aware of logic's limitations. Beyond logic there is intuition, and the creative scientist often is out there, rather than within the exquisitely arranged landscapes of rigorous logic.

For eighteen years before Newton wrote down the general law of gravitational attraction, he had an intuitive perception that the earth's gravitational force extended at least as far as the moon and was responsible for the moon's motion. Even then, another year passed before it became clear that an assumption basic to the whole idea had still not been proven—and the matter was brought to Newton's attention. He went to work on it at once. The next day he handed over a few sheets of paper containing the mathematical proof that a spherical mass, no matter how large—earth, moon, or sun—behaves gravitationally as if all its mass were concentrated into a single point at its center. Newton had assumed intuitively for years that something like this might be the case, and for all those years had never for a moment thought that everyone else did not share his perception.

A composer looked at me with surprise when I happened to mention that the scientist experienced creativity in exactly the same way as the artist. "But what does he create?" he asked. "I thought he dealt only with logical processes—deductions from experiment."

Creativity for the scientist does have certain characteristics that are unique. To begin with, the scientist picks his problem because he knows enough about it to know that no one knows very much about it—except that there are unanswered questions there. Out of insight or inspiration, he suggests a possible answer to one of the questions: for example, What *is* a possible structure for the atom? What *does* bind the atoms together to form molecules? By *what* means does the living cell store the chemical energy released within its walls? The creative moment occurs when the suggested answer is being formed. Naturally, the scientist would like to be proved right, and so the performance of the deciding experiment can never be the dispassionate exercise it is popularly thought to be. Experiment carries all the emotion of a contest. Objectivity lies in the scientist's willingness to accept, however reluctantly, evidence that his brilliant conception is wrong. Once Nature gives its decision, there is no appeal. In fairly short order then, the scientist is ruthlessly informed whether his creation is valid or not. The artist, on the other hand, has no such objective standard. He can always find, or invent, an aesthetic system to justify his creation.

There are several other important differences between creativity for the artist and for the scientist. If Shakespeare had never written *Hamlet*, if Beethoven had not lived to create *Eroica*, no one else would have brought these works into existence. Other artists would have created other works. In science, though, if Einstein had never lived to work out relativity, if Maarten Schmidt hadn't recognized the nature of the quasars in the sky, or if Crick and Watson had not solved the structure of DNA, other scientists would have done so. The world of art is infinite in creative possibilities, the world of science is restricted: there is only one Nature to be discovered.

Again, no work of art has ever had—ever can have—the revolutionary impact on man and his society the way the introduction of a new technology can. With the artist, a moment of history comes to an end when he finishes his particular work and the act of creation is completed. With the scientist, it is that precise moment that a new phase of history begins; even though he himself cannot possibly foresee what future generations will add to his contribution or choose to do with it. This is where he is the prisoner of his own time.

Faraday couldn't conceivably guess that dropping a small bar magnet down the center of a coil of wire would mean that a hundred years later millions of miles of electrical power lines would flash billions of kilowatt-hours back and forth across the earth. Nor could Semmelweis know that his campaign to save women from death by puerperal fever was one of the several steps that would help lead—five generations later—to the threat of such world overpopulation that mass starvation looms as one of man's possible fates.

Not long ago, I asked Otto Robert Frisch, who, with his aunt, Lise Meitner, had actually been the first to realize that uranium atoms were indeed undergoing nuclear fission with enormous emissions of energy, whether at that point (1939) he had any sense of what his work was to lead to. He had been a young man then, a refugee from Hitler Austria.

"My aunt and I spent the weekend together in the Swedish countryside," he said. "She told me what she had just heard from Hahn in Berlin. We discussed it over and over as we walked through the woods; and the more we talked, the more we became convinced that the uranium nuclei were indeed breaking up—*fission* was *her* word for it. We wrote up a short joint paper on this completely unsuspected nuclear process before we separated. She went back to Stockholm, and I went back to Copenhagen to the Bohr Institute. I had a vague sense that we were onto something that might be important, but I couldn't say how. I remember writing to my parents that we might have a tiger by the tail, but believe it or not I couldn't think of an experiment to do until Plazcek—do you remember him; the most skeptical man in the world?—Plazcek said he didn't believe any part of it, and that made me so angry that I said I'd prove it to him, and I did. But you see, that was all still months before Joliot in Paris detected the emission neutrons ejected during each fission which meant that a chain reaction was possible. I had no way of guessing that this would be so."

The inventors of radically new machines always judge the value of what they create, but their judgment is embedded in the standards and needs of their own times. Dr. Richard Gatling, a Union Army surgeon, appalled by the bloody cost of the American Civil War, reasoned that he could reduce the number of losses by reducing the size of armies. He developed a gun with a tenfold firing power so that one man could do the work of ten. The Gatling gun—the first modern machine gun—turned out to have a very different effect.

The Wright brothers seriously weighed the possible future effects of their invention. They saw their airplane as a sort of air scout able to fly over enemy lines and detect every movement. Military surprise would be impossible, and from then on wars would be useless.

When Einstein's work on relativity led him to the historic discovery of the convertibility of mass and energy, he did not foresee how his principle would act as a guide to the release of nuclear energy. Is he to be held responsible for the deaths at Hiroshima? Does history hold Newton guilty for every artillery barrage laid down by all the armies of the world in every war of the past three hundred years because one of the outcomes of Newton's laws of dynamics was the artillerist's science of ballistics?

Yet because of the scientist's inability to look over the walls of history and foresee what subsequent generations will do with the fruits of his discovery, society today blames the scientist for what it wrenched from his hand and turned into engines of evil, poisoning the earth's atmosphere, crust, and waters. The scientist is bewildered to find himself considered the villain. It is as if Prometheus were chained to the rock—not by the gods from whom he stole the fire, but by the men he tried to help, because, as they claim, he had now made it possible for them to burn one another to death. Nevertheless, the very scientists who are being considered the bogeymen are the ones who must still be called upon to use their ingenuity to help undo the damage which society has done to itself. They are more than anxious to meet the challenge.

Questions for Critical Analysis

1. What reasons did the scientists Wilson interviewed give for practicing their branch of science? Were any of their reasons convincing enough to make you consider switching your major? Can you give better reasons for why you selected your major?
2. Who are all these scientists Wilson mentions? How many of them had you already heard of? Write a list of their names and identify those you know by a phrase or two; look up the names of those you don't know. What is characteristic about the scientists Wilson includes in this essay?
3. Why does Wilson emphasize the human side of science? What's the point of including the statement about the Du Pont Corporation? "On Being a Scientist" first appeared in *Atlantic Monthly* magazine in 1970. What do you suppose was the attitude of his readers toward science? Why do you suppose that?
4. What does Wilson tell you about scientific creativity? How is scientific creativity different from artistic creativity? How is it the same?
5. Compare Wilson's discussion of science and scientific creativity to Sagan's definition of science and how scientists do their work.

Questions for Structural Analysis

1. What is the implied question of Wilson's first sentence? Does he ever answer it? How? and where?
2. What effect do Wilson's references to specific scientists and their comments have on you as you read this essay? Do you like hearing what the scientists say? Would you have paraphrased any of the quotations Wilson included? Why did Wilson include so many scientists?
3. Which of the stories about scientists did you like best? Why? What did the story reveal to you about that particular scientist? About science more generally?
4. Were you surprised by Wilson's assertion that scientists are intensely aware of words and their meanings? How does he explain this affinity? Why is it important to science? What about his statement of the scientist's visualization? Do you think three-dimensionally? According to Wilson, how does this dual way of thinking separate scientists from the rest of us? Do you agree?
5. Look at the final paragraph of the essay. Is Wilson referring to anything specific, or are these simply general statements? What is the damage that "society has done to itself"? Why are scientists bewildered to be considered villains? In what light do you consider them? Why?

*T*HE *S*EARCH FOR *U*NDERSTANDING

VANNEVAR BUSH

Vannevar Bush (1908–1974), an electrical engineering professor at the Massachusetts Institute of Technology, was noted for being a stimulating teacher who demanded excellence from his students: not only did he expect his engineering students to master the subject at hand, but he also expected them to write clear, precise sentences. In this essay, Bush presents a forceful case to the general reader that science is more than its results: science is inquiry—a search to find meaning. In a frenzy of antiscience feelings, people may want to abandon this need to know. If we abandon that, according to Bush, we abandon life itself.

Before you begin reading: *Consider the ways science affects your life every day. Write for ten minutes nonstop in your notebook about your relationship to science and technology.*

◆

IN THESE PAST FIFTY YEARS WE HAVE SEEN AN UNPARALleled advance of science. But we have seen much more. We have seen two great wars. We have seen a depression such that the repetition of it would shake the foundations of the republic. We have seen the splitting of the world into two armed camps, two philosophies, and two ways of life: on the one hand an oriental despotism in its modern form, and on the other hand a free world. We have even seen what may be the beginning of world order.

Science has had a part in the development of the form of the present schism. And I am not referring merely to the fact that science has made possible the A-bomb and the H-bomb. I am referring to something more fundamental, for political movements reflect the philosophy of peoples, and many old anchors have been torn loose since the turn of the century. Science has had much to do with this, for the way in which science has itself evolved has influenced our patterns of thought, our philosophy, and thus our political institutions.

Physics, which once could see the universe as made up entirely of two simple particles, now confronts some fifty particles, many of them far from simple. Its energy comes in discrete packages or quanta. The indeterminancy principle puts a limit to the knowable within its own domain. For most physicists, theory has become a convenience only. Physics does not mind having two entirely separate theories of light, quite contradictory when taken in their elements, but both useful. James Bryant Conant defines science as merely a series of inter-connected concepts and conceptual schemes arising from experiment and observation and fruitful of further experiments and observations.

If hypotheses are merely convenient tools, they may well be made convenient for other purposes than being guides to further experiment; they may be convenient for the state. In the U.S.S.R., scientists were long directed, in the interests of the state, to follow Lamarck and not Darwin. More important, a materialism on a scientific base encouraged a lust for conquest and an intractability in all international relations. There is danger in the intense emphasis upon science today, and upon the acceptance only of convenient and temporary working hypotheses; for this only too often carries with it an implied denial of any ultimate truth. We are likely to forget that an attitude, sound enough for the purposes of physics in its present state, may not be generalized without implying exceedingly broad assumptions. We are likely to forget, also, that we pursue science for other reasons than its mere utility. From a complete absorption in pragmatic science it is a short step, indeed, to full dialectical materialism—to a denial of all religion—to a denial of all virtue except that of strength.

Bertrand Russell wrote this as our century was getting under way: "That man is the product of causes which had no prevision of the end they were achieving; that his origin, his growth, his hopes and fears, his loves and his beliefs, are but the outcome of accidental collocations of atoms; that no fire, no heroism, no intensity of thought and feeling, can preserve an individual life beyond the grave; that all the labors of the ages, all the devotion, all the inspiration, all the noonday brightness of human genius, are destined to extinction in the vast death of the solar system, and that the whole temple of man's achievement must inevitably be buried beneath the debris of a universe in ruins—all these things, if not quite beyond dispute, are yet so nearly certain, that no philosophy which rejects them can hope to stand."*

This is the extreme view. Man, as he learns a little, is only too prone to believe that now he can know all or that he can know nothing. To separate scientific theory from our pondering on spiritual values is indeed sound practice. But to deny that there is any validity beyond the findings of science is absurd. In the realm of spiritual values we think more deeply today, even if perhaps no more soundly, because science has built a new conception of the cosmos by its measurements and its analyses.

This is a difficult world in which we live today, and scientific men do well to ponder their part in influencing the way in which we now proceed. But I

---

*Russell, Bertrand, "A Free Man's Worship," in *Basic Writings*, edited by Robert E. Egner and Lester E. Denonn (New York: Simon & Schuster, 1961).

believe that the extreme materialistic view is held mostly by those who become intoxicated by a bit of a grasp of material things. To pursue science is not to disparage the things of the spirit. In fact, to pursue science rightly is to furnish a framework on which the spirit may rise.

Fear is not new in the world, nor the problem of evil. The rabbit that crouches as the owl swoops knows terror, and the mother partridge dragging a wing to lure the invader from her chicks does so with a wildly beating heart. And that which is evil to the duck on her nest is good for the fox pups saved from starving. There are life and beauty in the world, but fear and evil are with them, for that is how the world was formed. And man, who gives these things names, wonders at his lot, and is baffled and confused.

There was no compassion in the world until man brought it. Nor was there beauty or virtue until he thought it so. His values do not all derive from his will to live, or from the sifting of selection. That a man will devote his life to the good of his fellows is not always a product of evolution, or self-seeking that is sublimated. Altruism is a product of his mind, not of his seamy history.

So too is his will to know. His yearning to understand reaches far beyond the control of nature for his bodily well-being. The shepherd on the hill at night views the stars and ponders, not that he can thus care better for his sheep, not just that he is idle and his mind roams, but because he wonders whether, beyond the stars, lies the reason why he can thus ponder.

The search for knowledge has always been under stress. The old geometer, manipulating his triangles in a quest for release from his perplexity, was never far from the barbarian and his spear. The shadow of the guillotine fell across the pages on which France recorded some of its most profound science. No man delves into the unknown who is not under sentence of death. The greatest work of man, a brain trained through the years to deal in wisdom, is destroyed in a moment by chance or malice. The inherited knowledge of the years endures, passed on and accumulated, but even that ends if free men fail.

A plane flies overhead on its peaceful mission. But it may some day be a plane which carries destruction such as the world has not yet seen. The edifices of the city may be consumed in a moment, and with them the edifices of the mind. The threat is very real.

It is well that we should band together in the resolve that the deadly plane shall not fly. It is even well that we should strive to ensure that, if it does, we shall still endure. The duty and the opportunity to struggle to preserve our lives, and our way of life, are not canceled just because the form of the threat has changed.

Do we exist just so that we can struggle to continue to exist? Or is there more to life than that? We understand so little, the universe is so great and so intricate, and beyond it lie things that we may never know. Is there real significance when man can observe a distortion of a galaxy which occurred long before dinosaurs roamed the swamps, or create a painting which conveys far more than is ever seen by the eye? Is all our ordering of what we think we know merely a fleeting guide to further search? Is there no real value in searching except to use? We, who think, are dedicated to the search for knowledge. Are we thus dedicated also to a search for truth? Has the word any meaning beyond convenience?

Because we must fail fully to understand, should we refuse to watch the galaxies as they seem to rush away toward oblivion? Should we probe toward the core of the earth only if it will help us find new ore? Does man speculate about his origin and his destiny merely because his mind developed the capacity to wonder as an incident to its capacity to help him compete, much as a toucan grew a fantastic bill as a chance product of genes that became combined for useful ends?

Does the mystery of our conscious thought lead us toward a greater mystery, beyond our feeble definition in terms of the marks on rules, or the ticking of a clock, which we cannot understand but which we cannot deny? Are we thus a part of something more profound than the knowledge we gain by the movement of needles on dials, or the tipping of a balance? Is there meaning in life beyond mere animal existence?

Science has a simple faith, which transcends utility. Nearly all men of science, all men of learning for that matter, and men of simple ways too, have it in some form and in some degree. It is the faith that it is the privilege of man to learn to understand, and that this is his mission.

If we abandon that mission under stress we shall abandon it forever, for stress will not cease. Knowledge for the sake of understanding, not merely to prevail, that is the essence of our being. None can define its limits, or set its ultimate boundaries. Our children's children may weight it more than we, may be able to lift the curtain just a bit, and believe they know why all this is so. We would leave them a heritage, even though we live in perilous days. Thus we would continue to delve and to ponder, even while we strive to keep the bombs from falling, even if we know that the bombs will fall and that the things we love may perish. For if we fail to struggle, and fail to think beyond our petty lot, we accept a sordid role. The light in our minds tells us that there is more to life than this.

That the threat is now intense is not a reason to abandon our quest for knowledge. It is a reason to hold it more tightly, in spite of the need for action to preserve our freedom, in spite of the distractions of living in turmoil, that it may not be lost or brushed aside by the demands of the hour. We would not neglect our duty to our country and our fellows to strive mightily to preserve our ways and our lives. There is an added duty, not inconsistent, not less. It is the duty to so live that there may be a reason for living, beyond the mere mechanisms of life. It is the duty to carry on, under stress, the search for understanding.

QUESTIONS FOR CRITICAL ANALYSIS

1. Bush wrote his essay in the context of 1965. What events does he refer to in the first paragraph? Consider his statement, "political movements reflect the philosophy of peoples," in historical terms and today's terms. Do you agree? How would you describe the philosophy of American people today? How is this philosophy reflected in political movements? (If you know something about late twentieth-century physics, what remarks does Bush make that identify the 1965 context of his essay?)
2. Compare James Bryant Conant's definition of science to Carl Sagan's in "Can We Know the Universe." Which definition is closer to your own? Why?
3. Many people believe that the role of science is to serve the public by creating technical and medical wonders. How does such an attitude limit or restrain scientific research? What is the relationship between basic research and technology?
4. Bush relates utilitarian justification for scientific research to a denial of all religion, to a denial of all virtue except strength. Why? Do you agree with him? What arguments would you advance to support Bush? oppose him?
5. Bush says, "no man delves into the unknown who is not under the sentence of death." Does he mean this literally? What does he mean? Do you agree in the context of the essays in this section?

QUESTIONS FOR STRUCTURAL ANALYSIS

1. What is the thesis for "The Search for Understanding"? When does the thesis become clear to you?
2. Bush quotes Bertrand Russell early in his essay. Why does he include this quotation? In what ways is Russell's statement crucial to Bush's essay?
3. Bush seems to go off on a tangent when he argues that science does not disparage or ignore the spiritual. What is he responding to? How do you react to this part of the essay? Do you agree with him? On what basis: your experiences, your reading, or what you've been told?
4. Toward the end of the essay, Bush uses a series of rhetorical questions to direct the reader's thoughts. How do you respond to these questions? Do they make you stop and think? Is this an effective device for the essay?
5. Describe Bush's language and vocabulary. What is his attitude toward his subject? toward his readers? Compare Bush's style with Sagan's. Which do you prefer, and why?

*T*HE *B*EAUTY OF *M*ATHEMATICS

HAROLD MOROWITZ

Harold Morowitz (1927–), a biophysicist at Yale University, is associate editor of the Journal of Biomedical Computing. *Morowitz describes the scientist's dependance upon mathematics in his essay, "The Beauty of Mathematics," showing how mathematics so naturally expresses what scientists know of the natural world. Writing to the general reader of* Science 82 *magazine, Morowitz suggests that mathematics is an important tool for all of us. Once we know mathematics we can bridge the communication gap between scientists and nonscientists and better understand the world.*

Before you begin reading: *How do you think and feel about mathematics? Write about your thoughts and feelings toward mathematics in your reading notebook and refer to experiences that led you to those feelings.*

◆

IN AN AGE DOMINATED BY SCIENTIFIC TECHNOLOGY, THERE is a continuing problem of communicating the content and meaning of science to a broader public. Researchers still find it difficult to translate the latest technical perspective into language that is understandable to nonspecialists. It often takes 50 years or more for novel theoretical ideas to become incorporated into the thinking of the greater intellectual community. The viewpoint of quantum mechanics, for example, put forward in the late 1920s, has still not had its full impact on humanistic thought. The material is that hard to digest. Yet there are few philosophers of science who doubt that this theory has and will continue to exert a deep effect on our views of man and nature.

The one aspect of science that is most enigmatic and difficult for outsiders to comprehend is the use of mathematical abstractions to describe events that are very concrete. A physicist sits at his desk writing a series of symbols and numbers, while out in space a planet orbits the sun. Exact instruments are used to take very careful measurements of the planetary positions, and *voilá*, the numbers obtained agree with the pencil-and-paper calculations. The whole space program, for example, depends on our ability to calculate exact orbits. Scientists' familiarity with this correlation between theory and experiment dulls us to the strangeness of the relation between the observed world and the little marks we put on paper.

There is a beautiful experience, available to physics students in their sophomore year of college, that illustrates the emotional impact of being able to deal with predictive mathematical theory. The first step in this exercise is to set down on a piece of paper, in mathematical form, Newton's second law of motion, which states that force equals mass times acceleration. Next, one writes the equation that means there is a universal force of gravity, an attraction between all bodies that is proportional to their masses and inversely proportional to the square of the distance between them. The final step is to carry out a few lines of mathematical manipulations that quickly yield equations for Johannes Kepler's laws of planetary motion.

The act of personally deriving the motion of the bodies of the solar system from a few simple assumptions is a profound experience. When the result emerges, there is in the minds of many students a sense of *déja vu*, the feeling of a return to some primordial knowledge.

Some scientists greeted with awe the act of predicting the future of celestial systems. Others responded with arrogance. After Pierre-Simon Laplace's *Celestial Mechanics* was published, for instance, the scientist met with Napoleon, who noted that he saw no mention of God in the book. Laplace is reported to have replied, "I have no need of that hypothesis."

The most noteworthy achievement of mathematics in celestial mechanics did not occur until more than 150 years after Newton's laws of motion and universal gravitation were published. Astronomers studying the planet Uranus were unable to explain its motion by the laws of mechanics. They postulated that the orbit was being influenced by an unknown planet farther out from the sun. Astrophysicists used the mathematical methods of Laplace to predict the path of the unknown object. This information was communicated to observers who in 1846 aimed their telescopes in the predicted direction and discovered the planet Neptune. This discovery remains one of the great triumphs of the human intellect and was totally dependent on the curious relation of the abstractions of mathematics to the concrete world of physics.

Once one understands and feels the power of the derivation of Kepler's laws and subsequent developments, he may become more mystical about mathematics, or he may become more committed to hard-nosed materialism. But one way or another the mathematical analysis is a moving experience.

Throughout physics, chemistry, and parts of biology, this strange relation between equations and real-world events keeps appearing. The scientist uses mathematics because it gives him both an abbreviated way of representing experience and a feeling of deep understanding. Nevertheless there remains a whimsical wonder about why mathematics works. Theoretical physicist and Nobel laureate Eugene Wigner once captured this feeling in an essay entitled, "The Unreasonable Effectiveness of Mathematics in the Natural Sciences."

Wigner's first argument begins with a statement of Einstein's that "the only physical theories which we are willing to accept are the beautiful ones." Mathematics seems to be the only study that generates sufficient beauty for the physicist. This tells us more about physicists than about physics, but in Eugene Wigner's view of science the subject material is, in any case, inseparable from the mind of the scientist.

After giving several examples of the applications of very abstract mathematics to specific problems of atomic structure and spectra, Wigner comes to the conclusion that "the unreasonable effectiveness of mathematics" in physics is an empirical law of epistemology. Somehow the structure of mathematics and the structure of the universe are close enough that one may represent aspects of the other with great precision.

Wigner's essay concludes with the following:

> Let me end on a more cheerful note. The miracle of the appropriateness of the language of mathematics for the formulation of the laws of physics is a wonderful gift which we neither understand nor deserve. We should be grateful for it and hope that it will remain valid in future research and that it will extend, for better or for worse, to our pleasure, even though perhaps also to our bafflement, to wide branches of learning.

Thus the scientist uses this wonderful gift of mathematics but, like the layman, remains puzzled as to why it works. Knowing that even the experts wonder will perhaps lessen the fear and loathing of mathematics on the part of so many people outside science. To some of us equations are objects of beauty, but to all of us they are tools of the trade.

A difficulty in coping with the mathematical side of science is worth overcoming if one wishes to be fully sympathetic with contemporary scientific thought. Even a rudimentary knowledge of mathematics will go a long way in getting a feel for the language of natural philosophy.

QUESTIONS FOR CRITICAL ANALYSIS

1. Describe the audience for this essay, which was originally published in *Science 82*, a popular science magazine. Does the "ideal reader" for this essay feel comfortable with mathematics? Do you like mathematics? How does your attitude toward mathematics affect your response to this essay?
2. Why does Morowitz consider the sophomore physics exercise a "beautiful experience"? What does this exercise reveal about mathematics? about nature? about the student? Have you performed this assignment? What did you think of it?
3. What is remarkable about the discovery of Neptune? What two opposing responses does Morowitz think possible? Which response do you feel more comfortable with? Why?

4. What did Einstein mean when he said, "the only physical theories which we are willing to accept are the beautiful ones"? Does this surprise you? What's beautiful about them?
5. Do you feel any differently toward mathematics after having read Morowitz? Why, or why not?

QUESTIONS FOR STRUCTURAL ANALYSIS

1. What is the thesis for this essay? Where is it stated? How is it stated?
2. How does Morowitz relate the theme of the first paragraph to his subject of mathematics?
3. Why does Morowitz include the story of Laplace and Napoleon? In what ways could the use of this illustration backfire? Would you have included it if you wrote this essay?
4. Toward the end of the essay, Morowitz describes Wigner's essay, "The Unreasonable Effectiveness of Mathematics in the Natural Sciences." (Notice how he introduces Wigner and, later, how he introduces the quotation.) Why does he spend so much time on Wigner's essay? Is his direct quote of Wigner's conclusion effective? Why, or why not?
5. What is Morowitz's conclusion? Is it appropriate to the rest of the essay? Is it consistent with the tone of the essay?

Searching Out Creation's Secrets

Carolyn Kraus

Carolyn Kraus teaches writing at the University of Michigan-Dearborn and publishes science features in general-interest magazines and newspapers. As she describes it, her goal is "to make complicated scientific subjects accessible to the general public by focusing on the human beings involved." "Searching Out Creation's Secrets," originally published in the Metropolitan Detroit Magazine, *has been collected in a forthcoming collection of essays,* Enormous Answers to Everything.

Before you begin reading: *Write a brief description of physicists in your reading notebook, answering questions such as, what type of people are they? what kinds of science do they do? how can you recognize one?*

◆

AT CASEY'S FAMILY RESTAURANT ON LAKE ERIE'S SHORE twenty miles east of Cleveland, breakfast regulars mull over local abuses in the free cheese distribution program, the at-large Middleberg kitten shooter, or the rich taste of Casey's own "bellybuster" pancakes. There is a lot of time to talk. Massive layoffs have left just a skeleton crew at the Morton salt mine just down the way. Local teenagers have devised their own timeless, low-budget adventures: They explore the mine grounds at night, sneaking by the Pinkerton detective at the gate to gather among the forty-foot salt pyramids stockpiled there.

Meanwhile, in a laboratory buried 2,000 feet beneath those salt mounds, a group of physicists ponders deep mysteries. They keep watch over 10,000 tons of water sealed in a giant bag. The bag lines a cavity the size of a five-story building, which has been dug below the floor of an adjacent chamber. Specially designed light sensors, strung on nylon fishing lines, descend into the water from a floating catwalk above the top rim of the cavity. The sensors peer through the eerie darkness and relay images to five computers in the laboratory. Here the scientists await a Sign—the blue flash of a single decaying proton that might illuminate the secrets of eternity.

"It's being called the experiment of the century," says Dr. Lawrence Sulak of the University of Michigan. He is one of twenty-nine physicists running the $5 million project, which is being funded by the Department of Energy. "At stake are some fundamental issues," he says. "Is matter essentially unstable? Are diamonds forever? Are we forever? Will we eventually turn into light instead of dust?"

These questions, which evoke both fairy tale and theology, also reflect the new physics. Just ten years ago, the notion that a proton was unstable seemed as absurd as the current choice of a salt mine for a laboratory. But then came the era of Grand Unified Theories, an ambitious, visionary quest to find unity and simplicity among the forces of nature. It is one of the foundations of the new physics.

Scientists have long believed that all the matter in the universe was created in a giant explosion fifteen billion years ago called the Big Bang. The set of theories that make up the Grand Unified Theories, constructed by physicists around the world over the past decade, is the most recent attempt to explain how everything came to exist from that explosion. One of its many daring predictions is that protons, which are in the nuclei of all atoms—all matter—*will not last forever.* Einstein's special Theory of Relativity told us early in this century that matter and energy are alternate forms of the same thing—that is, that one can be converted to the other. Now the Grand Unified Theories predict that this conversion of matter to energy will happen spontaneously over time, and that the universe of matter will eventually disappear—as if the movie of Creation were running backward in slow motion.

The regulars at Casey's restaurant need not worry, however, that their pancakes will disappear from plate to lip. Nothing will happen today, or next year, or in a billion years, even if protons do decay. The theory seeking physical proof beneath Lake Erie predicts that protons have a half-life of 10 to the 32nd years. In the language of physics, this means that half the protons in the universe will turn into energy within a timespan represented in years by a one with thirty-two zeros behind it. This is a future almost too remote for imagining, trillions of times longer than the life of the universe thus far.

How, then, can the theory be tested?

"You can test it out in one of two ways," says U-M post-doctoral researcher Dr. Steven Errede. "You can watch one proton for 10 to the 32nd years, in which case you have a family project. Or you can watch 10 to the 32nd protons for one year. . . ." That is, the more protons you watch, the sooner one can be expected to disintegrate.

Of course, no one has ever seen an atom, much less a proton, which is a tiny part of an atom. But with the help of sophisticated equipment, scientists can observe the effects of subatomic phenomena like protons and neutrons. The project to build a proton decay detector began in 1979, a collaboration among physicists from the University of Michigan, the University of California at Irvine, and the Brookhaven National Laboratory. They began on borrowed funds, since initially the Department of Energy found the project too bizarre to support. But money came through after three Nobel Prize-winning theoretical physicists—Steven Weinberg, Sheldon Glashow, and Abdus Salam—wrote letters of endorsement.

Dr. Sulak explains the Lake Erie proton detector this way: "Get a whole lot of matter that you can observe. Let's take water, because it is transparent and we can detect light given off by the particles decaying. Next, take it a half-mile underground to block out interference—for instance, from cosmic rays which continually bombard the earth from outer space [and could produce effects like those of proton decay]. Then, take 2,000 phototubes—light sensors—and paste them on the walls of the water tank so that they register the light that comes off the particles decaying. . . ." Dr. Sulak then explains that radiation given off by proton decay would be recorded in a particular, identifiable pattern.

"Now, 10,000 tons of water is 10 to the 32nd protons. At least *one* ought to pop off in a year."

Sulak smiles with boyish enthusiasm. "You can't do this experiment any better on earth. To improve it, you have to do it ten times bigger and on the moon."

It is early morning as a group of physicists, looking like moon men themselves, gear up to descend into the mine. They wear goggles, hardhats with miners' lights, and "self-rescuer" packs strapped to their belts in case of an oxygen shortage. "Break the seal and suck on the mouthpiece," one of the physicists instructs. "If it burns your lips, mouth and tongue, it's working." Then a drowsy Pinkerton, as if in an afterthought, distributes metal identification "body tags."

A primitive elevator carries the physicists to the mine floor. Ears pop from pressure changes and the darkness thickens. Everything is wet. Two thousand feet later, the elevator door opens to a rush of sulfurous air that stays in the back of the lungs all day.

Dodging puddles and slime-covered rocks, the physicists make their way along a subterranean path past idle mining equipment from which salt crystals hang like tiny stalactites. The elements are slowly reclaiming the cavern blasted twenty-four years ago into the 400-million-year-old salt deposit. On humid days, the vault drips like a tropical rain forest.

A shadowy figure appears at one turning and trudges toward the physicists. He identifies himself as Deward Curkendall, an old-timer. "Been working here since the mine opened," he says. "Longer than anybody." Curkendall smiles at the physicists with their *Star Wars* gear. "I was here when they were doing that other experiment," he chuckles, referring to a radioactive-decay study conducted here some twenty years ago. "I don't think one way or another about it. I've seen 'em come and go."

Curkendall's light fades into the distance again, veiled by falling rock salt. As the physicists round another turn, a headlight grazes over a rock wall where someone has painted in big red letters: "What time is it? What time is it?"

Suddenly, wind from an air vent whooshes into the mine. The physicists grab their hats and duck behind a heavy metal door which clangs shut against the ancient rock. An electric shoe polisher brushes the salt from their steel-toed boots and they enter an air-conditioned room stocked with refrigerators, microwave ovens, a Mr. Coffee, and a "high-energy" toilet ("Our destroilet," says a physicist) that bags the waste, zaps it to ashes, then blows it out into the depths of the mine.

Five computers at the far end of this laboratory are joined by a jungle of cables to the phototubes in the water-filled cavity beyond the back wall. The computers record every subatomic occurrence in the water onto printouts, which hang from the terminals like exhausted white tongues.

The physicists cluster around this latest data and begin sifting through it for evidence of two trails of light, moving apart at a forty-two-degree angle and triggering two circles of phototubes on opposite walls of the tank—the precise pattern expected from a spontaneously decaying proton.

On September 5, 1982, just one month after the detector began operating, the Lake Erie team thought they had "made a kill." Two circles came out on the computer. Someone breathlessly called the *New York Times*, but then the excitement subsided. The pattern was slightly off; the angle of light was wrong. The physicists nostalgically refer to the encounter as "the *New York Times* Event." There has not been a single strong candidate for proton decay since, although the phototubes blip away dutifully several times per second, registering cosmic rays which manage to penetrate into the water through the half mile of shielding rock.

Dr. Daniel Sinclair leaves the huddle around the computers and goes to the purification plant just outside the lab. Here the water is filtered through polyethylene bags under high pressure and made ultrapure so that the instruments can "see" subatomic events taking place in distant parts of the tank. Sinclair returns with two cups, one filled with purified water, the other with regular drinking water. Ironically, "the world's purest water" tastes bitter, metallic . . . actually terrible. But Sinclair is a devotee: "I always take my tea with ultrapure water," he says.

Sinclair is a mustachioed, slightly balding U-M professor with a gruff voice and a twinkle in his eye. On occasion, he has been known to leave his hat in the refrigerator. He is the "mad scientist" behind much of the detector's unorthodox assembly—a combination of sophisticated technology and inspired tinkering. Sinclair designed the reels to move the 2,058 light sensors into and out of the water, the beams to hold them in place, and the waterproof phototube housings to keep them dry and neutrally buoyant (i.e., they neither rise nor sink).

Smiling, he holds up his final version of the phototube housing or "beast," as the other physicists call it. It bears a strong resemblance to R2D2, the *Star Wars* robot. A $300 phototube is the "head," the "body" is constructed of plastic sewer piping from a hardware store, and plastic "arms" weighted with steel pellets emerge from both sides. Sinclair smiles again like a proud papa and admits, "I used to dream about different designs for this thing."

The detector has operated according to the physicists' plan, although one major setback occurred during construction. As the tank was being filled, its heavy plastic liner sprang a leak. Sinclair heard a deep rumbling as the water-soluble salt fill surrounding the detector melted and collapsed. The whole cavity threatened to cave in. "We've got a China Syndrome on our hands," someone shouted as people started to evacuate.

"If we leave now," Sinclair protested, "we can kiss those phototubes good-bye." He wasn't about to abandon his homemade beasts, even though the rumbling grew louder and cracks appeared on the laboratory floor. Sinclair rushed above ground, bought $500 worth of nylon rope, and, with several assistants, jerry-rigged the tubes and saved them as the leaking water was pumped out.

"I'll never forget that day," says Eric Shumard, a U-M graduate student who designed the detector's data-acquisition system and worked sixteen hours straight to save the tubes. "It was the same day Solidarity fell in Poland."

"Is that so?" asks Sinclair. "I didn't notice about Solidarity."

After checking the latest data, the physicists fit paper slipcovers over their shoes and enter the detector chamber. Some make repairs from the floating catwalk. Others prepare to dive into the water. Physicist/diver Karl Luttrell and his crew wear wetsuits with gloves and headgear glued on to avoid contaminating the water as they vacuum the bottom of the tank and check for leaks. From time to time, they have retrieved human relics from the watery depths—a wrench, two watches, a lone motel key.

With the elaborate electronics out of sight behind a wall, the scene appears both mysterious and simple—an immense pool contained within the world's largest plastic bag, and Sinclair's beasts that watch like thousands of eyes for the Sign from above. The bottom of the tank is sixty-five feet away, but appears much closer—the water's purity distorts one's sense of distance. "The first time you go in," says Luttrell, "it's like diving into midair."

"One day when I was diving in the tank," says Dr. Errede, "I started looking at all those tubes suspended weightlessly in the clear water. It was as if I was looking off into eternity. I couldn't work." These scientists, whose labors so often involve computers, complex equipment, or chalkboards covered with inscrutable symbols, are people who wonder at the universe. "You do physics," says Errede, "because you love to look at nature."

Here in the detector cavern, thick with humidity, the elements reign once more. Despite elaborate precautions to keep the water pure, slime covers the submerged cables and nylon fishing lines like thick jelly. "It gets in everywhere," says Sinclair. "Even if we killed it with $30,000 worth of chlorine, it would all come back."

When the door to the computer lab is closed and all light is eliminated so the phototubes may resume their silent search, one senses the pulse of the universe very close by. "One day I lay down and took a nap in the dark," says Shumard. "My watch dial seemed to glow. Pretty soon I was seeing Cerenkov light"—the eerie blue glow of a charged particle (in this case a decaying proton), traveling through water faster than the speed of light.

This blue flash, if actually detected, would prove the essential instability of all matter. It would follow that our earth, sky, selves—all is ephemeral and will eventually disintegrate into light.

But so far the blue flash has only come in dreams, and some of the physicists admit they no longer expect it. As more time passes, the theory seems less likely to be correct. Leaning from the catwalk and locating a faulty tube in the water, Sinclair speaks of proton decay in the past tense: "It would have been so breathtaking, so simple, so beautiful. How many miracles can you expect?"

He hauls up the tube and replaces it. Apparently phototubes die faster than protons. "We'll go on looking for proton decay for another five years," he says. "If we don't find it by then, we'll give it up."

If the project fails to "make a kill" in the next five years, this does not mean that protons don't decay, nor does it topple the Grand Unifying Theories which are pillars of the new physics. It may mean that protons decay differently than this particular theory predicts, or that their lifetime is longer than 10 to the 32nd years, perhaps many times longer. "We're experimentalists, not theorists," says Dr. Sulak. "We go out and look at nature and see how it works. We don't have any preconceived notions. . . .

"Still," he ventures, "I think the proton will eventually have to decay. It would be nice if we could discover it. But maybe nature made the world in such a way that the decay lifetime is ten times longer than we could see. So we're out of luck."

Meanwhile, a race to observe proton decay has developed worldwide. A dozen smaller detectors are operating in the United States, India, Japan, Switzerland and the U.S.S.R. The Indian experimenters claim to have seen proton decay already, though physicists here remain skeptical because they have not seen it on their own instruments.

In one low-budget variation of the Lake Erie detector, Dr. Marvin Marshak of the University of Minnesota has gone to the bottom of an iron mine, walled out the bats, set a computer on a chair, and stacked up slabs of concrete laced with iron to pack more protons into a smaller volume. The slabs form a thirty-one-ton cube wired to catch a proton in its last act.

The Lake Erie experimenters remain in the race, but they are beginning to eye more complicated theories that say protons decay in other ways. "Maybe proton decay isn't clear and distinctive," says Shumard. "These other theories predict decay events with less light, but basically you can use the same detection techniques and the same equipment."

The detector is also being used to study other phenomena. Ghostly, massless particles called neutrinos, rarely observed before, are appearing daily on the computer tapes. Several physicists are using the detector to observe the fast-moving particles from supernovas (exploding stars). Even the intrusive cosmic rays—merely a nuisance to the proton decay experiment—are being scrutinized by self-styled physicist trashpickers. "I came here to study what they're trying to get rid of," explains Dr. Robert Svoboda of the University of Hawaii.

But a year of disappointment in the search for proton decay has jarred the world of theoretical physicists and sent shock waves throughout the world's scientific community. "There's a sort of crisis building up," says Dr. Svoboda. "This theory predicting proton decay was very clear-cut, very simple. Now the theorists have run out of gas, and the ball goes into our court. We can look for things they haven't predicted, follow hunches, study the tapes for something that just looks funny." Such events, unclassified and unpredictable, are known in the world of physics as zoo-ons. "They're like animals in the zoo," Svoboda explains, "jumping from tree to tree."

So, along with disappointment has come a subversive sense of adventure among the physicists at the mine. They are experimentalists, traditionally charged with testing out the big ideas sparkling from the pencils of theorists. A healthy rivalry has long existed between the two interdependent breeds, but the idea men—the theorists—tend to walk off with the Nobel Prizes. Maybe this time the experimentalists can trump the theorists. "If you see something like this," reads a note above a diagram of X's, "call Maurice immediately."

Nearby, another message hangs in a frame, an Eighteenth Century poem by William Cowper:

God moves in a mysterious way
His wonders to perform
He plants his footsteps in the sea,
And rides upon the storm.

Deep in unfathomable mines
Of never failing skill
He treasures up his bright designs
And works his sovereign will.

No one is sure if the poem was posted as a joke or as a humbling reminder of the limits of rational thought. Perhaps both. Physicists operate on the edge of the unknown where logic, language—even the imagination—often fail.

Will the universe, which began as energy, end as energy? It is an irresistible question—one which has been asked a thousand ways since the ancient Babylonians pondered a world created in the fiery separation of land and sky. The search for proton decay is Twentieth Century science's latest attempt to fill in the blanks of our own cosmic epic.

Even if the round of experiments is unsuccessful, physicists will continue to search the invisible subatomic world for answers to the cosmic question. Plans are already brewing for a different kind of proton decay detector, one hundred times bigger than the Lake Erie setup, to operate in the open water off the shores of Hawaii.

As the sun sets over Lake Erie, the physicists leave the mine and return to their lodgings at the Mentor Country Inn. No one there seems to have heard of the "experiment of the century" going on down the road, though professors in steel-toed boots come and go.

Now cars filled with young people come out to cruise around No Help Wanted signs and idle machinery at the mine. Crickets begin to sing in the ragged lakeshore grass. Dr. Sinclair is still underground, tending his instruments as, in a burst of purple and orange, the sun disappears.

QUESTIONS FOR CRITICAL ANALYSIS

1. After reading Kraus's essay, look back at your prereading remarks about physicists. Explain how the physicists described in this essay conform to your ideas and how they break the stereotype. In your opinion, does Kraus "feed" the image of physicists as eccentric "mad scientists"? How?
2. Describe what's going on in the proton-decay experiment. What are the physicists trying to discover?
3. According to scientists Kraus quotes in the essay, physicists "do physics" because they "love to look at nature to see how it works." What does that mean? How does the physicists *look* at nature? (Compare them to Hardwick, Updike, Dillard, and others in Part One.) What is the physicists' attitude toward nature?
4. How do experimentalists conduct science? Why is it described as an adventure? Describe how the experimental approach differs from the theoretical approach. What did you learn about the experimentalist-theorist rivalry in this essay?
5. If proton-decay experiments are successful, what will scientists discover? How will this discovery affect our understanding of the universe? How will it affect our understanding of ourselves?

QUESTIONS FOR STRUCTURAL ANALYSIS

1. Describe the relationship between paragraphs one and two. Why did Kraus begin with a description of the townspeople? What was your reaction to the switch in the second paragraph?
2. On three occasions (other than the first paragraph) Kraus brings the townspeople into

the essay. Discuss why. Is each time effective? Why, or why not? Did you expect them to show up at any other time? When?

3. Look at the way Kraus describes the research station. How does her description extend beyond simply evoking the place?
4. Make a list of the political allusions, references to movies and literature. Why does Kraus use these devices? How do they affect your reading of the essay?
5. Reread the headnote and Kraus's description of why she writes science features. How does she succeed in this essay to convey information about the experiment? to show the human side of science?

*T*HE *B*AROMETER *S*TORY: *A*NGELS ON A *P*IN

ALEXANDER CALANDRA

Alexander Calandra (1911–), a professor of physics at Washington University in St. Louis, has been deeply involved in physics education. Calandra's interest in education extends beyond the schools and universities to include developing ways to teach science, and specifically physics, to the general public. His delight in teaching and in students is evident in "The Barometer Story" which was first published in Saturday Review, *a predominately literary magazine.*

Before you begin reading: *Think about your experiences in science classes and write a paragraph describing your best experience.*

◆

SOME TIME AGO, I RECEIVED A CALL FROM A COLLEAGUE who asked if I would be the referee on the grading of an examination question. He was about to give a student a zero for his answer to a physics question, while the student claimed he should receive a perfect score and would if the system were not set up against the student. The instructor and the student agreed to submit this to an impartial arbiter, and I was selected.

I went to my colleague's office and read the examination question: "Show how it is possible to determine the height of a tall building with the aid of a barometer."

The student had answered: "Take the barometer to the top of the building, attach a long rope to it, lower the barometer to the street, and then bring it up, measuring the length of the rope. The length of the rope is the height of the building."

I pointed out that the student really had a strong case for full credit, since he had answered the question completely and correctly. On the other hand, if full credit were given, it could well contribute to a high grade for the student in his physics course. A high grade is supposed to certify competence in physics, but the answer did not confirm this. I suggested that the student have another try at answering the question. I was not surprised that my colleague agreed, but I was surprised that the student did.

I gave the student six minutes to answer the question, with the warning that his answer should show some knowledge of physics. At the end of five minutes, he had not written anything. I asked if he wished to give up, but he said no. He had many answers to this problem; he was just thinking of the best one. I excused myself for interrupting him, and asked him to please go on. In the next minute, he dashed off his answer which read:

"Take the barometer to the top of the building and lean over the edge of the roof. Drop the barometer, timing its fall with a stopwatch. Then, using the formula $S = \frac{1}{2}at^2$, calculate the height of the building."

At this point, I asked my colleague if *he* would give up. He conceded, and I gave the student almost full credit.

In leaving my colleague's office, I recalled that the student had said he had other answers to the problem, so I asked him what they were. "Oh, yes," said the student. "There are many ways of getting the height of a tall building with the aid of a barometer. For example, you could take the barometer out on a sunny day and measure the height of the barometer, the length of its shadow, and the length of the shadow of the building, and by the use of a simple proportion, determine the height of the building."

"Fine," I said. "And the others?"

"Yes," said the student. "There is a very basic measurement method that you will like. In this method, you take the barometer and begin to walk up the stairs. As you climb the stairs, you mark off the length of the barometer along the wall. You then count the number of marks, and this will give you the height of the building in barometer units. A very direct method.

"Of course, if you want a more sophisticated method, you can tie the barometer to the end of a string, swing it as a pendulum, and determine the value of 'g' at the street level and at the top of the building. From the difference between the two values of "g," the height of the building can, in principle, be calculated."

Finally he concluded, there are many other ways of solving the problem. "Probably the best," he said, "is to take the barometer to the basement and knock on the superintendent's door. When the superintendent answers, you speak to him as follows: 'Mr. Superintendent, here I have a fine barometer. If you will tell me the height of this building, I will give you this barometer.'"

At this point, I asked the student if he really did not know the conventional answer to this question. He admitted that he did, but said that he was fed up with high school and college instructors trying to teach him how to think, to use the "scientific method," and to explore the deep inner logic of the subject in a pedantic way, as is often done in the new mathematics, rather than teaching him the structure of the subject. With this in mind, he decided to revive scholasticism as an academic lark to challenge the Sputnik-panicked classrooms of America.

QUESTIONS FOR CRITICAL ANALYSIS

1. Why did the professor want to give the student a zero for his exam? What had the student done incorrectly? How do you react to the student's first answer?
2. Why is Calandra reluctant to allow the student's answer, though correct, to be accepted?
3. What do you think about the student's second answer? Why was it accepted?
4. Which answer is your favorite one? Why?

QUESTIONS FOR STRUCTURAL ANALYSIS

1. How do you characterize the style of this essay?
2. What does the title mean: "Angels on a Pin"?
3. What is Calandra's point in telling this story?

*K*NOW *A*BOUT *O*UR *W*ORLD

TOPICS FOR WRITING ESSAYS

Many of the questions following each essay can serve as appropriate writing suggestions. The topics listed below expand the prereading exercises, but they can be used without completing that step first.

1. With your responses to the Morowitz prereading exercise serving as a base, interview some mathematicians on your campus. Why did they choose mathematics as a field of study? What do they find most fulfilling about their job? What do they do? If you have negative feelings towards mathematics, ask them to suggest ways for you to change your opinion. Write a profile for the student paper about mathematics and include what you discovered and learned in your interviews.
2. Interview professors in the branch of science you like best. What advice do they give for someone who wants to major in this branch of science? Why did they choose the subject? What do they like best about it? What opportunities are there for graduates in this major? Write an essay convincing someone to select this branch of science as a major.
3. Compare the way three of the authors in this section described science with your own ideas about science. Write your essay to a science faculty committee who is working to improve their courses in an effort to attract more majors.

RESEARCH POSSIBILITIES

1. Select one of the scientists named in Mitchell Wilson's essay. Find out as much as you can about why he or she decided to become a scientist and how that decision shaped his or her life. Write the story of this scientist's early life for junior high students, use vivid details and descriptions to make the biography come alive and to interest the young students in a possible science career.
2. Find out about the scientific research being conducted on your campus or in your community. Read as much as you can about the purpose of the work and what the research is designed to accomplish. If possible, interview some of the scientists involved in the work. Write a feature article about the research for a local magazine, capturing the excitement of the research as well as explaining the science to the lay reader.

THE MEANING OF SCIENCE

The essays in this section can be difficult reading on several levels: the ideas are challenging, the language is dense, and the author's tone can be disconcerting. Einstein's essay provokes us to examine the way we define our existence and the existence of the world around us. To begin to understand the essay you may need to read it several times. Feynman, certainly far more accessible as a writer, also challenges our ideas about science: how is it valuable? how do we know what we know? Nemerov, poet and essayist, provides a tongue-in-cheek comparison of scientists and priests, and in his comparison raises questions about how we understand our world. Mead explores the need for "human scientists" (social scientists) to dispel public distrust by instituting ethical standards and controls in their disciplines.

*P*HYSICS AND *R*EALITY

ALBERT EINSTEIN

Albert Einstein (1879–1955), a German-born American physicist whose contributions to modern science are unequalled, is best known for his theory of Relativity (described in a 1905 paper and developed in a 1916 paper) and his development of quantum theory. Through Einstein's work and that of the early developers of quantum mechanics, the world of predictable behavior based on physical laws changed and became less certain. In "Physics and Reality," Einstein examines the relationship between what our senses experience of the world and how we use these sense experiences to understand and think about the concepts on which the world is based.

Before you begin reading: *What is reality? How do you know something exists? What absolute proof do you have? Do you trust your senses? Have they ever failed you? Spend some time thinking on these questions, and then write in your notebook about how you know the world around you is real.*

◆

IT HAS OFTEN BEEN SAID, AND CERTAINLY NOT WITHOUT justification, that the man of science is a poor philosopher. Why then should it not be the right thing for the physicist to let the philosopher do the philosophizing? Such might indeed be the right thing at a time when the physicist believes he has at his disposal a rigid system of fundamental concepts and fundamental laws which are so well established that waves of doubt can not reach them; but, it can not be right at a time when the very foundations of physics itself have become problematic as they are now. At a time like the present, when experience forces us to seek a newer and more solid foundation, the physicist cannot simply surrender to the philosopher the critical contemplation of the theoretical foundations; for, he himself knows best, and feels more surely where the shoe pinches. In looking for a new foundation, he must try to make clear in his own mind just how far the concepts which he uses are justified, and are necessities.

The whole of science is nothing more than a refinement of every day thinking. It is for this reason that the critical thinking of the physicist cannot possibly be restricted to the examination of the concepts of his own specific field. He cannot proceed without considering critically a much more difficult problem, the problem of analyzing the nature of everyday thinking.

On the stage of our subconscious mind appear in colorful succession sense experiences, memory pictures of them, representations and feelings. In contrast to psychology, physics treats directly only of sense experiences and of the "understanding" of their connection. But even the concept of the "real external world" of everyday thinking rests exclusively on sense impressions.

Now we must first remark that the differentiation between sense impressions and representations is not possible; or, at least it is not possible with absolute certainty. With the discussion of this problem, which affects also the notion of reality, we will not concern ourselves but we shall take the existence of sense experiences as given, that is to say as psychic experiences of special kind.

I believe that the first step in the setting of a "real external world" is the formation of the concept of bodily objects and of bodily objects of various kinds. Out of the multitude of our sense experiences we take, mentally and arbitrarily, certain repeatedly occurring complexes of sense impression (partly in conjunction with sense impressions which are interpreted as signs for sense experiences of others), and we attribute to them a meaning—the meaning of the bodily object. Considered logically this concept is not identical with the totality of sense impressions referred to; but it is an arbitrary creation of the human (or animal) mind. On the other hand, the concept owes its meaning and its justification exclusively to the totality of the sense impressions which we associate with it.

The second step is to be found in the fact that, in our thinking (which determines our expectation), we attribute to this concept of the bodily object a significance, which is to a high degree independent of the sense impression which originally gives rise to it. This is what we mean when we attribute to the bodily object "a real existence." The justification of such a setting rests exclusively on the fact that, by means of such concepts and mental relations between them, we are able to orient ourselves in the labyrinth of sense impressions. These notions and relations, although free statements of our thoughts, appear to us as stronger and more unalterable than the individual sense experience itself, the character of which as anything other than the result of an illusion or hallucination is never completely guaranteed. On the other hand, these concepts and relations, and indeed the setting of real objects and, generally speaking, the existence of "the real world," have justification only in so far as they are connected with sense impressions between which they form a mental connection.

The very fact that the totality of our sense experiences is such that by means of thinking (operations with concepts, and the creation and use of definite functional relations between them, and the coordination of sense experiences to these concepts) it can be put in order, this fact is one which leaves us in awe, but which we shall never understand. One may say "the eternal mystery of the world is its comprehensibility." It is one of the great realizations of Immanuel Kant that the setting up of a real external world would be senseless without this comprehensibility.

In speaking here concerning "comprehensibility," the expression is used in its most modest sense. It implies: the production of some sort of order among sense impressions, this order being produced by the creation of general concepts, relations between these concepts, and by relations between the concepts and sense experience, these relations being determined in any possible manner. It is in this sense that the world of our sense experiences is comprehensible. The fact that it is comprehensible is a miracle.

In my opinion, nothing can be said concerning the manner in which the concepts are to be made and connected, and how we are to coordinate them to the experiences. In guiding us in the creation of such an order of sense experiences, success in the result is alone the determining factor. All that is necessary is *the statement* of a set of rules, since without such rules the acquisition of knowledge in the desired sense would be impossible. One may compare these rules with the rules of a game in which, while the rules themselves are arbitrary, it is their rigidity alone which makes the game possible. However, the fixation will never be final. It will have validity only for a special field of application (i.e., there are no final categories in the sense of Kant).

The connection of the elementary concepts of every day thinking with complexes of sense experiences can only be comprehended intuitively and it is unadaptable to scientifically logical fixation. The totality of these connections—none of which is expressible in notional terms—is the only thing which differentiates the great building which is science from a logical but empty scheme of concepts. By means of these connections, the purely notional theorems of science become statements about complexes of sense experiences.

We shall call "primary concepts" such concepts as are directly and intuitively connected with typical complexes of sense experiences. All other notions are—from the physical point of view—possessed of meaning, only in so far as they are connected, by theorems, with the primary notions. These theorems are partially definitions of the concepts (and of the statements derived logically from them) and partially theorems not derivable from the definitions, which express at least indirect relations between the "primary concepts," and in this way between sense experiences. Theorems of the latter kind are "statements about reality" or laws of nature, i.e., theorems which have to show their usefulness when applied to sense experiences comprehended by primary concepts. The question as to which of the theorems shall be considered as definitions and which as natural laws will depend largely upon the chosen representation. It really becomes absolutely necessary to make this differentiation only when one examines the degree to which the whole system of concepts considered is not empty from the physical point of view.

QUESTIONS FOR CRITICAL ANALYSIS

1. How has physics changed so that philosophizing is an acceptable behavior for physicists? Do you know what Einstein is talking about?
2. How does Einstein define science? What does he mean by this definition? What consequences result from such a definition?
3. What is "everyday thinking"? According to Einstein, how do we know the world around us? What makes our knowledge so uncertain?
4. What gives meaning to objects around us? How does Einstein's explanation compare with Cary's description of the artist's role? Are you surprised by the similarities between the artist's and the physicist's views of reality?
5. What are "primary concepts"? How do they differ from all other ideas? Can you give some examples of primary concepts?

QUESTIONS FOR STRUCTURAL ANALYSIS

1. Einstein begins by admitting that because he's a physicist many may not think he should write about subjects other than science. What is his subject? What reasons does he give for writing the essay?
2. Describe Einstein's sentence structure. Is his prose difficult to read and understand? Why? Rewrite a difficult sentence or two in a plainer style. How did you change the language?
3. Name the steps we take in thinking about the world around us. In what ways is our thinking arbitrary? What is more "real"—our sense experiences? or the objects? What does Einstein mean when he says that the "real world" has justification only as connected with sense impressions? Why does Einstein say that the fact that the world is comprehensible is a "miracle"?
4. Why is a "statement of rules" absolutely necessary in understanding the world? How does Einstein's allusion to a game help explain what he means? Can you make his statement even more concrete by expanding it?
5. What is the point of Einstein's essay? Had you thought of these ideas before? How has Einstein's essay altered your ideas about meaning?

*T*HE *V*ALUE OF *S*CIENCE

RICHARD P. FEYNMAN

When Richard P. Feynman (1918–1988) died, a Los Angeles Times *editorial stated: "Our community and the world are much poorer today for the loss of Richard Feynman, who until his death of cancer Monday night may have been the smartest person on earth." Feynman's life was one of achievement: He worked on the Manhattan Project* at Los Alamos, taught theoretical physics at Cornell University and California Institute of Technology, received the Nobel Prize in 1965 for the theory of quantum electrodynamics, served on the President's commission to investigate the Challenger disaster and dramatically illustrated a problem by dropping an O-ring into his ice water and showing its rigidity in the cold. Feynman preferred presenting a public image of himself as an iconoclast (as in his book,* Surely You're Joking, Mr. Feynman!*), and this posture is evident by the tone of this essay, "The Value of Science." Feynman's message, however, is serious: the "philosophy of ignorance" should be cherished for it leaves the world open to new insights and challenges.*

Before you begin reading: *Feynman quotes a Buddhist proverb in this essay: "To every man is given the key to the gates of heaven; the same key opens the gates of hell." Think about this proverb. What ideas does it bring to mind? What does it mean? Do you believe it to be true? Write down the ideas that come into your head while you think about its meaning.*

◆

FROM TIME TO TIME, PEOPLE SUGGEST TO ME THAT SCIENtists ought to give more consideration to social problems—especially that they should be more responsible in considering the impact of science upon society. This same suggestion must be made to many other scientists, and it seems to be generally believed that if the scientists would only look at these very difficult social problems and not spend so much time fooling with the less vital scientific ones, great success would come of it.

It seems to me that we do think about these problems from time to time, but we don't put full-time effort into them—the reason being that we know we

*The Manhattan Project was the designation of a secret scientific project begun in 1942 to develop atomic weapons.

don't have any magic formula for solving problems, that social problems are very much harder than scientific ones, and that we usually don't get anywhere when we do think about them.

I believe that a scientist looking at nonscientific problems is just as dumb as the next guy—and when he talks about a nonscientific matter, he will sound as naive as anyone untrained in the matter. Since the question of the value of science is not a scientific subject, this discussion is dedicated to proving my point—by example.

The first way in which science is of value is familiar to everyone. It is that scientific knowledge enables us to do all kinds of things and to make all kinds of things. Of course if we make good things, it is not only to the credit of science; it is also to the credit of the moral choice which led us to good work. Scientific knowledge is an enabling power to do either good or bad—but it does not carry instructions on how to use it. Such power has evident value—even though the power may be negated by what one does.

I learned a way of expressing this common human problem on a trip to Honolulu. In a Buddhist temple there, the man in charge explained a little bit about the Buddhist religion for tourists, and then ended his talk by telling them he had something to say to them that they would *never* forget—and I have never forgotten it. It was a proverb of the Buddhist religion:

"To every man is given the key to the gates of heaven; the same key opens the gates of hell."

What then, is the value of the key to heaven? It is true that if we lack clear instructions that determine which is the gate to heaven and which the gate to hell, the key may be a dangerous object to use, but it obviously has value. How can we enter heaven without it?

The instructions, also, would be of no value without the key. So it is evident that, in spite of the fact that science could produce enormous horror in the world, it is of value because it *can* produce *something*.

Another value of science is the fun called intellectual enjoyment which some people get from reading and learning and thinking about it, and which others get from working in it. This is a very real and important point and one which is not considered enough by those who tell us it is our social responsibility to reflect on the impact of science on society.

Is this mere personal enjoyment of value to society as a whole? No! But it is also a responsibility to consider the value of society itself. Is it, in the last analysis, to arrange things so that people can enjoy things? If so, the enjoyment of science is as important as anything else.

But I would like *not* to underestimate the value of the world view which is the result of scientific effort. We have been led to imagine all sorts of things infinitely more marvelous than the imaginings of poets and dreamers of the past. It shows that the imagination of nature is far, far greater than the imagination of man. For instance, how much more remarkable it is for us all to be stuck—half of us upside down—by a mysterious attraction, to a spinning ball that has been swinging in space for billions of years, than to be carried on the back of an elephant supported on a tortoise swimming in a bottomless sea.

I have thought about these things so many times alone that I hope you will excuse me if I remind you of some thoughts that I am sure you have all had—or this type of thought—which no one could ever have had in the past, because people then didn't have the information we have about the world today.

For instance, I stand at the seashore, alone, and start to think. There are the rushing waves . . . mountains of molecules, each stupidly minding its own business . . . trillions apart . . . yet forming white surf in unison.

Ages on ages . . . before any eyes could see . . . year after year . . . thunderously pounding the shore as now. For whom, for what? . . . on a dead planet, with no life to entertain.

Never at rest . . . tortured by energy . . . wasted prodigiously by the sun . . . poured into space. A mite makes the sea roar.

Deep in the sea, all molecules repeat the patterns of one another till complex new ones are formed. They make others like themselves . . . and a new dance starts.

Growing in size and complexity . . . living things, masses of atoms, DNA, protein . . . dancing a pattern ever more intricate.

Out of the cradle onto the dry land . . . here it is standing . . . atoms with consciousness . . . matter with curiosity.

Stands at the sea . . . wonders at wondering . . . I . . . a universe of atoms . . . an atom in the universe.

THE GRAND ADVENTURE

The same thrill, the same awe and mystery, come again and again when we look at any problem deeply enough. With more knowledge comes deeper, more wonderful mystery, luring one on to penetrate deeper still. Never concerned that the answer may prove disappointing, but with pleasure and confidence we turn over each new stone to find unimagined strangeness leading on to more wonderful questions and mysteries—certainly a grand adventure!

It is true that few unscientific people have this particular type of religious experience. Our poets do not write about it; our artists do not try to portray this remarkable thing. I don't know why. Is nobody inspired by our present picture of the universe? The value of science remains unsung by singers, so you are reduced to hearing—not a song or a poem, but an evening lecture about it. This is not yet a scientific age.

Perhaps one of the reasons is that you have to know how to read the music. For instance, the scientific article says, perhaps, something like this: "The radioactive phosphorous content of the cerebrum of the rat decreases to one-half in a period of two weeks." Now, what does that mean?

It means that phosphorus that is in the brain of a rat (and also in mine, and yours) is not the same phosphorus as it was two weeks ago, but that all of the atoms that are in the brain are being replaced, and the ones that were there before have gone away.

So what is this mind, what are these atoms with consciousness? Last week's potatoes! That is what now can *remember* what was going on in my mind a year ago—a mind which has long ago been replaced.

That is what it means when one discovers how long it takes for the atoms of the brain to be replaced by other atoms, to note that the thing which I call my individuality is only a pattern or dance. The atoms come into my brain, dance a dance, then go out; always new atoms but always doing the same dance, remembering what the dance was yesterday.

THE REMARKABLE IDEA

When we read about this in the newspaper, it says, "the scientist says that this discovery may have importance in the cure of cancer." The paper is only interested in the use of the idea, not the idea itself. Hardly anyone can understand the importance of an idea, it is so remarkable. Except that, possibly, some children catch on. And when a child catches on to an idea like that, we have a scientist. These ideas do filter down (in spite of all the conversation about TV replacing thinking), and lots of kids get the spirit—and when they have the spirit you have a scientist. It's too late for them to get the spirit when they are in our universities, so we must attempt to explain these ideas to children.

I would now like to turn to a third value that science has. It is a little more indirect, but not much. The scientist has a lot of experience with ignorance and doubt and uncertainty, and this experience is of very great importance, I think. When a scientist doesn't know the answer to a problem, he is ignorant. When he has a hunch as to what the result is, he is uncertain. And when he is pretty darn sure of what the result is going to be, he is in some doubt. We have found it of paramount importance that in order to progress we must recognize the ignorance and leave room for doubt. Scientific knowledge is a body of statements of varying degrees of certainty—some most unsure, some nearly sure, none *absolutely* certain.

Now, we scientists are used to this, and we take it for granted that it is perfectly consistent to be unsure—that it is possible to live and *not* know. But I don't know whether everyone realizes that this is true. Our freedom to doubt was born of a struggle against authority in the early days of science. It was a very deep and strong struggle. Permit us to question—to doubt, that's all—not to be sure. And I think it is important that we do not forget the importance of this struggle and thus perhaps lose what we have gained. Here lies a responsibility to society.

We are all sad when we think of the wondrous potentialities human beings seem to have, as contrasted with their small accomplishments. Again and again people have thought that we could do much better. They of the past saw in the nightmare of their times a dream for the future. We, of their future, see that their dreams, in certain ways surpassed, have in many ways remained dreams. The hopes for the future today are, in good share, those of yesterday.

EDUCATION, FOR GOOD AND EVIL

Once some thought that the possibilities people had were not developed because most of those people were ignorant. With education universal, could all men be Voltaires? Bad can be taught at least as efficiently as good. Education is a strong force, but for either good or evil.

Communications between nations must promote understanding: so went another dream. But the machines of communication can be channeled or choked. What is communicated can be truth or lie. Communication is a strong force also, but for either good or bad.

The applied sciences should free men of material problems at least. Medicine controls diseases. And the record here seems all to the good. Yet there are men patiently working to create great plagues and poisons. They are to be used in warfare tomorrow.

Nearly everybody dislikes war. Our dream today is peace. In peace, man can develop best the enormous possibilities he seems to have. But maybe future men will find that peace, too, can be good and bad. Perhaps peaceful men will drink out of boredom. Then perhaps drink will become the great problem which seems to keep man from getting all he thinks he should out of his abilities.

Clearly, peace is a great force, as is sobriety, as are material power, communication, education, honesty and the ideals of many dreamers.

We have more of these forces to control than did the ancients. And maybe we are doing a little better than most of them could do. But what we ought to be able to do seems gigantic compared with our confused accomplishments.

Why is this? Why can't we conquer ourselves?

Because we find that even great forces and abilities do not seem to carry with them clear instructions on how to use them. As an example, the great accumulation of understanding as to how the physical world behaves only convinces one that this behavior seems to have a kind of meaninglessness. The sciences do not directly teach good and bad.

Through all ages men have tried to fathom the meaning of life. They have realized that if some direction or meaning could be given to our actions, great human forces would be unleased. So, very many answers must have been given to the question of the meaning of it all. But they have been of all different sorts, and the proponents of one answer have looked with horror at the actions of the believers in another. Horror, because from a disagreeing point of view all the great potentialities of the race were being channeled into a false and confining blind alley. In fact, it is from the history of the enormous monstrosities created by false belief that philosophers have realized the apparently infinite and wondrous capacities of human beings. The dream is to find the open channel.

What, then, is the meaning of it all? What can we say to dispel the mystery of existence?

If we take everything into account, not only what the ancients knew, but all of what we know today that they didn't know, then I think that we must frankly admit that *we do not know*.

But, in admitting this, we have probably found the open channel.

This is not a new idea; this is the idea of the age of reason. This is the philosophy that guided the men who made the democracy that we live under. The idea that no one really knew how to run a government led to the idea that we should arrange a system by which new ideas could be developed, tried out, tossed out, more new ideas brought in; a trial and error system. This method was a result of the fact that science was already showing itself to be a successful venture at the end of the 18th century. Even then it was clear to socially-minded people that the openness of the possibilities was an opportunity, and that doubt and discussion were essential to progress into the unknown. If we want to solve a problem that we have never solved before, we must leave the door to the unknown ajar.

OUR RESPONSIBILITY AS SCIENTISTS

We are at the very beginning of time for the human race. It is not unreasonable that we grapple with problems. There are tens of thousands of years in the future. Our responsibility is to do what we can, learn what we can, improve the solutions and pass them on. It is our responsibility to leave the men of the future a free hand. In the impetuous youth of humanity, we can make grave errors that can stunt our growth for a long time. This we will do if we say we have the answers now, so young and ignorant; if we suppress all discussion, all criticism, saying, "This is it, boys, man is saved!" and thus doom man for a long time to the chains of authority, confined to the limits of our present imagination. It has been done so many times before.

It is our responsibility as scientists, knowing the great progress and great value of a satisfactory philosophy of ignorance, the great progress that is the fruit of freedom of thought, to proclaim the value of this freedom, to teach how doubt is not to be feared but welcomed and discussed, and to demand this freedom as our duty to all coming generations.

QUESTIONS FOR CRITICAL ANALYSIS

1. What three ways is science of value? Do any of these ways surprise you? Which one(s)?
2. Why does Feynman tell the story about his visit to the Buddhist temple? How does the proverb relate to his thesis?
3. Why does Feynman refer to "an elephant supported on a tortoise swimming in a bottomless sea"? What's the significance of that idea?
4. What experiences does Feynman believe are unavailable to unscientific people? Do you agree with him? Why, or why not? (If you disagree, give examples to illustrate your opinion.)
5. Why can't we "conquer ourselves," as Feynman puts it? What do we need to conquer? What does *meaning* have to do with our lives?

QUESTIONS FOR STRUCTURAL ANALYSIS

1. What is the point of Feynman's first three paragraphs? Reread the final sentence of the third paragraph. What does Feynman mean? How does that relate to the rest of the essay?
2. Describe Feynman's tone. Does his tone surprise you when you consider his scientific stature? Why, or why not?
3. Look at the section where Feynman describes his private thoughts about science. How do you react to this section? What makes these thoughts special to this time in history?
4. Feynman has divided this essay into five sections. What are the relationships among these sections? Why is there such a formal organization?
5. Why does Feynman conclude by saying, "We are at the very beginning of time for the human race"? How is this true? What is the scientist's responsibility? Is this an effective conclusion? Why, or why not?

On the *R*esemblances *B*etween *S*cience and *R*eligion

Howard Nemerov

Howard Nemerov (1920–), Poet Laureate of the United States, is also a novelist, essayist, critic, and teacher. He writes with wit and clarity, often deflecting the reader from his serious contemplation on the fundamental complexity of his subject. Nemerov compares science and religion with humor and intelligence in his essay "On the Resemblances Between Science and Religion," showing similarities between the ways science and religion are practiced, the people who devote themselves to each discipline, the specialized language of each, and, finally, how the general public responds to both enterprises.

Before you begin reading: *In your reading notebook, make two lists of ways that religion and science are similar and are dissimilar. Next, organize your lists into categories, and add at least one specific example to support each of your entries.*

◆

THIS IS A POETIC EXERCISE. I BEGIN BY ASSUMING THAT THE evident, large, and significant differences between science and religion, scientist and priest, have been amply acknowledged and endlessly elaborated, so that the characteristic relation between science and religion has been either enmity, that is, polar opposition, or no relation at all (the claim that they occupy mutually exclusive realms of discourse). It will be obvious at once that polar opposites must necessarily have much in common; and as to the other claim, that they divide the world between them, maintaining separate spheres of influence, that is a common interim and compromise solution for polar opposites and may be no more satisfactory or enduring here than it is seen to be in politics.

When two things are said to be opposites, it becomes a duty of the intelligence to look for their similarities.

When two things are said to have nothing in common, it becomes a pleasure of the intelligence to find out what they have in common.

The essential procedure of physical science is the experiment, a compound of hypothesis and observation which will produce the same results for anyone, anywhere, at any time, so long as the conditions and steps of the original are scrupulously and rigorously followed. If the same results are not obtained, either the hypothesis is incorrect or the person repeating the experiment repeated it inexactly in some way. In principle, the first alternative is always possible, for even the most adequately supported and long-established hypotheses are not supposed, quite, to become doctrine or dogma; but in practice, when the physics teacher sets up his apparatus before the class and the predicted result fails to occur he does not commonly announce a revolution in physics but apologizes for his error.

The essential procedure of religion is the ritual, a compound of explanation and observation which will produce the same results that have made the assertions of the original *quod semper, quod ubique, quod ab omnibus,* but only if the conditions and steps of the original are scrupulously and rigorously followed in the repetition. If the same results (prosperity at the harvest, victory in war, protection from calamity) are not produced the fault in principle is always thought to be an incorrect following of the procedures either technically or spiritually (in much the same way as prolonged investigation of almost every air disaster finds the cause in 'pilot error'), but in practice, over long periods, gods do disappear, rituals decay, become modified or transformed, are applied to allegedly different purposes.

The assertion that religious ritual is the product of observation may seem strange these days. But priesthood and its procedures were connected with astronomy (from the beginning), as among the Chaldeans; Lord Raglan tells us that what priests observably do (whatever they claim to be doing) is keep a sacred calendar; and, as Christopher Caudwell said of savages, they dance the rain dance at the approach of the rainy season, not in the dry.

Ideally, the scientific experiment can be performed by any sane person who goes about it in the right spirit, that is, a spirit of obedience to instructions. In practice, however, this is rarely possible, and then only with the simplest procedures. I can verify for myself, perhaps, the existence of interference patterns in light. But I do not own or have access to a particle accelerator and would not know what to do with it if I had. So it turns out that experiments are typically carried out by a separate class of persons trained from youth in experimental procedures; in theory, any young person may belong to this class, but in practice it is standard for applicants to be screened by aptitude tests and by a long, arduous novitiate, during which they learn the esoteric language of their vocation.

In certain sects of an allegedly ecumenical religion, especially those sects which refer their beliefs, correctly or not, to a return to primitive practices, anyone who feels moved by the spirit may say the rituals; in the Old Testament, for example, the establishment of one tribe, the Levites, as priest-specialists is relatively late; it occurs simultaneously with the rigorous codifying of doctrine and the forming of a nation. But after and apart from the primitive, the rituals of world religions are typically carried out by a separate class of persons trained from youth in the procedures of ritual; in theory, any young person may belong to this class, but in practice it is standard for applicants to be screened for signs of a vocation and, if they show such signs, by a long, arduous novitiate, in which they learn the esoteric language in which alone the rituals can be efficacious.

The language of science, mathematics, is esoteric and abstruse but international for its initiates; it refers to a supramundane or purely mental reality; it is in its purest form a language about itself, like music, refined of every worldly consideration and yet immensely powerful when applied to the world. The Fratres Arvali in Rome are said to have done their rites in a Latin so dead that they themselves did not know what its formulae meant (it is also said they winked at one another when they met in the street), and Bertrand Russell tells us plainly that 'Mathematics is a science in which we never know what we are talking about nor whether what we say is true' (quoted in Lucienne Felix, *The Modern Aspect of Mathematics*, p. 53), though the printed page will not record a wink.

Even when rituals are recited in the living language of the communicants, that language is highly specialized by archaic forms, lofty and traditional phrasing, and so on. But in our best example for the purpose of comparison, the Latin of the Catholic Church is esoteric and yet international for its initiates, refers to a supramundane or purely mental reality, is in its purest form a language about itself (note the linguistic problems involved in speaking of three persons as both one and three, or of bread and wine as becoming body and blood), ritually associated with music, and yet immensely powerful when applied to the world (as the same linguistic difficulties, when applied to the world, produced numerous bodies and a great deal of blood).

Scholium. We might pause here to look at music as the model language for both science and religion. Music is like that machine built a few years back by someone in California; it had thousands of moving parts and no identifiable function. The first digital computer (and pedal computer too, for that matter) was the cathedral organ, programmed by J. S. Bach, among others, to exhaust all the possible combinational resources of the tonal language as then understood. The musical language is in one respect observably unique, however: nobody died young and poor of Mozart, except Mozart.

Religion and science both have at least three ways of being understood (or not understood). These ways might be listed (for both) as aristocratic, bourgeois, and proletarian, or (also for both) as esoteric, exoteric, and superstitious. They might be diagrammatically set forth as follows:

1. Mysticism, vision, theology	**1.** Pure, or creative, science; philosophy of science
2. Morals, the good life, order	**2.** Technology, progress, order
3. The devil	**3.** The mad scientist

I should emphasize that my first description of the three possibilities as aristocratic, bourgeois, and proletarian does not assert these as fixed limitations of class; nothing in his own nature will prevent the child of a laborer from becoming a theologian or a theoretical physicist, but either will be a very aristocratic thing for him to become. Nor, obviously, is a member of the middle class condemned to be a bourgeois in religion or in science. Salvation to all that will is nigh, we might say, and so is damnation. Now to specify somewhat more elaborately the description of my three categories:

1. Here is the true source of what is generally and laughably called—with a straight face—the practical world: in the dreams and visions of gentle and profound and imaginative men whose word is peace. These men deal purely and in a humble spirit with the most immense and fundamental forces imaginable, with the simple and ineluctable mystery of The Word, The Logos, The Divine Name, Energy, Mass, Light, Number, and so on. They characteristically give utterance to brief, cryptic, world-transforming statements such as Know Thyself, I am the Light of the World, $E = mc^2$, or .000 000 000 000 000 000 000 006 6. . . . x frequency = quantum of energy. It seems rarely to occur to them that such announcements could ever become bloody instructions, and indeed the idea does look improbable. And they have their faithful followers, too, men generally regarded as either insane or disloyal by the establishment.

2. These great spirits have their equally faithful followers in the second realm, too. This is the so-called practical world referred to above, where the Logos descended into matter and crucified there becomes the weapon and the cause. This is the world where the great intuition that number is the nature of all things is translated to say that money is the number which is the nature of all things. It is the world of banners inscribed *Gott mit uns, Dieu et mon droit,* of coinage that reads on one side 'In God we trust' and on the other 'Five cents.'

This is not to say that we, who are largely the inhabitants of this second realm, are personally villainous; it is far more likely that we view ourselves, not incorrectly with respect to our situation in society, as driven by necessities beyond our control or understanding, impersonal necessities, compulsions to realize and exhaust all possibility, compulsions to incarnate in corruptible form everything divined for us by the dreamers of the realm above. Here, in our realm, even in metaphysical respects the middle class, live the great administrators of the Word: St. Paul, Innocent III, Ignatius Loyola, Luther, Calvin . . . I refrain from naming the scientific opposite numbers, who are still alive. But this is the realm in which the power of order is more important than anything else, where love another as thyself necessarily becomes the Albigensian Crusade and $E = mc^2$ is necessarily realized as a nuclear weapon.

But it is also and at the same time another realm, this second one, or it can be more benignly regarded: it is the world of that extremely active god from whom all blessings flow. In science these blessings are technological, and extend from the rather humble electric toaster through the remarkable or even miraculous invention of television and so on to splendors untold. In religion these blessings are a little more metaphorical but at least as real in their effects: our invisible identification with the Father above takes the visible form of our affiliation with the brothers below, and the regular iteration of forms of words that at least assure us we are talking about the same world has the effect of giving society a certain appearance of stability and meaningfulness surely as important to the good life as airplanes that run on time.

This is the exoteric realm, where both science and religion are taught as doctrines, or habits, concerning which no doubts exist that will not be cleared up sooner or later, somehow, by someone. It is the realm preeminently where human purpose is assumed to be known, so that no metaphysical nonsense is tolerated unless it is clearly understood to be exterior decoration.

3. The third realm is, at the simplest, where both religion and science are credited with immediate and magical powers, where their instrumentalities are hypostatized as 'beings'—the realm of overt and unsophisticated demonisms, dynamisms, projections, and introjections. As Bruno Bettelheim says, when electrical machines became familiar and important in daily life, 'influencing machines' became important in schizophrenia (see *The Informed Heart* [Glencoe, Illinois: The Free Press, 1960], pp. 52–61, for a discussion of the general theme). Here we have the more and less complicated idolatries, parodies of the ones in the second realm, dealing with mad scientists, death rays, machines turning on their makers—all these now within the practical realm, by the way—or, on the religious side, with getting in touch with the dead, with cosmic forces, lucky amulets, astrology, fortune-telling, and so forth. There is perhaps nothing more insane here than its equivalent in the second realm, but here it tends to affect individuals, not whole societies.

To the three ways of being (or not being) understood there correspond, in both science and religion, three teachings: I. Science for scientists, religion for the religious. 2. Science, or religion, for 'the intelligent layman.' 3. Science, or religion, for children.

1. Where the arcana are opened, much is in doubt; even the most fundamental things are left open to dispute.
2. That is largely left implicit, however, where the mysteries are explained 'in simple nontechnical language.'
3. 'The Wonderful Story of Religion.' 'The Wonders of Science.' Color pictures, enthusiasm.

Two final points of comparison may be briefly stated. I. Scientist and priest are both in the habit, though they regard it not as a habit but as a duty, of using their professional mastery to confer authority on their private opinions in matters concerning the common good. Religion and science both profess peace (and the sincerity of the professors is not being doubted), but each always turns out to have a dominant part in any war that is going or contemplated. 2. Both religion and science cost a great deal of money, much of which is spent on projects, realizable and not realizable, such as space ships and the Tower of Babel, of which the intelligence is not always or easily perceptible to people in other professions.

QUESTIONS FOR CRITICAL ANALYSIS

1. Why must polar opposites "necessarily have much in common"? Can you think of other examples to support this claim?
2. How are scientific experiments like religious rituals? How are they different? What do you think of Nemerov's characterization of scientific experiments? of religious rituals? What is his purpose in so characterizing them?
3. How are scientists and priests alike? Can you think of other ways they are similar? How are they different?
4. Parallel to Nemerov's comparison between science and religion is his comparison of theory and practice in both disciplines. What points does Nemerov make with these comparisons? How do these secondary comparisons develop the major comparison?
5. Nemerov defines three categories for understanding both science and religion. What are they? In what way(s) would you challenge Nemerov's explanations?

QUESTIONS FOR STRUCTURAL ANALYSIS

1. According to Nemerov, why is he examining this subject? What is his attitude toward the exercise? How do you respond to his tone? Why?
2. How does Nemerov organize his comparison? Write an informal outline of the essay.
3. What rhetorical devices does Nemerov use in writing this comparison? How do these devices enhance the essay? Do they affect his tone? How?
4. *Scholium* means a marginal annotation, an explanatory remark not essential to the train of thought. Why does Nemerov include this paragraph about music? What purpose does it have in his discussion of religion and science?
5. Nemerov concludes the essay with two final points of comparison. What are they? These two points reveal ways science and religion influence the public. Does Nemerov imply the contacts are beneficial or not? Why, or why not? How does this conclusion relate to the essay? Is it an effective conclusion? Why, or why not?

*T*HE *R*OLE OF THE *S*CIENTIST IN *S*OCIETY

MARGARET MEAD

Margaret Mead (1901–1979), an American psychological anthropologist, pioneered the research methods that helped turn social anthropology into a major science. Both respected and controversial, Mead's research of the relationships among races and between sexes helped promote social changes in racial harmony and sexual equality. "The Role of the Scientist in Society" was first presented at the 1947 Annual Meeting of the American Orthopsychiatric Association in a symposium for scientists concerned about problems relating to children.

Before you begin reading: *Think about science in its broadest terms: the natural sciences (physics, chemistry, biology, astronomy, geology), the social sciences (anthropology, psychology, sociology) and medicine. In your reading notebook write down two major headings: "How Science Benefits My Life" and "What I Fear Most about Science." Under each heading, make a list of at least 10 items.*

◆

I WANT TO DISCUSS THE PROBLEM OF HOW WE AMERICANS today feel about the scientist and the scientist's role, and what significance that feeling has for the contribution the scientist can make to the contemporary world crisis. This seems relevant because I am addressing an audience of practitioners. However much you may be devoting some part of your lives to research, most of you are giving most of your time to applying scientific insights to the problems of individuals, or occasionally, of groups. As practitioners, your every word and tone of voice become significant in conveying to those with whom you work, as patients, as collaborators, as members of the general public, the meaning and the promise, or the threat and the limitations of science. Perhaps even more potently than the stylizations of the scientist in the press and radio, the stage and film, the way in which the practitioner stylizes his own role, and sees his own role, tends to build up in the mind of the layman either a faith or a distrust in science. And to the degree that the practitioner sees the implications, the possible interpretations which may be placed upon his every act, he or she becomes the more aware and therefore the more effective as a communicator.

When science enters the realm of human relations, what will be the result? What, in fact, will happen to human relations and will they be seen as human at all? The problem can be approached from the standpoint of the scientist's picture of himself, as he sees himself mirrored in the conceptions of those around him. I would rather reverse this picture and explore some of the reasons why the layman entertains the various attitudes of fear, faith, hope, and distrust toward the scientist.

Central to this problem is the question of power. Science, as it has developed historically, has come to be associated with the idea of power, unlimited power over the forces of nature. Atomic discoveries have so enhanced this picture that it is safe to say that *power* is one of the first associations which the layman makes with the word *scientist*. A second association is the word *impersonal*. The scientist has been celebrated for his objectivity, his freedom from bias, his cool, aloof, impersonal—and almost by definition—inhuman behavior. This stereotype, frightening even when applied to someone who was experimenting with unrealizable entities, is extremely repellant when applied to human affairs. To treat another impersonally, coolly, aloofly, is to be lacking in warmth, in concern, in contact. The minute we are asked to think of the scientist in relation to human behavior, then this carefully built up picture of objectivity intervenes. The desire to make a split between this coolness and the human practitioner is seen in the contrast between the picture of the doctor—warm, and a little shabby, who sits by his patient's bedside—and the white-coated "scientist" who is pictured all alone with some shining piece of laboratory apparatus. One of the tasks of interpreting the meaning of science for human welfare becomes then to heal this split, to reunite the tired, friendly, country doctor, who knew and loved each patient as a person, and the cool impersonal man in a laboratory coat.

A second conflict centers around the fear that power over persons, even more than power over things, is blasphemous, is arrogating to man something which should be left to God. While this feeling is less strong in the United States, where man has come as an adult to deal with an unpatterned landscape, than it is in European countries where the works of man and the natural landscape both blend together in a past to which man adjusts, still the feeling is here. The phrase "playing God" comes readily to the lips when any specialist in human behavior seems too sure.

A third difficulty centers around the way in which the sciences of human behavior appear to restrict rather than expand the layman's sense of understanding and control of the world. The layman has no expectation of understanding, without expert help, the details of geological stratification, the movement of the stars, the wonders of embryology, or the operation of hormones and enzymes. Whatever the scientist discovers in these fields is felt to be added on to the layman's existing stock of knowledge, and the acquisition of wonderful new words like homeostasis, entropy, proton, adds to his sense of human dignity. But in the field of human relations each generation has characteristically thought of itself as well informed and well oriented. Parenthood and marriage, discipline and indulgence, love and hate, are matters which people think of themselves as "naturally" understanding. Every time a technical term, *affect* instead of love or hate, *ambivalence* for some simple phrase like mixed feelings, is developed in the sciences of human relations, the layman feels that part of his rightful inheritance as a social being has been snatched away from him, that what was simple and plain has been made mysterious and esoteric, that he is robbed of his dignity as a well-oriented human being.

This is perhaps especially likely to occur in a culture with a primary Protestant orientation, in which the insistence that each human being could read his Bible and deal directly with his God, without intervention of priest or sacrament, forms a natural background for a jealous guarding of individual choice and judgment in personal relations. The young Italian American graduate student who says "psychology is just the things my mother used to know, put in a way that no one can understand"; the jeering reaction of the press to the attempt of an educator to subsume all sorts of beatings, spankings, cuffings, ear boxings, and hand smackings under the heading of "manual discipline"—these are symptoms of this deep sense of loss and affront which the layman feels as the area of human relations is invaded, studied, classified, and labeled with new words which he must learn as he would have to learn the vocabulary of physics or chemistry.

It will probably be necessary to devise new educational methods which will set the student to wondering about human behavior first, before he is given any of this unwelcome knowledge, just as in the training of a natural scientist, the wondering curiosity of the student of natural history, of the child who holds a "cat's eye" in his hand and realizes that "this must have been alive," is the precursor of creative scientific curiosity. But too often expert knowledge in the field of human relations is offered to the layman and to the patient or client or student, not as an enlargement of a horizon which has first been opened up, but in response to what is technically called an expressed "need"—that is, a sense of individual inadequacy in solving one's psychological or social problems. If "need," a crying active awareness of trouble and inadequacy, is regarded as the appropriate setting for imparting expert knowledge in the field of personal relations, this practice is likely to reinforce the already existing sense of human outrage, that affairs which people should be able to think about and feel about as part of their adultness, must be handed over to specialists.

The position of the human relations scientist is further complicated by the current tendency to blame science and so scientists, for the plight to which our world has come. There is precedent in the history of human beliefs for expecting a cure from the one who causes the ailment, but when this occurs we classify it as "black magic." There are many primitive societies in which all disease, misfortune, and death are produced by men who are in special rapport with supernatural powers, and who may be persuaded by bribes, cajolery, threats or reversals of the behavior which induced them to start the train of evil, to undo what they have done. In such societies, power is to a degree undifferentiated, and reacted to with great ambivalence by those against whom it is exercised. (It is notable that witchcraft and black magic seem to increase in primitive societies in which the culture is disintegrating under contact with our civilization, and also where a village culture is giving place to an urban culture with the resulting atomization of the individual and increase in *anomie*.) A world in which the disintegration of all reliable values is attributed to the natural scientist, and the resulting disintegration of personality is then referred for treatment to the human relations scientist, is of course more complicated than a witch-ridden primitive society. Nevertheless useful parallels can be drawn. If the word scientist is used both for the men who discover the laws of thermodynamics and atomic fission and for the physician who must work day by day with individual breakdown, the possibility that the scientist will be seen as both the cause and the possible magical cure is very great. In this case, the success of the psychiatrist, especially with measures such as electric shock, drug or hypnotherapy, will also tend to be read backward and amalgamated with the attitudes toward the scientists who have produced the atomic bomb. The belief in the power of science will be increased, with a corresponding emphasis upon the malign nature of that power and an enhancement of the sense of individual helplessness of the layman.

The final and perhaps the central problem of the position of the human relations scientist in society concerns manipulation. Once the possibility of discovering and applying principles of human behavior is granted, what possible safeguard can society develop against the misuse of this power? The examples of recent decades in which a very little knowledge of human behavior has been used in commerce, in government, and in war to bemuse, befuddle, subjugate, corrupt, and disintegrate the minds of men, breed a very justified fear that a society with a real scientific grasp of human behavior would be a monstrous society in which no one would willingly live. It breeds the belief that it may be better to accept every human ill to which flesh is heir—disease, famine, war, insanity—than to risk the inevitable destruction of human dignity in a controlled world, in which those in absolute power have been absolutely corrupted by that power.

But while this fear is both justified and cogent, it is important to realize that the acceptance and incorporation of the science of human behavior is no longer a matter of choice. Atomic discoveries have introduced an order of urgency which the world has not hitherto faced, an urgency such that to neglect a single possible solution, no matter how difficult, becomes a treachery to the human race. In addition, the developments in domestic controls by totalitarian governments, in methods of opinion research and attitude testing by democratic governments, commercial undertakings, and in psychological warfare, especially of the "black" variety which introduces a final corrupting note in its denial of the source from which it emanates, have presented us with a degree of potentially destructive uses of the science of human behavior which we cannot eliminate by prayer or legislation or a refusal to face them. It is impossible to go back to an age of innocence; attempted returns to such earlier states invariably assume the unlovely aspect of political reaction and the oversimplifications of the near psychotic.

Our only course is to go forward and integrate the human sciences into the very fabric of our society. We must invent and introduce ethics and controls which will tie the hands of those with power, so that either by a self-denying ordinance or by carefully devised pressures, analogous to but much more complex than the "medical ethics" which have served mankind so well, or by controls which are in some way actually built into practice so that any manipulative behavior becomes self-defeating, manipulative behavior is impossible and human beings remain free in spite of having again eaten of the tree of knowledge. To do this, we need, most of all, a climate of opinion, a sense of the role of the scientist as the responsible expression of a new kind of civilization, a civilization to which disciplined self-awareness is the very breath of life. In developing such a climate of opinion, every practitioner, in every professional word and act, can contribute.

QUESTIONS FOR CRITICAL ANALYSIS

1. Describe the role of the scientist in society as Mead presents it. How does she see that role changing? How do your views on the subject differ from Mead's?
2. Reread the information in the headnote about the original audience for this paper. Why did Mead talk to them about this subject? How does she want the audience to respond? Do you think she was successful?
3. According to Mead, what are the ways science and scientists exert power over the general public? Do you agree with her? Why, or why not?
4. Throughout the essay, Mead reveals basic American beliefs and behaviors. Identify these and discuss whether you agree with Mead's characterization or not.
5. What is the nature of human, or social, sciences? How do they differ from the natural sciences? What is Mead's attitude toward each? How does she reveal her attitude?
6. Compare the picture of scientists Mead presents in her third paragraph with the scientists you encountered in Kraus's essay and with scientists you know.

QUESTIONS FOR STRUCTURAL ANALYSIS

1. Mead's paper was delivered to a professional audience. Point out ideas, words, and phrases that indicate the level of expertise she expects of her audience.

2. Look at the reasons Mead gives for why the general public distrusts science. How are they presented? Which ones are more clearly stated than others? What suggestions would you give Mead if you were to help her revise the paper?
3. What is Mead's stated purpose in this paper? Does she have a "hidden purpose"? What might that be?
4. Look at the following sentence: "While this feeling [fear that power over persons is blasphemous] is less strong in the United States, where man has come as an adult to deal with an unpatterned landscape, than it is in European countries where the works of man and the natural landscape both blend together in a past to which man adjusts, still the feeling is here." What does this mean? Do you agree? On what information or knowledge do you base your opinion?
5. What conclusion does Mead reach? Is it an effective conclusion?

The Meaning of Science

Topics for Writing Essays

Many of the questions following each essay can serve as appropriate writing suggestions. Some of the topics listed below expand the prereading exercises, but they can be used without completing that step first.

1. In clear, vivid language, write an explanation of Einstein's essay for someone who would not be able to understand the original. You may want to include more specific examples or allusions to enhance your explanation, but be sure you do not omit any of Einstein's original points.
2. In working out your class schedule for next semester, it has occurred to you that your college does not have an adequate science requirement for someone who has to earn a living in the scientific, technological 21st century. Write an open letter to the president of your college explaining why you think it is important for all graduates to study more science. Use Feynman's essay on the value of science as a reference, and also refer to points made in the essays included in the previous section, "Know About Our World."
3. Take the lists, categories, and examples you compiled in the Nemerov prereading exercise and write a paper comparing science and religion. Use Nemerov as a reference, but develop your own comparisons and contrasts. (A word of warning: If you hold strong religious beliefs and think this paper may turn into a sermon or diatribe, it would be better to select another topic.)

Research Possibilities

1. What is the value of science? Use the essays in this reader to analyze this question and develop a response. You will probably want to refer to essays in the previous section, "Know About Our World," and you may want to read ahead to the essays in the following section, "Is Science Evil?" Write your essay to a hostile audience. Be careful to include specific examples and reasons for your opinion.
2. You have read in earlier sections about how an artist must reveal reality through poems, paintings, plays, stories, or sculpture. In this section, you read about the arbitrary nature of reality: Do we know what is real and what isn't? Can you reconcile the two ideas? Write a paper that talks about the role of the artist (as discussed in these earlier essays) in a world in which meaning is meaningless. Be careful. Your audience is a reader who thinks that notion is ridiculous.

*I*s Science *E*vil?

Karl Jaspers essay responds directly to the question of this section, "Is Science Evil?" by defining science in terms of its relationship to us and to the world. Jaspers states, as others have previously in this textbook, that science itself is neither good nor evil: It has no moral nature and depends upon how human beings behave. Both Samuel Florman and Rachel Carson examine the ways we use science and technology in understanding our relationship to nature.

Karl Jaspers, "Is Science Evil?: Answering the Attack on Modern Knowledge and Technology"

Samuel C. Florman, "The Existential Engineer"

Rachel Carson, "The Obligation to Endure"

Is Science *Evil*?

Answering the Attack on Modern Knowledge and Technology

Karl Jaspers

Karl Jaspers (1883–1969), a philosopher, educator and one of the founders of twentieth-century existentialism, focused much of his work on how the individual's momentary choice defines his or her identity. "Is Science Evil?" argues that science can neither answer all questions nor distort the answers, is neither good nor bad, not human or inhuman, science is*; the human use of science determines its nature and gives it meaning. Through understanding the relationship of science, the quest for knowing, to God, the all-knowing, scientists stretch the limitations of science.*

Before you begin reading: *Is science evil? Think carefully about that question, listing reasons why you could call it "evil." What do you mean by "evil"? Next to each reason you listed, explain why calling it evil is inaccurate.*

◆

NO ONE QUESTIONS THE IMMENSE SIGNIFICANCE OF modern science. Through industrial technology it has transformed our existence, and its insights have transformed our consciousness, all this to an extent hitherto unheard of. The human condition throughout the millennia appears relatively stable in comparison with the impetuous movement that has now caught up mankind as a result of science and technology, and is driving it no one knows where. Science has destroyed the substance of many old beliefs and has made others questionable. Its powerful authority has brought more and more men to the point where they wish to know and not believe, where they expect to be helped by science and only by science. The present faith is that scientific understanding can solve all problems and do away with all difficulties.

Such excessive expectations result inevitably in equally excessive disillusionment. Science has still given no answer to man's doubts and despair. Instead, it has created weapons able to destroy in a few moments that which science itself helped build up slowly over the years. Accordingly, there are today two conflicting viewpoints: first, the superstition of science, which holds scientific results to be as absolute as religious myths used to be, so that even religious movements are now dressed in the garments of pseudoscience. Second, the hatred of science, which sees it as a diabolical evil of mysterious origin that has befallen mankind.

These two attitudes—both non-scientific—are so closely linked that they are usually found together, either in alternation or in an amazing compound.

A very recent example of this situation can be found in the attack against science provoked by the trial in Nuremberg of those doctors who, under Nazi orders, performed deadly experiments on human beings. One of the most esteemed medical men among German university professors has accepted the verdict on these crimes as a verdict on science itself, as a stick with which to beat "purely scientific and biological" medicine, and even the modern science of man in general: "this invisible spirit sitting on the prisoner's bench in Nuremberg, this spirit that regards men merely as objects, is not present in Nuremberg alone—it pervades the entire world." And, he adds, if this generalization may be viewed as an extenuation of the crime of the accused doctors, that is only a further indictment of purely scientific medicine.

Anyone convinced that true scientific knowledge is possible only of things that *can* be regarded as objects, and that knowledge of the subject is possible only when the subject attains a form of objectivity; anyone who sees science as the one great landmark on the road to truth, and sees the real achievements of modern physicians as derived exclusively from biological and scientific medicine—such a person will see in the above statements an attack on what he feels to be fundamental to human existence. And he may perhaps have a word to say in rebuttal.

In the special case of the crimes against humanity committed by Nazi doctors and now laid at the door of modern science, there is a simple enough argument. Science was not needed at all, but only a certain bent of mind, for the perpetration of such outrages. Such crimes were already possible millennia ago. In the Buddhist Pali canon, there is the report of an Indian prince who had experiments performed on criminals in order to determine whether they had an immortal soul that survived their corpses: "You shall—it was ordered—put the living man in a tub, close the lid, cover it with a damp hide, lay on a thick layer of clay, put it in the oven and make a fire. This was done. When we knew the man was dead, the tub was drawn forth, uncovered, the lid removed, and we looked carefully inside to see if we could perceive the escaping soul. But we saw no escaping soul." Similarly, criminals were slowly skinned alive to see if their souls could be observed leaving their bodies. Thus there were experiments on human beings before modern science.

Better than such a defense, however, would be a consideration of what modern science really genuinely is, and what its limits are.

Science, both ancient and modern, has, in the first place, three indispensable characteristics:

First, it is *methodical* knowledge. I know something scientifically only when I also know the method by which I have this knowledge, and am thus able to ground it and mark its limits.

Second, it is *compellingly certain.* Even the uncertain—i.e., the probable or improbable—I know scientifically only insofar as I know it clearly and compellingly as such, and know the degree of its uncertainty.

Third, it is *universally valid.* I know scientifically only what is identically valid for every inquirer. Thus scientific knowledge spreads over the world and remains the same. Unanimity is a sign of universal validity. When unanimity is not attained, when there is a conflict of schools, sects, and trends of fashion, then universal validity becomes problematic.

This notion of science as methodical knowledge, compellingly certain, and universally valid, was long ago possessed by the Greeks. Modern science has not only purified this notion; it has also transformed it, a transformation that can be described by saying that modern science is *indifferent to nothing.* Everything—the smallest and meanest, the furthest and strangest—that is in any way and at any time *actual,* is relevant to modern science, simply because it *is.* Modern science wants to be thoroughly universal, allowing nothing to escape it. Nothing shall be hidden, nothing shall be silent, nothing shall be a secret.

In contrast to the science of classical antiquity, modern science is *basically unfinished.* Whereas ancient science had the appearance of something completed, to which the notion of progress was not essential, modern science progresses into the infinite. Modern science has realized that a finished and total world-view is scientifically impossible. Only when scientific criticism is crippled by making particulars absolute can a closed view of the world pretend to scientific validity—and then it is a false validity. Those great new unified systems of knowledge—such as modern physics—that have grown up in the scientific era, deal only with single aspects of reality. And reality as a whole has been fragmented as never before; whence the openness of the modern world in contrast to the closed Greek cosmos.

However, while a total and finished world-view is no longer possible to modern science, the idea of a unity of the sciences has now come to replace it. Instead of the cosmos of the world, we have the cosmos of the sciences. Out of dissatisfaction with all the separate bits of knowledge is born the desire to unite all knowledge. The ancient sciences remained dispersed and without mutual relations. There was lacking to them the notion of a concrete totality of science. The modern sciences, however, seek to relate themselves to each other in every possible way.

At the same time the modern sciences have increased their claims. They put a low value on the possibilities of speculative thinking, they hold thought to be valid only as part of definite and concrete knowledge, only when it has stood the test of verification and thereby become infinitely modified. Only superficially do the modern and the ancient atomic theories seem to fit into the same theoretical mold. Ancient atomic theory was applied as a plausible interpretation of common experience; it was a statement complete in itself of what might possibly be the case. Modern atomic theory has developed through experiment, verification, refutation: that is, through an incessant transformation of itself in which theory is used not as an end in itself but as a tool of inquiry. Modern science, in its questioning, pushes to extremes. For example: the rational critique of appearance (as against reality) was begun in antiquity, as in the concept of perspective and its application to astronomy, but it still had some connection with immediate human experiences; today, however, this same critique, as in modern physics for instance, ventures to the very extremes of paradox, attaining a knowledge of the real that shatters any and every view of the world as a closed and complete whole.

So it is that in our day a scientific attitude has become possible that addresses itself inquisitively to everything it comes across, that is able to know what it knows in a clear and positive way, that can distinguish between the known and the unknown, and that has acquired an incredible mass of knowledge. How helpless was the Greek doctor or the Greek engineer! The ethos of modern science is the desire for reliable knowledge based on dispassionate investigation and criticism. When we enter its domain we feel as though we were breathing pure air, and seeing the dissolution of all vague talk, plausible opinions, haughty omniscience, blind faith.

But the greatness and the limitations of science are inseparable. It is a characteristic of the greatness of modern science that it comprehends its own limits:

1. Scientific, objective knowledge is not knowledge of Being. This means that scientific knowledge is particular, not general, that it is directed toward specific objects, and not toward Being itself. Through knowledge itself, science arrives at the most positive recognition of what it does *not* know.
2. Scientific knowledge or understanding cannot supply us with the aims of life. It cannot lead us. By virtue of its very clarity it directs us elsewhere for the sources of our life, our decisions, our love.
3. Human freedom is not an object of science, but is the field of philosophy. Within the purview of science there is no such thing as liberty.

These are clear limits, and the person who is scientifically minded will not expect from science what it cannot give. Yet science has become, nevertheless, the indispensable element of all striving for truth, it has become the premise of philosophy and the basis in general for whatever clarity and candor are today possible. To the extent that it succeeds in penetrating all obscurities and unveiling all secrets, science directs us to the most profound, the most genuine secret.

The unique phenomenon of modern science, so fundamentally different from anything in the past, including the science of the Greeks, owes its character to the many sources that were its origin; and these had to meet together in Western history in order to produce it.

One of these sources was Biblical religion. The rise of modern science is scarcely conceivable without its impetus. Three of the motives that have spurred research and inquiry seem to have come from it:

1. The ethos of Biblical religion demanded truthfulness at all costs. As a result, truthfulness became a supreme value and at the same time was pushed to the point where it became a serious problem. The truthfulness demanded by God forbade making the search for knowledge a game or amusement, an aristocratic leisure activity. It was a serious affair, a calling in which everything was at stake.
2. The world is the creation of God. The Greeks knew the cosmos as that which was complete and ordered, rational and regular, eternally subsisting. All else was nothing, merely material, not knowable and not worth knowing. But if the world is the creation of God, then everything that exists is worth knowing, just because it is God's creation; there is nothing that ought not to be known and comprehended. To know is to reflect upon God's thought. And God as creator is—in Luther's words—present even in the bowels of a louse.

The Greeks remained imprisoned in their closed world-view, in the beauty of their rational cosmos, in the logical transparency of the rational whole. Not only Aristotle and Democritus, but Thomas Aquinas and Descartes, too, obey this Greek urge, so paralyzing to the spirit of science, toward a closed universe. Entirely different is the new impulse to unveil the totality of creation. Out of this there arises the pursuit through knowledge of that reality which is not in accord with previously established laws. In the Logos itself [the Word, Reason] there is born the drive toward repeated self-destruction—not as self-immolation, but in order to arise again and ever again in a process that is to be continued infinitely. This science springs from a Logos that does not remain closed within itself, but is open to an anti-Logos which it permeates by the very act of subordinating itself to it. The continuous, unceasing reciprocal action of theory and experiment is the simple and great example and symbol of the universal process that is the dialectic between Logos and anti-Logos.

This new urge for knowledge sees the world no longer as simply beautiful. This knowledge ignores the beautiful and the ugly, the good and the wicked. It is true that in the end, *omne ens est bonum* (all Being is good], that is, as a creation of God. This goodness, however, is no longer the transparent and self-sufficient beauty of the Greeks. It is present only in the love of all existent things as created by God, and it is present therefore in our confidence in the significance of inquiry. The knowledge of the createdness of all worldly things replaces indifference in the face of the flux of reality with limitless questioning, an insatiable spirit of inquiry.

But the world that is known and knowable is, as created Being, Being of the second rank. For the world is unfathomable, it has its ground in another, a Creator, it is not self-contained and it is not containable by knowledge. The Being of the world cannot be comprehended as definitive, absolute reality, but points always to another.

The idea of creation makes worthy of love whatever is, for it is God's creation; and it makes possible, by this, an intimacy with reality never before attained. But at the same time it gives evidence of the incalculable distance from that Being which is not merely created Being but Being itself, God.

3. The reality of this world is full of cruelty and horror for men. "That's the way things are," is what man must truthfully say. If, however, God is the world's creator, then he is responsible for his creation. The question of justifying God's ways becomes with Job a struggle with the divine for the knowledge of reality. It is a struggle against God, for God. God's existence is undisputed and just because of this the struggle arises. It would cease if faith were extinguished.

This God, with his unconditional demand for truthfulness, refuses to be grasped through illusions. In the Bible, he condemns the theologians who wish to console and comfort Job with dogmas and sophisms. This God insists upon science, whose content always seems to bring forth an indictment of him. Thus we have the adventure of knowledge, the furtherance of unrestricted knowledge—and at the same time, a timidity, an awe in the face of it. There was an inner tension to be observed in many scientists of the past century, as if they heard: God's will is unconfined inquiry, inquiry is in the service of God—and at the same time: it is an encroachment on God's domain, all shall not be revealed.

This struggle goes hand in hand with the struggle of the man of science against all that he holds most dear, his ideals, his beliefs; they must be proven, newly verified, or else transformed. Since God could not be believed in if he were not able to withstand all the questions arising from the facts of reality, and since the seeking of God involves the painful sacrifice of all illusions, so true inquiry is the struggle against all personal desires and expectations.

This struggle finds its final test in the struggle of the scientist with his own theses. It is the determining characteristic of the modern scientist that he seeks out the strongest points in the criticism of his opponents and exposes himself to them. What in appearance is self-destructiveness becomes, in this case, productive. And it is evidence of a degradation of science when discussion is shunned or condemned, when men imprison themselves and their ideas in a milieu of like-minded savants and become fanatically aggressive to all outside it.

That modern science, like all things, contains its own share of corruption, that men of science only too often fail to live up to its standards, that science can be used for violent and criminal ends, that man will steal, plunder, abuse, and kill to gain knowledge—all this is no argument against science.

To be sure, science as such sets up no barriers. As science, it is neither human nor inhuman. So far as the well-being of humanity is concerned, science needs guidance from other sources. Science in itself is not enough—or should not be. Even medicine is only a scientific means, serving an eternal ideal, the aid of the sick and the protection of the healthy.

When the spirit of a faithless age can become the cause of atrocities all over the world, then it can also influence the conduct of the scientist and the behavior of the physician, especially in those areas of activity where science itself is confused and unguided. It is not the spirit of science but the spirit of its vessels that is depraved. Count Keyserling's dictum—"The roots of truth-seeking lie in primitive aggression"—is as little valid for science as it is for any genuine truth-seeking. The spirit of science is in no way primarily aggressive, but becomes so only when truth is prohibited; for men rebel against the glossing over of truth or its suppression.

In our present situation the task is to attain to that true science which knows what it knows at the same time that it knows what it cannot know. This science shows us the ways to the truth that are the indispensable precondition of every other truth. We know what Mephistopheles knew when he thought he had outwitted Faust:

Verachte nur Vernunft und Wissenschaft
Des Menschen allerhöchste Kraft
So habe ich Dich schon unbedingt.
(Do but scorn Reason and Science
Man's supreme strength
Then I'll have you for sure.)

Questions for Critical Analysis

1. How is science under attack? What historical events fuel this attack? Why does Jaspers write that scientific corruption is not an argument against science?
2. Jaspers offers two defenses of science. What are they? Which one is the more persuasive to you? How do the three indispensable characteristics of science relate to these defenses?
3. What does Jaspers mean when he says that the foundation for modern science is Biblical religion?
4. Explain the difference between the Greek closed-world view and the modern open-world view.

5. Compare Jaspers' discussion of appearance and reality with Einstein's discussion in "Physics and Reality."
6. Margaret Mead presented many reasons why people distrust scientists and blame them for their problems in her essay, "The Role of the Scientists in Society." How do Jaspers' comments relate to Mead's? In what ways would they agree with each other? in what ways disagree?

QUESTIONS FOR STRUCTURAL ANALYSIS

1. Jaspers has divided this essay into six major sections. What is the topic of each section and how does it relate to the other sections?
2. Describe Jaspers' transitions from one section to another. What techniques does he use to make his argument coherent? Do his numbered lists make it easier or harder to understand him? Why?
3. How does Jaspers define modern science? How does his definition affect his argument?
4. In this essay, how does Jaspers describe the relationship between religion and science? The two are often thought to be mutually exclusive. What is Jaspers' point in bringing God into the discussion? (Compare Jaspers' discussion with Nemerov's essay, "On the Resemblances Between Science and Religion.")
5. What is the significance of the final quotation by Mephistopheles to Faust? Who is Mephistopheles? Who is Faust? What do these lines mean? Why would Jaspers use them to conclude his essay?

*T*HE *E*XISTENTIAL *E*NGINEER

SAMUEL C. FLORMAN

Samuel C. Florman (1925–) combines his engineering expertise with a great love and ability for writing. Co-owner of Kreisler Borg Florman Construction Company, partner of Borg Florman, Consulting Engineers, Florman is an excellent advocate for technology. "The Existential Engineer" was written in part to refute the notions that science and technology were inherently evil and destructive. America has long had a love-hate relationship with technology: on the one hand, Americans love progress and technical wizardry, while on the other hand, they rail against the evils. Florman expounds on the creative dimension of engineering, emphasizing the interdependence of the artist and the engineer. This essay not only defines the engineer, but also the culture that has given rise to the engineer. "The Existential Engineer" appeared in The Existential Pleasures of Engineering *(1976). Like Jaspers, he responds to the common opinion after the Second World War that both the evils of Hitler and his Nazi medical experimentation on the Jews and the destructive powers of the atomic and nuclear bombs were clear evidence of the depravation of science and technology.*

Before you begin reading: *Go into one room of your home and look around you. Make a list of all the objects you see that did not exist in 1850. Next to each item, state whether or not you would be willing to live without it.*

◆

SISYPHUS WAS CONDEMNED BY THE GODS TO FOREVER ROLL a huge stone up a mountain, only to see it fall back to the bottom each time he reached the summit. Albert Camus has depicted this mythical figure as the archetypical existential hero. Sisyphus has no illusions to sustain him, no hope that some day his labors will end. But he has pride and courage and the satisfaction that comes instinctively to a person undertaking a task. "The struggle itself toward the heights is enough to fill a man's heart," concludes Camus. "One must imagine Sisyphus happy."

Theodore Roszak has expressed dismay that Camus, "the most great-hearted of our humanist heroes," cannot find in life "a project any less grotesquely absurd than the labor of Sisyphus taking his stone once again up the hill." But Roszak is taking the symbol of the stone too literally. Of course we aim for more than rolling a stone up a hill. But we are beginning to realize that for mankind there will never be a time to rest at the top of the mountain. There will be no new arcadian age. There will always be new burdens, new problems, new failures, new beginnings. And the glory of man is to respond to his harsh fate with zest and ever-renewed effort.

This is why Sisyphus can serve as a symbol of the modern engineer. Today's engineer has lost faith in the utopia that engineers of an earlier age thought they were bringing to mankind. Yet his work, springing as it does from the most basic impulse of humanity, can fill him with existential joy.

That there will be no utopia has become clear beyond questioning. Human beings are too varied, too fickle, and too willful. Technologically oriented optimists like Buckminster Fuller may excite us with visions of glass-domed paradises humming with computers. Humanists like René Dubos may enchant us with tales (featured on *The New York Times* Op-Ed page) of isolated human societies living rich and happy lives under conditions of primitive simplicity. These ideals are interesting, inspiring, and comforting. But we know that they are ideals—perhaps only mirages—that cannot become reality for us. In fact, they are evidence of the differences that surface whenever people start to consider what constitutes the good life.

We have, in our new wisdom and humility, stopped talking about "progress." Except for a few elemental humanitarian concepts, such as not wanting anyone to starve or freeze, we simply cannot agree on which way we want to go. We are talking a lot about "trade-offs," since we have learned that the pursuit of many different worthy objectives results inevitably in conflicts, and that these conflicts can only be resolved by compromise—or by force. The engineer does not underestimate the importance of his contributions to society; but he has abandoned all messianic illusions. He acknowledges that he has made mistakes; but he rejects totally the image of himself as villain, false prophet, or sorcerer's apprentice. He is a human being doing what human beings are created to do: fulfilling his human destiny both biologically and spiritually, and finding his reward in existential pleasure.

This pleasure is not solely the instinctual satisfaction of a lion on the hunt or a beaver building his dam. Pure instinctual gratification is involved, but only as a part of a complex world. *Homo faber* does not merely putter around, nor is he interested only in survival and comfort. He shares the values and ideals of the human race—mercy, justice, reverence, beauty, and the like. But he feels that these abstract concepts become meaningful only in a world where people lead authentic lives—struggling, questing, and creating.

We have seen the existential pleasures of engineering illuminated by the poetry and myth of Homer and the Old Testament. The question occurs naturally: Where are the poets of the modern era who chant such verses and tell such tales? Where is the poetic evidence that these pleasures still exist? A total absence of artistic verification would not invalidate the claims of the engineer. But such a state of affairs would inevitably make these claims suspect. It is hard to believe that there can exist any valid human experience which does not find its celebration in art.

On this score the engineer need have no apprehensions. The artistic evidence does exist. Perhaps not in voguish movements that occupy the spotlight in fashionable centers of culture. But contemporary creative writers have not been blind to the existential pleasures of engineering. A consideration of this artistic evidence can hardly fail to be a crucial element in our search for a philosophy of engineering to supplant the discredited utopian beliefs of our youth.

For those of us who are engineers, the poetic vision of our profession can serve to reinterpret and refine our own rough-hewn feelings. For young engineers, or would-be engineers, it can give some intimations of the glorious inheritance that is theirs. For those who hold to the view that engineering is soul-deadening and antiexistential (and for those who have never given the matter much thought one way or the other) perhaps the words of poets, novelists and philosophers will open some new and unexpected prospects.

Humanists may be pleased to see us relying upon the creative artist. They may even consider it an embarrassment to us that we find it necessary to look to the poet to give expression to our innermost feelings. But of course we rely upon the artist! He is our cousin, our fellow creator. The artist, in turn, relies upon us. We help to make the world which it is his destiny to interpret. And we give him the materials without which he would be almost totally mute. For the poet we have created pen and ink, the revolutionary printing press, the typewriter, and more lately electronic communications media. For the musician we have created his marvelous instruments and concert halls. ("We have yet sufficiently to realize," according to Lewis Mumford, "that the symphony orchestra is a triumph of engineering.") The history of the fine arts is inextricably intertwined with changing technology, from the introduction of oil paints and lost-wax bronze casting to the cinema and electric arc welding. Right now at the interface between technology and the fine arts there is a frenzy of activity in which it is often difficult to tell the engineers from the artists. In museums and galleries viewers are confronted with restless kinetic sculptures, welded steel forms, flashing neon tubes, inflated plastic shapes, glowing laser beams, pulsing electronic sounds, and a variety of computer-operated multimedia displays. To work with artists—to *become* artists—has been the existential pleasure of several thousand engineers.

Most engineers, of course, are not involved in creating works of art (except as their functional creations may fortuitously emerge as art). But the relationship of engineering to the arts has been one of kinship rather than, as is sometimes suggested, of unrelieved hostility. This is all by way of assuring the humanist that it is no embarrassment for the engineer to look to the creative writer for elucidation of the satisfactions inherent in engineering. Lovers, after all, have never resented Shakespeare for putting into verse those sentiments which can be felt by the ordinary man, but expressed best by the artist.

◆

The first and most obvious existential gratification felt by the engineer stems from his desire to change the world he sees before him. This impulse is not contingent upon the need of mankind for any such changes. Doubtless the impulse was born from the need, but it has taken on a life of its own. Man the creator is by his very nature not satisfied to accept the world as it is. He is driven to change it, to make of it something different. Paul Valéry, in his poetic drama, *Eupalinos*, has expressed this impulse with a romantic flourish:

> The Constructor . . . finds before him as his chaos and as primitive matter, precisely that world-order which the Demiurge wrung from the disorder of the beginning. Nature is formed and the elements are separated; but something enjoins him to consider this work as unfinished, and as requiring to be rehandled and set in motion again for the more special satisfaction of man. He takes as the starting point of his act the very point where the god left off . . . the masses of marble should not remain lifeless within the earth constituting a solid night, nor the cedars and cypresses rest content to come to their end by flame or by rot, when they can be changed into fragrant beams and dazzling furniture.

This desire to change the world is brought to a fever pitch by the inertness of the world as it appears to us, by the very *resistance* of inanimate things, to use the concept expressed by Gaston Bachelard in *La Terre et les Rêveries de la Volonté:*

> The resistant world takes us out of static being. . . . And the mysteries of energy begin. . . . The hammer or the trowel in hand, we are no longer alone, we have an adversary, we have something to do. . . . All these *resistant* objects . . . give us a pretext for mastery and for our energy.

The existential impulse to change the world stirs deep within the engineer. But it is a vague impulse that requires particular projects for its expression. Here the engineer cannot help but be enthralled by the countless possibilities for action that the world presents to him. In *A Family of Engineers*, Robert Louis Stevenson has told of the allure that the profession of engineering had for his grandfather:

> . . . the perpetual need for fresh ingredients stimulated his ingenuity. . . . The seas into which his labours carried the new engineer were still scarce charted, the coast still dark. . . . The joy of my grandfather for his career was as the love of woman.

The engineer today, for all his knowledge and accomplishment, can still look out on seas scarce charted and on coasts still dark. Each new achievement discloses new problems and new possibilities. The allure of these endless vistas bewitches the engineer of every era.

For many engineers, the poetic image of seas and coasts can be taken literally. Water and earth are the substances that engaged the energies of the first engineer—the civil engineer. Civil engineering is the main trunk from which all branches of the profession have sprung. Even in this age of electronics and cybernetics, approximately 16 percent of American engineers are civil engineers.

If we add mining, basic metals, and land and sea transportation, fully a quarter of our engineers are engaged in the ancient task of grappling with water and earth. Civil engineering has traditionally included the design and construction of buildings, dams, bridges, railroads, canals, highways, tunnels—in short, all engineered structures—and also the disciplines of hydraulics and sanitation: water supply, flood control, sewage disposal, and so forth. The word "civil" was first used around 1750 by the British engineer, John Smeaton, who wished to distinguish his works (most notably the Eddystone Lighthouse) from those with military purposes. The civil engineer, with his hands literally in the soil, is existentially wedded to the earth, more so than any other man except perhaps the farmer. The civil engineer hero of James A. Michener's novel, *Caravans*, cries out, "I want to stir the earth, fundamentally . . . in the bowels." The hydraulic engineer hero of Dutch novelist A. Den Doolaard's book, *Roll Back the Sea*, stares across the flood water rushing through broken dikes and feels "a strange and bitter joy. This was living water again, which had to be fought against."

Living water. Nature, which appears at one moment to be inert and resistant, something which the engineer is impelled to modify and embellish, in the next instant springs alive as a flood, a landslide, a fire, or an earthquake, becomes a force with which the engineer must reckon. Beyond emergencies and disasters, through the environmental crisis of recent years, nature has demonstrated that she is indeed a living organism not to be tampered with unthinkingly. Nature's apparent passivity, like the repose of a languid mistress, obscures a mysterious and provocative energy. The engineer's new knowledge of nature's complexities is at once humbling and alluring.

Another dichotomy with which nature confronts the engineer relates to size. When man considers his place in the natural world, his first reaction is one of awe. He is so small, while the mountains, valleys and oceans are so immense. He is intimidated. But at the same instant he is inspired. The grand scale of the world invites him to conceive colossal works. In pursuing such works, he has often shown a lack of aesthetic sensibility. He has been vain, building useless pyramids, and foolish, building dams that do more harm than good. But the existential impulse to create enormous structures remains, even after he has been chastened. Skyscrapers, bridges, dams, aqueducts, tunnels—these mammoth undertakings appeal to a human passion that appears to be inextinguishable. Jean-Jacques Rousseau, the quintessential lover of nature undefiled, found himself under the spell of this passion when he came upon an enormous Roman aqueduct:

> I walked along the three stages of this superb construction, with a respect that made me almost shrink from treading on it. The echo of my footsteps under the immense arches made me think I could hear the strong voices of the men who had built it. I felt lost like an insect in the immensity of the work. I felt, along with the sense of my own littleness, something nevertheless which seemed to elevate my

soul; I said to myself with a sigh: "Oh! that I had been born a Roman!" . . . I remained several hours in this rapture of contemplation. I came away from it in a kind of dream. . . .

The rapture of Rousseau for "the immensity of the work" survives in the midst of our most bitter disappointments with technology. A 1964 photo exhibition at The Museum of Modern Art in New York, entitled "Twentieth-Century Engineering," brought home this truth to a multitude of viewers. The introduction to the exhibition catalogue directed attention to the fact that the impact of enormous engineering works is sometimes enhanced by the "elegance, lightness, and the apparent ease with which difficulties are overcome," and sometimes by the opposite, the monumental extravagance that appears when "the engineer may glory in the sheer effort his work involves." Ada Louise Huxtable of the *New York Times* reacted to the show with an enthusiasm that even the proudest of civil engineers would hesitate to express:

It is clear that in the whole range of our complex culture, with its self-conscious aesthetic kicks and esoteric pursuit of meanings, nothing comes off with quite the validity, reality, and necessity of the structural arts.

Other art forms seem pretty piddling next to dams that challenge mountains, roads that leap chasms, and domes that span miles. The kicks here are for real. These structures stand in positive, creative contrast to the willful negativism and transient novelty that have made so much painting and literature, for example, a kind of diminishing, naughty game. The evidence is incontrovertible: building is the great art of our time.

"The kicks here are for real." And if they are for real to the observer of photographs, imagine what they are like to the men who participate in creating the works themselves. *Roll Back the Sea*, the Dutch novel already mentioned, has a scene describing the building of the Zuyder Zee wall which gives some slight taste of the excitement surrounding a massive engineering work:

The great floating cranes, dropping tons of stiff clay into the splashing water with each swing of the arm. Dozens of tugboats with their white bow waves. Creaking bucket dredges; unwieldy barges; blowers spouting the white mass of sand through long pipelines out behind the dark clay dam; and the hundreds of polder workmen in their high, muddy boots. An atmosphere of drawing boards and tide tables, of megaphones and jingling telephones; of pitching lights in the darkness, of sweat and steam and rust and water, of the slick clay and the wind. A dike in the making, the greatest dike that the world had ever seen built straight through sea water.

The mighty works of the civil engineer sometimes appear to be conquests over a nature that would repel mankind if it could. Thus Waldo Frank perceived the Panama Canal slashing through the tropical jungle:

> Its gray sobriety is apart from the luxuriance of nature. Its wilfulness is victor over a voluptuary world that will lift no vessels, that would bar all vessels.

At other times the civil engineer's structures appear to grow out of the earth with a natural grace that implies the fulfillment of an organic plan. Pierre Boulle, in *The Bridge Over the River Kwai*, writes: "An observer, blind to elementary detail but keen on general principles, might have regarded the development of the bridge as an uninterrupted process of natural growth." The bridge rose day by day, "majestically registering in all three dimensions the palpable shape of creation at the foot of these wild Siamese mountains. . . ." Fifty years after the construction of the Eiffel Tower a Parisian recalled: "It appeared as if the tower was pushing itself upward by a supernatural force, like a tree growing beyond bounds yet steadily growing. . . . Astonished Paris saw rising on its own grounds this new shape of a new adventure."

From the organic implications of the civil engineer's structures it is but a short step to the spiritual. Mighty works of concrete, steel, or stone, seeming alive but superhuman in scope, inevitably invoke thoughts of the divine. The ultimate material expressions of religious faith are, of course, the medieval cathedrals. They are usually defined as the material creations of religious men. But they can also be considered as magnificent works of engineering which, through their physical majesty and proportion, impel the viewer to think lofty thoughts. In *Mont Saint-Michel and Chartres* Henry Adams has conveyed a sense of the way in which these physical structures both reflect and evoke a spiritual concept:

> Every inch of material, up and down, from crypt to vault, from man to God, from the universe to the atom, had its task, giving support where support was needed, or weight where concentration was felt, but always with the condition of showing conspicuously to the eye the great lines which led to unity and the curves which controlled divergence; so that, from the cross on the fleche and the keystone of the vault, down through the ribbed nervures, the columns, the windows, to the foundation of the flying buttresses far beyond the walls, one idea controlled every line.

William Golding, in his novel *The Spire*, has explored the theme of the interrelationship between construction and religion. Set in medieval England, the novel relates the story of the building of a cathedral tower, a tower which threatens to cause the collapse of the structure on which it rests. Priest and master builder confront each other, and the construction is accompanied by their dialogue, the dialogue between faith and technology. At one point the priest addresses the master builder in these words:

> My son. The building is a diagram of prayer; and our spire will be a diagram of the highest prayer of all. God revealed it to me in a vision, his unprofitable servant. He chose me. He chooses you, to fill the diagram with glass and iron and stone, since the children of men require a thing to look at. D'you think you can escape? You're

> not in my net—. . . It's His. We can neither of us avoid this work. And there's another thing. I've begun to see how we can't understand it either, since each new foot reveals a new effect, a new purpose.

Not only cathedrals, but every great engineering work is an expression of motivation and of purpose which cannot be divorced from religious implications. This truth provides the engineer with what many would assert to be the ultimate existential experience.

I do not want to get carried away on this point. The age of cathedral building is long past. And, as I have already said, less than one-quarter of today's engineers are engaged in construction activities of any sort. But every manmade structure, no matter how mundane, has a little bit of cathedral in it, since man cannot help but transcend himself as soon as he begins to design and construct. As the priest of *The Spire* expresses it: "each new foot reveals a new effect, a new purpose."

In spite of the many ugly and tasteless structures that mar our cities and landscapes, public enthusiasm for building has survived relatively unscathed through the recent years of disenchantment with technology. The engineer, in company with architects, artists, and city planners, has kept alive the public faith in the potentiality for beauty, majesty, and spirituality in construction.

At a time when we are embarrassed to recall the grandiose pronouncements of so many of our predecessors, the First Proclamation of the Weimar Bauhaus, dating from 1919, retains its dignity and ability to inspire. It was the concept of architect Walter Gropius that great art in building grew out of craftsmanship, was in fact nothing other than craftsmanship inspired. His concept of craftsmanship included necessarily the essentials of civil engineering. "We must all turn to the crafts," he told his followers:

> Art is not a "profession." There is no essential difference between the artist and the craftsman. The artist is an exalted craftsman. In rare moments of inspiration, moments beyond the control of his will, the grace of heaven may cause his work to blossom into art. *But proficiency in his craft is essential to every artist.* Therein lies a source of creative imagination.
>
> Let us create a *new guild of craftsmen*, without the class distinctions which raise an arrogant barrier between craftsman and artist. Together let us conceive and create the new building of the future, which . . . will rise one day toward heaven from the hands of a million workers like the crystal symbol of a new faith.

Enough, then, of the civil engineer and his wrestling with the elements, his love affair with nature, his yearning for immensity, his raising toward heaven the crystal symbol of a new faith. His existential bond to the earth, and expression of his own elemental being, need no further amplification, no additional testimonials.

QUESTIONS FOR CRITICAL ANALYSIS

1. Who is Sisyphus? Why does Florman begin his essay with a reference to the myth? How does Sisyphus serve as a symbol of the modern engineer?
2. What quarrel does Florman have with Theodore Roszak over the meaning of Sisyphus' task?
3. How has the engineer's role changed? How has his perception of his role changed? Why are these not the same thing?
4. How does his desire to change the world sustain the engineer? Describe ways this desire can be realized. Explain Florman's comments about the engineer's response to size.
5. Why does Florman feel he needs to justify engineering? What is he responding to? What do you think of engineers? Why?

QUESTIONS FOR STRUCTURAL ANALYSIS

1. In the first paragraph Florman refers to Albert Camus' analysis of the myth of Sisyphus. Do you know what Florman is talking about? What does Florman expect of his reader? (Do some research to find out why Florman began his essay like this.)
2. What does "the existential engineer" mean? Look up the definition of existential. Explain the meaning of the title based on the definition as well as Florman's essay.
3. What is the implied antipathy between humanists and engineers? (Who are humanists?) Why should such a feeling exist? Do you know about these feelings from first-hand experience? Name ways the arts depend upon engineers. Name ways engineers depend upon the arts.
4. Florman includes more than 10 directly quoted passages in this essay. Evaluate these quotes in terms of (1) their effect on the development of Florman's ideas, (2) how well they enhance Florman's text, and (3) whether you think Florman made the right choice to quote rather than paraphrase.
5. Is Florman's conclusion effective? Why, or why not? How does it relate to the rest of the essay?

*T*HE OBLIGATION TO *E*NDURE

RACHEL CARSON

Rachel Carson (1907–1964) began her college career as an English major, but switched to biology and graduated in science. Carson's Silent Spring *(1962) was a major impetus for the environmental concerns of the late 1960s–early 1970s. Described as "a book about death which exalts life,"* Silent Spring *showed the public how much harm had been caused to the earth by the indiscriminate use of pesticides. "The Obligation to Endure," a chapter from the book, reveals how mankind has destroyed the environment thoughtlessly and predicts that change will occur only when the public discovers all the facts and demands a reversal of life-threatening behavior.*

Before you begin reading: *In what ways that you know about has humanity destroyed its environment? Make a list of five major environmental problems, and next to each problem write what you know about ways to solve them.*

◆

THE HISTORY OF LIFE ON EARTH HAS BEEN A HISTORY OF interaction between living things and their surroundings. To a large extent, the physical form and the habits of the earth's vegetation and its animal life have been molded by the environment. Considering the whole span of earthly time, the opposite effect, in which life actually modifies its surroundings, has been relatively slight. Only within the moment of time represented by the present century has one species—man—acquired significant power to alter the nature of his world.

During the past century this power has not only increased to one of disturbing magnitude but it has changed in character. The most alarming of all man's assaults upon the environment is the contamination of air, earth, rivers, and sea with dangerous and even lethal materials. This pollution is for the most part irrecoverable; the chain of evil it initiates not only in the world that must support life but in living tissues is for the most part irreversible. In this now universal contamination of the environment, chemicals are the sinister and little-recognized partners of radiation in changing the very nature of the world—the very nature of its life. Strontium 90, released through nuclear explosions into the air, comes to earth in rain or drifts down as fallout, lodges in soil, enters into the grass or corn or wheat grown there, and in time takes up its abode in the bones of a human being, there to remain until his death. Similarly, chemicals sprayed on croplands or forests or gardens lie long in soil, entering into living organisms, passing from one to another in a chain of poisoning and death. Or they pass mysteriously by underground streams until they emerge and, through the alchemy of air and sunlight, combine into new forms that kill vegetation, sicken cattle, and work unknown harm on those who drink from once pure wells. As Albert Schweitzer has said, "Man can hardly even recognize the devils of his own creation."

It took hundreds of millions of years to produce the life that now inhabits the earth—eons of time in which that developing and evolving and diversifying life reached a state of adjustment and balance with its surroundings. The environment, rigorously shaping and directing the life it supported, contained elements that were hostile as well as supporting. Certain rocks gave out dangerous radiation; even within the light of the sun, from which all life draws its energy, there were short-wave radiations with power to injure. Given time—time not in years but in millennia—life adjusts, and a balance has been reached. For time is the essential ingredient; but in the modern world there is no time.

The rapidity of change and the speed with which new situations are created follow the impetuous and heedless pace of man rather than the deliberate pace of nature. Radiation is no longer merely the background radiation of rocks, the bombardment of cosmic rays, the ultraviolet of the sun that have existed before there was any life on earth; radiation is now the unnatural creation of man's tampering with the atom. The chemicals to which life is asked to make its adjustment are no longer merely the calcium and silica and copper and all the rest of the minerals washed out of the rocks and carried in rivers to the sea; they are the synthetic creations of man's inventive mind, brewed in his laboratories, and having no counterparts in nature.

To adjust to these chemicals would require time on the scale that is nature's; it would require not merely the years of a man's life but the life of generations. And even this, were it by some miracle possible, would be futile, for the new chemicals come from our laboratories in an endless stream; almost five hundred annually find their way into actual use in the United States alone. The figure is staggering and its implications are not easily grasped—500 new chemicals to which the bodies of men and animals are required somehow to adapt each year, chemicals totally outside the limits of biologic experience.

Among them are many that are used in man's war against nature. Since the mid-1940's over 200 basic chemicals have been created for use in killing insects, weeds, rodents, and other organisms described in the modern vernacular as "pests"; and they are sold under several thousand different brand names.

These sprays, dusts, and aerosols are now applied almost universally to farms, gardens, forests, and homes—nonselective chemicals that have the power to kill every insect, the "good" and the "bad," to still the song of birds and the leaping of fish in the streams, to coat the leaves with a deadly film, and to linger on in soil—all this though the intended target may be only a few weeds or insects. Can anyone believe it is possible to lay down such a barrage of poisons on the surface of the earth without making it unfit for all life? They should not be called "insecticides," but "biocides."

The whole process of spraying seems caught up in an endless spiral. Since DDT was released for civilian use, a process of escalation has been going on in which ever more toxic materials must be found. This has happened because insects, in a triumphant vindication of Darwin's principle of the survival of the fittest, have evolved super races immune to the particular insecticide used, hence a deadlier one has always to be developed—and then a deadlier one than that. It has happened also because, for reasons to be described later, destructive insects often undergo a "flareback," or resurgence, after spraying, in numbers greater than before. Thus the chemical war is never won, and all life is caught in its violent crossfire.

Along with the possibility of the extinction of mankind by nuclear war, the central problem of our age has therefore become the contamination of man's total environment with such substances of incredible potential for harm—substances that accumulate in the tissues of plants and animals and even penetrate the germ cells to shatter or alter the very material of heredity upon which the shape of the future depends.

Some would-be architects of our future look toward a time when it will be possible to alter the human germ plasm by design. But we may easily be doing so now by inadvertence, for many chemicals, like radiation, bring about gene mutations. It is ironic to think that man might determine his own future by something so seemingly trivial as the choice of an insect spray.

All this has been risked—for what? Future historians may well be amazed by our distorted sense of proportion. How could intelligent beings seek to control a few unwanted species by a method that contaminated the entire environment and brought the threat of disease and death even to their own kind? Yet this is precisely what we have done. We have done it, moreover, for reasons that collapse the moment we examine them. We are told that the enormous and expanding use of pesticides is necessary to maintain farm production. Yet is our real problem not one of *overproduction*? Our farms, despite measures to remove acreages from production and to pay farmers *not* to produce, have yielded such a staggering excess of crops that the American taxpayer in 1962 is paying out more than one billion dollars a year as the total carrying cost of the surplus-food storage program. And is the situation helped when one branch of the Agriculture Department tries to reduce production while another states, as it did in 1958, "It is believed generally that reduction of crop acreages under provisions of the Soil Bank will stimulate interest in use of chemicals to obtain maximum production on the land retained in crops."

All this is not to say there is no insect problem and no need of control. I am saying, rather, that control must be geared to realities, not to mythical situations, and that the methods employed must be such that they do not destroy us along with the insects.

The problem whose attempted solution has brought such a train of disaster in its wake is an accompaniment of our modern way of life. Long before the age of man, insects inhabited the earth—a group of extraordinarily varied and adaptable beings. Over the course of time since man's advent, a small percentage of the more than half a million species of insects have come into conflict with human welfare in two principal ways: as competitors for the food supply and as carriers of human disease.

Disease-carrying insects become important where human beings are crowded together, especially under conditions where sanitation is poor, as in time of natural disaster or war or in situations of extreme poverty and deprivation. Then control of some sort becomes necessary. It is a sobering fact, however, as we shall presently see, that the method of massive chemical control has had only limited success, and also threatens to worsen the very conditions it is intended to curb.

Under primitive agricultural conditions the farmer had few insect problems. These arose with the intensification of agriculture—the devotion of immense acreages to a single crop. Such a system set the stage for explosive increases in specific insect populations. Single-crop farming does not take advantage of the principles by which nature works; it is agriculture as an engineer might conceive it to be. Nature has introduced great variety into the landscape, but man has displayed a passion for simplifying it. Thus he undoes the built-in checks and balances by which nature holds the species within bounds. One important natural check is a limit on the amount of suitable habitat for each species. Obviously then, an insect that lives on wheat can build up its population to much higher levels on a farm devoted to wheat than on one in which wheat is intermingled with other crops to which the insect is not adapted.

The same thing happens in other situations. A generation or more ago, the towns of large areas of the United States lined their streets with the noble elm tree. Now the beauty they hopefully created is threatened with complete destruction as disease sweeps through the elms, carried by a beetle that would have only limited chance to build up large populations and to spread from tree to tree if the elms were only occasional trees in a richly diversified planting.

Another factor in the modern insect problem is one that must be viewed against a background of geologic and human history: the spreading of thousands of different kinds of organisms from their native homes to invade new territories. This worldwide migration has been studied and graphically described by the British ecologist Charles Elton in his recent book *The Ecology of Invasions.* During the Cretaceous Period, some hundred million years ago, flooding seas cut many land bridges between continents and living things found themselves confined in what Elton calls "colossal separate nature reserves." There, isolated from others of their kind, they developed many new species. When some of the land masses were joined again, about 15 million years ago, these species began to move out into new territories—a movement that is not only still in progress but is now receiving considerable assistance from man.

The importation of plants is the primary agent in the modern spread of species, for animals have almost invariably gone along with the plants, quarantine being a comparatively recent and not completely effective innovation. The United States Office of Plant Introduction alone has introduced almost 200,000 species and varieties of plants from all over the world. Nearly half of the 180 or so major insect enemies of plants in the United States are accidental imports from abroad, and most of them have come as hitchhikers on plants.

In new territory, out of reach of the restraining hand of the natural enemies that kept down its numbers in its native land, an invading plant or animal is able to become enormously abundant. Thus it is no accident that our most troublesome insects are introduced species.

These invasions, both the naturally occurring and those dependent on human assistance, are likely to continue indefinitely. Quarantine and massive chemical campaigns are only extremely expensive ways of buying time. We are faced, according to Dr. Elton, "with a life-and-death need not just to find new technological means of suppressing this plant or that animal"; instead we need the basic knowledge of animal populations and their relations to their surroundings that will "promote an even balance and damp down the explosive power of outbreaks and new invasions."

Much of the necessary knowledge is now available but we do not use it. We train ecologists in our universities and even employ them in our governmental agencies but we seldom take their advice. We allow the chemical death rain to fall as though there were no alternative, whereas in fact there are many, and our ingenuity could soon discover many more if given opportunity.

Have we fallen into a mesmerized state that makes us accept as inevitable that which is inferior or detrimental, as though having lost the will or the vision to demand that which is good? Such thinking, in the words of the ecologist Paul Shepard, "idealizes life with only its head out of water, inches above the limits of toleration of the corruption of its own environment . . . Why should we tolerate a diet of weak poisons, a home in insipid surroundings, a circle of acquaintances who are not quite our enemies, the noise of motors with just enough relief to prevent insanity? Who would want to live in a world which is just not quite fatal?"

Yet such a world is pressed upon us. The crusade to create a chemically sterile, insect-free world seems to have engendered a fanatic zeal on the part of many specialists and most of the so-called control agencies. On every hand there is evidence that those engaged in spraying operations exercise a ruthless power. "The regulatory entomologists . . . function as prosecutor, judge and jury, tax assessor and collector and sheriff to enforce their own orders," said Connecticut entomologist Neely Turner. The most flagrant abuses go unchecked in both state and federal agencies.

It is not my contention that chemical insecticides must never be used. I do contend that we have put poisonous and biologically potent chemicals indiscriminately into the hands of persons largely or wholly ignorant of their potentials for harm. We have subjected enormous numbers of people to contact with these poisons, without their consent and often without their knowledge. If the Bill of Rights contains no guarantee that a citizen shall be secure against lethal poisons distributed either by private individuals or by public officials, it is surely only because our forefathers, despite their considerable wisdom and foresight, could conceive of no such problem.

I contend, furthermore, that we have allowed these chemicals to be used with little or no advance investigation of their effect on soil, water, wildlife, and man himself. Future generations are unlikely to condone our lack of prudent concern for the integrity of the natural world that supports all life.

There is still very limited awareness of the nature of the threat. This is an era of specialists, each of whom sees his own problem and is unaware of or intolerant of the larger frame into which it fits. It is also an era dominated by industry, in which the right to make a dollar at whatever cost is seldom challenged. When the public protests, confronted with some obvious evidence of damaging results of pesticide applications, it is fed little tranquilizing pills of half truth. We urgently need an end to these false assurances, to the sugar coating of unpalatable facts. It is the public that is being asked to assume the risks that the insect controllers calculate. The public must decide whether it wishes to continue on the present road, and it can do so only when in full possession of the facts. In the words of Jean Rostand, "The obligation to endure gives us the right to know."

QUESTIONS FOR CRITICAL ANALYSIS

1. Why is Carson concerned about the power humans exert over the environment? What examples does she give to illustrate her concern?
2. What is the essential cause for the destruction of the environment? Why is it an almost impossible situation to change?
3. Why did humans start using chemicals against insects? What environmental problems has this practice caused? Do you think that using an aerosol spray to kill a roach in your kitchen is the same thing? What dangerous chemicals do you contribute to the environment?
4. Carson claims that much of the necessary knowledge for changing the cycle of destruction is known. Why don't we use this knowledge? Why do we resign ourselves to living in a world "just not quite fatal"? Carson wrote this essay in 1962. Do you think our situation has improved since then? worsened? Why do you think so?

5. What does the final statement, a quotation from Jean Rostand, mean? Is this an effective conclusion to the essay?

QUESTIONS FOR STRUCTURAL ANALYSIS

1. What is the thesis of Carson's essay? How does the introductory paragraph set the stage for the essay that follows?
2. Carson is deeply committed to her subject. How does she make the reader feel her sense of urgency?
3. Carson switches early from discussing man's "heedless" destruction of the environment to "man's war against nature." How does Carson's language reflect her attitude toward man's behavior? Compare Carson's attitude toward and descriptions of man's relationship with nature to Florman's in the previous essay.
4. At the end of the essay, Carson makes several contentions. What are they? How does she want her reader to respond?
5. Several authors of essays in this textbook have made the point that science and technology is neither good nor bad in itself. Do you think Carson agrees with that idea? Why, or why not? Support your answers with examples and explanations.

Is Science *Evil*?

Topics for Writing Essays

Many of the questions following each essay can serve as appropriate writing suggestions. Some of the topics listed below expand the prereading exercises, but they can be used without completing that step first.

1. How is the world today different from the world into which your grandparents were born? Which world is better? Describe the ways science and technology have changed your grandparents' world, arguing either that (1) they had a better world or (2) you have a better world. Write your essay to a reader unlikely to agree with your position.
2. Select one of the environmental problems you included in your list in response to the Carson prereading exercise. What is being done in your community about this problem? Interview people who are working to solve the problem; find out about the history of the problem and the community's response; determine the possibility of future solutions. How can students help solve this problem? Write a report of the problem and how the community is working toward a solution for your local newspaper, with the intention of not only educating but also involving more members of the community.
3. Refer to both Carson's attitude toward the man-nature relationship and Florman's when you write an essay describing ways humans can coexist with the world around them. Be careful not to rely on vague generalizations or emotional appeals with no support. Include specific examples and information to document your ideas. Your essay should be written to new members of the Students for a Safe Environment Committee who are only beginning to think about the subject.

Research Possibilities

1. In Richard Feynman's essay, "The Value of Science," (in the previous section, "The Meaning of Science"), he quotes a Buddhist proverb: "To every man is given the key to the gates of heaven; the same key opens the gates of hell." How does this proverb apply explicitly to twentieth-century science? Narrow the focus of your research to a single scientific concern: atomic energy, nuclear weapons, biotechnology, and so on, and read both pro and con arguments. Write a paper to the general public explaining the proverb in light of your research.
2. Rachel Carson's book, *Silent Spring* (in which "The Obligation to Endure" appeared), was one of the primary sources of information that spurred national environmental

policy. The book was published in 1962. Find out how people responded to the book: read reviews, articles, newspaper stories. Can you trace pro-environment policies and involvement to Carson's work? Write a report on Carson's influence on environmental issues.

3. What is the worst environmental problem you know about? Find out what the government and private agencies are doing to solve the problem. In a feature article written for a college magazine, describe the problem to students who may not be concerned about it, and describe why the problem scares you. Be sure to include proposed solutions, and discuss how the college student population can work toward solving the problem.

4. Read and compare the treatments of engineers and engineering in Samuel Florman's book, *The Existential Engineer* (1976), and John McPhee's book, *The Control of Nature* (1989). You may want to focus on how the authors describe the engineer's relationship to nature, the influence of engineers on human society, or the changing roles of engineering. Address your comparison to a sympathetic audience of students pursuing a degree in engineering.

*T*HE *T*HREAT OF *P*EACE

Since 1945, when the bomb was dropped on two cities in Japan, we have struggled with the question of how to avoid nuclear war. This collection of essays, included in the Science and Mathematics section because the creation and maintenance of atomic and nuclear weapons depend in large measure upon the support of the scientific community, provide a bleak look at our future. Erikson, in describing how the United States reached the point of dropping an atomic bomb, warns that, unless we learn a better decision-making process, nuclear war will be hard to avoid. Rabi identifies the scientific and political power unleashed by atomic weapons and, although he is hopeful that nations will find peaceful ways to use this power, he knows our nation chose the "easy path" to weapons build-up. Schell advocates nuclear freeze by describing the fate of the earth when a decision to use nuclear weapons is made. And, after criticizing alternative solutions to peace, Krauthammer claims that deterrence is "the only reasonable attitude toward nuclear weapons."

Of Accidental Judgments and Casual Slaughters

Kai Erikson

Kai Erikson (1931–), a sociologist, educator, and author, published "Of Accidental Judgments and Casual Slaughters" in The Nation *(1985) on the fortieth anniversary of dropping the atomic bomb on Hiroshima and Nagasaki. After examining the elements historically advanced as crucial to making the decision to use the bomb, Erikson concludes that, in fact, no true decision was made in August 1945. Using an atomic weapon against Japan was the natural consequence of developing the weapon. Erikson uses these conclusions to fuel his closing argument for disarmament.*

Before you begin reading: *In your reading notebook, make a list of world events that indicate to you that nuclear war is inevitable. Next to each item, suggest a way to change its impact.*

◆

THE BOMBINGS OF HIROSHIMA AND NAGASAKI, WHICH took place forty years ago this month, are among the most thoroughly studied moments on human record. Together they constitute the only occasion in history when atomic weapons were dropped on living populations, and together they constitute the only occasion in history when a decision was made to employ them in that way.

I want to reflect here on the second of those points. The "decision to drop"—I will explain in a minute why quotation marks are useful here—is a fascinating historical episode. But it is also an exhibit of the most profound importance as we consider our prospects for the future. It is a case history well worth attending to. A compelling parable.

If one were to tell the story of that decision as historians normally do, the details arranged in an ordered narrative, one might begin in 1938 with the discovery of nuclear fission, or perhaps a year later with the delivery of Einstein's famous letter to President Roosevelt. No matter what its opening scene, though, the tale would then proceed along a string of events—a sequence of appointees named, committees formed, reports issued, orders signed, arguments won and lost, minds made up and changed—all of it coming to an end with a pair of tremendous blasts in the soft morning air over Japan.

The difficulty with that way of relating the story, as historians of the period all testify, is that the more closely one examines the record, the harder it is to make out where in the flow of events something that could reasonably be called a decision was reached at all. To be sure, a kind of consensus emerged from the sprawl of ideas and happenings that made up the climate of wartime Washington, but looking back, it is hard to distinguish those pivotal moments in the story when the crucial issues were identified, debated, reasoned through, resolved. The decision, to the extent that one can even speak of such a thing, was shaped and seasoned by a force very like inertia.

Let's say, then, that a wind began to blow, ever so gently at first, down the corridors along which power flows. And as it gradually gathered momentum during the course of the war, the people caught up in it began to assume, without ever checking up on it, that it had a logic and a motive, that it had been set in motion by sure hands acting on the basis of wise counsel.

Harry Truman, in particular, remembered it as a time of tough and lonely choices, and titled his memoir of that period *Year of Decisions*. But the bulk of those choices can in all fairness be said to have involved confirmation of projects already under way or implementation of decisions made at other levels of command. Brig. Gen. Leslie R. Groves, military head of the Manhattan Project, was close to the mark when he described Truman's decision as "one of noninterference—basically, a decision not to upset the existing plans." And J. Robert Oppenheimer spoke equally to the point when he observed some twenty years later: "The decision was implicit in the project. I don't know whether it could have been stopped."

In September of 1944, when it became more and more evident that a bomb would be produced in time for combat use, Franklin Roosevelt and Winston Churchill met at Hyde Park and initialed a brief *aide-mémoire*, noting, among other things, that the new weapon "might, perhaps, after mature consideration, be used against the Japanese." This document does not appear to have had any effect on the conduct of the war, and Truman knew nothing at all about it. But it would not have made a real difference in any case, for neither chief of state did much to initiate the "mature consideration" they spoke of so glancingly, and Truman, in turn, could only suppose that such matters had been considered already. "Truman did not inherit the question," writes Martin J. Sherwin, "he inherited the answer."

What would "mature consideration" have meant in such a setting as that anyway?

First of all, presumably, it would have meant seriously asking whether the weapon should be employed at all. But we have it on the authority of virtually all the principal players that no one in a position to do anything about it ever really considered alternatives to combat use. Henry L. Stimson, Secretary of War:

> At no time, from 1941 to 1945, did I ever hear it suggested by the President, or by any other responsible member of the government, that atomic energy should not be used in the war.

Harry Truman:

> I regarded the bomb as a military weapon and never had any doubt that it should be used.

General Groves:

> Certainly, there was no question in my mind, or, as far as I was ever aware, in the mind of either President Roosevelt or President Truman or any other responsible person, but that we were developing a weapon to be employed against the enemies of the United States.

Winston Churchill:

> There never was a moment's discussion as to whether the atomic bomb should be used or not.

And why should anyone be surprised? We were at war, after all, and with the most resolute of enemies, so the unanimity of that feeling is wholly understandable. But it was not, by any stretch of the imagination, a product of mature consideration.

"Combat use" meant a number of different things, however, and a second question began to be raised with some frequency in the final months of the war, all the more insistently after the defeat of Germany. Might a way be devised to demonstrate the awesome power of the bomb in a convincing enough fashion to induce the surrender of the Japanese without having to destroy huge numbers of civilians? Roosevelt may have been pondering something of the sort. In September of 1944, for example, three days after initialing the Hyde Park *aide-mémoire*, he asked Vannevar Bush, a trusted science adviser, whether the bomb "should actually be used against the Japanese or whether it should be used only as a threat." While that may have been little more than idle musing, a number of different schemes were explored within both the government and the scientific community in the months following.

One option involved a kind of *benign strike*: the dropping of a bomb on some built-up area, but only after advance notice had been issued so that residents could evacuate the area and leave an empty slate on which the bomb could write its terrifying signature. This plan was full of difficulties. A dud under those dramatic circumstances might do enormous damage to American credibility, and, moreover, to broadcast any warning was to risk the endeavor in other ways. Weak as the Japanese were by this time in the war, it was easy to imagine their finding a way to intercept an incoming airplane if they knew where and when it was expected, and officials in Washington were afraid that it would occur to the Japanese, as it had to them, that the venture would come to an abrupt end if American prisoners of war were brought into the target area.

The second option was a *tactical strike* against a purely military target—an arsenal, railroad yard, depot, factory, harbor—without advance notice. Early in the game, for example, someone had nominated the Japanese fleet concentration at Truk. The problem with this notion, however—and there is more than a passing irony here—was that no known military target had a wide enough compass to contain the whole of the destructive capacity of the weapon and so display its full range and power. The committee inquiring into likely targets wanted one "more than three miles in diameter," because anything smaller would be too inadequate a canvas for the picture it was supposed to hold.

The third option was to stage a kind of *dress rehearsal* by detonating a bomb in some remote corner of the world—a desert or empty island, say—to exhibit to international observers brought in for the purpose what the device could do. The idea had been proposed by a group of scientists in what has since been called the Franck Report, but it commanded no more than a moment's attention. It had the same problems as the benign strike: the risk of being embarrassed by a dud was more than most officials in a position to decide were willing to take, and there was a widespread feeling that any demonstration involving advance notice would give the enemy too much useful information.

The fourth option involved a kind of *warning shot*. The thought here was to drop a bomb without notice over a relatively uninhabited stretch of enemy land so that the Japanese high command might see at first hand what was in store for them if they failed to surrender soon. Edward Teller thought that an explosion at night high over Tokyo Bay would serve as a brilliant visual argument, and Adm. Lewis Strauss, soon to become a member (and later chair) of the Atomic Energy Commission, recommended a strike on a local forest, reasoning that the blast would "lay the trees out in windrows from the center of the explosion in all directions as though they were matchsticks," meanwhile igniting a fearsome firestorm at the epicenter. "It seemed to me," he added, "that a demonstration of this sort would prove to the Japanese that we could destroy any of their cities at will." The physicist Ernest O. Lawrence may have been speaking half in jest when he suggested that a bomb might be used to "blow the top off" Mount Fujiyama, but he was quite serious when he assured a friend early in the war: "The bomb will never be dropped on people. As soon as we get it, we'll use it only to dictate peace."

Now, hindsight is too easy a talent. But it seems evident on the face of it that the fourth of those options, the warning shot, was much to be preferred over the other three, and even more to be preferred over use on living targets. I do not want to argue the case here. I do want to ask, however, why that possibility was so easily dismissed.

The fact of the matter seems to have been that the notion of a demonstration was discussed on only a few occasions once the Manhattan Project neared completion, and most of those discussions were off the record. So a historian trying to reconstruct the drift of those conversations can only flatten an ear against the wall, as it were, and see if any sense can be made of the muffled voices next door. It seems very clear, for example, that the options involving advance notice were brought up so often and so early in official conversations that they came to *mean* demonstration in the minds of several important players. If a James Byrnes, say, soon to be named Secretary of State, were asked why one could not detonate a device in unoccupied territory, he might raise the problem posed by prisoners of war, and if the same question were asked of a James Bryant Conant, another science adviser, he might speak of the embarrassment that would follow a dud—thus, in both cases, joining ideas that had no logical relation to each other. Neither prisoners of war nor fear of failure, of course, posed any argument against a surprise demonstration.

There were two occasions, however, on which persons in a position to affect policy discussed the idea of a nonlethal demonstration. Those two conversations together consumed no more than a matter of minutes, so far as one can tell at this remove, and they, too, were off the record. But they seem to represent virtually the entire investment of the government of the United States in "mature consideration" of the subject.

The first discussion took place at a meeting of what was then called the Interim Committee, a striking gathering of military, scientific and government brass under the chairmanship of Secretary Stimson. This group, which included James Byrnes and Chief of Staff Gen. George C. Marshall, met on a number of occasions in May of 1945 to discuss policy issues raised by the new bomb, and Stimson recalled later than at one of their final meetings the members "carefully considered such alternatives as a detailed advance warning or a demonstration in some uninhabited area." But the minutes of the meeting, as well as the accounts of those present, suggest otherwise. The only exchange on the subject, in fact, took place during a luncheon break, and while we have no way of knowing what was actually said in that conversation, we do know what conclusion emerged from it. One participant, Arthur H. Compton, recalled later:

> Though the possibility of a demonstration that would not destroy human lives was attractive, no one could suggest a way in which it could be made so convincing that it would be likely to stop the war.

And the recording secretary of the meeting later recalled:

> Dr. Oppenheimer . . . said he doubted whether there could be devised any sufficiently startling demonstration that would convince the Japanese they ought to throw in the sponge.

Two weeks later, four physicists who served as advisers to the Interim Committee met in Los Alamos to consider once again the question of demonstration. They were Arthur Compton, Enrico Fermi, Ernest Lawrence and Robert Oppenheimer—as distinguished an assembly of scientific talent as could be imagined—and they concluded, after a discussion of which we have no record: "We can propose no technical demonstration likely to bring an end to the war; we see no acceptable alternative to direct military use." That, so far as anyone can tell, was the end of it.

We cannot be sure that a milder report would have made a difference, for the Manhattan Project was gathering momentum as it moved toward the more steeply pitched inclines of May and June, but we can be sure that the idea of a demonstration was at that point spent. The Los Alamos report ended with something of a disclaimer ("We have, however, no claim to special competence. . . ."), but its message was clear enough. When asked about that report nine years later in his security hearings, Oppenheimer said, with what might have been a somewhat defensive edge in his voice, "We did not think exploding one of those things as a firecracker over the desert was likely to be very impressive."

Perhaps not. But those fragments are telling for another reason. If you listen to them carefully for a moment or two, you realize that these are the voices of nuclear physicists trying to imagine how a strange and distant people will react to an atomic blast. These are the voices of nuclear physicists dealing with psychological and anthropological questions about Japanese culture, Japanese temperament, Japanese will to resist—topics, we must assume, about which they knew almost nothing. They did not know yet what the bomb could actually do, since its first test was not to take place for another month. But in principle, at least, Oppenheimer and Fermi reflecting on matters relating to the Japanese national character should have had about the same force as Ruth Benedict and Margaret Mead reflecting on matters relating to high-energy physics, the first difference being that Benedict and Mead would not have presumed to do so, and the second being that no one in authority would have listened to them if they had.

The first of the two morals I want to draw from the foregoing—this being a parable, after all—is that in moments of critical contemplation, it is often hard to know where the competencies of soldiers and scientists and all the rest of us begin and end. Many an accidental judgment can emerge from such confusions.

But what if the conclusions of the scientists had been correct? What if some kind of demonstration had been staged in a lightly occupied part of Japan and it *had* been greeted as a firecracker in the desert? What then?

Let me shift gears for a moment and discuss the subject in another way. It is standard wisdom for everyone in the United States old enough to remember the war, and for most of those to whom it is ancient history, that the bombings of Hiroshima and Nagasaki were the only alternative to an all-out invasion of the

Japanese mainland involving hundreds of thousands and perhaps millions of casualties on both sides. Unless the Japanese came to understand the need to surrender quickly, we would have been drawn by an almost magnetic force toward those dreaded beaches. This has become an almost automatic pairing of ideas, an article of common lore. If you lament that so many civilians were incinerated or blown to bits in Hiroshima and Nagasaki, then somebody will remind you of the American lives thus saved. Truman was the person most frequently asked to account for the bombings, and his views were emphatic on the subject:

> It was a question of saving hundreds of thousands of American lives. I don't mind telling you that you don't feel normal when you have to plan hundreds of thousands of complete, final deaths of American boys who are alive and joking and having fun while you are doing your planning. You break your heart and your head trying to figure out a way to save one life. The name given to our invasion plan was "Olympic," but I saw nothing godly about the killing of all the people that would be necessary to make that invasion. I could not worry about what history would say about my personal morality. I made the only decision I ever knew how to make. I did what I thought was right.*

Veterans of the war, and particularly those who had reason to suppose that they would have been involved in an invasion, have drawn that same connection repeatedly, most recently Paul Fussell in the pages of *The New Republic.* Thank God for the bomb, the argument goes, it saved the lives of countless numbers of us. And so, in a sense, it may have.

But the destruction of Hiroshima and Nagasaki had nothing to do with it. It only makes sense to assume, even if few people were well enough positioned in early August to see the situation whole, that there simply was not going to be an invasion. Not ever.

For what sane power, with the atomic weapon securely in its arsenal, would hurl a million or more of its sturdiest young men on a heavily fortified mainland? To imagine anyone ordering an invasion when the means were at hand to blast Japan into a sea of gravel at virtually no cost in American lives is to imagine a madness beyond anything even the worst of war can induce. The invasion had not yet been called off, granted. But it surely would have been, and long before the November 1 deadline set for it.

---

*Merle Miller notes, in *Plain Speaking: An Oral Biography of Harry S. Truman*, that Truman may have had moments of misgiving: "My only insight into Mr. Truman's feeling about the Bomb and its dropping, and it isn't much, came one day in his private library at the Truman Memorial Library. In one corner was every book ever published on the Bomb, and at the end of one was Horatio's speech in the last scene of *Hamlet*." Truman had underlined these words:

> And let me speak to the yet unknowing world
> How these things came about. So shall you hear
> Of carnal, bloody, and unnatural acts,
> Of accidental judgments, casual slaughters,
> Of deaths put on by cunning and forced cause,
> And, in this upshot, purposes mistook
> Fall'n on the inventors' heads.

The United States did not become a nuclear power on August 6, with the destruction of Hiroshima. It became a nuclear power on July 16, when the first test device was exploded in Alamogordo, New Mexico. Uncertainties remained, of course, many of them. But from that moment on, the United States knew how to produce a bomb, knew how to deliver it and knew it would work. Stimson said shortly after the war that the bombings of Hiroshima and Nagasaki "ended the ghastly specter of a clash of great land armies," but he could have said, with greater justice, that the ghastly specter ended at Alamogordo. Churchill came close to making exactly that point when he first learned of the New Mexico test:

> To quell the Japanese resistance man by man and conquer the country yard by yard might well require the loss of a million American lives and half that number of British. . . . Now all that nightmare picture had vanished.

It *had* vanished. The age of inch-by-inch crawling over enemy territory, the age of Guadalcanal and Iwo Jima and Okinawa, was just plain over.

The point is that once we had the bomb and were committed to its use, the terrible weight of invasion no longer hung over our heads. The Japanese were incapable of mounting any kind of offensive, as every observer has agreed, and it was our option when to close with the enemy and thus risk casualties. So we could have easily afforded to hold for a moment, to think it over, to introduce what Dwight Eisenhower called "that awful thing" to the world on the basis of something closer to mature consideration. We could have afforded to detonate a bomb over some less lethal target and then pause to see what happened. And do it a second time, maybe a third. And if none of those demonstrations had made a difference, presumably we would have had to strike harder: Hiroshima and Nagasaki would still have been there a few weeks later for that purpose, silent and untouched—"unspoiled" was the term Gen. H. H. Arnold used—for whatever came next. Common lore also has it that there were not bombs enough for such niceties, but that seems not to have been the case. The United States was ready to deliver a third bomb toward the end of August, and Groves had already informed Marshall and Stimson that three or four more bombs would be available in September, a like number in October, at least five in November, and seven in December, with substantial increases to follow in early 1946. Even if we assume that Groves was being too hopeful about the productive machinery he had set in motion, as one expert close to the matter has suggested, a formidable number of bombs would have been available by the date originally set for invasion.

Which brings us back to the matter of momentum. The best way to tell the story of those days is to say that the "decision to drop" had become a force like gravity. It had taken life. The fact that it existed supplied its meaning, its reason for being. Elting E. Morison, Stimson's biographer, put it well:

> Any process started by men toward a special end tends, for reasons logical, biological, aesthetic or whatever they may be, to carry forward, if other things remain

> equal, to its climax. [This is] the inertia developed in a human system. . . . In a process where such a general tendency has been set to work it is difficult to separate the moment when men were still free to choose from the moment, if such there was, when they were no longer free to choose.

I have said very little about Nagasaki so far because it was not the subject of any thought at all. The orders of the bomber command were to attack Japan as soon as the bombs were ready. One was ready on August 9. Boom. When Groves was later asked why the attack on Nagasaki had come so soon after the attack on Hiroshima, leaving so little time for the Japanese to consider what had happened to them, he simply said: "Once you get your opponent reeling, you keep him reeling and never let him recover." And that is the point, really. There is no law of nature that compels a winning side to press its superiority, but it is hard to slow down, hard to relinquish an advantage, hard to rein the fury. The impulse to charge ahead, to strike at the throat, is so strong a habit of war that it almost ranks as a reflex, and if that thought does not frighten us when we consider our present nuclear predicament, nothing will. Many a casual slaughter can emerge from such moods.

If it is true, as I have suggested, that there were few military or logistic reasons for striking as sharply as we did and that the decision to drop moved in on the crest of an almost irreversible current, then it might be sensible to ask, on the fortieth anniversary of the event, what some of the drifts were that became a part of that larger current. An adequate accounting would have to consider a number of military, political and other matters far beyond the reach of this brief essay, the most important of them by far being the degree to which the huge shadow of the Soviet Union loomed over both official meetings and private thoughts. It is nearly impossible to read the remaining record without assuming that the wish to make a loud announcement to the Russians was a persuasive factor in the minds of many of the principal participants. There were other drifts as well, of course, and I would like to note a few of the sort that sometimes occur to social scientists.

For one thing, an extraordinary amount of money and material had been invested in the Manhattan Project—both of them in short supply in a wartime economy—and many observers thought that so large a public expense would be all the more willingly borne if it were followed by a striking display of what the money had been spent for.

And, too, extraordinary investments had been made in men and talent, both of them in short supply in a wartime economy. The oldest of the people involved in the Manhattan Project—soldiers, engineers and scientists—made sacrifices in the form of separated families, interrupted careers and a variety of other discomforts, and it makes a certain psychological sense that a decisive strike would serve as a kind of vindication for all the trouble. The youngest of them, though, had been held out of combat, thus avoiding the fate of so many men of their generation, by accidents of professional training, personal skill and sheer timing. The project was their theater of war, and it makes even more psychological sense that some of them would want the only shot they fired to be a truly resonant one.

The dropping of such a bomb, moreover, could serve as an ending, something sharp and distinct in a world that had become ever more blurred. The Grand Alliance was breaking up, and with it all hope for a secure postwar world. Roosevelt was dead. The future was full of ambiguity. And, most important, everybody was profoundly tired. In circumstances like that, a resounding strike would serve to clarify things, to give them form, to tidy them up a bit.

There are other matters one might point to, some of them minor, some of them major, all of them strands in the larger weave. There was a feeling, expressed by scientists and government officials alike, that the world needed a rude and decisive shock to awaken it to the realities of the atomic age. There was a feeling, hard to convey in words but easy to sense once one has become immersed in some of the available material, that the bomb had so much power and majesty, was so compelling a force, that one was almost required to give it birth and a chance to mature. There was a feeling, born of war, that for all its ferocity the atomic bomb was nevertheless no more than a minor increment on a scale of horror that already included the firebombings of Tokyo and other Japanese cities. And there was a feeling, also born of war, that living creatures on the other side, even the children, had somehow lost title to the mercies that normally accompany the fact of being human.

The kinds of points I have been making need to be stated either very precisely or in some detail. I have not yet learned to do the former; I do not have space enough here for the latter. So let me just end with the observation that human decisions do not always emerge from reflective counsels where facts are arrayed in order and logic is the prevailing currency of thought. They emerge from complex fields of force, in which the vanities of leaders and the moods of constituencies and the inertias of bureaucracies play a critical part. That is as important a lesson as one can learn from the events of 1945—and as unnerving a one.

The bombings of Hiroshima and Nagasaki supply a rich case study for people who must live in times like ours. It is not important for us to apportion shares of responsibility to persons who played their parts so long ago, and I have not meant to do so here: these were unusually decent and compassionate people for the most part, operating with reflexes that had been tempered by war. We need to attend to such histories as this, however, because they provide the clearest illustrations we have of what human beings can do—this being the final moral to be drawn from our parable—when they find themselves in moments of crisis and literally have more destructive power at their disposal than they know what to do with. That is as good an argument for disarming as any that can be imagined.

Questions for Critical Analysis

1. What is the point of Erikson's essay? How does the historical event of bombing Hiroshima and Nagasaki illustrate this point? What response does Erikson want from his readers?
2. Name two questions that were raised about using the atomic bomb. How were these questions answered?
3. What reasons does Erikson give for why the fourth option, a warning shot, was not considered acceptable? How does Erikson describe the official attitude toward this option? What was the Los Alamos report? What does Erikson think of the report? of the "decisions"?
4. Erikson refers to many public officials and scientists and alludes to historical events in telling this story. Who did you know about already? Make a list of the names and write a brief description of those you know; look up the names you don't recognize. Why does Erikson include so many of the key players and events?
5. Erikson argues that no "sane power, with the atomic weapon securely in its arsonal, would hurl a million or more of its sturdiest young men on a heavily fortified mainland." Do you agree with him? Discuss the implications of Erikson's claim on U.S. involvement in the Korean War and Vietnam conflict or USSR involvement in Afghanistan.

Questions for Structural Analysis

1. In his introduction, Erikson describes this essay as a parable, a case history. In what ways is this an accurate description? Write an informal outline of the essay to show the organization and development of its major points.
2. Look carefully at Erikson's word choice, images, and metaphors. How does his language reveal his political point of view? What is his attitude toward the subject he's writing about?
3. Erikson proposes two morals to be learned from this parable. What are they? How do they relate to the title of the essay? Based on the evidence presented in the essay, do they seem reasonable morals?
4. How does Erikson respond to the common argument (given by Truman and others) on why Americans dropped the atomic bombs on Japan? Describe his attitude. How does his language reveal this attitude? Discuss his reasoning. Does it make sense to you? Why, or why not?
5. Does Erikson convince you by his argument? Why, or why not?

*A*PPROACHES TO THE *A*TOMIC *A*GE

I. I. RABI

Isidor Isaac Rabi (1898–1988) apprenticed in physics in the Europe of Niels Bohr, Arnold Sommerfeld, Wolfgang Pauli, Werner Heisenberg, and Otto Stern. When he returned to the United States in 1929, he established a molecular beam laboratory at Columbia University, measuring the magnetic properties of atoms and molecules. He received the 1944 Nobel Prize in Physics for this work. During the Second World War, Rabi was Associate Director of the MIT Radiation Laboratory, which developed microwave radar used in both the European and Pacific wars. Rabi was one of two advisors (the other was Niels Bohr) to J. Robert Oppenheimer during the Manhattan Project at Los Alamos, New Mexico, developing the atomic bomb. Present at the first explosion of an atomic bomb, Rabi has been committed to using atomic and nuclear energy for peaceful means and curtailing the presence and development of nuclear weapons. Rabi's concern with the philosophical questions of physics is apparent in "Approaches to the Atomic Age," originally a lecture delivered to the Boston Institute for Religious and Social Studies on January 3, 1946.

Before you begin reading: *In your notebook make a list of world events you see as hopeful in eliminating the possibility of nuclear war. Next to each item, jot down reasons why you think it is a positive sign.*

◆

IT IS MY BELIEF THAT THE SCIENTIST'S VIEW OF THE WORLD is very much like the spiritual view of the world. They both stem from the same source, from human aspiration, from the depths of the soul, from deep thinking and feeling.

On July 16, 1945, I was out in the desert in New Mexico; not many yards away was Mr. James B. Conant, then President of Harvard University. There were other men there, also. We were awaiting the tests of the first large-scale release of atomic energy.

In the desert there, the site chosen had been named "Journey of Death" hundreds of years ago. This site was chosen because it was supposed to be far away from human habitation. Nine miles away from where we were, there was a tower about one hundred feet high. On the top of that tower was a little shack about ten by ten. In that shack was a bomb. The whole experiment had been in preparation for almost a year. Hundreds of men took part in it. There were many rehearsals, and this particular morning it was to go off. At first, the announcer said: "Thirty seconds"—"Ten seconds"—and we were lying there, very tense, in the early dawn, and there were just a few streaks of gold in the east; you could see your neighbor very dimly. Those ten seconds were the longest ten seconds that I ever experienced. Suddenly, there was an enormous flash of light, the brightest light I have ever seen or that I think anyone else has ever seen. It blasted; it pounced; it bored its way into you. It was a vision which was seen with more than the eye. It was seen to last forever. You would wish it would stop; altogether it lasted about two seconds. Finally it was over, diminishing, and we looked toward the place where the bomb had been; there was an enormous ball of fire which grew and grew and it rolled as it grew; it went up into the air, in yellow flashes and into scarlet and green. It looked menacing. It seemed to come toward one.

A new thing had just been born; a new control; a new understanding of man, which man had acquired over nature.

That was the scientific opening of the atomic age.

Naturally, we were very jubilant over the outcome of the experiment. While this tremendous ball of flame was there before us, and we watched it, and it rolled along, it became in time diffused with the clouds. This ground was the umbilical cord connected with it; then it was washed out with the wind. We turned to one another and offered congratulations, for the first few minutes. Then, there was a chill, which was not the morning cold; it was a chill that came to one when one thought, as for instance when I thought of my wooden house in Cambridge, my laboratory in New York, and of the millions of people living around there, and this power of nature which we had first understood it to be—well, there it was.

This bomb was made and given to the military; and the President of the United States and the Secretary of War, the Secretary of State, and the Joint Chiefs of Staff were to decide what to do with it. No scientist was called in to join in making this decision. To the politician, the scientist is like a trained monkey who goes up to the coconut tree to bring down choice coconuts. If he is successful in bringing down a very choice one, the owner of the monkey begins to worry, lest somebody else learn the trick. And the priest is in the same position. He is asked to bless the arms of the nation; he is not asked what the nation should do with those arms. So that we are exactly in the same place.

The decision was made. Three weeks later, a single B-29, in the clear blue morning, flew over the beautiful city of Hiroshima. There was not a cloud in the sky. There was not a shot fired against it. The men in the B-29 took careful aim, and they dropped this bomb. It veered off sharply. The story they tell is exactly the same story that I have told you except for this, that this great cloud and its umbilical cord of dust was the city of Hiroshima, rather than the sands of the desert.

That decision was not made by the scientists. As a matter of fact, a large number of them in the project protested against the use of it.

Now, the dark pall which has fallen over Hiroshima and its thousands of dead and dying has spread over all the world, and has entered our hearts and minds with a paralyzing fear.

The President of the United States, on hearing the news of Hiroshima, went from one part of his ship to another, announcing this great event.

We who were connected with this thing, when we heard of the bombing of Hiroshima, were pleased that the details had been successful. We did not feel gay over it. We did not feel gay over it then, and we do not feel gay over it today. Fear has dominated the whole history of the atomic bomb and atomic energy. It was the fear of the triumph of Nazi brutality which made a gentle soul like Albert Einstein, a saint of science, urge upon the President of the United States, Franklin D. Roosevelt, the necessity of developing this new form of destruction, lest the enemy get it first. It was fear that made this peace-loving country lavish such huge sums of money on the rapid development of the bomb. It was fear that made the scientists of the United States band themselves together with representatives from scientists of other civilized nations to develop this instrument of destruction.

I very well remember the time when I was in New Mexico, seated in the room with some of the top scientists there. The question was asked: Should the laboratory be extended?

The big problem was: Where was the enemy in this field of work?

We went over the history of this discovery, from 1939, when the first announcement of uranium was made.

What did the Nazis have? Who were the Nazi scientists?

We knew them all. Where were they? What were they doing? What means did they have at their command? How could a nation like Germany, then engaged in a life-and-death struggle with Russia, spare the resources for this sort of development? We went over the whole thing again, and looked at the history of our own development and tried to see where they could have been cleverer, where they might have had better judgment and avoided this error or that error.

What then?

We finally arrived at the conclusion that they could be exactly as advanced as we were, or perhaps further. We felt very solemn.

I thought of London, from which I had returned six months previously, and the devastation in London.

Then we went back to work and the laboratory was expanded. This was a very special piece of work, because no bomb had ever been made. In fact, the research for the process of making the bomb actually was developed before the material itself out of which the bomb was made. The research on how to make the bomb was being done and carried on during the time when the factory for making the materials was being built.

One did not know what the enemy had. One did not want to lose a single day, a single week. And certainly, a month would be a calamity. The production of the material out of which the bomb was made, and its delivery to an enemy, should have first priority. That is one of the reasons why this was tried out in the wilds of New Mexico.

We now know that the Nazis were nowhere in the race. At the end of World War II, they had not advanced to the point where we were in 1941; in spite of all the talk, they never got very far at all.

But it takes time to get under way, to make the spiritual resource effective. By the time the bomb was perfected, the war in Europe had been won. We now know that the Japanese war was over.

Why did this humanitarian, peace-loving country, headed by President Truman, a man of the people, an average American if ever there was one, set the example of superman's destruction? This is a question which will be argued for years to come. But I think I can understand it. The atomic bomb is a very easy and convenient weapon. The man who gave the "go ahead" signal did not have to think of exposing thousands of American boys to the hazards of battle. One, and only one, bomber, manned by ten men, carried this bomb. In the possession of such overwhelming power, it is only human for those who can wield it to become impatient and exasperated over the delay in our position.

The signal was given, and Hiroshima went up in brown smoke. We now have more than the results of Hiroshima and Nagasaki. In each case, thousands of people were killed instantly and thousands more died a lingering death over a period of a few weeks.

In Dr. Morrison's testimony before the Senate committee, he stated that twenty-four hundred nurses, orderlies, and trained first-aid workers were in Hiroshima, and eighteen hundred were made casualties in a single instant. Somehow this is more striking to me than the total figure of one hundred thousand people killed and ten square miles destroyed. This bomb destroys equally the just and the unjust, the wise and the foolish, the nurse and the soldier with his gun. And yet, the actual release of the weapon concerned ten men in one airplane.

What are the consequences of this unprecedented condition of destruction, with ten men in one airplane? It simply means that we are living in a world where material power has become so strong that it must be powerful. There is only one way to conquer it. The lesson which I draw from Hiroshima and Nagasaki is that this simply must not happen again. It should not happen to ourselves or to any of our countrymen or to people anywhere else in the world.

The atomic bomb is an instrument of evil, which even the righteous people found themselves capable of using in the heat of war. It must be abolished. But, to abolish it, we must abolish all wars, and the possibility of waging war, and the sovereign right of any nation or state to wage war. We must be forthright and bold about this. No time or use policy based on fear and suspicion and pursued in a small-minded, picayune fashion will abolish the bomb. The Court of Peace must be as strong as a call to arms. A call to peace can only be had by a clear return to the basic values upon which this country was founded, and only by such return to the basic values can we get the fall of Hiroshima out of our hearts.

On this concept, thirteen very diverse states formed a voluntary union, based on broad human aspirations. There was also the courage to fight a war to preserve that union, and those broad human principles upon which it was based are not pacifism but a militant desire for peace, and that must be the inspiration of our policy.

I now want to say a few things on the technical side. If an atom of uranium were expanded a billionfold, it would be about the size of a large round watermelon. In the very center of this, you would find a small kernel called the nucleus, about the size of a very small grain of sand. This is the nucleus of the uranium atom. If the weight were increased proportionately to this expansion in size, the whole thing would weigh about one thousand pounds. You now have this one thousand pounds; and the outer electrons, outside this kernel, would weigh one-quarter of a pound; and the small kernel, the nucleus, would weigh the rest of the one thousand pounds.

What we call atomic energy is really nuclear energy, ordinary chemical energy, like the explosion of dynamite coming from a rearrangement of the outer electrons, which are very much like a tenuous gas or smoke, prepared for the nucleus. A rearrangement of the particles may blow up the nucleus, release energy a million times greater than the rearrangement of the outside electrons.

We learned much from nuclear physics—radioactivity, its application for the cure of cancer and other diseases, and, for its utilization in industry; how, for example, to paint the dials of watches. These were the two principal practical applications of nuclear physics.

Then came World War II, the call to be of some help, and the request came to the scientists. Then there was the social consciousness, the feeling of the scientist that he must do something for his country which was so unprepared. And thus we witnessed the accelerated practical development. And now we have the atomic bomb.

If the atomic bomb were the end of the story, perhaps ways could be found to cope with the problem in a somewhat less drastic manner than that which I propose. But the reader must realize that the atomic bomb is just the first version. It is the first automobile, the first airplane, and it compares with the atomic bomb of the future the way the Wrights' first airplane compares with the V-2 rocket. There is much more to come. And the progress of the art of destruction has reached the point where we could destroy this very planet.

The most serious thing about the atomic bomb, even today, is its amazing cheapness. It costs less than one-tenth as much money in dollars to destroy a square mile by atomic bombing as it does by ordinary bombing. Even the poor nation can afford to be destructive.

What peaceful uses can we find for atomic energy? We have been promised a brilliant future for the application of atomic energy. It will be cheap power. We will have more gadgets in the home, and places which are poor in coal, oil, and water power will have the possibility of utilizing atomic energy.

That is not an appealing prospect when we realize that this atomic energy carries with it an adverse star. Any system which can be devised for making atomic energy also makes the raw material for an atomic bomb. The energy which made the atomic bomb is the energy which allows the heat of the sun to bestow its warmth from the heavens. And there are even more violent forms of energy transformation in some of the stars. We do not know the exact nature of those energy transformations. There are new discoveries made almost yearly in the fundamental structure of matter. In the cosmic rays, there is a tremendous amount of energy and properties, far beyond our understanding.

A new world is unfolding before us, and it keeps on unfolding before us. The scientist wants to understand this. He wants to take pleasure in understanding it. He wants to take pleasure in telling his fellow man about it until he broadens his mind; he even taunts him by letting him see how wonderfully the world is constructed. But he wants to do this now, unhampered by the military at his side. He wants to be a peaceful citizen on the globe. He does not want to be the servant of evil and of destruction. It is only by the control of this thing that he can fulfill his wish.

It is very appropriate that the scientist should take the lead in this. Science has done it from the very beginning; it has organized itself along hopeful lines, because the whole position of science from the time of Galileo has been an international tradition. Scientists have communicated their results to one another freely. They visit back and forth.

The Book of Nature is not written in any one language; it is written in universal language. Scientists read that book together and have always read that book together.

When the danger of World War II came to civilization, the scientists in this country, of Great Britain, of Canada, of Denmark, yes, even the best ones of Germany and Austria, worked together to perfect this thing. They were not against anybody; they worked for the protection of civilization, for making the world habitable, and in a way that free science would still be possible.

We have taken the first step toward that, in winning the Second World War, and not only by the creation of the bomb but by the other contributions of science; and now, by virtue of the terrible nature of this weapon, and the terrible promise of the future, we are fortunate that these very men, these scientists, have had this tradition of international understanding and cooperation which has extended for many centuries; they love that world, and have stood up ready to awaken their fellow men to the dangers that threaten it, and to point out the only path on which security lies, enabling us to pursue our spiritual and material lives in peace and in hope.

We have arrived at a stage in our history where we are forced to choose between two paths. One is a simple path, advocated by many senators, the path of becoming strong nationally, increasing our stock of atomic bombs, and engaging in newer research for their improvement, together with other weapons of war. But in this direction lies ultimate disaster, since all other peoples will be forced to follow the same road. The other path is a thorny one and beset with great initial difficulties.

How can we get together into a strong union with other peoples of different languages, histories, and traditions?

How can we overcome the suspicions, jealousies, and even hatreds in ourselves and in others?

The problems seem insurmountable. Their solutions are almost too much to expect of human nature. But we are strengthened in our task through the knowledge that this task has been accomplished before on this continent. If we can recover the spirit and depth of vision of Washington, Franklin, Jefferson, and Lincoln, we can lead the world into a millennium of peace and perhaps even of grace.

QUESTIONS FOR CRITICAL ANALYSIS

1. Rabi expresses the belief that "the scientist's view of the world is very much like the spiritual view of the world." What does he mean? How would you compare his view with that of Nemerov ("On the Resemblances Between Science and Religion") and Jaspers ("Is Science Evil?")?
2. Compare Rabi's account of the scientists' response to the bomb to that described by Erikson. How does each discuss the decision-making process? What does each have to say about the scientists' responsibility?
3. Summarize Rabi's analysis of creating and using the bomb. What is his attitude toward this operation? How do you know?
4. Rabi first gave this lecture to the Boston Institute for Religious and Social Studies in January 1946 (four months after Hiroshima and Nagasaki). What do you think was Rabi's purpose in making this speech? What response did he expect from his audience?
5. Compare Rabi's description of witnessing the explosion to Laurence's ("Atomic Bombing of Nagasaki Told by Flight Member") and to the Japanese as described by Hersey ("A Noiseless Flash") in Part Four. How were their responses to the event similar? How were they dissimilar?

QUESTIONS FOR STRUCTURAL ANALYSIS

1. What lessons did Rabi draw from Hiroshima and Nagasaki? What are his arguments, how does he support them, and how effective are they?
2. What does Rabi mean by "The Book of Nature is not written in any one language"? What role does Rabi see for scientists? What difference does it make that Rabi, a world-renowned atomic physicist, is the author of this essay?
3. Rabi begins with a vivid description of what he saw at the test explosion of the first atomic bomb. How did you respond to this description? Why does Rabi begin this way?
4. Does Rabi assume that his audience knows much about physics? How well does he explain the science to a general reader? What techniques does he use? How do you characterize his language and word choice?
5. How does Rabi's conclusion relate to his title, "Approaches to the Atomic Age"? Why is he hopeful about the future? Are you? Why, or why not?

A REPUBLIC OF *I*NSECTS AND GRASS

JONATHAN SCHELL

Jonathan Schell (1943–) is a member of the New Yorker *staff and author of early books on the Vietnam War (*The Village of Ben Suc*, 1967, and* The Military Half*, 1968), a book on American politics from 1969 to 1974 (*The Time of Illusion*, 1975), and two books on the prospect of nuclear war (*The Fate of the Earth*, 1982, and* The Abolition*, 1984). This essay, "A Republic of Insects and Grass," is excerpted from an early section of* The Fate of the Earth*, originally serialized in the* New Yorker. *By showing how the existence of life would be destroyed through a nuclear holocaust, Schell argues that the fear of extinction should make us willing to abolish nuclear weapons.*

Before you begin reading: *Think about how you would live differently if you really believed the extinction of the human race were likely. Write a paragraph in your notebook describing the changes that would occur in your daily life if you thought we would soon all be killed.*

◆

IN RECENT YEARS, SCIENTISTS IN MANY FIELDS HAVE ACcumulated enough knowledge to begin to look on the earth as a single, concrete mechanism, and to at least begin to ask how it works. One of their discoveries has been that life and life's inanimate terrestrial surroundings have a strong reciprocal influence on each other. For life, the land, oceans, and air have been the environment, but, equally, for the land, oceans, and air life has been the environment—the conditioning force. The injection of oxygen into the atmosphere by living things, which led to the formation of an ozone layer, which, in turn, shut out lethal ultraviolet rays from the sun and permitted the rise of multicellular organisms, was only one of life's large-scale interventions. The more closely scientists look at life and its evolution, the less they find it possible to draw a sharp distinction between "life," on the one hand, and an inanimate "environment" in which it exists, on the other. Rather, "the environment" of the present day appears to be a house of unimaginable intricacy which life has to a very great extent built and furnished for its own use. It seems that life even regulates and maintains the chemical environment of the earth in a way that turns out to suit its own needs. In a far-reaching speculative article entitled

"Chemical Processes in the Solar System: A Kinetic Perspective," Dr. McElroy has described the terrestrial cycles by which the most important elements of the atmosphere—oxygen, carbon, and nitrogen—are kept in proportions that are favorable to life. He finds that in each case life itself—its birth, metabolism, and decay—is chiefly responsible for maintaining the balance. For example, he calculates that if for some reason respiration and decay were suddenly cut off, photosynthesis would devour all the inorganic carbon on the surface of the ocean and in the atmosphere within forty years. Thereafter, carbon welling up from the deep ocean would fuel photosynthesis in the oceans for another thousand years, but then "life as we know it would terminate." Dr. McElroy also observes that the amount of ozone in the stratosphere is influenced by the amount of organic decay, and thus by the amount of life, on earth. Nitrous oxide is a product of organic decay, and because it produces nitric oxide—one of the compounds responsible for ozone depletion—it plays the role of regulator. In the absence of human intervention, living things are largely responsible for introducing nitrous oxide into the atmosphere. When life is exceptionally abundant, it releases more nitrous oxide into the atmosphere, and may thus act to cut back on the ozone, and that cutback lets in more ultraviolet rays. On the other hand, when life is sparse and depleted, nitrous-oxide production is reduced, the ozone layer builds up, and ultraviolet rays are cut back. These speculative glimpses of what might be called the metabolism of the earth give substance to the growing conviction among scientists that the earth, like a single cell or a single organism, is a systemic whole, and in a general way they tend to confirm the fear that any large man-made perturbation of terrestrial nature could lead to a catastrophic systemic breakdown. Nuclear explosions are far from being the only perturbations in question; a heating of the global atmosphere through an increased greenhouse effect, which could be caused by the injection of vast amounts of carbon dioxide into the air (for instance, from the increased burning of coal), is another notable peril of this kind. But a nuclear holocaust would be unique in its suddenness, which would permit no observation of slowly building environmental damage before the full—and, for man, perhaps the final—catastrophe occurred. The geological record does not sustain the fear that sudden perturbations can extinguish all life on earth (if it did, we would not be here to reflect on the subject), but it does suggest that sudden, drastic ecological collapse is possible. It suggests that life as a whole, if it is given hundreds of millions of years in which to recuperate and send out new evolutionary lines, has an astounding resilience, and an ability to bring forth new and ever more impressive life forms, but it also suggests that abrupt interventions can radically disrupt any particular evolutionary configuration and dispatch hundreds of thousands of species into extinction.

The view of the earth as a single system, or organism, has only recently proceeded from poetic metaphor to actual scientific investigation, and on the whole Dr. Thomas's observation that "we do not really understand nature, at all" still holds. It is as much on the basis of this ignorance, whose scope we are only now in a position to grasp, as on the basis of the particular items of knowledge in our possession that I believe that the following judgment can be made: Bearing in mind that the possible consequences of the detonations of thousands of megatons of nuclear explosives include the blinding of insects, birds, and beasts all over the world; the extinction of many ocean species, among them some at the base of the food chain; the temporary or permanent alteration of the climate of the globe, with the outside chance of "dramatic" and "major" alterations in the structure of the atmosphere; the pollution of the whole ecosphere with oxides of nitrogen; the incapacitation in ten minutes of unprotected people who go out into the sunlight; the blinding of people who go out into the sunlight; a significant decrease in photosynthesis in plants around the world; the scalding and killing of many crops; the increase in rates of cancer and mutation around the world, but especially in the targeted zones, and the attendant risk of global epidemics; the possible poisoning of all vertebrates by sharply increased levels of Vitamin D in their skin as a result of increased ultraviolet light; and the outright slaughter on all targeted continents of most human beings and other living things by the initial nuclear radiation, the fireballs, the thermal pulses, the blast waves, the mass fires, and the fallout from the explosions; and, considering that these consequences will all interact with one another in unguessable ways and, furthermore, are in all likelihood an incomplete list, which will be added to as our knowledge of the earth increases, one must conclude that a full-scale nuclear holocaust could lead to the extinction of mankind.

To say that human extinction is a certainty would, of course, be a misrepresentation—just as it would be a misrepresentation to say that extinction can be ruled out. To begin with, we know that a holocaust may not occur at all. If one does occur, the adversaries may not use all their weapons. If they do use all their weapons, the global effects, in the ozone and elsewhere, may be moderate. And if the effects are not moderate but extreme, the ecosphere may prove resilient enough to withstand them without breaking down catastrophically. These are all substantial reasons for supposing that mankind will not be extinguished in a nuclear holocaust, or even that extinction in a holocaust is unlikely, and they tend to calm our fear and to reduce our sense of urgency. Yet at the same time we are compelled to admit that there *may* be a holocaust, that the adversaries *may* use all their weapons, that the global effects, including effects of which we are as yet unaware, *may* be severe, that the ecosphere *may* suffer catastrophic breakdown, and that our species *may* be extinguished. We are left with uncertainty, and are forced to make our decisions in a state of uncertainty. If we wish to act to save our species, we have to muster our resolve in spite of our awareness that the life of the species may not now in fact be jeopardized. On the other hand, if we wish to ignore the peril, we have to admit that we do so in the knowledge that the species may be in danger of imminent self-destruction. When the existence of nuclear weapons was made known, thoughtful people everywhere in the world realized that if the great powers entered into a nuclear-arms race the human species would sooner or later face the possibility of extinction. They also realized that in the absence of international agreements preventing it an arms race would probably occur. They knew that the path of nuclear armament was a dead end for mankind. The discovery of the energy in mass—of "the basic power of the universe"—and of a means by which man could release that energy altered the relationship between man and the source of his life, the earth. In the shadow of this power, the earth became small and the life of the human species doubtful. In that sense, the question of human extinction has been on the political agenda of the world ever since the first nuclear weapon was detonated, and there was no need for the world to build up its present tremendous arsenals before starting to worry about it. At just what point the species crossed, or will have crossed, the boundary between merely having the technical knowledge to destroy itself and actually having the arsenals at hand, ready to be used at any second, is not precisely knowable. But it is clear that at present, with some twenty thousand megatons of nuclear explosive power in existence, and with more being added every day, we have entered into the zone of uncertainty, which is to say the zone of risk of extinction. But the mere risk of extinction has a significance that is categorically different from, and immeasurably greater than, that of any other risk, and as we make our decisions we have to take that significance into account. Up to now, every risk has been contained within the frame of life; extinction would shatter the frame. It represents not the defeat of some purpose but an abyss in which all human purposes would be drowned for all time. We have no right to place the possibility of this limitless, eternal defeat on the same footing as risks that we run in the ordinary conduct of our affairs in our particular transient moment of human history. To employ a mathematical analogy, we can say that although the risk of extinction may be fractional, the stake is, humanly speaking, infinite, and a fraction of infinity is still infinity. In other words, once we learn that a holocaust *might* lead to extinction we have no right to gamble, because if we lose, the game will be over, and neither we nor anyone else will ever get another chance. Therefore, although, scientifically speaking, there is all the difference in the world between the mere possibility that a holocaust will bring about extinction and the certainty of it, morally they are the same, and we have no choice but to address the issue of nuclear weapons as though we knew for a certainty that their use would put an end to our species. In weighing the fate of the earth and, with it, our own fate, we stand before a mystery, and in tampering with the earth we tamper with a mystery. We are in deep ignorance. Our ignorance should dispose us to wonder, our wonder should make us humble, our humility should inspire us to reverence and caution, and our reverence and caution should lead us to act without delay to withdraw the threat we now pose to the earth and to ourselves.

In trying to describe possible consequences of a nuclear holocaust, I have mentioned the limitless complexity of its effects on human society and on the ecosphere—a complexity that sometimes seems to be as great as that of life itself. But if these effects should lead to human extinction, then all the complexity will give way to the utmost simplicity—the simplicity of nothingness. We—the human race—shall cease to be.

Questions for Critical Analysis

1. What point does Schell make in his introduction about the relationship between life and the environment? Why does he spend so much time on this? How would Rachel Carson ("The Obligation to Endure") respond to Schell's argument?
2. Which among the many details or examples did you find especially convincing or compelling? Why?
3. Schell's essay describes the environmental aftermath of nuclear war, but to what purpose? Of what is he trying to convince the reader? Do you agree or disagree with Schell about the necessity of eliminating nuclear weapons? Why?
4. Compare Schell's concerns over the fate of the earth with Carson's. How are their ideas similar? How are they dissimilar? Which scenario scares you more? Why?
5. How close does Schell think we are to extinction? Do you agree with him? Why, or why not?

Questions for Structural Analysis

1. How does Schell use Dr. McElroy's research in his introductory paragraph? In what ways does McElroy's research help Schell develop his thesis? What is his thesis?
2. This is a dense, information-filled essay, written in four long paragraphs. Did you have trouble following it? Why, or why not? Why do you think he chose this style?
3. This essay combines narration and description to develop an argument against nuclear weapons. How do these devices work together? Note narrative and/or descriptive examples that you think are especially effective.
4. Schell writes that: "although, scientifically speaking, there is all the difference in the world between the mere possibility that a holocaust will bring about extinction and the certainty of it, morally they are the same, and we have no choice but to address the issue of nuclear weapons as though we knew for a certainty that their use would put an end to our species." How does he support this argument? If you agreed with it, how would you respond? What reasons could you give for not agreeing?
5. What is the tone of Schell's final paragraph? Is it different from the other three paragraphs? How? What were your feelings when you finished reading this essay?

In Defense of Deterrence

Charles Krauthammer

After graduating from Harvard Medical School with a specialty in psychiatry, Charles Krauthammer (1950–) served as chief resident of the Psychiatric Consultation Service at Massachusetts General Hospital. His interest in politics led him to a career change as speech writer for Vice-President Walter Mondale, and he soon became a political writer for Time *magazine and* The New Republic. *"In Defense of Deterrence," collected with other writings in* Cutting Edges: Making Sense of the 80s *(1985), first appeared in* The New Republic *under the title "The Real Way to Prevent Nuclear War."*

Before you begin reading: *What steps do you think the United States should take to avoid the risk of nuclear war? Write your ideas in your reading notebook during ten uninterrupted minutes.*

◆

"SAFETY WILL BE THE STURDY CHILD OF TERROR, AND survival the twin brother of annihilation." That was Winston Churchill's description of what he called "the balance of terror." Each superpower has the ability to incinerate the defenseless population of the other many times over; each refrains from attacking because it fears retaliation in kind; each knows that aggression is tantamount to suicide. That is deterrence. Sometimes deterrence is called MAD, mutual assured destruction. By whatever name, deterrence has prevented the outbreak of nuclear war, indeed any war, between the United States and the Soviet Union for a generation.

Living in a world of deterrence is very uncomfortable. Every American and Soviet city dweller knows that he is targeted for destruction by nuclear weapons five thousand miles away. But the physical danger is only part of the problem. The world of deterrence is a world of paradoxes. Weapons are built in order never to be used. Weapons purely for defense of helpless populations, like the antiballistic missile systems, become the greatest threat to peace. Weapons aimed at people lessen the risk of war; weapons aimed at weapons, increase it.

The strains of living in such a world are enormous. A vast antinuclear movement is now rising in the U.S., animated principally by weariness and revulsion with this arrangement. Why now? Ronald Reagan is much of the answer. He helped defeat the SALT II treaty before his election, and has been reluctant to engage the Soviets in strategic arms talks since. For the first time in more than a decade, the U.S. and the Soviet Union are not engaged in negotiations to control strategic nuclear weapons. Worse, Mr. Reagan and some of his advisers have spoken in frighteningly offhand ways about "limited nuclear war" and nuclear warning shots. The Carter Administration's mobile MX plan played a part, too. It appeared such an enormously cumbersome and expensive contrivance that people began to wonder if the experts had not lost touch with reality. So millions of Americans have decided it is time for them to take the problem into their own hands,and an antinuclear grass-roots crusade has emerged.

Like all crusades, it has its bible: Jonathan Schell's . . . *The Fate of the Earth* . . . and its banner: "the freeze." Recently it even acquired an auxiliary brigade, four members of the American foreign policy establishment who opened a wholly new front by calling for a U.S. renunciation of any first use of nuclear weapons. The bible, the banner, and the brigade approach the nuclear dilemma from different directions, but they all challenge the established doctrines of deterrence. The brigade wants to limit deterrence; the freeze proponents want to ignore it; and Jonathan Schell wants to abolish it. Each deserves the closest scrutiny.

Jonathan Schell flatly rejects deterrence. That is the source of his originality. Otherwise his three-part thesis is unremarkable. Part I restates, albeit elegantly, the awful details of a nuclear holocaust, and concludes that it would lead to the extinction of the human race. (That is the view of some scientists, though not of the National Academy of Sciences' study which Schell used in reaching many of his conclusions.) Part II, an interminable rumination on the meaning of human extinction, comes to the unsurprising conclusion that extinction would be monstrous.

"From the foregoing it follows," Schell writes, after delivering his message in a reiterative style that constitutes its own kind of overkill, "that there can be no justification for extinguishing mankind." The real interest in Schell's book lies in Part III, "The Choice." Here he argues that traditional approaches to nuclear peril, like strategic arms limitation treaties, are mere gestures, aspirin given to a dying patient. He argues that deterrence is a logical fraud because the leaders of a country that had sustained a first strike would have no reason to retaliate, indeed, no country in whose name to retaliate.

What Schell refuses to acknowledge is that any potential aggressor would be deterred—and for over thirty years has been deterred—from striking first because he must anticipate not only the logical responses of the victim, but all possible human responses. Revenge, for example, is one motive to launch a second strike. Paul Warnke, President Carter's arms control chief, gives another. He argues that "our moral commitment" would "require that the leaders who had perpetrated this enormity not be allowed to inherit the earth and bend its people to their will." Soviet leaders reading Warnke (a nuclear dove and a supporter of the freeze) are highly unlikely to calculate that a first strike would meet with no response because that would be "illogical." Furthermore, no one knows what would happen in the confused, unimaginably strained atmosphere of a nuclear crisis. To act—to attack—under the assumption that the other side is constrained to follow purely "logical" courses of action is itself totally illogical. It is precisely because of these calculations that nuclear deterrence has succeeded in preventing nuclear war. That is not to say that deterrence can never fail, but the argument from history is a powerful one. An even more powerful one is the absence of an alternative.

Not that Schell shies away from providing one: a world graced by total disarmament (nuclear and conventional), the abolition of violence, the eradication of national boundaries, the renunciation of sovereignty, and the founding of a new world political order for the peaceful settlement of international disputes. How does he propose to bring this about? That is a detail he could not work into his 231-page treatise. That "awesome, urgent task," he graciously concedes, "I have left to others."

Although he does not explain how we are to bring about a lion-and-lamb scenario which even Isaiah had the audacity only to predict and not to mandate, he does give us a clue as to what the operating principle of his post-messianic world will be. Here we come directly to the critical center of Schell's thinking, to the force that not only underlies his passion today but will save mankind tomorrow—fear. In his world, Schell writes, "Fear would no longer dictate particular decisions, such as whether or not the Soviet Union might place missiles in Cuba; rather, it would be a moving force behind the establishment of a new system by which every decision was made. And, having dictated the foundation of the system, it would stand guard over it forever after, guaranteeing that the species did not slide back toward anarchy and doom." I have my doubts.

Fear is not just the saving principle of Schell's new world order; it is the animating force behind a new mass movement—the freeze campaign. The movement demands a mutual halt in the development, production, and deployment of all nuclear weapons, "because," as the campaign slogan puts it, "no one wants a nuclear war." Like Schell, freeze proponents are deeply concerned, and rightly so, about the prospect of living in a world in which we have the capacity to blow ourselves to bits at any moment. The freeze crusade has enlisted hundreds of thousands of Americans by showing what happens if the Sword of Damocles ever drops. Thus the graphic stills of Hiroshima victims and the maps with concentric circles radiating from ground zero in everyone's hometown. Schell recognizes that removing this sword requires renunciation not just by overkill, but of minimal deterrence, of the simple capacity to destroy the other side *once*. But very few freeze proponents advocate reducing levels below "sufficiency," because they recognize that in a pre-messianic world this would destabilize the nuclear balance and increase the chances of war. Under a freeze—indeed, under even the most radical of arms proposals, such as former Ambassador George Kennan's proposal to cut nuclear levels in half—the superpowers would still retain the capacity for the total destruction of the other society. Insofar as people support the freeze because they can't stand the thought of being a target for Soviet missiles, they have joined the wrong movement. The freeze offers no solution to that problem. They should be with Jonathan Shell's total disarmament movement, working on the "awesome, urgent task" of remaking human nature.

Some might argue that there is another way, short of universal brotherhood, to remove the Sword of Damocles. That is unilateral disarmament. But quite apart from the fact that such a move would mean the surrender of our values, it would do little to secure our survival. The historical record does not support the proposition that helplessness is a guarantee of safety. There has been one nuclear war on record; in it a nonnuclear Japan lost Hiroshima and Nagasaki. So far there has been only one biological war, the one going on today in Laos and Cambodia. These weapons, now used against helpless tribesmen, were never used against American troops fighting the same Vietnamese forces in the same place. The Hmong, unlike the Americans, lack the capacity to retaliate in kind.

The freeze is not unilateralist, nor do many of its advocates reject deterrence. They say they reject overkill. "Enough is enough," they say. "Why waste billions on useless weapons if all they will do, as Churchill said, is to make the rubble bounce?" (It is sometimes also argued, somewhat anomalously, that having useless, rubble-bouncing weapons is at the same time dangerous.)

The problem is that in their zeal to curb overkill, freeze advocates ignore the requirements of deterrence and, in particular, the requirement for survivability of the deterrent. Our weapons must be able to withstand a first strike and penetrate Soviet defenses in a retaliatory strike (and vice versa). If either side finds the survivability of its weapons systems declining, the world becomes less safe. In an international crisis, each side, particularly the more vulnerable side, has incentive to strike first: the invulnerable side to use its advantage, the vulnerable side to strike before it is too late.

What would happen under a freeze? The U.S. retaliatory capacity depends on the three legs of its strategic triad: the land-based ICBMs, the bomber force, and submarines. Because of the increasing accuracy, power, and numbers of Soviet missiles, the U.S. land-based missile force will soon become vulnerable to a first strike. (It is precisely to eliminate that vulnerability that President Carter proposed hiding the MX in multiple shelters, a scheme now abandoned.) That leaves the bomber and submarine forces. The bomber force consists of aging B-52s that are increasingly vulnerable to attack while still on the ground, and to being shot down while trying to penetrate Soviet air space. Hence President Carter's decision to deploy air-launched cruise missiles, which would be better able to penetrate Soviet defenses and would allow the B-52s to remain outside Soviet air space. The freeze proposal would prevent deployment of these missiles. It would also prevent production and development of a new bomber, either the B-1 or the Stealth, which would be better able to elude destruction on the ground and Soviet defenses in the air. Note that the B-1 or the Stealth would not be any more destructive than the B-52. They would not make the rubble bounce any higher. They would simply be more likely to get to the target, and therefore present the Soviets with a very good reason never to launch a first strike.

That leaves the submarine force, which the U.S. is now in the process of modernizing to make more survivable. The new Tridents are quieter than existing subs, and because they have longer-range missiles they can hide in larger areas of the ocean. The freeze would stop their deployment.

The freeze, a proposal devised for its simplicity, does not deal very well with paradox. It is one of the paradoxes of deterrence that defensive weapons (the ABM, for example) can be more destabilizing and therefore more dangerous to peace than offensive weapons. The freeze fixates on nuclear weapons because they appear more terrible than others. And indeed they are. But they are not necessarily more destabilizing. As former Under Secretary of the Navy James Woolsey points out, the freeze does nothing to prevent nonnuclear antisubmarine and antiaircraft advances, which weaken deterrence. But it does prevent modernization of nuclear systems designed for survivability, which enhances deterrence.

What exactly does it mean to say that if survivability declines, war becomes more likely? One quick fix for a vulnerable deterrent is to adopt a policy of launch-on-warning: as soon as we detect enemy missiles leaving their silos, we launch our missiles before they can be destroyed. (Some officials unsuccessfully urged President Carter to adopt launch-on-warning as an alternative to building the mobile MX.) But this creates a hair-trigger situation, where the time for the world's most important decision is not a matter of minutes but of seconds, too short to check out a faulty radar reading or a misinterpretation of data. That's the price of ignoring deterrence.

This analysis looks simply at what would happen if the freeze were already a reality. But however fervently American citizens may wish it, they cannot vote a "mutual verifiable freeze" into existence. Unfortunately, that must be negotiated with the Soviets. And bad as a freeze would be as an end point, it would be worse as a U.S. negotiating position—which is exactly what it would be if, say, the Kennedy-Hatfield amendment were adopted. First, it is certain to delay other arms control initiatives. The freeze appeals to American voters because of its simplicity, but a mutual freeze would involve complex negotiations with the Soviets. What exactly would be frozen? At what stage? How would it be verified? The production, stockpiling, and qualitative upgrading of nuclear weapons cannot be detected by satellite, and the Russians have always refused on-site inspection. That problem alone turns the freeze into either a nonstarter or a source of interminable negotiation.

Ironically, there does exist an arms control proposal which, though very complicated, poorly understood by the American people, and unsuited for two-hour ratification by town meetings, is very well understood by the Soviets: SALT II. They have already signed it. If the aim of the freeze movement is a quick, simple, bold move in arms control that would allow us to proceed to real reductions, then the answer is not a freeze, but SALT II. Representative Les Aspin has already pointed out with dismay the American penchant for reinventing the arms control wheel every four years. In 1977 President Carter rejected the Vladivostok Accords negotiated by President Ford and proposed drastic reductions instead. The Soviets rejected his proposal out of hand. It took more than two years to renegotiate SALT II on the original lines of Vladivostok. President Reagan in turn rejected SALT II and called for as yet unspecified START talks. The freeze proponents are doing precisely the same thing. It simply makes no sense to propose a freeze that would require years of negotiations when SALT II is at hand, has already been approved by the Soviets, and could be adjusted in small details and ratified quickly. Of course, SALT is not as catchy a slogan as the freeze. But it is certainly a better, quicker, and more serious path to arms control.

Another aim of the freeze campaign is to move to real reductions. But to arm a U.S. negotiating team with a freeze offer is to ensure that it will have no leverage with which to bargain the Soviets into reductions. We will have unilaterally announced our willingness to forgo all our modernization programs, like the Trident, the cruise missile, and the Stealth bomber. The theory is that this gesture will elicit from the Soviets a more conciliatory negotiating position. The theory is in conflict with history. The Soviets do not have a good record of responding to unilateral gestures. At the Glassboro Summit in 1967, President Johnson tried to interest Premier Kosygin in ABM negotiations. Kosygin demurred. A year later, the Senate defeated an amendment to deny funds for an American ABM system. Three days later Soviet Foreign Minister Andrei Gromyko announced the Soviets' willingness to negotiate arms control. Eventually they agreed to an almost total ban on ABMs. We are using the same strategy today in Geneva, offering systems that we propose to build as bargaining chips. We offer to forgo deployment of the Pershing II and ground-launched cruise missiles in Europe if the Soviets dismantle their SS-20s. Under a freeze, our position in Geneva would collapse and the SS-20s would remain in place. (Brezhnev calls *that* arrangement a freeze.) In strategic arms talks, any attempts on our part to, say, bargain away one of our new systems against the Soviets' destabilizing silo-killing ICBMs would fail.

The freeze is not a plan; it is a sentiment. (Montana's proposed freeze resolution, for example, opposes "the production, development and deployment of nuclear weapons by any nation." It will unfortunately not be binding on

President Zia of Pakistan.) The freeze reflects the deeply felt and wholly laudable wish of millions of Americans that something be done to control nuclear weapons. But when taken seriously as a plan, the freeze continually fails on its own terms. It seeks safety, but would jeopardize deterrence; it seeks quick action, but would delay arms control; it seeks real reductions, but removes any leverage we might have to bring them about.

Finally, it mistakes the most likely cause of an outbreak of nuclear war. In its fixation on numbers, the freeze assumes that somehow high weapons levels *in themselves* make war more likely. True, an uncontrolled arms race breeds suspicion between the superpowers and can increase the risk of war; but arms control measures (like SALT I or II) can allow higher levels, and still decrease the risk by building confidence on both sides and letting each know precisely what the other is doing. If nuclear war ever comes, it most likely will be not because the weapons fire themselves, but because some national leader, in order to preserve some national interest, orders them fired. When did we come closest to nuclear war in the last thirty-six years? In October 1962, when President Kennedy decided to threaten Khrushchev with war unless he obeyed our ultimatum on the Cuban missiles. In 1962 the level of nuclear arms was much lower than it is today. And when was the chance of nuclear war smallest? Probably at the height of detente, during the Apollo-Soyuz love fest, when U.S.-Soviet relations were good, even though each side had the capacity for multiple overkill.

The absolute level of nuclear weapons is only one factor, and a relatively small one at that, in determining the likelihood of nuclear war breaking out. (It is certainly less important than the balance of vulnerabilities on each side, i.e., the stability of deterrence.) The most likely source of nuclear war is from a regional conflict between the superpowers, where one or the other has important interests, but finds itself at a conventional disadvantage. That is the American situation today in Europe and in the Persian Gulf. To prevent the Soviets from taking advantage of their superiority in conventional arms, the U.S. has reserved the option of using nuclear weapons to respond to a nonnuclear Soviet attack. This policy of extending nuclear deterrence to conventional conflicts has kept the peace. But it is dangerous. It blurs the line between conventional and nuclear war, and by threatening "limited" nuclear war it opens the door to a nuclear holocaust since no one knows whether a limited nuclear war can be kept limited. The most effective way to eliminate that danger, and thus eliminate the greatest existing risk of nuclear war, is to make this kind of extended deterrence unnecessary: to right the conventional balance by radically bolstering allied forces, particularly on the West European frontier. NATO could then deter a conventional attack without having to threaten to wage nuclear war.

One of Schell's dictums is that compared to the peril of a nuclear holocaust, all other human values pale into insignificance, indeed, lose their meaning because they lose their context. If the antinuclear crusaders really believe that, they should be clamoring for increased conventional forces to reduce the European imbalance. They aren't. The reason is that the freeze crusade, which springs from deeply felt antiwar and antiarmament sentiments, is not comfortable with the thought that preventing nuclear war may require a radically enlarged conventional defense. Furthermore, one of the major appeals of the antinuclear movement is the promise to halt the economic drain caused by "useless" nuclear weapons and to redirect resources to human needs. But a shift away from strategic to conventional weapons would be very expensive. Our reliance on nuclear weapons—and the current conventional balance in Europe—results in large part from a desire to *reduce* defense spending. In the 1950s we decided to buy defense in Europe on the cheap. Rather than match the vast armies and tank forces of the Warsaw Pact, we decided to go nuclear, because, as John Foster Dulles put it, it offered "more bang for the buck."

But the European defense balance has become more unstable since Dulles's day. In the 1950s the U.S. threatened "massive retaliation." If the Soviets crossed into Western Europe, we would attack the Russian homeland with a strategic nuclear strike. When the Russians acquired the same capacity against the U.S., that threat lost its credibility. The Kennedy Administration adopted a new policy of "flexible response," a euphemism for a limited nuclear war. Under the new doctrine, the U.S. reserved the right to use theater nuclear weapons on the battlefield to thwart a conventional Soviet attack. That has been our policy ever since. (Ronald Reagan did not invent it, although he has the habit of throwing it around more casually and publicly than other Presidents.) This doctrine has troubled many Americans, but as long as the U.S. was not prepared to challenge the Soviet conventional superiority in Europe, nor prepared to abandon its European allies, there seemed no other choice.

Enter the auxiliary brigade of the antinuclear movement: four former high Administration officials, two of whom, under President Kennedy, gave us "limited nuclear war" (Robert McNamara and McGeorge Bundy); one of whom gave us "containment" (George Kennan); and one of whom gave us SALT I (Gerard Smith). Two weeks ago they opened an entirely new front in the crusade. They called for the adoption of a "no-first-use" policy on nuclear weapons. It was a renunciation of "flexible response" and of "extended deterrence." (They would retain extended deterrence in one restricted sense: as a retaliation for a Soviet *nuclear* attack on Western Europe, an unlikely possibility since the Soviets are prepared to renounce first use, and since with their conventional advantage they have no reason to attack with nuclear weapons.)

The problem with folding our nuclear umbrella, as the four wise men themselves acknowledged, is that, unaccompanied by conventional rearmament, it means the end of the Western alliance and the abandonment in particular of West Germany to Soviet intimidation and blackmail. The other problem with a no-first-use policy is that it might paradoxically increase the chances of nuclear war. Today a war between the U.S. and the Soviets is deterred at its origin: since even the slightest conventional conflict between them carries the threat of escalating into a nuclear one, neither happens. The no-first-use policy moves the "firebreak" from the line dividing war from peace to the line dividing conventional war from nuclear war. It trades the increased chance of conventional war (because now less dangerous and more "thinkable") for a decreased chance of such a war becoming nuclear. But no one can guarantee that *in extremis*, faced with a massive Soviet invasion of Western Europe, the U.S. would stick to its no-first-use pledge. Thus, by making a European war thinkable, this policy could, whatever its intentions, lead to a nuclear war.

Unless, that is, we have the conventional forces to preserve the original firebreak between war and peace. Thus, to prevent both political and (possibly) nuclear calamity, a no-first-use pledge must be accompanied, indeed preceded, by a serious conventional buildup of Western forces on the European frontier. The problem with McNamara et al. is that although they acknowledge this need, they treat it very casually—certainly with nothing like the urgency with which they call for abandoning extended deterrence. They speak only vaguely of the need for "review" and "study" of conventional military needs, of whether the political will exists in the West for such a buildup, and of "whether we Americans have a durable and effective answer to our military manpower needs in the present all-volunteer active and reserve forces" (they cannot quite bring themselves to say the word "draft"). Their eagerness to be the first off the blocks with a no-first-use policy is obvious. Their reluctance to urge on their antinuclear allies the only responsible and safe (and costly) means of achieving it is lamentable. The result of their highly publicized, grossly unbalanced proposal is predictable: another support in the complex and highly vulnerable structure of deterrence has been weakened. The world will be no safer for it.

Despite the prophesies of Schell, the pandering of the freeze-riding politicians, and the posturing of the four wise men—and the good intentions of millions of concerned Americans caught up in the antinuclear maelstrom—there is no need to reinvent nuclear policy. There *is* a need for arms control: SALT II is the best transition to real reductions. There *is* a need to avoid limited nuclear war: rebuilding our conventional strength and perhaps reintroducing the draft would reduce that risk. These proposals are neither new nor exciting. Unlike Schell's crusade, they don't promise to restore "the wholeness and meaning of life." They don't suggest that "the passion and will that we need to save ourselves would flood into our lives. Then the walls of indifference, inertia, and coldness that now isolate each of us from others, and all of us from the past and future generations, would melt, like snow in the spring." They don't promise to set right "our disordered instinctual life." That is because working to reduce the chances of nuclear war is not an exercise in psychotherapy. It is not a romance. It is mundane work in pursuit of mundane objectives: a modest program of nuclear modernization, SALT II, and a bigger conventional defense. These measures will not cure anomie, but will help to maintain deterrence, that difficult abstraction on which our values and our safety depends.

QUESTIONS FOR CRITICAL ANALYSIS

1. Several times Krauthammer makes the point that defense weapons threaten peace while weapons of aggression assure peace. Write a paragraph exposing such an idea as doublespeak. Write a second paragraph defending the idea. Which paragraph more accurately reflects your opinion?
2. What political events have happened since Krauthammer wrote the essay? Point out some of his references that are outdated or no longer valid.
3. What does Krauthammer mean when he says, "The freeze is not a plan; it is a sentiment"? What connotations does the word "sentiment" have? Describe Krauthammer's tone in this and other instances when he describes opposing views. How does his tone affect your reading of the essay?
4. What is Krauthammer's opinion of Jonathan Schell and his arguments? How does he treat Schell's views? Which author do you agree with? Why?
5. *The People's Guide to National Defense,** pointing out that many people feel once a country has the ability to destroy another, it does not need to increase its nuclear arsenal, quoted Admiral Rickover: "One missile-carrying submarine carries enough thermonuclear warheads to devastate every Russian city of more than 100,000. The 160 MIRVs on one Pøseidon submarine could kill 30 million Soviets." How many nuclear weapons do you think we need to deter war?

QUESTIONS FOR STRUCTURAL ANALYSIS

1. Why does Krauthammer open his essay with the Churchill quote? What does it mean? How does it relate to the point Krauthammer makes in the essay?
2. Restate the thesis in your own words. Do you agree with Krauthammer's point of view? Why, or why not?
3. Describe Krauthammer's argument style. (To follow the argument better, make an outline of his major points and the supporting evidence for each point.) What opposing views does he present? How does he deal with them? Do you think he is fair? Why, or why not?
4. What evidence does Krauthammer use to support his thesis? Are you convinced by his arguments?
5. How does Krauthammer's use of military and political terms and acronyms affect your reading of the essay? What do the acronyms stand for?

---

*By Sheila Tobias, Peter Goudinoff, Stefan Leader, Shelah Leader. New York: William Morrow, 1982.

The Threat of Peace

Topics for Writing Essays

Many of the questions following each essay can serve as appropriate writing suggestions. The topics listed below expand the prereading exercises, but they can be used without completing that step first.

1. Rabi describes the successful explosion of the atomic bomb as "a new understanding of man." What does he mean by that? Explain how man's understanding of himself changed through the creation of the atomic bomb. When you write your essay, you may find it useful to refer to several of the essays from this reader. (Appropriate ones include those by Rabi, Erikson, and Schell in this section, as well as those by Mojtabai, Hersey, Laurence, Bush, Wilson, Einstein, Feynman, Jaspers, and Carson in other sections.) Write your essay for a thoughtful reader who is concerned but not very clear about the differences between scientific and military approaches to atomic energy.
2. Is nuclear war the provence of politicians and the military alone? What is a citizen's responsibility? Write an essay for the student paper in which you examine what the average person can do with respect to nuclear war. You may want to use material referred to by Krauthammer as well as his essay and those by Mojtabai, Schell, Erikson, and Rabi.
3. Write an essay to your grandchild explaining how your generation worked to avoid the holocaust of nuclear war. You may want to focus on specific world events, on abstract arguments, on activist groups, and so forth.

Research Possibilities

1. Krauthammer, among others, does not agree with Schell's analysis of post-nuclear war America. Read essays and articles both in support of and critical of Schell's argument (which was published in *The Fate of the Earth*, 1982). Compare and analyze the arguments of each side and write a paper explaining why you agree with one side or the other. Address your essay to a politically astute reader, concerned about nuclear war but not familiar with Schell's views.
2. At the end of his essay, Rabi suggests two paths people could take after August 1945: (1) building up an arsenal of atomic and nuclear weapons, and (2) nations cooperating in an effort to find peaceful uses of atomic energy. Find out what kinds of activities have been pursued along the second path and how successful they have been. Write a report to a reader who does not think that anything has been done to encourage international cooperation in such activities.

3. Krauthammer argues that it does not make sense to keep reinventing arms control initiatives when SALT II has been signed by the Soviet Union and offers a path toward peace. What do you know about SALT II? When was it proposed? Why did the U.S. government reject it? Conduct library research to find out the background, content, and context of the SALT II negotiations. You may also want to interview a professor who specializes in U.S.-Soviet relations. Write a report on the U.S. response to SALT II for a reader who does not know much about SALT II but has read Krauthammer's essay. You will want either to agree with Krauthammer and support SALT II or refute his arguments.
4. In his first message to Congress, 1789, President George Washington said: "To be prepared for war is one of the most effective means of preserving peace." Obviously, Krauthammer uses this reasoning to support maintaining nuclear arsenals in the late twentieth century. Examine America's military policies historically—selecting a specific time period or event—and argue in support of or against Washington's statement. Try to convince your reader to agree with your position.

PART FOUR
JOURNALISM

*T*HE *P*OWER OF THE *N*EWS

Politically aware people base their knowledge on facts read in the newspapers. Where do newspapers get their stories? Can we trust them to give us the real *news? How do they control our behavior through their presentation of events? MacNeil's essay states the problem: the public does not trust the news media. The other essays in this section offer some answers: Lapham asserts that the media is defined by the expectations and assumptions of its audience; Goldstein believes that reporters sometimes bankrupt journalistic ethics; and Parenti claims the media is controlled by a conspiracy of the ruling class.*

*T*HE *M*EDIA AND THE *P*UBLIC *T*RUST

ROBERT MACNEIL

Troubled by the time limitations on television news reporting, Robert MacNeil (1931–) developed the idea of presenting daily in-depth analyses of major news stories and, since October 1975, he has worked as coanchor of the MacNeil/Lehrer News Hour *on public television. MacNeil's dissatisfaction with news coverage was the focus of* The People Machine: The Influence of Television on American Politics *(1968), his indictment of network television's preoccupation with entertainment rather than news. As reprinted below, "The Media and the Public Trust" is an adaptation of a speech presented to an audience of executives and engineers at Edison Electric Institute's 1985 annual convention.*

Before you begin reading: *Think about your attitude toward the media. Do you trust them to tell you the truth about news events? Write as many questions as you can think of to ask a major journalist about the ethical standards of the media.*

◆

IF I WERE IN YOUR SHOES, ONE OF THE THINGS THAT MIGHT concern me today would be how to communicate to the American public through the filter of the mass media. If you were in my shoes you might be concerned about how to be serious and how to be fair in an environment when your competition often seems to be a lot more successful not worrying about seriousness or fairness.

It seems to me that the difficulty of being fair and serious in today's competitive media world is one of the realities behind the present friction between the news media and the public. Let me explain.

There is a pretty general feeling in the news media at present that their relations with the public are in something like a crisis state.

Just how grave the situation is and what, if anything, should be done about it, is a matter of debate. But there is plenty of evidence that it is grave, evidence that the public trust is an ebbing tide.

There is the large number of libel suits, a growing trend for juries to find against journalist defendants and to award huge damages to the plaintiffs. They are not always upheld on appeal but they reveal an attitude. Eugene Patterson, editor of the *St. Petersburg Times*, says, "Juries are the American people. They want to punish us."

Then there are the megaton libel suits, like General William Westmoreland's, Ariel Sharon's and Senator Paul Laxalt's, brought, the media defendants believe, with punitive or intimidating intent.

There are the opinion surveys which can be read to indicate some decline in public confidence, or can be read the other way. The glass can often seem two-thirds full and one-third empty. The findings are inconsistent and sometimes contradictory.

They also show distressing assumptions about what government could or should do to the press and amazing ignorance of the First Amendment—all coupled with a general applause for the abstract idea of a free press.

There is a proliferation of groups of aroused citizens wanting to discipline or curb or regulate journalists. One of them, Fairness In Media, was trying to buy equity control of CBS to become Dan Rather's boss and is now applauding Ted Turner's takeover bid.

There is an unquantifiable, but, to all of us working in the media, evident spirit of rancor abroad in the land. When the Reagan Administration initially excluded the press from Grenada, and the public applauded, *Time* magazine reported that its letters ran eight-to-one against the press and the opposition "was expressed in gleeful, even vengeful terms."

David Gergen, then White House communications director, commented, "Unfortunately, kicking the press is a sure-fire applause line with almost any audience."

So, why, editors began to ask, do they hate us?

Survey after survey shows specific irritants turning up consistently. Significant parts of the public—minorities, true, but large minorities—think the media are often inaccurate, unfair, biased, intrusive of privacy, unethical, arrogant, and preoccupied with bad news.

It is a verdict pretty well summed up in a pop song "Dirty Linen," sung by Don Henley:

> Dirty little secrets
> Dirty little lies
> We got our dirty little fingers
> In everybody's pie.
> We love to cut you down to size.

And the refrain:

> Kick 'em when they're up
> Kick 'em when they're down.

And there is the Anne Murray song:

> There's a local paper rolled up in a rubber band.
> One more sad story's one more than I can stand.
> Just once how I'd like to see the headlines say:
> 'Not much to print today,
> Couldn't find nothin' bad to say.'

And the bulletin of the American Society of Newspaper Editors, which printed those songs, also pointed out that in novels, plays, movies, and television shows recently, the public sees journalists in a very unfavorable light.

Why do they hate us?

Daniel Schorr, until recently chief correspondent of Cable News Network, said last year, "The words 'power of the press' always carried a white hat connotation of power exercised for good. But 'power of the media' has a black hat sound of power exercised against people."

According to opinion surveys, many Americans resented the behavior of some television crews intruding on the grief of bereaved families after the Marine barracks were blown up in Lebanon. The public seems to discount the defense of journalists that some such families find release and catharsis in exposing their grief.

I remember very hesitantly approaching the father of a boy killed in Vietnam for permission to film his funeral. His son's name was Ron. He said he was glad: "It will give Ron's death some meaning."

People felt like that after Lebanon. But the public remembers the crews that staked out houses and filmed as Marine officers delivered the news of a loved one's death. The public remembers the shrieks. The public may even want to hear them and then feel ashamed of voyeurism.

When the *Washington Post* returned a Pulitzer Prize because its young reporter, Janet Cooke, confessed to inventing an eight-year-old heroin addict, 61 percent of Americans sampled by Gallup said they believed "very little" or "only some" of the news we print or broadcast. Only 33 percent said they believed most news reports.

Why do they hate us?

Some thoughtful journalists suggest we may have been wearing the First Amendment too brazenly, not as a shield, but as a challenge.

Michael O'Neill, former editor of the *New York Daily News*, said two years ago, "We have to be careful not to claim more than we have a right to claim in the public interest. After all, it is the public's interest, not ours."

Lou Boccardi, president of the Associated Press, points out that the media occupy a different place in this society than they used to and he wonders, "Have we reached a point where we must recognize an obligation not to do some of the things the First Amendment gives us every right to do?"

Many other explanations are offered, for example, that we are the purveyors of bad news.

Some think that journalism, the media, has become just another big institution, like the others Americans suspect of too much power. Interestingly, the surveys often show that people love their local paper or news show, but hate newspapers or television in general.

Everyone in the media has his own explanation for what is going on, and I would like to offer a partial explanation of my own this afternoon.

I believe that there is a rising public expectation of fairness, that a higher standard of fairness is demanded of our profession now than in the old days when journalism was local, pointed, and hot. The rise of a national journalism has long ago cooled off the partisanship. The days have gone when a paper like the *Los Angeles Times* could deny access to political opponents. The trend today is to open up access, to broaden the range of views printed.

From the beginning, broadcasters, using limited public airways, could not be sharply partisan, first out of practicality, later by regulation. Some feel that broadcasters, who have influenced print in so many other ways, thus created expectations of fairness among readers and that made newspapers more objective, as did declining competition and probably a better educated public.

Fairness—even-handedness, balance, objectivity—is the demand I hear more consistently from the public than anything else, and the greatest complaint I hear is lack of it. The public defines fairness very broadly and is spurred on by people with axes to grind who want to define fairness their own way.

I see a danger that unless the journalism profession redefines fairness and its importance to us, others will increasingly try to define it for us—and perhaps succeed.

I see a number of ways in which the news media today may be unconsciously working against fairness, or stimulating a public perception of unfairness.

I think there is, frankly, scorn for fairness in some quarters. It may be left over from the new journalism, which died because it excused mediocre practitioners from the drudgery of gathering facts, and because people got tired of reality filtered through perceptions no more interesting than their own. In some quarters, it is clearly a yearning for straight advocacy journalism, which regards fairness as effete and unmanly and thinks telling both sides of a story and letting the public decide the merits is wimpy and even irresponsible.

There is an attitude common in the media that any good journalist can apply common sense and quickly fathom what is right and what is wrong in any complicated issue and that professional pride demands that he say so. The targets of this often facile journalism—the company, the school, the military, the hospital—see the superficiality, the shallowness of the story and consider it unfair.

Coupled with this attitude is one in which a reporter or a camera crew act as though their presence, their action in covering a story, is more important than the event they are covering. People love that!

Then there is the more cynical belief that the American public loves the myths of good guys and bad guys and wants the real world fitted into such molds, so someone always has to be the bad guy.

I also see what the public may perceive as unfairness in the aggressive negativism, sometimes of a rather theatrical, posturing kind, that has pervaded so much reporting, especially from Washington, since Vietnam and Watergate. It is as though the media has not yet digested these events but still felt obliged to duel with ghosts.

There is a difference between skepticism and disbelief. It is true that all the icons of our beliefs trembled on the walls in the decade from 1965 to 1975. Scarcely an institution went untouched. Most of them have been rehabilitated in the public mind, including the presidency.

Yet in Washington, I feel that some media representatives are continuing to act out a ritual hostility learned when they thought government was lying to them everyday about virtually everything. It may have started as a collective professional attitude of "Boy, they're never going to pull the wool over our eyes again."

It may be frustration over their increasingly smooth manipulation by recent administrations.

It may be the influence of television exposure, which feeds on adversarial confrontation. Never ignore how the values fashionable in entertainment programs inform the journalistic end of the medium. All television gravitates towards drama, and what passes for drama is often belligerence, people barking at each other, like soap opera actors, sounding vehement to make up for cardboard characters or too little rehearsal time.

So we have the media sounding vehement, belligerent, barking at President Reagan, who responds by grinning ruefully. Who is going to win that kind of contest?

Perhaps reporters feel the climate of the time requires that they sound hostile so that they will appear to be tough.

But what if that merely feeds a perception the surveys show that the press is simply being rude—in the words of a Citizens Choice study, being "too hard" on government, in this case the president. What if the effect is to substitute in the public mind, and perhaps in the press' own, this rather theatrical toughness for the real thing?

Few people in the business think the news media are tougher on this president than on his recent predecessors. Yet the public thinks so. They think we are picking on him. So we may be reinforcing public perception of unfairness without any corresponding trenchancy to back it up. It would be like being hanged for rape when the only crime was a little necking.

But another effect could be to strengthen the hand of government, any administration, in manipulating the media, to have the public think that we are unfair to government.

It must be puzzling to the public, then, to see the increasing use of unnamed sources, which implies some complicity with government. Does it strain credibility to have us barking at the administration like a watchdog outside while licking hands and eating scraps from every stray official inside?

But broaden the definition of fairness even farther. It is very difficult to be fair when you have to squeeze complex reality into too small a space or time. It is a criticism more often made of television than print but not exclusively. Time and space are arbitrarily parcelled out by assumptions about the importance of a story and the degree of public interest. But if the slot is too small, all but the newest facts or opinions get left out—the context, the qualifications, the contrary views, the explanations, extenuations—all the things which tend to make the treatment fair, or seem unfair if they are left out.

By an even wider conception of fairness still, some might argue that it is unfair to the public because such a story gives too simple or lopsided a view of reality.

Well, I am now skating on thinner ice, but I suggest each of these points is a plausible ingredient, if a small one, in the discontent we face.

But the overall question of fairness is not small, and I will conclude with a far more obvious example.

Of course the reason all this is so much in our minds right now is because the macho arm of American journalism—the commandos of the Fourth Estate, the investigative reporters—have recently been on trial in the most spectacular way.

There has been a lot of media relief that *Time* magazine was only found guilty of an inaccuracy, not libel, and that General Westmoreland withdrew his case against CBS. Clearly that relief is justified in the sense that neither case advanced or encouraged the use of the court system by public officials for punitive revenge on journalists who have attacked their reputations. They may even have served the purpose of clarifying the need for some restraint in damage awards.

That is looking at it from the press point of view—the press anxious to preserve its clear and necessary right to criticize public officials.

But look at it from the public point of view, and take the CBS-Westmoreland case because it was an American official involved and, not irrelevantly, a man many admired for his long and distinguished career of service to this country.

The trial judge and the CBS lawyer said early on to the jury and to the public, the issue is not fairness. And to prove libel it was not. The general had to prove not that CBS was unfair but that it knowingly, maliciously, and recklessly broadcast a false report. And yet outside the confines of the courtroom, for most of the American people, I strongly suspect the issue was fairness.

By its own admission, CBS had not treated General Westmoreland by its own internal standards of fairness. Since the aborted trial, CBS says the documentary* was fair and accurate, but that is not quite what CBS said in the internal investigation conducted by Burton Benjamin.

He said the issue of whether General Westmoreland cooked the books on enemy troop strength in Vietnam for political reasons was "obviously and historically controversial," meaning there were two sides, it was not a proved case, and that there was imbalance in presenting the two sides. General Westmoreland and his one defender got a total of 5 minutes and 59 seconds. Sam Adams, the former CIA official who was his chief accuser, and his eight supporting witnesses got 19 minutes and 19 seconds. Sympathetic witnesses were coddled, one was interviewed twice to improve his testimony, and there were other violations of CBS news standards.

Benjamin also pointed out that the documentary had not included portions of an interview with President Johnson in which he said he was fully aware of the size of the enemy force that confronted the U.S. in the TET offensive—which would have detracted significantly from the impression that he was kept in the dark by Westmoreland.

To its credit, CBS acknowledged the Benjamin report and finally released it in full. The network said it would have been better if the word "conspiracy" had not been used, if more people who disagreed with the premise had been interviewed and if there had been strict compliance with CBS news standards. Those are pretty big "ifs."

If those "ifs" had been followed, the documentary would have been perceived as a fair, objective inquiry, charges made and charges denied, not a trial on television, with CBS in full control of the evidence, playing prosecutor, judge, and jury. Perceived as a fair inquiry, it would have been much harder for General Westmoreland to dismiss as a hatchet job. More to the point, it seems very unlikely there would have been a libel suit at all.

Perhaps CBS' conclusions about General Westmoreland's conduct were completely correct. The network says so and late testimony in the trial was clearly pointing in that direction. Perhaps the reality was a good deal more complicated than they made it seem. It was certainly a legitimate if not a very new piece of Vietnam history to subject to this dramatic inquiry. But it can be argued that it was a public service. The war was tragically expensive for the United States, and the judgments good and bad that prosecuted the war deserve the fullest airing.

But why is it necessary in a piece of journalism, however right it thought it was, to treat a distinguished American—or anyone else—less fairly than he would be treated in a court of law if charged with a criminal offense?

It makes ordinary people ask, what was the motive? What was the animus? Was it intended to be a serious effort to contribute to the nation's knowledge of

*"The Uncounted Enemy: A Vietnam Deception," one-hour documentary aired by CBS television on January 23, 1982.

the war while some principal characters were still around? Or was it the jungle motive—to get him?

I single CBS out because they are a great news organization and they had the courage to single themselves out in this case by insisting that this hot piece of journalism be tested against CBS traditions and experience. And I suggest that those traditions encompass and assume a sense of fairness that would satisfy most reasonable people.

It is a good example because the frailties of the mighty make us all tremble.

I hope "The Uncounted Enemy: A Vietnam Deception" does not become a model for American journalism emulated by others, taught in journalism schools, as what you can get away with.

The First Amendment does not require fairness but I think the American public is beginning to.

In one of the Federalist Papers, Alexander Hamilton asks, "What is the liberty of the press? . . . Its security, whatever fine declarations may be inserted in any constitution respecting it, must altogether depend on public opinion, and on the general spirit of the people and the government." And so the liberty of the American press has depended for two centuries. And I believe that journalistic carelessness or arrogance that ignores basic fairness—a decent respect for the opinions of mankind—will invite attacks on that liberty, and turn the general spirit of the people more hostile.

One survey found majorities of 70 to 80 percent of the American people in favor of laws requiring newspapers and television to give political opponents of major parties and opponents on controversial issues equal coverage. In other words, the public would support laws which are transparently unconstitutional.

Until now, American journalists have ignored or laughed off such views, confident that the right-thinking majority would protect them, and when their enemies had them surrounded, the First Amendment cavalry would gallop up just in time.

Perhaps it always will and perhaps it will not. But if the media want to buy more insurance against public indifference to the First Amendment—fairness is a small price to pay.

QUESTIONS FOR CRITICAL ANALYSIS

1. What evidence does MacNeil offer to support his position that the public trust in the news media is subsiding? Is his evidence compelling?
2. How do you define the role of the news media? According to MacNeil, what contradictory notions does the public hold about this role? Why are these ideas contradictory?
3. How does MacNeil define the "rising public expectation of fairness"? Do you agree

with his premise that the public expects the press to be fair? What do you base your opinion on?

4. Why does the news media sometimes exhibit an "aggressive negativism"? How does that attitude come across to the public? How does the public react?
5. Where do "unnamed sources" come from? Does it color your response to a news story when you read that it is based on these sources? Why, or why not?

QUESTIONS FOR STRUCTURAL ANALYSIS

1. It is clear from the first sentence that MacNeil is delivering a speech. How do the first two paragraphs establish his topic? If you were in the audience, how would you respond to this introduction?
2. Early in the article, MacNeil repeats the refrain, "Why do they hate us?" three times. What different answers does he give each time?
3. What attitudes are revealed by the lyrics MacNeil quotes? Why did he illustrate his point by popular songs? Name some unflattering portrayals of journalists in novels, plays, movies, or television shows.
4. MacNeil presents scenarios which he can later reject. Look, for example, at his two-paragraph discussion beginning, "I think there is, frankly, scorn for fairness in some quarters." How does he present these journalists? Can you think of examples to support this characterization? Is it fair? Why, or why not?
5. MacNeil refers to the news media's treatment of the Ronald Reagan administration (pre-1985), *Time*'s article on Israeli Defense Minister Ariel Sharon and CBS's documentary, "The Uncounted Enemy," about General William Westmoreland. What is his point in mentioning these reports? Why does he include the *Time* magazine and CBS stories? Do you know anything about these incidents, and were you able to follow his analysis?
6. What is MacNeil's conclusion? Is it effective? If you had attended the lecture, how would you describe it to a friend?

GILDING THE NEWS

LEWIS LAPHAM

Lewis Lapham (1935–) has been a reporter with the San Francisco Examiner *and the* New York Herald Tribune, a contributor to Saturday Evening Post *and* Life, *and editor of* Harper's. *"Gilding the News," which appeared in* Harper's *in July 1981, analyzes the nature of the news media by studying the expectations and assumptions of its audience. Society makes contradictory demands on reporters, expecting news to be entertaining as well as true, and, as a result, the line between fiction and fact becomes difficult to distinguish.*

Before you begin reading: *What role does the press serve in a democratic society? In your reading notebook list five verbs to describe that role. Write a short paragraph expanding each verb into a description of the press's responsibility.*

◆

I really look with commiseration over the great body of my fellow citizens who, reading newspapers, live and die in the belief that they have known something of what has been passing in the world in their time.
HARRY TRUMAN

I don't hold with high falutin' talk. . . . I'm a newspaperman. I tell stories.
DEREK JAMESON, Former Editor, The *Daily Express* (London)

IN NEW YORK THESE DAYS THE LAWYERS ADVISING BOOK publishers on libel matters ask for revisions in the fiction. The lawyers no longer make much of a distinction between what is true, what might be true, what a plaintiff will say is true. If the author of a lascivious novel has portrayed an actress living in California, and if somebody knows a woman who vaguely fits the description and can afford the price of a lawsuit, maybe it is safer to change the character into a man and move his story to Connecticut. With works of nonfiction the lawyers take even more elaborate precautions. The anonymous source of information becomes as adept as a secret agent at moving his place of residence, acquiring a new occupation, revising his nationality and date of birth.

Given the dubious composition of the stuff sold in the literary markets as imitations of reality, the indignant denunciations of the *Washington Post* in April seemed slightly forced. The *Post* had received a Pulitzer Prize for a news story that proved to be a work of fiction, and for a period of several days alarmed editorial writers in newspapers around the country felt called upon to defend the honor of the profession. Yet, it was true that the once glorious *Post* had defiled the holy places of journalism, and it was a terrible sight to behold, but let nobody think that such blasphemy had become habitual among the ladies and gentlemen of the fourth estate. No, no, said the collective editorial voice of the nation, we are good boys and girls; some of us are statesmen, and we never tell lies.

The offending story, a melodramatic account of an eight-year-old black child addicted to heroin, had been written by a young black reporter named Janet Cooke. It appeared on the front page of the *Post* in September of last year under the headline JIMMY'S WORLD. The boy was not further identified on the grounds that the reporter had promised to protect her sources of information. When the editors of the *Post* learned that Miss Cooke had received the Pulitzer Prize, they sent her notes of fond congratulation.

That was on Tuesday. Within twenty-four hours it was discovered that Miss Cooke had invented Jimmy. The boy was a composite figure, a fictional device pasted together out of Miss Cooke's notes in order to personify her impressions of drug addiction in the slum of southeast Washington. Her editors abruptly declared their praise inoperative. Benjamin Bradlee, the executive editor of the *Post*, characterized Miss Cooke as "a pathological liar," and compared her treachery to that of the infamous Richard Nixon.

The *Post* returned the prize, and on the Sunday after its disgrace the paper published an 18,000-word act of contrition written by its own ombudsman. The confession took up almost as much space as the news of the attempted assassination of a president, and the inflated self-importance of the writing (implying that the United States might relapse into barbarism because a newspaper had trifled with the facts) was characteristic of the "agony" suffered by the press as a whole. As might have been expected, it was the *New York Times* that achieved the most finely articulated tone of unctuousness. Every other reputable newspaper, said the *Times* (assuming without question its own comfortable place among the company of the elect), had sustained an affront to its dignity and loss of its credibility because "the fabricated event, the made-up quote, the fictitious source . . . debases communication, and democracy."

On the heathen side of the reaction, people bearing grudges against the media expressed an ill-concealed delight in the *Post*'s humiliation. Mr. Nixon was rumored to have smiled when told of the sham in Washington. Commodores of yacht clubs were reported to be gleefully beating their hands on tables. Here was proof of everything they had been saying for years about the contemptible falsehoods circulated by the media in the name of conscience. How apt that the *Post* should have been cast as the villain of the piece. It was the *Post* that had hounded poor Mr. Nixon out of the White House; it was the *Post* that had been memorialized in a Hollywood romance starring Dustin Hoffman and Robert

Redford; it was the *Post* that embodied all Spiro Agnew had meant to imply about the sanctimonious hypocrisy of the liberal Eastern establishment. And now here was the *Post* passing off the counterfeit stuff of fiction as the coin of truth. God's will had been done, and to people envious or resentful of the media it was once again possible to believe that justice had not vanished from the earth.

ARS LONGA, VITA BREVIS

Whether reading the high-minded explanations in the papers, or listening to the sermons of corporate vice presidents once grievously wronged by a correspondent from *Newsweek*, I noticed that relatively few people took the trouble to wonder about the nature of the media. They wished to assign to the newspapers and television networks an almost magical omnipotence, and it didn't occur to them that much of the information they received in the course of a week or a year—in newsletters, stock-market analysis, gossip, medical diagnosis, State Department announcements, scientific journals—sooner or later proved to be a figment of somebody's imagination. Within a few weeks of Miss Cooke's fall from grace, a columnist for the New York *Daily News* by the name of Michael Daly resigned his space because he had been accused of publishing a fraudulent report from Belfast. Mr. Daly apparently made use of quotations from a pseudonymous British gunner named "Christopher Spell" and then went on to pretend that he had been present when a British army patrol came under attack from Irish youths throwing gasoline bombs. Michael J. O'Neill, the editor of the paper, deplored the use of what were called "questionable journalistic practices." Mr. Daly said that he had employed those techniques in "300 columns over two years."

The confusion about the media seems widely distributed, and maybe people need to be reminded that the media tell stories. There is nothing reprehensible about telling stories. Some are more complicated than others. Gibbon told a story, and so did Einstein. Almost everything presented in the theater of the news constitutes a kind of story, and to some extent all the principal players, whether identified as Henry Kissinger, Billy Martin, or Jean Harris, appear as composite figures, their quotations fitted into a context suitable to the occasion, their images made up of fragments as easily transposed as the bits and pieces of a mosaic or a documentary film. Less than six weeks after Jean Harris had gone to prison for killing Dr. Herman Tarnower, NBC made a television movie of her trial, with Ellen Burstyn in the part of an imagined Jean Harris.

The distinctions between the degrees of fabrication have less to do with the chicanery of editors than with the desires of an audience that pays for what it wants to hear and stands willing to accept the conventions proper to its place and time. We are all engaged in the same enterprise, all of us caught up in the making of analogies and metaphors, all of us seeking evocations and representations of what we can recognize as appropriately human. Stories move from truths to facts, not the other way around, and the tellers of tales endeavor to convey the essence of a thing. Given the perspective of centuries and ten years to write a book, the historian finds it hard enough to discover the meaning of a single event. The journalist usually has a few hours to write and the perspective of last week. Why then expect the poor fellow to revise the history of the world? Journalists have less in common with diplomats and soothsayers than they do with vagabond poets.

Unfortunately for Mr. Daly and Miss Cooke, the literary conventions of the daily newspaper forbid the use of fictitious characters. It is permissible to rely on the anonymous source, i.e., an informant who may or may not exist and who may or may not have said what the reporter eventually attributes to him in the paper. If a reporter telephones an acquaintance at the Defense Department and asks for information about events in El Salvador or the State Department, the acquaintance can elect to speak "off the record." Protected by an invisible cloak, the acquaintance can then repeat as fact the gossip overheard the day before yesterday about Secretary Haig's wish to make himself emperor of all the Americas. The anonymous source thus moves even further offstage, and what appears in the next day's paper is a quotation of a quotation dressed up in the rubric of authority.

It is also permissible in a daily newspaper to sustain those myths that its audience wishes to believe. During the presidential campaign of 1976 the media wanted to believe that Jimmy Carter was a romantic figure embodying the rural virtues of the imaginary South. The media's belief reflected the wish of their audience. An influential audience in 1976 felt that the country needed to be pardoned for the sins committed in Vietnam and Washington. Who better to play the part of the redeemer than an unknown evangelist from Plains, Georgia? The media thoughtfully left out of its accounts those aspects of Mr. Carter's character that might have confused the image.

The conventional definitions of reality suffer little contradiction because the media have neither the resources nor the desire to prove them wrong. The connection between the use of drugs and the committing of crimes, for instance, rests on a mythopoeic interpretation of the facts; so do the conceptions of *Realpolitik* and détente; so also do the explications of the Vietnam war, the justifications for profit and loss, the discussions of the grand abstraction known as the third world. Speaking through the personae of the appropriate officials, a newspaper can lend its voice to the pieties of the age. What it cannot do, at least not yet, is resort to such a crude device as the fabrication of a composite figure.

Other instruments of the media have been playing on the device at least since the early 1960s, with varying degrees of success. So many of the books and magazine articles of the last twenty years have been shaped out of an alloy of fact and fiction that even the libel lawyers have trouble separating the truth into its component elements. *All the President's Men*, a book written in part by Robert

Woodward, Miss Cooke's metropolitan editor, introduced the character of "Deep Throat," a source of information otherwise unidentified, to whom the authors assigned quotations inimical to the interests of President Nixon. It is possible that the *nom de presse* represented an individual well placed within the White House at the time of the drama in question; it is also possible that the name served as a disguise for several informants. Given the mythical requirements of the year in which the book was published, it didn't much matter whether "Deep Throat" had descended to earth in the body of a man. People believed that he existed, and that was sufficient to the purposes of the moment.

For many years a substantial number of people believed that Carlos Castaneda had discovered a sorcerer in the Mexican desert and that his name was Don Juan. In 1966, Truman Capote published *In Cold Blood*, a book that he described as a nonfiction novel because he had rearranged the objects of scene and character in such a way as to improve the interior decor of what he called reality. Gail Sheehy established her reputation as an investigative reporter by writing a magazine article about a prostitute and a pimp, both of them collages pasted together in much the same way that Janet Cooke made the pastiche of Jimmy. In David Halberstam's book *The Best and the Brightest*, few of the quotations from or about his cast of public men bear the weight of attribution. In 1977 Alex Haley won a Pulitzer Prize for *Roots*, a romance passing as history. In 1980 Norman Mailer won a Pulitzer Prize for *The Executioner's Song*, a supposedly factual account of Gary Gilmore's death, submitted to the prize committee as fiction.*

None of these observations has anything to do with literary merit. They address the questions of technique. When I first went to work for the *San Francisco Examiner* in 1957, the oldest reporter in the city room occupied the desk next to mine, and I often marveled at the ease with which he wrote the accounts of routine catastrophe. In the drawer, with a bottle of bourbon and the manuscript of the epic poem he had been writing for twenty years, he kept a looseleaf notebook filled with stock versions of maybe fifty or sixty common newspaper texts. These were arranged in alphabetical order (fires; homicides; ship collisions; etc.) and then further divided into subcategories (fires—one-, two-, and three-alarm; warehouse, apartment building; etc.). The reporter had left blank spaces for the relevant names, deaths, numbers, and street addresses. As follows: "A——alarm fire swept through a——at——St. yesterday afternoon, killing——people and causing $——in property damage."

At the *Examiner* in the late 1950s the corps of correspondents understood that what appeared in the paper constituted a kind of stage play in which cops,

*For the purposes of example I have mentioned only a few of the more well-known books of the last generation. The list could be extended through a long series of titles—books about the Bermuda Triangle or the secrets of the Pyramids, David Rorvik's clone, novels of espionage, *The Spike*, by Robert Moss and Arnaud de Borchgrave, the *romans à clef* by Harold Robbins and Irving Wallace, books about faith healers and mystics of various powers and denominations.

politicians, Russians, war heroes, and ladies of doubtful virtue all played traditional roles. The reporters further understood that the most satisfying stories (about the mayor's sexual perversities or the park commissioner's deal with the governor) never made the paper. Nobody objected to these omissions because it was assumed that the newspaper language still could more or less accurately portray the world of events. The disjunction between reality and its evocation gave the reporters a sense of their importance of "being on the inside." In the absence of decent pay, the flattery compensated them for the work of writing pageants.

TRUTH IS RELATIVE

The conventions changed in the early 1960s, shortly after the election of John F. Kennedy and the disappearance of what used to be called the avant-garde. Even in the spring of 1961, by which time I had come to New York as a reporter for the *New York Herald Tribune*, it was possible to take substantial liberties with the facts. The editor of that paper assigned me to the rewrite desk, and for nights on end I would listen to the wavering voices of correspondents at the other end of a bad phone connection in Algeria or the Congo, taking down dictation and then revising their texts in a way that conformed to the editor's expectations of the world.

On one occasion the *Tribune*'s man in Moscow telephoned a dispatch about a meeting of the Soviet Academy of Sciences at which a few scientists had made a few inoffensive remarks about the uses of technology. My editor interpreted the dispatch to mean that First Secretary Nikita Khrushchev's initiatives toward détente had been defeated by the well-known militarists in the Politburo. He instructed me to seek guidance from a professor at Columbia University who knew enough about Russian affairs to explain why the meeting heralded the advent of World War III. (It is my distinct recollection that the professor was Zbigniew Brzezinski, but I cannot be sure of this, and I doubt whether Mr. Brzezinski would remember the conversation.) Once the professor understood what was wanted he supplied the missing explanation, and the story appeared on the front page of the next day's paper under a Moscow dateline.

I did the same with the news arriving over the phone from the paper's operatives in the metropolitan police bureaus, making notes about citizens found dead in cars or arrested for homicide. Almost always I was writing about people whom I had never seen, sometimes furnishing them with motives and characterizations at which I could only guess, arranging the acceptable abstractions of the day (cold war, missile gap, new frontier) into the equations of social or political meaning. I find myself doing the same thing in the writing of this essay. Never having met Miss Cooke, and not having read her portrayal of Jimmy's World, I know only what I've read about her in the press, primarily the ombudsman's account in the *Washington Post.* Nor have I met Mr. Daly or read more than ten or twelve of his columns in the *Daily News.* On at least one level of meaning, I have only a formal or theoretical grasp of what I'm talking about; Miss Cooke and Mr. Daly appear to me as characters in a play of ideas. The same thing could be said of most of the news from Poland or the White House.

Thus abstraction doth make theologians of us all, and we exhaust ourselves in passionate arguments about things that few of us have ever seen. We talk about the third world as if it were a real place rather than a convenient symbol, about the gears of the national economy as if they were as intelligible as the gears on a bicycle. People became lifelong enemies because they disagree about the military strategy of the Soviet Union; on further investigation it generally turns out that neither antagonist speaks Russian or has been to Russia.

Within a year of President Kennedy's election the profession of journalism began to recruit apprentices from Harvard and Yale. Having enjoyed the privileges of both affluence and education, the new generation of journalists felt inhibited by the older conventions. They thought of themselves as "creative," as the possessors of "the truth" brought down from Cambridge in bound volumes, as novelists *manqués*, as the social equals of the politicians or popular celebrities about whom they were obliged to make romances. At university they had been introduced to competing theories of reality, and they had heard rumors of discoveries in the sciences that called into question the structure of knowledge, reality, and matter. Apparently matter was a force that cohered, not a substance; physicists deduced the presence of subatomic particles, otherwise invisible, by tracking their passage through a bubble chamber. Einstein's notion of relativity did to Newton's mechanics what Cubism had done to Impressionism, and it was conceivable that a man's perception of the universe depended on the intensity of his belief in that perception. If the techniques of literary criticism could be applied to the canon of weapons in Robert McNamara's Pentagon, then maybe the devices of literary fiction could be applied to the data bases of the news.

What came to be called "the new journalism" made its gaudy debut in the magazines—in *New York, Esquire, Life,* and the *Saturday Evening Post.* The form was not, in the strict sense, new. *Time* magazine had been contriving an artificial reality for years: so had the makers of newsreels and Hollywood epics. But the form seemed new when contrasted with the stodginess of the 1950s and the old doctrine that journalism concerned itself only with facts.

The techniques of the new journalism had more in common with the making of documentary films than with the writing of novels. The writer seeks to make an image, not a work of art. He begins with an attitude of mind and a mass of random observations—notes on the weather; tones of voice; landscapes; fragments of conversation; bits and pieces of historical incident; descriptions of scene; impressions of character. These materials correspond to the film maker's unedited film or the raw information received every week by the newsmagazines.

In order to impose a form on the chaos of his notes the writer decides on a premise and a point of view. He then can arrange the materials into a coherent design, as if he were fitting small stones into the pavement of a mosaic.*

It was, after all, a scientific age, supposedly capable of subtle measurement and highly technical analysis. Truth-tellers of all descriptions stood in anxious need of clothing their figures in the lineaments of reality. Otherwise, who would listen to them? Novelists and sociologists borrowed the forms of the empirical sciences, dressing up their stories in the costumes of "case histories," forcing the narrative into whatever language would carry with it the impression of truth. It was not enough to have grasped the essence of a thing; it was necessary to give it an age, a name, an address, a set of circumstances.

Janet Cooke apparently had a talent for the genre, but so also did Gail Sheehy, Norman Mailer, and Hunter Thompson. Before writing her account of Jimmy's World she mentioned to her city editor that in traveling through southeast Washington she had been told of an eight-year-old boy addicted to heroin. "That's the story," said the city editor. "Go after it. It's a front-page story." Miss Cooke obliged. If she couldn't find the boy in question, she knew that such children had been reported to exist. She invented a plausible speech for the child (plausible, at least, to the editors of the *Post*), and she described in detail the furniture of an imaginary house. Her account was not too dissimilar from the travel writing that used to appear in *National Geographic*. The explorer goes to darkest Africa and returns with an amalgam of scientific and anecdotal observation—photographs of the explorer standing with his wife and pet dik-dik, published in conjunction with reports about what the animal has been known to do or what the witch doctor might have said.

The uses of the new journalism escape the blame of critics and the resentment of prize committees if the author makes it clear to the reader that he has violated the sanctities of the facts. This can be done either with a brief digression into the first person singular, with a summary statement of method, or with a tone of voice sufficiently unique to defy classification as that of a disembodied narrator. In the hands of the less accomplished practitioners, the devices of the

---

*The similarity of the new journalism and the documentary-film technique was made plain to me in the summer of 1974, when I was invited by NBC to consider the possibility of writing a film on the multinational oil companies. The price of oil had been going up, and the Arab states had combined into a cartel known as OPEC that apparently was making trouble. The network had collected, at huge expense, fifty or sixty hours of film on Armand Hammer, the chairman of Occidental Petroleum. The trouble was that the producers didn't know what the film meant. They had all these pictures—Armand Hammer in Los Angeles; Armand Hammer talking to Edwin Newman in a corporate jet somewhere over Poland; Armand Hammer at the Hermitage in Moscow; Armand Hammer with the Libyans; miscellaneous footage of oil tankers lying at anchor in New York harbor, refineries, the Persian Gulf, Arabs carrying hawks—but what in God's name was the story? Were the oil companies good or bad? Was Armand Hammer a scoundrel or the savior of Western civilization? What was the meaning of the Russian connection?

The producers had assembled the pieces of the puzzle, but without an image in mind, how were they going to put the pieces together into fifty-two minutes of coherent narrative? I didn't accept the offer, because I could foresee nothing but meetings.

new journalism serve the purposes of evasion, and it becomes possible to present a reality of one's own invention as if it corresponded to an objective description of events. The newsmagazines do this every week.

Several years ago a writer employed by *Time* published in *Harper's* an essay written almost entirely in the omniscient third person. Toward the end of the last paragraph the author permitted himself a conclusion and went so far as to write the words, "I think." When he saw the galley proofs of the article he was horrified by his recklessness, and he changed the phrase to read "millions of people think."

Under the technical and epistemological pressures of the 1960s, the lines between fiction and fact became increasingly difficult to distinguish. The previously distinct genres of journalism, literature, and theater gradually fused into something known as media. The amalgam of forms resulted in a national theater of celebrity. If in 1965 the academic critics were beginning to notice that nobody was writing serious plays, the literary critics observed that the novelists had wandered off into the wilderness of self. Who could compete with the continuous performance on the stage of events? Network television presented a troupe of celebrities transported with the ease of a Shakespearean scene change to Dallas, Vietnam, Chicago, Vienna, Washington, and the Afghan frontier. The technical and lighting effects were astonishing, the verisimilitude of the characters so startling as to make them seem almost lifelike. By 1972 the tropes of the new journalism had become so commonplace that an anonymous writer for the *Economist*, a London weekly known for its rectitude, could begin his account of the American elections that year with the sentence, "It was raining in America on election day." The writer obviously didn't mean to say that it was raining everywhere in the United States. He wished to say something about the state of mind of the American people, and he used the rain as a metaphor to express his intimations of doubt and melancholy.

A similar sleight of hand governs the use of quotation from the secretary of state, the chairman of the Chase Manhattan Bank, or any of the other players in the national repertory company. The writer already has in mind the shape of the story, but he needs to give it a plausible authority or office of origin. He cannot possibly depict the matter at hand in all of its complexity, and so he asks a question that will carry along the plot in the direction of melodrama. Would the secretary say that the reports of Syrian troops east of Beirut mean war or peace? Is it true, Mr. Rockefeller, that your bank sustains the racist economy of South Africa?

The actors experienced in the theater of the news know what the prompters want to hear. People drawn into the play for a single performance, usually as minor or supporting characters when their businesses collapse or their children commit suicide, never know what to say. They make the mistake of trying to explain, at some length and in boring detail, and they wonder why the account in the papers the next morning bears so little resemblance to their understanding of the facts.

MORE IS LESS

If the media succeed with their spectacles and grand simplifications, it is because their audiences define happiness as the state of being well and artfully deceived. People like to listen to stories, to believe what they're told, to imagine that the implacable forces of history speak to them with a human voice. Who can bear to live without myths? If people prefer to believe that drug addiction causes crime, that may be because they would rather not think that perfectly ordinary people commit crimes, people not too different from themselves, people living in the same neighborhoods and sending their children to the same schools.

The media thus play the part of the courtier, reassuring their patrons that the world conforms to the wish of the presiding majority. The media advertise everything and nothing. Yes, say the media, our generals know what they're doing (no, say the media, our generals are fools); the energy crisis was brought down on our innocent heads by the Arabs (the energy crisis is the fault of our profligacy and greed); Vietnam was a crusade (Vietnam was imperialism); homosexuality is a "lifestyle" (homosexuality is a disease); the Kennedys were demigods (the Kennedys were beasts); the state is invincible (the state has lost its nerve); yes, Virginia, there is a reality out there, and not only can it be accurately described but also it looks just the way you always wanted it to look.

By telling people what they assume they already know, the media reflect what society wants to think of itself. The images in the mirror compose the advertisement for reality. Janet Cooke's story received a Pulitzer Prize because it confirmed what the committee, most of whose members were both ambitious and white, wished to believe about people who were alienated and black. If blacks were lost to heroin at the age of eight, how could they mount a revolution? We are safe, my dear Trevor, for at least another generation.

Although notoriously inept at the art of disguise, the FBI agents dressed up to look like Arabs succeeded in their charade against the congressmen filmed in the ABSCAM screenings because the congressmen wanted to believe that a sheik was somebody in a robe who had nothing better to do than bestow $50,000 in cash on the princes of Christendom.

The simplicities of the media enjoy the further advantage of a much vaunted "communications revolution" that has had the paradoxical effect of lowering the norm of literacy. The immense increase of available information over the last generation has so fragmented the literate audience that instead of bringing people together the sophistication of the new technologies has forced them further apart and deprived them of the capacity to speak a common language. As recently as 1960 there was such a thing in the United States as a fairly unified field of informed opinion. More or less the same people read more or less the same newspapers and magazines. They comprised an educated audience that was still small enough to talk to itself and that could agree, at least in rough outline, as to the country's history, character, and hope of the future.

After 1965, this single audience dispersed into a thousand audiences, each of them preoccupied with its own interests and realities, each of them speaking the jargon of a particular speciality or profession. The diaspora followed, in part, from the rise in the population after the Second World War and the subsequent multiplication of graduates of the nation's universities during the 1960s; in part, the diaspora reflected the wealth and dynamism of a society that could afford to pursue so many lines of random inquiry.

Who now can make sense of the surfeit of information? Even a middle-level executive at a middle-level brokerage firm receives 500 household advisories a week (not to mention subscriptions to trade journals, the daily and financial press); dossiers of equivalent bulk circulate at every level of authority within the corridors of any American institution large enough to boast of its presence in the twentieth century. What then must be the data base provided for the officials holding the higher places in a bureaucracy the size of the State or Treasury departments? Who has the time to read what they have to read?

The more people know, the less they know. To the extent that society as a whole expands and complicates its acquisition of knowledge, so the individual members of society find less and less to say to one another on any level of meaning beyond the reach of Mike Wallace. They escape the burden of their anxieties by retreating into the magic shows of the national celebrity theater. The gaudiness of the television spectacle, which so obviously shifts the weight of personality against the subtlety of mind, imposes a kind of numb silence on people who might otherwise have had something useful to say.

In the autumn of 1977, I taught a seminar at Yale on the art of the press, and I noticed that of the eighteen students in the class five or six of them hoped to make careers in journalism; they were as ambitious as Janet Cooke, and their questions about Peter Zenger and the First Amendment served as preambles to requests for an introduction to a deputy editor at the *New York Times*. The other students in the class paid relatively little attention to the media. Their interest was that of an anthropologist or a student of comparative mythology. The media presented them with portraits of reality they thought inauthentic, a reality of a kind, but one without the dimension of insight or wisdom. Brought up with the wonders of the communications revolution, they somehow understood that the news had moved out of the newspapers. If, in the 1930s, Bernard Baruch could speculate in the financial markets on the basis of what he read in the *Times*, by the late 1960s anybody who wanted seriously to follow events (whether in finance, foreign affairs, or the sciences) had to depend on more detailed sources of information.

Janet Cooke, like Michael Daly and the generation of correspondents raised on the principles of the new journalism, understood that the media had become a theater. Apparently she wanted to be a star, and the résumés she submitted both to the *Post* and then to the Pulitzer Prize committee read like the list of credits that producers receive from unemployed actors. I've never yet met an actor who, when trying out for a part, doesn't answer yes to every question asked. Can he sing? Like Sinatra. Can he dance? Like Astaire. Does he know languages? His mother was French. Thus, when applying for a job at the *Post*, Miss Cooke conferred on herself a degree from Vassar and a fluency in French and Spanish. Her advertisement to the Pulitzer Prize committee was further elaborated with a graduate degree from the University of Toledo, a year's study at the Sorbonne, and a fluency in Italian and Portuguese. It was this pathetic forgery of her life, not the fabrication of her story in the paper, that led to the discovery of her fraud.

If Miss Cooke had not won the Pulitzer Prize, perhaps the journalists who condemned her, both inside and outside of the *Post*, would not have been so harsh in their judgments. When Mr. Daly resigned from the *Daily News*, effectively pleading *nolo contendere* to the charge of having faked a dispatch from Belfast, nobody felt obliged to denounce him as a pathological liar and a disgrace to the profession. But the Pulitzer Prize is not something to be trifled with; like the Academy Award, it denotes grandeur. "Applause," remarked Ambrose Bierce, "is the echo of a platitude," and even a brief study of the Pulitzer Prizes awarded over a period of years suggests that they sustain the passions of the moment. Thus William Styron receives a prize for *The Confessions of Nat Turner* in 1968, at just about the point in time when sentiment on behalf of civil rights had become thoroughly respectable; Frances FitzGerald wins a prize for *Fire in the Lake* in 1973, by which time it had become correct to bemoan the American presence in Vietnam; Herman Wouk wins a prize for *The Caine Mutiny* in 1952, when the country was far enough into the cold war to think that naval officers showed virtue and maturity by obeying the orders of a demented captain.

If the prizes raise the politically expedient into the realm of authority and beauty, so also they maintain the pomp and majesty of a profession constantly in need of reassurance. The ladies and gentlemen of the fourth estate know that they have been living beyond their moral and intellectual means, and their desire to establish themselves as a social class reflects their anxiety about being discovered as bankrupts. The prizes might impress the groundlings on the public side of the curtain, but within the profession they shore up the confidence of the younger members of the troupe who might otherwise begin to question the validity of their claims to privilege. The continued credibility of the press, not to mention its hope of profit, rests on the popular belief that it deals in the currency of fact. If the reality of the press were seen to be as arbitrary as that of the government or the Mobil Oil Corporation, what would happen then? No wonder Miss Cooke was driven from the temple, followed by stones.

The custodians of the press undoubtedly have a point. As has been said, people like to believe in myths, and the extravagance of the libel awards recently bestowed on Carol Burnett and a former Miss Wyoming suggests that the audience has begun to grow restive. The *National Enquirer* published a silly gossip item about Miss Burnett in a Washington restaurant with Henry Kissinger. The gossip was false, as is most gossip published in even the most reputable of newspapers, but a jury in Los Angeles awarded Miss Burnett $1.3 million in punitive damages, a sum equivalent to half the *Enquirer*'s assets. The former Miss Wyoming claimed that a work of fiction published in *Penthouse* magazine (a story about an imaginary Miss Wyoming) caused her immeasurable suffering and embarrassment, and a jury in Cheyenne presented her with $12.5 million.

The disproportionate levy of punishment further suggests that people may expect too much of journalism. Not only do they expect it to be entertaining, they expect it to be true. It isn't so much that people insist on believing in the accuracy of the media (the *Enquirer*, after all, regularly announces cures for cancer and sightings of UFOs); the mistakes and distortions they will forgive if they can retain their faith in the underlying honesty of the enterprise. But once let them suspect that the difference between fact and fiction may be as random as a number drawn in a lottery, and their resentment will wreak an expensive vengeance. More than once I have heard the media described as "an army of occupation," and Congress has been besieged with bills offering redefinitions of the liberties granted under the First Amendment.

Once there was a religious theater in which God staged cataclysmic floods, plagues, and heavenly fires with the effortless aplomb of ABC's "Wide World of Sports." Now that God has been pronounced dead, it is conceivable that people would like to transfer His powers and dominions to the media. What else do they have to put in His place? To a large extent the media have had the roles of judge and inquisitor thrust upon them because so many other institutions have proved themselves inadequate to the tasks of omniscience. The media disguise their lack of knowledge with the quality of knowingness, their weakness with the power to forge the metal of celebrity and transmute a political issue into a salable commodity.

If the individual can be flattered into believing that he is present at all important public occasions, he may also be tricked into believing that he has no story of his own. The man who substitutes what Saul Bellow once called the nonstory of the news for the line of his own narrative condemns himself to an unending contemplation of the images that crowd across the media's many mirrors, a man forever suspended in the revolving light-show of names, issues, events, votes, hearings, treaties, wars, scandals, and final scores. The resulting loss of identity leads to the familiar chronicle of confused conflict, which in turn can be reprocessed into tomorrow's broadcast or next year's best-selling murder.

The huge image of the media expands in a vacuum, and before it engulfs all other forms of authority, it might be useful to ask what is meant by the old proverb about truth making men free. If people seek knowledge in the hope that it will grant them freedom and power, and if the media can satisfy neither of those desires, maybe that is because the customers expect the media to include those favors in the price of admission. The truth unfortunately has to be discovered every day, by each individual working with the tools of his own thought, imagination, and patient study. If we are all engaged in the same endeavor, seeking the representations of the truly human, then probably we should not assign so much belief to the contrived mythologies of the media. In the same editorial in which it admonished the *Washington Post*, the *New York Times* expressed the complacent notion that "great publications magnify beyond measure the voice of any single writer." This is not quite accurate. The instruments of the media multiply or amplify a voice, serving much the same purpose as a loudspeaker in a ball park or a prison. The amplification leaches the soul out of the voice, squeezing it into the institutional sound that pays the enormous costs of the big media. What magnifies a voice is its human character—its compassion, honesty, and moral intelligence. The great institutions of the day did everything they could to suppress the voice of Thomas Paine's *Rights of Man*; so also did the resident authorities try to muffle the voices of Freud and Marx and Christ. The human voice ceaselessly renews itself, evolving into the future with a force far greater than that of the old magic shows.

QUESTIONS FOR CRITICAL ANALYSIS

1. What is the story about Janet Cooke and the *Washington Post*? What did Cooke do that was unethical? Do you think it was bad? Why, or why not?
2. What does Lapham say is the "nature of the media"? Do you agree? What does he think is permissible for the press to do? Would you add limitations? Why, or why not?
3. Who was "Deep Throat"? How is Deep Throat different from Jimmy in Cooke's article? How are they the same? Why is one acceptable and one not?
4. What is "new journalism"? How does it "create an impression of truth"? How does Lapham's attitude toward new journalism compare with MacNeil's attitude?
5. Compare Lapham's attitude toward the press and its responsibility with MacNeil's attitude. What would Lapham think of MacNeil's premise that the press needs to acquiesce to the public's demand for fairness? What is Lapham's attitude toward the public?

QUESTIONS FOR STRUCTURAL ANALYSIS

1. Lapham begins his essay with two quotations. Why? What do these quotations do for the essay? How did you respond to these quotes?
2. What is the relation of the first paragraph of the essay to the discussion that follows? Why is the first paragraph important to the essay?
3. What is Lapham's attitude toward the *Washington Post*? How does he reveal his feelings? Describe Lapham's tone throughout the essay.
4. If you read a news story written by Lapham, would you trust it to be accurate? Why, or why not?
5. What is Lapham's conclusion? Is it optimistic? pessimistic? How does the larger context of the conclusion extend his comments on the public and the media?

*J*OURNALISTS *W*HO *M*ASQUERADE

TOM GOLDSTEIN

Tom Goldstein, a legal affairs reporter for the New York Times *between 1973–79, teaches journalism at the University of California-Berkeley. "Journalists Who Masquerade," a chapter from* The News at Any Cost *(1985), describes the debilitating effect of deception not only on society's perception of the news media but also on journalism itself. In this essay which first appeared in the* Washington Journalism Review, *a magazine published for those involved in gathering and disseminating the news, Goldstein tackles the ethical implications of reporters relying on everything from passive deception to active impersonation in search of the story.*

Before you begin reading: *What is an ideal reporter? In your notebook write a list of characteristics. Use that list to write a paragraph that describes the ideal journalist and the way he or she reports the news.*

◆

CARLA CANTOR, A YOUNG REPORTER STARTING HER SECond year at the *Daily Record* of Morristown, New Jersey, sought to talk to the brother of Dierdre O'Brien, a New Jersey waitress who had been stabbed to death in December 1982. She went about this in a straightforward way, asking for the interview. She was unsuccessful. Eight months later, there was another sordid murder in Morris County. A 24-year-old go-go dancer was stabbed to death, and this time, according to court records, in her attempt to add depth and color to her story, Carla Cantor allegedly resorted to means that were less than straightforward.

She says that she told the stepfather of the dead go-go dancer that she was a reporter but did not tell anything to the mother, whose native tongue was not English. The family of the dead woman disputed this and said Cantor had told them she was "from the morgue" in an attempt to obtain personal information about the victim. In 1983, Cantor was prosecuted for impersonating a government official, and a local judge found that she had violated a New Jersey statute that forbids someone from posing as a government official. At the very least, based on the testimony at the trial, Cantor was aware at an early point in her interview that the dead woman's parents misunderstood who she was and that she apparently did nothing to correct this misunderstanding.

The article that emerged from her interview was full of chilling detail. It made good copy, and although not calculated to do so, it hurt the dead woman's family. It told of how the victim was born out of wedlock, how, according to her mother, she liked the "good times—wild crowds, drink and drugs," and how her mother had not seen her in the past three years. The most telling quote in her article, however, did not come from a family member but from an unnamed neighbor who spoke to the reporter on the condition that her name not be used: "Adele was the saddest child I knew. When other kids would get Good Humor bars, she would lick the wrappers."

At the trial Judge Aldan Markson found the story "artfully and manipulatively written; it was calculated to bring tears to the eyes of susceptible readers." As a witness, he said, Cantor appeared "naive, soft-spoken, shy, absent-minded and fearful." He found her "educated, able and intelligent." But "she was not a truthful witness," and Judge Markson fined her $500 and sentenced her to do 30 days of community work. [In late 1984, another judge overturned the conviction and ordered a new trial. This July 22, Cantor was found guilty by Morristown Municipal Judge William Boffa, Jr. of impersonating a government official while conducting an interview for a newspaper article. She has said she will appeal the ruling.]

Was the story worth doing? Clearly. A murder in a small community deserves a follow-up; and this story, no matter how painful to the victim's family, outlined the dark side of the victim's past. Could the story have been done without the reporter posing (as the first judge determined she had done) or without her partially withholding her identity (as she herself conceded)? Most likely, yes. The victim's background could have been reconstructed using traditional reporting techniques—the searching of public records and interviews with friends, old acquaintances and neighbors (keep in mind the potency of the neighbor's quote in the article). It would have taken longer that way, but it is hard to see why a delay of a few days would have been detrimental to the public interest.

From a purely practical calculus, the results gained from misrepresentation and posing hardly seem to warrant the risks. Pragmatism aside, there are fundamental reasons against masquerading. In the long term, posing mortgages the credibility of the press. The notion of truthfulness is so essential to journalism that it should not be trifled with. It is important that people know to whom they are talking, and impersonation undercuts an implicit trust between journalists and those whom they interview. Some stories will surely be harder to get if a reporter does not pose. Others will be impossible to get. But not so many as one might suppose.

In the context of the number of stories appearing each day, stealth or impersonation is used sparingly. Outright posing is generally condemned by today's editors, but this disapproval manifests itself more in word than in deed. When posing is considered in a written code, it is usually criticized. But few of the 50 largest newspapers ban it altogether. A survey of television stations, conducted by Charles Burke of the University of Florida in 1983, showed that undercover reporting was relatively common. More than a quarter of the 299 network affiliates in the top 100 markets that responded said that in the previous two years reporters had gone undercover, representing "themselves as other than journalists." Another survey showed that two-thirds of journalists approved of the practice.

Still, most journalists feel there are limits to posing. Some will pose only in a public place as, say, a bartender. Some will not lie on an employment form. Others say they will not impersonate a policeman or anyone who is authorized to compel information. (Most likely, that impersonator would be subject to criminal prosecution, as Carla Cantor was.)

These distinctions, however, are often blurred. At the 1984 meeting of IRE (Investigative Reporters & Editors) Bob Greene of *Newsday* drew a line on impersonation and said he would never pose as a policeman. Yet, with particular relish, he told the story of how he and a colleague, in the aftermath of the drowning of Mary Jo Kopechne off Chappaquiddick Island in 1969, rented a black car, put an antenna on it to suggest they were policemen, wore black rain coats, went to a motel where the dead woman's friends were staying, and demanded to see the record of their toll telephone calls. "We never said we were cops," said Greene. "We never said we were reporters." If they had been asked who they were—and they were not asked—they would have answered: "People investigating Chappaquiddick."

This is passive deception, which occurs far more frequently than active impersonation. Greene and his colleague never misrepresented themselves. But they certainly tried to leave the impression that they were not reporters. The distinction between what Greene did and a reporter posing as a bartender is a fine one, but it is the type of distinction that journalists try to draw.

Probably the most elaborate and best-known recent example of posing bore fruit in a 25-part series that appeared in the Chicago *Sun-Times* in 1978. The paper went one step beyond ordinary undercover work and engaged in the equivalent of a sting operation. For four months, the paper operated a bar—playfully called the Mirage—in order to document the day-to-day official corruption that plagued Chicago's small-business owners. Some reporters worked as bartenders while photographers worked from a hidden room, snapping pictures of payoffs. Payoffs of $10 to $100 were made to city inspectors so they would disregard health and safety hazards. Shakedowns by state liquor inspectors were observed. Tax fraud by accountants was uncovered.

In a book published shortly after the series ran, the two main reporters, Zay N. Smith and Pamela Zekman, explained their thinking as they prepared to go undercover. By owning a tavern, they said, "we could see how the system actually works." In their own eyes they would avoid technical entrapment. They interpreted this self-imposed mandate to mean that "it was all right to give somebody a chance to show off his normal talent for lawbreaking. It was not all right to nudge that person into committing crimes that were new to him." They distinguished what they would do from what they considered to be improper undercover work: "It would be an invasion of privacy if a reporter worked undercover, say, as a politician's valet or housemaid. But a tavern was a licensed public place."

The reaction to the series was mostly positive. The story received national attention, in large part because the *Sun-Times* permitted the television show "60 Minutes" to join the scheme, and the undercover operation was shown on the television show as the first item after the 1978 Superbowl. It created a predictable stir in journalistic circles, and it won many prizes. The Chicago paper was expected to win the Pulitzer prize in 1979, and a Pulitzer jury recommended that it receive the award.

But two prominent journalists sitting on the Pulitzer advisory board, the body that determines the winners, blocked the *Sun-Times* from winning the prize. Objections were lodged by Benjamin Bradlee, executive editor of the *Washington Post*, and Eugene Patterson, who had once been managing editor at the *Post* and was then managing editor of the *St. Petersburg Times*. They argued that reporters needed to operate in the open. Patterson said the reporters should have interviewed bar owners. That, he said, "would have been the hard way to get the story." Several years later, speaking to an audience of students at the University of Florida, Patterson said he voted as he did because he "did not want other reporters to follow suit." At the time, Bradlee asked: "How can newspapers be for honesty and integrity when they themselves are less than honest in getting a story? We instruct our reporters not to misrepresent themselves, period."

Part of the reason the rejection of the *Sun-Times* entry came as such a surprise was that in prior years the Pulitzer board had often given its imprimatur to posing, signaling to thousands of journalists across the country that the premier award in journalism could be won if reporters showed enough ingenuity and courage in camouflaging the fact they were journalists. On at least four occasions in the preceding two decades, a Pulitzer prize had been awarded to stories in which reporters posed:

- In 1961, Edgar May, a *Buffalo Evening News* reporter who exposed laxity and mismanagement in New York State's welfare services, had posed as a social caseworker.
- Ten years later, in 1971, William Hugh Jones, a *Chicago Tribune* reporter, posed as an ambulance driver to expose collusion between the police and private ambulance companies to restrict service in low-income areas.
- In 1974, William Sherman, a *New York Daily News* reporter, wrote a series in which, posing as a Medicaid recipient, he uncovered major abuses in the administration of Medicaid in New York City.

- That same year, *Newsday* carried a 32-part series that followed the trail of heroin traffic from Turkey to France to the New York metropolitan area. Bob Greene was a member of the winning *Newsday* team. In France he impersonated a lawyer. (Ten years later, he said of his role in this series: "I lied. I cheated. I damn near stole. The result obviously was good. I'd do it again. Our fine sense of ethics diminishes in proportion to the importance of the story.")

The 1979 rejection of the Mirage series marked a change in the Pulitzer policy, and by the early 1980s, the message that the Pulitzer board looked on undercover reporting with disfavor had apparently spread. Robert Christopher, administrator of the prizes, said that relatively few entries based on undercover reporting had been submitted between 1981 and 1983. Two reporters—one for the *Los Angeles Herald-Examiner* who posed as an illegal alien in a sweatshop in 1981, the other from the *Wall Street Journal* who posed as a day laborer in 1983—were finalists in the competition, but neither won.

Even though it has lost the blessing of the Pulitzer board, posing seems still to be as entrenched among journalists as it has been for at least a century. An early impersonator was Nellie Bly, who rose quickly in journalism at the end of the 1800s at the *New York World* by engaging in a series of adventures. In the tradition of the intrepid participant-observers, she explored the depths of the ocean in a diving bell and went around the world beating the mythical record established by Phileas Fogg in Jules Verne's *Around the World in Eighty Days*. She gained admittance to Blackwell's Island Insane Asylum in the East River off Manhattan (it is now Roosevelt Island) by posing as a madwoman, and she then exposed the filthy conditions inside.

In the late 1930s, Dorothy Kilgallen, the energetic and hardedged reporter and columnist for Hearst's *New York Evening Journal*, was based in Hollywood, and there she wrote a series of gimmick columns. In one of them, she tried to find out whether it was possible for a plain girl from Peoria—Mary Warren was her disguised name—to crash the formidable studio gates. To each studio guard, she repeated, "I'm Mary Warren from Peoria, and I'm looking for a job as an extra." Each time, she was referred to Central Casting, and then was turned down. In her column Kilgallen advised all the Mary Warrens from Peoria to stay and work at home, while nurturing the hope of being discovered there. "What was possible ten years ago in this town is no longer possible," she concluded about her rejection in Hollywood.

In the early 1960s Gloria Steinem first gained wide attention for an article she wrote for *Show* magazine: "I Was a Playboy Bunny." The article required her to lie repeatedly—about her age, her name and her background—and to pose. In applying for the job, she said she was 24 years old rather than 28. A supervisor came by and looked over the application. "'You don't look 24,' she said. Well, that's that, I thought. 'You look much younger.' I smiled in disbelief."

Steinem let herself be flattered. Her undercover observations reveal a predictably unpleasant working environment. The glamour that was promised in the advertisement that she answered did not materialize. Some of her observations seem particularly thin. She found that most of the customers "seemed to be middle-aged businessmen"—a revelation that hardly seems worth her going undercover to unearth. (In 1985, a television movie, "A Bunny's Tale," based on her article, was shown. In the film the 17 days she spends working as a Playboy Bunny radicalize her. In fact, she said, "It took me longer in reality to reach that conclusion.")

Probably the most respectable, or at least the most defensible, use of posing, in terms of what can be accomplished, involves the investigation of what the sociologist Erving Goffman called "total institutions"—mental homes, prisons, nursing homes, boarding schools and monasteries. In this type of posing, the reporter masks his identity and is a participant-observer.

Prisons appear to be the institutions most sought out by contemporary journalist-infiltrators. There are logical reasons for this. They house the outcasts. They are forbidden places that ordinarily inquisitive reporters cannot plumb. They are often dangerously overcrowded. How are prisoners treated? Are there programs to help them? Or do prisons merely teach them to be still more-hardened criminals? What causes disturbances and riots? Few newspapers have a reporter exclusively assigned to cover prisons (I am aware of one paper, the *Jacksonville Times Union*, which has a reporter stationed near Florida's death row in Starke), and few reporters have much expertise in penology. It is hard for them to get a fix on what is going on inside.

In most jurisdictions, prison officials are willing to let reporters interview inmates, but these are often the model prisoners—the best behaved and the most articulate—and these interviews can lead to a slanted Potemkin-village portrayal of life inside. In a 1974 opinion, *Pell v. Procunier*, the United States Supreme Court set limitations on what reporters could do inside prisons. Under the court's ruling administrators need not grant them interviews with specific inmates.

In the past several years, some administrators have allowed reporters to masquerade as inmates to get an eyewitness view from the inside. This has led to some good writing, and occasionally to shrewd insights. But overall the conclusions that have been drawn rarely seem worth the effort.

In 1982, an ambitious examination of prison life was undertaken by a group of reporters at the *Arizona Daily Star* in Tucson. During the project, one reporter worked undercover as a guard, another as an inmate. Their assignments were authorized by prison officials, but their identity was kept secret from other guards and inmates. This was done, the paper said, so that "the *Star* could report more accurately and vividly about the conditions inside Arizona's prisons."

Ten days after the reporter, R. H. Ring, entered prison as an inmate, he was cornered in a stairwell and beaten by four other inmates because he refused to give one of them his belt. Six of his teeth were broken, and he suffered a bruise the size of a softball on his hip. (A photograph of him showing off the bruise accompanied his story.) He was sent back to Tucson later that night after he and prison officials decided that his safety was in jeopardy. Ring, something of an adventurer, had served a short period of time in a jail a decade earlier, and he was anxious to do this assignment: "I wanted to see what prison was like, firsthand, to feel it and hear it and smell it and eat the bad food. . . . In a more professional stance, I told the appropriate officials that, to write an accurate news story on prison, I had to be there. No number of interviews with cons and guards would provide the same strength of reality." The result was a 10,000-word article, which lapses in and out of stream of consciousness. It bespeaks a rebellious reporter, and while powerfully written, it tells more about Ring and his feelings than about the prison. Such self-conscious writing seems to be the common failing of this genre of first-person undercover reporting.

The *Arizona Daily Star* series demonstrates the severe limitations of undercover reporting. Capturing the reality of prison life is as elusive and difficult for the undercover reporter as it is for the reporter who identifies himself. But finding out what goes on in prisons is not impossible.

The Carson City *Nevada Appeal* came up with an unconventional—and aboveboard—approach: In 1982, it began carrying a weekly column, "Being There," written by Gerald Crane, who was not a reporter but a high school dropout serving a 35-year sentence for kidnapping and bank robbery. He was at the Northern Nevada Correctional Center in Carson City. In a column in July 1984, Crane wrote: "We'd like to imagine riots are well planned by participants possessing a clear objective in mind. Of the several I have attended, all were the direct result of random events colliding. Because the casual chemical soup of prison changes its composition moment to moment, there is no way to anticipate the catalyst that will ignite the stagnant pond into the boiling bog. Where there is fire there need not have been smoke first."

Probably the best contemporary picture of prison life was contained in the official report of the state commission that studied the Attica prison riot and the bloody takeover by the New York State Police. That commission had a large staff and subpoena power to force witnesses to testify, but many of the insights in its final report resulted from sensitive observation over a period of time and determined reporting.

For many years in the 1970s, without resorting to posing, the magazine *Corrections* gave a valuable look at the inside of prisons. Before it folded in 1983, the magazine dealt with a variety of topics—inmate capitalism, privately owned prisons, pretrial diversion, the problems of transsexuals in prisons, preventing suicides in prisons, inmate grievance procedures, the plight of retarded offenders, bail reform, the question of women guards working in male prisons, Vietnam veterans in prisons and the possibility that pastel walls prevent jailhouse brawls.

Few, if any, newspapers will, or should, go into the kind of detail on prisons that *Corrections* magazine did, but what is necessary in thoroughly covering prisons—and other beats like prisons—is a long-term investment in manpower and dogged reporting. Posing is a shortcut that may be cheaper and may produce results faster. But, at its best, it can lead only to splashy "one shot" stories.

The most common justification among editors for permitting reporters to pose is that, in limited doses, it is acceptable when there is no other way to ferret out an important story.

"I would limit role-playing to situations where the information to be gained is of *substantial* public interest, and when the information sought would not be available in the same form if reporters were required to use secondhand accounts," says John Seigenthaler, editorial director of *USA Today* who is also publisher and editor of the *Tennessean* in Nashville. In 1984, the policy of the McClatchy newspapers in California, according to Frank McCulloch, then the executive editor, "emphasized our distaste for posing but pulls up just short of forbidding it under any circumstances." In 1985, a reporter from the paper did, in fact, go undercover to do a story on sweat shops.

Most of the time, there is an alternative to posing. "We stopped the practice," says Eugene Patterson of the *St. Petersburg Times*, who had been instrumental in blocking the granting of the Pulitzer prize to the Mirage series. "We reserve the right to resume it if a specific case arises wherein an important public interest can only be served by disguising a staffer. But such cases will be rare indeed. We pay a prize in lost credibility each time we sneak. Hard work and burnt shoe leather can produce the facts the old-fashioned way—cleanly."

At NBC, misrepresentation is permissible only in "isolated and infrequent situations where, for example, failure to conceal one's identity would make it impossible to investigate and disclose an impropriety of major significance." At ABC, reporters "should not disguise their identity or pose as someone with another occupation" without the approval of management. In its production standards, CBS says: "In approaching individuals or organizations for interviews or coverage, misrepresentation should be avoided. Misrepresentation is unnecessary and in any event, candor on the part of the reporters and producers most often would better achieve the purpose." The drafters of the standards leave room for an exception—"when there is clear reason to believe that an improper activity could *otherwise not be reported*."

What sometimes happens, though, is that journalists skip over the tough intermediate steps and reach the "last resort" justification too hastily. In fact, most stories where impersonation has been used and the "last resort" justification has been cited could, with some ingenuity and hard work, have been done without posing.

For example, in 1979, the Strand, a large cluttered bookstore on the edge of Greenwich Village in Manhattan, which is well known for selling new volumes at sharp discounts, sent out a letter soliciting copies of books from reviewers. One of these letters was passed along to an executive of the Gannett chain, who happened to be chairman of the Professional Standards Committee of the Associated Press Managing Editors Association (APME). The editor was upset, and a reporter with the *Rochester Democrat and Chronicle*, a Gannett paper, was assigned to do a story on the bookstore for the Gannett News Service. He was sent to work at the store for 14 days.

In an editor's note that accompanied the article, the undercover approach was never really justified. "We had to do it from the inside to be effective and accurate," was the only explanation given at the time by Richard B. Tuttle, the Gannett executive who was chairman of the Professional Standards Committee of the APME.

In Rochester, the article appeared on a Sunday in early August 1979 at the top of the front page. There were three sidebars to boot, thus deluging newspaper readers in Rochester with a story of far more interest to the paper's executives than it possibly could have been to upstate New Yorkers. (The editor's note, in fact, said the articles would be part of a report to the APME's October convention that year.)

The story, by Michael Cordts, began: "In private transactions with a New York City bookstore, reporters across the nation have been pocketing thousands of dollars by selling complimentary copies of books sent to their newspapers." Cordts said ten newspaper book reviewers had "admitted" selling copies to the bookstore. In his story, Cordts told how he had confronted reviewers with his knowledge that he had seen crates bearing their return addresses at the bookstore.

If indeed as many reviewers were selling their books as the story claimed, it seems that a lot of phone calls strategically placed around the country would have led to the same result as the undercover reporting. The likelihood is that some reviewers would have lied on the phone and that others would have confessed. It is unethical for reviewers to sell copies of books that were given to them, but it is hardly the worst transgression committed by journalists. The articles in the Rochester paper overplayed the rather trivial matter. (Many newspapers forbid their reviewers from profiting personally on the sale of books. Often, they will auction off review copies and donate the proceeds to charity.)

The Strand continues to do a flourishing business in selling reviewers' copies. In 1985, the store still advertised that it had "tens of thousands of new reviewers' copies"; earlier, in an interview, Fred Bass, the president of the store, said he received thousands of reviewers' copies a week—more copies than ever. Cordts' article, he said, actually had helped his business.

Some newspapers that prohibit the type of posing engaged in by Michael Cordts permit reporters to mask their identity or merely to withhold mentioning their occupation unless questioned.

At the *Denver Post*, Tim Kelly, the managing editor in early 1984, said that while posing is "judged on a case by case basis, a reporter is not permitted to deny he's a reporter if questioned." At the *Seattle Times*, James B. King, the editor, reports: "Years ago we allowed a reporter to be hired as a nurse's aid in a nursing home suspected of fraud and poor treatment of patients. We had been barred from inspecting the facility. I'm not sure we would do the same again. We have, however, allowed reporters to not identify themselves unless asked. If asked, they are instructed to identify themselves."

The *New York Times* takes an unambiguously hard line in forbidding journalists to misrepresent themselves. "I don't believe in journalists' masquerading," A. M. Rosenthal told me in an interview. "I don't think it is illegal. But I don't think it is in the spirit of the First Amendment." But the *Times* permits reporters to mask their occupation and behave as ordinary members of the public when covering consumer stories, such as reviewing restaurants. (Mimi Sheraton, who had been the longtime restaurant reviewer, occasionally wore wigs and other disguises; her picture was posted in kitchens in some of the city's better-known restaurants.)

There are other occasions where the lack of disclosure works well enough. Reporters do not wish to disclose their identity immediately so that they can more accurately get the "feel" of a situation. In the summer of 1983, Philip Shenon of the *Times* wrote a diary about three days he spent in a welfare hotel. In *Winners & Sinners*, an internal publication of the *Times*, Shenon was properly credited for his ingenuity and was asked to share his techniques in getting the story. "Don't reveal yourself too soon," he said. "I feared that the hotel management would learn about me from some gossipy tenant and throw me out. For most of the first day and a half, I just wandered around the hotel, watched the tenants and observed their living conditions. I began my interviews late in the afternoon of the second day. I always identified myself as a *Times* reporter. People were usually willing to talk; by then, many were used to seeing me in the hotel. There is another advantage to remaining incognito for a time: You don't have to worry what events are being staged for your benefit. I wore a Walkman, which often sparked conversation. The young kids kept pulling the earphones from my neck to listen to the music. As they listened, I talked to their parents."

In other special instances, lack of full disclosure may be acceptable. For many years, Nicholas Gage was an investigative reporter for the *Wall Street Journal* and the *New York Times*. He left the *Times* in 1980 to devote himself full-time to writing a book about his mother, Eleni, and how she had died. The book became an obsession. As if he were an actor in one of the great Greek tragedies, he embarked on a successful search for his mother's killer. She had been executed in 1948 by Communist rebels during the Greek Civil War. The book was a huge success, and Gage became a hero among Greek-Americans.

In the spring of 1984, when I was teaching at the University of Florida, Gage spoke to a group of 150 or so Greek-Americans in a crowded, windowless room. He spoke about Greece and about the book. The audience was attentive and well informed.

"I used all the techniques I have learned over two decades," he said in a barely audible monotone. He said that he had taped all interviews, some secretly, and once, when he confronted his mother's murderer, a gun was hidden in the back of his pants and a tape recorder was hidden in a sock. ("As an investigative reporter," he writes in *Eleni*, "I had used this mini-recorder many times when interviewing criminals and informants.") In gathering material for the book, he did not fully disclose his intentions. He told people he was a Greek writer doing a book on the civil war, and he gained valuable material from former guerrillas who thought Gage was sympathetic to them.

Eventually, Gage did not kill his mother's assassin: "I realized my mother had made me, and she had not made me a killer," Gage told the Florida audience. In his quest he violated all sorts of journalistic rules. But in contrast to his investigative reporting at the *Wall Street Journal* or the *Times*, his book is really not presented as a piece of conventional journalism at all. It is a first-person adventure and, in a sense, a journal. He records a personal mission of such intensity that in his mind he was prepared to kill. In this context he could hardly be bound by the rules of journalistic ethics.

In Florida he said: "As Tom Goldstein, a former colleague at the *Times* can tell you, you have to tell the truth, but nothing says you have to tell the whole truth." But there are great problems with adopting his advice as a general rule.

It is a deception when a reporter pretends not to be one. At Chappaquiddick, Bob Greene of *Newsday* was careful never to say what he was, but he wanted others to think that he was a law enforcement agent. The distinction between active posing and passive deception is subtle. Benjamin Bradlee of the *Washington Post*, who vehemently objected to the posing in the Mirage tavern series, takes the view that it is not always necessary for a reporter to identify oneself as a reporter. At the *Post* it is all right for reporters to dress and act like someone else as long as they do not give another identity or say they are not reporters.

For example, in 1983, in an account of how men from the streets of Washington seek work in the fields of North Carolina, Neil Henry posed as a destitute drifter "with a scraggly beard" who carried with him a social security card for identification along with a notebook and a *Washington Post* press pass. Some of his companions knew his real identity. In another series in the *Post*, in 1984, on how easily drugs could be smuggled into a prison near Washington, a *Post* reporter did not disclose her identity. The reporter, Athelia Knight, sat silently on a bus that was headed for Lorton Reformatory to observe ways in which marijuana and other illegal drugs were surreptitiously brought into the facility. She said about the bus ride, "I must have seemed like just another woman with a husband or boyfriend locked up."

In defending the two series, Bradlee told me: "I see a really seminal distinction between planning any kind of a deception, however much the end might seem to justify the means, and embarking on a project where your occupation as a journalist is not advertised.

"In the first instance the journalist is actually posing as someone else, be it a bartender or be it a doctor or whatever. In the second instance there is no pose.

There may be no sign around the reporter's neck, but at no time did Neil Henry or Athelia Knight lie."

Yet, it is by no means certain that the reporters needed to mask their identity to come up with these stories. In his series Neil Henry came up against the same problems that the reporters in Boston and Arizona who posed as prison inmates faced. There is a real question of just what he was observing. At one point, Henry self-consciously says, "Having come to North Carolina without a change of clothes, and having neither the means nor opportunity to acquire another set, I was ughsome, foul-smelling, and exhausted." But, of course, this was make-believe, since Henry was, in fact, a reporter and could, had he wished, easily have acquired another set of clothes.

The larger problem with stories like this is that they rely exclusively on the integrity of reporters. Bradlee says his reporters do not lie. But it is asking a lot of readers to accept this as a general rule, since readers know that some reporters sometimes lie. At trial, under oath, Carla Cantor said that all she did was fail to reveal to the dead go-go dancer's mother the fact that she was a reporter. At the first trial, the judge did not believe her.

The question of credibility was also at the heart of an undercover story by Agnes Palazzetti, a veteran reporter for the *Buffalo Evening News*. In 1981, she wrote a story on how getting caught for shoplifting can be "a traumatic and terrifying experience." The headline was: "Posing as Shoplifter Works Too Well." The overline to the headline bore this message: "Embarrassed Reporter Learns a Lesson." But the headline is misleading. She did not merely masquerade as a shoplifter; she *shoplifted*, and when caught she claimed she did so because she was a reporter.

In her first-person account, Palazzetti wrote how she sought to test out the rather tepid hypotheses that retail stores do not have the proper security or enough sales personnel to curb shoplifting. "In order to learn exactly what shoplifting is all about, this reporter, working outside of the boundaries of truly ethical journalism, decided that after almost 30 years' experience as a reporter, I would find out if what had been written on shoplifting was really so. I didn't even tell my editors, because I knew they wouldn't allow me to break the law for a story."

Perhaps not, but after she did so, they ran her story, and played it prominently. Palazzetti recounts: "Eventually, it dawns on you, you're being arrested and you are not being believed—at least by some. One feeling is more bewildering than the other, but finally you sort it out and realize that all of this nightmare will make an even better story." Eventually, she was released from custody.

Palazzetti's explanation of her arrest is limp, and there is absolutely no evidence, beyond her own word, that she was not in fact shoplifting and would have said nothing had she not been caught. The reader cannot independently know if the reporter is telling the truth. A newspaper needs the trust of the reader, and one of the problems of selective posing is that this trust is undermined.

A common thread runs through many of the stories where reporters pose or fail to disclose their identities. They wish to take the law into their own hands, or at least to help law enforcement—which they sometimes view as inefficient.

This was the case at the *Miami Herald*, which did a major series on drugs in South Florida schools in 1982. Illegal drugs are a serious problem in Miami. In the early 1980s, three-quarters of the cocaine and three-quarters of the marijuana that entered this country did so through Florida, according to Stanley Marcus, United States attorney for the southern district of Florida. The *Herald* is an aggressive paper, deeply concerned about its community, and it wants to do something about curbing drugs. In the fall of 1983, the *Herald* stepped beyond the normal role of a newspaper as recorder of events on its news pages. Along with the Junior League of Miami, a local television station and a group called Informed Families of Dade County, it sponsored what an advertisement called a "media campaign"—"EPIDEMIC: South Florida Fights Drugs."

A year earlier a team of reporters from the paper had spent two months preparing a major series of stories in which they explored the drug culture in south Florida high schools. Initially, the editors were going to have youthful-looking reporters buy drugs in school yards to show how easy it was. The paper had no intention of letting the local prosecutor, whom the ranking editors distrusted, know of their plans. In early March the paper was poised for the mass buy. (I know this because I had informally applied for a job there and was spending part of an afternoon with three top editors. Our conversation was interrupted when they held a conference call with one of the newspaper's outside lawyers to talk through the story a final time. Several months after this, I discussed the incident with an editor at the *Herald* and was authorized to write about the private conversation.)

At the paper, the policy is to discourage active posing, but there had been instances where it has been allowed, says Pete Weitzel, the current managing editor, "where there was no misrepresentation, simply no representation as a reporter." Ultimately, the undercover buys in the drug series did not happen. "We decided it was not wise," says Weitzel. "We initially thought we would make purchases, verify they were drugs, then write our stories. It raised all the obvious questions. Suppose someone got arrested? There are real problems in aiding and assisting, of witnessing a crime, in gathering a story."

Reporters did not pose, but they dressed like high school students to blend in with their surroundings. The main story that was finally published focused on a young man named Rob Cappello, the son of a former policeman. He was brash and a braggart, and he is quoted directly and extensively, and was the only offender identified by his full name. At the time, he was 18 years old, just beyond being protected by Florida's juvenile offender laws. He was the only person the reporters talked to who was 18. The article said that he sold about 30 marijuana joints a morning from his territory, which was pinpointed unambiguously in the article. He was dealing boldly, in plain view, and had no right to expect privacy. Pictures of him were snapped by a photographer hiding behind a bush.

He knew he was talking to reporters. They had identified themselves. He was also naive, and the reporters said afterward that Cappello probably was not aware that the reporters were witnessing all that was happening or that what he said would be quoted directly in the paper. When they chatted with him, the reporters did not take notes. After a conversation, they rushed to their car to take down what he had said. The reporters did not pose. They disclosed their identity, but they still were being deceptive, and even though Cappello was a wrongdoer, their deception undercut an otherwise fine story. The day the story ran Cappello did not show up at school. He never returned.

The *Miami Herald* stopped short of stepping over into the domain of law enforcement. Other journalists have not. Sometimes, as in the Mirage series, journalists set up a sting operation. In its guidelines, ABC acknowledges that in some "exceptional circumstances" it will sanction cooperation with police. "These involve occasions when ABC News is invited to accompany and observe police in undercover or 'sting' operations."

But this approach can result in a reporter's becoming a willing pawn of law enforcement. In 1982, Danny Garcia, a reporter for the *San Antonio Light*, posed as an illegal alien to experience, according to an editor's note, "the real-life ordeal of an illegal alien crossing into the United States."

Posing as a Mexican, Garcia infiltrated an operation that smuggled aliens into the United States. He floated across the river from Mexico in a tire tube. (He wrote of this experience: "I had been overcome by a feeling of terror, fearing that I would either drown or be robbed by my crossers. But at the same time, those fears had been outweighed by a strange sense of fascination. 'So this is what it's like. *This* is what it's like to be a wetback,' I thought to myself.") Eventually, he was caught by "La Migra"—the U.S. Border Patrol—on the way to San Antonio with a group of real aliens. He was then charged as a co-conspirator in the trafficking of undocumented aliens.

His role was an ambiguous one. He told his arresting officers that he was really a reporter. They didn't believe him. Then, he wrote in his story, he "explained to the officers that I would provide information if they helped protect my cover." They still did not believe him. But the reporter felt secure for he knew that he "had already implicated a major smuggler in an organized felony offense." The charges against him were eventually dropped. Garcia had taken on the role of informant for the government. That is a role a journalist should never willingly play. A journalist is paid to write stories, not assist the government.

One of the obvious dangers of reporters posing as illegal aliens, as prisoners or as prison guards or of their taking on the role of law enforcement agents is that others may then use this as a pretext to pose as journalists. There is no way of knowing how common this "reverse-posing" is, but examples are cited with sufficient frequency to suggest that this subterfuge is employed often. This, too, undercuts the ability of journalists to do their job.

Members of the organization of Lyndon H. LaRouche, Jr., the sometimes presidential candidate, often have been accused of disguising themselves as reporters representing well-known media outlets in order to gather information and gain access where they might not otherwise be accepted. LaRouche's politics swing from the far left to the far right, and the fringe group he leads has remarkable staying power. In 1984, he ran for president as the head of the National Democratic Policy Committee, a misleading name because that committee had nothing whatsoever to do with mainstream Democratic Party politics. His group used to be the U.S. Labor Party, but it was no friend of organized labor.

At the AFL-CIO convention in 1983, a LaRouchite who pretended to represent *Business Week* was barred. "Our experience with the LaRouche group has been entirely negative," said Murray Seeger, director of the department of information of the AFL-CIO. "We, by tradition, operate an open policy in dealing with the media. At our 1983 convention, for instance, we granted press credentials to American newspapers and magazines ranging from the Communist Party's *Daily World* to *Forbes*, the 'capitalist tool.' We admitted representatives from East Germany and the Soviet Union. Only those from the LaRouche publications—*New Solidarity* and *Executive Intelligence Review*—were barred automatically.

"The reason for that unusual position is that the representatives of these publications do not meet the barest minimum standards of journalistic behavior. The same persons who purport to be reporters are also pamphleteers and salesmen for the various LaRouche products. They agitate. Since President Lane Kirkland is one of the targets for their abuse, LaRouche representatives come to our meetings and hand out their papers or slap stickers on meeting room walls in the early morning hours when the rooms are empty." Seeger said that he has been approached by "Atlantic Business Week" and "other pseudo publications" and traced the telephone numbers to LaRouche headquarters.

In the fall of 1984, LaRouche lost a $150 million libel action he brought against NBC for having characterized him as the extremist leader of a political cult. Instead, the jury awarded damages to NBC, which had countersued. [An appeal in both cases is pending.] A main contention in the countersuit was that LaRouche followers had tried to sabotage an NBC interview with Senator Daniel P. Moynihan (D-New York). They impersonated network reporters and called his office to say that the interview had been canceled.

Even more serious than the activities of LaRouche's followers are the occasions when law enforcement officials cloak themselves in the wrappings of reporters. In the late 1970s, officers from the Public Disorder Intelligence Division of the Los Angeles Police Department would sometimes show up at news conferences at the Los Angeles Press Club wearing civilian clothes and taking notes, and in 1978 members of that unit were caught posing as a television crew in order to videotape spectators and speakers at a city council meeting on a nuclear power plant. That same year Utah police attempted to arrest a man by posing as reporters from the *Los Angeles Times*.

In 1981, while pretending to be working for WCBS-TV, an investigator hired by the New York City Health and Hospital Corp. made videotapes of municipal hospital doctors who were on strike. He was collecting evidence to be used in a court action under the state's Taylor Law, which prohibits strikes by public employees.

That subterfuge, said Mark Lieberman, then a reporter for the *New York Daily News* and president of the New York Press Club, "poses a dire threat to the ability of honorable professional journalists to retain their credibility. Reporters must have the ability to gather information without the public feeling it is being duped or entrapped."

In 1983, deputy sheriffs in Portland, Oregon, induced a man to leave a barricaded shed by saying they were a television crew and wished to interview him. That same year, in Athens, Georgia, a United States marshal went to serve a summons on a member of an organization planning to hold a demonstration at the nearby Savannah River Plant, which produces fuel for nuclear weapons. In trying to identify the person to whom the court papers were addressed, one marshall said he was a reporter from Greenville, South Carolina.

Several months later, the Justice Department closed its inquiry of the incident by clearing the marshal. The department's Office of Professional Responsibility determined that the marshal did not engage in any "ongoing effort to masquerade as a reporter," but merely had "agreed that he was a reporter when another individual . . . suggested that he was." In its statement, the Justice Department unit said it was not aware that the marshal had violated any regulation or law. "His actions were limited in scope and undertaken to accomplish a bonafide law enforcement mission which he had been assigned."

A bill introduced in the Senate in 1983 would have set standards for Justice Department agents who impersonate reporters or others. That bill would have required that before an undercover operation involving impersonation of a reporter—or of a lawyer, doctor or clergyman—could be carried out, a determination would have to be made that there is "probable cause to believe that the operation is necessary to detect or prevent specific acts of criminality."

That legislation, which was not enacted in 1983 or 1984 (and now most likely is dead), was opposed by news organizations. In May 1984, John Seigenthaler of the *Nashville Tennessean* and *USA Today* and himself a former official of the Department of Justice, testified on behalf of several news groups that this legislation would "disastrously interfere with the independence and objectivity" of the press. "If the government infiltrates a news organization or impersonates a reporter, then that organization or reporter is the unwitting partner of the government," he said. "Once the news media become known as anything less than an independent chronicler of news and events, its vital role in the democracy is weakened." He said, "Once infiltration and impersonation are legitimized, the principle of independence for the news media is lost, the damage is done."

Posing, either by journalists or by others as journalists, leads to the erosion of boundaries between who has legitimate claim as a journalist and who does not. If reporters pose as others, it is only a matter of consistency that their moral authority to protest when others pose as journalists is undermined.

In May 1984, nine months after Carla Cantor, the New Jersey reporter, was accused of posing as a morgue employee, six young people were arrested at a "smoke in" staged at the town green in Morristown to protest laws forbidding the use of marijuana. They were passing around a substance that they said was marijuana, but was in fact an herb. (Under the state's "look-alike" law, a substance need only look like a forbidden drug, and therefore these arrests were apparently valid.) A "cameraman" and an "interviewer" who wore T-shirts and windbreakers that said they were from Channel 6, "New Jersey Morning News," covered the demonstration. There is no such station. The cameraman was a deputy sheriff, the interviewer an assistant county prosecutor. (By posing as television journalists, they reaped the benefit of having ready evidence on videotape.) In New Jersey there is no statute forbidding police officers to pose as news gatherers.

After the arrests, David Corcoran, the president of the New Jersey chapter of the Society of Professional Journalists, Sigma Delta Chi, recalled Carla Cantor's conviction in her first trial. In view of that case—then under appeal—he said, "it comes with particularly bad grace for law enforcement to do the same thing."

But he missed the point by half. Cantor's conviction at that time for impersonating a government official gave the law enforcement officials the very pretext they need for doing so.

Questions for Critical Analysis

1. How does posing mortgage the credibility of the press?
2. What is the difference between passive deception, as practiced by Bob Greene, and active impersonation by a reporter? Is either practice justified? Why, or why not?
3. Why did the reporters of the Chicago *Sun-Times* run a bar for four months? How was it successful? Why did they not receive a Pulitzer Prize for their story? Do you think what they did was proper?
4. What are the advantages of reporters posing to get stories? What are the disadvantages?

Under what conditions do you think Goldstein would approve of posing? Under what conditions would you pose to get information you wanted?

5. What are the dangers of others posing as reporters? What do you think of the AFL-CIO policy against LaRouche's group? Defend your opinion.

QUESTIONS FOR STRUCTURAL ANALYSIS

1. What is Goldstein's thesis? Why does he open the essay with the story of Carla Cantor instead of a clearly defined thesis statement? What effect did Carla Cantor's story have on you?
2. Goldstein advances his thesis through a series of examples. What major points does he develop through the story of the *Sun-Times* reporters? Are all of these examples useful? Which ones were particularly effective for you, and why?
3. What does Goldstein mean by the phrase: "slanted Potemkin-village portrayal"? What is he referring to? Why use the phrase?
4. Why does Goldstein include a quotation by Nicholas Gage quoting Goldstein? How does that quote relate to the subject of the essay? Does it affect your response to the essay?
5. Goldstein returns to the Cantor's story in his conclusion. How does he relate his concluding remarks to his introduction? What is his conclusion? Is it effective?

*T*HE *N*EWS *M*EDIA AND *C*LASS *C*ONTROL

MICHAEL PARENTI

Michael Parenti (1933–), a political scientist, is active in civil rights and anti-war organizations. Parenti has written several books, including Democracy for the Few *(1974),* Power and Powerlessness *(1978) and* Inventing Reality: Politics and the Mass Media *(1986). "The News Media and Class Control" is adapted from a speech Parenti made as the keynote address to a meeting of the Marxist Scholars Conference. Parenti acknowledges that the criticism leveled at the press from both the political right and left is justified, but he argues that the blame is being placed inaccurately on either the nature of media or the reporter. According to Parenti, the distortions of the media are the result of a deliberate and concerted effort to support social and economic class power. Parenti's audience, both at the conference and through* Political Affairs, *the journal in which this essay was published, is sympathetic to a Marxist interpretation of what's wrong with the press.*

Before you begin reading: *Do you think you are manipulated by the media? Before you respond, look briefly at each item on the list below:*

- *drug pusher*
- *someone riding in a limousine*
- *homeless person*
- *migrant farm worker*
- *basketball star*
- *president of a university*

If you were casting these characters in a movie, who would you ask to play the parts? Look carefully at the list of actors you named. Circle the ones which move beyond the stereotypical image created by the media. Next to your first list of actors, write an alternative name that would surprise the viewing public.

◆

THE U.S. NEWS MEDIA OPERATE UNDER A WELL-ESTABlished ideology which claims they have no established ideology, no racial, gender or class biases. Supposedly the media just report things as they see them. But more than ever we hear complaints to the contrary. There are the salvos from

Rightwingers, from whose ideological perspective the media appear as atheistic, liberal and soft on Communism. And the business community attacks the media for "failing to show business's side of things" and for running occasional reports about corporate pollution, wasteful defense contracts and the like. The occasional negative story that appears in the news, along with TV dramas like "Dynasty" and "Dallas" which have portrayed individual tycoons as ruthless cutthroats, convince corporate conservatives that the media are liberal tools bent on portraying business in the worst possible light.

These Rightist attacks help the media maintain an appearance of neutrality and objectivity. Being attacked by "extremists both on the Left and the Right," the broadcast and print news media see this as proof that they must be free of ideology and political bias. The truth is that while the press may not be totally uncritical or totally adulatory toward the Big Business community, it is not an autonomous adversary, independent of the corporate class. As we know, the big media are themselves a part of the business class, owned and controlled by the same individuals, conglomerates and banks that own most of America (and much of the rest of the world). If anything, the print and broadcast media underplay most of the more damaging information and commentary about corporate doings. What is reported is but the tip of the iceberg, but even this is more than business cares to endure and is seen as an attack on the entire business system.

If the Right had its way, the mainstream media would be dedicated exclusively to a glowing portrayal of American business, complete with upbeat reports on the economy, the blessings of the American Way of Life, and anti-Communist horror tales.

Not all the criticism is from conservatives. "Moderates" and liberals, including some journalists, have criticized the press for failing to inform the public about the crucial issues. Criticism from the political Center focuses less on content than on the lack of it. The critics complain that the news is superficial and trivial, focusing on personalities rather than issues, on surface happenings rather than substantive matters. I agree with such observations, but I want to point out that this mainstream criticism of the media remains more of a complaint than an analysis. When these critics get around to explaining why stories are so poorly reported, they are likely to blame the journalists. Again and again, we are told that reporters are misled by their sources, inept, poorly informed, too reliant on officialdom, and riddled with personal prejudices.

These kinds of criticisms are often true, but they place too much blame on the weakest, lowliest link in the news-manufacturing chain: the reporters. The critics say nothing about the editors who cut and rewrite the reporters' copy and control their jobs, and nothing about the head executives who hire, fire, pay and promote the editors and who exercise ultimate control over them.

The Centrist-liberal critique fails to note that while the journalist's product may be gravely wanting in depth and accuracy, it remains acceptable copy to the reporter's superiors. Journalists who produce more penetrating stories, ones that reveal too much about the exploitative, undemocratic nature of corporate capitalism at home and abroad, will run into difficulties with superiors. By fingering the working journalist as the main or only culprit, liberal critics are implicitly treating reporters as free agents when in fact they are not. The working press work for someone other than themselves.

Sometimes media critics will fault not the journalists or anyone else involved in manufacturing the news but the technologies of the media themselves. In this day and age, it's all the rage to blame technology. By its nature, we are told, television emphasizes the visual over the ideational. Action events, national leaders and political candidates have visual appeal; issues and policy analysis do not. Hence there is bound to be more surface than substance. This problem is also said to exist—to a lesser extent—with the print media, which have limited space and time to frame vastly complex events on a daily basis. So, it is said, news organizations latch onto simple images in order to reduce their subject matter to easily manageable components.

There is no denying that stereotyping and reductionism are the common tools of shallow thinking, but why must such shallowness be treated as inevitable? That the media so frequently resort to slick surface treatment does not mean such treatment is the only way the media can function. Rather than being a criticism, this "blaming the technological nature of the media" is a disguised defense. It gets everyone off the hook and treats television, or whatever medium, like a disembodied technological force all its own. *However, it is not television as such that chooses to cling to surface events but the people who run it.* With the right script and right intentions, visual media can offer engrossingly penetrating presentations on vital subjects, as demonstrated by the many fine independently produced documentaries which the major networks do not deign to carry.

The basic distortions in the media are not innocent errors, for they are not random; rather they move in the same overall direction again and again, favoring management over labor, corporatism over anticorporatism, the affluent over the poor, private enterprise over socialism, whites over Blacks and other minorities, males over females, officialdom over protestors, conventional politics over dissidence, and anti-Communism and military buildups over disarmament, national chauvinism over internationalism, U.S. dominance of the Third World over revolutionary change. The press does many things and serves many functions, but its major role and irreduceable responsibility is continually to recreate a view of reality supportive of existing social and economic class power.

Money, or the lack of it, is another excuse given by those who prefer innocent explanations that avoid questions of power and interest. All sorts of vital issues go unmentioned in the broadcast and print media, they argue, because it would be too expensive to try to cover all that is happening in the world. But the truth is, the major news organizations compose a vast newsgathering structure with correspondents and stringers throughout much of the world. There are more than 1,000 correspondents in Washington, D.C., tripping all over themselves trying to "develop sources" in the White House. Every four years some 12,000 newspeople cover each of the major party national conventions to report on nominations that are known in advance. As Adam Hochschild pointed out, "The press competes all right, but over ridiculous things."

With television evening news limited to 22 minutes (8 minutes for commercials) and with prime time being so expensive, there simply is not enough opportunity for more than "snapshot and headline service," media apologists have argued. And newspaper production costing what it does, there supposedly is not enough affordable print space. In truth, if one were to count the political daytime talk shows, late night news shows, local and national evening news, and hourly news programs on commercial and public radio and television, there is something close to round-the-clock news programming—but almost all of it is thin and repetitious in content. Although the network evening news has only a scant 22 minutes, it finds time for plenty of frivolous subjects. If the evening news were expanded to one hour, this would not guarantee more depth of coverage. If anything, the surface quality of broadcast news would become even more evident, and an hour of it more unsatisfying—as has been the case with the local television news programs that have gone to an hour format.

Time is not an ironclad factor in determining how indepth one might go. In five minutes one could make some devastating revelations and connections on any number of issues. But how often would a network news team attempt to do so?

Similarly, it is not true that our leading newspapers lack the space or staff for more comprehensive coverage. Left publications with only a fraction of the material resources and staff available to the major press organizations probe into controversial issues with far more depth and persistence. The startling news that the CIA was funding cultural, academic and student organizations was first publicized by the now-defunct *Ramparts* magazine. Ralph Nader's widely received work on automobile safety was ignored by the mainstream press and first began appearing in the *Nation*, a low-budget publication. Journalist Seymour Hersh sent his account of the My Lai massacre to an outfit almost nobody had heard of, Dispatch News Service, after none of the major wire services would pick it up.

Stories about hunger in America, the chemical poisoning of our environment and our people, the illegal activities of the CIA at home and abroad, U.S. sponsored torture and assassinations in Latin America and Iran (under the Shah), the dangers of nuclear power plants, revelations about the real nature of the KAL

007 flight, and other such shockers were uncovered by radical and progressive publications long before they were finally picked up—if ever—by the mainstream press.

News production is not a purely autonomous process, responsive only to its own internal conditions. Most distortions are more political than productional. What is it about the interior dynamics of newsgathering and the foibles of reporters that obliges the press to treat capitalism as a benign system and socialism as a pernicious one? Not much. But there is plenty in the pattern of ownership and control, the vested class interests, the financial muscle of big advertisers and in the entire capitalist social and cultural order which explains that bias. News producers—from owners to reporter—are so immersed in the dominant political culture that they may not be fully aware of how they misrepresent, evade and suppress the news. From this, some people have concluded that distortions in the news are due to cultural factors rather than to deliberate manipulation, and that to argue otherwise is to lapse into conspiracy theory.

Some comments are in order. First it should be noted that while much of the "mobilization of bias" is indeed built into the political culture, we can not treat every communicational evasion and distortion simply as the product of a tainted culture. Nor can we assume there is no such thing as conspiracy. Just because some people have fantasies about conspiracies does not mean every conspiracy is a fantasy—as Watergate, the Pentagon Papers, the FBI's COINTELPRO campaign, and the CIA's daily doings have demonstrated. Like most other cultural institutions, the media exercise their influence through overt means. Given the nature of the institution, it would be hard to imagine *secret* mass media. But there may be something secret and conspiratorial, something deliberately slanted and politically motivated, about news production, as found in the unpublicized owner and advertiser dominance over news personnel and editorial content, and in the instances of government interference and manipulation.

The existence of a common pool of culturally determined (systemic, nonconspiratorial) political values can not be denied, but where did this common pool come from? Who or what determines the determining elements in the culture itself? And can we reduce an entire culture, including its actively struggling political components, to a set of accumulated habituations and practices that simply build up over time?

In any case, the values and dominant opinions of our political culture are not all that ingrained and ubiquitous. Major portions of the public, often majorities, do not support present levels of taxation, military spending, military interventionism, the cold war, the arms race, nuclear power, and various domestic policies harmful to the environment, the poor, and to working people. In other words, it may be true that most media elites (and political elites) share common views on these subjects, but much, and sometimes most, of the public—and much of the working press—do not. The "dominant shared values and beliefs" which are supposedly the natural accretions and expressions of our common political culture, are not shared by all or most—certainly not at the issue level—although they surely are dominant in that they tend to preempt the field of opinion visibility because their proponents own and control so much of the communications universe.

Like any other social group, media elites consciously pursue their self-interest and try to influence others in ways that are advantageous to themselves. They treat information and culture as vital instruments of class power. Even if they never put it in those words, they keep control of the command posts of communication systems. Regardless of what their academic and journalistic apologists say on their behalf, they have no thought of leaving political discourse and mass communication openly accessible to an unrestricted popular development. Why recognition of these unexceptional facts should brand one a "conspiracy theorist" is not clear.

Can it really be argued (as it often is in the academic literature) that elites have no power over the news organizations they own and finance? Or that if they do have power, they never use it? Or that they use it only in the belief they are fostering the common interest? Certainly all modern ruling classes justify their rule in universalist terms—and have a way of believing their own propaganda. But whether they think of themselves as patriots or plotters is not the point. No doubt they like to see themselves as the defenders of American democracy even as they bolster their class privileges. Like everyone else, they believe in the virtue of their cause and equate the pursuit of their class interests with the pursuit of the general interest. Indeed, much of their propaganda is designed to treat these two things as coterminous.

The question is not how they see themselves, but how we see them. *That a particular class has achieved cultural hegemony over the entire society does not mean it has created a democratic culture.* Nor need we struggle with the question of whether the causal factor is "class" or "culture," as if these terms were mutually exclusive; for class dominance both helps to create and is fortified by cultural hegemony.

News distortion is *both* a product of shared cultural values *and* deliberate acts of disinformation. Political beliefs do not automatically reproduce and sustain themselves. They must be (at least partly) consciously propagated. And with time and repetition yesterday's propaganda becomes today's "shared cultural values and beliefs."

Consider a specific example: the untruth repeated in the press about the Soviet Union being unable to feed its people. Stories about the starving Russians are as old as the Bolshevik Revolution itself (and indeed, during the years of foreign invasion and civil war, immediately after the Revolution, there was some truth to them). Uttered today, the assertion is false. The USSR is the world's leading producer of milk and other dairy products. It produces more than enough grain to feed its people, but it imports grain for fodder in order to increase its meat supply. Western Europe imports more grain from the U.S. than does the Soviet Union, yet no one accuses West Germany or the Benelux nations of being unable to feed their people. But through unchallenged and ubiquitous repetition, be it Flora Lewis in the *New York Times*, Dan Rather on CBS, Marvin Kalb on NBC or *Time* magazine, the falsehood about the starving Russians becomes part of conventional wisdom—especially in the absence of contrary information of equal currency.

Whether or not newspeople are deliberately lying when they circulate such misinformation is less significant than that they feel free to make such statements without checking the facts. Often they do believe what they say, in large part because such beliefs are not a personal invention but are shared by almost all the opinion manufacturers of the capitalist press, and also because there are rewards for orthodox belief and penalties for ideological deviation.

Like everyone else, reporters and editors either sincerely share in the political ideology that makes it so easy for them to believe the news they produce or they go along with things because they know which side their bread is buttered on. It is difficult to know at what exact psychological point an individual's self-serving rationalization turns into sincere belief, but we do know there are variations among members of the working press; some are consciously aware of the coercive controls exercised over them in the news hierarchy—even if the ideologists of pluralism deny the existence of such things.

If the dominant culture were a mystically self-sustaining *deus ex machina*, there would be nothing left for us to do but throw up our hands and wait for the natural, gradual process of change to unfold across the centuries. But neither history nor society work that way. In fact, there is an element of struggle and indeterminancy in all our social life and political culture. Along with institutional stability we have popular agitation; along with elite manipulation we have widespread skepticism; along with ruling class coercion we have mass resistance (at times). Things are not as innocent and inevitable as the apologists of this system (including some of the critics of the media) would have us believe.

It being their goal to disguise the class nature of capitalist society, the apologists are forever looking for innocent causalities. The problems we face are caused by technology, we are told (as indeed some of our problems are). Or, it turns out, we are supposedly enveloped by "cultural forces" about which we can do little. And to suggest otherwise, to suggest that conscious interests and power are part of present social arrangements, is to be a "conspiracy theorist"—a charge which is supposed to drive us to instant denial out of fear that we are being "reductionist" and "simplistic" in our thinking. But what is more simplistic and reductionist than to reduce the actualities of class struggle and class dominated cultural formations to a problem of "technology" and "culture"?

Who cares whether the ruling class and its representatives do or do not sincerely believe their own propaganda? Sometimes they do and sometimes they don't. The question is an urgent one only for their apologists, who forever seek to demonstrate the innocence of the system under which we live. But the rest of us need not fall for that game. We do not have to deny the evidence before us. We don't have to think of the liars, manipulators, oppressors and aggressors who rule this country and control its communicational universe to be nothing more than well-intentioned actors on the social stage. It used to be said that the British empire grew in a state of absentmindedness. And so today the apologists would have us believe that the existing system is sustained in a state of absentmindedness. But no oppressive class order was ever so sustained and the claim is no truer today than it was during the time of the British empire.

By becoming aware of the conscious and deliberate elements of our oppression, we are less awed by its seemingly ubiquitous and omnipotent quality, and can better appreciate how conscious struggle leads to betterment. The rulers of this society, who try to keep history from happening, have a keen sense of our potential power and the possibilities for change. So too can we—when we see ourselves as not only the victims of technology and culture but as the makers of history.

QUESTIONS FOR CRITICAL ANALYSIS

1. According to Parenti, what proof does the media offer to justify its claim of neutrality and objectivity? Why does he discount these claims?
2. How do moderates and liberals criticize the press? What does Parenti think of their criticisms? Do you agree with him? Why, or why not?
3. What conspiracy does Parenti see implicit in the media? What evidence does he offer to support his ideas? Does he convince you of his opinion? Why, or why not?
4. In what ways does Lapham, in "Gilding the News," agree with Parenti's claims? In what ways does he disagree?
5. Parenti states that "liars, manipulators, oppressors and aggressors" rule this country and "control its communicational universe." What support does he provide for this statement? Do you agree with him? Is he partially right? Defend your response.

QUESTIONS FOR STRUCTURAL ANALYSIS

1. This article is a revised version of a speech. Are there clues to indicate that this was a speech? What are they? Is his audience sympathetic? neutral? antagonistic? How do you know?

2. Early in the essay, Parenti's political stance is clear. What are Parenti's politics? How do you know? Does his tone enhance his message? or detract from his message? Why?
3. Parenti italicizes two sentences in the essay. Why does he highlight these sentences? How are they important to his thesis? Is it effective to use italics? How did you respond to these statements?
4. Who are the "elites" Parenti refers to? What do they do? How do they influence the media? What is your response to them? Why does Parenti use that word, "elites," to refer to these people?
5. What is Parenti's conclusion? How does he expect his audience to respond? How do you respond to the conclusion? to the essay as a whole?

The Power of the News

Topics for Writing Essays

Many of the questions following each essay can serve as appropriate writing suggestions. Some of the topics listed below expand the prereading exercises, but they can be used without completing that step first.

1. What is the underlying purpose of a newspaper? To inform the public and report the news? or to sell papers and make a profit as a business? Write an essay about a newspaper's responsibility to its public and its publisher, using examples from at least two newspapers to illustrate your analysis. Address your essay to the editor of one of the newspapers you read.

2. What purpose does the campus newspaper serve? Does it keep you informed? offer opinions on campus activities and administrative policy? Do the stories reflect an attitude or bias? Interview members of the paper staff, readers, and administrators and write an evaluation of the paper, offering recommendations for its improvement, in an open letter to the editor.

3. Compare the essays by Lapham and Parenti. How does each writer define the responsibility of the press? What are their attitudes toward the media? the public? the news? What does each say that helps you define the American media? What do they say that you don't agree with? Use your comparison of these essays to write a paper to a journalism professor defining the responsibility of the American press.

Research Possibilities

1. Select a controversial news event. Find stories that cover this event in at least two different ideologically oriented papers or magazines. Find a story of the event in a more traditional paper. Compare the ways the reporters covered the story. Which version do you think is accurate? Write an analysis of the news reports on the event.

2. Do you trust the media? Develop a survey to determine how people on campus and in your community feel about the press. Conduct your survey, questioning at least 25–35 people. Interview others—professionals, students, professors, workers, and so forth. Develop questions that will require more than yes or no answers. (You could ask questions like, What do you trust about the media? For example, are sports scores recorded accurately? games described adequately? Where do you begin to distrust the media? news coverage? editorials? features? Why don't you trust the press? And so on.) Write a report about the attitude in your community toward the media that could be featured in the local newspaper.

*R*EPORTING *W*AR

The wars we study in history books are often wars of strategy and politics, and we forget that people are the ones firing the guns, dropping the bombs, and dying. Each of these essays reports a personal and often emotional response to a war experience.

STUDS TERKEL, "EVELYN FRASER"

JOHN HERSEY, "A NOISELESS FLASH"

WILLIAM L. LAURENCE, "ATOMIC BOMBING OF NAGASAKI TOLD BY FLIGHT MEMBER"

PHILIP CAPUTO, "EPILOGUE TO *A RUMOR OF WAR*"

*E*VELYN *F*RASER

STUDS TERKEL

Studs Terkel (1912–   ) is an interviewer and author who provides a mirror by which America can see itself. For each book, Terkel focuses his interviews on a single theme, recording from Americans their impressions, memories, and opinions of past and present events. "Evelyn Fraser," a selection from Terkel's The Great War *(1984), is the first-hand account of the Second World War from a woman's point of view. Fraser's narration reveals both the daily routine of those involved in the war and her feelings toward her work and her country.*

Before you begin reading: *Fantasize about the day that you receive a notice from your government to join the military for active duty. Write a brief account of how the next few days would go.*

◆

Her gray hair is bobbed, Dorothy Parker fashion: "I'd probably have had an Afro if I had enough hair." She has, this week, retired after twenty-three years as a proofreader for the *Chicago Tribune*.

I WAS A WAC, YES. A CAPTAIN IN PUBLIC INFORMATION. I HAD two tours of duty in Germany. The shocking thing was to walk among Germans and see them as human beings, and then see Dachau. It was so difficult to put together. My translator, a survivor of the Holocaust, had such a sense of guilt because he survived.

I'd been a reporter in Evansville, Indiana. I did a story on the WACs in training at Fort Oglethorpe. I thought it would be an even better story if I volunteered. I never thought they'd accept me because I'm so neurotic. I'd be a woman 4-F and that would be another story.

So I'm having these examinations with about sixteen others, big, healthy girls. This psychiatrist is mad as the very devil. I couldn't understand it. Finally it's my turn: "Are you pregnant?" I said, "I wasn't when I came in." It turns out I was the only one that passed. The other sixteen weren't accepted because they got mad at him for asking such questions. It just amused me. I was in the army. Jeez, now I have to go all the way through with this.

At camp in Georgia, where I had done this story, I'd been treated as an important reporter by the colonel. Now I was in fatigues, doing KP. The colonel didn't recognize me. When I reminded him, he was really flustered. (Laughs.)

You wake up one morning in this barracks, with all these people. You've never been able to sleep without the shades down. And here I am. What have I done?

I'm heading for my duty station in Camp Breckenridge, Kentucky. I have this bundle of orders. I'm the only woman on the train. This sailor sits down by me: "Hey, honey, where you going?" I said, "I can't tell you. Classified orders." (Laughs.) Naturally he laughed, he and the others. They didn't take us very seriously.

It was awkward for the men. I'd been brought into Camp Atterbury for administrative work. This lieutenant wouldn't tell me a thing about the job. He was afraid I was going to replace him and he'd have to go overseas. I beat him to it: "Look, you can put everything on the desk now. I'm going overseas and you can stay here." (Laughs.) When we came along, the men in clerical jobs were none too happy. We replaced them for combat overseas. That was the whole idea. Nobody wants to go overseas to fight.

I went in in September of '43 and was commissioned in May of '44. In basic training we were around all these women. You seldom encountered a male. When I got on the bus with a weekend pass, I heard male voices and little children's. You didn't realize how much you missed those voices.

I was a recruiting officer in Cleveland. I had to find out what the resistance to the WACs was about. There were stories that our women were promiscuous and it wouldn't be a nice place for a nice girl. We took only high school graduates, so few of the women passed. You'd be surprised the number of women we had to reject for physical reasons. There were lots of high school graduates with syphilis who didn't know they had it. Black and white. It was incredible to me. I had thought everybody was fairly healthy.

When I was in Paris I met this black WAC captain. They had a segregated detachment over there. They were beautiful girls, well qualified. I said, "I guess you girls are having an awful lot of fun over here." Because there were so many black soldiers in Paris. She says, "No, they're having a terrible time. All the black soldiers are taking out the white French girls."

At that time VD was rampant among our soldiers. It was an epidemic. The officers couldn't understand why the men didn't stop at the stations for treatment, after they had contact with the women. This was in Germany. It seemed obvious to me. I took my bars off and went to an enlisted club. I found out. These fellas, if they were out after bed check, would not stop at the pro station. So I suggested to the general, why not put a pro station in the barracks? They wouldn't have to worry about being late for bed check. He told his male officers it's funny that they had to have a WAC suggest such a practical thing. (Laughs.)

In late '45, I was in Vienna. The four powers were there. I wanted to see the Danube. We get in our jeep and we're crossing the bridge and this Russian soldier holds a rifle at us. Then I saw some husky-looking Russian gals with real thick stockings walking across the street. They glared at us. I couldn't understand where this had broken down, see? Maybe if we had handled it better in some way and tried to be more cordial, it might have helped. But we were so busy selling them watches. All the Russians wanted watches, and our people were so busy getting all the black-market Micky Mouse watches from the United States.

I was there, near the Saar, the French zone, when we had taken over the occupation. Of course, the French had taken all the latrines and everything back to France. They took all this old junk, and the Russians took all this old junk. We had to completely rebuild it. That's why Germany has got such nice new facilities. (Laughs.) Our money. The French and Russians took all the obsolete stuff.

I had to give every officer a Why We Fight orientation. I used to give them one where I'd say how the Russians were our friends and how we were fighting together. Next minute, they expected us to give a lecture about the communists. A complete reversal, a change of gears. This really was disillusioning.

I saw all those cemeteries in Europe of eighteen-year-old boys, with all the little crosses. I talked to mothers who came over to see those crosses. I tried to persuade them not to bring the body home. Truthfully, I don't think they know, in many cases, what remains are in that grave. You'd get an arm here, a leg there.

If it weren't for the war, I'd have probably stayed in Evansville as a newspaperwoman. Maybe got a job in Indianapolis or Chicago. (Laughs.) I wouldn't have traveled as extensively as I did. It really changed my life. A young woman my age never had an apartment away from her parents. My mother would have thought I was a fallen woman. This way, I could gloriously go off on my own and be on my own.

I used part of the GI Bill to go to Northwestern and then full time to Roosevelt U. I'd never had accounting and all those dull subjects. I thought it would be a good exercise. It helped. I can balance my checkbook now. (Laughs.)

Dachau? I saw the lampshades made out of skin. I saw a lot of the children who had been in the camps. We had Christmas parties for them. They didn't even know how to open a package. It was incredible. Then you looked at these Germans, and they were people like—(laughs)—everybody.

What we've learned, I think, is that we should examine everything very carefully before we get into any kind of conflict. They design a weapon. We design a weapon. Where's it going? I don't know what the answer is. Unfortunately, the dead can't speak. I wonder what they'd say.

QUESTIONS FOR CRITICAL ANALYSIS

1. What sort of person is Evelyn Fraser? How do you know?
2. Why did the men resent the Women's Army Corps? Does this surprise you? Does it match your opinion of soldiers?
3. Fraser says she was disillusioned by the changes in the U.S. policy toward Russia.

Why? What changes? How does Fraser think U.S.-Russian relations could have started in a different direction? Is she naive?

4. What opportunities did serving in the WACs give Fraser? What did she learn from her experiences?
5. Twice Fraser refers to Germany and Dachau. How do you know she was deeply affected by seeing the people from the concentration camps? Why didn't she say more about her feelings and observations?

QUESTIONS FOR STRUCTURAL ANALYSIS

1. Studs Terkel's *The Good War*, like many of his other books, is a collection of first-person interviews with people directly involved in the subject. What elements in "Evelyn Fraser" identify the selection as a transcript of an interview? What is the benefit of this approach to a subject? What are the deficiencies of such an approach?
2. What is the point of Fraser's story? Is there a thesis? Since it's an oral expression, its development and coherence are not tightly maintained. How effective is this story?
3. What is the connection between paragraphs one and two? What about the composition of these two paragraphs identifies them as oral rather than written communication? How would you rewrite these two paragraphs if you were using Fraser's interview as the basis for an essay?
4. Notice the times Fraser switches between present and past tense (for example, see the final two sentences of paragraph three). How is this effective in the retelling of the story? Should Terkel have edited the interview to make it more consistent? Why, or why not?
5. In the conclusion Fraser echoes comments she made about Dachau made in the first paragraph. What connects the introduction to the conclusion? Is it an accident that she moves from comments about the concentration camps to her final paragraph?

A Noiseless Flash

John Hersey

John Hersey (1914–) was a war and foreign correspondent during the Second World War, from 1942–45, for Time, Life, *and the* New Yorker. *Two of his books tell his experiences covering the war in the Pacific (*Men on Bataan, *1942, and* Into the Valley, *1943) and several novels present the war in Europe (*A Bell for Adano, *1944, and* The War, *1950, among others). In 1946 Hersey visited Hiroshima and wrote an account of how the atomic bomb, dropped on that city on August 6, 1945, radically changed the lives of six victims. By telling the story from the point of view of individuals who experienced atomic war firsthand, Hersey personalizes the atrocities—making them easier for us to understand and, therefore, more overpowering than a mere recitation of statistics would provide. "A Noiseless Flash" is the opening section of the resulting book,* Hiroshima. *The* New Yorker *devoted its entire August 1946 issue to the publication of* Hiroshima.

Before you begin reading: *Most of us were born and have lived under the shadow of nuclear weapons. Have you ever felt afraid because of the threat of nuclear war? Focus on the idea of nuclear war and transcribe into your reading notebook whatever thoughts and feelings come to your mind.*

◆

AT EXACTLY FIFTEEN MINUTES PAST EIGHT IN THE MORNING, on August 6, 1945, Japanese time, at the moment when the atomic bomb flashed above Hiroshima, Miss Toshiko Sasaki, a clerk in the personnel department of the East Asia Tin Works, had just sat down at her place in the plant office and was turning her head to speak to the girl at the next desk. At that same moment, Dr. Masakazu Fujii was settling down crosslegged to read the Osaka *Asahi* on the porch of his private hospital, overhanging one of the seven deltaic rivers which divide Hiroshima; Mrs. Hatsuyo Nakamura, a tailor's widow, stood by the window of her kitchen, watching a neighbor tearing down his house because it lay in the path of an air-raid defense fire lane; Father Wilhelm Kleinsorge, a German priest of the Society of Jesus, reclined in his underwear on a cot on the top floor of his order's three-story mission house, reading a Jesuit magazine, *Stimmen der Zeit*; Dr. Terufumi Sasaki, a young member of the surgical staff of the city's large, modern Red Cross Hospital, walked along one of the hospital corridors with a blood specimen for a Wassermann test in his hand; and the Reverend Mr. Kiyoshi Tanimoto, pastor of the Hiroshima Methodist Church, paused at the door of a rich man's house in Koi, the city's western suburb, and prepared to unload a handcart full of things he had evacuated from town in fear of the massive B-29 raid which everyone expected Hiroshima to suffer. A hundred thousand people were killed by the atomic bomb, and these six were among the survivors. They still wonder why they lived when so many others died. Each of them counts many small items of chance or volition—a step taken in time, a decision to go indoors, catching one streetcar instead of the next—that spared him. And now each knows that in the act of survival he lived a dozen lives and saw more death than he ever thought he would see. At the time, none of them knew anything.

The Reverend Mr. Tanimoto got up at five o'clock that morning. He was alone in the parsonage, because for some time his wife had been commuting with their year-old baby to spend nights with a friend in Ushida, a suburb to the north. Of all the important cities of Japan, only two, Kyoto and Hiroshima, had not been visited in strength by *B-san*, or Mr. B, as the Japanese, with a mixture of respect and unhappy familiarity, called the B-29; and Mr. Tanimoto, like all his neighbors and friends, was almost sick with anxiety. He had heard uncomfortably detailed accounts of mass raids on Kure, Iwakuni, Tokuyama, and other nearby towns; he was sure Hiroshima's turn would come soon. He had slept badly the night before, because there had been several air-raid warnings. Hiroshima had been getting such warnings almost every night for weeks, for at that time the B-29s were using Lake Biwa, northeast of Hiroshima, as a rendezvous point, and no matter what city the Americans planned to hit, the Superfortresses streamed in over the coast near Hiroshima. The frequency of the warnings and the continued abstinence of Mr. B with respect to Hiroshima had made its citizens jittery; a rumor was going around that the Americans were saving something special for the city.

Mr. Tanimoto was a small man, quick to talk, laugh, and cry. He wore his black hair parted in the middle and rather long; the prominence of the frontal bones just above his eyebrows and the smallness of his mustache, mouth, and chin gave him a strange, old-young look, boyish and yet wise, weak and yet fiery. He moved nervously and fast, but with a restraint which suggested that he was a cautious, thoughtful man. He showed, indeed, just those qualities in the uneasy days before the bomb fell. Besides having his wife spend the nights in Ushida, Mr. Tanimoto had been carrying all the portable things from his church, in the close-packed residential district called Nagaragawa, to a house that belonged to a rayon manufacturer in Koi, two miles from the center of town. The rayon man, a Mr. Matsui, had opened his then unoccupied estate to a large number of his friends and acquaintances, so that they might evacuate whatever they wished to a safe distance from the probable target area. Mr. Tanimoto had had no difficulty in moving chairs, hymnals, Bibles, altar gear, and church records by pushcart himself, but the organ console and an upright piano required some aid. A friend of his named Matsuo had, the day before, helped him get the piano out to Koi; in return, he had promised this day to assist Mr. Matsuo in hauling out a daughter's belongings. That is why he had risen so early.

Mr. Tanimoto cooked his own breakfast. He felt awfully tired. The effort of moving the piano the day before, a sleepless night, weeks of worry and unbalanced diet, the cares of his parish—all combined to make him feel hardly adequate to the new day's work. There was another thing, too: Mr. Tanimoto had studied theology at Emory College, in Atlanta, Georgia; he had graduated in 1940; he spoke excellent English; he dressed in American clothes; he had corresponded with many American friends right up to the time the war began; and among a people obsessed with a fear of being spied upon—perhaps almost obsessed himself—he found himself growing increasingly uneasy. The police had questioned him several times, and just a few days before, he had heard that an influential acquaintance, a Mr. Tanaka, a retired officer of the Toyo Kisen Kaisha steamship line, an anti-Christian, a man famous in Hiroshima for his showy philanthropies and notorious for his personal tyrannies, had been telling people that Tanimoto should not be trusted. In compensation, to show himself publicly a good Japanese, Mr. Tanimoto had taken on the chairmanship of his local *tonarigumi*, or Neighborhood Association, and to his other duties and concerns this position had added the business of organizing air-raid defense for about twenty families.

Before six o'clock that morning, Mr. Tanimoto started for Mr. Matsuo's house. There he found that their burden was to be a *tansu*, a large Japanese cabinet, full of clothing and household goods. The two men set out. The morning was perfectly clear and so warm that the day promised to be uncomfortable. A few minutes after they started, the air-raid siren went off—a minute-long blast that warned of approaching planes but indicated to the people of Hiroshima only a slight degree of danger, since it sounded every morning at this time, when an American weather plane came over. The two men pulled and pushed the handcart through the city streets. Hiroshima was a fan-shaped city, lying mostly on the six islands formed by the seven estuarial rivers that branch out from the Ota River; its main commercial and residential districts, covering about four square miles in the center of the city, contained three-quarters of its population, which had been reduced by several evacuation programs from a wartime peak of 380,000 to about 245,000. Factories and other residential districts, or suburbs, lay compactly around the edges of the city. To the south were the docks, an airport, and the island-studded Inland Sea. A rim of mountains runs around the other three sides of the delta. Mr. Tanimoto and Mr. Matsuo took their way through the shopping center, already full of people, and across two of the rivers to the sloping streets of Koi, and up them to the outskirts and foothills. As they started up a valley away from the tight-ranked houses, the all-clear sounded. (The Japanese radar operators, detecting only three planes, supposed that they comprised a reconnaissance.) Pushing the handcart up to the rayon man's house was tiring, and the men, after they had maneuvered their load into the driveway and to the front steps, paused to rest awhile. They stood with a wing of the house between them and the city. Like most homes in this part of Japan, the house consisted of a wooden frame and wooden walls supporting a heavy tile roof. Its front hall, packed with rolls of bedding and clothing, looked like a cool cave full of fat cushions. Opposite the house, to the right of the front door, there was a large, finicky rock garden. There was no sound of planes. The morning was still; the place was cool and pleasant.

Then a tremendous flash of light cut across the sky. Mr. Tanimoto has a distinct recollection that it travelled from east to west, from the city toward the hills. It seemed a sheet of sun. Both he and Mr. Matsuo reacted in terror—and both had time to react (for they were 3,500 yards, or two miles, from the center of the explosion). Mr. Matsuo dashed up the front steps into the house and dived among the bedrolls and buried himself there. Mr. Tanimoto took four or five steps and threw himself between two big rocks in the garden. He bellied up very hard against one of them. As his face was against the stone, he did not see what happened. He felt a sudden pressure, and then splinters and pieces of board and fragments of tile fell on him. He heard no roar. (Almost no one in Hiroshima recalls hearing any noise of the bomb. But a fisherman in his sampan on the Inland Sea near Tsuzu, the man with whom Mr. Tanimoto's mother-in-law and sister-in-law were living, saw the flash and heard a tremendous explosion; he was nearly twenty miles from Hiroshima, but the thunder was greater than when the B-29s hit Iwakuni, only five miles away.)

When he dared, Mr. Tanimoto raised his head and saw that the rayon man's house had collapsed. He thought a bomb had fallen directly on it. Such clouds of dust had risen that there was a sort of twilight around. In panic, not thinking for the moment of Mr. Matsuo under the ruins, he dashed out into the street. He noticed as he ran that the concrete wall of the estate had fallen over—toward the house rather than away from it. In the street, the first thing he saw was a squad of soldiers who had been burrowing into the hillside opposite, making one of the thousands of dugouts in which the Japanese apparently intended to resist invasion, hill by hill, life for life; the soldiers were coming out of the hole, where they should have been safe, and blood was running from their heads, chests, and backs. They were silent and dazed.

Under what seemed to be a local dust cloud, the day grew darker and darker.

At nearly midnight, the night before the bomb was dropped, an announcer on the city's radio station said that about two hundred B-29s were approaching southern Honshu and advised the population of Hiroshima to evacuate to their designated "safe areas." Mrs. Hatsuyo Nakamura, the tailor's widow, who lived in the section called Nobori-cho and who had long had a habit of doing as she was told, got her three children—a ten-year-old boy, Toshio, an eight-year-old girl, Yaeko, and a five-year-old girl, Myeko—out of bed and dressed them and walked with them to the military area known as the East Parade Ground, on the northeast edge of the city. There she unrolled some mats and the children lay down on them. They slept until about two, when they were awakened by the roar of the planes going over Hiroshima.

As soon as the planes had passed, Mrs. Nakamura started back with her children. They reached home a little after two-thirty and she immediately turned on the radio, which, to her distress, was just then broadcasting a fresh warning. When she looked at the children and saw how tired they were, and when she thought of the number of trips they had made in past weeks, all to no purpose, to the East Parade Ground, she decided that in spite of the instructions on the radio, she simply could not face starting out all over again. She put the children in their bedrolls on the floor, lay down herself at three o'clock, and fell asleep at once, so soundly that when planes passed over later, she did not waken to their sound.

The siren jarred her awake at about seven. She arose, dressed quickly, and hurried to the house of Mr. Nakamoto, the head of her Neighborhood Association, and asked him what she should do. He said that she should remain at home unless an urgent warning—a series of intermittent blasts of the siren—was sounded. She returned home, lit the stove in the kitchen, set some rice to cook, and sat down to read that morning's Hiroshima *Chugoku*. To her relief, the all-clear sounded at eight o'clock. She heard the children stirring, so she went and gave each of them a handful of peanuts and told them to stay on their bedrolls, because they were tired from the night's walk. She had hoped that they would go back to sleep, but the man in the house directly to the south began to make a terrible hullabaloo of hammering, wedging, ripping, and splitting. The prefectural government, convinced, as everyone in Hiroshima was, that the city would be attacked soon, had begun to press with threats and warnings for the completion of wide fire lanes, which, it was hoped, might act in conjunction with the rivers to localize any fires started by an incendiary raid; and the neighbor was reluctantly sacrificing his home to the city's safety. Just the day before, the prefecture had ordered all able-bodied girls from the secondary schools to spend a few days helping to clear these lanes, and they started work soon after the all-clear sounded.

Mrs. Nakamura went back to the kitchen, looked at the rice, and began watching the man next door. At first, she was annoyed with him for making so much noise, but then she was moved almost to tears by pity. Her emotion was specifically directed toward her neighbor, tearing down his home, board by board, at a time when there was so much unavoidable destruction, but undoubtedly she also felt a generalized, community pity, to say nothing of self-pity. She had not had an easy time. Her husband, Isawa, had gone into the Army just after Myeko was born, and she had heard nothing from or of him for a long time, until, on March 5, 1942, she received a seven-word telegram: "Isawa died an honorable death at Singapore." She learned later that he had died on February 15th, the day Singapore fell, and that he had been a corporal. Isawa had been a not particularly prosperous tailor, and his only capital was a Sankoku sewing machine. After his death, when his allotments stopped coming, Mrs. Nakamura got out the machine and began to take in piecework herself, and since then had supported the children, but poorly, by sewing.

As Mrs. Nakamura stood watching her neighbor, everything flashed whiter than any white she had ever seen. She did not notice what happened to the man next door; the reflex of a mother set her in motion toward her children. She had taken a single step (the house was 1,350 yards, or three-quarters of a mile, from the center of the explosion) when something picked her up and she seemed to fly into the next room over the raised sleeping platform, pursued by parts of her house.

Timbers fell around her as she landed, and a shower of tiles pommelled her; everything became dark, for she was buried. The debris did not cover her deeply. She rose up and freed herself. She heard a child cry, "Mother, help me!," and saw her youngest—Myeko, the five-year-old—buried up to her breast and unable to move. As Mrs. Nakamura started frantically to claw her way toward the baby, she could see or hear nothing of her other children.

In the days right before the bombing, Dr. Masakazu Fujii, being prosperous, hedonistic, and at the time not too busy, had been allowing himself the luxury of sleeping until nine or nine-thirty, but fortunately he had to get up early the morning the bomb was dropped to see a house guest off on a train. He rose at six, and half an hour later walked with his friend to the station, not far away, across two of the rivers. He was back home by seven, just as the siren sounded its sustained warning. He ate breakfast and then, because the morning was already hot, undressed down to his underwear and went out on the porch to read the paper. This porch—in fact, the whole building—was curiously constructed. Dr. Fujii was the proprietor of a peculiarly Japanese institution: a private, single-doctor hospital. This building, perched beside and over the water of the Kyo River, and next to the bridge of the same name, contained thirty rooms for thirty patients and their kinfolk—for, according to Japanese custom, when a person falls sick and goes to a hospital, one or more members of his family go and live there with him, to cook for him, bathe, massage, and read to him, and to offer incessant familial sympathy, without which a Japanese patient would be miserable indeed. Dr. Fujii had no beds—only straw mats—for his patients. He did, however, have all sorts of modern equipment: an X-ray machine, diathermy apparatus, and a fine tiled laboratory. The structure rested two-thirds on the land, one-third on piles over the tidal waters of the Kyo. This overhang, the part of the building where Dr. Fujii lived, was queer-looking, but it was cool in summer and from the porch, which faced away from the center of the city, the prospect of the river, with pleasure boats drifting up and down it, was always refreshing. Dr. Fujii had occasionally had anxious moments when the Ota and its mouth branches rose to flood, but the piling was apparently firm enough and the house had always held.

Dr. Fujii had been relatively idle for about a month because in July, as the number of untouched cities in Japan dwindled and as Hiroshima seemed more and more inevitably a target, he began turning patients away, on the ground that in case of a fire raid he would not be able to evacuate them. Now he had only two patients left—a woman from Yano, injured in the shoulder, and a young man of twenty-five recovering from burns he had suffered when the steel factory near Hiroshima in which he worked had been hit. Dr. Fujii had six nurses to tend his patients. His wife and children were safe; his wife and one son were living outside Osaka, and another son and two daughters were in the country on Kyushu. A niece was living with him, and a maid and a manservant. He had little to do and did not mind, for he had saved some money. At fifty, he was healthy, convivial, and calm, and he was pleased to pass the evenings drinking whiskey with friends, always sensibly and for the sake of conversation. Before the war, he had affected brands imported from Scotland and America; now he was perfectly satisfied with the best Japanese brand, Suntory.

Dr. Fujii sat down cross-legged in his underwear on the spotless matting of the porch, put on his glasses, and started reading the Osaka *Asahi*. He liked to read the Osaka news because his wife was there. He saw the flash. To him—faced away from the center and looking at his paper—it seemed a brilliant yellow. Startled, he began to rise to his feet. In that moment (he was 1,550 yards from the center), the hospital leaned behind his rising and, with a terrible ripping noise, toppled into the river. The Doctor, still in the act of getting to his feet, was thrown forward and around and over; he was buffeted and gripped; he lost track of everything, because things were so speeded up; he felt the water.

Dr. Fujii hardly had time to think that he was dying before he realized that he was alive, squeezed tightly by two long timbers in a V across his chest, like a morsel suspended between two huge chopsticks—held upright, so that he could not move, with his head miraculously above water and his torso and legs in it. The remains of his hospital were all around him in a mad assortment of splintered lumber and materials for the relief of pain. His left shoulder hurt terribly. His glasses were gone.

Father Wilhelm Kleinsorge, of the Society of Jesus, was, on the morning of the explosion, in rather frail condition. The Japanese wartime diet had not sustained him, and he felt the strain of being a foreigner in an increasingly xenophobic Japan; even a German, since the defeat of the Fatherland, was unpopular. Father Kleinsorge had, at thirty-eight, the look of a boy growing too fast—thin in the face, with a prominent Adam's apple, a hollow chest, dangling hands, big feet. He walked clumsily, leaning forward a little. He was tired all the time. To make matters worse, he had suffered for two days, along with Father Cieslik, a fellow-priest, from a rather painful and urgent diarrhea, which they blamed on the beans and black ration bread they were obliged to eat. Two other priests then living in the mission compound, which was in the Nobori-cho section—Father Superior LaSalle and Father Schiffer—had happily escaped this affliction.

Father Kleinsorge woke up about six the morning the bomb was dropped, and half an hour later—he was a bit tardy because of his sickness—he began to read Mass in the mission chapel, a small Japanese-style wooden building which was without pews, since its worshippers knelt on the usual Japanese matted floor, facing an altar graced with splendid silks, brass, silver, and heavy embroideries. This morning, a Monday, the only worshippers were Mr. Takemoto, a theological student living in the mission house; Mr. Fukai, the secretary of the diocese; Mrs. Murata, the mission's devoutly Christian housekeeper; and his fellow-priests. After Mass, while Father Kleinsorge was reading the Prayers of Thanksgiving, the siren sounded. He stopped the service and the missionaries retired across the compound to the bigger building. There, in his room on the ground floor, to the right of the front door, Father Kleinsorge changed into a military uniform which he had acquired when he was teaching at the Rokko Middle School in Kobe and which he wore during air-raid alerts.

After an alarm, Father Kleinsorge always went out and scanned the sky, and in this instance, when he stepped outside, he was glad to see only the single weather plane that flew over Hiroshima each day about this time. Satisfied that nothing would happen, he went in and breakfasted with the other Fathers on substitute coffee and ration bread, which, under the circumstances, was especially repugnant to him. The Fathers sat and talked awhile, until, at eight, they heard the all-clear. They went then to various parts of the building. Father Schiffer retired to his room to do some writing. Father Cieslik sat in his room in a straight chair with a pillow over his stomach to ease his pain, and read. Father Superior LaSalle stood at the window of his room, thinking. Father Kleinsorge went up to a room on the third floor, took off all his clothes except his underwear, and stretched out on his right side on a cot and began reading his *Stimmen der Zeit*.

After the terrible flash—which, Father Kleinsorge later realized, reminded him of something he had read as a boy about a large meteor colliding with the earth—he had time (since he was 1,400 yards from the center) for one thought: A bomb has fallen directly on us. Then, for a few seconds or minutes, he went out of his mind.

Father Kleinsorge never knew how he got out of the house. The next things he was conscious of were that he was wandering around in the mission's vegetable garden in his underwear, bleeding slightly from small cuts along his left flank; that all the buildings round about had fallen down except the Jesuits' mission house, which had long before been braced and double-braced by a priest named Gropper, who was terrified of earthquakes; that the day had turned dark; and that Murata-*san*, the housekeeper, was nearby, crying over and over, "*Shu Jesusu, awaremi tamai!* Our Lord Jesus, have pity on us!"

On the train on the way into Hiroshima from the country, where he lived with his mother, Dr. Terufumi Sasaki, the Red Cross Hospital surgeon, thought over an unpleasant nightmare he had had the night before. His mother's home was in Mukaihara, thirty miles from the city, and it took him two hours by train and tram to reach the hospital. He had slept uneasily all night and had wakened an hour earlier than usual, and, feeling sluggish and slightly feverish, had debated whether to go to the hospital at all; his sense of duty finally forced him to go, and he had started out on an earlier train than he took most mornings. The dream had particularly frightened him because it was so closely associated, on the surface at least, with a disturbing actuality. He was only twenty-five years old and had just completed his training at the Eastern Medical University, in Tsingtao, China. He was something of an idealist and was much distressed by the inadequacy of medical facilities in the country town where his mother lived. Quite on his own, and without a permit, he had begun visiting a few sick people out there in the evenings, after his eight hours at the hospital and four hours' commuting. He had recently learned that the penalty for practicing without a permit was severe; a fellow-doctor whom he had asked about it had given him a serious scolding. Nevertheless, he had continued to practice. In his dream, he had been at the bedside of a country patient when the police and the doctor he had consulted burst into the room, seized him, dragged him outside, and beat him up cruelly. On the train, he just about decided to give up the work in Mukaihara, since he felt it would be impossible to get a permit, because the authorities would hold that it would conflict with his duties at the Red Cross Hospital.

At the terminus, he caught a streetcar at once. (He later calculated that if he had taken his customary train that morning, and if he had had to wait a few minutes for the streetcar, as often happened, he would have been close to the center at the time of the explosion and would surely have perished.) He arrived at the hospital at seven-forty and reported to the chief surgeon. A few minutes later, he went to a room on the first floor and drew blood from the arm of a man in order to perform a Wassermann test. The laboratory containing the incubators for the test was on the third floor. With the blood specimen in his left hand, walking in a kind of distraction he had felt all morning, probably because of the dream and his restless night, he started along the main corridor on his way toward the stairs. He was one step beyond an open window when the light of the bomb was reflected, like a gigantic photographic flash, in the corridor. He ducked down on one knee and said to himself, as only a Japanese would, "Sasaki, *gambare!* Be brave!" Just then (the building was 1,650 yards from the center), the blast ripped through the hospital. The glasses he was wearing flew off his face; the bottle of blood crashed against one wall; his Japanese slippers zipped out from under his feet—but otherwise, thanks to where he stood, he was untouched.

Dr. Sasaki shouted the name of the chief surgeon and rushed around to the man's office and found him terribly cut by glass. The hospital was in horrible confusion: heavy partitions and ceilings had fallen on patients, beds had overturned, windows had blown in and cut people, blood was spattered on the walls and floors, instruments were everywhere, many of the patients were running about screaming, many more lay dead. (A colleague working in the laboratory to which Dr. Sasaki had been walking was dead; Dr. Sasaki's patient, whom he had just left and who a few moments before had been dreadfully afraid of syphilis, was also dead.) Dr. Sasaki found himself the only doctor in the hospital who was unhurt.

Dr. Sasaki, who believed that the enemy had hit only the building he was in, got bandages and began to bind the wounds of those inside the hospital; while outside, all over Hiroshima, maimed and dying citizens turned their unsteady steps toward the Red Cross Hospital to begin an invasion that was to make Dr. Sasaki forget his private nightmare for a long, long time.

Miss Toshiko Sasaki, the East Asia Tin Works clerk, who was not related to Dr. Sasaki, got up at three o'clock in the morning on the day the bomb fell. There was extra housework to do. Her eleven-month-old brother, Akio, had come down the day before with a serious stomach upset; her mother had taken him to the Tamura Pediatric Hospital and was staying there with him. Miss Sasaki, who was about twenty, had to cook breakfast for her father, a brother, a sister, and herself, and—since the hospital, because of the war, was unable to provide food—to prepare a whole day's meals for her mother and the baby, in time for her father, who worked in a factory making rubber earplugs for artillery crews, to take the food by on his way to the plant. When she had finished and had cleaned and put away the cooking things, it was nearly seven. The family lived in Koi, and she had a forty-five-minute trip to the tin works, in the section of town called Kannonmachi. She was in charge of the personnel records in the factory. She left Koi at seven, and as soon as she reached the plant, she went with some of the other girls from the personnel department to the factory auditorium. A prominent local Navy man, a former employee, had committed suicide the day before by throwing himself under a train—a death considered honorable enough to warrant a memorial service, which was to be held at the tin works at ten o'clock that morning. In the large hall, Miss Sasaki and the others made suitable preparations for the meeting. This work took about twenty minutes.

Miss Sasaki went back to her office and sat down at her desk. She was quite far from the windows, which were off to her left, and behind her were a couple of tall bookcases containing all the books of the factory library, which the personnel department had organized. She settled herself at her desk, put some things in a drawer, and shifted papers. She thought that before she began to make entries in her lists of new employees, discharges, and departures for the Army, she would chat for a moment with the girl at her right. Just as she turned her head away from the windows, the room was filled with a blinding light. She was paralyzed by fear, fixed still in her chair for a long moment (the plant was 1,600 yards from the center).

Everything fell, and Miss Sasaki lost consciousness. The ceiling dropped suddenly and the wooden floor above collapsed in splinters and the people up there came down and the roof above them gave way; but principally and first of all, the bookcases right behind her swooped forward and the contents threw her down, with her left leg horribly twisted and breaking underneath her. There, in the tin factory, in the first moment of the atomic age, a human being was crushed by books.

Questions for Critical Analysis

1. Could Hersey have observed all the events, including the dialogue, that he reports here? Is he using explicitly fictional techniques to tell his story? What difference does it make? What are your thoughts and feelings about it?
2. Why did Hersey select six survivors to present his story? Why not include stories about some of the people who died? How would the effect be different?
3. Compare the stories of the six individuals. In what ways were they similar? How were they different?
4. Compare William Laurence's article (on page 508) written from the bomber at the time the bomb was dropped with this selection written a year later from the perspective of those who were on the ground.
5. Hersey's *Hiroshima* was very popular and widely read after it was published in 1946. From this selection, can you see why? Analyze its effectiveness, in 1946 and today.
6. How does this essay and Laurence's "Atomic Bombing of Nagasaki Told by Flight Member" relate in substance and tone to Kai Erikson's "Of Accidental Judgments and Casual Slaughter" (from Section III)?

QUESTIONS FOR STRUCTURAL ANALYSIS

1. Why did Hersey organize this selection as he did—with a general introduction followed by six individual accounts of the bombing. Is it effective? Would you have written it differently? How?
2. Hersey relies heavily on description to portray the devastation of the bombing. What descriptive techniques does he use?
3. What is the effect of the focus on Mr. Tanimoto and the other individuals? What use is it, argumentatively and rhetorically?
4. How is Hersey's attitude toward the United States' use of the atomic bomb evident in this essay? What is his attitude? What clues do you find that reveal it?
5. What is the function of the final anecdote about the woman crushed by books? How well does the conclusion serve the entire selection?

*A*TOMIC *B*OMBING OF *N*AGASAKI *T*OLD BY *F*LIGHT *M*EMBER

WILLIAM L. LAURENCE

William L. Laurence (1888–1977), a New York Times *journalist, was known as "the dean of science writers." Using familiar, nontechnical language, he described scientific subjects so that the ordinary reader could understand the extraordinary scientific events of this century. Laurence, assigned to the Manhattan Project*, knew many of the scientists involved in atomic research during the Second World War and he knew of its military application. Although disappointed not to be included in the first bombing mission to Hiroshima, Laurence joined the crew on the second flight and won his second Pulitzer Prize (in 1946) for this account of the bombing of Nagasaki. "Atomic Bombing of Nagasaki as Told by Flight Member" appeared in the* New York Times *on August 9, 1945. The second atomic bomb was dropped on Nagasaki on August 8, 1945, and Laurence's story was delayed by one day.*

Before you begin reading: *Where does your information about the Second World War come from? Think about the stories you've been told, you've read or seen on television or at the movies. In your notebook, make a list of images that come into your mind when you think of that war. Next to each image on your list, write a word or phrase that conveys the emotion of the event.*

◆

WITH THE ATOMIC BOMB MISSION TO JAPAN, AUG. 9 (DElayed)—We are on our way to bomb the mainland of Japan. Our flying contingent consists of three specially designed B-29 "Superforts," and two of these carry no bombs. But our lead plane is on its way with another atomic bomb, the second in three days, concentrating in its active substance an explosive energy equivalent to 20,000 and, under favorable conditions, 40,000 tons of TNT.

We have several chosen targets. One of these is the great industrial and

*The Manhattan Project was the designation of a secret scientific project begun in 1942 to develop atomic weapons.

shipping center of Nagasaki, on the western shore of Kyushu, one of the main islands of the Japanese homeland.

I watched the assembly of this man-made meteor during the past two days, and was among the small group of scientists and Army and Navy representatives privileged to be present at the ritual of its loading in the "Superfort" last night, against a background of threatening black skies torn open at intervals by great lightning flashes.

It is a thing of beauty to behold, this "gadget." In its design went millions of man-hours of what is without doubt the most concentrated intellectual effort in history. Never before had so much brainpower been focused on a single problem.

This atomic bomb is different from the bomb used three days ago with such devastating results on Hiroshima.

I saw the atomic substance before it was placed inside the bomb. By itself it is not at all dangerous to handle. It is only under certain conditions, produced in the bomb assembly, that it can be made to yield up its energy, and even then it gives only a small fraction of its total contents—a fraction, however, large enough to produce the greatest explosion on earth.

The briefing at midnight revealed the extreme care and the tremendous amount of preparation that had been made to take care of every detail of the mission, to make certain that the atomic bomb fully served the purpose for which it was intended. Each target in turn was shown in detailed maps and in aerial photographs. Every detail of the course was rehearsed—navigation, altitude, weather, where to land in emergencies. It came out that the Navy had submarines and rescue craft, known as Dumbos and Superdumbos, stationed at various strategic points in the vicinity of the targets, ready to rescue the fliers in case they were forced to bail out.

The briefing period ended with a moving prayer by the chaplain. We then proceeded to the mess hall for the traditional early morning breakfast before departure on a bombing mission.

A convoy of trucks took us to the supply building for the special equipment carried on combat missions. This included the "Mae West," a parachute, a lifeboat, an oxygen mask, a flak suit and a survival vest. We still had a few hours before take-off time, but we all went to the flying field and stood around in little groups or sat in jeeps talking rather casually about our mission to the Empire, as the Japanese home islands are known hereabouts.

In command of our mission is Maj. Charles W. Seeney, 25, of 124 Hamilton Avenue, North Quincy, Mass. His flagship, carrying the atomic bomb, is named The Great Artiste, but the name does not appear on the body of the great silver ship, with its unusually long, four-bladed, orange-tipped propellers. Instead it carried the number 77, and someone remarks that it was "Red" Grange's winning number on the gridiron.

BOMBARDIER AN 8TH A. F. VETERAN

Major Seeney's co-pilot is First Lieut. Charles D. Albury, 24, of 252 Northwest Fourth Street, Miami, Fla. The bombardier, upon whose shoulders rests the responsibility of depositing the atomic bomb square on its target, is Capt. Kermit K. Beahan of 1004 Telephone Road, Houston, Tex., who is celebrating his twenty-seventh birthday today.

Captain Beahan has the awards of the Distinguished Flying Cross, the Air Medal and one Silver Oak Leaf Cluster, the Purple Heart, the Western Hemisphere Ribbon, the European Theatre Ribbon and two battle stars. He participated in the first Eighth Air Force heavy bombardment mission against the Germans from England on Aug. 17, 1942, and was on the plane that transported Gen. Dwight D. Eisenhower from Gibraltar to Oran at the beginning of the North African invasion. He has had a number of hair-raising escapes in combat.

The navigator on The Great Artiste is Capt. James F. Van Pelt Jr., 27, of Oak Hill, W. Va. The flight engineer is M/Sgt. John D. Kuharek, 32, of 1054 Twenty-second Avenue, Columbus, Neb.; S/Sgt. Albert T. De Hart of Plainview, Tex., who celebrated his thirtieth birthday yesterday, is the tail gunner; the radar operator is S/Sgt. Edward K. Buckley, 32, of 529 East Washington Street, Lisbon, Ohio. The radio operator is Sgt. Abe M. Spitzer, 33, of 655 Pelham Parkway, North Bronx, N. Y.; Sgt. Raymond Gallagher, 23, of 572 South Mozart Street, Chicago, is assistant flight engineer.

The lead ship is also carrying a group of scientific personnel, headed by Comdr. Frederick L. Ashworth, USN, one of the leaders in the development of the bomb. The group includes Lieut. Jacob Beser, 24, of Baltimore, Md., an expert on airborne radar.

The other two Superfortresses in our formation are instrument planes, carrying special apparatus to measure the power of the bomb at the time of explosion, high speed cameras and other photographic equipment.

Our "Superfort" is the second in line. Its commander is Capt. Frederick C. Bock, 27, of 300 West Washington Street, Greenville, Mich. Its other officers are Second Lieut. Hugh C. Ferguson, 21, of 247 Windermere Avenue, Highland Park, Mich., pilot; Second Lieut. Leonard A. Godfrey, 24, of 72 Lincoln Street, Greenfield, Mass., navigator; and First Lieut. Charles Levy, 26, of 1954 Spencer Street, Philadelphia, bombardier.

The enlisted personnel of this "Superfort" are: T/Sgt. Roderick F. Arnold, 28, of 130 South Street, Rochester, Mich., flight engineer; Sgt. Ralph D. Curry, 20, of 1101 South Second Avenue, Hoopeston, Ill., radio operator; Sgt. William C. Barney, 22, of Columbia City, Ind., radar operator; Corp. Robert J. Stock, 21, of 415 Downing Street, Fort Wayne, Ind., assistant flight engineer, and Corp. Ralph D. Belanger, 19, of Thendara, N. Y., tail gunner.

The scientific personnel of our "Superfort" includes S/Sgt. Walter Goodman, 22, of 1956 Seventy-fourth Street, Brooklyn, N. Y., and Lawrence Johnson, graduate student at the University of California, whose home is at Hollywood, Calif.

The third "Superfort" is commanded by Maj. James Hopkins, 1311 North Queen Street, Palestine, Tex. His officers are Second Lieut. John E. Cantlon, 516 North Takima Street, Tacoma, Wash., pilot; Second Lieut. Stanley C. Steinke, 604 West Chestnut Street, West Chester, Pa., navigator; and Second Lieut. Myron Faryna, 16 Elgin Street, Rochester, N. Y., bombardier.

The crew are Tech. Sgt. George L. Brabenec, 9717 South Lawndale Avenue, Evergreen, Ill.; Sgt. Francis X. Dolan, 30-60 Warren Street, Elmhurst, Queens, N. Y.; Corp. Richard F. Cannon, 160 Carmel Road, Buffalo, N. Y.; Corp. Martin G. Murray, 7356 Dexter Street, Detroit, Mich., and Corp. Sidney J. Bellamy, 529 Johnston Avenue, Trenton, N. J.

On this "Superfort" are also two distinguished observers from Britain, whose scientists played an important role in the development of the atomic bomb. One of these is Group Capt. G. Leonard Cheshire, famous Royal Air Force pilot, who is now a member of the British military mission to the United States. The other is Dr. William G. Denny, Professor of Applied Mathematics, London University, one of the group of eminent British scientists that has been working at the "Y-site" near Santa Fe, N. M., on the enormous problems involved in taming the atom.

Group Captain Cheshire, whose rank is the equivalent to that of colonel in the United States Army Air Forces, was designated as an observer of the atomic bomb in action by Winston Churchill when he was still Prime Minister. He is now the official representative of Prime Minister Clement R. Attlee.

IN STORM SOON AFTER TAKE-OFF

We took off at 3:50 this morning and headed northwest on a straight line for the Empire. The night was cloudy and threatening, with only a few stars here and there breaking through the overcast. The weather report had predicted storms ahead part of the way but clear sailing for the final and climactic stages of our odyssey.

We were about an hour away from our base when the storm broke. Our great ship took some heavy dips through the abysmal darkness around us but it took these dips much more gracefully than a large commercial airliner, producing a sensation more in the nature of a glide than a "bump," like a great ocean liner riding the waves, except that in this case the air waves were much higher and the rhythmic tempo of the glide much faster.

I noticed a strange eerie light coming through the window high above the navigator's cabin and as I peered through the dark all around us I saw a startling phenomenon. The whirling giant propellers had somehow became great luminous disks of blue flame. The same luminous blue flame appeared on the plexiglass windows in the nose of the ship, and on the tips of the giant wings it looked as though we were riding the whirlwind through space on a chariot of blue fire.

It was, I surmised, a surcharge of static electricity that had accumulated on the tips of the propellers and on the di-electric material in the plastic windows. One's thoughts dwelt anxiously on the precious cargo in the invisible ship ahead of us. Was there any likelihood of danger that this heavy electric tension in the atmosphere all about us might set it off?

I expressed my fears to Captain Bock, who seems nonchalant and imperturbed at the controls. He quickly reassures me:

"It is a familiar phenomenon seen often on ships. I have seen it many times on bombing missions. It is known as St. Elmo's Fire."

On we went through the night. We soon rode out the storm and our ship was once again sailing on a smooth course straight ahead, on a direct line to the Empire.

Our altimeter showed that we were traveling through space at a height of 17,000 feet. The thermometer registered an outside temperature of 33 degrees below zero centigrade, about 30 below Fahrenheit. Inside our pressurized cabin the temperature was that of a comfortable air-conditioned room, and a pressure corresponding to an altitude of 8,000 feet. Captain Bock cautioned me, however, to keep my oxygen mask handy in case of emergency. This, he explained, might mean either something going wrong with the pressure equipment inside the ship or a hole through the cabin by flak.

The first signs of dawn came shortly after 5 o'clock. Sergeant Curry, who had been listening steadily on his earphones for radio reports, while maintaining a strict radio silence himself, greeted it by rising to his feet and gazing out the window.

"It's good to see the day," he told me. "I get a feeling of claustrophobia hemmed in in this cabin at night."

He is a typical American youth, looking even younger than his 20 years. It takes no mind-reader to read his thoughts.

"It's a long way from Hoopeston, Ill.," I find myself remarking.

"Yep," he replies, as he busies himself decoding a message from outer space.

"Think this atomic bomb will end the war?" he asks hopefully.

"There is a very good chance that this one may do the trick," I assure him, "but if not, then the next one or two surely will. Its power is such that no nation can stand up against it very long."

This was not my own view. I had heard it expressed all around a few hours earlier, before we took off. To anyone who had seen this man-made fireball in action, as I had less than a month ago in the desert of New Mexico, this view did not sound overoptimistic.

By 5:50 it was real light outside. We had lost our lead ship, but Lieutenant Godfrey, our navigator, informs me that we had arranged for that contingency. We have an assembly point in the sky above the little island of Yakoshima southeast of Kyushu, at 9:10. We are to circle there and wait for the rest of our formation.

Our genial bombardier, Lieutenant Levy, comes over to invite me to take his front-row seat in the transparent nose of the ship and I accept eagerly. From that vantage point in space, 17,000 feet above the Pacific, one gets a view of hundreds of miles on all sides, horizontally and vertically. At that height the vast ocean below and the sky above seem to merge into one great sphere.

I was on the inside of that firmament, riding above the giant mountains of white cumulous clouds, letting myself be suspended in infinite space. One hears the whirl of the motors behind one, but it soon becomes insignificant against the immensity all around and is before long swallowed by it. There comes a point where space also swallows time and one lives through eternal moments filled with an oppressive loneliness, as though all life had suddenly vanished from the earth and you are the only one left, a lone survivor traveling endlessly through interplanetary space.

My mind soon returns to the mission I am on. Somewhere beyond these vast mountains of white clouds ahead of me there lies Japan, the land of our enemy. In about four hours from now one of its cities, making weapons of war for use against us, will be wiped off the map by the greatest weapon ever made by man. In one-tenth of a millionth of a second, a fraction of time immeasurable by any clock, a whirlwind from the skies will pulverize thousands of its buildings and tens of thousands of its inhabitants.

Our weather planes ahead of us are on their way to find out where the wind blows. Half an hour before target time we will know what the winds have decided.

Does one feel any pity or compassion for the poor devils about to die? Not when one thinks of Pearl Harbor and the Death March on Bataan.

Captain Bock informs me that we are about to start our climb to bombing altitude.

He manipulates a few knobs on his control panel to the right of him and I alternately watch the white clouds and ocean below me and the altimeter on the bombardier's panel. We reached our altitude at 9 o'clock. We were then over Japanese waters, close to their mainland. Lieutenant Godfrey motioned to me to look through his radar scope. Before me was the outline of our assembly point. We shall soon meet our lead ship and proceed to the final stage of our journey.

We reached Yakoshima at 9:12 and there, about 4,000 feet ahead of us, was The Great Artiste with its precious load. I saw Lieutenant Godfrey and Sergeant Curry strap on their parachutes and I decided to do likewise.

We started circling. We saw little towns on the coastline, heedless of our presence. We kept on circling, waiting for the third ship in our formation.

It was 9:56 when we began heading for the coastline. Our weather scouts had sent us code messages, deciphered by Sergeant Curry, informing us that both the primary target as well as the secondary were clearly visible.

The winds of destiny seemed to favor certain Japanese cities that must remain nameless. We circled about them again and again and found no opening in the thick umbrella of clouds that covered them. Destiny chose Nagasaki as the ultimate target.

We had been circling for some time when we noticed black puffs of smoke coming through the white clouds directly at us. There were fifteen bursts of flak in rapid succession, all too low. Captain Bock changed his course. There soon followed eight more bursts of flak, right up to our altitude, but by this time were too far to the left.

We flew southward down the channel and at 11:33 crossed the coastline and headed straight for Nagasaki about 100 miles to the west. Here again we circled until we found an opening in the clouds. It was 12:01 and the goal of our mission had arrived.

We heard the prearranged signal on our radio, put on our arc-welder's glasses and watched tensely the maneuverings of the strike ship about half a mile in front of us.

"There she goes!" someone said.

Out of the belly of The Great Artiste what looked like a black object went downward.

Captain Bock swung around to get out of range; but even though we were turning away in the opposite direction, and despite the fact that it was broad daylight in our cabin, all of us became aware of a giant flash that broke through the dark barrier of our arc-welder's lenses and flooded our cabin with intense light.

We removed our glasses after the first flash, but the light still lingered on, a bluish-green light that illuminated the entire sky all around. A tremendous blast wave struck our ship and made it tremble from nose to tail. This was followed by four more blasts in rapid succession, each resounding like the boom of cannon fire hitting our plane from all directions.

Observers in the tail of our ship saw a giant ball of fire rise as though from the bowels of the earth, belching forth enormous white smoke rings. Next they saw a giant pillar of purple fire, 10,000 feet high, shooting skyward with enormous speed.

By the time our ship had made another turn in the direction of the atomic explosion the pillar of purple fire had reached the level of our altitude. Only about forty-five seconds had passed. Awe-struck we watched it shoot upward like meteor coming from the earth instead of from outer space, becoming ever more alive as it climbed skyward through the white clouds. It was no longer smoke, or dust, or even a cloud of fire. It was a living thing, a new species of being, born right before our incredulous eyes.

At one stage of its evolution covering millions of years in terms of seconds, the entity assumed the form of a giant square totem pole with its base about three miles long, tapering off to about a mile at the top. Its bottom was brown, its center was amber, its top white. But it was a living totem pole, carved with many grotesque masks grimacing at the earth.

Then, just when it appeared as though the thing has settled down into a state of permanence, there came shooting out of the top a giant mushroom that increased the height of the pillar to a total of 45,000 feet. The mushroom top was even more alive than the pillar, seething and boiling in a white fury of creamy foam, sizzling upward and then descending earthward, a thousand Old Faithful geysers rolled into one.

It kept struggling in an elemental fury, like a creature in the act of breaking the bonds that held it down. In a few seconds it had freed itself from its gigantic stem and floated upward with tremendous speed, its momentum carrying into the stratosphere to a height of about 60,000 feet.

But no sooner did this happen when another mushroom, smaller in size than the first one, began emerging out of the pillar. It was as though the decapitated monster was growing a new head.

As the first mushroom floated off into the blue it changed its shape into a flowerlike form, its giant petal curving downward, creamy white outside, rose-colored inside. It still retained that shape when we last gazed at it from a distance of about 200 miles.

Questions for Critical Analysis

1. Laurence wrote his news account within the context of the Second World War in 1945. What references that you may have had to look up were clearly understood by his readers? In what other ways does the story reveal its historical context?
2. Laurence has a reputation for explaining complicated technical information so that the average person can understand it. How well do you think he succeeds in this article?
3. Using the first person is unusual in a news story. Why did Laurence choose that approach to the story? He describes a nuclear bombing from inside the bomber. How does this point of view affect your reading of the story? What were your thoughts and feelings about it?
4. Laurence describes his sensations on the plane, hearing motors and feeling "oppressive loneliness." How does this section relate to the rest of the account?
5. Did you learn anything unexpected from this account of how the second atomic bomb was dropped?

Questions for Structural Analysis

1. This is a news story written when the United States was at war and when many of its citizens were killed daily. How does the tone of the article reflect this situation? How would this story be told now, with more than 40-years perspective on the events?

2. Laurence's account is very detailed. What details are the most compelling and memorable, and why? What is the effect of providing the names, ages, and addresses of the flight members? How would the effect be different if you were reading the story on August 9, 1945?
3. Look carefully at the language Laurence uses to describe what he saw and felt. Some examples include: "thing of beauty," "riding the whirlwind through space on a chariot of blue fire," "it changed its shape into a flowerlike form, its giant petal curving downward, creamy white outside, rose-colored inside." This is unusual language for a news account. What is the significance of Laurence's language? How does it affect you while you read the essay?
4. Why does Laurence ask the question, "Does one feel any pity and compassion for the poor devils about to die?" What is the purpose of using this device? He answers in the negative. Does he provide persuasive evidence? What is the effect of this paragraph on you? How would a typical reader in 1945 have responded differently?
5. Laurence discusses only his experience from the plane and makes no mention of events from the ground. Why do you think he did this? What is the effect? How do you think you would have reported the event?

*E*PILOGUE TO *A R*UMOR OF *W*AR

PHILIP CAPUTO

Philip Caputo (1941–), Chicago Tribune *journalist, served as a foreign correspondent to Rome (1972–74), Beirut (1974–76), and Moscow (1976–77). Caputo's experience as a Marine in Vietnam from 1964–67 and as a journalist covering the fall of Saigon to the North Vietnamese forces in April 1975 formed the foundation of his book* A Rumor of War *(1977). In this "Epilogue" to the book, Caputo provides a first-hand account of the chaotic exit by American troops leaving Saigon to the oncoming North Vietnamese. With an intensity echoed in other accounts of the Vietnam Conflict, Caputo shows us the confusion felt by the Americans who "were both opposed to the war and yet emotionally tied to it."*

Before you begin reading: *If you have served in the military, think of an event that you witnessed or took part in that deeply affected you. Focus on the event, the place, the people involved and write your memories in your reading notebook. If you have not served in the military, write a paragraph discussing your opinion of joining the military as a way of serving your country.*

◆

> But the past is just the same—and War's a bloody game . . .
> Have you forgotten yet? . . .
> Look down and swear by the slain of the War that you'll
> never forget.
>
> SIEGFRIED SASSOON, "AFTERMATH"

WE WERE CROUCHED IN THE SECOND-FLOOR CORRIDOR of the Continental Palace Hotel, wondering if the North Vietnamese Army had finally invaded Saigon, hoping it had not. The century-old walls trembled slightly from the concussion of the seven-hundred-pound bombs enemy planes were dropping on Tan Son Nhut airbase, five miles away. Every policeman and soldier in the city seemed to be firing a rifle or machine gun. The noise was deafening. Cringing in the hallway, we had no way of knowing whether the shooting was still directed at the planes or if a full-scale, street-to-street battle for the capital had begun. Having spent the past month observing the South Vietnamese Army losing one battle after another, there was no doubt in our minds that they would lose this one too. There was considerable doubt about our own future. As we listened to the thud of bombs and the rattle of small-arms fire, we asked each other unanswerable questions. Would there be enough time for an evacuation? If not, how would we, American correspondents, be treated by the Communist victors? In the final moments of chaos, would the South Vietnamese, feeling betrayed by Washington, turn their weapons on every American they saw?

It was useless to speculate under the circumstances. One of our more practical members suggested that we forgo debating what might happen and find out what was happening. After some hesitation, we left the shelter of the corridor and walked downstairs to the lobby. It was filled with frightened civilians and weeping children who had been driven in off the streets by the gunfire. The hotel's high, wooden door was now barred, like the gate to a medieval castle. Four of us opened it cautiously and went outside.

The small-arms fire was still heavy, but it seemed aimed at the enemy jets that whined over the city, heading with their bombs for the airbase. We saw no green-clad soldiers in pith helmets—the enemy's distinctive headgear. There were quite a few policemen, ARVN soldiers, and other newsmen running down the streets. They were as confused as we. Together with my colleague from the *Chicago Tribune*, Ron Yates, I jogged over to the UPI offices, a block from the hotel.

We found confusion there as well. One reporter was melodramatically typing out a story while dressed in a helmet and flak jacket. Teletype machines clacked urgently. After reading the wire services' dispatches, Yates and I decided that the final crisis, though near, had not yet arrived. Enemy units were still a day's fighting from the city. Assuming that the American embassy would order an evacuation the following day, Yates and I went back to the hotel to pack our gear. It was dark by the time we finished. The air raid was over. Through the window of my top-floor room, I could see the flames of a burning fuel dump. Gekko lizards clung to the room's white walls, the walls quaking from the secondary explosions set off by the bombs, the lizards immobile in their reptilian indifference.

I dragged my gear down to Nick Proffitt's room, which was two floors below. Proffitt, the correspondent for *Newsweek*, had taken me in the week before when an enemy rocket had devastated the top floors of the nearby Metropole Hotel. Having survived one month of the 1975 offensive in Vietnam, I had no intention of being blown to bits in bed. Proffitt had kidded me about my fears. I didn't mind. He could kid me all he wanted. At thirty-three, with a wife and two children to support, I no longer felt the need to prove anything to anyone.

Proffitt and I stayed up half the night, drinking the last of our beer, smoking the last of his dope, reminiscing about the past and speculating about tomorrow. Although we hoped the embassy would order an evacuation, we had our doubts. So far, it had refused to surrender its illusions that the ARVN could stop the North Vietnamese advance.

Like me, Proffitt was an "old" Indochina hand. He had been a correspondent in Vietnam in the late sixties and early seventies. When the final Communist offensive began, we were both in Beirut, based as Middle East correspondents for our respective publications. It was after reading about the fall of Danang in a dispatch coming over the newswire in my Beirut office that I had volunteered to go to Saigon. Reading the story resurrected long-buried memories of men and battalions, fire-fights and assaults, of nameless, numbered hills and joyless, rainy dawns on the line. Even after a decade's absence, I could clearly picture the part of Vietnam I knew best: the expanse of rice paddy and jungle west of Danang. It was as if a mental curtain had been raised, revealing a detailed battle map, with the dangerous places marked in grease pencil and the names of certain places underlined, names that meant something to me because men had died there. Hoi-Vuc, Binh Thai, Hill 270 and Charlie Ridge and Purple Heart Trail. It was difficult to accept the idea that they were now all in enemy hands.

I felt restless all that day and kept checking the teletype for the latest developments. It soon became clear that even ten years had not been long enough to break the emotional embrace in which the war held me. I *had* to go back, whatever the risks. I *had* to see the war end, even though it looked as if it was going to end in a defeat of the cause I had served as a soldier. I cannot explain this feeling. It just seemed I had a personal responsibility to be there at the end. So I sent a message to the *Tribune*'s home offices, offering to assist Yates—the paper's regular correspondent in the Far East—in covering the enemy's offensive. The editors said that was fine with them. The next morning I was on an Air France jet.

I landed at Tan Son Nhut on April 2, ten years and one month after I had landed at Danang with the 9th Expeditionary Brigade.

An accurate description of the final month of North Vietnam's final campaign would require a book in itself. I am not even sure if what occurred could be called a campaign; a migration, rather. The North Vietnamese Army simply rolled over the countryside, driving on Saigon. Except for a brief, hopeless stand made by a single division at the provincial capital of Xuan Loc, the ARVN offered no significant resistance. The South Vietnamese Army broke into pieces. It dissolved. There were terrible scenes of panicked soldiers beating and trampling civilians as they fled from the advancing enemy. Late in the month, the atmosphere of disintegration became palpable. Not just an army, but an entire country was crumbling, collapsing before our eyes. The roads were jammed with refugees and routed soldiers. Some of the columns were twenty miles long, winding out of the hills and rubber plantations toward the flat marshlands around Saigon. They stretched along the roads for as far as we could see, processions that seemed to have no beginning and no end. They shambled in the rain and heat: barefoot civilians; soldiers whose boots were rotting on their feet, some still carrying their weapons and determined that their little bands would stick together, most without weapons, broken men determined only to escape;

lost children crying for their parents, parents for their children; wounded men covered with dried blood and filthy battle dressings, some walking, some lying in heaps in the backs of ambulances; trucks, buses, herds of water buffalo, and oxcarts creaking on wooden wheels. They were packed densely and stretched down the roads, solid, moving masses that rolled over barricades and flowed past the hulks of burned-out tanks, past the corpses and pieces of corpses rotting in the fields at the roadsides. And from behind those retreating columns came the sound of bombs and shellfire, the guttural rumbling of the beast, war, devouring its victims.

There was so much human suffering in these scenes that I could not respond to it. It was numbing. Regardless of the outcome, I wanted to see it end. At the same time, a part of me did not want to see it end in a North Vietnamese victory. I kept thinking about Levy, about Sullivan, about all of the others, and something in me cried out against the waste of their lives. The war was lost, or very nearly lost. Those men had died for no reason. They had given their all for nothing.

I think these ambivalent feelings were typical of American veterans who, like me, were both opposed to the war and yet emotionally tied to it. After my discharge from the Marine Corps in mid-1967, I had drifted into the antiwar movement, though I was never passionately involved in it. I eventually joined the Vietnam Veterans Against the War, but my most explicit gesture of protest was made in 1970, when I mailed my campaign ribbons to President Nixon, together with a long and bitter letter explaining why I was opposed to American policies in Indochina. I thought, naïvely, that such a personal, individual act would have more effect than mass marches. About a month later, I received in the mail an envelope bearing the return address "The White House." It contained my medals and a curt note, written by some obscure functionary, which said that the Executive Branch of the United States government was not authorized to receive or hold military decorations; therefore, my ribbons were being returned to me. The writer concluded with the ominous phrase: "Your views about U.S. policies in South Vietnam have been noted and brought to the attention of the proper authorities." That episode sums up my career as an antiwar activist. My grand gesture of personal protest had been futile, as futile as the war itself. I seemed to have a penchant for lost causes.

Proffitt and I fell asleep in the early-morning hours. Lying on the floor behind the furniture with which I had barricaded the window, I was jarred awake when the North Vietnamese began shelling Tan Son Nhut and part of the city with rockets and 130-mm field guns. It was April 29. The bombardment went on for six hours. Around ten-thirty, a reporter who had a citizens' band radio tuned to the American embassy's frequency announced, "They've just passed the word. That's it. It's one-hundred-percent evacuation. It's bye-bye everybody."

A hasty, undignified exit followed. Crowds of newsmen, embassy officials, Vietnamese civilians, and various other "evacuees" stumbled down the half-deserted streets toward the evacuation points. I passed a group of ARVN militiamen and smiled at them wanly. "You go home now?" one of them asked. "Americans di-di?"

"Yes," I said, feeling like a deserter, "Americans di-di."

Our motley column was eventually directed to a staging area across the street from a hospital. Columns of smoke were rising from the city's outskirts, and someone said that North Vietnamese troops had been spotted only two miles from where we were standing. We stood about, dripping sweat and listening to the steady thud of the incoming one-thirties. Finally, two olive-drab buses, led by a car with a flashing mars light, pulled up. We piled on board, some sixty or seventy crammed on each bus, the small convoy heading for Tan Son Nhut.

We were just passing through the airport's main gate as a South Vietnamese plane took off from the smoking, cratered runway. An old C-119 cargo plane, it had not climbed more than a few hundred feet when a spiraling fireball rose up behind it. There was a great boom as the anti-aircraft missile slammed into the C-119 and sent it crashing into the city. Our nervousness turned to fear, for we were to be evacuated by helicopter. Easy targets.

The buses stopped in front of a complex of buildings known as the Defense Attaché's Office. During the height of American involvement in the war, the complex had been called Pentagon East. It had served as Westmoreland's headquarters. The tennis courts nearby were to be the landing zone for the helicopters. We clambered off the buses, spurred on by a heavy shell that banged into the tarmac seventy-five yards away. "Don't panic," someone said in a voice several octaves higher than normal.

Inside the building, we were lined up, divided into helicopter teams, and tagged. Every foot of every long corridor in the building was filled with Americans, Vietnamese refugees, newsmen from a dozen different countries, even a few old French plantation owners. The walls shook from the blasts of the shells hitting the runway. Small-arms fire crackled at the perimeter of the airbase. It was going to be a hot LZ. I hoped it would be my last one, and I tried not to think about those anti-aircraft missiles.

We sweated it out in there until the late afternoon, when the first of the Marine helicopters arrived. They were big CH-53s, each capable of holding as many people as a small airliner. "Okay, let's go!" yelled a Marine sergeant from the embassy guard. "Let's go. Drop all your luggage. No room for that. Move! Move! Move!" I dropped the valise I had lugged around all day and dashed out the door, running across the tennis courts toward the aircraft. Marine riflemen were crouched around the LZ, their weapons pointed toward the trees and rice paddies at the fringes of the airfield. Together with some sixty other people, half of them Vietnamese civilians and ARVN officers, I scrambled on board one of the CH-53s.

The helicopter lifted off, climbing rapidly. Within minutes, we were at six thousand feet, the wreckage of the South Vietnamese cargo plane burning far below. It was all so familiar: the deafening racket inside the helicopter; the door gunners crouched behind their machine guns, muzzles pointed down at the green and brown gridwork of the Mekong Delta through which flooded rivers spread like a network of blood vessels; and the expectant waiting—terrifying and yet exhilarating—as we looked for tracers or for the bright corkscrewing ball of a heat-seeking missile. One started to come up, but the lead helicopter in our flight diverted it with a decoy flare that simulated an aircraft engine's heat. We took some ground fire—fire from South Vietnamese soldiers who probably felt that the Americans had betrayed them.

My mind shot back a decade, to that day we had marched into Vietnam, swaggering, confident, and full of idealism. We had believed we were there for a high moral purpose. But somehow our idealism was lost, our morals corrupted, and the purpose forgotten.

We reached the coast about twenty minutes later. We were out of danger, out of range of the missiles, removed from all possibility of being among the last Americans to die in Vietnam. Relaxing their grip on the .50-caliber machine guns, the door gunners grinned and flashed the thumbs-up sign. Swooping out over the South China Sea, over the thousands of fishing junks jammed with refugees, the CH-53 touched down on the U.S.S. *Denver*, a helicopter assault ship that was part of the armada the Seventh Fleet had assembled for the evacuation. There was some applause as the aircraft settled down on the flight deck and as we filed out, a marine slapped me on the back and said, "Welcome home. Bet you're glad to be out of there." I was, of course. I asked him which outfit he was from. "Ninth MEB," he answered. The 9th Expeditionary Brigade, the same unit with which I had landed at Danang. But the men who belonged to it now seemed a good deal more cynical than we who had belonged to it ten years before. The marine looked at the faint blue line marking the Vietnamese coast and said, "Well, that's one country we don't have to give billions of dollars to anymore."

The evacuees were processed and sent down to the scorching mess deck for a meal. Most of us were giddy with relief, but one disconsolate diplomat from the American Embassy just sat and muttered to himself, "It's over. It's the end. It's the end of an era. It was a lousy way to have it end, but I guess it had to end some way." Exhausted and sweating, he just shook his head. "The end of an era." I supposed it was, but I was much too tired to reflect on the historical significance of the event in which I had just taken part: America had lost its first war.

The next day, April 30, the ship's captain announced that the Saigon government had surrendered to the North Vietnamese. We took the news quietly. It was over.

QUESTIONS FOR CRITICAL ANALYSIS

1. Caputo served in Vietnam with the 9th Marine Expeditionary Brigade in 1965 and 1966. He returned to Vietnam in 1975 as a newspaper correspondent. How does his earlier experience as a Marine influence his coverage of the fall of Saigon?
2. Caputo states that "even ten years had not been long enough to break the emotional embrace in which the war held me." How does he explain this phenomenon? In what ways does America seem to be still held in an "emotional embrace" with the Vietnam War today?
3. This Vietnam veteran and journalist terms his feelings about the end of the war "ambivalent." What are his conflicting feelings? What examples does he use to make them understandable?
4. Caputo writes about those who died in the war, "Those men had died for no reason." If you have read, thought, or studied about the Vietnam War, how do you respond to Caputo's statement? What are your own thoughts and feelings about the meaning of the war? Are you aware of how your opinions influenced your experience with this essay?
5. The "Epilogue" opens with lines from Siegfried Sassoon's poem, "Aftermath": "Look down and swear by the slain of the War that you'll never forget." Why did Caputo select these lines to preface his epilogue? Could these lines serve as an epigram for this entire section? Why, or why not?

QUESTIONS FOR STRUCTURAL ANALYSIS

1. The first paragraph sets the stage with a sense of danger and uncertainty. How do these feelings develop throughout the selection? Is this an effective introduction?
2. This article is a narrative, but it contains a "flashback" to ten years earlier. Why does Caputo interrupt his chronology? What effect does it have on you, the reader?
3. Caputo's essay is very personal—and yet this is also an account of a great international drama of tragic dimensions. How different is this from a "standard" news story? Caputo could have written such an account. What difference does it make to you that he did not?
4. What details and anecdotes in this account of the last hours of the war are most memorable and compelling? Where does Caputo use them and to what effect?
5. What feelings, attitude, tone are evident in the conclusion? How does the conclusion relate to the introduction?

*R*EPORTING *W*AR

TOPICS FOR WRITING ESSAYS

Many of the questions following each essay can serve as appropriate writing suggestions. Some of the topics listed below expand the prereading exercises, but they can be used without completing that step first.

1. Interview five or more people on campus about their thoughts and fears concerning the proliferation of nuclear weapons. Are you surprised by either their awareness or lack of concern? Include information you learned about yourself through the Hersey prereading exercise, and write an essay to the student newspaper which describes your findings, analyzes them, and comes to a conclusion.
2. Would you be willing to fight for your country under all circumstances? under no circumstances? under some circumstances? Use ideas that came to you during the prereading experiences, and write a defense of your decision to a hostile audience of your peers.
3. Conduct library research about a war first, then interview some veterans about their experiences in that war. Ask questions about their feelings at the time they served in the military and about their feelings as they look at the experience in retrospect. Write a feature article for the local newspaper about that war, keeping in mind the veterans' reliability as sources.
4. Select the essay from this section that most impressed you. Write an analysis of this essay, explaining why you want the reader of your paper to read the essay, and what you expect her (or his) response to be.
5. Have you served in the military and been involved in a war or conflict? Use details of the event you wrote about in the Caputo prereading exercise in an essay that shows someone who has never been to war what it was like for you.

RESEARCH POSSIBILITIES

1. The decision made at the beginning of America's involvement in the Second World War to create atomic weapons was fueled by the scientists' fear that German physicists were working on the same project. Do you agree with the decision to create an atomic bomb? Government and scientific leaders were not as concerned that Japan could develop their own atomic weapons. Do you agree with Truman's decision to drop the atomic bombs on Japan? Write an essay defending your answers. Assume that your

reader does not understand the concerns of the scientists or the politicians. You will need to conduct research beyond the essays in this section to write a thoughtful essay. (Among others, you may want to consult Richard Rhodes' *The Making of the Atomic Bomb*, 1986.)

2. Begin with the essays from this section as well as those from the previous section, "The Threat of Peace," and write a report designed to get college students involved in the discussion of war and peace—either by promoting a strong military or by actively supporting the anti-war movement. You may want to explore approaches to the subject made by young people in other countries, or look at the war-and-peace turmoil in the American 1960s. To be effective, your report needs to explain why citizens should be involved in such policy issues, how they already take part in the debate, results of their involvement and ways they can further their involvement.

PART FIVE
EDUCATION

*T*HE *P*ROBLEM OF *I*LLITERACY

America is a democratic nation, founded on the principle of participatory government. With a third of the nation unable to read or write—and that number increasing—our form of government is jeopardized. Kozol, Bettelheim and Zelan, and Larrick address the problem of illiteracy in America: what the situation is, how we got to this point, and what we can do about it. Berry extends the definition of literacy, broadening it to include not only reading and writing skills but the ability to define ourselves and our civilization through knowledge and mastery of the language. By Berry's broader definition, a greater number of citizens can be described as illiterate, and our democracy is on even shakier ground.

JONATHAN KOZOL, "A THIRD OF THE NATION CANNOT READ THESE WORDS"

BRUNO BETTELHEIM AND KAREN ZELAN, "WHY CHILDREN DON'T LIKE TO READ"

NANCY LARRICK, "ILLITERACY STARTS TOO SOON"

WENDELL BERRY, "IN DEFENSE OF LITERACY"

A Third of the Nation Cannot Read These Words

Jonathan Kozol

Jonathan Kozol (1936–) describes himself as split between the academic world of literary scholarship and the realities of poverty, ignorance, and illiteracy that he encounters in America's inner-cities and in many public schools. In "The Crippling Intelligence," Kozol wrote that literacy is "the issue that obsesses me," and he has presented eloquent books to stir his readers to the same pitch of anger that he feels. In 1967 Kozol's Death at an Early Age: The Destruction of the Hearts and Minds of Negro Children in the Boston Public Schools *described the inability of the school system to educate poor black children. This essay is the opening chapter of* Illiterate America *(1985), Kozol's revealing portrait of how illiteracy weakens our nation. In 1988, Kozol published* Rachel and Her Children, *a book describing the cycle of poverty and homelessness in which the illiterate are trapped.*

Before you begin reading: *Think about how reading gives you freedom and power. Carry your reading notebook with you an entire day and record every time you read during that time.*

◆

> You have to be careful not to get into situations where it would leak out . . . If somebody gives you something to read, you make believe you read it . . .*

HE IS METICULOUS AND WELL-DEFENDED.

He gets up in the morning, showers, shaves, and dresses in a dark gray business suit, then goes downstairs and buys a New York *Times* from the small newsstand on the corner of his street. Folding it neatly, he goes into the subway and arrives at work at 9 A.M.

He places the folded New York *Times* next to the briefcase on his desk and sets to work on graphic illustrations for the advertising copy that is handed to him by the editor who is his boss.

*For this and all other items of quotation, documentation, or public record, see Notes beginning on page 532.

"Run over this with me. Just make sure I get the gist of what you really want."

The editor, unsuspecting, takes this as a reasonable request. In the process of expanding on his copy, he recites the language of the text: a language that is instantly imprinted on the illustrator's mind.

At lunch he grabs the folded copy of the New York *Times*, carries it with him to a coffee shop, places it beside his plate, eats a sandwich, drinks a beer, and soon heads back to work.

At 5 P.M., he takes his briefcase and his New York *Times*, waits for the elevator, walks two blocks to catch an uptown bus, stops at a corner store to buy some groceries, then goes upstairs. He carefully unfolds his New York *Times*. He places it with mechanical precision on a pile of several other recent copies of the New York *Times*. There they will remain until, when two or three more copies have been added, he will take all but the one most recent and consign them to the trash that goes into a plastic bag that will be left for pickup by the truck that comes around during the night and, with a groaning roar, collects and crushes and compresses all the garbage of the occupants of this and other residential buildings of New York.

Then he returns upstairs. He opens the refrigerator, snaps the top from a cold can of Miller's beer, and turns on the TV.

Next day, trimly dressed and cleanly shaven, he will buy another New York *Times*, fold it neatly, and proceed to work. He is a rather solitary man. People in his office view him with respect as someone who is self-contained and does not choose to join in casual conversation. If somebody should mention something that is in the news, he will give a dry, sardonic answer based upon the information he has garnered from TV.

He is protected against the outside world. Someday he will probably be trapped. It has happened before; so he can guess that it will happen again. Defended for now against humiliation, he is not defended against fear. He tells me that he has recurrent dreams.

"Somebody says: WHAT DOES THIS MEAN? I stare at the page. A thousand copies of the New York *Times* run past me on a giant screen. Even before I am awake, I start to scream."

If it is of any comfort to this man, he should know that he is not alone. Twenty-five million American adults cannot read the poison warnings on a can of pesticide, a letter from their child's teacher, or the front page of a daily paper. An additional 35 million read only at a level which is less than equal to the full survival needs of our society.

Together, these 60 million people represent more than one third of the entire adult population.

The largest numbers of illiterate adults are white, native-born Americans. In proportion to population, however, the figures are higher for blacks and

Hispanics than for whites. Sixteen percent of white adults, 44 percent of blacks, and 56 percent of Hispanic citizens are functional or marginal illiterates. Figures for the younger generation of black adults are increasing. Forty-seven percent of all black seventeen-year-olds are functionally illiterate. That figure is expected to climb to 50 percent by 1990.

Fifteen percent of recent graduates of urban high schools read at less than sixth grade level. One million teenage children between twelve and seventeen cannot read above the third grade level. Eighty-five percent of juveniles who come before the courts are functionally illiterate. Half the heads of households classified below the poverty line by federal standards cannot read an eighth grade book. Over one third of mothers who receive support from welfare are functionally illiterate. Of 8 million unemployed adults, 4 to 6 million lack the skills to be retrained for hi-tech jobs.

The United States ranks forty-ninth among 158 member nations of the U.N. in its literacy levels.

In Prince George's County, Maryland, 30,000 adults cannot read above a fourth grade level. The largest literacy program in this county reaches one hundred people yearly.

In Boston, Massachusetts, 40 percent of the adult population is illiterate. The largest organization that provides funds to the literacy programs of the city reaches 700 to 1,000 people.

In San Antonio, Texas, 152,000 adults have been documented as illiterate. In a single municipal district of San Antonio, over half the adult population is illiterate in English. Sixty percent of the same population sample is illiterate in Spanish. Three percent of adults in this district are at present being served.

In the State of Utah, which ranks number one in the United States in the percent of total budget allocated to the education sector, 200,000 adults lack the basic skills for employment. Less than 5 percent of Utah's population is black or Hispanic.

Together, all federal, state, municipal, and private literacy programs in the nation reach a maximum of 4 percent of the illiterate population. The federal government spends $100 million yearly to address the needs of 60 million people. The President has asked that this sum be reduced to $50 million. Even at the present level, direct federal allocations represent about $1.65 per year for each illiterate.

In 1982 the Executive Director of the National Advisory Council on Adult Education estimated that the government would need to spend about $5 billion to eradicate or seriously reduce the problem. The commission he served was subsequently dismissed by presidential order.

Fourteen years ago, in his inaugural address as governor of Georgia, a future President of the United States proclaimed his dedication to the crisis of Illiterate America. "Our people are our most precious possession . . . Every adult illiterate . . . is an indictment of us all . . . If Switzerland and Israel and other people can end illiteracy, then so can we. The responsibility is our own and our government's. I will not shirk this responsibility."

Today the number of identified nonreaders is three times greater than the number Jimmy Carter had in mind when he described this challenge and defined it as an obligation that he would not shirk.

On April 26, 1983, pointing to the literacy crisis and to a collapse in standards at the secondary and the college levels, the National Commission on Excellence in Education warned: "Our Nation is at risk."

Notes

529 Epigraph: All quotations not taken from author's interviews are drawn from two sources:

(1) *Foresight*, vol. 1, no. 3, Southern Growth Policies Board, Research Triangle Park, North Carolina, September 1983.

(2) *The Adult Illiterate Speaks Out*, by Anne Eberle and Sandra Robinson, National Institute of Education, Washington, D.C., September 1980.

The second document, one of the most moving and insightful I have seen, derives from the experience of people who have been involved in Vermont Adult Basic Education. Despite my reservations in regard to many of the techniques employed by ABE, this remarkable paper is a tribute to the capability of some extraordinary literacy workers to listen closely to the needs of those they serve. Many of the viewpoints I have stated in this chapter were provoked by my initial reading of this data several years ago. The authors draw some of these words from interviews conducted by other authors. Passages have been condensed and edited for clarity.

Nonreader purchases New York *Times*: This and later anecdotes without citation are drawn from interviews conducted by the author between 1979 and 1984. Interviews were not tape-recorded and therefore represent the author's reconstructions. Names and circumstances have been altered to protect the anonymity of individuals.

530 Numerical breakdown, 60 million illiterate adults: U.S. Department of Education, first estimate: Far West Laboratory for Educational Research and Development, San Francisco, September 1983.

Office of Vocational and Adult Education, second estimate: U.S. Department of Education, Washington, D.C., June 1983.

White House, third estimate: press release, September 7, 1983.

National Institute of Education, fourth estimate: Dr. Manuel J. Justiz, U.S. Department of Education, Washington, D.C., January 18, 1984; *Newsweek*, July 30, 1984.

U.S. Bureau of the Census, fifth estimate: "Literacy: Current Problems and Current Research," in *Fifth Report of the National Council on Educational Research*, National Institute of Education, Washington, D.C., 1979.

Illiteracy, ethnic breakdown: *Final Report of Adult Performance Level Project*, University of Texas, Austin, 1977. Also see: Illinois Senator Paul Simon, cited in *Adult and Continuing Education Today*, Bethesda, 1983.

531 Percentiles by age levels and by other categories: San Francisco *Examiner*, December 12, 1983. See also: Boston *Globe*, March 26, 1983; and "Adult Illiteracy, Selected Statistics," California State Library, Sacramento, 1983.

531 Secretary of Education Terrel Bell is quoted by the Washington *Post*, November 27, 1982: "The U.S. Labor Department estimates that up to 75 percent of [the unemployed] lack the basic skills . . . that would enable employers to train them for the jobs that will open up in the next few years."

531 Juvenile illiterates before the courts: "Eighty percent of the new criminals who pass my desk would not be here if they had graduated from high school and could read and write." (Florida Judge Charles Phillips, cited by Laubach Literacy International, 1982)

United States, forty-ninth among 158 members of the United Nations: Washington *Post*, November 25, 1982; *Foundation News*, January/February 1983.

Prince George's County: Washington *Post*, November 26, 1982.

A lead editorial in the Boston *Sunday Globe*, March 11, 1984, estimates that 40 percent of the city's adult population is functionally illiterate. An op-ed article in the New York *Times*, August 19, 1982, estimates that 800,000 adults in the New York City area are illiterate. Unless NewYork is three times better educated than the rest of the U.S., this estimate should be approximately 2 million people. For detailed information on literacy needs and programs in the Boston area, contact Tomas Kalmar, Adult Literacy Resource Center, Roxbury Community College, Boston, Massachusetts.

San Antonio: *The Status of Illiteracy in San Antonio*, by José A. Cardena et al., United San Antonio Literacy Committee, August 1983. Author's interviews with Marguerita Huantes, United San Antonio Literacy Committee, and with Carolina Rodriguez, Multilingual Education, Research and Training, San Antonio, March 1984.

Utah: "Adult Literacy in Utah," by Garth L. Mangum, paper prepared for National Institute of Education, November 1, 1983.

Present levels of federal funding and President's request for their reduction: author's interview with Gary Eyre, Executive Director of American Association for Adult and Continuing Education, December 14, 1983.

Executive Director of National Advisory Council on Adult Education, estimate of $5 billion needed to address the problem: "Illiterate? Who, Us?" by Rosa Williams, *Foundation News*, January/February 1983.

Former President Carter. *Addresses of Jimmy Carter*, Department of Archives and History, Atlanta, 1975.

532 *Report of the National Commission on Excellence in Education*, U.S. Government Printing Office, Washington, D.C., April 26, 1983.

QUESTIONS FOR CRITICAL ANALYSIS

1. The opening story in Kozol's essay illustrates how a man hides his illiteracy from others. List the methods he uses to fool others. Who does he have to watch out for? How does he feel about what he does?
2. Kozol includes many statistics and facts about illiteracy in America. Which fact surprised you the most? Why?

3. What do you think is the federal government's responsibility toward the 60 million functionally illiterate Americans? What does Kozol think? What role do you think state and local governments should take toward the problem?
4. Does the individual who can read and write have any responsibility toward those citizens who cannot? Why, or why not?
5. Why is the number of illiterate Americans growing?

QUESTIONS FOR STRUCTURAL ANALYSIS

1. Why did Kozol begin this essay with the story about the illiterate man? How did you react to the story? Describe the man in the story: What kind of job does he have? What sort of person does he seem to be?
2. How does Kozol present the information in the rest of the essay? How did you respond to his presentation?
3. What is Kozol's point of view toward illiteracy in America? What are his feelings? How do you know?
4. This essay is a chapter from a book entitled *Illiterate America.* In what ways can you identify the essay as part of a longer work? From reading this chapter, are you interested in reading more of the book? Why, or why not?
5. Do you think the conclusion of this essay is effective? Why, or why not?

*W*HY *C*HILDREN *D*ON'T *L*IKE TO *R*EAD

BRUNO BETTELHEIM AND KAREN ZELAN

Bruno Bettelheim (1903–), a widely acclaimed child psychologist and educator, began his work with emotionally disturbed children. His interest in their dreams and fantasies led to his study of children and fairy tales, The Uses of Enchantment *(1976), written with Karen Zelan. "Why Children Don't Like to Read," written for the general reader and originally published in* The Atlantic Monthly *(1981), describes how the way reading is taught and the books used to teach reading work against a child's natural curiosity and predisposition to like reading. Bettelheim developed these ideas further in his book,* On Learning to Read: The Child's Fascination with Meaning *(1982).*

Before you begin reading: *Picture a 6-year-old who hates books and reading class. In your reading notebook, make two lists: (1) methods you would use to encourage the child to read and (2) books you would make sure the child reads. Use these lists to write a brief argument you would make to the child encouraging him to read.*

◆

A CHILD'S ATTITUDE TOWARD READING IS OF SUCH IMPORtance that, more often than not, it determines his scholastic fate. Moreover, his experiences in learning to read may decide how he will feel about learning in general, and even about himself as a person.

Family life has a good deal to do with the development of a child's ability to understand, to use, and to enjoy language. It strongly influences his impression of the value of reading, and his confidence in his intelligence and academic abilities. But regardless of what the child brings from home to school, the most important influence on his ability to read once he is in class is how his teacher presents reading and literature. If the teacher can make reading interesting and enjoyable, then the exertions required to learn how will seem worthwhile.

A child takes great pleasure in becoming able to read some words. But the excitement fades when the texts the child must read force him to reread the same word endlessly. Word recognition—"decoding" is the term used by educational theorists—deteriorates into empty rote learning when it does not lead directly to the reading of meaningful context. The longer it takes the child to advance from decoding to meaningful reading, the more likely it becomes that his pleasure in books will evaporate. A child's ability to read depends unquestionably on his learning pertinent skills. But he will not be interested in learning basic reading skills if he thinks he is expected to master them for their own sake. That is why so much depends on what the teacher, the school, and the textbooks emphasize. From the very beginning, the child must be convinced that skills are only a means to achieve a goal, and that the only goal of importance is that he become literate—that is, come to enjoy literature and benefit from what it has to offer.

A child who is made to read, "Nan had a pad. Nan had a tan pad. Dad ran. Dad ran to the pad," and worse nonsense can have no idea that books are worth the effort of learning to read. His frustration is increased by the fact that such a repetitive exercise is passed off as a story to be enjoyed. The worst effect of such drivel is the impression it makes on a child that sounding out words on a page—decoding—is what reading is all about. If, on the contrary, a child were taught new skills as they become necessary to understand a worthwhile text, the empty achievement "Now I can decode some words" would give way to the much more satisfying recognition "Now I am reading something that adds to my life." From the start, reading lessons should nourish the child's spontaneous desire to read books by himself.

Benjamin S. Bloom, professor of education at the University of Chicago, has found that who will do well in school and who will do poorly is largely determined by the end of the third grade. Thus, reading instruction during the first three grades is crucial. Unfortunately, the primers used in most American schools up to and sometimes through the third grade convey no sense that there are rewards in store. And since poor readers continue to be subjected to these primers well past the third grade, their reading can only get worse as their interests and experience diverge further from the context of the books.

That rote learning is the wrong way to teach reading was recognized more than seventy years ago. In the first important treatise on the teaching of reading published in this country, *The Psychology and Pedagogy of Reading* (1908), the author, Edmund Burke Huey, urged that drills be kept separate from the activity of reading. He wrote: "The school should cease to make primary reading the fetich [sic] it has long been. The child should never be permitted to read for the sake of reading, as a formal process or end in itself. The reading should always be for the intrinsic interest or value of what is read. . . . Word-pronouncing will therefore always be secondary to getting whole sentence-meanings, and this from the very first. . . . School readers, especially primers, should largely disappear, except as they may be competent editings of the real literature of the mother tongue, presented in literary wholes, or as they may be records of the children's own experiences and thoughts."

For many decades, textbooks have been used as the basis for reading instruction by the vast majority of elementary school teachers, and they are much worse today than the ones Huey objected to. According to one study, first readers published in the 1920s contained an average of 645 new words. By the late 1930s, this number had dropped to about 460 words. In the 1940s and 1950s, vocabulary declined further, to about 350 words. The vocabularies of primers in seven textbook series published between 1960 and 1963 ranged from 113 to 173 new words. More recent primers, compared with the 1920s editions, also have small vocabularies. For example, *Let's See the Animals*, published in 1970 by Bowmar/Noble, introduces 108 new words; *May I Come In?*, published in 1973, by Ginn & Company, introduces 219 new words; *Finding Places*, published by the American Book Company, in 1980, introduces 192 new words. Although in the 1920s few children went to kindergarten and little preschool reading instruction was given, by the 1970s, when many children were attending kindergarten and reading was consistently taught there, the first-grade primers contained only a quarter of the vocabulary presented to first-graders fifty years ago.

When they enter school, most children already know and use 4,000 or more words. Nobody has to make a deliberate effort to teach them these words, with the exception of the first few learned in infancy. Children make words their own because they want to, because they find them pleasing and useful. Even the least verbal group of first-graders has mastered well over 2,000 words, thus invalidating the claim that children of culturally deprived families would be unfairly burdened by primers of larger vocabulary. This condescending assumption ignores the richness of daily life in even the poorest households. By encouraging the adoption of less challenging books, it has helped to deprive most children at school just as poverty deprives many children at home.

The Scholastic Aptitude Test (SAT) is a particularly reliable measure of an age group's intellectual accomplishment, because, unlike most of the various achievement tests administered in schools, its standards do not change from one year to the next. The mean score on the verbal SAT (which registers reading comprehension) has been declining for the past ten years. Although it would be difficult to establish a cause-and-effect relationship between the declining verbal ability of college-bound high school juniors and seniors and the decline in vocabulary of primers over the past several decades, there can be no doubt that the scores reflect diminishing regard for the written word.

Research in the teaching of reading, far from justifying the continuous reduction in the number of words used in primers, fails to show any reason for it. It is therefore hard to understand why textbook publishers have pursued this course, and why educators have not rebelled. One possible explanation is that as primers become simpler, children, because they are bored, read them with less and less facility. The publishers, in response, make the books even simpler and, thus, even less effective.

Primers have no authors. Many people help to create the books, and the financial investment required runs into the millions. (The sizable staff of one large publishing house worked for five years to produce a first-grade program alone.) Yet despite such prodigious effort and expense, all basic series are more or less alike. To recoup the large investment in a series, a publishing house must be able to sell it to schools all over the country. It cannot risk controversy.

We can cite two examples from our own experience. One publisher, in an effort to improve a first-grade reader, came up with a story in which children bring a balloon home from a fair, whereupon a cat leaps on it and it bursts. The story would seem harmless enough to most people, but when the book was tested in an Illinois school system, cat-lovers were outraged: the story had maligned their pets, turned children against animals, and so on. The local school superintendent, who was coming up for re-election, decided to withdraw the book, and the publisher, fearing similar setbacks elsewhere, decided to drop the story.

Another publishing house was preparing a new edition of its widely used series. One of us, asked to consult, objected in detail to the blandness of the stories proposed. The company's vice-president in charge of textbooks confessed that he, too, thought the stories would bore young readers, but he was obliged to keep in mind that neither children nor teachers buy textbooks: school boards and superintendents do. And their first concern is that no one mind their choices. Fairy tales, for example, would never do. Some people would complain that the stories insult stepmothers; others would find the punishment of evildoers too cruel.

The result of such constraints is a book full of endlessly repeated words passed off as stories. Many teachers have told us that they don't like such a book, but assume that since a primer has been put together by experts, and approved by experts, it must be appropriate for children even if it is obnoxious to an adult. In the course of our research on the teaching of reading we have talked to children who were not so credulous. Many told us that their teachers must have faked an interest in the stories, or that they must think children are not very smart.

Fourth- and fifth-graders who had left the beginners' books behind described their resentments to us quite clearly. One rather quiet boy, who preferred to read or work by himself and rarely participated in class, spoke up all on his own and with deep feeling. He had felt so ashamed to say the things written in primers that he could not bring himself to do it. And although he now liked reading a lot, he said, he still had a hard time reading aloud.

The first- and second-graders were as unhappy with their books as the older children remembered being. They said they read only because they had to, and that on their own they would never choose such "junk." "It's all impossible," one of them said. When he was asked why, answers came from around the room: "The children aren't real!" "They aren't angry!" When one child exclaimed, "They aren't anything!" all agreed that there was nothing more to be said.

Textbook writers and publishers know that their books are dull, and they have tried to make them more attractive by commissioning many colorful illustrations. For example, the number of pictures in primers of the Scott, Foresman series doubled between 1920 and 1962, from about one picture per one hundred words to nearly two per hundred words. The trouble with pictures is that the printed text becomes even less appealing in comparison. Words seem to be less vivid and to convey less information. Worse, being able to guess from the pictures what the text is about, a child who is reluctant to read has no incentive to learn.

The publishers' advice to teachers reinforces this syndrome. Typically, the elaborate teachers' guides for each book in a series suggest that the class be asked questions about the pictures before reading the story. Yet there is evidence that pictures retard or interfere with learning to read. Consider the following report by a psychologist of reading, Eleanor J. Gibson: "Children in the second term of kindergarten were given practice with three-letter common words ('cat,' 'bed,' 'dog,' etc.) on flash cards. In one group, the word on the card was accompanied by the appropriate picture. In another, it appeared alone. Training trials, in which the experimenter pronounced the word as it was displayed to the child, alternated with test trials [in which] the child was shown the word alone and asked to say what it was. The picture group made significantly more errors and took longer . . . than the group without pictures. The pictorial redundancy appeared to be distracting rather than useful." Yet in most of the preprimers and primers in classrooms today, words are used primarily as labels and captions.

Learning to read is not an entertainment but hard work. Rather than face this directly, publishers seek to distract children with references to play. But allusions to strenuous physical activities make a child want to move, not think. Worse, a first-grader knows from his own experience just how complex a ball game can be. So a weak story about a ball game is most likely to convince the child that reading about a ball game is dull compared with playing in one.

In Harper & Row's "Janet and Mark" series (1966), school makes its first appearance in second grade in *All Through the Year.* The last section of the book is titled "Too Much Is Too Much of Anything," and the first story about the things that are too much, "A Feeling in the Air," is about school. "Everyone was waiting. . . . It was the last day of school. A little while, and it would be all over." The children are "daydreaming . . . of baseball and swimming and bicycle rides." In the last picture of the story, we see them streaming out of the school building, joyful to be released.

Psychoanalytic studies of the so-called "double bind" have shown that nothing is more confusing and disturbing to a child, or has more detrimental effects, than contradictory messages from an adult about important issues. Almost every preprimer and primer bears such contradictory messages. Tacitly, they say that the educational system, which requires the child to go to school and presents him with a book so that he may learn to read, holds that school and learning are serious business. But the explicit message of the text and pictures is that the child should think—that is, read—only about playing. The idea seems to be that a suggestion of what books are really for—to open new worlds of thought and imagination—would have the most undesirable consequences for the child's reading achievement.

From a psychoanalytic perspective, the primers' emphasis on play ensures that the books will be addressed solely to the child's pleasure-seeking ego—the earliest, most basic, but also most primitive motivating force in man. But as the child reaches school age, around age five, he should have learned to exchange (at least to some extent) living by the pleasure principle for making choices in accord with the reality principle. The primers, by presenting him almost exclusively with images of fun, throw the child back to the developmental phase he is trying, with difficulty, to outgrow. Such primers insult the child's intelligence and his sense of worth, and the offense goes far to explain why children reject their reading books as empty. The books talk down to children; they do not take children's aspirations seriously.

In class, children read aloud. For some time to come, even if the child does not voice what he is reading, he will form the words with his lips. Reading aloud feels to a child as if he were speaking to his teacher, or whoever might be listening to him. For that matter, it is not unusual for a child to think that his teacher wrote the book, and has planted messages for him in it. In a conversation, we wish to hold our listener's attention and impress him with what we have to say. But the teacher is oblivious of the child's impression that reading aloud is a sort of conversation; instead, the teacher listens carefully to make sure that the child reads the words as they are printed in the book, and corrects him when he fails. To do so is a teacher's duty, according to the teaching methods favored in this country; it may also be the only way a teacher can remain alert through the near-hypnotic effect of the words. In any case, the child experiences the teacher's interruptions as rejection, which certainly does not make reading more attractive to him.

Furthermore, a child may have good reason to make a mistake. Reading for meaning is anything but passive, even when the content is absorbed exactly as presented. And the more intent a reader is on taking in the meaning, the more active he is in his reading. In order for a child to maintain the minimal interest necessary for reading a story, he may try to correct the story or improve it by misreading it. The barrenness of the text may tempt the child to project meaning where there is none.

The texts of preprimers and primers consist of words that can be readily sounded out. But these words are often combined in sentences that no one would ever say. Such a text is actually harder for the beginner to read. For example, because the child usually learns early to recognize the words "store"and "man," one widely used basal text (*People Read*, one of the Bank Street readers) tells about a "store man" when referring to a salesman. Out of a wish to make learning to read easy, children who know the word that the text of this story means to convey are asked to recognize and use in their reading a phrase that rarely comes up in writing or speech. To compound the irony, the phrase appears in a book whose title by implication promises to tell how everybody reads and what they read. The result is that children may be provoked to errors by the discrepancy between ordinary language and the uncommon language of the book.

We have spent a number of years observing school reading lessons, and have learned that children make mistakes for many reasons, in addition to the obvious one of ignorance. For example, a first-grade boy was reading "Van's Cave," a story in the 1969 J. B. Lippincott series about a hunter and his dog, Spot. The story goes that the hunter shoots five ducks, which the dog retrieves. They then return to the cave, where they live. The man starts a fire on which he plans to roast the ducks. The text says: "Spot must not leave the ducks. He can see a wolf near the cave." This, inexplicably, is accompanied by a picture showing the dog asleep. The boy reversed the meaning of the sentence by reading, instead, "He can't see a wolf near the cave." It is possible that the boy did so because the picture shows the dog asleep. But it is more likely that the boy's knowledge of dog behavior made it seem unreasonable to him that a dog would sleep when it saw a wolf lurking nearby. A first-grader might also wish to believe that his dog would safeguard him. So the misreading of "can't" for "can," seemingly a simple error, reflects on one level the child's attempt to bring what the text says into accord with the picture. On another level, it may register the boy's protest against a dog that sleeps when its master needs protection. Finally, the misreading is a statement correctly describing normal dog behavior.

One first-grade girl complained about a story in McGraw-Hill's Sullivan Storybook series which told of a ball falling into a patch of tar. She thought it should have said that the ball fell into a puddle. The teacher, knowing that this phonics-based text used "patch of tar" in preference to "puddle" because these words are pronounced as printed, while "puddle" is pronounced "puddel," said that perhaps the author of the story thought children would have difficulty in recognizing "puddle." By this she meant difficulty in decoding and reading the word. But the girl fastened on the exact words the teacher had used. She was indignant, and angrily exclaimed, "I know 'puddle' when I see it." We cannot say for sure that her remark did not simply reflect the fact that the word "puddle" was in her active vocabulary, while the words "patch of tar" were not, but the way she expressed herself suggests a more subtle reason for her sense of insult. She made it clear that she saw puddles in everyday life, not tar patches; and her reaction entailed the wish that teachers and those who write for children show respect for a child's experiences of the world.

Another smart first-grader puzzled his teacher because all year he had balked at reading, despite evidence that he knew how. On the day we observed him, the boy made numerous errors—for example, reading "stick" for "chick." This, the teacher told him, showed he had not mastered word beginnings and endings, and that he should therefore continue with his exercises. The boy refused.

The teacher then suggested that we read with him, upon which the boy strenuously protested that the workbook the teacher had assigned to him was boring. (The book, part of McGraw-Hill's Sullivan Programmed Reading series, is typical of most workbooks, in that the exercises require the student to fill in missing letters.) With our encouragement, the boy made one more attempt;

again he read "stick" for "chick." But this time, before anyone had time to react, he corrected himself and angrily blurted out: "Fill in the blanks, that's all I get! Witch, witch, witch . . . ditch, ditch, ditch . . . stick, stick, stick . . . chick, chick, chick!" And that was it. He would not do any more reading with us that day. The boy had made error upon error, in this way giving vent to his negative feelings. But by pairing "witch" with "ditch," and "stick" with "chick," he showed that he understood well the different word beginnings and endings, and that his substitutions were not made in ignorance.

A couple of days later, we again asked the boy to read. He refused the Sullivan series but was willing to try something more interesting. We settled on *The Bear Detectives*, by Stan and Jan Berenstain. The story tells how Papa Bear and his children hunt for a missing pumpkin, using a detective kit. Although the small bears discover various clues to the pumpkin's whereabouts, they can't find it. After reading the story eagerly for some thirty pages, the boy substituted the word "defective" for "detective": "He's in the barn. This is it! Hand me that defective kit." Earlier he had read "detective" correctly, demonstrating that he was well able to read the word—that he knew what it designated and how it fit into the story. It seemed to us that the boy, having read for so many pages that the detective kit was no help in the search for the pumpkin, and carried away by the excited wish of the bears to find it, was once more expressing his frustration with a text.

A few days later, this boy's workbook again required him to read a list of words that, bereft of context, made no sense. He then read "dump" for "jump." Responding to the feelings this misreading suggested, we asked, "Who wants to dump this?" The boy immediately read the correct word, "jump," and then nodded at us. When we asked him why he wanted to dump the workbook, his unhesitating reply was, "'Cause it's garbage."

Just as children are likely to change the words of a dull story in order to make it more interesting, they are also likely to change the words of an interesting story because they have a personal stake in the meaning. For example, one competent first-grader read a story to us smoothly and with interest and comprehension in her voice. The story was about tigers, and the little girl made only one mistake: she consistently read "tigger" for "tiger." It is easy to understand why this child would shy away from thinking about dangerous tigers in favor of contemplating the harmless character of Tigger in the Pooh books, which were favorites of hers. Her switch in thought seemed to relieve her fear about what the ferocious beast would do next as the story unfolded.

It requires considerable ingenuity on the part of first-graders to make radical alterations in meanings by only the slightest change of letters. In the examples of the boy reading about the dog and the wolf and the girl reading about the tiger, the children retained all the letters of the printed word, adding to them a single letter. By adding a "t," the boy substituted correct animal behavior for an incorrect description of it, and by adding a "g," the girl replaced an animal threatening danger and destruction with one symbolizing safety and pleasure.

In the third example, by substituting one letter for another in a nine-letter word, the child expressed his dissatisfaction with the uselessness of an object that played a central role in the story he was reading.

When a child utters a word entirely different from the one printed in the book, teachers are likely to assume, correctly, that the child's attention has wandered, or that he may have given up on reading a word that is hard for him. When what the child reads is only slightly different from what is printed, teachers are also likely to conclude that the child has a problem—faulty discrimination between letters—even though the error may change the meaning of the sentence radically. They assume this despite the fact that the child has already read most letters as printed, suggesting that he was paying attention to the page and could recognize the letters correctly. But what if a child's substitution of one or a few letters makes good—though altered—sense within the context of a story? Perhaps he has perceived what the printed word signifies, decided that it is unacceptable, and found a solution that suits his purposes.

A teacher's reflex to catch and correct mistakes is but one example of a situation that occurs over and over again in schools, and not only where beginners are taught to read: the educator's faith in abstract theories about how learning must proceed blinds him to the sophistication of the child's mind. The teacher's insistence on accuracy often barely hides the fact that what is involved is also a power play, in which the teacher uses her superior knowledge and her authority to gain her point. The child—consciously or, more often, subconsciously—reacts to being the victim of such a power play, and is antagonistic. Unfortunately, many children manage to defeat the teacher by refusing to learn; their victory robs them of their chance to be educated, and it deprives society of competent citizens.

It is not impossible to teach children to read while respecting their intelligence and dignity. The primers used in Europe are generally far more difficult than those in use in this country. We believe their success is proved by the fact that at the end of the first grade, the average European child has a larger reading vocabulary than that of the average American child. Moreover, reading retardation, the curse of so many young Americans, is much less common among European children and, when it occurs, is rarely as severe.

The most recent series of basic readers published in Switzerland stands as a notable alternative to the American textbooks that we have complained about. The early reading program consists of three preprimers and one primer. The preprimers are loose-leaf booklets, each page (with a single exception) comprising a few short lines of text and an illustration. Since there are no pictures on the covers of the booklets, the child is encouraged to form his own opinion of what each booklet is about by reading.

The first preprimer is entitled *We are all here*, meaning "here to read together." Its first page has only two words: "I am." And on this page there is no picture, no face to rival the child's own. The Swiss child's reading thus begins with the strongest statement of self-assertion imaginable. After sixteen more pages, each with a few words for the child to learn, there follow twenty-eight pages devoted either to snatches of well-known songs or to a few lines from popular fairy tales. In this way, the first preprimer leads easily to the next, *Once upon a time*, which is composed of five fairy tales from Grimm. Though quite simple, these versions are nonetheless faithful in all essentials to the originals.

The third Swiss preprimer, *Edi*, is about a little boy who might be the peer of the children reading about him. The first page shows Edi with his school satchel on his back, standing between his father and mother. The story goes that Edi, who has eaten something that disagrees with him, gets sick and is sent to the country to stay with relatives and get well. We follow Edi's experiences on the farm until the end of the book, when he returns home, his health fully restored. There he finds that while he was away, his mother had a baby; Edi has a sister. Edi's story deals with two of the most critical events in a child's life: sickness and the birth of a sibling.

The primer of the Swiss series, *It's your turn*, meaning "it's your turn to read," begins with counting rhymes and songs typically sung by children as accompaniment to their games. Since Swiss children know all these rhymes and songs, they know how the words they are decoding ought to sound, and so it is likely that at this more difficult level of reading, their attempts will be error-free. Thus the children's confidence in their ability to read this new, thicker, rather scary-looking book is supported, and they are ready for the remaining sections, which are longer and a little harder.

It's your turn has many colorful pictures that embellish the text without giving away its meaning; the child *must* read in order to understand. For example, a poem by Christian Morgenstern, "Winternight," is illustrated by a picture of a town at night, covered with falling snow; the picture conveys the spirit of the poem but permits no conclusion about its substance. In addition to the Morgenstern poem, the book contains a number of other poems and short stories, many by famous German authors. The selection represents all periods of German literature: contemporary, Romantic, classical, and medieval, and legendary folktales, rhymes, and riddles.

This first Swiss reader, like its American counterparts, tries to introduce children to reading by means of attractive and fairly easy material. The chief difference is that none of the pieces in the Swiss reader patronize the child; there is no deviation from ordinary language or ordinary usage. Children have been reciting the counting rhymes to each other for hundreds of years. No words are avoided because they might be difficult (as is done constantly in American primers)—and they prove not to be too hard, because the child who uses them in everyday conversation already knows what they mean, and is thus eager to master whatever technical obstacles they present on the page. In one way or another, all the stories appeal to children of primary age, but in none of them is there even the mention of active play. If anything, the pieces are on the contemplative side, though with a light touch. The most impressive difference between this book and American primers is the literary quality of many of its selections. The Swiss primer manages to introduce the child to literacy at the same time that it teaches him the rudiments of reading.

These primers, used in the German-speaking parts of Switzerland, have a special lesson to teach American educators and publishers. It has been argued that our primers have to employ unnaturally simple words because many minority children speak a different language at home: Spanish, Chinese, "black English," and so on. But the language that *all* children growing up in the German parts of Switzerland speak—a dialect called *Schweizer Deutsch*, or Swiss German—is very different from the High German they must speak and read in school. Although during the first few months of school the children are allowed to speak to the teacher in their dialect, from the start they learn to read only the High German in which their primers are published. For some reason, Swiss children do not find this enforced bilingualism such a handicap that they fail to become able readers. We believe that their lack of difficulty is explained to a great extent by the fact that they like what they are given to read.

QUESTIONS FOR CRITICAL ANALYSIS

1. How do Bettelheim and Zelan characterize the language used in reading books for the early grades?
2. What do Bettelheim and Zelan think of the content of these readers? If there are samples of these textbooks in the education section of the library, take a look at them. Do you agree or disagree with Bettelheim and Zelan?
3. Neither the teacher nor the publisher wants to hinder a child from learning to read. What's going on here? What reasons does a publisher have for publishing textbooks like those described in this essay? Why does a teacher try to teach reading using these books as well as the teaching methods Bettelheim and Zelan find counter-productive? If you were superintendent of a school district, what would you do to make sure your students learned to read?
4. Describe the differences between the Swiss method of teaching reading and the American method. Why is one more effective than the other?
5. Several states have mandated reading programs for elementary school children based on literature, not basal reading textbooks. What evidence from Kozol's essay and the Bettelheim-Zelan essay will you use to convince your governor to change reading requirements for your state?

QUESTIONS FOR STRUCTURAL ANALYSIS

1. Look carefully at the first paragraph of this essay. What is its tone? How do you respond to the paragraph? Do you want to continue reading? Why, or why not?

2. What reasons do Bettelheim and Zelan give for children not liking to read? What is the progression in how the reasons are presented to the reader?
3. What support do the authors provide for their thesis? Are you convinced by their evidence? How do they bring this support into the article?
4. Why did the authors include a comparison with the way children are taught to read in Switzerland? What points did they make through this comparison? Was their conclusion to the essay effective? Why, or why not?
5. In what ways do Bettelheim and Zelan define the problem of illiteracy? What solutions do they offer?

*I*LLITERACY *S*TARTS *T*OO *S*OON

NANCY LARRICK

Nancy Larrick (1910–) is an educator, writer, and editor who has devoted much of her life to teaching children how to read. Larrick, the author of A Parent's Guide to Reading, *has received many awards including a citation of merit from the International Reading Association (1977), a citation for distinguished contributions to children's literature from Drexel University (1977), and membership to the Reading Hall of Fame. "Illiteracy Starts Too Soon," first published in the teacher's magazine* Phi Delta Kappan, *presents the case for better books in the classroom to an audience of elementary and secondary school teachers.*

Before you begin reading: *Try to remember the first time you read a book, or an early reading experience. How did you feel about reading? In your reading notebook, make a list of words or phrases that capture your experience. Use that incident and your list as a starting point to write a paragraph about reading.*

◆

THE U.S. POSTAL SERVICE IN 1984 ISSUED A NEW COMMEMOrative stamp. "A Nation of Readers," which depicted Abraham Lincoln reading to his son Tad. Perhaps, someone suggested, the postal authorities had to go back 100 years to find a picture of a father reading to his son. Doubtless the modern father and his son, instead of reading, would be watching "The Cosby Show" or perhaps "Wheel of Fortune."

When 1987 was designated "The Year of the Reader," the Ad Council swung into action with a three-year media blitz that reportedly "has increased citizen awareness of functional illiteracy from 21.4% to 30% of the population in one year." However, I have seen no claim that functional illiteracy itself has declined as a result. Nor do I expect to.

It will take more than a media blitz to transform the American public into a nation of readers. Jonathan Kozol, relentless gadfly of U.S. education, reports in *Illiterate America* that 25 million American adults cannot read the poison warning on a can of pesticide or a letter from their child's teacher. An additional 35 million read at a level below the full survival needs of our society. Together, these 60 million people represent more than one-third of the entire adult population of this country.

Of the 159 members of the United Nations, the U.S. ranks 49th in its level of literacy. In terms of books produced per capita, the U.S. ranks 24th. Moreover, the incidence of illiteracy in the U.S. is rising, with an estimated 2.3 million adults annually joining the ranks of the functionally illiterate.

To date, thousands of articles, reports, studies, surveys, and community projects have addressed the matter of adult literacy in the U.S. Not so much has been said about the juvenile illiterate. Yet every report on adult illiterates makes at least passing reference to the fact that high school dropouts and high school pushouts failed to learn to read in school. How can a child painlessly master oral language without any formal educational program and then fail to master written language despite years of instruction?

More than 50 years ago, Frances Clarke Sayers, a distinguished children's librarian, gave an answer that is equally applicable today. "If the majority of students cannot read," she wrote, "there must be something basically wrong with present-day methods of teaching." She continued, "In an effort to enliven and enrich the business of teaching reading, the mechanics of reading has encroached upon the ultimate purpose of reading, the art of reading."

One of those who has steadfastly promoted the mechanics of reading is Rudolf Flesch, whose book *Why Johnny Can't Read and What You Can Do About It* created such a storm on the education scene more than 30 years ago that the ripples are still lapping at our feet. Flesch launched a vitriolic attack on teachers and the educational system in general, and he advocated a rigid program of phonics as the guaranteed way to teach every child to read. Explaining the ease with which phonics can lead to mastery of a language, he told of teaching himself to read a Czechoslovakian newspaper. "I can read it," he wrote, "but of course I don't understand it."

In 1981 Flesch published another book, *Why Johnny Still Can't Read.* This time around Flesch concluded that the trouble was that his earlier admonitions had not been followed. His renewed demand: more phonics in systematic programming.

Although Flesch found no improvement in the literacy level among children, he certainly cannot blame this lack of improvement on any lack of systematic phonics drill. If he were to visit the exhibit hall of the annual convention of the International Reading Association, he would see nearly 500 exhibits of national and international conglomerates promoting "print ware, hardware, and software" as aids to a traditional program of reading as decoding.

At one booth I saw a crowd of teachers watching a computer demonstration in which a rabbit's ears went up when the operator gave the correct answer, down when the answer was wrong. Bells rang. Computer voices cried out, "Good work!" or "Not quite! Try again!" Hucksters explained their wares, extolling their elaborate combinations of publications for every child. Often they offered free trial copies, easy-payment plans, and constant updating (virtually guaranteeing the obsolescence of the materials then being offered for sale).

As an example of the complexity and sheer bulk of these educational programs, let me repeat Frank Smith's list of one publisher's complete package of primary-grade reading materials for the 18 reading levels from kindergarten through fourth grade: 10 student texts, seven workbooks, nine practice books, 10 sets of practice masters, seven sets of "comprehension and writing masters," three readiness tests, seven initial placement inventories, 10 assessment tests (A and B forms), four testing/management resource books, three achievement tests, plus class-size sets of student profile cards at each level. Supplementary materials across the 18 levels include: seven skill development charts, four vocabulary development charts, 10 solo books, 10 "Extras! For Reinforcement," three sets of ABC cards, five sets of cards containing phonic pictures, five sets of word cards, three sets of story cards, three packs of games, seven records or cassettes, and five tutorial programs.

Ten teacher's editions exist, along with 10 sets of letters for teachers to send to parents.[1]

In 1980 textbook sales in the United States, from kindergarten to college, totaled $1.5 billion, an average of $40 per student. The primary-grade package cited by Smith is only one of many, which, taken together, make up the most lucrative segment of book publishing in this country.

All these plans begin with reading as decoding of fragments. Kozol calls this the mechanization of reading, a sort of vivisection of language by which children begin, not with sentences or even words, but with letters—one at a time. First the initial consonants, at the beginning of kindergarten, then the short vowels. Long vowels begin at the primer level, and so on. Initial clusters of consonants must wait until the start of second grade. So the sentence "Charlie chased the chipmunk" is off-limits for at least the first year and a half.

But no one has been able to prove that children learn in this way. The 4-year-old who could spot his mother's Honda in the parking lot before she could did not begin by learning what the hubcap looked like, then the wheel, then the fender, and so on. Instead, he identified her car by the complete contour and later noted that its hubcaps were different from those on the neighbor's earlier model.

Both reading workbooks and computer software emphasize fragmented learning. Match words that are identical. Draw a line from the words in Column A to the matching words in Column B. Fill in missing letters, then missing words. Unscramble misspelled words. Rearrange words in a sentence so they make sense. Combine segments into whole sentences. In short, begin with what is incomplete or wrong, and try to make sense of it! If you do this successfully on a computer program, bells will ring, the rabbit's ears will go up, and the voice will declare, "Congratulations! You're a winner!"

---

[1]Frank Smith, *Insult to Intelligence: The Bureaucratic Invasion of Our Classrooms* (New York: Arbor House, 1986), p. 4.

So that the bells can ring out more joyfully and the rabbit's ears go up more often, these first reading materials are so simplified in many cases as to be meaningless. Words are few, combined into unnatural segments, and repeated over and over. Teachers are directed to dissect, analyze, repeat, review, and repeat again.

Surely this is what the English critic Richard Hoggart referred to when he spoke of the "trivialization" of reading matter. According to Hoggart, "Reading, which in other settings promoted intellectual growth, now threatens it."

Let me share with *Kappan* readers a few vivid examples of reading matter that has been trivialized. These samples are taken from a basal-reader series—those books that come in packs: for instance, six levels before grade 1 and for each level a textbook, a skillpack, a studybook, and much more. These books cover the country like acid rain. The language is "basal reader" language, of course—what someone once called the only language in print that was never spoken by any human. Note the first page of each of two mini-stories in *Pre-primer #4* in the Ginn series:

"I will go out," the dog thought.
"I will see what I can see."
What will the dog see?
What do you see here?

Now consider this page from a second mini-story in the same book:

Where Are Wheels? (title)
Where are wheels?
Here are wheels.
Wheels are on a van.
Wheels are on a truck.
Wheels are on the go!

On that one page, 10 different words are recombined to make a total of 24 for the child to read. Two hundred thirty-three words of explanation are provided to show the teacher how to have students read that page, repeat, drill, and repeat again.

Can you think of any child aged 5 or 6 who would want to learn to read after this opening sampler? How can we expect a child to relate to this stilted, unnatural, meaningless conglomeration of words?

Suppose, instead, a child meets these lines from a trade book:

And then
Something went BUMP!
How that bump made us jump!

Does that stir your curiosity and make you want to turn the page and read on? If so, you are plunged into *The Cat in the Hat*, by Dr. Seuss—an early reading book that uses the simple words of the basal readers to create something intriguing.

Now consider this verse from a recent book by Karla Kushkin:

> There was a hog
> who ate a dog
> and then he ate
> a grass-green frog
> and then he was so full
> he cried.
> And then he lay down—
> *bang*—and died.[2]

Notice that in this little sample the words say something, in this case something funny, to the child. It is a mini-story that builds its tiny plot from nothing to a ludicrous climax: "And then he lay down—*bang*—and died." Furthermore, the language follows the familiar rhythm of everyday speech—not the awkward plod of "Where are wheels? Here are wheels."

It is interesting to note that the first great literacy campaign of modern times was directed by Martin Luther in the 16th century. The reading materials he offered came from his own very rhythmical translation of the Bible, as well as from the hymns that he wrote and for which he composed the music. (Surely nearly everyone can hum "A Mighty Fortress Is Our God.")

Two hundred years later, when English convicts were shipped out to colonize Australia, they were taught to read the King James version of the Bible. On many of the ships, meticulous records were kept of the reading progress of each prisoner—records now treasured by historians as well as reading specialists.

In the U.S. we offer reading instruction to our prisoners, too. But, if Kozol is right, the typical reading fare is:

> Jim gets a job.
> Jack gets a car.
> Jane gets a baby.

Modern literacy campaigns in both Cuba and China have made use of materials that reflect the political ideologies and passions of the leaders of those countries. Unlike the adult literacy materials used in the U.S., this is reading matter to sharpen the intellect and stir the soul, to win the compassion and commitment of the reader.

With our children we seem to stick to mechanistic skill-and-drill, which appeals neither to the intellect nor to the emotions. The preprimers and primers

[2]Karla Kushkin, *Something Sleeping in the Hall* (New York: Harper, 1985), pp. 34–35.

don't include anything that can be called literature, even watered-down literature. Teachers are not directed to read aloud each day from good literature. Nor are they expected to draw children into recording or dictating their responses to experiences or situations. Oral language—the natural language of everyday speech—is not provided for children to read.

If we start young children on such drivel as "Where are wheels? Here are wheels," how can we expect them to want to read? And if teachers follow the detailed directions in the teacher's guides, ask the specified questions, and accept only the answers deemed "correct" for scoring purposes (though other answers may be equally appropriate), their pupils will know that reading is something to be avoided.

In advertising their wares, publishers use the word *fun* ad nauseam. Reading is *fun*. Workbook pages are *fun*. Supplying words for blanks in sentences is *fun*. Rearranging words to make a sentence is *fun*. Fun is what the publishers promise, all right, but I never see any signs of pupils having fun when I visit a class using basal readers and workbooks.

It is no wonder that American children (ages 6-11) rush home from school to watch a weekly average of 23 hours and 19 minutes of television, year round. Twenty-eight percent of these children's viewing occurs during prime time (8 p.m. to 11 p.m.): 2% occurs after 11 p.m.[3] Television provides fast-paced action and a steady emotional pull in language that is familiar—all of which are missing from the preprimers and primers.

Think of the children who have watched "The Cosby Show" (children's favorite show, according to the Nielsen ratings) and on the following morning must face, "Where are wheels? Here are wheels." How will they respond? How would you or I respond?

Probably these children will shift their thoughts to other things, very much as they switch TV channels when one program is disappointing. Teachers tell me that this happens in many situations in which children are told to sit still, keep quiet and listen, or work silently—or perhaps to draw lines to connect related words or to fill blanks in printed sentences. "Then that glazed look comes on," said one teacher, "and I know they've switched channels."

While the basal-reader juggernaut rolls on, delivering truckloads of printed materials to schools and pulling in millions of dollars, more and more teachers are looking for effective ways to encourage children's love of reading while they are developing reading skills.

One of the most revealing research studies was conducted by Dorothy Cohen.[4] Working with 20 classes of second-graders in the Bronx, Cohen divided

[3] *Television: 1987 Nielsen Report* (Northbrook, Ill.: Nielsen Media Research, 1987), p. 9.

[4] Dorothy Cohen, "The Effect of Literature on Vocabulary and Reading Achievement," *Elementary English*, vol. 45, 1968, pp. 209–13, 217.

them into two groups. Ten classes were read to systematically each day and had many library books in the classroom. Each day they had activities to make the books that were read to them memorable dramatization, discussion, illustrations, and so on. The other 10 classes (the control group) were taught in the usual basal-reader mode. At the end of the year, the 10 experimental classes were significantly ahead of the control classes in reading, vocabulary, and comprehension.

Bernice Cullinan, Angela Jaggar, and Dorothy Strickland replicated Cohen's study with second-graders from low socioeconomic backgrounds in New York City.[5] Many of the books used with these children had urban settings and recounted stories of black or Hispanic characters. The same procedures were used as in Cohen's study, and once again those children who had been read to, who had become involved in stories and poems, and who had had books to explore on their own were far ahead of the control groups that had not been given such opportunities.

By this time there have been innumerable classroom projects and research studies pointing out more appealing—and more successful—ways to teach reading that will last a lifetime. Some of the most revealing of these projects have been developed at Ohio State University by students of Charlotte Huck. She has long advocated the teaching of reading through trade books instead of lock-step approach of the basals and their skill/drill workbooks, activity books, and computer software.

In her talk at the 1985 annual convention of the National Council of Teachers of English, Huck spoke of the urgent need to win the support of administrators and primary teachers in implementing such a program. "I have learned," she said, "the key words to make them listen. You simply say, 'Research now proves that the more literature children are exposed to and the earlier they are exposed, the better will be their reading scores.' Then you have them."

Let me tell you of a school in which the children *are* learning to read with children's literature instead of basal readers and workbooks. The school is P.S. 192 in New York City, located on the West Side, just south of the George Washington Bridge. This district has more aliens—legal and illegal—than any other in the New York area. In P.S. 192 the American Reading Council has set up the Open Sesame Program, a demonstration project that begins with kindergartners.

The school building itself is a great, dank fortress, which was packed to the rafters with 1,900 children until the summer of 1985, when 10 prefabricated classrooms were set up in the bleak schoolyard to accommodate 10 kindergarten

---

[5]Bernice E. Cullinan, Angela Jaggar, and Dorothy Strickland, "Language Expansion for Black Children in the Primary Grades: A Research Report," *Young Children*, vol. 29, 1974, pp. 98–112.

classes. When I visited the school in October 1985, the kindergartners had been in their new quarters only a few weeks. Electricians, carpenters, and their tools were still evident in the corridors, but it was obvious that good things were already happening under Open Sesame leadership.

The Open Sesame plan is operating with the agreement of the principal, the school district officials, and the American Reading Council. The goal is to offer children the opportunity to read in an unpressured, pleasurable way. The curriculum, built on the work of Jean Piaget, Frank Smith, and Sylvia Ashton-Warner, employs language experience and immersion in children's literature. There are no basal readers, workbooks, activity sheets, or practice books. I saw quantities of library books—"real books," the children often call them—displayed with their colorful covers showing and being used continuously by the children.

In these classrooms, words are everywhere. They are pasted on windows, doors, floors, and chalkboards. Each child collects favorite words: key words are written on cards and dangle from key rings; big words, such as *helicopter* or *television*, never found on a basal-reader list, are quickly mastered by triumphant children.

Ninety-two percent of these children come from non-English-speaking homes; 96% come from homes below the poverty level; 80% could speak no English on entering school in September.

When I visited these kindergartens, I was impressed with the informal, relaxed atmosphere and the freedom with which children moved about the room to get materials or consult with the teacher. Occasional Spanish phrases or questions from the teacher eased the silent ones into using English to talk about their drawings or about the story being read or told. Other students dictated phrases or sentences to go with pictures they had drawn. Several in need of help or commendation turned quite naturally to me when they saw that the teacher was occupied.

From time to time a teacher made a point about identification of letters, but it was always in a natural context. One teacher, who had begun reading what was evidently one of the children's favorite books, put the title on the low chalkboard on an easel beside her. The title, *Pickle, Pickle, Pickle Juice*, by Patty Wolcott, provided an opportunity to note the letter P and its sound. What other words begin with that sound? Pedro's name. Yes. And Pauletta's. What else? Pumpkin! Of course, it's Halloween.

Reading aloud to the children from the very simple books in the classroom library is a part of every day. One young teacher sat cross-legged on a low stool surrounded by children who sat on the carpeted floor. At one point, several children retold parts of the story she had just read to them. Again, they chimed in on repeated words and phrases. Everyone seemed to be involved. It was an exciting project to be part of, even for one morning. That was Halloween 1985.

By the close of school the following June, all 225 kindergartners were able to read their dictated stories and the books by Dick Bruna and Patty Wolcott. Some were even reading on a second-grade level. Best of all, they loved to read stories and were proud to be readers. Even children in the special education section of the kindergarten listened eagerly to stories read aloud; all of them could read their own key words, and three were reading the Wolcott books.

The first year's success of the kindergarten project at P.S. 192 impressed school officials so favorably that they made a written commitment to extend the Open Sesame Program gradually through the sixth grade. In 1986-87, 350 first-graders, as well as all kindergarten groups, were part of Open Sesame. By late spring of 1987 all 350 first-graders were reading in English with excitement and enthusiasm. Sixty percent of these 6-year-olds were reading on or above grade level; some were reading at the third-grade level. When a school district evaluator gave all first-graders a simple test of comprehension, only three of the 350 could not read and comprehend the passage. Those three had been in this country less than six months.

Of course, one basic problem is that standardized tests for first grade stress phonics, not comprehension. Open Sesame teaches phonics only as children ask for help with their writing. From the first days in kindergarten, children are encouraged to use their own invented spelling in their writing. However, they quickly move to conventional or "correct" spelling largely because of their saturation with print materials.

How will these youngsters get along on the second-grade standardized test mandated by the New York City Board of Education? Is it possible that they can read and comprehend but still fail the phonics-based test? The Open Sesame leaders are taking no chances. As preparation for the second-grade standardized test, the children will be given a series of 10- to 15-minute sessions in "test-taking skills," so that they will understand the language of phonics ("underline the long *a* in the following words," etc.). These special coaching sessions will not be called reading and will not take time from reading "real books."

To facilitate the Open Sesame Program, publishers of trade books have contributed a classroom library of 250 books for each of the 20 kindergarten and first-grade classrooms in the program. A Lowenstein Grant has made possible the purchase of another 17,940 books for the upper grades. Enthusiasm is running high at P.S. 192, a school that in 1984 was classified by New York State as one of its 50 worst schools.

Schoolpeople in New York City are watching P.S. 192. At the same time, educators nationwide are looking toward California, where State Superintendent Bill Honig has launched the California Reading Initiative, a statewide literature-based program to improve students' reading ability and reading habits. This comprehensive plan includes components such as curriculum development, teacher training, and the development of accurate assessment tools.

A special committee has assembled a recommended list of more than 1,000 trade books for use with the three million California children in kindergarten through eighth grade. These books will be available throughout the state in many bookstores, supermarkets, retail outlets, and, it is hoped, in all classrooms. The California Department of Education has indicated that at least 20% of California's K-8 textbook budget can be spent on the purchase of trade titles in order to implement the initiative, which has been described as "a major new thrust of the Honig administration's reform efforts."

In 1932 a remarkable little book titled *Les Livres, les Enfants, et les Hommes* was published in Paris. It was written by Paul Hazard, an eminent French scholar who was on the faculty of the Sorbonne, who held honorary degrees from Harvard and Columbia, and who became a member of the French Academy in 1940. The English translation, *Books, Children, and Men*, was published in Boston by *The Horn Book* in 1944. It remains an inspired revelation of the role of adults who, in their infinite wisdom, have oppressed children by "robbing imagination of its rightful place and declaring war on dreams." How have they done this? Hazard explains:

> They have offered him books that oozed boredom, that were likely to make him detest wisdom forever; silly books and empty books, pedantic books and heavy books, books that paralyzed the spontaneous forces of his soul; absurd books by tens and by hundreds, falling like hail on the springtime. The sooner they stifled the young heart, the sooner they effaced from a young spirit the sense of freedom and pleasure in play . . . the more men were pleased with themselves for having raised children without delay to their own state of supreme perfection.[6]

I hope we will not repeat—or continue to repeat—such oppression. Instead, let us heed what Hazard declares to be the cry of the children: "Give Us Books! Give Us Wings!"

QUESTIONS FOR CRITICAL ANALYSIS

1. What does the title, "Illiteracy Starts Too Soon," mean?
2. What is implicit in America's attitude toward teaching children in all communities? Why don't we "shape the intellect and stir the soul"?
3. Larrick maintains that watching television is more interesting and fun for most children. Why? How does this idea relate to Hoggart's statement: "Reading, which in other settings promoted intellectual growth, now threatens it"? What would you do to reverse this situation?

---

[6]Paul Hazard, *Books, Children, and Men* (Boston: The Horn Book, 1944), pp. 3–4.

4. In the last section of her essay, Larrick spends considerable time describing the reading program, Open Sesame, for kindergarten students in a New York inner city public school. Why is this program remarkable? What is the significance of its name, "Open Sesame"?
5. Compare Larrick's essay with the comments made in the Introduction of this textbook. Would Larrick agree with the idea of "active reading"? Do you think young children can be taught to read actively? How?

QUESTIONS FOR STRUCTURAL ANALYSIS

1. Were you surprised to see a reference in Larrick's third paragraph to Jonathan Kozol's essay ("A Third of the Nation Cannot Read These Words")? Why did she use his information? How does she incorporate Kozol in her essay? Why did she decide not to quote him directly?
2. What do you think of Rudolf Flesch's ideas, based on the references to him in Larrick's essay? What does Larrick think of Flesch and his conclusions? What is Larrick's point in quoting Flesch's comment on reading Czechoslovakian: "I can read it, but of course I don't understand it"?
3. What is reading by decoding? Do you think Larrick teaches this method? Why, or why not? Notice Larrick's analogy of a child recognizing the family car. Is this a good analogy? Why, or why not?
4. Larrick's feelings often are apparent through the similes and metaphors she uses in describing how reading is taught. Find some of figures of speech and discuss the implicit emotion behind them.
5. Why does Larrick conclude her essay on teaching methods by quoting a 1932 book? Is this an effective conclusion? Why, or why not?
6. Both Bettelheim and Zelan and Nancy Larrick discussed the problem of children not learning how to read. Compare the way they presented the issue. Which essay did you think was more effective? Which one did you enjoy reading better? Explain your answers.

*I*N *D*EFENSE OF *L*ITERACY

WENDELL BERRY

Wendell Berry (1934–), a poet, novelist, and essayist, resigned from the academic world to farm his family's land and reinstate pre-industrial farming techniques. Berry holds that our understanding of language and literature depends upon a shared "sense of place" focused sharply on the land. "In Defense of Literacy," published in A Continuous Harmony: Essays Cultural and Agricultural (1972)*, defines literacy as "the mastery of language and the knowledge of books" and argues that literacy, thus defined, is a necessity to life.*

Before you begin reading: *How are you culturally illiterate? Write several headings on a page of your reading notebook: Science, History, Literature, Music, Industry, Art, Economics, Geography. Now write lists of people, ideas, things, and events you think you should know more about under each category.*

◆

IN A COUNTRY IN WHICH EVERYBODY GOES TO SCHOOL, IT may seem absurd to offer a defense of literacy, and yet I believe that such a defense is in order, and that the absurdity lies not in the defense, but in the necessity for it. The published illiteracies of the certified educated are on the increase. And the universities seem bent upon ratifying this state of things by declaring the acceptability, in their graduates, of adequate—that is to say, of mediocre—writing skills.

The schools, then, are following the general subservience to the "practical," as that term has been defined for us according to the benefit of corporations. By "practicality" most users of the term now mean whatever will most predictably and most quickly make a profit. Teachers of English and literature have either submitted, or are expected to submit, along with teachers of the more "practical" disciplines, to the doctrine that the purpose of education is the mass production of producers and consumers. This has forced our profession into a predicament that we will finally have to recognize as a perversion. As if awed by the ascendency of the "practical" in our society, many of us secretly fear, and some of us are apparently ready to say, that if a student is not going to become a teacher of his language, he has no need to master it.

In other words, to keep pace with the specialization—and the dignity accorded to specialization—in other disciplines, we have begun to look upon and to teach our language and literature as specialties. But whereas specialization is of the nature of the applied sciences, it is a perversion of the disciplines of language and literature. When we understand and teach these as specialties, we submit willy-nilly to the assumption of the "practical men" of business, and also apparently of education, that literacy is no more than an ornament: when one has become an efficient integer of the economy, *then* it is permissible, even desirable, to be able to talk about the latest novels. After all, the disciples of "practicality" may someday find themselves stuck in conversation with an English teacher.

I may have oversimplified that line of thinking, but not much. There are two flaws in it. One is that, among the self-styled "practical men," the practical is synonymous with the immediate. The long-term effects of their values and their acts lie outside the boundaries of their interest. For such people a strip mine ceases to exist as soon as the coal has been extracted. Short-term practicality is long-term idiocy.

The other flaw is that language and literature are always *about* something else, and we have no way to predict or control what they may be about. They are about the world. We will understand the world, and preserve ourselves and our values in it, only insofar as we have a language that is alert and responsive to it, and careful of it. I mean that literally. When we give our plows such brand names as "Sod Blaster," we are imposing on their use conceptual limits which raise the likelihood that they will be used destructively. When we speak of man's "war against nature," or of a "peace offensive," we are accepting the limitations of a metaphor that suggests, and even proposes, violent solutions. When students ask for the right of "participatory input" at the meetings of a faculty organization, they are thinking of democratic process, but they are *speaking* of a convocation of robots, and are thus devaluing the very traditions that they invoke.

Ignorance of books and the lack of a critical consciousness of language were safe enough in primitive societies with coherent oral traditions. In our society, which exists in an atmosphere of prepared, public language—language that is either written or being read—illiteracy is both a personal and a public danger. Think how constantly "the average American" is surrounded by premeditated language, in newspapers and magazines, on signs and billboards, on TV and radio. He is forever being asked to buy or believe somebody else's line of goods. The line of goods is being sold, moreover, by men who are trained to make him buy it or believe it, whether or not he needs it or understands it or knows its value or wants it. This sort of selling is an honored profession among us. Parents who grow hysterical at the thought that their son might not cut his hair are *glad* to have him taught, and later employed, to lie about the quality of an automobile or the ability of a candidate.

What is our defense against this sort of language—this language-as-weapon? There is only one. We must know a better language. We must speak, and teach our children to speak, a language precise and articulate and lively enough to tell the truth about the world as we know it. And to do this we must know something of the roots and resources of our language; we must know its literature. The only defense against the worst is a knowledge of the best. By their ignorance people enfranchise their exploiters.

But to appreciate fully the necessity for the best sort of literacy we must consider not just the environment of prepared language in which most of us now pass most of our lives, but also the utter transience of most of this language, which is meant to be merely glanced at, or heard only once, or read once and thrown away. Such language is by definition, and often by calculation, not memorable; it is language meant to be replaced by what will immediately follow it, like that of shallow conversation between strangers. It cannot be pondered or effectively criticized. For those reasons an unmixed diet of it is destructive of the informed, resilient, critical intelligence that the best of our traditions have sought to create and to maintain—an intelligence that Jefferson held to be indispensable to the health and longevity of freedom. Such intelligence does not grow by bloating upon the ephemeral information and misinformation of the public media. It grows by returning again and again to the landmarks of its cultural birthright, the works that have proved worthy of devoted attention.

"Read not the Times. Read the Eternities," Thoreau said. Ezra Pound wrote that "literature is news that STAYS news." In his lovely poem, "The Island," Edwin Muir spoke of man's inescapable cultural boundaries and of his consequent responsibility for his own sources and renewals:

> Men are made of what is made,
> The meat, the drink, the life, the corn,
> Laid up by them, in them reborn.
> And self-begotten cycles close
> About our way; indigenous art
> And simple spells make unafraid
> The haunted labyrinths of the heart . . .

These men spoke of a truth that no society can afford to shirk for long: we are dependent, for understanding, and for consolation and hope, upon what we learn of ourselves from songs and stories. This has always been so, and it will not change.

I am saying, then, that literacy—the mastery of language and the knowledge of books—is not an ornament, but a necessity. It is impractical only by the standards of quick profit and easy power. Longer perspective will show that it alone can preserve in us the possibility of an accurate judgment of ourselves, and the possibilities of correction and renewal. Without it, we are adrift in the present, in the wreckage of yesterday, in the nightmare of tomorrow.

QUESTIONS FOR CRITICAL ANALYSIS

1. When Berry uses the term "literacy," what does he mean? How is his definition different from the other authors in this section? Is it a less valid definition?
2. In what ways does Berry feel that universities are failing? How do English teachers contribute to this failure? Do you agree with Berry? Why, or why not?
3. Discuss the "first flaw," short-term practicality, as it influences the way reading is taught (described in other essays in this section) or the way journalists conduct their business (in the previous section).
4. What point does Berry make about the importance of valuing language? Do you agree with him? Make a list of other common terms that Berry might consider examples of devalued language?
5. Why does Berry believe literacy is a necessity? Do you agree with him? Why, or why not?

QUESTIONS FOR STRUCTURAL ANALYSIS

1. Look carefully at the first paragraph. What is Berry's thesis? How does he feel about his subject? How do you know?
2. What are the two sides of Berry's argument about literacy? How does Berry set up the argument of his opposition? Is he fair to his opponent? Why, or why not?
3. What examples does Berry use to support his belief that language is used as a weapon? Does he convince you to agree with him? How? or why not?
4. Why does Berry refer to Jefferson's ideas and quote Thoreau, Pound, and Muir? Who are these people? Are these sources important to the essay? In what ways?
5. Look at Berry's language in this essay. How does he use images, patterns, and rhythm? Does his language support his point of view? How?

*T*HE *P*ROBLEM OF *I*LLITERACY

TOPICS FOR WRITING ESSAYS

Many of the questions following each essay can serve as appropriate writing suggestions. Some of the topics listed below expand the prereading exercises, but they can be used without completing that step first.

1. Write an essay which explains to an educated reader what reading means to you. Be careful when you write this not to slip into vague, over-generalized, platitudinous thinking or writing. Personalize the essay with specific examples, or a single important incident. (In preparing for this essay, you may reread Eudora Welty's "A Sweet Devouring" from Part One.)
2. Interview one or two professors in the teacher education department of your school who specialize in elementary education or in the teaching of reading. What methods do they use to teach reading? What do they think of Bettelheim and Zelan's research? Use your interview material as well as the essays in this section to write an article for the alumni magazine describing how your college instructs reading teachers.
3. Have you read *Cultural Literacy* by E. D. Hirsch? If you have, write a review of Hirsch's book using the ideas in Berry's essay, "In Defense of Literacy," as a point of comparison.

RESEARCH POSSIBILITIES

1. Find out about adult literacy programs in your community. How long have they been working? Who is their clientele? How are reading teachers selected and trained? Interview those who run the program, those who recommend clients, and, if possible, some graduates of the program. Write a feature story on the program for your local newspaper.
2. Interview professors and students from the eight discipline areas listed in the Berry prereading exercise. What do they think an educated person (*not* someone majoring in the discipline) should know about their subject? Read books and articles about liberal education (for example, Alfred North Whitehead's *The Aims of Education*, or Hirsch's book, *Cultural Literacy*, mentioned above). Using the information you gather, write a definition of a literate person for publication in the alumni magazine.

Can We Improve the Schools?

The assumption of each of the authors in this section is that American public schools are in bad shape and need to be improved. Mitchell and Magnet offer the most compelling pictures of the problems of the schools, and Sizer and Boyer the clearest advice on how to change the system. Kolderie takes exception with those who think that schools can be improved through funding grants and programs and insists that before the schools can change, the people most deeply involved in the schools—the board members, superintendents, principals and teachers—must be convinced that change is necessary and possible. He maintains that business has a responsibility to convince school leaders and the community that improving the schools is in their best interest. Clendenin, chairman of BellSouth Corporation, describes the willingness of the business community to accept that responsibility.

*T*HE COLUMBUS GAP

RICHARD MITCHELL

Richard Mitchell (1929–   ), professor of English at Glassboro State College, is the editor and publisher of a controversial monthly publication, The Underground Grammarian, *which examines our misuse of language. Through three books,* Less than Words Can Say *(1979),* The Graves of Academe *(1981), and* The Leaning Tower of Babel *(1984), Mitchell blames the public schools (the teachers and the teachers of teachers) for producing a population of muddled speakers and thinkers. "The Columbus Gap," a chapter from* Less than Words Can Say, *ridicules educators' emphasis on teaching "values clarification" rather than language skills.*

Before you begin reading: *Can you remember a course you took in high school in which you learned virtually nothing? In your notebook, describe what made that course worthless.*

◆

AMERICAN PUBLIC EDUCATION IS A REMARKABLE ENTERprise; it succeeds best where it fails. Imagine an industry that consistently fails to do what it sets out to do, a factory where this year's product is invariably sleazier than last year's but, nevertheless, better than next year's. Imagine a corporation whose executives are always spending vast sums of money on studies designed to discover just what it is they are supposed to do and then vaster sums for further studies on just how to do it. Imagine a plant devoted to the manufacture of factory seconds to be sold at a loss. Imagine a producer of vacuum cleaners that rarely work hiring whole platoons of engineers who will, in time, report that it is, in fact, true that the vacuum cleaners rarely work, and who will, for a larger fee, be glad to find out why, if that's possible. If you discover some such outfit, don't invest in it. Unfortunately, we are all required to invest in public education.

Public education is also an enterprise that regularly blames its clients for its failures. Education cannot, after all, be expected to deal with barbarous and sometimes even homicidal students who hate schools and everything in them, except, perhaps, for smaller kids with loose lunch money. If the students are dull and hostile, we mustn't blame the schools. We must blame the parents for their neglect and their bad examples. If the parents are ignorant and depraved, then we must blame "society." And so forth—but not *too* far. Those who lament thus seem not inclined to ask how "society" got to be that way, if it *is* that way, and whether or not public education may have made it so.

The theme of the educators' exculpation, in its most common terms, goes something like this: We educators are being blamed for the corporate failures of a whole society. Our world is in disarray, convulsed by crime, poverty, ignorance, hatred, and institutionalized materialism and greed. The public expects us to cure all these ills, but that's just impossible. We are being given a bum rap. Besides, we're not getting enough money to do the job.

Well, it is a terrible thing to be held accountable for the sins of the world, and even worse that such a fate should be visited on such a noble and self-sacrificing bunch. We'd all feel much better, surely, if we could only pin all the pains and disorders of the human condition on some institution better suited to take the rap—General Motors, perhaps, or the Mafia. Come to think of it, however, General Motors never claimed that it could cure those pains and disorders; even the Mafia was not so bold. Public education *has* made such claims.

Our educators have said that they would teach love and the brotherhood of mankind as well as the importance of brushing after meals. They have promised to teach social consciousness and environmental awareness, creativity, ethnic pride, tolerance, sensitivity to interpersonal/intercultural relationships, and the skills of self-expression, provided, of course, that such skills didn't involve irrelevant details like spelling and the agreement of subjects and verbs. They have said that they will straighten everybody out about sex and venereal disease and the related complications of family life, and about how to operate voting machines and balance checkbooks. They have invited Avon ladies to rap with third graders about their career objectives. They have undertaken to engender in naturally self-centered and anarchic children a profound respect for the folkways of migrant workers and the peculiarities of octogenarians. All of this, and much more, they promise us.

General Motors did not presume to promise us those things. Even the Mafia, perhaps the only enterprise in the country that could actually achieve such results in its own peculiar fashion, refrained from making such offers. Unlike public education, General Motors and the Mafia are modest, medium-sized enterprises fully aware of their limitations. Furthermore, each of them, in its own way, does have to do some palpable work for its money, but public education is guaranteed a handsome income whether it works or not. In fact, the less it works, the larger the income it can demand. What kind of nation would this be, after all, if we refused to invest more and more money in the pursuit of such noble and splendid goals?

Very few Americans will recall asking the educators to pursue such goals. It was the educators who decided not only that such an enterprise was mandated by the people but that it belonged properly in the public schools. They are experts, right? Who are we to say what they should or shouldn't—or could or couldn't—do? Who are we to go against the will of the people? Anyway, all of those things are just wonderful. It is possible, though, that we wouldn't now be blaming educators for not doing them if they hadn't assured us that they could and would do them. We hold no grudge against the crackpot next door who is working on a perpetual-motion machine unless he has told us that he could make one and separated us from lots of our money to buy custom-made magnets and extra-large rubber bands.

Most of us *will* recall that somewhere in our history, maybe it was back in Jefferson's time, we *did* ask the schools to teach everybody to read and write and cipher. Somehow, as hard as it may be to teach those things, it does seem a more modest undertaking than teaching love and tolerance and the brotherhood of all mankind. We may have expressed a few other desires—that the children should learn something of history, their own history especially, and of the literature and art that have not solved the ills of the human condition at all, but have made them clear and concrete and all too human. We did hope that the children would learn something of science and its methodology, by which we can understand and work at least some of the things in the world. We did ask a few other little things, most of them matters of fact and knowledge, silly things sometimes, like the names of the states and their capitals, and the length of the Nile and the Amazon, and the author of Gray's "Elegy."

Those few things that we do seem to have asked of public education are remarkably possible to teach. It is faddish nonsense to say that we don't know how, for instance, to teach reading and writing to the ignorant and must spend lots of money on studies and experiments before we can begin. All children are ignorant. All children who have ever learned to read and write have begun that task in ignorance. We know how to teach reading and writing—it's been done successfully millions and millions of times. It does require exactitude and discipline, and somewhat more of those things in the teacher than in the learners. It requires drill and recitation and memorization and practice, but these things can be made to happen. In one way, it is easy to teach reading and writing and arithmetic because it's possible to achieve concrete and measurable results through regular and practicable methods. In that respect, it is very difficult to teach the brotherhood of all mankind because we don't know exactly what that is or how we would measure it. In another way, however, it's much harder to teach reading and writing and arithmetic because we do have to know those things if we are to teach them, and we do have to be continuously rigorous and exact. To teach the brotherhood of mankind seems to be mostly the presentation of attractive but untestable assertions and the reiteration of pious slogans and generalizations. If you'd like to be a teacher, but you don't want to work too hard, by all means set up as a teacher of the brotherhood of mankind rather than as a teacher of reading and writing and arithmetic. Such a career has the further advantage that no one knows how to decide whether you have actually taught anyone anything, whereas teachers of reading and writing and arithmetic are always being embarrassed when their students are shown not to have learned those things.

It takes a very simple fellow not to be a little suspicious when he notices that all this teaching of "values" and "attitudes" seems to be at once much easier and more profitable than teaching things like the chief exports of New Zealand or the trade routes of the ancient Greeks, to say nothing of reading, writing, and arithmetic. Even an idiot will grow suspicious should he behold all of the implications of the values-teaching business. The profits are indeed enormous. You can't just go and teach values. You have to study *how* to teach values. You need money, and time, and questionnaires, and duplicating machines to duplicate the questionnaires, and keypunch operators to tabulate the replies to the questionnaires, and computer time to collate the data punched by the keypunch operators, and probably a new Mr. Coffee machine so that everybody can take a break once in a while. You need to figure out how to teach both the values themselves and the art of values-teaching to those who are eager to become values teachers. You need to devise the strategies by which values teachers can be sold to the schools in the disguises of social studies teachers and language arts teachers.

Here is how values-teaching works in the classroom. This is what they call a "values clarification strategy"—later on we'll have a sensitivity module. This values clarification strategy is suggested for use with students of all ages, and, as you'll see, it is equally relevant to the subject matter of any course taught in any school in America, which is to say, not at all.

The teacher writes two words—one at either end of the blackboard. "Cadillac" and "Volkswagen" are recommended; the first probably ought to go on the *right* end of the blackboard, thus suggesting, even in a home economics course, something useful about the eternal verities of politics and money. Having written "Cadillac" and "Volkswagen" in the neat block capitals that are actually *taught* in education courses, the teacher asks the student which of those brands they "identify with" and to get up and move to the corresponding side of the room. After some puzzled looks and shrugs, and one smart aleck in the back of the room drawing circles around his temple, and lots of milling and shuffling, the students end up standing in bunches on either side of the room, wondering what the hell can happen next. It's worse than they imagine, for the teacher now instructs them to choose partners of their own persuasion and to hold a serious discussion of the values that have sent them into the one camp or the other. The serious discussion is to last for two minutes. Then they all go back to their places and watch for the next pair of words.

Now you can imagine how they feel. It's like finding yourself at a party where a bubble-brained hostess wants everybody to play Truth or Consequences or else! Of course, even in the worst of our schools, there are no students as stupid as the teacher who would do such a thing, so they probably manage to find something less inane to talk about for those two minutes, giving thanks the while that at least it beats the Congress of Vienna or the square of the hypotenuse. Furthermore, if they shuffle back to their seats as slowly as possible, the bell might ring before they have to choose between a rose and a daisy or between an electric typewriter and a quill pen. Unlike the teacher, they know that anyone who "identifies" with an electric typewriter is crazy, just about as crazy as anyone who "identifies" with a quill pen.

Take a few moments wondering what it means "to identify" with a Cadillac. Only one thing is clear: the man who identifies with a Cadillac probably does not imagine that he *is* a Cadillac. Everything else is vague. It could be any or several of these: he wants a Cadillac; he admires a Cadillac; he deserves a Cadillac; he needs a Cadillac . . . add some more for yourself. The list will probably be very long and very boring. Without such a list of possibilities, however, the little game of values clarification would be impossible. The students and the teacher can play it only because they *don't* know what they mean by "identifying with" something. Nor is it the point of the game to *define* that term. The game is simply a self-indulgent wallowing in ignorance with only one clear result: It takes up some time that might have been spent in studying something concrete and useful but admittedly more difficult.

Grammar, for instance. Notice that such a futile exercise is made possible, and even made futile, because a transitive verb, "identify," has been twisted into an intransitive form. It is *not* a "rule" of English grammar that some verbs must have objects. It is simply the *fact* that some verbs evoke relationships that don't make any sense without an object. When someone asks you "How do we see?" you understand him well enough to answer, although the answer may be either a neurological disquisition or "through a glass, darkly." When he asks you "How do we view?" you need more information if you are to answer him, because the idea evoked by the word "view" is not complete in itself. This, like so many things that we think of as arbitrary rules, is actually a clue to how the mind works in English. The "identify with" values clarification game assures that, for a while at least, no mind will work.

Things like that really do happen in our schools. Although it may not seem so at first, it is just that sort of thing that causes the corruption of language that, in its turn, causes just that sort of thing. In fact, it is only the preachers and practitioners of such nonsense who take it seriously. Imagine for the moment that the students could be persuaded to take it seriously. There you are—remember, this is suitable for all ages—standing on your side of the room. You *do* choose a partner, let's say, and you settle down to the serious business of discussing, for two minutes, the tremendous values and heartfelt convictions that have led you to identify with "Cadillac." What do you say? What *can* you say? No matter how seriously you take it, can you do much more than recite a slogan or two, put forth some well-known generalization, enunciate some vague impression or casual opinion? And your partner, obviously not in need of conviction, can do only the same. So there you stand, muttering desultorily about resale value and roominess and pointing out that a careful driver can save gasoline by not accelerating too fast. Great. Should you find yourself in such a predicament, of course, you *won't* take it seriously. Like any right-thinking human being, you will pick the best-looking partner you can reach and spend those two minutes arranging something for later. Now *that* might clarify some values. Vaporizing about Cadillacs can only air some prejudices, and not even strong ones at that.

Consider now what happens to language in an exercise like that. Are quill pens and electric typewriters values? To prize one, must we despise the other? Should we be doing any of this stuff at all in a school, where we are supposed to learn some arithmetic and the intelligent use of language? If a student is to take any learning at all from such an exercise, leaving aside the revelation that his teacher is a nitwit, it is that what we say doesn't much matter. Idle rapping is called the clarification of values. Any old thing at all, anything a teacher can *name*, becomes a value. Unreal polarities are suggested by the pairings of such "values," and students are given to understand that through discourse they have discovered that "value" in them that has led them to one pole or the other. This little game will hardly suggest to any student that a "clarification of values" must, if it is to take place at all, proceed through discursive statements and logical analysis. It leaves the impression that vague opinions and the suggestions of environment are "clarifications." Students usually *do* learn something in class, but it's seldom what the teacher had in mind. In this class, the students will learn to be content with empty talk and to accept random reflection as though it were knowledge.

This "values clarification" business is very popular in the schools, and an educationist named Simon has written, with a couple of pals, a nifty handbook chock-full of "values clarification strategies." The examples mentioned are not, as you probably thought, silly exaggerations—they're from the book. A wily teacher could spend a whole year playing those fun games in class and still have enough examples left over for summer session. They are all designed not only to stay as far as possible from hypotenuses but to reduce the power of language in the players. They achieve that result by offering the students experiences rather than study and feelings rather than knowledge. The experiences and feelings, however, exist as words only. It is hard to imagine the student suggestible and feebleminded enough to think that he does, in fact, feel more empathy for Arabs after eating a sheep's eye.

Eating a sheep's eye, of course, is not a values clarification strategy. It is what Simon would call a "sensitivity module," and here is a more likely example:

> In teaching elementary children about the early world explorers, one teacher had her children go out and actually "discover" new parts of the city. One instruction was to "find a new and faster route to the ball field." The gap between the world of Columbus and their own world in the city was narrowed.

By "elementary children" he means, probably, children in elementary school, unless, perhaps, he thinks that "elementary" means something like "simple-minded." It would take a simple-minded child, indeed, to get sucked into a silly project like this. And what makes the project silly is also what brought it to pass in the first place—bad language.

People who can use language accurately can make useful analogies and learn to understand things. They can also tell—through language, for there is no other way—just how far an analogy can be pushed before it becomes useless. That "sensitivity module" is drawn from a silly analogy, which suggests that what Columbus did is comparable to finding a better way to get to the ball field. To make such an analogy requires both ignorance and misunderstanding of history. That's not "discovery," and even Simon feels uncertain enough about it to put those quotation marks around the word. In fact, the search for some hitherto unimagined route to the ball field is so absurd on the face of it that the students who undertook it must surely have spent their time in the nearest snack bar. A teacher silly enough to give such an assignment has to be humored, of course, so the students must have spent a few minutes concocting a good story, maybe something about monsters and the edge of the known world.

Notice that this exercise is called a "sensitivity module." Such is the power of language that nonsensical time wasters like this become significant educational processes when given the right name, and money is spent to design them. In what sense this can be called a "module," there is no understanding. If this is a "module," then lunch might just as well be called a "module." In fact, lunch *is* a "module" in many schools. Just as in Dallas, buses are "motorized attendance modules." A module, therefore, is anything you please. There's no profit in worrying about the module, however; it's the "sensitivity" part that's important.

Schools are in favor of sensitivity and opposed, naturally, to insensitivity. In the traditional curriculum there are still some outdated things that cause insensitivity. Historical dates cause insensitivity. The square of the hypotenuse instills callousness. Untempered grammar and spelling produce ruthless elitism. The multiplication table can engender inhumanity, and precise diction has been known to result in fascism. Since we have not yet managed to persuade the public that such studies should be discontinued utterly, the best we can do is mitigate them, wherever possible, with expeditions into the mists of what is called noncognitive learning. If we make children learn mere facts about the difficulties of navigation in the fifteenth century, they may well grow up to be cutthroats and boors, totally lacking in sensitivity. Far better it is to send them wandering the streets of the city and pretending to search for *terra incognita*. That way, you see, they'll get the "feel" of exploration. Well, let's say that they can at least pretend to get the feel. When they get back, they won't know any dehumanizing things about the nasty economic implications of exploration in the Renaissance or those silly and irrelevant political struggles of fifteenth-century Europe, but they will have "narrowed the gap" between themselves and Columbus.

And what can that mean—to narrow the gap between us and Columbus? Those things that separate us from Columbus—can they be taken all together and understood as a "gap"? If so, in what way, *exactly*, is the gap "narrowed" when we find a quicker way to get to the ball field? When we eat blubber, do we narrow the gap between us and the Eskimos? When we walk around blindfolded for an hour, do we narrow the gap between us and the blind? They do things like this in school—not just in the public schools but even and especially in the schools that produce the teachers for the public schools. All such "gaps" are very large and complex, and to understand them and to have knowledge about them will require that we first make many statements of fact. To "feel" like an Eskimo and to know what being an Eskimo involves are utterly different things. The former is probably impossible for non-Eskimos. The latter can be achieved by anyone who will attend to statements of fact. Ten thousand sensitivity modules will not teach us how it is with men who sail into the utterly unknown; to read their words just may give us an inkling.

People who worry about teaching sensitivity have little use for exactitude in statements of fact. The vagueness of narrowing gaps and identifying with Volkswagens seems to them somehow "humanistic," and precise statements of fact and matters of knowledge seem the opposite of "humanistic," whatever that might be. This attitude can survive and flourish only where language is diffuse and imprecise. The accurate statement of empirical propositions would destroy it.

It is possible, of course, to clarify values. Whether that is the proper business of the schools is another matter, but it surely can be done. It can be done, however, only through language, only through a chain of logical discourse. Logical discourse requires exactitude. If we *do* want to teach morality or at least the thoughtful examination of our deeds and their apparent meanings, we can do this only through teaching exactitude. It is no accident that thought, word, and deed keep company together in prayer books. To clarify our values must mean to make fine distinctions. To make fine distinctions means to see how different things are similar and how similar things are different. This calls for many finely tuned words and subtle grammatical devices and the ability to put them all together with precision. The finer the distinctions we can make in words and, therefore, in our thoughts, the finer the judgments we can make about the nature of our deeds. Contrariwise, careless and blunted words conceal the nature of our deeds.

I had read—and I believe it—that the Nazi bureaucracy generated thousands and thousands of pages of routine paperwork related to the business of killing Jews, but in all that paperwork the word "killing" appears nowhere. Those who think that a concern for precision in language is finicky and pedantic should ponder that for a while. The people who say to each other "Let's kill the Jews" have indubitably clarified their values. Having done so, they may find them repellent and decide to seek others, but I wouldn't count on it. The people who say that a sensitivity module will narrow the gap between us and Columbus have *not* clarified their values or anything else. If our values happen to be abhorrent, as they often are, we can know that only through stating them plainly. It's not impossible that thousands of Germans could have done what they did only because they spoke carefully of "transportation" and "resettlement" and "solution" rather than of "killing."

It is not only possible to clarify values but obviously desirable. It is also possible, and desirable, to balance budgets. To teach people how to balance budgets, it just isn't enough to let them play with fat wads of Monopoly money. We have to teach them arithmetic. To teach them how to clarify values, we must teach them mastery of the system with which we express values and the only device we have for "knowing" them. That's language.

The values of "values clarification" stand in need of some clarification. To *see* that requires enough skill in language to recognize the abuse of language. To *do* it requires even more. It would help, too, to remember the words of Hobbes: "For words are wise men's counters, they do but reckon with them; but they are the money of fools that value them . . . by authority." "Clarification" is a word. When a teacher in his authority tells his students that they will now clarify their values by rapping about Cadillacs and Volkswagens, what are the poor kids to do? They have not been taught the skills of language, and they have no choice but to believe or to pretend that they believe. In either case, they must grow up believing that the clarification of values is a silly game played in dreary places by preposterous people to no useful end. They become a herd and live, perforce, the unexamined life.

There is more clarification of values in a single sentence of Bacon than in all the strategies of Simon. Consider the rest of that line: "Reading maketh a full man; conference a ready man; and writing an exact man." We have read that line so often, of course, that we seldom do more than nod at it. When we give it some thought, we can discover (and this time the "discovery" is real) the power of that mind and the power of language in the meticulous choice of the words "full," "ready," and "exact." That's exact language and the expression of an exact thought. The words tell us not only that a well-read man is "full" but that an ill-read man is "empty," as empty as the student whose study of Columbus took him to the ball field. They tell us that the man who cannot "confer," who is not fluent and practiced in his speech, is uncertain and inept, like the student just returned from the ball field and needing desperately to convince his teacher that his sensitivity has been heightened—really! They tell us that the man who cannot "write" is imprecise and unclear in his mind, like Simon, who tells us that the Columbus gap has been narrowed through a sensitivity module.

There is no need, of course, to ferret out the fact that the schools are in the business of teaching "values" at the expense of reading, writing, and ciphering. They boast of it publicly. Here are the words of a professor of educational psychology explaining to the public why they ought to accept with equanimity the fact that students do so poorly on tests of reading, writing, and ciphering. Those tests, you must understand,

> do not attempt to quantify such crucial concerns as students' self-perception; their attitude toward, and relationship with, people whose culture and social class differ from their own; their ethical behavior, values, personal philosophy and moral commitments; their creativity, emotional health and sense of ethnic identity—precisely the areas that schools have been emphasizing.

So. We have traded skill in language and number for ethical behavior, personal philosophy, moral commitment, creativity, and emotional health. Not at all a bad deal. But wait. What has become of those millions of young people deeply schooled in morality? These are the "areas" the schools have been "emphasizing" for decades now. How is it that Earth is not yet fair and all men glad and wise? How is it that creativity and emotional health lead to the beating of teachers and the destruction of file cabinets? What personal philosophy calls forth the smashing of toilet bowls with sledgehammers?

Children are much smarter than we think. They know when they are being deceived and defrauded. Unless they can utter what they know, however, they know it only in part and imperfectly. If we do not give them the language and thought in which they might genuinely clarify some values, they will do their clarifying with sledgehammers. None of the lofty goals named above can be approached without the skillful practice of language and thought, and to "emphasize" those "areas" in the absence of that practice is to promulgate thought control rather than the control of thought.

Questions for Critical Analysis

1. What is Mitchell's opinion of public education? What led him to this opinion? Based on your experiences in elementary and high school, do you agree with him? Why, or why not?
2. Why does Mitchell use General Motors and the Mafia as examples? What does each organization represent? What point does he make by referring to them?
3. In what ways have the schools failed? Why is America trapped into supporting a failing institution?
4. What is a student supposed to learn by the values-education exercises Mitchell describes? How does he suggest students could really be taught values?
5. What do you suppose Simon, quoted in Mitchell's essay, meant when he said his

sensitivity module would narrow the gap between Christopher Columbus and the student? What does Mitchell think of such a goal? What do you think of it? How would you respond if your child was taught by such methods?

QUESTIONS FOR STRUCTURAL ANALYSIS

1. State Mitchell's thesis. Describe how he develops his argument to support this thesis.
2. What is Mitchell's attitude toward the schools? List words and phrases that reveal this attitude. Does Mitchell think teachers are doing a good job? In what ways? When do teachers fail? Show how Mitchell's language reveals his attitude toward teachers.
3. Evaluate Mitchell's comparison of teaching subjects versus teaching values. How does this comparison support his thesis? Is Mitchell's long illustration of "values-teaching" a digression, or is it critical to the development of his ideas? Did any teacher ever teach your class in this way? What did you think of the exercise then? Has your opinion changed?
4. Explain the point Mitchell makes in his discussion of grammar and language. What does he assume of his reader? How do the educational exercises he describes "reduce the power of language"?
5. How does Mitchell apply Francis Bacon's statement to his discussion? Why is this quotation especially pertinent to his argument?

*B*ETTER *S*CHOOLS

THEODORE R. SIZER

Theodore R. Sizer (1932–) makes headlines by criticizing the state of high schools, proposing reforms, and establishing a network of high schools, the Coalition of Essential Schools, through which reforms can take place. Horace's Compromise: The Dilemma of the American High School *(1984) offers radical proposals for school reform; "Better Schools," a chapter from this book, outlines Sizer's "five imperatives for better schools," which are the focus of his "crusade to remake the American high school." In his introduction, Sizer says: "We know that the game of school learning is won or lost in classrooms and we feel that America's present system of schooling makes winning often very difficult indeed."*

Before you begin reading: *In your reading notebook list five recommendations to improve elementary and secondary education. Next to each item, provide (1) a possible argument against your recommendation and (2) a plan for implementing your suggestion.*

◆

THERE ARE FIVE IMPERATIVES FOR BETTER SCHOOLS:

1. Give room to teachers and students to work and learn in their own, appropriate ways.
2. Insist that students clearly exhibit mastery of their school work.
3. Get the incentives right, for students and for teachers.
4. Focus the students' work on the use of their minds.
5. Keep the structure simple and thus flexible.

Giving teachers and students room to take full advantage of the variety among them implies that there must be substantial authority in each school. For most public and diocesan Catholic school systems, this means the decentralization of power from central headquarters to individual schools. For state authorities, it demands the forswearing of detailed regulations for how schools should be operated. It calls for the authorities to trust teachers and principals—and believe that the more trust one places in them, the more their response will justify that trust. This trust can be tempered by judicious accreditation systems, as long as these do not reinfect the schools with the blight of standardized required practice.

The purpose of decentralized authority is to allow teachers and principals to adapt their schools to the needs, learning styles, and learning rates of their particular students. The temptation in every school will be to move toward orderly standardization: such is the instinct, it seems, of Americans, so used as we are to depending on structure. Good schools will have to resist this appeal of standardization: the particular needs of each student should be the only measure of how a school gets on with its business. Greater authority is an incentive for teachers, one that will attract and hold the kind of adults which high schools absolutely need on their staffs.

The requirement for *exhibitions of mastery* forces both students and teachers to focus on the substance of schooling. It gives the state, the parents, prospective employers, and the adolescents themselves a real reading of what a student can do. It is the only sensible basis for accountability.

Effective exhibitions will be complicated to construct and time-consuming to administer. To be fair, they need to be flexible: not all students show themselves off well in the same way. They cannot, then, merely be standardized, machine-graded, paper-and-pencil tests.

The process of constructing and overseeing these exhibitions can be threatening, because it will force teachers to see and to deal with the gaps and redundancies that arise from the traditional curriculum. Teachers find it safe to work in the privacy of their classrooms, delivering the credits their courses bestow on each student. A commonly constructed exhibition invades this privacy—a step that is as necessary as it may be intimidating.

The existence of specific exhibitions is itself a strong *incentive* for both students and teachers. Exhibitions clarify ends. The student knows what she or he has to do in order to progress and graduate. If pursuit of that high school graduation diploma is voluntary, the adolescent is left on his or her own; the games attendant on compulsory attendance can no longer be used as excuses. To the young person who has met the minimal competencies in literary, numeracy, and civic understanding, the high school says, Here is what our diploma means; join us and we'll help you master the knowledge it represents, but the work is basically yours to do. The challenge of such an arrangement is powerful. There is self-esteem to be gained from being the key worker, and if wise teachers appropriately adjust the study to the pace of each student, success will breed success. The personalization inherent in such adjusted pacing is also rewarding; it signals to the student that he or she is important as an individual.

Not all adolescents will find any one school setting congenial. Some students respond well to judicious prodding. Others wilt under it, but flourish in gentler places. The claim for personalization extends to a variety of school settings (separate schools or schools-within-schools), and the opportunity for choice among them itself is a spur to energy. Loyalty roots only with difficulty, if at all, in places forced on us; commitment readily follows from free choice.

The focus of high school should be on *the use of the mind*. Although young citizens need to learn about and be exposed to many sides of life, the mind is central, and the school is the principal institution that society has for assisting adolescents in its use. High schools cannot be comprehensive and should not try to be comprehensive; there are some aspects of an adolescent's life in which a school has no right to intrude, and helping students to use their minds well is a large enough assignment, in any case.

The only way to learn to think well and usefully is by practice. The way a teacher assists this learning is by coaching. What a student chooses or is asked to think about is important, obviously, but secondary to the skills of observing and imaginatively using knowledge. A self-propelled learner is the goal of a school, and teachers should insist that students habitually learn on their own. Teacher-delivered knowledge that is never used is temporary.

Issues concerning values inevitably arise in every school, and learning to use one's mind involves making decisions of conduct and belief. How one uses one's mind, and how one accordingly behaves, raise questions about character: Is this fair? Is it thoughtful? Is it generous? Is it *decent?* Schools should not teach merely pure thinking; they must also promote thoughtfulness, at core the qualities of decency. Schools should accept that obligation, not only because it is important, but because it is inescapable. A school *will* affect its students' character, willy-nilly. It should do so carefully, in a principled way.

Personalization of learning and instruction requires a flexible school structure. A flexible structure implies *a simple structure*. A school day segmented into seven or eight time units, each with its own set of imperatives, is almost impossible to bend. A curriculum represented by six or seven autonomous subjects quickly freezes hard: if each gets what its teacher feels is its due, all lose substantial freedom. Furthermore, such a fractionated and specialized set of subjects distorts knowledge for young minds; a simpler, more cogent organization of subject matter is wise.

Any effort to simplify the curriculum will be as threatening to teachers as will be the creation of general graduation exhibitions. We have been trained in our specializations, and we step outside them with trepidation. Our university mentors may often mock these forays, too; for many of them "specialization" and "standards" are synonymous—a false equation, but one that they will nonetheless scathingly defend. Reconstituting the shape of the curriculum—strengthening it by simplifying it and making it cogent to adolescents—will be a lonely, politically rocky effort.

Fortunately, each of these five imperatives governs the work of one or another existing school. There is no novelty here. However, pressing them ahead *together* would be novel, a school reconstruction effort of considerable scope and risk.

We hope that many schools will find one or more of these imperatives persuasive enough to push them vigorously. We also hope that some will have the courage to embrace them all, simultaneously. We need new model schools, ones resting on imperatives, like these five, that appear to serve well modern conditions and adolescents. The imperatives interlock, and as they are engineered into practical forms, their interconnection will become a source of strength—and of efficiency. The financial costs of better schools can be justified if the pretentious practices of comprehensiveness are stalwartly eliminated.

Better schools will come when better structures are built. Those structures have no inherent merit, however: their sole function will be to provide apt and nurturing conditions that will attract students and teachers and make their work together worthwhile and efficient.

QUESTIONS FOR CRITICAL ANALYSIS

1. What five methods does Sizer propose to improve the schools? Do you agree with each of his suggestions? Which do you think is most important? Why?
2. Sizer states that schools must insist on "exhibitions of mastery" but he doesn't say what those should be. Think of your school experiences and make a list of suggestions.
3. What is the contract between student and school? What must each party agree to? Does this arrangement describe how things were at your high school? Why, or why not?
4. Who do you think Sizer assumes is his audience? What does Sizer want his reader to do after reading his essay?
5. What would Richard Mitchell ("The Columbus Gap") think of Sizer's imperatives? Which ones would he like, and why? Which ones would he dislike, and why? Which ones do you like, and why? Which ones do you dislike, and why?

QUESTIONS FOR STRUCTURAL ANALYSIS

1. Write an outline of Sizer's essay. Evaluate how well he develops each of his imperatives.
2. Describe Sizer's tone. How does he feel about the schools? Compare his attitude with Mitchell's. What are the similarities between them? What are the differences?
3. What words and phrases does Sizer use that strike you as specialized or jargonistic? Rewrite these phrases so that they are not "educationese."
4. Does one of Sizer's imperatives seem better presented than the others? Select one idea and evaluate the way Sizer develops it. What would you add or subtract from the discussion?
5. What is Sizer's conclusion? After reading his proposals carefully, do you agree with this conclusion? What would you suggest differently?

*H*OW TO *S*MARTEN *U*P THE *S*CHOOLS

MYRON MAGNET

Myron Magnet, in a special report for Fortune *magazine, proposes that American schools are falling so quickly behind those in other nations that business can no longer stand on the sidelines in school reform. Using data from the Department of Education and information published in popular books on the state of American education, Magnet suggests ways the schools can improve and how business can support that improvement.*

Before you begin reading: *Do you think your elementary and secondary education prepared you adequately for college and/or the work force? Write two paragraphs in your reading notebook: one describing the strengths of your precollege education and one describing the weakness of your education.*

◆

SO IGNORANT AND BENIGHTED ARE MANY YOUNG RE-cruits to the U.S. work force that one executive after another has recoiled in horror, gasping with astonishment. *These* are the troops we're supposed to win the global competition with? How can such a work force dominate the knowledge-intensive industries where the future will be made? What use are modern management techniques that draw on the worker's talents and initiative when he has no dogged, practical Yankee ingenuity to tap? And if two of every five new jobs that the Labor Department expects to be created by the turn of the century will call for more than basic skills, where will the ten million qualified workers come from to fill them? Presumably not all from Hong Kong.

Little wonder that many executives are joining the education reform movement sweeping America. They fear that if we can't count on public schools to produce workers who can read, think, calculate, and communicate, we can kiss our economic preeminence goodbye.

The failure of U.S. public education from kindergarten through high school is vast and ominous. Its most notorious measure is the plunge in College Board test performance. Combined scores on the verbal and math exams fell almost yearly from 980 points out of a possible 1600 in 1963 to a nadir of 890 in 1980, before gradually recovering to 906 by 1986. On another series of national tests, science performance of 9-, 13-, and 17-year-olds worsened steadily from 1970 to

1982, the last year for which data are available. Math performance by 17-year-olds has also deteriorated.

Comparison with other nations disheartens. U.S. eighth-graders on an international math test in 1982 answered an average of only 46% of the questions correctly, compared with top-scoring Japan's 64%. The American kids couldn't even top the average score (52%) for the 11 competing nations. Worse, the top 5% of the U.S. 12th-graders who took international calculus and algebra tests in 1982 came in dead last among the top 12th-graders of nine developed countries, squelched not only by first-ranked Japan but also by Finland, New Zealand, Hungary, and others. That 5% is the *crème de la crème*, since few enough U.S. high school seniors take advanced math at all. Contends University of Illinois education professor Herbert J. Walberg: "People often say that our best and brightest can compare with Japan's best and brightest—who only memorize. But it's simply not true."

How literate are American students—not in the sense of being able to declaim Shakespeare or write like George Will, but rather being able to understand an instruction manual or compose a comprehensible memo for the suggestion box? A congressionally mandated study found in 1984 that fewer than a fifth of approximately 2,000 11th-graders could adequately write a note applying for a summer job at a swimming pool. The average 11th-grader, who only just made it into the realm of meaningful discourse, couldn't do a wide range of writing tasks well enough to ensure he would be understood.

Not surprisingly, average young adults are weak readers and reasoners too—but the scope of what they can't do takes your breath away. Of 23,000 young adults who took a simple qualifying exam for entry-level jobs at New York Telephone, 84% flunked. A government-sponsored study estimated that only 37% of the 21- to 25-year-olds tested could be counted on to comprehend material as complex as a New York *Times* article on the downing of KAL Flight 007. Just 38% could dependably carry out such tasks as using a chart to pick the right grade of sandpaper or figuring their change from $3 if they had a 60-cent cup of soup and a $1.95 sandwich. Don't expect more than one young adult in five to read a schedule well enough to say when a bus will reach the terminal.

Reform leaders—executives, governors, educators, and Secretary of Education William J. Bennett and his staff—are worried not just because many young Americans lack the basic skills needed to build quality cars or even run cash registers. Many new graduates also lack a solid core of the knowledge that makes America work as a country, that common culture that turns a pluralistic hodgepodge into a unified nation without depriving anyone of his distinctive identity. They lack that modicum of political judgment, based on at least a smattering of history, that makes democracy authentic and not a masquerade. Missing too is the historical and literary knowledge that shows the vastness and variety of human aspiration and achievement, strengthening character and values and enlarging one's sense of the possibilities and worth of one's life.

How much is missing grows dismayingly clear from a recent influential book, *What Do Our 17-Year-Olds Know?* by assistant secretary of education Chester E. Finn Jr. and Columbia Teachers College professor Diane Ravitch. Based on tests of a representative national sample of 8,000 17-year-olds, the book reports that fewer than a third of these high school seniors knew in which half-century the Civil War occurred, or what the Magna Carta is or the Reformation was, or that the Declaration of Independence is the document that marked the separation of the colonies from Britain, or that Lincoln wrote the Emancipation Proclamation. A third of them—this is not a joke—didn't know that Columbus discovered America before 1750 or what *Brown* v. *Board of Education* was about. A third couldn't recognize the best-known passage from either the Constitution or the Declaration of Independence. Just over half knew that Stalin led Russia in World War II and—wait for it—that Russia did not invade Israel during that conflict.

Literature questions uncovered a vaster wasteland of ignorance. For these kids, the modern novel is deader than Marley's ghost: Fewer than one 17-year-old scholar in five could match Dostoevski or Conrad or James Joyce with appropriate book titles, and Hemingway and D. H. Lawrence fared little better. Since each question carried four possible answers—and "I don't know" was not among them—this is a worse result than random guessing would produce and suggests an almost militant ignorance. Fewer than half the students knew that Byron, Keats, and Wordsworth were poets.

More happily, the average student scored 68% on the Shakespeare questions and 67% on the Bible ones—poor enough, but passing grades compared with a flunking average for the tests as a whole. As for the Greek myths also central to our cultural heritage, just over half the students knew who Oedipus was or what an Achilles' heel is. Fewer than half could identify Don Quixote or the main theme of *Walden* or the author of a well-worn pair of Poor Richard's maxims.

How did America come to commit "unthinking, unilateral educational disarmament," as the Department of Education's attention-grabbing *Nation at Risk* report termed it? To begin, blame that tattered orthodoxy, "progressive" education. Repeatedly discredited, it nevertheless doesn't die, thanks primarily to the schools of education that are its life-support apparatus. Whatever freshness might once have sparkled in its child-centered approach, its commitment to social utility and "effective living," its rejection of the tyrannies of facts and memorization, of pressure and competitiveness, that freshness has long since turned to stone.

Just one example of the aridity: the "expanding environments" social studies curriculum most schools use from kindergarten through the third grade. Proceeding like those addresses young children write that move from "Mary Jones, Elm Street" to "U.S.A., the Earth, the Universe," this program starts with the child as a family member and moves through his membership in a school, neighborhood, community, even (inevitably) a global community. The four-year sequence, says education professor Ravitch, "is virtually content-free."

For children living at the end of the 20th century—viewers of TV news, observers of modern life, some even visitors to outer space via *Star Wars* or *E.T.* on the VCR—the triviality of this curriculum anesthetizes the mind. "You belong to a family," explains a popular, representatively vacuous first-grade text analyzed by University of Georgia education professors A. Guy Larkins and Michael L. Hawkins. "Some families have two parents . . . Families do things together." Ditto for families in Canada, England, and Japan—the global approach, you see, based on the belief that if we all stress the many things we have in common instead of our supposedly unimportant differences and conflicts, there would be no wars.

Other equally empty textbooks add that children have birthdays, birthdays are fun, and American Indians and Chinese people have them too. Third-graders—these are 8-year-olds—soporifically discover that "all communities have homes . . . buildings where people work, play, learn, and worship . . . parks where people go to have fun . . . stores where people shop . . . roads." All four grades learn how milk gets from the cow to the kitchen, each time with the same numbing simple-mindedness. When Benjamin Franklin appears in one book, it is as a Philadelphia post-office improver and college and library founder. Children aren't told he was a diplomat and nation builder, community roles evidently too heady and interesting for the environment expanders who compiled this text.

Obvious, superficial, and unfailingly boring, the Georgia professors judge, these wan texts utterly displaced red-blooded fare that put muscle on children's minds and imaginations—Greek myths, Robinson Crusoe, stories of national heroes like Washington and Lincoln, of Pilgrims, Indians, and pioneers, of heroes of legend and history from Moses and Ulysses to King Arthur and Joan of Arc. Says Diane Ravitch of this older curriculum: "Children *enjoy* it. They learn painlessly when their lively minds and their sense of romance and adventure are engaged." And they learn something other than that school is dumb.

The progressive preference for utility and "effective living" over the inspiring and instructive richness of our cultural heritage works its way all through the curriculum and powerfully shapes what high-schoolers learn, or don't learn. These days cooking and driving courses count as much toward a high school diploma as English, history, or science courses. While it's fine to teach kids to cook and drive, 13 states let high-schoolers earn at least half their graduation credits from electives like these or like Bachelor Living, where presumably they can learn condom etiquette and that communities have singles bars.

Though progressive education has been doing its work for more than 60 years, it took the upheavals of the Sixties and early Seventies to exaggerate all its tendencies and hasten the evacuation of learning from the schools. A revealing case in point: the trivialization of American history textbooks. While schoolbook publishers are used to dancing tactfully among the sometimes contradictory demands of text-buying authorities wedded to fundamentalism or secular humanism or the free market, the contentions of the Sixties overwhelmed their suavity. That became clear in a report of an expert panel sponsored by the New York–based Educational Excellence Network.

With blacks, Hispanics, American Indians, other ethnic groups, feminists, homosexuals, and nuclear disarmers all clamoring for due mention of the dignity of their accomplishment or injustice of their suffering, history books have resorted to what the report calls "a kind of textual affirmative action." This often crowds out the more important parts of the story and turns texts into dead catalogues of disjointed facts or "distort[s] in order to mention and appease." In the pictures in one leading high school text, the report says, "Texas cowboys, World War I soldiers, and Civilian Conservation Corps surveyors are represented [only] by blacks. In its index, Women's Rights is a longer entry than the Revolutionary War."

Since such texts must not offend interest groups, you can guess how forceful the writing is. Deadly too is that the committees that write these books prefer thinking sociologically about communities and social classes rather than thinking in the traditional historical terms of stories filled with passion and conflict and peopled by vivid characters whose bold or devious or wise actions change the world. So much for drama. Since the texts mustn't use too difficult a vocabulary or carry too heavy a "concept load," they end up even more vapid and colorless.

Progressive education has always tried to replace teacher authoritarianism with teacher-pupil cooperation. But the Sixties' shakeup of education reduced the distance between teacher and pupil so drastically that it fatally subverted teacher authority. Teachers lost confidence that they really knew what pupils should learn, even that they as teachers had something worth teaching. Popular songs might well contain as much wisdom and poetry as Melville, went the cant of the day, and spontaneity might be more valuable than knowledge.

At the college level, where this tendency was most pronounced, the consequence was a reduction in course requirements and admission requirements. High schools in turn reduced graduation requirements, figuring that if colleges didn't require applicants to know foreign languages or sciences for admission, maybe they weren't important. Trivial electives and texts crowded out solid fare in the name of a specious relevance, so that today, 20 years later, students read a biography of onetime teen tennis player Tracy Austin, say, instead of the life of Marie Curie or Pocahontas.

Required homework went the way of required courses. The proportion of high school seniors who did at least five hours a week declined 30% between 1972 and 1980. Says assistant education secretary Finn: "Kids tend to learn that which they study, and to learn it in proportion to the amount of study they do—and up to the level they are obliged to learn it to by the adults in their lives." Not only does less homework produce less learning, but it also fails to instill the work ethic that the U.S. economy needs. Even as teachers were demanding less from students in every way, they were inflating grades, further eroding the incentive to work hard.

Such authority as the schools left themselves the courts helped take away. Principals cannot suspend pupils without a formal hearing, the Supreme Court ruled in 1975, invoking the 14th Amendment's due-process guarantee and thereby turning school discipline from an extension of parental discipline into a quasi-adversarial proceeding on the legal model. Weeks later the Court subverted school order further by ruling that pupils could sue individual teachers and principals for damages for infringing their civil rights. How much do you want to discipline a troublemaker who can make a federal case of it?

The Court broadly impaired learning with the forced busing that followed its 1971 *Swann* ruling. Views differ on whether busing is sound social policy, but it is hard to disagree that its educational costs have been high. In many districts race relations for years became at least as much the focus of school life as education. Angry mobs, frightened or hostile children, and policemen in school hallways did not foster an atmosphere conducive to learning. For a federal judge like W. Arthur Garrity Jr., who ran the Boston school system like a commissar for 11 years, the first priority could not be education. The white flight that busing accelerated often deprived urban schools of the most motivated pupils, whose mainstream values helped set a tone of order and relative respect for school.

Americans like to think that schools can be used to change society, but the influence goes both ways. From the Sixties onward vast social and cultural changes twisted schools out of shape. Families grew unstable, what with the increasing divorce rate and, in a small sliver of society, an emerging underclass pathology. Says University of Chicago sociologist James Coleman, author of the well-known 1966 Coleman Report on education: "Schools were never successful with children from families who didn't have a high level of educational aspirations and strong support for those aspirations." Faced with an influx of children from weak families, schools reduced their demands. They did so especially since the weak families included minority families whose advocates persuaded courts that the high failure and suspension rates among their children were evidence not of pupil shortcomings but of discrimination. Public education reduced itself to the lowest common denominator. Coleman's conclusion: "Weak families have created weak schools, which are not good for kids from strong families." Nor are they good for children from weak families, who arguably need education the most.

If U.S. education were like a run-down factory that required only a little sprucing up and modernizing, the situation wouldn't be so troubling. Instead, with the notable exception of some suburban schools and urban magnet schools, it more resembles an overgrown garden where weeds are beginning to choke out the wholesome growth and supplant it. The forces that have devastated traditional schooling have left not a vacuum but something like a new American culture that is disquietingly resistant to learning.

This culture is producing a new democratic character, minutely anatomized in Allan Bloom's *The Closing of the American Mind*, whose runaway sales attest to the surge of national concern about the bankruptcy of education. At the center of this distinctive modern American personality is a profound belief that truth and values are relative and that therefore the proper attitude toward the world is an indiscriminate openness, a willingness to accept without judging. Students learn this in part from an education whose unthinking global pluralism tells them that different cultures are all much alike deep down, that the differences don't matter, that the most divergent ways of doing and believing and valuing are equally worthy of respect. It is an openness that by making all things equal makes them equally unimportant and therefore not very interesting to learn.

Nothing else in the spirit of this age gives learning any hold on the young. They know that progress has made the past obsolete, with nothing to teach them. They are isolated in a complacent egoism fostered partly by progressive education's emphasis on the child's spontaneous feelings, partly by the emotional remoteness often engendered by the divorce of their parents or the evident impermanence of all the relationships around them, partly by an inability to attach themselves emotionally to a national community that they've been taught is no better than any other one, partly even by their omnipresent rock music's glorification of each adolescent impulse. You can certainly teach such children basics like math and science. But it will take skillful teachers, and especially teachers who are not immersed in this same culture, to get them at all fired up about the rest of our neglected cultural inheritance.

Where to start to fix this mess? The education reformers offer an array of ingenious answers, some of which have begun to sprout programs. Their first helpful idea is that everyone involved—students and especially every level of education authority—must be held accountable for student performance. This means finding out how the students really are doing and publicizing the results. Is the individual student learning what he or she is supposed to learn? Twenty-four states make sure by demanding that he or she pass a competency exam for high school graduation, and 11 states require competency exams for promotion from grade to grade. Some states are mindful that a passing grade, designed to represent minimum acceptable performance, can turn into the norm, depressing standards rather than raising them. These states keep the hurdle high.

How do the students of each school perform? Over a dozen states publish a report card that grades and compares schools, allowing taxpayers and parents to hold authorities accountable by opposing higher taxes for schools or by voting out elected administrators or by complaining to teachers and principals. In Prince George's County, Maryland, Superintendent John A. Murphy makes his 172 principals answerable for their pupils' test scores by posting in his conference room bold graphs of each school's annual scores, prominently labeled with the principal's name. Murphy's school reforms get plenty of credit for the recent economic turnaround of this racially mixed area straddling the Washington Beltway. He came into office in 1984 vowing to raise his schools' scores from the 50th percentile range nationwide to the top quarter in 1990. The goals he sets for his principals go up annually in order to meet that mark, which he thinks he will reach a year ahead of schedule.

So far, just knowing that the boss is watching has proved incentive enough. Says he: "As in any business, if you're going to measure people to see whether or not they're performing, they're going to perform—even if you can't reward them." But he already has started talking about including principals and teachers in a bonus pay plan, based—to foster teamwork within each school—on the success of a school's test scores, attendance rates, advanced course enrollment, and so on. Making each school responsible for its own results will of course require moving authority from the central school district bureaucracy to the principal, a move education reformers urge. Says William Kristol, chief of staff to Secretary of Education Bennett: "The problem now is schools are overregulated but underaccountable. We should free up the principal and then reward him if he does well and change him if he does poorly."

Accountability also extends to school boards and school superintendents, who in a handful of states can be placed under the thumb of a state monitor in case of gross incompetence. The Department of Education has been publicizing state-by-state College Board scores, often with the enthusiastic applause of governors. Says Richard P. Mills, chief education aide to New Jersey Governor Thomas Kean: "You cannot be a governor without being an education advocate right now. If you're concerned about regional development, you have to be concerned about the quality of the graduates." Governors have also realized that education is their biggest budget item, swallowing around 40% of state revenues.

You can't get far without improving the quality of teachers. Today's talented young people rarely choose the classroom as a career, especially now that smart, ambitious women are hardly restricted to traditional "women's work" like teaching. Last year's high school seniors who intended to major in education posted combined verbal and math College Board scores of 845, 61 points below the already dismal average of all seniors. Only 58% of these prospective teachers—compared with 68% of all college-bound seniors—had chosen an academic track in high school. The rest took general or vocational programs heavy in courses of the Bachelor Living ilk.

In response, New Jersey has upped admission requirements for the education programs in its state colleges, and Missouri has set up grants and loans designed to attract into teacher-training programs students with high grades and SAT scores. Dismayed by teacher certification exams that often test little more than basic literacy, the Washington-based Carnegie Forum on Education and the Economy has organized a National Board of Professional Teaching Standards, which will issue certificates to teachers who pass the rigorous tests it is now devising. Says foundation executive director Marc Tucker: "You won't need it to get a job at first, but as in every other profession, people will want a board-certified professional."

Universally contemptuous of the education major as a vapid and inadequate program, reformers agree that teachers need a four-year liberal arts education, with a major in whatever subject they plan to teach. The reformers recommend a further year or two learning teaching techniques, perhaps as an apprentice supervised by a master teacher.

New Jersey has proved that teachers educated this way can succeed resoundingly in the classroom. It hires teachers who haven't taken the usual education courses required for certification if they have a BA in the subject they want to teach, can pass the Educational Testing Service's National Teacher Exam in it, and successfully complete a year's residency, which includes a sort of pedagogical boot camp. The 800 teachers New Jersey has hired by these criteria—including retired business and military people, musicians, less well paid parochial school teachers, and recent college grads who have decided they'd like to teach—have higher SAT scores and college grades than teachers with education degrees.

Now New Jersey is trying to set up a new route to the certification of principals. Instead of three years' teaching experience and three specialized courses, you will get certified with an MBA or any master's degree in management. All you'll need to do is take a management test, go through an assessment center, and work for a year under supervision. Wall Street casualties, look across the river.

You can't attract better teachers without increasing their pay. But, says Prince George's superintendent Murphy, "taxpayers are sick and tired of giving across-the-board raises and letting those people who aren't doing the job get more and more money." After all, per-pupil education expenditures between 1950 and 1986, adjusted for inflation, more than tripled to around a breathtaking $4,000, with most of the rise coming in the period when SAT scores plummeted. But taxpayers will tolerate increased spending tied to results, like Murphy's planned performance-based bonus or like Rochester, New York's new teacher career ladder. As teachers grow in competence through four defined ranks, their pay will go up to a peak for the very best of $60,000.

Reformers like to point with fascination to the slums of Spanish Harlem, where Community School District 4 pulled itself from 32nd place out of 32 New York City school districts in test scores in 1973 to 16th today. Students reading at grade level rose from 16% to 63%. The secret: a network of elementary and junior high schools from which parents are free to choose the one they like best for their children, regardless of where they live in the district.

Each school, headed by a director without tenure, has its own distinctive twist—a focus on music or math, say, or a rigorous, traditional curriculum—and so students separate themselves into groups according to their own or their families' ambitions for their future. Each school is small enough so that students aren't anonymous. Directors of these schools make their pitches to prospective students and their parents in the spring before students enter. The market mechanism operates: Schools get better and more various by competing to offer what people want. Those that offer it successfully flourish; the others dwindle.

Warm fans of District 4 include some reformers who favor a voucher system for education. This would let parents send a child to either a public or an accredited *private* school, with the $4,000 or so of tax money earmarked for his education paid out accordingly. Competition would improve all the schools, these reformers say, probably correctly. The need to perform or go out of business would beat down vested interests resisting public school reform—especially the National Education Association, the largest teachers' union, which vehemently opposes merit pay, alternate teacher certification, and teacher competency testing.

But if one object of education reform is to restore a shared cultural core to Americans, the centrifugal tendency of a voucher system seems a push in the wrong direction. The system inevitably would proliferate sectarian schools and so promote separateness rather than commonality. It would be justified as a last resort only if public education were bankrupt beyond repair, or if schools bent on satisfying every interest group developed curricula that were all periphery and no core, or if children who wanted to learn were prevented from getting a decent education by a disruptive population required to attend school. Most public schools haven't reached that point, though, and the reform movement is likely to keep them from it.

A better solution is what California school authorities have been doing to the school curriculum. They have tried to come to grips with just what the core culture includes—that shared national knowledge that E. D. Hirsch Jr. defined in the title of his best-selling book, *Cultural Literacy*. The state education department has drawn up a list of a thousand mainstream books—from *Cinderella* to *Great Expectations*—that ideally children should have read or listened to between kindergarten and high school graduation. The department also has just drawn up an extensive framework for a history and social studies curriculum that will begin in kindergarten with stories about how people lived in the past and with the simplest preliminary discussions of democratic values. From grades five through 12 students will alternate each year between courses in world history and American history, moving from earliest times to the present. California's state testing program will ensure that local schools teach what these curricula prescribe.

Though the history curriculum celebrates cultural diversity, there's nothing relativistic about it; it aims to inspire a high respect for democracy. Unlike a high school in New York's Westchester County that, for fear of offending secularists, failed to tell pupils who was thanked on Thanksgiving, and defined a pilgrim as one who takes a very long journey, the California courses will deal straightforwardly with controversial or difficult issues, explaining their historical significance and outlining the current fuss over them.

Says California superintendent of education Bill Honig: "In a free country, where you have free choice, you have to choose from an educated perspective. Our teachers never make the most important point about education: It helps you lead a better life." If reformers can ensure such an education to the majority of Americans, it will be a famous victory.

Questions for Critical Analysis

1. Why is American business worried about the schools? What data does Magnet give to explain their concern?
2. Did Magnet's evidence of problems in the schools surprise you? What was the most startling fact? What was the least surprising fact? Why?
3. Magnet lists historical and literary facts that a survey revealed 17-year-olds didn't know. Do you know the answers to those questions? Why is it important to know such things?
4. Compare Magnet's comments on textbooks with the analysis in essays by Larrick and Bettelheim and Zelan (in the previous section). How does Magnet extend their concerns? Compare Magnet's comments on teaching "living skills" versus academic skills with points made in Richard Mitchell's essay. Are they concerned about the same thing? How does Magnet's tone and approach differ from Mitchell's?
5. What three reforms does Magnet suggest for improving the schools? What evidence makes him believe it's possible to improve the current situation?

Questions for Structural Analysis

1. What is Magnet's thesis? Describe the organization of this essay. Is it effective?
2. This essay was originally published in *Fortune* magazine. Who is its audience? What is Magnet's purpose in writing about this subject to that audience? How does his presentation reflect his understanding of his audience?
3. How does Magnet's word choice reveal his attitudes toward students? textbooks? textbook authors? teachers? What is the tone of this essay? How do you respond to Magnet's tone?
4. Magnet cites several authorities in this essay. Name them and explain why he uses them to support his argument.
5. How does Magnet conclude his essay? Are you convinced by his argument? Why, or why not?

*W*EAVING THE *I*NVISIBLE *T*APESTRY

JOHN L. CLENDENIN

John L. Clendenin (1934–) worked throughout the Bell Telephone network since graduating from Northwestern University in 1955, and has been chairman and chief executive officer of BellSouth Corporation since 1982. Clendenin's interest in the impact of education on economic development spurred education reform in his home state of Georgia during the early to mid-1980s. "Weaving the Invisible Tapestry" is a speech delivered to the Southern Governors' Association at their annual meeting in September, 1988.

Before you begin reading: *Think about the implications of an uneducated or badly educated populace for American business and industry. In your notebook make a list of 10 ways America loses when its citizens are not well-educated.*

◆

THANK YOU, GOVERNOR HARRIS, FOR THAT KIND INTRO-duction, and thank you, members of the nation's oldest and largest Governors' Association, for the chance to meet with you here in this beautiful setting, with the goal of making our South a better place to live and work. It's an honor to address such a distinguished group, and I appreciate your invitation.

I'm here to share a businessman's view of education, and—inescapably, for me, I'm afraid—a bit of a grandfather's view of education, too. I'll tell you right off the bat I'm no optimist about the issue—but I'm no pessimist, either.

What I *am* is a *realist* with some very *real* concerns and hopes. And those concerns and hopes spring from my firm belief that the future of education is the future of everything else. That's true of business, and that's true of grandkids. Nowhere is it more true than right here in our own backyard. And *that*, Governors and ladies and gentlemen, is why I cannot in good conscience leave here today without asking for your help . . . for your leadership . . . for action on the educational problem we face in this country today.

It's not a new concern. The ancient Greek Socrates said: "Pay attention to the young, and make them as good as possible."

Well, just *how* good the young can be is perhaps most dramatically demonstrated by another ancient Greek idea—the Olympics. But as our modern version of those games unfolds in Korea, I can't help but think that for every Phidippides . . . or for every Greg Louganis . . . there always have been and there always will be another million kids out there less blessed. In fact, in America, a million kids drop out of school every year just as effortlessly and routinely as Louganis drops off the diving board. Will we pay attention to *them*? Will we make *them* as good as possible?

On a philosophical level, I'm concerned about them because they're the future. And I'm concerned about education because education's the invisible tapestry these young people will use to *weave* their world . . . to fasten it together . . . and to drape themselves with possibility. And yes—you've guessed it—*that's* my perspective as a man with eight grandchildren.

My practical businessman's perspective, though, is also charged with concern over these young people, because I'm CEO of a very large high-tech company, with some 100,000 employees, mostly Southerners, and our business is absolutely dependent on an educated—and an educable—workforce to survive and to thrive in the age of information.

That's an increasingly elusive resource these days. We're not producing enough young people who can turn information into insight into productivity. Far from it. But the fact is, we've got an even more *basic* problem. Namely—Johnny. Or, really—a whole *lot* of Johnnys.

Because as you well know, here in the South perhaps more than elsewhere in this country, there are a lot of Johnnys who can't read or write. Johnnys who don't know where Athens, Greece is, or—sad to say—even *what* Athens, Greece is. Johnnys who can't figure out how much they owe when they order a burger and fries.

But none of this is any news to you. And it's no news to anyone who's been paying attention that you Southern Governors have been working hard to provide the steps in education reform that will move Johnny up the learning ladder. But the process is painfully slow . . . the problem is enormously complex . . . and guess what? Johnny's knocking at the doors of the IBMs, the GEs, the AT&Ts, the RJR-Nabiscos, the Deltas, the Burroughs-Wellcomes, the Coca-Colas, the Belks, the Federal Expresses, the Norfolk-Southerns, the First Wachovias, the Humanas and the BellSouths of the world—and Johnny's looking for work. Today.

Well, I have bad news for him: He probably won't find it at BellSouth—or at any of these major corporations.

Because as much as we want them, and as much as we desperately need them, workers qualified to fill the 20 million new information-age jobs this country will create before the century turns are becoming so scarce it's scary.

Things have changed. Jobs have changed. Sweat and good hands aren't enough any more. According to the *Wall Street Journal*, even *auto mechanics* today need the equivalent of a two-year electrical engineering degree *just to get by* fixing a modern car.

So what happens to those million kids across this nation who quit school every year? Obviously, they can't turn to auto mechanics any more, or to any of the great variety of jobs that used to be within the reach of a dropout. Collectively unemployed or underemployed, these young people pack an enormous economic punch, and unfortunately, it's a potential social knockout. Here's why.

First of all, jail's a whole lot more expensive than school. And the odds have been shown to be pretty strong that you go to either one or the other.

And second, the less school you take, the less money you make. Undereducation undercuts. Pure and simple. It undercuts our tax base. It undercuts the spirit of our welfare system. It undercuts our productivity. In fact, each year's crop of American dropouts costs this country an estimated 240 billion dollars of lost earnings and taxes over their lifetimes.

Notice I said earlier that we need not only an educated workforce—but also an *educable* workforce, because stepping out of high school . . . into high tech . . . is like stepping onto a moving sidewalk: You've got to be prepared for the jolt of acceleration. In other words, you've got to be taught to learn.

And the frightening truth is that even though our nation spends 185 billion dollars annually on public education, we're turning out a bumper crop of functional illiterates. And the additional 30 billion dollars business spends each year on remedial training—even when it's added to the 180 billion *more* that business spends for on-the-job training—it's *still* not enough to stem the tide.

We must all face the chilling reality that our nation is losing ground, and losing it fast, in the world economic race. And we're losing it, to a significant degree, because of Johnny.

And although it's preposterous to lay the blame entirely at the steps of our schools, what all this means is this: It really hurts when our educational system fails someone. It's a failure with several layers of repercussions.

At a tragic, individual level, educational failure hurts a *person*. A human being. And it can also hurt the extended family.

At an economic level, educational failure hurts our collective wallet. It drains money from us as individuals and as citizens of collective enterprises.

And perhaps most disturbing for the long term—at a dangerously deep social level, educational failure threatens to polarize our nation and to tear apart our society's whole cloth.

Now, I'm *not* saying nothing's being done about it:

- Concern over the issue is certainly elevated. Virtually every major news magazine has had a cover story on the subject in the past six months, and the presidential campaign is full of rhetoric about education.
- And it's true that a lot of money and energy are being expended in education's behalf.
- We're also generating some creative thinking on education's behalf. Vivid examples abound all around the country, and quite noticeably right here in the South.

In fact, some of the most encouraging news I've read in a long time is contained in your report, "Success from the South"—a report which is a focal point of this gathering here today. That report makes it clear that collectively, we *are* making significant, incremental progress in certain key areas.

But the pace of our progress, in the face of our problem, is like charting the universe as it expands.

We must do more. We *can* do more. And the unique power—the leadership—to make a meaningful difference is concentrated right here in this room.

We need *action*. We need the action *your leadership alone* can generate.

Your *National* Governors' Association's 1991 Report on Education says:

> The Governors are ready to provide the *leadership* needed to get results on the hard issues that confront the better schools movement. We are ready to lead the second wave of reform in American public education.

That hits the nail on the head. *You* are in a unique position of *leadership*.

Frankly, that's why each of you is in office. Your constituents demand leadership and action. And that's why it's a pleasure to work with energetic leaders like you at the state level. Armed with a vision, you can make things happen.

So I'm *not* here to suggest specific reforms, because you each have special situations in your home states which you're well aware of and are tackling aggressively.

But in the interest of *action*, I *am* here to challenge you to intertwine that *political* leadership quality you uniquely possess . . . to intertwine it with the leadership of the *education* community, and with that of the *business* community. Together, we can create a formidable braid of *three* threads . . . combined, woven together into one unit much stronger than any single strand could ever be.

I firmly believe that working together, we can build up enough educational momentum to launch this nation's brainpower into the next century—on an improving trajectory. But time is running critically short.

That's why, just two weeks ago in Washington, I challenged my CEO colleagues who make up the Policy Council of the Business Round Table to personally commit their companies to aggressive support for education reform. I told them I believe that as an organization and as a nation, we're beyond task forces . . . we're beyond studies . . . we're beyond reports. While those were necessary and useful, I believe we're finally primed for action.

So I challenged them to roll up their sleeves and do something about education in this country. I was pleased to hear their positive response, and I hope to see tangible improvement in specific cities across the country as these CEOs gear up their visible business support. I hope for progress such as we've seen in Indianapolis, Cincinnati, Portland, Baltimore, Albuquerque, Rochester and other American cities where government, education and business have joined forces in specific community-wide partnerships, thanks to committed and influential *leaders*. Government, and education and business *leaders*.

I think it's an approach that can work. I believe we can make real *progress* through such partnerships.

But progress will come hard—perhaps particularly hard for us here in the South . . . because here in the South, we start with some especially crippling problems.

The frightening news crossed my desk recently that according to the U.S. Department of Education, *not one* of the nine Southern states which the BellSouth companies serve with local telephone service—*not one* even cracks the top *half* in rankings in a *single major category* of the latest report card on public schools. Not in ACT scores. Not in SAT scores. Not in spending per student. Not in teachers' salaries. Not in high-school graduation rates. And these nine states are among *your* states, too.

And though I, like Governor Harris, resent the negative cast toward the South some of these reports contain, and though I have doubts that this report-card approach provides an accurate picture, the fact is, businesses can't ignore the economic fallout from such statistics. So it doesn't surprise me that, according to a recent survey conducted by The Conference Board, education has replaced local economic development as *the* top community-affairs issue with major corporations. Nearly two-thirds of the 130 companies polled listed primary and secondary education as their number-one community concern, up from 42 percent in 1985. The Conference Board summed it up: "The (findings) reflect a widespread belief that the quality of U.S. education has dire economic implications."

So businesses are concerned. And businesses in the South are *especially* concerned. I hear it every day.

They're awakening to the fact that answers to some of our educational challenges lie in *cooperative efforts*—creative alliances between education and commerce. In fact, I got some good news recently from The Carnegie Foundation. They polled some 14,000 teachers nationwide about partnerships between education and business. The survey is called "The Report Card on School Reform: The Teachers Speak," and it asked teachers from all fifty states to describe the relationship between schools and business today, compared to five years ago. Is it worse or better than it used to be?

Across the country, only 45% rated the relationship as "better" in their state; that obviously is *not* the good news. The good news for *me* is the fact that among the states reporting improvement, all nine BellSouth states—all of them SGA states—*all nine appear in the top eleven.*

So it would seem that Southern businesses are rediscovering the age-old link between education and economics, and are joining educators to strengthen that link.

It's a crucial link, and it's one that state government can help nurture.

You can help nurture it by weaving together the strands of government, education and business. You can create a climate where the three communities trust each other . . . solicit each other . . . support each other. After all, we can't blame just the education community for all our education woes. The fact is, their system's creaking under peripheral stresses that aren't their fault . . . the stresses of the poverty cycle and all its attendant hemorrhages . . . the stresses of drug abuse, teenage pregnancy, medical neglect, unemployment, poor housing, adult illiteracy, and so on and so on and so on. These tragedies have obvious impact on our schools, and they aren't equipped to resolve them.

So what can you, as our political leaders, do to help? How can you bring these three communities to an integrated view of the problem? And how can you fold their special resources into integrated solutions? Well, as leaders you can foster collaboration, and one possibility is creating tough-minded, practical, action-oriented, state-sponsored blue-ribbon advisory panels on education, guided by leaders from the three communities. And then—challenge them.

Challenge them to suggest practical solutions to perennial problems, such as distributing funds fairly—without sacrificing kids. Such as creating standards—without creating straitjackets. Such as enhancing teacher workpools with alternative talent—without compromising accreditation. You're called on to conjure such alchemy each day. Why not harness some extra horsepower to help?

Why not? States don't have all the answers. Neither do educators, and neither do businesses. But we all have leaders. And it's obvious to everyone we don't have forever to fix Johnny's problem. As the comedian says, there's a fine line between fishing and just standing on the shore like an idiot. Well, ladies and gentlemen, it's time to fish or cut bait.

I mentioned earlier that simple thing we call the braid. You know—it's actually an amazing design. It may *look* simple, but it's not.

In fact, the deceptive structure's so strong that nature *itself* braids for strength. It braids root systems on craggy mountainsides. It braids molecular structures in chemical compounds. It braids number-chains in such advanced mathematics as topology. Braids show up a lot in nature, from geology to genetics. In fact, scientists call the braid "the elemental fabric" because it's nature's first step toward weaving.

Well, I propose we consider the *braid of cooperation* among government, education and business the elemental fabric, too, because it's the first step to weaving the invisible tapestry of education and that social fabric called knowledge.

There's a true story about braids, and it has to do with the largest wooden roof in the world. It's a very old roof, and covers an enormous Buddhist temple in Kyoto, Japan. The monks who built it centuries ago didn't have any rope to hoist its massive beams into place. So their thousands of followers grew their hair long . . . cut it . . . and wove it into massive braids—ropes of human hair twelve inches thick. With these braids, the carpenters raised high the roof.

A strong braid. A strong personal commitment. And if, as leaders, we're to live up to Socrates' admonishment to make our young as good as possible, we're compelled to weave such a braid, compelled to join such a commitment. We have a debt to our children called the future. And it's a debt much bigger than any wooden roof.

You know, Socrates was quite an educator himself, and in fact inspired much of our Western learning tradition. And as you're well aware, he had a habit of asking tough questions demanding honest answers. So it's no coincidence his last thought was a tough question, too.

As he lay on his deathbed, his last words were: "Will you remember to pay the debt?"

It's a tough question, all right, particularly when turned to us . . . who hold the future of today's young Americans in our hands.

"Will you remember to pay the debt?"

Will we?

QUESTIONS FOR CRITICAL ANALYSIS

1. The September 1988 meeting of the Southern Governors' Association, with its theme "Success in the South," was one of celebration as each governor talked about economic progress in his state. What message did Clendenin bring these governors? Why would the governors pay attention to his message? How do you think he wanted them to respond?
2. What issues does Clendenin bring before his audience? How does his presentation of the issues compare with the essays in this section?
3. Why would education be a crucial issue for the governors?
4. Why does Clendenin think the work toward progress is especially hard in the South? Think about news stories you've read and heard about urban inner city schools (in New York, Chicago, Detroit, Newark, Miami and so forth) and compare the problems with those Clendenin describes. What are the underlying social problems affecting schools in all areas of the country?
5. Based on points made in Clendenin's speech, what proposals would you, as the education aide to the governor, make to your state for action?

QUESTIONS FOR STRUCTURAL ANALYSIS

1. What elements clearly identify this as a speech? Describe the language and sentence patterns. Point out rhetorical devices, references, tone, attention to audience and so forth. Compare Clendenin's speech with other speeches in this text: Martin Luther King, Jr.'s "On Being a Good Neighbor," Robert MacNeil's "The Media and the

Public Trust," or Felix Rohatyn's "Commitment." Do you think this was an effective speech? Why, or why not?

2. How does Clendenin use the tapestry mentioned in his title as a recurring image throughout the speech? Is it an effective device? Why, or why not? How does the story of the braid reinforce the image?
3. Describe the structure of this speech: Where does the thesis occur? How are illustrations used? Write an outline of the speech to show how the ideas develop.
4. Clendenin quotes Socrates twice in the speech—at the beginning: "Pay attention to the young, and make them as good as possible" and at the end: "Will you remember to pay the debt?" Why does he use Socrates as a source? What does each quote mean, and how does it enhance the speech?

EDUCATION THAT WORKS: THE RIGHT ROLE FOR BUSINESS

TED KOLDERIE

Ted Kolderie, a senior fellow at the Center for Policy Studies at the University of Minnesota, has been involved with educational policy issues since 1967 and has been a member of educational task forces for both Governor Albert Quie and Governor Rudy Perpich. This essay, published in the Harvard Business Review, *is addressed to the business community and presents school/business partnerships from the point of view of business. Kolderie laments the failure of educational reform movements to attack the roots of the problem; media, corporate and philanthropic foundations have focused on "quick fixes" and public relations projects at the expense of long-range programs that could result in substantial change.*

Before you begin reading: *What if public schools had to compete for students? Imagine what the schools in your community would be like if parents and students could choose which one to support. Make two lists in your notebook. In the first, list five or more ways the schools would improve if they were in competition with each other for students. In the second, list five or more ways the schools would be hurt by parental choice.*

◆

WHY IS BUSINESS SO NICE TO THE SCHOOLS? IT IS NOT hard to understand the impulse to help. Business knows the importance of public education. It recognizes the schools' problems. It knows it has money and influence that can make a difference. What's curious is the *way* businesses have been responding—with what one student of corporate involvement calls "fuzzy altruism" rather than with a tough-minded, though sympathetic, thinking through of the situation of this large, complex, and troubled public enterprise.[1]

Stripped to its essentials, the situation is this: an old institution, long accustomed to stability, now faces growing outside competition, major changes in the nature of its customers, and a deepening internal crisis in the quality of its

[1]See the studies by Professor Dale Mann of Teachers College, Columbia University.

professional work force. Its managers' response has essentially been to point to outside changes beyond their control, to resist changing the nature of the operation, and to insist that problems could be resolved if only they could have loyal support and additional resources.

Faced with this situation, most business executives would probably prescribe a hard challenge to the traditional ways of thinking, followed quickly by decisive action to change the basics of the operation. Very little of the present business involvement in public education, however, can be called either challenging or decisive. Rather, "partnerships" are the order of the day. Business has come in offering to help and wanting to be liked. So the problem gets framed by the people who run the schools. And business gets involved not with the central issues in education but with a classroom here, a school there, a district somewhere else.

This tinkering at the margin is not the way to help public education out of its problems. In the long term, it will hurt rather than help a critically important institution that desperately needs to change but that—without the pressure of some necessity—cannot generate internally the will to face the hard decisions that change requires.

Business's involvement today is roughly the equivalent of doing your daughter's homework. It is a kindness, but a misdirected kindness. Business should help the schools. But not that way.

YOU CAN'T "DO" IMPROVEMENT

Nothing has been as useful to me in thinking about this issue as a conversation with William Andres late in 1984. He was just then leaving as chairman of Dayton-Hudson Corporation and about to chair a task force on productivity in Minnesota state government.

When we sat down he said, "You're in the public sector. I'm not. So you tell me: Is productivity in government something you do? Or is it something that happens if you do the fundamentals right?"

I paused to think. "I'm in retailing," he said. "In retailing turnover is very important. Stores that turn over their inventory rapidly are more profitable. Every so often some store manager decides to try to *do* turnover. And all of a sudden the store isn't profitable any more. So we decided long ago that turnover isn't something you do. We concentrate on doing the fundamentals right. Now tell me: Is productivity in the public sector something you do, or something that happens if you do the fundamentals right?"

The point was clear. Productivity in government ought to be something that happens naturally because the fundamentals have been set right. So is improvement in the schools. It ought not to have to be forced in from the outside piece by piece.

Yet much of business's attempt to help the schools amounts precisely to "doing" improvement. Donating computers. Giving science teachers summer training. Recognizing outstanding teachers. Motivating students to graduate by promising them a college education. Helping pass a law extending the school year or toughening teachers' tests. It is hard to criticize such efforts. Presumably they are well-intentioned—good at least for the students, teachers, schools, and districts lucky enough to be chosen. But resources are always limited. So the test is always whether these efforts change the system. The critical questions are: Do the improvements last? Do the improvements spread? Too often the experience is that isolated, episodic improvements do not spread. And that they last only as long as the external financing lasts.

Business should be tougher. When approached for support, executives should ask the central question: "If these things are so important, why aren't they important enough for the system to do itself? Why are they done only when we finance them?"

Something is wrong with the fundamentals of a system that does not do the things it says are most important and in which improvements do not spread and do not last. If business were thinking strategically, it would be helping to see that the schools get opportunities and incentives to innovate on their own.

THE STATIC FUNDAMENTALS

Education has not had to innovate in order to survive. People in business may not welcome competition, but they accept the reality of it. So increasingly they assume the need for change. People in education have not been similarly exposed to competition—to the risk of failure. So like any managers comfortable in a cartel, they cling tightly to the traditional "givens" of their system.

Education *is* a kind of cartel.

- Customers have to use the service. School is compulsory, roughly between ages 7 and 16.
- The service is offered free. On principle, the public schools will not charge fees.
- Each state and each large urban area is divided into discrete service areas. Children go to school in the district in which they live.
- Within each district, there is one and only one public teaching organization ("franchised," in effect).
- Competition is suppressed. Some state laws literally say districts may not compete for the enrollment of students.
- A family may choose not to send its children to the schools of the teaching organization in the district in which it lives. But it then must pay privately either the cost of moving its residence or the cost of tuition—to a nonpublic school or (an option most people overlook) to another public school district.
- The equity problems are serious. There is no right to move between districts. Choice depends on private wealth. Tracking is pervasive. As Professor John Goodlad reported in *A Place Called School*, children are commonly

grouped by ability; the abler students are assigned the abler teachers, and the lower track children never catch up.[2]

- The system is rewarded, and is accountable, politically. Revenues are appropriated to districts from local taxes and from state aids on the basis of students enrolled or programs offered. Users only indirectly discipline the system. The idea is that a teacher who does not perform will be dismissed by the principal; a principal who does not perform will be dismissed by the superintendent; a superintendent who does not perform will be dismissed by the board; and a board that does not perform will be dismissed by the voters.
- The system resists efforts to measure and report student performance wherever this would lead to comparisons among schools and districts. Measurement exposes differences and requires explanations. Differences are hard for a system built on the idea of the common school and of a "general and uniform system of public education." Often they can be reasonably explained. But it is easier to avoid them, and so avoid having to declare the underlying belief that in the end the schools are not responsible for what the student learns.
- The school board plays dual and potentially conflicting roles. It is a buyer of education on its citizens' behalf. It is also the sole "franchised" operator of a public teaching business within its district.
- The school administration is typically organized as a classic public bureau. Teachers—the professionals in direct contact with the students—are employees in a hierarchy, working for administrators. Advancement is through administration or through political efforts to lift the salary scale generally. There is essentially no concept of a teacher being promoted.
- Students are grouped by age into grade levels. At the high school level, the day is divided into periods of about 50 minutes each. Students move from subject to subject, from hour to hour. Time is a constant; so, given differences among students, learning is a variable. In the upper grades, the time is spent mainly with teachers talking, students listening.

This system took its present form in the 1890s. It has not changed much since. It has grown in size: more children attend, and more children graduate. The number of districts has been greatly reduced. Desegregation and collective bargaining have appeared. But the traditional pattern of schooling persists: one teacher in a classroom, with 30 students, six times a day. "Cell and bell" is the way some educators describe the teacher's life. In his candid moments, one of the good principals I know says, "Frankly, my task is to motivate as far as possible and for as long as possible people who are in essentially dead-end jobs."

There is little need to change. When schools and teachers do try to improve (and many do), nothing very good happens to them. When they do not (and

---

[2]John I. Goodlad, *A Place Called School* (New York: McGraw-Hill, 1984).

some do not), nothing very bad happens to them. Stability and security can easily become the cherished values. Comparisons of districts, schools, and teachers are often taken as criticism. Criticism is often taken as hostility. "Don't use the term *change*," the president of a major Minnesota education association urged the Governor's Discussion Group. "Why not?" someone asked. "To talk about change," he said, "implies that what went on before was not OK."[3]

The policy variable is resources. Money is quality, quality is money. More of one, more of the others. The way of doing things remains a given. "The cards are stacked against innovation," Goodlad wrote.

BUSINESS AS RESUSCITATOR

For any country serious about excellence in its system of public education, this is an absurd arrangement.

There has to be some reasonable connection between the success of the system and the success of its students, some reward for schools that do improve and some sanction for those that do not try to improve. Educators are right that children cannot be made to learn and that it is unfair to lay on teachers the full responsibility for the performance of children who are in school only 11% of the time between ages 5 and 16. But we can still insist that it is foolish to have no connection at all.

Broadly, two ways to make this connection are now coming into the national discussion. Both would significantly change the traditional givens of education. Business needs to understand and to encourage both of them.

The first is a buyer-side strategy involving a switch from assignment to choice as the method by which the student gets to the school. A strategy that takes down the fences now surrounding districts (and many schools) would permit students to enroll in the public district or school they and/or their parents believe will best meet their needs.

It is important to stress *public* school. In the past two years—largely as a result of policy developments in Minnesota—it has become clear that choice does not have to involve the private schools, as the conventional voucher debate has assumed. Choice can be made available simply among public schools and school districts.

The American public supports this opening up of the system. In 1986, in its annual survey for the *Kappan* magazine, the Gallup Poll for the first time asked public school parents, "Would you like to be able to choose the public school your children attend in this community?" Some 68% said yes.[4]

---

[3]Notes from the 18 months of meetings of the discussion group convened by Governor Rudy Perpich to develop a strategy for school improvement in Minnesota are available from the author.

[4]*Phi Delta Kappan*, September 1986, p. 56.

The nation's governors and some presidential aspirants have quickly begun to understand the way in which this idea makes it possible to be for public education and for the people's power to choose at the same time.[5]

Introducing an element of competition will have an effect. Schools and school districts do not like to lose students and the revenue that comes with them. Faced with that prospect, they will respond with improvements.

The second of the possible changes is to create some disengagement, some dynamics, on the seller side, by moving to an essentially contract relationship between the school boards and their teaching organizations. This can be done in the following three ways:

DIVESTITURE The school administration could be spun off into a free-standing public corporation. Even if there were still only the one teaching organization, the roles of board and administration would change dramatically. Questions about whether to buy china or plastic dishes for the lunchroom would shift to the agenda of the new school-management corporation. The board would be obliged to concentrate on what students should learn, on who should teach them, and on whether the learning is progressing satisfactorily.

Once the board had become clearly a buyer, other teaching organizations, public and private, would almost certainly appear, offering to run one or more of its schools. And once out of its operating role, the board might be tempted to see what somebody else could do. That kind of competition, too, should stimulate change.

SCHOOL-SITE MANAGEMENT Individual schools could be given a contract relationship with their district. Study after study has concluded that the school, not the district, should in fact be the unit of improvement and that more authority should be delegated to the school.

Decision making needs to be decentralized in education. Very large central-office bureaucracies have built up over the years. Schools today have quite limited authority to change on their own. Business executives today should see this immediately but often do not—perhaps because they know and talk mainly with superintendents. Principals are not often invited to meetings about education policy.

Decentralization via school-site management would permit decisions about how to use time, people, and money to be made in some new and more collegial way by the principal, the teachers, and the parents at the school site. Their autonomy would be connected to their ability to improve.

---

[5]See *A Time for Results* (Washington, D.C.: National Governors' Association, 1986).

A PRIVATE PRACTICE OPTION Professional teachers in small groups could be given the opportunity to work for themselves, on contract to their school or district. There is a growing interest today in making teaching truly professional. Yet the system does not let teachers work in the way that defines a professional. They are paid for their hours on the job, not for what they do. If you want to be a teacher, you have to be an employee.

School districts could link pay with performance by letting groups of public school teachers work for themselves. A group of math teachers, for example, could form a small professional practice. The teachers would decide on their own approach to learning. They would select their colleagues. They would pick the learning materials. They would make the work assignments. They would decide when to use what technology. They would be paid a lump sum to cover salaries, fringes, and other costs. They would decide how the money would be shared among them. If their practice were successful, they could take contracts with other schools or districts. They would have an opportunity to grow in professional responsibility and income.

All three of these disengagements would increase both opportunities and incentives in the system. No school or district would have to change or to improve. But all would be freer to do so. If one did not, another might. Students would be able to move between the two. Create these countervailing opportunities and you will have created the necessity for improvement. Create this necessity and you will have, in Bill Andres's terms, done the fundamentals right.

MODELS FROM MINNESOTA

Appealing, perhaps obvious, as this strategy is, it will not easily win business support. It challenges much of what the educational system takes as given. It would be resisted. So it would bring business into conflict with the major groups in public education.

And business would rather not fight the schools. It is not fun for a CEO to find himself or herself at a meeting—or, worse, on television—confronted by the superintendent saying, "I'm trying to row this boat. Why are you trying to tip it over?" The unwritten rule has been, in the words of one CEO, "You don't take on anything you might lose, especially if you have to do it in public."

The prospect of controversy presents, however, one of those basic tests of commitment. Business has to decide whether it is serious or not. If the central issues are going to be raised and addressed, somebody is bound to be upset, and some conflict is inevitable. No pain, no gain.

With proper handling, the fundamentals can be changed. One encouraging example is in Minnesota, where a business community known for its charitable giving has also been developing some considerable sophistication about what is required for major public system change.

From 1966 to 1967, Donald Dayton, chairman of Dayton-Hudson Corporation, Earl Ewald, chairman of Northern States Power Company, and Philip Nason, chairman of the First National Bank of Saint Paul, played key roles in the design and advocacy of a new approach to metropolitan government in the Twin Cities region. Much of that effort was indirect, through the urban program of the Upper Midwest Council. Its leaders understood the fundamental importance of giving the Twin Cities region some political unity with which to manage its essential social and economic unity. The council sponsored research. It helped get the key bill drafted. It organized the St. Thomas Conference at which the policy consensus emerged.

On the day of the critical legislative hearing, Dayton, Ewald, and Nason did not send a governmental affairs officer to represent them. They came. They did not read a statement and leave. They stayed, listening, all morning. Legislative opponents of the bill, who had hoped to kill the proposal, immediately began to pressure the corporate lobbyists. But within 48 hours those opponents were offering an alternate version.

From that point on, it was simply a question of what form the new arrangement would take. A compromise was enacted, and the Twin Cities Metropolitan Council went on to become, in the opinion of many, the most innovative and successful effort at metropolitan governance in the nation.

Business leaders in Minnesota, concerned about the cost of health care, came early to understand the importance of dealing with the way that system was structured and rewarded—which meant, with the way doctors were paid. No meaningful cost control would be possible so long as physicians' decisions about patient care were not related to the real cost of ordering resources into use.

So in the 1970s, corporate representatives supported an effort by the insurance industry to expand prepayment as an alternative to fee-for-service medicine and insisted that this effort include competition among the prepaid plans as well. Today almost half the Twin Cities area's two million residents are enrolled in prepaid medical plans.

In 1983, at the urging of Lewis Lehr, chairman of 3M Company, the Minnesota Business Partnership intervened in the debate about public education. It retained Berman/Weiler Associates to study elementary and secondary education in Minnesota. The $250,000 study proposed a dramatic redesign of the system: elementary school through grade 7 and high school ending after grade 10; mastery learning, diagnostic tests, site management, and some family choice. It was a bolder proposal than many business executives had expected to have to defend. But they swallowed hard and supported the report—and Governor Rudy Perpich when he sent an even broader open-enrollment bill to the legislature in 1985.

Business, like the governor, was vigorously attacked by some education organizations. But in 1987 the partnership, headed by the former chairman of First Bank System, George Dixon, was still insisting on the need for choice, the need for measurement, and the need for differentiating the teaching staff. "I expected business to come into the education debate," a teachers' union lobbyist said. "But I did not think they would stay in it the way they have."

Today business's critics are more restrained. The Minnesota Education Association changed its leadership early in 1986. The new president, Robert Astrup, made overtures early to the Business Partnership. At Astrup's invitation, Dixon spoke at the MEA's summer conference and stood firmly by the partnership's proposals.

A step at a time, the givens are changing in Minnesota. In 1985, eleventh and twelfth graders were given the option of finishing high school in any college to which they could get admitted. An option to start again in some other district or in some special alternative program was extended in 1987 to students at the other end of the curve, who have dropped out or who are behind in age or grade level or are otherwise at risk. Uniform rules were written for interdistrict enrollment, and Governor Perpich continues to urge school boards to voluntarily give students greater access to programs.

Changing public systems in fundamental ways is not easy. But it can be done. You develop your own independent understanding of the situation. You find strong staff, committed to change. You look for the points of leverage, where a one-time action will change the system for good. You concentrate not on enacting particular changes but on increasing the system's capacity for change. You work together to pool the risk. You find individuals willing to master the brief. You work through organizations that are not so vulnerable to pressure. You recognize that even a single strategic change may take several years to accomplish. And you do not give up.

MOUNTING PRESSURES

The pressure from the education system not to do this will be intense. No institution welcomes change, and when change has been postponed too long it seems more frightening still. If choice and competition are proposed, there will be pleas to help all schools instead. And someone will suggest that students and their families cannot make educationally sound choices.

Educators are right to be concerned. The changes in the school's clientele and political situation are real. Students in the public schools today are poorer, more likely to be of color, less advantaged by help and support at home, and more likely to be working part- or full-time. Drugs and discipline are big problems, which students more than anyone want corrected. Education's base of political support has deteriorated with the decline in the proportion of households with children of school age.

Choice will disrupt settled routines, though only a small proportion of the students is likely to move. The need for good information will be real. Equity will need to be protected. And there are social as well as individual objectives for learning that will have to be maintained.

But so is the need to change the institution real. Two forces are threatening the public schools, partly with problems, partly with opportunities. One is the impending retirement of half the nation's teachers within the next eight years. The other is the appearance of an entrepreneurial sector of education, much of it built around new technologies of learning, ready to move in if the public schools stand pat.

The country will probably lose something like a million teachers by 1995 through retirements and resignations. The issue is not whether they can be replaced. Somebody can always be found. The issue, as Linda Darling-Hammond of the Rand Corporation's Center for the Study of the Teaching Profession points out, is quality.[6]

To attract that many quality replacements back from other careers and from the top half of the graduating class in that period of time, simply raising salaries would not be enough. Public education would have to outbid all the other institutions that want them—all of American business and industry and all of the other professions.

Albert Shanker, the president of the American Federation of Teachers, says simply that "with our traditional answers the job cannot be done." The risk (perhaps the prospect) is that low-quality replacements will be hired. States and districts, concerned about performance, would then want to control teachers even more closely. This would make teaching still less attractive to persons with opportunities elsewhere. As the spiral wound downward, the country would turn away from public education.

And the public would find alternatives. Partly these would be the traditional nonpublic schools. But most would likely appear from the growth of the "learning business."

This new business is a coming together of the commercial tutoring programs, the businesses developing and marketing computer and videodisc hardware and software, the publishing houses as they pick up electronic technology, the training companies, the commercial vocational schools, and a day-care industry that is adding more and more education to the custody it offers, all day long, all year long.

These new vendors are already finding markets in the military, in corrections institutions, in adult-literacy programs, in manpower-training centers, in programs bought by adults for their children and for their own self-development, and in the $40 billion spent each year by corporations for training and staff development.

Nothing about the emergence of this learning business will enhance social equity or preserve America's common-school tradition. But that will not stop

[6]See *Beyond the Commission Reports: The Coming Crisis in Teaching* (Washington, D.C.: Rand Corporation's Center for the Study of the Teaching Profession, 1984).

its growth if the public schools continue to believe they can stonewall the pressure for fundamental change.

Strategically, public education has to make a major move. Thoughtful leaders inside the institution sense the implications of the forces at work. But they face tremendous inertia internally. They need the pressure of some necessity to make clear to their staffs and to their members what would happen to public education should it try to go protectionist.

These leaders will need help from good friends of public education on the outside. Business should not comfort the schools with partnerships that simply give the standpatters inside public education new reason to claim there is no need to change after all. It should press the schools to deal with the challenges they face and then offer to help them when they do.

LIFE WITHOUT LIFE SUPPORT

Calls to introduce the dynamics that will require the schools to change have started to appear, most notably in two major private-sector reports issued in 1986. Albert Shanker played a prominent role in both.

The report of the Committee for Economic Development from its Task Force on the Teaching Profession saw the coming problem in teaching and recommended that more authority for decisions be given to teachers and administrators in the schools.

Unfortunately, it drew back from recommending any choice or competition among schools to create incentives for schools to use that authority. In that sense, the CED report did not move to the fundamentals.

The Carnegie Forum Task Force on Teaching as a Profession did move heavily to fundamentals. It envisioned a system "in which school districts can offer the pay, autonomy, and career opportunities necessary to attract to teaching highly qualified people who would otherwise take up other professional careers. In return, teachers would agree to higher standards for themselves and real accountability for student performance."

Marc Tucker, the forum's staff director, calls that quid pro quo the heart of the report. The report defined accountability. It offered a choice between an administrative approach (tests, merit pay) and a market approach (choice among schools, contracting).

Unfortunately, this focus on fundamentals has faded. Media attention concentrated on the task force's proposals for improving the pay, administrative support, decision-making authority and education of teachers, and especially on the idea of a system of national specialty boards to certify or accredit outstanding professional teachers—an idea in which the Carnegie Corporation is now investing heavily. Interest in the real accountability for student performance that would be expected of teachers in return has continued to decline even within the Carnegie Forum itself.

In part this reflects Shanker's influence and his interest in the proposals that, in trade union terms, call for a big increase in wages, a big improvement in working conditions, and a big increase in worker control of the enterprise. As a member of the task force said recently, the forum is trying to sell the specialty boards to teachers, and it is not helpful to talk to teachers about other proposals teachers do not favor.

In part, too, the pressure now to redefine the improvement of education as simply the improvement of teaching was inevitable. It is always difficult to get beyond money and beyond people, down to the fundamentals that determine how effectively the money and the people can be used. This was difficult even for the National Governors' Association, important as its contribution to the national discussion was last year.

Business's best contribution will be to insist that the debate get the fundamentals right. Business executives and business organizations should concentrate on finding ways to introduce those opportunities and incentives, those consequences for improving and not improving, that will motivate districts and schools to improve on their own.

It is time to be strategic. It is time to stop trying to "do" improvement. We should not and we cannot hook up public education permanently to an external life-support system, dependent on a continuing flow of business and foundation help for the improvements that a healthy institution would be making in its own interest, from its own resources.

QUESTIONS FOR CRITICAL ANALYSIS

1. What does Kolderie mean when he describes business' involvement with the schools as "the equivalent of doing your daughter's homework"? Would Clendenin or Magnet agree with him? Why, or why not? Why does Kolderie question the role business plays and can play in school reform?

2. Most of the points in Kolderie's list of 12 fundamentals focus on a single issue. What is it? Which of these points have been made in other essays? How do the various authors agree and disagree with each other?

3. What reforms does Kolderie propose for the schools? Which ones are similar to those proposed by Sizer, Boyer, and Magnet? Which ones are different? What rate of success do you think these reform proposals will have? Why?

4. What reason does Kolderie give for business' reluctance to support substantial educational reforms? How does the Minnesota experience serve as a model in his discussion?

5. Kolderie's essay was published in the *Harvard Business Review*. Is his audience different from Magnet's? How? Describe his approach to his audience and compare it with Magnet's. How would Kolderie need to change his essay for publication in *Fortune*?

QUESTIONS FOR STRUCTURAL ANALYSIS

1. What points does Kolderie establish in his introduction? How did you respond to this introduction? Did it make you want to continue reading? Why, or why not?
2. Kolderie has organized his argument into seven major sections. Why? How do these sections relate to one another?
3. Explain how Kolderie's conversation with William Andres helped him develop a perspective on the role business can play in education reform. How does this anecdote support the thesis of the essay?
4. How does Kolderie present the problems inherent in reforming education? What problems does he mention? Do you think this discussion strengthens or weakens his essay? Why?
5. In practical terms, what does Kolderie think business should do to help public education? If you were the CEO of a major corporation, how do you think you would respond to Kolderie's argument? Is his conclusion convincing? Why, or why not?

*F*OUR *E*SSENTIAL *G*OALS

ERNEST L. BOYER

Ernest L. Boyer (1928–), president of the Carnegie Foundation for the Advancement of Teaching, is one of the country's leading spokesmen on why American education needs improvement and how we can go about improving it. In High School: A Report on Secondary Education in America *(1983), he evaluated American high schools, calling for major private and public commitment to education. Boyer called for American colleges "to renew themselves" in* College: The Undergraduate Experience in America *(1987). To complete his overview of American education, Boyer published* The Early Years *(1988), an examination of preschool and early elementary education. This essay, a chapter in* High School, *clearly sets out four goals which should serve to guide our efforts at school reform. Boyer looks hard at the problems on all levels of the American educational system; he is optimistic that we can rejuvenate our declining educational system.*

Before you begin reading: *What was the best, or the worst, school you have attended? In your reading notebook, write a paragraph that describes what made that school the best or worst. Then write a second paragraph describing ways you would improve the school (even if it was "the best") if you were principal.*

◆

A HIGH SCHOOL, TO BE EFFECTIVE, MUST HAVE A CLEAR and vital mission. Students, teachers, administrators, and parents at the institution should have a shared vision of what, together, they are trying to accomplish. But is it possible to serve all students and also find a coherent purpose for our schools?

In preparing this report, we looked at the education laws in all fifty states. We discovered a numbing hodgepodge of rules and regulations. In the State of California the education code is four volumes and 3,700 pages long, and in New York it takes five volumes and 4,000 pages to print the education law.

More troublesome are the vague and wide-ranging mandates the states have imposed on public education. Many of these requirements are pushed by special-interest groups. Frequently, they trivialize the mission of public education and, therefore, are rarely taken seriously by schools. Here is a sampling of what state laws say the schools should do.

Idaho: "The school programs shall be organized to meet the needs of all pupils, the community, and to fulfill the stated objectives of the school."[1]

Mississippi: The purpose of education is "to provide appropriate learning experiences to promote the optimum growth and development of youth and adults throughout life."[2]

Oregon: "Each individual will have the opportunity to develop to the best of his or her ability the knowledge, skills, and attitudes necessary to function as an individual . . . a learner . . . a producer . . . a citizen . . . a consumer . . . and a family member."[3]

Maine: The public schools must teach virtue and morality for not less than one-half hour per week. This includes "principles of morality and justice and a sacred regard for truth, love of country, humanity, a universal benevolence, sobriety, industry and frugality, chastity, moderation and temperance, *and all other virtues that ornament human society*" (emphasis added).[4]

California: "Each teacher shall endeavor to impress upon the minds of the pupils the principles of morality, truth, justice, patriotism, and a true comprehension of the rights, duties, and dignity of American citizenship, including kindness toward domestic pets and the humane treatment of living creatures, to teach them to avoid idleness, profanity, and falsehood, and to instruct them in manners and morals and the principles of a free government."[5]

Illinois: All graduates are required by law "to have had adequate instruction in honesty, justice, moral courage, humane education, [and] safety education."[6]

Arizona: A half-unit course is required on the "Essentials and Benefits of the Free Enterprise System."[7]

Rhode Island: Provision must be made for instruction in physiology and hygiene, with special reference to the effects of alcoholic liquors, stimulants, and narcotics on the human system.[8]

Wisconsin: "Every public school shall provide instruction in kindness to and the habits, usefulness, and importance of animals and birds, and the best methods of protecting, preserving and caring for all animal and bird life." And in what can only be described as enthusiastic local boosterism, Wisconsin also requires that every public and private elementary and high school give instruction in "the true and comparative vitamin content and food and health values of dairy products and their importance for human diet."[9]

At the district level we found school leadership frequently preoccupied with administrative procedures. Educational goals appeared to be of only marginal concern. In one district, for example, principals were called together by the superintendent to produce "performance standards" for the year. All schools in the district were expected to accomplish the following objectives:

- Raise the attendance rate
- Reduce teacher absence to 1.5 days per year (which, incidentally, was less than the sick days allowed in the contract)
- Improve parent participation[10]

We also visited schools that were focused on keeping track of the "Carnegie units" earned by students rather than the larger issue of what students should be learning. The Carnegie unit was born about seventy years ago. At that time, there was much confusion about what a high school transcript meant. "Classics" could mean Ancient History twice a week at one high school, or it could mean Latin every day at another.

To rectify the situation, the Carnegie Foundation proposed a standard unit to measure high school work based on time. A total of 120 hours in one subject—meeting 4 or 5 times a week, for 40 to 60 minutes, for 36 to 40 weeks each year—earns for the student one "unit" of high school credit. "The Carnegie unit," became a convenient, mechanical way to measure academic progress throughout the country. And, to this day, this bookkeeping device is the basis on which the school day, and indeed the entire curriculum, is organized. And, at some schools, adding up Carnegie units seems to be the main objective.

Other high schools we visited had written goals. Often they were vaguely stated, offering little guidance as to what schools should teach and students learn. They were generally ignored. At Sands High School, a comprehensive school in the Southeast, we were handed the teachers' manual, which included seven "goals":

- To provide substantial and varied learning experiences that will facilitate life in a multi-cultural changing society.
- To develop programs that are consistent with student interest, ability, and potential.
- To encourage each student to know his worth and to use this sense of worth to productively participate in the school and the larger community.

- To provide a body of learning that will encourage the cohesion of the student body.
- To provide an atmosphere of cooperative interdependence.
- To encourage the student to understand his rights and responsibilities.
- To teach skills that will enable the student to function both effectively and affectively in a changing society.[11]

At Prairie View, a small high school on the western plains, we found this so-called "Statement of Objectives":

> The Prairie View Public School is vitally aware that the school of today is the school of the people it serves. The school provides educators who are knowledgeable in their subject matter and who are dedicated to serving all students and their needs.[12]

When we asked teachers, principals, and students about school goals, their response frequently was one of uncertainty, amusement, or surprise. "What do you mean?" "Goals for what?" Some teachers just smiled. Others apologized for not knowing. Some referred us to the teachers' manual. One faculty member told us he thought goals and objectives were something "to be learned in teacher education courses and then forgotten." Another put it more bluntly: "If we had goals, we wouldn't follow them anyway."

When school people did talk to us about objectives, comments differed sharply from group to group. Students said they wanted to "get out," "be with friends," "get into a good college," "pass the competency exam," "get a job." Others were more cynical: "The school is here to keep you off the street and out of trouble until you're old enough to get out there and deal with it."

The principals we talked with spoke of other aims: "develop school spirit," "graduate as many students as possible," "help students pass the state-required exams," "improve relations between different races," "maintain order," "build a sense of community," "improve students' opportunities in life," "successfully mainstream handicapped students."

In one large urban academic school, however, we met a principal who had a special vision of what he was trying to accomplish. In his words:

> I have a dream for the school and for what goes on in the classroom. I'd like every teacher to focus on problem-solving, to make the *process* of learning—not factual recall—the center of instruction. I'd like us to challenge our students to think.[13]

Teachers, on the other hand, spoke frequently about preparing kids to get into a "good" college. Many teachers we talked with shared deeply their students' concerns about "getting good grades" and "getting into an Ivy League institution or to the prestigious state university." These same teachers also expressed nagging doubts about the pressure. As one put it, "All middle-class kids here want to go to college, and it's what their parents want for them, whether or not they have the ability. Many of them frankly don't have it. But if they don't get into college, then we feel we've failed."[14]

Vocational education teachers, on the other hand, said their goal was to "help the kids get jobs." The measure of their success was job placement. The depressed economy seemed to have many teachers worried. As one business education instructor put it: "It's our job to prepare students for jobs. But if there aren't any jobs for them when they graduate, if they wind up on unemployment, then what have we accomplished? What are we doing here?"[15]

A few teachers had distressingly low aspirations for their students. One admitted:

> Our goal is to get our students so that they can function adequately in blue collar society. You wouldn't write that down and it would be real embarrassing if someone from the University saw it written, but our goal is to get these kids to be like their parents. We're not really satisfied with their aspirations, but that's our goal.[16]

Still another put it this way:

> The goal, I guess, is to keep things quiet and have kids come to school and get their ADA (Average Daily Attendance) . . . have a good team (whatever sport we're doing) . . . and to get through the year.[17]

Not surprisingly, many teachers we met were often confused about new demands confronted by the school. One high school teacher said:

> We no longer are expected to just teach a subject. We have to be psychiatrists. We have to take care of the drug problems. Too many demands are being placed on the school by the state.[18]

Another agreed:

> We are called upon to act on behalf of many social agencies. We are taking care of human problems every single minute. Just where education fits into that is a very difficult thing.[19]

After visiting schools from coast to coast, we are left with the distinct impression that high schools lack a clear and vital mission. They are unable to find common purposes or establish educational priorities that are widely shared. They seem unable to put it all together. The institution is adrift.

We recommend that every high school have clearly stated goals and purposes that are understood and supported by the students, teachers, administrators, and parents of the institution. But where do we begin? Do we reach back to the Latin Grammar School, to prepare young men—and women—for Harvard and Yale, or for one of three thousand other colleges and universities? Do we recapture the vision of Calvin Woodward, to prepare young people more effectively for the work place? Do we follow the Americanizing impulses of the new immigrations? Or should high schools continue to take over the work of other troubled institutions—the family, the neighborhood, the church?

Garfield High School seems to have found the answer. Garfield is a comprehensive high school in the middle of one of the largest and most distressed cities in the United States. It has a student body of 2,000 students, 80 percent of whom are black or Hispanic. Most students live in a high-rise public housing project.

Just a few blocks north of Garfield, the black and white neighborhoods are not integrated. A few blocks south the neighborhood is all black: middle class, poor, and rich, an integration of class but not race. A half mile west, the community is depressed and dangerous; no place for strangers.

According to its thirteen-year record, Garfield is one of the best high schools in the city. A tradition of success is suggested by high SAT scores and placement of its students into top-flight colleges; daily attendance rates of 96 percent; a student newspaper that wins national awards; and a mathematics team that, in the words of the students, "beats the pants off" the suburban teams.

Garfield's success is reinforced by students who consider the school a special place, by parents who are deeply involved in school affairs, and by a staff who say it is "one of the few schools in the city where teachers work with students and care about learning." One parent caught the spirit we felt at Garfield when she said:

> You know why I like Garfield? It is a no nonsense school. Teachers expect the child to work here, and more than that, they care about your child. My daughter's music teacher, for example, checks up on how she is doing in her other courses. Yesterday, before the first grading period, I decided to call all my daughter's teachers and they were all available. It's not that my daughter is that good in class, always; she has had some trouble in school. But the troubles have always been able to be worked out because the teachers can explain what they are doing and because they obviously care. As a parent you know something is right when your daughter is getting up early and getting you up early so she can get to school. Before Garfield, I had trouble getting her out of bed, now she gets me up.[20]

Classes are focused and challenging at Garfield High. In a mathematics class, we heard students ask questions like "What does *X* to the two-thirds power plus *Y* to the two-thirds power minus one look like?" The teacher in a physics class was heard saying: "You have been told the initial velocity and the rate of acceleration, that it is constant, and the time of the acceleration. Write an equation to tell us how far the object has traveled." In an English class, students were discussing their favorite poets; in a social studies class, a new city law was being skillfully critiqued.

Near the end of a busy day at Garfield High, we chatted briefly with a middle-aged science teacher in the hall. When asked to comment on her own experience, she spoke easily of her feelings:

> You know, I think Garfield is the best an inner city school can be. Not that the staff or the circumstances are perfect; in fact, I'm sure the staff was better eight years ago, when I first came to Garfield. I never saw such professionals, such smart people, in my life as when I arrived here! Of course, many of those have left; a few have stayed and a few new ones have kept Garfield going. When you think about it, this school is resilient. I don't know why exactly, except it must be many things together—the parents, the kids, the teachers, the administration, the tradition. Yes, "resilient" is the best word to describe Garfield today.[21]

Garfield is not trouble-free. One student complained to us about "too much pressure." A mother said, "There is no social program for white students at the school. They are intensely conscious of being in a minority, a new experience." Another mother reported: "One of the greatest problems at Garfield is people's perception of the security problem. Lots of people are antsy because they think it's dangerous." Teachers talk about a shortage of supplies and complicated student scheduling that takes hours of their time.

Still, Garfield is a school that works. There is a shared sense of mission. People know where they are going. What happens there matches well-understood objectives. When we talked to Garfield parents, teachers and students, the following purposes emerged. *First*, develop critical thinking; *second*, prepare students for further education; *third*, increase students' career options; and *fourth*, build a spirit of community and service.

One faculty member spoke movingly, even eloquently, about the need to preserve the value of the common culture, to broaden the horizons of the students to arouse their curiosity, and to teach them to think critically. In his words:

> First, we have to teach students what I'll call survival skills; in other words, the basics. These are absolutes, for any further learning is impossible without them. But beyond those survival skills, there is a cultural and ethical body that binds us all. A culture requires that this body of knowledge be taught, if it's going to survive. Remember, Yeats in one of his poems warned us that a society must not disintegrate into randomness. I think the schools have a critical role to play in seeing that that doesn't happen. We need to put students in touch with knowledge in a coherent way so that they are contributing members of a common culture.[22]

High schools to be effective must have a sense of purpose, with teachers, students, administrators, and parents sharing a vision of what they are trying to accomplish. The vision must be larger than a single class in a single day. It must go beyond keeping students in school and out of trouble, and be more significant than adding up the Carnegie units the student has completed.

We propose four essential goals and the ways these goals can be achieved.

> First, the high school should help all students develop the capacity to think critically and communicate effectively through a mastery of language.

Second, the high school should help all students learn about themselves, the human heritage, and the interdependent world in which they live through a core curriculum based upon consequential human experiences common to all people.

Third, the high school should prepare all students for work and further education through a program of electives that develop individual aptitudes and interests.

Fourth, the high school should help all students fulfill their social and civic obligations through school and community service.

Today, many proposals for school reform are heatedly debated. But, unguided by a larger vision, they amount to little more than tinkering with an elaborate and complex system. What is needed—and what we believe these four goals constitute—is a clear and coherent vision of what the nation's high schools should be seeking to accomplish.

NOTES

1. Ernie Knee, *Accreditation Standards and Procedures for Secondary Schools* (Boise: Idaho State Department of Education, Idaho State, 1981), p. 3.
2. "Standards for Accreditation of Teachers and Secondary Schools," *Mississippi State Department of Education Bulletin*, no 171, July 1981, p. 2.
3. *Elementary-Secondary Guide for Oregon Schools, 1980: Standards for Public Schools* (Salem, Oregon: Department of Education, 1981), p. viii.
4. Maine Revised Statutes Annotated, Title 20-SS 1221, 1980.
5. California State Board of Education, Curriculum Development and Supplemental Materials Commission. History–Social Science Framework Committee. *History, Social Science Framework for California Public Schools, Kindergarten through Grade 12* (Sacramento: California State Department of Education, 1981), pp. 38–39.
6. Illinois Revised Statutes, 1981, ch. 122, para. 27–12ff.
7. National Association of Secondary School Principals, *State-Mandated Graduation Requirements*, 1980 (Reston, Virginia: National Association of Secondary School Principals, 1980), p. 5.
8. Rhode Island State Department of Education, *Rhode Island Laws Relating to Education*, Title 16 of the General Laws, 1975.
9. *Wisconsin State Statutes*, SS-18.01, 1977, pp. 519–520.
10. Carnegie Foundation High School Visits, 1982.
11. Ibid.
12. Ibid.
13. Ibid.
14. Ibid.
15. Ibid.
16. Ibid.
17. Ibid.
18. Ibid.
19. Ibid.
20. Ibid.
21. Ibid.
22. Ibid.

QUESTIONS FOR CRITICAL ANALYSIS

1. What research prompted Boyer's essay? What was discovered through this research? Did any of these findings remind you of the situation in your high school? Which ones? Why?
2. Describe a typical school goal as described by Boyer. Why are the goals generally written in such vague terms? What is characteristic about the language of these goals? How could they be improved?
3. Did any of the statements by teachers and principals surprise you? How? Did any sound familiar? Which ones?
4. Which student responses sounded like something you would say about your high school experience? Explain why you would respond that way.
5. What are Boyer's four essential goals? How do they compare with Sizer's five imperatives ("Better Schools")? How are they better goals than those presented by the schools Boyer quotes in the essay? What would Richard Mitchell ("The Columbus Gap") think of these goals? What do you think of them?

QUESTIONS FOR STRUCTURAL ANALYSIS

1. How does Boyer begin his essay? Were you interested in this essay, or bored by it? Why? How did Boyer's style contribute to your response?
2. Boyer's essay opens with a description of state rules and regulations and then moves into a discussion of local goals. How does Boyer relate these two topics? Describe the ways he develops his points.
3. Boyer depends upon data and anecdotes from extended research. Evaluate his incorporation of this information into the essay. Select examples of research material used in an effective way. If you can, select examples of material that does not work especially well in the essay. Be ready to defend your selections.
4. How does the example of Garfield High School serve Boyer's essay? Why does he spend so much time on it? Would you like to have attended Garfield High? Why, or why not?
5. The essays by Sizer and Boyer exemplify two very different methods of organization. Describe the way each essay is organized. Which method did you think was more effective? Why?

Can We Improve the Schools?

Topics for Writing Essays

Many of the questions following each essay can serve as appropriate writing suggestions. Some of the topics listed below expand the prereading exercises, but they can be used without completing that step first.

1. At a recent district meeting in a small midwestern town, a 75-year-old woman stood up and, to rousing applause, announced, "I have no interest in seeing any of my money spent on education. It's not my problem." Write an argument for public and private support of education, explaining to this woman and her supporters why it is in her interest to support the public schools.
2. Evaluate a school you attended in view of points raised in these essays. In what ways was the school succeeding? How was it failing? How were its problems being addressed? Make recommendations for ways to improve the school. (Your recommendations should be serious ones and closely tied to the issues raised by these articles. If you spend your time talking about better food in the cafeteria, you've missed the point of the assignment.) Write your essay to be sent to both the superintendent and school board who oversee the school as well as the parent-teachers organization.
3. Using points raised in the essays in this section by Mitchell and Magnet as a starting place, write an argument on (1) why "value education" is important, (2) why it should be part of the school curriculum, and (3) how it could be better taught. Address your essay to Mr. Mitchell, a hostile but intelligent reader.

Research Possibilities

1. What knowledge have freshmen in your college brought from their high school educations? Get a copy of Chester E. Finn Jr. and Diane Ravitch's book, *What Do Our 17-Year-Olds Know?*, and write a survey of your own to administer to college freshmen. Be sure to include questions about literature, history, art, physics, biology, chemistry, mathematics, political science, economics, and business. (You may want to consult other books and articles as you create your survey.) Try to get a representative sample of the freshman class (you'll need to base your sample on information from the admissions office) and write a report on the state of knowledge among students in your freshman class. This report should be written for the president of the college and the dean of undergraduate studies. (Be sure to include in your report a copy of the survey.)

2. What is the university's responsibility toward the local public schools? In what ways is your college helping to improve the schools? Interview members of the arts and sciences faculty, members of the school of education, and administrators in the school district to find out what programs are already in place and what needs might be met through school-university partnerships. Write a report on the local situation for the school and college leaders, recommending ways they can strengthen their relationship.
3. What kind of support does the governor of your state provide education? (In order to direct your research better, you need to focus on either higher education or the schools.) Find out about legislation that affects education, budget decisions, partnerships among government, business, and education leaders and programs designed to improve education. Write a report on the state's activities to be published as a promotion piece for the state.

PART SIX
*B*USINESS

*T*HE *B*USINESS OF *B*USINESS

The four authors in this section paint a gloomy picture of America: its economy, people, business and government leaders. Galbraith and Lamb both seem to offer little hope that business leaders will have the vision to stop America's economic decline; Rostow and Rohatyn, while describing an equally depressing state of affairs, do suggest ways that business leaders can be instrumental in altering the situation.

JOHN KENNETH GALBRAITH, "THE 1929 PARALLEL"

ROBERT BOYDEN LAMB, "THE BATTLEFIELD MEDICS"

WALT W. ROSTOW, "DANGER AND OPPORTUNITY"

FELIX ROHATYN, "COMMITMENT"

*T*HE 1929 *P*ARALLEL

JOHN KENNETH GALBRAITH

John Kenneth Galbraith (1908–), a Harvard economist, professor, and author, writes about economics so the lay reader can understand its implications. "The 1929 Parallel," published in The Atlantic Monthly, *compares the situation on Wall Street in early 1987 to that of pre-depression Wall Street in 1929. When you consider that this essay was published only nine months before the October crash on Wall Street, Galbraith's warnings seem prophesy. America's love for easy money on Wall Street is the topic of many Galbraith works including* The Great Crash of 1929 *(1955) which described the last days of the 1920s boom and* The Affluent Society *(1958), a depiction of America's addiction to consumerism.*

Before you begin reading: *Think about what you know or have learned about the Wall Street Crash of 1929. In your reading notebook, write a description of what happened economically and socially as a result of the crash.*

◆

Senator Couzens:	*Did Goldman, Sachs and Company organize the Goldman Sachs Trading Corporation?*
Mr. Sachs:	*Yes, sir.*
Senator Couzens:	*And it sold its stock to the public?*
Mr. Sachs:	*A portion of it. The firms invested originally in ten per cent of the entire issue for the sum of ten million dollars.*
Senator Couzens:	*And the other ninety per cent was sold to the public?*
Mr. Sachs:	*Yes, sir.*
Senator Couzens:	*At what price?*
Mr. Sachs:	*At a hundred and four. That is the old stock . . . the stock was split two for one.*
Senator Couzens:	*And what is the price of the stock now?*
Mr. Sachs:	*Approximately one and three quarters.*

from the Senate Hearings on Stock Exchange Practices, 1932

IN MARCH OF 1929 PAUL M. WARBURG, A FOUNDING PARENT of the Federal Reserve System and an immensely prestigious banker in his time, called attention to the current orgy, as he said, of "unrestrained speculation" in the stock market and added that were it not brought to an end, there would be a disastrous collapse. His warning was badly received. It was made clear that he did not appreciate the new era in economic well-being that the market was so admirably reflecting; he was said by one exceptionally articulate critic to be "sandbagging American prosperity." Less eloquent commentators voiced the thought that he was probably short in the market.

There was a decidedly more sympathetic response somewhat later that year to the still remembered observation of Professor Irving Fisher, of Yale, one of the most diversely innovative scholars of his time. Fisher said, "Stock prices have reached what looks like a permanently high plateau." Fisher was, in fact, long in the market and by some estimates lost between eight and ten million dollars in the almost immediately ensuing crash.

There is here a lesson about the larger constant as regards financial aberration and its consequences. There is a compelling vested interest in euphoria, even, or perhaps especially, when it verges, as in 1929, on insanity. Anyone who speaks or writes on current tendencies in financial markets should feel duly warned. There are, however, some controlling rules in these matters, which are ignored at no slight cost. Among those suffering most will be those who regard all current warnings with the greatest contempt.

The first rule—and our first parallel with 1929—has to do with the stock market itself and, as it may somewhat formally be called, the dynamics of speculation.

Any long-continued increase in stock prices, such as preceded the 1929 crash and such as we experienced at least until last September, brings a change in the purposes of the participants in the market. Initially the motivating force is from institutions and individuals who buy securities (and bid up prices) because of some underlying circumstance, actual or imagined, that is judged to affect values: The economy as a whole is improving. Inflation as a threat is pending or perhaps receding. The tax prospect seems favorable. Or, mercifully, a business-oriented Administration has come to power in Washington. Most of all, in a time when common-stock dividends are largely a fixed dole to stockholders, interest rates are thought likely to decline. This calls for a compensating increase in the value of stocks if they are to earn only the new going return. On such matters virtually all comment concerning the market, informed and often otherwise, centers.

But as a stock-market boom continues (the same can be true as regards a boom in real estate or even art), there is increasing participation by institutions and people who are attracted by the thought that they can take an upward ride with the prices and get out before the eventual fall. This participation, needless to say, drives up prices. And the prices so achieved no longer have any relation to underlying circumstance. Justifying causes for the increases will, also needless to say, be cited by the sadly vulnerable financial analysts and commentators and, alas, the often vulnerable business press. This will persuade yet other innocents to come in for the loss that awaits all so persuaded.

For the loss will come. The market at this stage is inherently unstable. At some point something—no one can ever know when or quite what—will trigger a decision by some to get out. The initial fall will persuade others that the time has come, and then yet others, and then the greater fall will come. Once the purely speculative component has been built into the structure, the eventual result is, to repeat, inevitable.

There will previously have been moments of unease from which there was recovery. These are symptoms of the eventual collapse. In 1928 and through the winter, spring, and summer of 1929 the stock market divorced itself from all underlying reality in the manner just cited. Justification was, of course, asserted: the unique and enduring quality of Coolidge and Hoover prosperity; the infinitely benign effects of the supply-side tax reductions of Secretary of the Treasury Andrew W. Mellon, who was held to be the greatest in that office since Alexander Hamilton; the high-tech future of RCA, the speculative favorite of the time, which so far had not paid a dividend.

But mostly speculators, amateur and otherwise, were getting on for the ride. In the spring of 1929 came the initial indication of instability—a very sharp break in the market. Prices recovered, and in the summer months they rocketed up. There was another bad break in September and further uneasy movements. Then, at the end of October, came the compelling rush to get out and therewith the crash. No one knows what precipitated it. No one ever will. A few—Bernard Baruch and, it has long been said, Joseph P. Kennedy—got out first. Most went down with the mob; to an extraordinary degree, this is a game in which there are mainly losers.

The question now, in the winter of 1987, is whether the stock market is or has been repeating its history. There was, early last year, a period of very sharply appreciating prices following an earlier, slower ascent. Then, on September 11 and the days following, came a severe slump, the worst in any recent period. So far (as this is written) there has been no significant recovery. As to the further prospect, no one knows, despite the extreme willingness to say otherwise on the part of many who do not know. What is certain, however, is that once again there existed a speculative dynamic—of people and institutions drawn by the market rise to the thought that it would go up more, that they could ride the rise and get out in time. Perhaps last September signaled the end; perhaps it was an episode in a continuing speculative rise with a worse drop yet to come. What we do know is that speculative episodes never come gently to an end. The wise, though for most the improbable, course is to assume the worst.

Another stock-market collapse would, however—one judges—be less traumatic in its larger effect than was the one in October of 1929. The Great Crash had a shattering effect on investment and consumer spending and eventually on production and employment, leading to the collapse of banks and business firms. Now there are safety nets, as they are called. Unemployment compensation, pensions, farm-income support, and much else would have a general cushioning effect, along with government fiscal support to the economy. There is insurance of bank deposits and the further certainty that any large corporation, if in danger, would be bailed out. Modern socialism, as I've elsewhere said, is when the corporate jets come down on National and Dulles airports.

A second, rather stronger parallel with 1929 is the present commitment to seemingly imaginative, currently lucrative, and eventually disastrous innovation in financial structures. Here the similarity is striking and involves the same elements as before. In the months and years prior to the 1929 crash there was a wondrous proliferation of holding companies and investment trusts. The common feature of both the holding companies and the trusts was that they conducted no practical operations; they existed to hold stock in other companies, and these companies frequently existed to hold stock in yet other companies. Pyramiding, it was called. The investment trust and the utility pyramid were the greatly admired marvels of the time. Samuel Insull brought together the utility companies of the Midwest in one vast holding-company complex, which he did not understand. Similarly, the Van Sweringen brothers built their vast railroad pyramid. But equally admired were the investment trusts, the formations of Goldman, Sachs and Company and the United Founders Corporation, and—an exceptionally glowing example of the entrepreneurial spirit—those of Harrison Williams, who assembled a combined holding-company and investment-trust system that was thought to have a market value by the summer of 1929 of around a billion dollars. There were scores of others.

The pyramids of Insull and the Van Sweringens were a half dozen or more companies deep. The stock of the operating utility or railroad was held by a holding company. This company then sold bonds and preferred stock and common stock to the public, retaining for itself enough of the common stock for control. The exercise was then repeated—a new company, more bonds and stock to the public, control still retained in a majority or minority holding of the stock of the new creation. And so forth up the line, until an insignificant investment in the common stock of the final company controlled the whole structure.

The investment trusts were similar, except that their ultimate function was not to operate a railroad or a utility but only to hold securities. In December of 1928 Goldman, Sachs and Company created the Goldman Sachs Trading Corporation. It sold securities to the public but retained enough common stock for control. The following July the trading corporation, in association with Harrison Williams, launched the Shenandoah Corporation. Securities were similarly sold to the public; a controlling interest remained with the trading corporation. Then Shenandoah, in the last days of the boom, created the Blue Ridge Corporation. Again preferred stock and common were sold to the public; the controlling wedge of common stock remained now with Shenandoah. Shenandoah, as before, was controlled by the trading corporation, and the trading corporation by Goldman Sachs. The stated purpose of these superior machinations was to bring the financial genius of the time to bear on investment in common stocks and to share the ensuing rewards with the public.

No institutions ever excited more admiration. The creators of the investment trusts were men of conceded as well as self-admitted genius, and were believed to have a strong instinct for the public interest. John J. Raskob, the chairman of the Democratic National Committee in those days, thought an investment trust might be created in which the toiling masses would invest from their weekly earnings. He outlined the proposal in a *Ladies' Home Journal* article titled "Everybody Ought to Be Rich."

In all these operations debt was incurred to purchase common stock that, in turn, provided full voting control. The debt was passive as to control; so was the preferred stock, which conferred no voting rights. The minority interests in the common stock sold to the public had no effect of power either. The remaining, retained investment in common stock exercised full authority over the whole structure. This was leverage. A marvelous thing. Leverage also meant that any increase in the earnings of the ultimate companies would flow back with geometric force to the originating company. That was because along the way the debt and preferred stock in the intermediate companies held by the public extracted only their fixed contractual share; any *increase* in revenue and value flowed through to the ultimate and controlling investment in common stock.

It was a grave problem, however, that in the event of failing earnings and values, leverage would work fully as powerfully in reverse. All income and value, and in practice more, would be absorbed by the outer debt and preferred shares; for the originating company there would remain literally—very literally—nothing. But of this in 1929 no one, or not many, thought; a rising market combined with the managerial and investment genius of the men who built these structures made any such concern seem irrelevant in the extreme.

Here the parallel: after fifty-seven years investment trusts, called closed-end funds, are now coming back into fashion, although still, I would judge, in a rather modest way as compared with 1929. The more exciting parallel is in the rediscovery of leverage. Leverage is again working its wonders. Not in utility pyramids: these in their full 1929 manifestation are forbidden by law. And the great investment houses, to be sure, still raise capital for new and expanding enterprises. But that is not where the present interest and excitement lie. These lie in the wave of corporate takeovers, mergers, and acquisitions and the *leveraged* buy-outs. And in the bank loans and bond issues, not excluding the junk bonds, that are arranged to finance these operations.

The common feature of all these activities is the creation of debt. In 1985 alone some $139 billion dollars' worth of mergers and acquisitions was financed, much of it with new borrowing. More, it would appear, was so financed last year. Some $100 billion in admittedly perilous junk bonds (rarely has a name been more of a warning) was issued to more than adequately trusting investors. This debt has a first claim on its earnings; in its intractable way, it will absorb all earnings (and claim more) at some astringent time in the future.

That time will come. Greatly admired for the energy and ingenuity it now and recently has displayed, this development (the mergers and their resulting debt), to be adequately but not unduly blunt, will eventually be regarded as no less insane than the utility and railroad pyramiding and the investment-trust explosion of the 1920s.

Ever since the Compagnie d'Occident of John Law (which was formed to search for the highly exiguous gold deposits of Louisiana); since the wonderful exfoliation of enterprises of the South Sea Bubble; since the outbreak of investment enthusiasm in Britain in the 1820s (a company "to drain the Red Sea with a view to recovering the treasure abandoned by the Egyptians after the crossing of the Jews"); and on down to the 1929 investment trusts, the offshore funds and Bernard Cornfeld, and yet on to Penn Square and the Latin American loans—nothing has been more remarkable than the susceptibility of the investing public to financial illusion and the like-mindedness of the most reputable of bankers, investment bankers, brokers, and free-lance financial geniuses. Nor is the reason far to seek. Nothing so gives the illusion of intelligence as personal association with large sums of money.

It is, alas, an illusion. The mergers, acquisitions, take-overs, leveraged buy-outs, their presumed contribution to economic success and market values, and the burden of debt that they incur are the current form of that illusion. They will one day—again, no one can say when—be so recognized. A fall in earnings will render the debt burden insupportable. A minor literature will marvel at the earlier retreat from reality, as is now the case with the Penn Square fiasco and the loans to Latin America.

The third parallel between present and past, which will be vividly and also painfully revealed, concerns one of the great constants of capitalism. That is its tendency to single out for the most ostentatious punishment those on whom it once seemed to lavish its greatest gifts.

In the years before the 1929 crash the system accorded fortune and prestige to a greatly featured group of men—to Arthur W. Cutten, M. J. Meehan, Bernard E. ("Sell'em Ben") Smith, and Harry F. Sinclair, all market operators of major distinction; also to Charles E. Mitchell, the head of the National City Bank as it then was, and Albert Wiggin, the head of the Chase National Bank, both deeply involved in the market on their own behalf; to Ivar Kreuger, the Match King, international financier (and sometime forger of government bonds); and to Richard Whitney, soon to become president of the New York Stock Exchange and its most uncompromising public defender.

All suffered a fearful fall after the crash. Called before a congressional committee, Cutten, Meehan, and Sinclair all had grave lapses of memory.

Mitchell and Wiggin, the great bankers, were both sacked; Mitchell went through long and tedious proceedings for alleged income-tax evasion, and the large pension Wiggin had thoughtfully arranged for himself was revoked. Ivar Kreuger went out one day in Paris, bought a gun, and shot himself. Harry Sinclair eventually went to jail, and so, for embezzlement, did Richard Whitney. Whitney's passage into Sing Sing, in dignified, dark-vested attire, wearing, it has been said, the Porcellian pig of his Harvard club, was one of the more widely circulated news portraits of the time.

The young professionals now engaged in much-admired and no less publicized trading, merger takeover, buy-back, and other deals, as they are called, will one day, we can be sadly sure, suffer a broadly similar fate. Some will go to jail; some are already on the way, for vending, buying, and using inside information. Given the exceptionally oblique line between legitimate and much-praised financial knowledge and wrongfully obtained and much-condemned inside information, more are known to be at risk. But for most the more mundane prospect is unemployment and professional obloquy, and for some, personal insolvency. Expensive apartments will become available on the upper East Side of Manhattan; there will be property transfers in the Hamptons. David Stockman, said by the press to have a car sent out for him to Connecticut each morning by his employer, may end up taking the train.

S. C. Gwynne, a young onetime banker, tells in his excellent book *Selling Money* of his services in the late seventies and early eighties to the international division of Cleveland Trust, now AmeriTrust, a relatively conservative player on the world scene. He journeyed from Manila to Algiers and Riyadh in search of loans. It was a time of admiring reference to the recycling of funds on deposit from the OPEC countries to the capital-hungry lands. And he tells us that

> by December 31, 1982, more than $200 million in loans would be in trouble in Mexico, Brazil, Venezuela, Poland, and the Philippines. . . . By 1984, thirteen of the seventeen officers who had staffed the [international] division in 1980 would be gone, and Ben Bailey, [the] deputy manager, and most of the members of the senior credit committee that approved the foreign loans would take early retirements.

The end for those in the present play will come when either recession or a tight-money crunch to arrest inflation makes the debt load they have so confidently created no longer tolerable. Then there will be threats of default and bankruptcy, a drastic contraction in operations, no bonuses, a trimming of pay and payrolls, and numerous very, very early retirements. And from many who did not themselves foresee the result, there will be a heavy-handed condemnation of the failure to see that this would be the result. For those who engage in trading operations at the investment houses the day of reckoning could be when the market goes down seemingly without limit. Then will be rediscovered the oldest rule of Wall Street: financial genius is before the fall.

The final parallel with 1929 is a more general one; it has broadly to do with tax reduction and investment incentives. In the Coolidge years, as noted, Andrew Mellon reduced taxes on the affluent. The declared purpose was to stimulate the economy; more precise reference to saving, investment, and economic growth was for the future. The unannounced purpose was, as ever, to lessen the tax bite on the most bitten. By the summer of 1929 the economy was, nonetheless, stagnant—even in slight recession. (To this, rather than to the built-in inevitabilities of speculation, some economists looking for deeper substance later attributed the crash.) There is every likelihood that a very large part of the enhanced personal revenues from the tax reduction simply went into the stock market, rather than into real capital formation or even improved consumer demand.

So again now. Funds have been flowing into the stock market to be absorbed by the deals aforementioned or the cost of making them. Some, perhaps much, of this money—no one, to be sure, knows how much—is from the supply-side tax reductions. Real capital spending is currently flat, even declining—a depressing fact.

From the mergers, acquisitions, and buy-backs, it is now reasonably well agreed, comes no increase at all in industrial competence. The young men who serve in the great investment houses render no service to investment decisions, product innovation, production, automation, or labor relations in the companies whose securities they shuffle. They have no real concern with such matters. They do float some issues for new ventures or expanded operations; one concedes this while noting again how dismal is the present showing on real capital investment. Mostly their operations absorb savings into an inherently sterile activity.

History may not repeat itself, but some of its lessons are inescapable. One is that in the world of high and confident finance little is ever really new. The controlling fact is not the tendency to brilliant invention; the controlling fact is the shortness of the public memory, especially when it contends with a euphoric desire to forget.

QUESTIONS FOR CRITICAL ANALYSIS

1. What happened in the Stock Market Crash of 1929? What does Galbraith's title, "The 1929 Parallel," mean?
2. What was the first cause for the 1929 crash? Why was loss inevitable in a market such as the one in 1929? What is the parallel risk in today's market?
3. Describe the second major cause for the 1929 crash. Why is it a risky innovation? List some examples of this form of investment.
4. What financial innovation threatened the stock market in 1987? Why was it dangerous?
5. Describe the professionals involved in the Stock Market in the 1980s. What does

Galbraith think of them? How does Galbraith's characterization compare with what you know about them?

QUESTIONS FOR STRUCTURAL ANALYSIS

1. Why does Galbraith begin his essay with dialogue from the 1932 Senate Hearings on Stock Exchange Practices? What does the dialogue mean? What do you learn from this dialogue that is important to the rest of the essay?
2. List words and terms that relate directly to the stock market and to investment. Do you know what they mean? How does the context help define their meaning?
3. How does Galbraith organize his comparison? Write an informal outline of his analysis.
4. List the individual points of comparison Galbraith makes between the Stock Market in 1929 and 1987. Are you convinced by his analysis that there is cause for concern?
5. What is Galbraith's conclusion? Is it an effective or a disappointing conclusion? How does your knowledge of the October 1987 Stock Market Crash affect your reading of the essay? Do you own stock? Does your experience with investments affect your response to the essay?

*T*HE *B*ATTLEFIELD *M*EDICS

ROBERT BOYDEN LAMB

Robert Boyden Lamb (1941–), writer, consultant on economics and business, and professor of finance and management at New York University School of business, is the author of Running American Business: Top CEOs Rethink Their Major Decisions *(1987). In "The Battlefield Medics," published in* Business Month, *he indicts corporate America's chief operating officers as unwilling to take risks and develop long-range programs to solve the problems facing business and industry. According to Lamb, CEOs are more eager to hire fast-talking lawyers than to work on problems; they have no vision and they are willing to pay for the present on the basis of expected future earnings.*

Before you begin reading: *What qualities make a leader? Are business leaders different from political or military leaders? Think about the concept of leadership and write your definition of the ideal leader.*

◆

FOR AMERICAN CHIEF EXECUTIVES, THE RECENT WALL Street crash came as the culmination of a decade or more of rude surprises: the oil shocks of the 1970s, ferocious global competition, waves of deregulation, sharp swings in interest rates and a surge in takeover-related activity that has left the mightiest corporations vulnerable. Alas, if history is any guide, the reaction of most CEOs to the stockmarket crisis will deepen the dislocation and uncertainty in the long run.

Harsh? Perhaps. But the actions of American chief executives amid the chaos of the past decade—a low, dishonest decade if there ever was one—hardly fill one with confidence. Granted, they have often been as much the victims as the perpetrators of this age of uncertainty. But they have reacted to events like battlefield medics, concerned not with living to a ripe old age but with surviving until tomorrow. For some time now, they have been consumed with finding short-term solutions to long-term problems.

As a result, CEOs, like the federal government and the yuppies, have been paying for the present with future earnings. Instead of scouting out and investing in the kind of productive activities that power corporate growth, they have been much more comfortable either buying back their own company's stock—a ploy that proved shortsighted indeed on October 19, when the market crash wiped out $500 billion of equity values in a day—or overpaying to buy someone else's business. Given this emphasis on asset shuffling and financial management, it is no surprise that finance, rather than production or marketing or engineering, has become the spawning ground for CEOs in the 1980s.

Fear and uncertainty also have bred bogeymen upon whom all troubles can be blamed. We know who they are: Japan, politicians, regulators, Wall Street, the raiders. Consider the takeover game, which many chief executives blame for their increasingly short-term focus on earnings. Raiders, despite their motives, recognized one salient fact: Many companies *were* loaded with undervalued and underutilized assets. And many CEOs showed more concern for their own careers than for the fortunes of shareholders, employees or the company itself.

Indeed, as the takeover wars heated up, CEOs of target companies found it easier to hire expensive lawyers and investment bankers, or to shoulder debt or pay greenmail, than to improve their own operations. Some CEOs were even eager to join the battle, either as raiders—remember the Bendix-Martin Marietta travesty—or as participants in leveraged buyouts.

More seriously, most CEOs are neither trained nor equipped to thrive in turbulent times. They reach the top job by slowly moving up the corporate ladder for 25 years, a process that inhibits risk-taking, encourages the formation of old-boy networks and creates a sort of tunnel vision. As John Kenneth Galbraith has pointed out, corporations are essentially bureaucratic organizations. And for years, American managers rode the tide of U.S. military and economic dominance insulated from an unruly world; they rarely had to cope with intense external pressure or even with defections from their ranks.

As a result, chief executives generally tend to be little more than skilled technicians, able to pull levers and push buttons but poor at designing a new machine, a new organization or a new product. Corporate hierarchies do not welcome change or embrace new opportunities; imagination and creativity are rarely rewarded. CEOs as a group do not possess a complex or subtle view of the world. The record of big companies in developing new businesses has been dismal, in part because most CEOs are caretakers of an older patrimony, not builders of new ones.

There are, of course, exceptions to the run-of-the-mill CEO in corporate leaders such as Jack Welch, who has remade General Electric in a few short years, or Donald Petersen, who has revived the fortunes of Ford Motor. In the drug industry, Richard Furlaud has restructured Squibb into a pharmaceutical money machine, and Roy Vagelos has transformed Merck from a company living on past triumphs to one bursting with new ones. In computers, John Sculley has gotten Apple moving again, and Kenneth Olsen has turned Digital Equipment into a powerhouse. Then there is Lee Iacocca, the man and the phenomenon.

The emergence of Iacocca as a celebrity has as much to do with the general desire to discover a dynamic, imaginative corporate leader as with the realities of the Chrysler story.

But for every Welch, Olsen or Iacocca, there are dozens of CEOs trapped in a world they do not understand, managing for retirement or drifting along with the newest fashion pitched by the trendiest consultant: this year financial services, next year high technology; this year factory automation, next year quality circles.

Who are they? Just think of the industries in which the United States has had difficulty competing: cars, consumer electronics, steel, machine tools, semiconductors. Or look at former conglomerates—Gulf + Western, ITT, Beatrice, LTV—suffering through spasms of acquisition and divestiture. Or consider companies trapped by legal and regulatory nightmares of their own creation: A.H. Robins, Union Carbide, Texaco, Manville.

The decline of a company is not a pleasant sight, particularly in the current economic and business climate. Problems left unattended feed on themselves. Intense pressures and competition trigger the quick fix—an acquisition, say—and the company loads up with debt. Earnings slip, morale suffers and good managers drift away. As uncertainty increases, the former collegiality vanishes; CEOs become autocratic, firing executives, flailing about. Suddenly, only drastic alternatives offer themselves: closing factories, laying off workers, selling off divisions. The stock price falls, raiders stir and a leveraged buyout begins to look attractive.

To turn it around takes wisdom, imagination and leadership. These are rare commodities in the corporate world—although there are glimmers of them out there, like gold in a gravel pan. But I am reminded of something William May, the former chairman of American Can, said to me several years ago: "It was not so long ago that the American management style stood, in the eyes of the world, as a mighty colossus—so formidable, so accurate, so impregnable that all the rest of the world could do was imitate its workings. But now, it is true, American business is in terrible trouble."

May's words seemed shocking then. It is a sign of the times that one no longer feels much surprise.

QUESTIONS FOR CRITICAL ANALYSIS

1. What three practices does Lamb accuse chief executive officers (CEOs) of performing? Why does Lamb disapprove of these actions?
2. What is Lamb implying when he says "It is no surprise that finance, rather than production or marketing or engineering, has become the spawning ground for

CEOs"? Why is this not a compliment? (Lamb is a professor of finance. Does that surprise you? Why?)

3. Who are the "good guys" Lamb mentions? Why are they good CEOs? Can you name some of the bad CEOs he refers to?
4. Look up one of the companies or events Lamb lists as problematic: Bendix-Martin Marietta, Gulf + Western, ITT, Beatrice, LTV, A.H. Robins, Union Carbide, Texaco, Manville. Explain why Lamb lists that company.
5. Compare Lamb's CEOs with Galbraith's investment professionals. In what ways are they similar? In what ways dissimilar?

QUESTIONS FOR STRUCTURAL ANALYSIS

1. What is Lamb's attitude toward CEOs? How is it expressed? How early in the essay do you know how he feels? List words and phrases that reveal his feelings.
2. Why does Lamb refer to CEOs as "Battlefield Medics"? What images does that phrase evoke? Is it an accurate label? fair?
3. Lamb published this essay in *Business Month*, a magazine directed to business executives. How do you suppose his initial audience responded? How do you think Lamb wants them to respond?
4. Lamb quotes William May, retired CEO from American Can, at the conclusion of his essay. Is the quotation effective? Why, or why not? How does the conclusion relate to the introduction?
5. Is this essay a fair analysis of CEOs? Why, or why not?

*D*ANGER AND *O*PPORTUNITY

WALT W. ROSTOW

Walt W. Rostow (1916–), economist and educator, served as a top White House advisor to both Presidents Kennedy and Johnson. Published in Business Month *(January 1988), "Danger and Opportunity" is written for an audience interested in American business. Rostow is optimistic about America's future because he can identify cooperative efforts to meet the problems at the local and state levels. However, for America to survive its industrial crisis, business must not only keep up with the fast pace of technological change, but also develop economic relationships with third world countries.*

Before you begin reading: *Keeping in mind America's changing position in the world, write a paragraph describing what you think someone your age in Japan thinks of the United States. Next write a paragraph describing your views of the United States. (You may want to try writing additional paragraphs giving the points of view of a Russian student, a Latin American student, a German student, and others.)*

◆

I AM AWARE THAT CHIEF EXECUTIVES LIVE IN A WORLD where they bear an inescapable responsibility for profits and must therefore concern themselves with costs, markets and output next month and next year. In looking down the road to the year 2000, I shall have to consider more distant forces; but I shall try to say something along the way, and in the end, about the meaning of the picture I draw for the operating world of the chief executive officer.

Two reservations. First, John Maynard Keynes once wrote: "The inevitable never happens. It is the unexpected always." That proposition should remain firmly before the reader as well as the writer of an article that ventures to look a dozen years ahead.

Second, one of my conclusions as both a historian and a former public servant is that it is dangerous to separate the long run from the short run. The long run is powerfully shaped by what happens from day to day.

That proposition has a particular meaning right now. The United States is in the midst of a deeply rooted economic crisis caused by a sustained effort to live beyond its means. We have been running this country the way Mayor John Lindsay ran New York City. The symptoms of the crisis are known to us all: the federal deficit; the related but even more dangerous trade deficit; the shift from a surplus to a debtor nation; a greatly weakened dollar, which may help with the trade deficit but at the certain cost of our standard of living and increased inflationary pressure. Much depends on our wage discipline in handling that pressure. If we are to get the benefit in expanded exports from the devalued dollar, we shall have to avoid wage increases in excess of productivity increases.

In general, how things look in the year 2000 will be greatly affected by the manner, the timing and the degree of success with which we work our way out of this crisis. That process could leave us more unified at home and strengthened abroad, or it could lead to a corrosion of our domestic life, the fragmentation of our alliances across the Atlantic and Pacific and heightened tension with the Soviet Union. It is not difficult to construct the scenario either way.

I shall build this article on the optimistic assumption that the United States will work its way out of the crisis in pretty good style. Not only is that assumption necessary if I am to focus on the long-run forces at work, but I believe that it is probably correct. Despite the fact that neither national political party has yet faced up fully to the challenges posed by our current situation, I believe, on balance and without naïveté, that our great continental society remains vital and resilient. My first conclusion is that this underlying resilience will assert itself politically before the year 2000, and that a new phase in our national political life will be installed by that time.

I hold this temperately optimistic view not out of simple faith but because the politics of partnership can be observed alive and well at the state and local levels. There are, of course, states and cities where politics and social life are dominated by tension and raw confrontation. But the dominant trend outside Washington is toward cooperation in an effort to solve problems that, it is widely appreciated, can be solved only by cooperation.

This process can be perceived in relations between business and labor as both face the reality of brutal international competition and the consequent choice of either closing down the plant or cutting costs and raising productivity. The reconstruction of the centers of many American cities has been the product of even more complex partnerships embracing the private sector (including banks, insurance companies and pension funds) and state and local government, with the universities and labor often lending a hand.

Most important of all have been the partnerships between the universities and the private sector in generating and diffusing new technologies, with state and local governments and financial institutions sometimes getting into the act with new forms of venture capital. There are now some 50 high-tech concentrations in the United States built by such partnerships. Not all will flourish, but each represents a form of cooperation not to be found in either economics or government textbooks. And I rate as one of the most powerful positive forces in the country the intense competition among the states to attract and expand high-tech firms.

That competition has carried with it a renewed realization that first-rate educational institutions are vital to the bottom line. I say "renewed" because land-grant colleges were built on that realization starting more than 120 years ago, and the tradition of collaboration they inaugurated between the universities and the private sector represents a major advantage for the United States relative to most of the rest of the world at a time of technological revolution.

In any case, I believe that, as often in American history, developments in the states now herald the shape of national politics, and that we will see the politics of partnership and cooperation dominant at the national level by the year 2000—probably well before.

I believe this will happen not because the American people will experience an infusion of brotherly love or a reduction in our particular national dose of original sin. I believe that the process is under way because we remain a society with a will to survive and the energy to grapple with the problems that the flow of history places before us. We will continue to behave at home as we often (and dangerously) have behaved on the world scene—in conformity with Samuel Johnson's 18th-century dictum: "Depend upon it, sir, when a man knows he is to be hanged in a fortnight, it concentrates his mind wonderfully." The gallows in this case are the shift in the Atlantic world from the politics of dividing an expanding pie to the politics of dealing with a protracted competitive test of our viability as nation-states.

For more than a century now—since, say, Bismarck outflanked the German Socialists with the first modern social-welfare legislation—the politics of the Western world have focused (like the recent budget debates in Washington) on the division of a nation's resources between social-welfare outlays (and income redistribution in favor of the disadvantaged) and the claims of the private sector. Occasionally, allocations to the military entered what was essentially a running zero-sum debate, softened by the underlying assumption that the pie was more or less automatically expanding. Social-welfare outlays rose from 4 percent in 1913 (an average for the United States, the United Kingdom and Germany) to about 14 percent for the major advanced industrial countries by 1960 and 24 percent by the mid-1970s.

The central question before the United States and the Western world generally is whether the resources to be divided will continue to increase. The question arises because of two great historical developments: first, the emergence around the mid-1970s of the technological revolution embracing microelectronics, genetic engineering, a new batch of manufactured industrial materials and the increasingly ubiquitous laser; second, the rise toward technological competence, over the full spectrum of possibilities, of the major countries of Latin America, a substantial group of countries in the Pacific and, most significant of all, China and India.

Each of these developments—like the two Chinese characters for the word *crisis*—is both a danger and an opportunity.

The new technological possibilities represent the fourth such concentration over the past two centuries. The first, which came on stage in Britain in the 1780s, consisted of new textile machinery, the fabrication of good iron with coke rather than charcoal and Watt's improved steam engine. The second, the steam railroad, emerged in a big way in the 1840s and led to the manufacture of cheap steel by the 1870s. The third, occurring around the turn of the century, embraced electricity, the internal combustion engine and a batch of new chemicals.

As opposed to the earlier technological revolutions, this one is marked by close links to areas of basic science that are themselves evolving in a revolutionary way. Business leaders will have to operate in an environment of extremely rapid change. Our business schools and textbooks on administration are not geared to, say, an obsolescence rate of 30 percent a year.

The danger posed by the new technological revolution can, then, be quite precisely defined. It does not lie in the likelihood that we will be outstripped by others in the pace at which we generate new technologies. It lies in the fact that in certain key sectors of the economy, neither management nor labor has fully accepted the proposition that both profits and real wages—indeed, economic survival—now depend on the pace of technological change.

We were and remain quite competitive in three sectors that, in effect, arose out of laboratories: electronics, chemicals and aerospace. We fell dangerously behind in steel, motor vehicles, machine tools and textiles, where the links between management and research and development were weak. Henry Ford's creation of the moving assembly line was a major act of creative engineering. But it did not arise from basic science; it was built on direct analogy to a slaughterhouse. Henry Ford wouldn't have been caught dead talking to a professor. We still need engineering imagination, but we need a great deal more.

Certainly the most confident of my predictions about the year 2000 is that successful American leaders will have to understand how to handle the links between science, invention, management and the work force. This means that labor retraining will be a major endless task. Put another way, whether we face danger or opportunity hinges on the pace at which we efficiently apply the new technologies across the whole face of the economy.

The importance of this task of business leadership is heightened by the second challenge we confront. [There is a chart that] shows the approximate historical timing of the entrance of four "graduating classes" (of nations) into what I call takeoff and what the economist Simon Kuznets called the beginning of modern economic growth. Most of the fourth class (which includes other countries of Latin America and the Middle East besides those named) is now in what I call the drive to technological maturity. That is the stage at which a society's capacity to absorb new technologies radically expands, its growth rate reaches its maximum and it learns to produce competitively the full range of modern manufactures. In the course of that process, it becomes at once an enlarged market for the technologically sophisticated exports of advanced industrial countries and a competitor in sectors of lesser sophistication.

Right now our major anxiety is focused on the trade surpluses built up mainly at our expense by Japan and West Germany. But, as the Japanese are fully aware, their primacy in the manufacture of motor vehicles and durable consumer goods is already being undermined by South Korea, Taiwan and other aspiring countries of the Pacific Basin, while U.S. airlines are using Brazilian-manufactured aircraft in increasing numbers on feeder lines. Quite conscious of the new trend, Japan is using its surplus now to invest abroad, so that its earnings from dividends and profits can support its balance of payments as the United States recovers its poise and the fourth graduating class moves on to technological maturity.

For this process to proceed to full term, evidently, the Latin American countries will have to work their way out of their debt problems (with the help of the world community), and the Middle East will have to at last find stable peace. But what about India and China? Do these two vast countries with low levels of income per capita really belong among the likely challengers in this round?

I believe they do. They may be among the poorest of the developing countries, but they are also among the technologically most sophisticated. They can already produce atomic weapons, rockets, aircraft, motor vehicles and machine tools. At a talk I gave in Hong Kong in 1969, I made what seemed to local listeners to be a bad joke. When asked about the turning over of the city to China in the 1990s, I said I thought it would be a close thing whether China took over Hong Kong or Hong Kong took over China. Right now, the south of China is alive with factories manufacturing all manner of consumer goods under Hong Kong's tutelage. Hong Kong (and Taiwan) will leave a deep imprint on Chinese history.

But the deeper reason for taking the fourth graduating class, including India and China, seriously lies in the educational revolution in these countries. As the current situation in the Soviet Union suggests, it takes more than a critical mass of educated men and women to absorb sophisticated modern technology efficiently.

It also requires a system that provides strong incentives for technological change plus institutional arrangements that make the scientist, engineer, businessman and worker an effective interacting team. It would be most unwise for American business to assume that the fourth graduating class, despite the current vicissitudes of a good many of its members, will not fulfill those conditions over the next generation. The Chinese universities, for example, were gravely set back by the Cultural Revolution. But surely this loss will be fully made up by the year 2000.

The problem posed by this prospect is not new. Academics may argue legitimately as to who deserves the title of the first modern economist, but the name of David Hume would have to appear on any list of contestants. His essays in economics have been called "the Cradle of Political Economy," and one of Adam Smith's major biographers said: "But for Hume, Smith could never have been."

Writing in 1758, Hume asked what would happen to front-runners that first developed the skills of large-scale trade—the specializations that go with the exploitation of comparative advantage, including improvement in "the mechanic arts"—when their success stirred a "fermentation" in less advantaged societies, which proceeded to imitate the more advanced but with the advantage of lower wage rates. His answer, in response to the mercantilist instinct to throttle the latecomers in the cradle, was that a front-runner could enjoy the advantages of expanded two-way trade with the aspiring country if it maintained an open trading system, but that to sustain the inevitably intensified competition it would have to remain "industrious and civilized."

Hume's summation: "Nor needs any state entertain apprehensions that their neighbors will improve to such a degree in every art and manufacture as to have no demand from them. Nature, by giving a diversity of geniuses, climates and soils to different nations, has secured their mutual intercourse and commerce, as long as they all remain industrious and civilized. Nay, the more the arts increase in any state, the more will be its demands from its industrious neighbors."

What, then, are the implications of future developments for American business in its dealings with Japan, Western Europe, the Soviet Union and the developing nations?

There is a good deal of talk about a loosening of U.S. ties across the Atlantic and Pacific. And there is some basis for this view: for example, strong isolationist impulses still alive in American political life; chronic anti-Americanism in Western Europe; the self-inflicted wounds on the international economic position of the United States since 1981; and, whether justified or not, less fear on both sides of the Atlantic of a Soviet Union now preoccupied with the restructuring of its domestic life and international arrangements. And, as I noted at the beginning, it is not difficult to write a scenario of fragmentation and international chaos.

But I am inclined to think it a bit more probable that the ties across the Atlantic and Pacific will remain for certain abiding reasons and that they will intensify for certain new ones. The abiding reasons are the deeply rooted common interests of Western Europe and the United States in maintaining a balance of power in Europe, and of Japan, China and the United States in maintaining a balance of power in Asia. In a nuclear age, this requires the presence of substantial U.S. conventional military force in both regions. Most Americans understand that there is no security for us in isolationism, although it is quite possible that a more united Europe and Japan will assume a larger share of common tasks by the year 2000.

These transoceanic ties may well intensify for economic and technological reasons. Every television viewer in the United States is now aware of the heightened financial interdependencies dramatized since October 19 by the intimate interaction of capital markets in New York, Tokyo, Hong Kong, Sydney and London.

The high-tech interdependencies are not yet as well understood. Beneath the surface—and the reality—of technological competition, a rather subtle fact is asserting itself: Each of the major new areas of technology is so diversified that lines of comparative advantage are emerging within each. These are leading to expanding levels of trade in high-tech products and an extraordinary network of binational and multinational high-tech ventures. I have no doubt that sufficiently unwise policies could once again fragment and impoverish the world economy. But it is a harder world to pull apart than that of the 1930s.

Finally, the coming of the Soviet Union into the central affairs of the world economy, and the foreseeable emergence of India, China, Brazil and others, is likely to heighten rather than dilute the common interests of the industrialized world.

So far as the Pacific is concerned, this tendency will be strengthened if the governments of the region, without interfering with the extraordinary private trade and payments network now operating, set up a Pacific Basin intergovernmental organization embracing the region's advanced industrial and developing countries to deal with an increasingly recognized group of supplementary problems and possibilities.

The Soviet Union is obviously undergoing its most profound changes since Lenin seized power in 1917. Gorbachev may or may not succeed in his current effort to restructure Soviet society, but the Soviet Union, like the United States, cannot escape from the reality of the current technological revolution or from the emergence of the new group of technologically competent industrial powers. To deal with these phenomena it must overcome the fact that its noncompetitive system is poorly geared to the task of absorbing new technologies. It must face the fact that neither it nor any other nation is capable of controlling a world of increasingly diffuse power and nationalist assertiveness, and it must do so at a time when awareness of the virtues of competitive markets and aspiration for political democracy are rising in many parts of the world, including the Soviet empire.

Gorbachev appears to understand all this. He is quite explicit that his policies at home are required to prevent the Soviet Union from losing its status as a superpower, and he has concluded that the Soviet economy cannot be fully modernized unless it joins the world economy and becomes internationally competitive. That is why the Soviet Union is in the process of joining the General Agreement on Tariffs and Trade, seeking observer status in the World Bank and the International Monetary Fund, beginning joint ventures, planning a politically precarious price reform and talking, at least, about a future convertible ruble.

I certainly cannot predict precisely where this quite revolutionary adjustment to reality will stand in the year 2000. But in one way or another these are the directions in which powerful historical forces are pushing the Soviet Union. And for an American chief executive, the opportunity for mutually advantageous business arrangements is likely to expand gradually, with many headaches along the way. Should the Soviet Union prove capable of restructuring its political, social and economic institutions in such a way as to permit its talented pool of scientists and engineers to absorb efficiently the large backlog of unapplied technologies available, it may experience a surge of growth like that of Japan after 1955. But slower, uneven progress appears more likely down to the year 2000.

As I argued in the Spring 1987 issue of *Foreign Affairs* ("On Ending the Cold War"), there are good reasons in the emerging world environment for the cold war as we have known it for more than 40 years to wither away; but a poor performance by the United States at home and abroad could unnecessarily revive it.

After a decade of not-so-benign neglect, and another of narrow concentration on Central America, it is time to build a new relationship with Latin America. The essential instruments already exist: the Organization of American States and the Inter-American Development Bank. But the relationship cannot be an exercise in nostalgia for the Alliance of Progress; neither Latin America nor the United States is as it was when President Kennedy made his Alliance speech in March 1961. Latin America is a more mature if hard-pressed region, with wider global interests.

But we share problems and possibilities on which a new agenda could be built (quite aside from a definitive settlement of the debt question): the new technologies, environmental protection, patient joint efforts on some of the hard cases (Bolivia and Haiti, for example) and combined support for subregional efforts in the Caribbean and Central America. There is every reason to revive a dignified dialogue among partners with a Latin America moving toward technological maturity and struggling to sustain democracies consistent with a humane culture.

We will, of course, face other important problems down to the year 2000—problems in the Middle East and Africa and, quite possibly, another phase of relative energy shortage. And Keynes will be at least partially right; unexpected things will certainly happen.

But my central conclusion is quite simple. If we make good my optimistic assumption and face the two challenging revolutions—new technology and the maturation of a good many third-world countries—in an "industrious and civilized" manner, we can go into the new century in a more prosperous and peaceful world than the one we know. As for CEOs, they had better learn more about science and technology and administering in an environment of rapid obsolescence. And an extra foreign language or two won't hurt, because the interaction between our economy and others will surely intensify.

The greatest task of CEOs is not to guess or await the outcome but to play a vigorous role in making the optimistic assumption come true. And this means working much more closely with universities, the labor force, the political process—in short, with the whole community of which they are a critical part.

QUESTIONS FOR CRITICAL ANALYSIS

1. What are the ingredients of the "current crisis" Rostow describes? Have any of these ingredients changed since this essay was published in 1988? Rostow decides to remain optimistic and to believe that the United States will work its way out of the crisis. Do you agree with him? Why, or why not? Does Lamb's analysis of CEOs affect your response to Rostow?
2. Why is cooperation at the state and local level evidence of national success? Can you think of specific examples to support Rostow's theory?
3. What are the two historical developments Rostow notes? How do these developments present both danger and opportunity to America?
4. In what areas has America remained strongly competitive? In what areas does America fall behind other countries? What reasons can you give for both these conditions?
5. According to Rostow, what are the implications of future developments for American businesses dealing with other countries?

QUESTIONS FOR STRUCTURAL ANALYSIS

1. Rostow begins his essay with an italicized statement of purpose and two reservations. Why? How did you react to such an introduction? Is it an effective way to begin the essay?
2. Rostow wrote this essay for the readers of *Business Month*, an audience of executives. If you hadn't been told that, how would you know he expected a business-savvy audience? List and define words, images, and phrases that relate specifically to his intended audience.
3. This essay is organized into three major sections. Describe each section and discuss its relationship to the other two.
4. Rostow uses quotations and historical details effectively in the essay. Make a list of the people he refers to and, next to each name write a brief description of who he is. Why does he refer to them? Did you find that his references detracted from or enhanced his essay? Why?
5. In his conclusion, what specific suggestion does Rostow give to CEOs facing the year 2000? How does the conclusion relate to the rest of the essay? Do you think this is an effective conclusion? Why, or why not?

COMMITMENT

FELIX ROHATYN

Felix Rohatyn (1928–), an investment company executive, has worked with Lazard Freres & Co. since 1948. "Commitment," originally delivered to the French-American Chamber of Commerce on December 1, 1978, warns that America is in danger of losing her democratic ideals because of a cynical, lazy, irresponsible citizenry. The nation faces problems of increasing debt, a bad economy, ineffective schools, racial discrimination, and high adult illiteracy. According to Rohatyn, the commitment of business leaders is a crucial element toward developing solutions for these problems.

Before you begin reading: *What does "democracy" mean? Think about the concept in relation to your life in the United States. In your reading notebook, write a definition of democracy. Then write another paragraph explaining your responsibilities as a citizen toward keeping democracy healthy.*

◆

THE HOLIDAY SEASON IS IN FULL SWING. THANKSGIVING IS over, election day is behind us, Christmas is around the corner; everybody feels optimistic. We have much to be thankful for. New York has survived. Peace may come to the Middle East. The economy is still strong.

But we live in unusual, confusing times, and bizarre things are happening. Washington tries to save the dollar by selling our gold, and to control inflation by a guaranteed-to-be-mild recession. We will try to balance the budget while we increase defense spending by cutting back our spending on the poor and the cities, even though the decay of urban America could be more dangerous than Soviet ambitions. We begin our negotiations with the oil-producing countries, which have already bankrupted the Western world, with the proposition that a further 7 percent price increase would be modest and would make up for the erosion of the dollar which the oil producers have already helped erode in the first place. A theological argument takes place among economists (who, like dermatologists, never seem to solve anybody's problems, but always travel first-class) as to whether we are headed for a mild recession, or a rolling readjustment, or stagflation, or anything that doesn't sound serious and frighten anybody. Howard Jarvis, whose Proposition 13 is as effective a method for dealing with our problems as a neurosurgeon operating with a meat-axe, is acclaimed in Washington as a modern Moses down from the mountain. Just as in the 1960s all truth and wisdom were supposed to reside in that segment of our population barely beyond the age of puberty, so today wisdom comes to us from self-styled conservatives whose economic notions are out of *Alice in Wonderland*. If all of this seems a little strange, it should not be surprising when we look at how we elect our government, and how our leaders, once elected, then govern.

In the last election almost two out of three people of voting age did not exercise their franchise, while the 37 percent of the people who voted were sold candidates the way Procter & Gamble sells detergent. During news programs and football games, *The Mary Tyler Moore Show* and Monday night movies, we were bombarded with thirty-second spots that turned each candidate into an actor. With opinion polls telling the candidates what the voters wanted to hear, and ample money to make sure the voters heard it over and over again, men and women who, with few exceptions, follow rather than lead were given power by a minority of the electorate. Once in office, the same process continues; if saying what the polls tell you to say gets you elected, why not do what the polls tell you to do to stay in office? The trouble is that polls cannot teach you to lead in a crisis; in 1939 when a backbencher screamed at Neville Chamberlain, "Speak for England," he wasn't asking him to take a poll, he was asking him to lead.

Today, despite our current prosperity, we face dangers and uncertainties ahead, fully as deadly as those England faced in 1939. Our economy is out of control, our currency is in danger, our institutions of government unresponsive or inept. The interaction, at every level, between the executive and legislative branches of government produces fewer and fewer solutions to greater and greater problems. We are engaged in a world-wide competition with a brutal, totalitarian ideology, but whether we win or lose depends on whether we can show that our system works, and not on the size of our cruise missiles or the killing range of the neutron bomb. This means not only controlling inflation for the housewife in Columbus but providing education and employment for the young black in Harlem, and providing a hard dollar for the gnome in Zurich.

We are, by any standard, the richest country in the world. We carry the heritage of democracy handed down from Pericles through the great figures of French enlightenment to our founding fathers. Yet we treat this heritage, the most precious of our possessions, with contempt when we abdicate our responsibility to vote, contempt in the way we manage our affairs, contempt in our acceptance of mediocre leadership.

I traveled recently to Israel for the first time. From a jumble of impressions, one came through most strongly: commitment. Commitment to freedom, commitment to survival, commitment to a way of life. People from all backgrounds, from all over the world, clawed a country out of rock and desert, fought for it against great odds, prevailed, and fight to keep it every day. We, on the other hand, with more to fight for than anyone else, seem unwilling to make the slightest effort. Commitment is not fashionable. Cool is the order of the day. Today men with blood as thin as water flaunt their passions as cold as ice. But Pericles was not cool—neither was Thomas Jefferson, nor Winston Churchill, and they made and preserved our world.

Commitment is not a museum piece. A great Frenchman, Jean Monnet, changed the face of postwar Europe when, through sheer personal willpower, he brought about first the European Coal and Steel Authority and then the European Common Market.

Commitment saved New York City from a bankruptcy that many cool and sophisticated people precipitated. New York survived because some of its committed citizens would not let it fail, because these New Yorkers willed it not to. At a time of visible, palpable crisis, people rallied around: private citizens and politicians, Democrats and Republicans, union leaders and bankers, first with a program to stem the tide, second with a program to rebuild the foundation, third with a program for recovery. Recovery may still be a long way off, but we have stemmed the tide and rebuilt the foundation.

America's strength can be enormous—moral, economic, military. In the last twenty years, peaceful revolutions have transformed our society: civil rights and human rights, the emergence of women as an economic and political force, the concern for the environment. Our economy recovered from the last recession and is still going strong. But underneath it all, there are weaknesses, economic and social, which, if not contained, will sap our strength.

The situation of America today is not so different from that of New York City in 1975. The similarities are striking:

- increasing deficits, internal and external, year after year, papered over with accounting gimmicks to allow politicians to sidestep politically difficult decisions
- increasing reliance on borrowed money to finance those deficits (New York financed itself with short-term notes; the United States does it with borrowed Arab oil money) while neglecting capital formation, with resulting dramatic deterioration of physical plant
- creating greater and greater hidden liabilities in the form of unfunded private and public pensions, Social Security, etc.
- losing private-sector jobs, driven out by high taxes and low productivity
- continuing to absorb large numbers of illegal immigrants at a time of high unemployment

New York City was required to prepare a comprehensive multiyear program to cope with our crisis. We had the good fortune to have a governor willing to put his neck on the line and provide leadership, since the program demanded sacrifice from everyone—a reduced labor force, a stretched-out debt, higher transit fares, City University tuition, some rolled-back pension costs and temporarily increased taxes. Our future in New York is still bleak because the country's future is unclear, but we averted a catastrophe because, in a time of need, we were able to act together, we were able to commit, and leadership lived up to our commitment.

What the country faces is not a bigger or smaller recession, more or less inflation, a stronger or weaker dollar. Those are all effects; they are not causes. We face the possible loss of our most precious asset, democracy, surely the most magnificent form of organized life, because we are lazy, cynical and unwilling to make the effort, unwilling to demand the kind of leadership democracy requires. It is easy to blame the politicians, but we put them in office by our votes or our failure to vote. It is easy to blame the unions, but we in the business leadership have exercised no greater restraint. It is easy to blame the press, the academicians, almost anybody but ourselves.

We are at war today: with inflation, with unemployment, with lack of education, with racial discrimination. We are, furthermore, not winning. If we lose, our system of government may not survive. Whether we wind up with left-wing or right-wing authoritarianism is irrelevant; poison is as lethal served from the left as from the right.

New York City found itself at war and put in motion the equivalent of a wartime austerity program and coalition government. A coalition government should manage a similar program on a national scale. If this means gas rationing in order to reduce oil imports, so be it; if it means wage and price restraints, voluntary or mandatory, for some time, so be it; if it means temporarily limiting imports from Japan, so be it.

The President must mobilize the country's dreams as well as its muscle and demand that the people and the Congress support a true wartime program. The hour is very late, almost as late for the United States as it was for New York in 1975. In the city we fought against bankruptcy; Washington is now fighting the same thing but calls it controlling inflation, protecting the dollar, avoiding a recession.

The real question is whether a democracy can find leadership, nobility of purpose and sacrifice only in a time of crisis, at the brink of disaster. Or can it face up to its problems in times that appear to be normal, when the crisis is still only dimly perceived on the horizon? We will soon have the answer, but if the President loses this fight—if collectively we cannot create the climate to help him win—the result will not be a moratorium imposed upon our noteholders or a wage freeze imposed on the unions, but possibly the end of a form of government that since the days of the French Revolution has done more for more people than any other system ever invented. There will be no winners or losers then, simply the story of another nation that was unable to count its blessings and lost sight of its values.

Questions for Critical Analysis

1. Make a list of the seven events Rohatyn mentions in the second paragraph to describe the state of the U.S. economy in 1978. Next to each item write a note indicating the change in its status since 1978.

2. What does Rohatyn think about our election process? Do you agree with him? Why, or why not? What is the connection between our election process and the state of the economy?
3. What dangers does Rohatyn see in America's future? He wrote this essay over ten years ago. Have any of his warnings come true? How?
4. What did Rohatyn learn from his visit to Israel? How does he compare the Israeli attitude to America's? Do you agree? Why, or why not?
5. Why does Rohatyn mention the New York City's bankruptcy in 1975? What do you know about that economic crisis? Why is it appropriate to use New York City as an example?

QUESTIONS FOR STRUCTURAL ANALYSIS

1. Describe Rohatyn's opening paragraph. What is his tone? What is he referring to? Does the reader anticipate the "But" which opens the next paragraph? Why, or why not?
2. What is the thesis of this essay? Where is it stated? Why doesn't Rohatyn state it clearly at the beginning of the essay?
3. In the first half of the essay Rohatyn presents his views of America. Describe his assessment in your own words. What does he offer to support his opinion? How does he feel about America? What clues help you discover his feelings?
4. Rohatyn delivered "Commitment" as a speech before the French-American Chamber of Commerce in New York City in December 1978. What indications can you find to reveal that this was a speech? How does the language reflect its audience of business leaders? How do you suppose the audience reacted?
5. Rohatyn concludes that at issue is not economic growth, or maintaining a standard of living, but protecting America's democratic form of government. Has he convinced you of the urgency of the situation? How?

The Business of Business

Topics for Writing Essays

Many of the questions following each essay can serve as appropriate writing suggestions. Some of the topics listed below expand the prereading exercises, but they can be used without completing that step first.

1. Create a survey on American Business and interview at least 20 people on campus (professors, students, administrators, and staff) to discover their attitudes toward business. Write an analysis of your survey for the student newspaper, making recommendations to the School of Business based on your findings.
2. Compare Lamb's portrait of current CEOs with ideas expressed by both Rostow and Rohatyn. Develop a definition of a leader from these essays, and write an essay on leadership in business.
3. According to Rohatyn, what role must the ordinary citizen play in keeping democracy alive in the United States? Do you agree with him? Does he overstate the negative aspects of citizens' behavior? Check newspapers and other sources to find out how many eligible voters in your community voted in the last election. Interview students and others to see how seriously they considered their voting rights. Use both your research findings and Rohatyn's comments to analyze how people in your community regard their responsibility of citizenship. Write your analysis for publication in the local paper.

Research Possibilities

1. The entrepreneurial spirit has long been considered one of the strengths of American business and industry. Recently, however, studies are suggesting that entrepreneurialism is draining good engineers and managers from major industries and weakening America's economic future. Read articles and books on this subject and write an analysis for an educated audience concerned about retaining America's competitive edge in a global economy.
2. Use John Kenneth Galbraith's essay, published in January 1987 (and written at least a month or two before then) as the basis for a comparison between the Stock Market Crash of October 1987 and his predictions. Is there reason to be concerned that an even greater crash will occur? Write your essay to young investors who want to begin playing the market.

BUSINESS FOR THE TWENTY-FIRST CENTURY

The writers in this section look to America's economic future with cautious optimism, suggesting specific ways to bring about a revitalized, productive society. Kanter focuses on corporate restructuring, Weinig on better educating engineers, Enslow on using "expert systems," and Thurow on changing the context in which free enterprise can function. Although each proposes a different solution, as a group they are encouraged by the belief that America can change downward economic trends and become, once again, the leader on the international stage.

ROSABETH MOSS KANTER, "REAWAKENING THE SPIRIT OF ENTERPRISE: TOWARD AN AMERICAN CORPORATE RENAISSANCE"

SHELDON WEINIG, "MANAGING BETTER"

BETH ENSLOW, "THE PAYOFF FROM EXPERT SYSTEMS"

LESTER THUROW, "CREATING A WORLD-CLASS TEAM"

*R*EAWAKENING THE *S*PIRIT OF *E*NTERPRISE: *T*OWARD AN *A*MERICAN *C*ORPORATE *R*ENAISSANCE

ROSABETH MOSS KANTER

Rosabeth Moss Kanter (1943–), a professor at Yale University's School of Management, serves as a consultant to many Fortune 500 companies. Kanter has earned a reputation as a writer who defines and explains the state of American business and shows the way to productive change. The Change Masters: Innovations and Entrepreneurship in the American Corporation *(1982) demonstrates how successful businesses today are characterized by openness and "participative management." "Reawakening the Spirit of Enterprise" is the final chapter of that book.*

Before you begin reading: *What do you know about the business world? What are your feelings toward corporate leaders? Where do you get your opinions? In your notebook, write two lists, one of 10 positive thoughts about business and one of 10 negative thoughts about business. Next, write an example of a person, company or event (real or fictional) next to each idea.*

◆

> The Renaissance, which bridged medieval and modern times, is not considered a unique blooming, but part of a process of development. Just the same, something happened; it happened by way of contact of cultures, it happened through the reacquisition of classical learning, it happened as the age of exploration doubled the extent of the known world, it happened as new classes of people thrust their way into the political process, and as curious natural philosophers began to ask questions.
>
> ELIZABETH JANEWAY, *POWERS OF THE WEAK*

RIP VAN WINKLE WENT TO SLEEP FOR TWENTY YEARS. When he awakened, the American landscape had changed dramatically, and his bones creaked with age. The world around him was no longer one he understood or in which he could function well.

Will history someday see that classic story as a parable for much of corporate America today—falling asleep in the 1960s and waking up too old, too tired in the 1980s? Or can more organizations learn to operate in the integrative and highly people-centered ways of the innovating companies I have identified?

If American organizations use this opportunity to arouse the potential entrepreneurs in their midst—the people at all levels with new ideas to contribute—then, unlike Rip van Winkle, they could be renewed, refreshed, and readied for a changed world. The spirit of enterprise could thus be reborn, heralding a kind of Renaissance for corporate America.

The first question about a "corporate Renaissance" is its feasibility, especially for older, troubled industries. Doubters wonder whether the existence of more corporate entrepreneurs would really make much of a difference for them. They question whether the success of high-technology firms is really due to better management rather than to growing markets that will absorb virtually anything. In short, are practices characteristic of companies like Hewlett-Packard, "Chipco," and high-tech sectors of GE really transferrable to matured corporate giants?

At extremes of market conditions, of course, the quality of the organization probably does not matter much. Having the right product in a world hungry for it masks a large number of organizational sins: the company can get away with being poorly managed and still do well financially. At the other extreme, where the product is clearly the wrong thing at the wrong time, then no amount of organizational change by itself is likely to guarantee success.

We would search in vain for the organizational alchemy to transform a smokestack industry into a high-technology firm; and attempts to effect a "transmutation" via divestitures and acquisitions deflect important managerial attention from improving the quality of internal operations. Companies take on their shape, and in part become locked into it, from their industry and their history. More recently founded companies can adapt practices from a more modern era and can support more change while their basic systems are still being developed, making it more likely that computer and electronics companies will indeed have more innovation-stimulating practices, while industries with ample time to experience hardening-of-the-organizational-arteries, such as autos and insurance, will have fewer.

Yet despite these broad tendencies, individual firms even within the same industry still vary, and there is a range of differences with respect to investment in people and the encouragement of employees' participation in innovative problem solving. In my comparative study, those firms with early and progressive human-resource practices, when compared with a similar company in the *same industry*, had been significantly more profitable over the last twenty years.

Similarly, it is not only high-technology firms that are characterized by the kinds of practices that keep innovation alive for long periods of time. Procter and

Gamble operates within one of the oldest industries, but has continued to break new ground in product introductions as well as workplace practices. (Indeed, the company considers information about its team-oriented manufacturing facilities "proprietary.") Cummins Engine, well known for its quality-of-work-life programs, occupies a spot in one of the so-called declining industries, but has performed consistently better than other diesel-engine manufacturers. And an even more striking illustration of the potential for transformation of older industries is the speed with which many banks are trying to reorient and develop new products and services as the rules governing financial institutions change. If banks, long considered among the most traditionbound of American corporations, can do it, then so can other industries.

Constraints and environmental conditions count; they make it more or less difficult to carry out organizational objectives, and they present leaders with problems as well as opportunities. It would be naive to fail to recognize this. But within those boundaries, it is the capacity to engage and use human energies effectively that sorts successes from failures, in the long run if not always in the short. Innovations such as new products or market applications, as well as effective organizational problem solving at all levels, depend on people—and the need for these competitive advantages grows with environmental turbulence and a less expansive economy.

Today more than ever, because of profound transformations in the economic and social environment for American business, it should be a national priority to release and support the skills of men and women who can envision and push innovations. This requires, in turn, corporations that operate integratively, that help individuals make the connections and get the tools to move beyond preestablished limits and break new ground, working through coalitions and teams. Making the power available to people at all levels of organizations to take action to introduce or experiment with new strategies and practices, often seen as a luxury of rich times, is in fact a *necessity* for survival and success in difficult times.

"Corporate entrepreneurs" are often the authors not of the grand gesture but of the quiet innovation. They are the ones who translate strategy—set at the top—into actual practice, and by doing so, shape what strategy turns out to mean. Top leaders' general directives to open a new market, improve quality, or cut costs mean nothing without the ability of relevant managers and professionals to design the systems to carry them out or redirect their staffs' activities accordingly. So the meaning of change and the extent to which it can significantly affect an organization can be, in many cases, determined almost exclusively by the initiative and enterprise of people at middle levels and below, who themselves design new ways of carrying out their routine operations that may quickly or eventually add up to an altered state for the organization.

Indeed, without sufficient flexibility to permit random creativity in unexpected—and nonpreferred—places in the organization, many companies would not have developed new programs, new products, or new systems that were eventually adopted as organizationwide initiatives, to the great benefit of the whole. Because innovators have their finger on the pulse of operations, they can see, suggest, and set in motion new possibilities that top strategists may not have considered—until a crisis or galvanizing event makes them search for a successful departure from tradition in the company's own experience.

In short, individuals do not have to be doing "big things" in order to have their cumulative accomplishments eventually result in big performance for the company.

It is in this sense that individuals in the right circumstances are the keys to innovation. They are only rarely the inventors of the "breakthrough" system. They are only rarely doing something that is totally unique or that no one, in any organization, ever thought of before. Instead, they are often applying ideas that have proved themselves elsewhere, or they are rearranging parts to create a better result, or they are noting a potential problem before it turns into a catastrophe and mobilizing the actions to anticipate and solve it.

By being able to get the power to act, individuals are helping the organization stay ahead of change.

The environment—e.g., industry conditions—and history—e.g., a company's past investments—constrain the *arenas* in which corporate entrepreneurs can maneuver, but they do not eliminate the *possibility* for productive innovations in *some* arena.

If the physical or product side of the organization cannot be quickly modified, for example, owing to capital investment and other heavy sunk costs, there is still room for innovation in the organization itself—in modifying production methods, in changing product details to be more responsive to customers, in identifying novel uses, in improving quality, or in taking advantage of the knowledge of the organization's people to respond better and more quickly to the environment—to improve service, to improve relationships, to reduce labor conflict or other forms of costly friction in the company. Repeated studies of innovation in American companies make clear that it need not decline as the company ages or as a product matures but that the domain shifts away from rapid technical changes to changes in method or form of organization.

Even so, one should not rule out the possibility of a dramatic breakthrough in product form or use itself. It is when a company stops believing that it can always do better, regardless of the domain in which excellence is sought, that innovation is stifled.

Thus, the innovating organization needs the people ready to see and act on these possibilities. It needs the people capable of adapting as circumstances change because they already have a broader base of skills, of organizational knowledge, and of relationships in advance of any demand for change. They are flexible and deployable, with retraining time reduced.

In short, a company can make itself adaptable by removing more of the barriers to major changes in *advance* of external crisis or threat. It can have people familiar with problem solving and with working through others in teams, who will be ready to step forward as innovators when they see a need and a possibility. These skills are less necessary in routine operations, of course, where segmentalism can work—units separated from each other, levels working independently, individuals pursuing defined-in-advance jobs without looking for or thinking about improvements other than incremental ones. But under circumstances demanding change, demanding new responses, then an adaptable, cooperative, and even entrepreneurial work force is required.

It is in this sense that modifications in organization design and improvements in human-resource systems constitute innovation-promoting innovations. They make the organization ready to both stimulate and take advantage of unprogrammed innovations that come from participating teams at the bottom and entrepreneurial managers in the middle and higher.

What is important to note about the "failures" of older companies with respect to innovation is not the utter impossibility of change, but rather, how easily it *could* have been done. In both the smaller example of the "Petrocorp" Marketing Services Department and the larger example of General Motors, the pieces are there for transforming changes—toward a more integrative form—with the potential to solve major problems for the company. But if the organization's leaders do not recognize this, and do not put the pieces together, then the potential for innovation-enhancing innovations is lost. If there is any "failure" in these accounts, it is not in the impossibility of transforming change but in the lack of ability on the part of those guiding the systems to understand the change process sufficiently well to take advantage of the innovation in their midst. Maybe these isolated instances of microchanges would not, one by one, "save" the company—but they might change the odds; they might tip the balance.

The true "tragedy" for most declining American companies struggling to keep afloat in this environment is not how far they are from the potential for transformation but rather how close they might come and not know it. How many quiet corporate entrepreneurs have put forward the seeds of ideas for major improvements? How many of them have silently improved their own operations, or slightly shifted production methods, or raised quality standards, or involved their workers in problem-solving teams, and gained in the process an important kind of learning for the company, if leaders had only known? How many quality-of-work-life programs have shown so much potential and yet been limited in their application and spread? How many people *know* that they could contribute more but feel that their company does not care about their efforts?

All any company has to do to explore its own potential to become a more innovating organization is to see what happens when employees and managers are brought together and given a significant problem to tackle, along with the power tools—the resources, information, and support—to help them meet the challenge. The energy and excitement that are unleashed, the ideas that come bubbling forth, the zest for work that suddenly appears in employees who had looked like "deadwood" are just a few of the indications that there is more "entrepreneurial spirit" to be tapped in most organizations, more willingness to cooperate in solving problems when the roadblocks stemming from segmentalism are removed.

Many executives who are otherwise hard-boiled and tough-minded evaluate the impact of their innovation-stimulating organizational change efforts in just such qualitative terms. When I push them for measures, they counter with intuitive yardsticks. For example: "All I have to do is walk through the factory and I know it feels different around here. People say hello in a different way. They smile. They are tackling their work with energy. They push back. I hear from them. There are ideas bubbling up from the bottom. . . . I used to avoid walking through the plant if I could help it, but now it's a pleasure."

The executive who spoke those words was clear that there would be a payoff in both productivity and innovation to his support for a more integrative, participative organization, and it would clearly show up in financial results. But he did not feel that he had to justify the creation of an energetic organization merely on the basis of bottom-line results. After all, that would defeat one of the purposes of his new style of organization: to begin to treat people as contributing individuals rather than an anonymous mass whose primary purpose was fitting into the slots the company had made available.

Thus, if there is a realm where economic and human interests coincide, it is here, in the creation of innovating organizations. Reporting the impact only in terms of numbers is to deny a very important part of the reality of these kinds of changes. After all, as people, we live out our work lives not only through abstractions like numbers but rather through the numerous daily encounters that give us opportunities for contributing—or not—as the organization's structure and culture allow.

HOW TO BEGIN

Obviously, not everybody in an organization should be involved in innovation and change all, or even much, of the time. Even while considering change, companies have to manage a wide range of ongoing operations where efficiencies may require repetitive and routinized tasks, tightly bounded jobs, and clearly defined authority. Specialization of organization segments and limited contact between them can be an excellent strategy where no change is required, where repeating what is known *works* because both the demands and the activities to meet them are predictable. So innovation is not the *only* task of a successful company; the structure must also allow for maintenance of ongoing routines.

When trying to visualize the kind of organization that has *both* an array of routine jobs and opportunities for innovation, I am reminded of a common magician's truck using a set of large "magic rings." To set the stage, the magician hands five separate rings perhaps 8 to 10 inches in diameter to a volunteer from the audience for inspection. The rings each appear perfectly smooth and unbroken, and try as he or she might, the volunteer cannot get the rings to connect. Then the magician takes the rings back and tosses them into the air, and they immediately interlock. For the next few minutes, the magician dazzles the audience with displays of all the possible configurations of interlocking rings.

This provides an intriguing metaphor for the innovating organization. For a large part of its ongoing operations, an innovating organization may look on the surface just like a segmented one. It has a clear structure; its organization charts may show a differentiation into departments or functional units, there may be stated reporting relationships, and people may occupy specific jobs with specific job descriptions and bounded responsibilities. Just like the magic rings, the parts can be separated and, for routine purposes, dealt with separately. But with the toss of a problem, the additional connections between and across segments become clear: executive teams considering decisions together; "dotted line" reporting relationships to another area or more; multidisciplinary project teams; regular meetings of councils representing several areas; crosscutting task forces; territories shared by more than one function; teams of employees pulling together to improve performance; networks of peers who exchange information and support each other's projects.

It is the possibility that the separate rings can indeed be easily connected, when the need arises, that gives the organization its potential for innovation.

Integrative, participative mechanisms do not *replace* the differentiation of definable segments that carry out clear and limited tasks; they supplement it. They prevent the existence of segments from turning into segmentalism. This is the idea behind a "parallel" organization presented earlier, a second organization that links the separate rings of the maintenance-oriented organization in flexible and shifting ways to solve problems and guide changes. There is a clear structure for routine operations overlaid with vehicles for participation. There is a predictable routine punctuated by episodes of high involvement in change efforts.

Top executives, whose mandate is to define the organization's structure, are the appropriate "magicians" in this case. They are the ones who can allow the tossing of the rings to connect people in new ways, across segment boundaries, so that they can participate in solving problems.

The idea behind having a second, or parallel, organization alongside routine operations only makes explicit what is already implicit in an integrative, innovating company: the capacity to work together cooperatively regardless of field or level to tackle the unknown, the uncertain. In a formal, explicit parallel organization, this is not left to happenstance but is guided—managed—to get the best results for both the company and the people involved.

Note that the parallel organization is not itself another specific "program" to temporarily solve an immediate local problem (isolating bits and pieces of problems from each other in segmentalist fashion and not allowing solutions to affect the whole system) but rather a means for managing innovation, participation, and change to ensure a *continuing* adaptive organization and an adaptive population within it. But under the leadership of the parallel organization may be any number of specific "programs," improvements, R&D efforts, and problem-solving groups. Its steering committee may manage an array of integrative vehicles—from standing committees linking parts of the organization on issues of major policy concern to temporary problem-solving groups or teams to innovative projects initiated by corporate entrepreneurs.

As the issues and problems change, so does the configuration of the "rings" making up the parallel organization. The steering committee, as manager of this flexible and responsive system, makes the links among the rings, creating new links in new circumstances—and connects the parallel organization to ongoing operations. This connection is important, in both directions. It helps make the problem-solving efforts responsive to the needs of the rest of the system, and it helps ensure that they in turn can take full advantage of the innovations derived from parallel-organization efforts.

There is a parallel organization guiding change at the divisions making up Honeywell's Defense and Marine Systems Group, for example. There the steering committee is chaired by each division general manager and consists of all his direct reports plus other key operations heads. At different times, the steering committee is managing different projects; in mid-1982 they included an advisory committee monitoring the implementation of a new performance communication system it had designed; a standing committee on community relations; nine task teams on major employee concerns; a study group considering how to involve the union on the steering committee; and a number of individuals to whom divisionwide tasks had been assigned. At the same time, the steering committee continued to take a broad view of policy and to examine long-range goals.

What is striking about Honeywell's participative activities is their careful *management*. The steering committee, with its staff, was watching over budgets, writing guidelines for proposals, establishing accountabilities, communicating to the rest of the organization, and generally handling all the logistics needed to make the parallel organization function effectively. In short, the parallel organization at Honeywell is a coherent vehicle for ensuring that the conditions supporting innovation and productive change are present in the division. (People still do their regular jobs in the routine hierarchy, but they also have a second way to contribute, through teams and task forces, above and beyond the limits of their job.) It is not surprising that Richard Boyle, the division general manager leading this activity, is known as an "entrepreneur" around Honeywell. For him the division's outstanding financial results, well above plan, and its future projections are inextricably connected to the commitment to participative management; besides, "it saves us [the executives] time when we can get more of the organization involved in helping us be ready for the future."

Thus, an appropriate place to begin replacing segmentalism with the integrative approaches that support innovation is with the creation of a second structure, a structure for change, parallel to and connected with the company's ongoing structure for doing business as it has already learned how to do. Building a steering committee to guide this structure for change is itself an integrative step: the team at the top working cooperatively across functional lines to view their territory as a whole and combine data about needed changes from many perspectives—problem seeking as well as problem solving. This group can look for and reward innovations that already exist—the departures from tradition that suggest new options—as well as stimulate and encourage other innovations. It can set broad guidelines that give direction to action, channeling the entrepreneurial instincts of innovators in productive directions. And it can decide whether and how to change the way ongoing activities are handled.

Top management has many options for stimulating more innovation. It can assure that a portion of each job definition is loose, that roles and interests overlap enough to force people to work together across disciplinary or hierarchical boundaries, through multiple connections fostering cross-segment initiatives and teamwork. It can support and coordinate the actions of innovators, providing legitimacy, information, and resources to potential corporate entrepreneurs. By seeing the connection of decisions to one another, and encouraging and supporting coalitions, it can avoid segmentalism and make changes that will help support valuable initiative so that it does not slide away. It can make sure that all kinds of people and all kinds of levels in the organization feel included in an integrated whole, with the chance to participate in making a difference for the organization.

And then, the new approach can cascade downward. Teamwork to guide a parallel organization at the top can be matched by similar teams at the head of each major operation, serving integrative functions on more local levels, and moving downward to create integrative mechanisms for middle management, across level, across function, across barriers of race, sex, or employment category. When this occurs, the opportunity for lower echelons to participate in improvement-oriented teams (such as quality circles or committees or task forces or simply staff meetings) can be related appropriately to a consistent organizational culture and coherent strategic directions—not detached pieces handled segmentally but integrated groups connected to an organizational style that begins at the top and that supports local flexibility and initiative.

With my findings about innovating organizations in mind, it is not hard to imagine an action program to remove roadblocks to innovation at a "Southern Insurance," a "Meridian Telephone," or a Petrocorp. These would be among the important elements to be managed by the executive team or its designated steering committee:

Encouragement of a culture of pride. Highlight the achievements of the company's own people, through visible awards, through applying an innovation from one area to the problems of another—and letting the experienced innovators serve as "consultants."

Enlarged access to power tools for innovative problem solving. Provide vehicles (a council? an R&D committee? direct access to the steering committee?) for supporting proposals for experiments and innovations—especially those involving teams or collaborators across areas.

Improvement of lateral communication. Bring departments together. Encourage cross-fertilization through exchange of people, mobility across areas. Create cross-functional links, and perhaps even overlaps. Bring together teams of people from different areas who share responsibility for some aspect of the same end product.

Reduction of unnecessary layers of hierarchy. Eliminate barriers to resource access. Make it possible for people to go directly after what they need. Push decisional authority downward. Create "diagonal" slices cutting across the hierarchy to share information, provide quick intelligence about external and internal affairs.

Increased—and earlier—information about company plans. Where possible, reduce secretiveness. Avoid surprises. Increase security by making future plans known in advance, making it possible, in turn, for those below to make their plans. Give people at lower levels a chance to contribute to the shape of change before decisions are made at the top. Empower and involve them at an earlier point—e.g., through task forces and problem-solving groups or through more open-ended, change-oriented assignments, with more room left for the *person* to define the approach.

Before these kinds of organizational changes can be made, of course, corporate leaders must make a personal commitment to do what is needed to support innovation. They must believe that times are different, understand that the transforming nature of our era requires a different set of responses. They need a sense of sufficient power themselves that they can be expansive about sharing it. They need a commitment to longer-term objectives and longer-term measures. And they as individuals must think in integrative rather than segmentalist ways, making connections between problems, pulling together ideas across disciplines, viewing issues from many perspectives. In short, top executives need at least some of the qualities of corporate entrepreneurs in order to support this capacity at lower levels in the organization.

If there is any domain over which top executives have control, it is organizational culture and structure, the setting of the context for others around and below them. Even if ideas bubble up, as I showed at Chipco and other innovative organizations, organizational style bubbles down. Even the most effective of corporate entrepreneurs soon reach the limit of their own ability to push innovative improvement when the environment set at the top does not support their activities for the use of their results. Indeed, until corporate leaders see the nature of this environment in its full-blown implications, they are doomed to make segmental, and therefore ultimately less effective, responses.

Instead of continuing to think that they can run the organization from the top, effective leaders will be those who know how to take advantage of the capacity of those below. They will be those who appreciate the fundamental transformation in the way organizations and the people in them must work to fit the economic and social challenges of our time. And thus, they can help contribute to a resurgence of the entrepreneurial spirit even within large organizations, a virtual Renaissance for corporate America.

THE AMERICAN WAY TO A CORPORATE RENAISSANCE

The models for the innovating organization are not particularly new, although they have received greater public attention and legitimacy in just the last few years, when the news reached us that certain of our successful foreign competitors might be beating us because of more people-conscious, commitment-producing workplaces. During the last twenty years, a large number of tools have been made available to American companies to stimulate the highest performance from their employees and managers, from more meritocratic performance-appraisal systems that reward individual achievement to cross-level problem-solving teams.

The tools are there—if we care to use them.

To me, that is the central issue: not inventing still another fancy new management system with its own acronym or alphabet label, but using what we already have. The issue is to create the conditions that enable companies to take advantage of the good ideas which already exist, by taking better advantage of the talents of their people. By encouranging innovation and entrepreneurship at all levels, by building an environment in which more people feel included, involved, and empowered to take initiative, companies as well as individuals can be the masters of change instead of its victims.

New ideas will "save the American economy." New ideas will provide our competitive advantage.

The source of new ideas is people. That's why an organization's way of educating and involving people, distributing them among assignments, and rewarding their efforts are so critical in its ability to innovate. Selecting "good" people, certainly. But there are not enough creative geniuses to go around. And there are too many problems in most American companies in this era for them to be able to afford to have only a handful of people thinking about solutions.

Individuals make a difference. That's the positive side of "American individualism"—entrepreneurs not afraid to break the mold in seeking to break a record or competing to win a game. In organizations, this initiative is best expressed through teamwork, and thus we saw that managerial entrepreneurs with innovative accomplishments were most likely to have participative/collaborative styles, to involve a team of others to bring their idea to fruition. Innovation and participation are linked. Strong individuals, along with a tradition of teamwork, bring productive accomplishments into being.

It is hard to mention "teams" or "participation" anymore without someone's labeling them "Japanese-style management." In the first place, this is faintly ridiculous, because it is just as American to use teams, and when American companies do it, they are doing it as Americans, out of their own organizational priorities and images. But if we stopped there, with the idea of participation, we might indeed be missing a distinctively American strength: the initiative of individuals. Innovating companies emphasize teamwork, but they also reward individuals, and they give internal entrepreneurs free rein to pioneer—as long as they can also work with the team. So "American-style" participation does not and should not mean the dominance of committees over individuals, the submergence of the individual in the group, or the swallowing of the person by the team, but rather *the mechanism for giving more people at more levels a piece of the entrepreneurial action.*

Thus, companies need to be encouraged to *invest* in people rather than paying them off—that is, to channel more of their "rewards" into budgets for projects or new ventures and less into after-the-fact bonuses for executives. Tax incentives could help; e.g., by a combination of deferred compensation for individuals and write-offs for the company, pools of working capital could be made available to support innovative projects inside a corporation.

Indeed, Harry Olson, a former senior executive of American Express, has proposed that severence pay for personnel laid off during a recession could be treated this way, as "venture capital" rather than a payoff to the individuals terminated. He argued that the company could use the same amount of money that would otherwise be paid directly to the individuals to set each of them up in a business; this in turn might create long-term gain for the company. Even if only a small proportion of the businesses paid off, the company would be no worse off than it is by the present system of cash payments that are not reinvested for its benefit. A similar reasoning is behind the efforts of companies like 3M and Levi-Strauss to set up internal venture-capital banks to fund new ventures developed by internal entrepreneurs.

Investment in internal human-resource systems is also related to the encouragement of corporate entrepreneurship in the interests of productivity and innovation. To the extent that innovation and change can save jobs through better company performance, and to the extent that an investment in human resources creates a better labor pool not only for the current company but also for the society at large should people change companies, then it is in the public interest as well as the company's interest to support investments in these areas. There could be tax credits, for example, for the development of training programs or other internal educational efforts meeting certain standards—in part a way of acknowledging the important educational role increasingly played by major corporations in today's society.

While not all aspects of a company's human-resource practices are reducible to concrete manifestations that could be supported in this fashion, a surprising number would lend themselves to this: e.g., the start-up costs of improving labor-management cooperation or beginning a joint labor-management committee; the R&D costs of a program to encourage more innovation in manufacturing methods; the retraining costs of shifting workers from one manufacturing sector to another or giving them skills to be more adaptable in the face of the changing technical environment. (It is striking to contemplate what kinds of changes could be encouraged by this method. For the most part, government interventions in the human-resource realm, e.g., safety and affirmative action, have been negative—threatening companies with punishment if they do not comply with regulations but not providing any rewards for quick compliance and creative change.)

If more companies are encouraged to increase their investment in their people, following the lead of the innovating companies I have described by replacing segmentation with integration, then this could in fact turn out to be a transforming era—one that might even be termed an American "corporate Renaissance" because of its humanistic as well as economic benefits.

In an American corporate Renaissance, we could see the reawakening of a dormant spirit of enterprise at all levels of organizations, among all kinds of workers. Entrepreneurship and initiative would be rewarded in large as well as small companies, and there would be a sense of shared purpose—almost a missionary zeal—with which people approached their work. The humanistic thrust inherent in the idea of a Renaissance would be manifested in corporate attention toward ending the "miseries" of earlier corporate work systems, integrating quality-of-life concerns with productivity. The potential for doing this already exists, in countless offices and factories all over America beginning to see the virtues of a more participative workplace.

The Renaissance analogy suggests a growing "intellectuality" surrounding the American corporation. No longer the mindless machine, the corporation could be the instrument for meaningful intellectual exploration. There is already a growing trend toward self-conscious corporate examination of purpose and philosophy, sometimes expressed in the narrower and more technical idea of a corporate "mission" but increasingly being expressed in more philosophical statements of operating principles that stress human concerns. I have participated in the drafting of several such statements by groups of executives, including phrases such as "work life and home life have interacting needs that will be recognized." What is striking is not the mechanics of producing such statements (talk is cheap, after all) but the self-reflective discussions that take place among corporate leaders who are now participating in perhaps their first chance to examine their own and others' values. I am not suggesting that such statements of philosophy always result in immediate action or solve all of the workplace problems to which they are addressed, but they are an important starting point for a corporate Renaissance.

This growing concern with corporate purpose and long-term responsibilities would be aided by a quest for leaders characterized by long-range, integrative thinking. And by their encouragement to operate, once in executive office, toward long-term objectives. Perhaps it would even be possible to build these encouragements into corporate charters, the very framework for the corporation itself.

Corporate governance—e.g., the shape and composition of the Board of Directors and the officer group—has been much discussed over the last few decades as a means to ensure that the public interest, as well as that of key groups such as employees, is reflected in corporate decisions. But there has been practically no discussion of the use of such mechanisms to encourage investment in the long term, including in its traditional form of R&D expenditures. But what if, for example, there were tax incentives, or even requirements, for publicly chartered firms to withhold a proportion of an officer's or a director's compensation until five years after retirement? Would this decrease the tendency to manage against stock price or quarterly income statements and encourage investment in activities that might not pay off until after the executive's term? Would this encourage more careful succession planning and development of successors?

At this point, of course, such suggestions seem fanciful, and we can only speculate about their likely results. But consider that entrepreneurs who *found* companies often have to be willing to wait years for a return, trying to build a long-term capacity rather than just make a quick killing. Why shouldn't corporate executives too have to wait for rewards until the ultimate results of their actions are known?

A long-term view and concern with corporate philosophy and mission is only one part of a Renaissance-style intellectual awakening. The intellectual dimension of a possible corporate Renaissance is represented in more mundane ways by the increasing numbers of "knowledge workers" whose task performance is linked to the quality of their intellect, a rapid growth in "intellectual" staff functions such as planning departments, and a general increase in the amount of education carried on by and within corporations. There are even some companies hiring historians and cultural anthropologists to help them grasp ineffable dimensions of the corporate experience.

We could see a potential Renaissance in the flowering of literature highlighting the drama and excitement of activities within the new-style innovating corporations. Most great literature about business in the past seemed to fall into one of two camps: muckracking treatments of the corporation as oppressor of the human spirit, or cynical accounts of how someone beat the system. But otherwise, great art has not come out of the corporate sector; only dull monotony and Babbitry. (The great executive/poet Wallace Stevens did not write about his insurance company.) Between Horatio Alger and the recent past, we have only Willy Loman and the man in the gray flannel suit—and stories about the smothering of creativity . . . But today business stories are beginning to be told for their dramatic qualities as well as their immediate news value. The corporation is being seen as a human arena, and thus one out of which great tragedy and great comedy might be crafted—or gripping adventure stories like *The Soul of a New Machine*, about the design of a new computer.

There is drama in innovation and change that does not exist in a segmentalist environment. Out of the new high-tech companies in the Silicon Valley and Route 128, populated by the generation that gave us beads and plumage, has come a more colorful and expressive kind of existence, full of Friday parties-by-the-company-pool, tales of legendary heroes who found important companies but occupy the smallest office, and rituals like a "boot camp" to teach new managers about company culture. Thus, business life in an innovating company may be seen not only as a necessity, but as *interesting*—a life through which people can express themselves.

This Renaissance could also be signaled by the beginning of an end of a "Dark Ages" of insularity, closed boundaries, and chauvinism of all kinds. The potential for this is clear, though we still have a distance to go. With awareness and acknowledgment of the successes of foreign competition, American companies have become less smug and insular, willing to learn from other countries and other companies, integrating their overseas operations into the domestic mainstream—but respecting the differences of other cultures, and not automatically assuming American superiority. A greater sense of community and social responsibilities would also bring about a corporate Renaissance. Indeed, I nominate Minneapolis as the capital city for the corporate Renaissance because of the pioneering efforts of companies like Dayton-Hudson, General Mills, Honeywell, Control Data, and others to break down boundaries between company and community, behave responsibly, develop new work systems, and join together to promote these values.

Other forms of chauvinism and insularity would have to be overcome to warrant the Renaissance label, of course: assumptions of managerial superiority, male superiority, white superiority. But companies *could* do it—we have models of successful work systems that are more integrative environments—if they chose to put a commitment into the effort. Models exist.

Finally the potential for an American corporate Renaissance would be enhanced by the kinds of people developed and rewarded in leading-edge innovating companies: broader-gauged, more able to move across specialist boundaries, comfortable working in teams that may include many disciplines, knowledgeable about how to manage ambiguous assignments and webs of interdependencies. In short, Renaissance people—men and women of skill and cultivation who could function simultaneously in several organizational worlds.

The style of thought and problem-solving capacity associated with such Renaissance people are encouraged by a strong, affordable educational system that combats narrow vocationalism and permits people the luxury of studying a variety of fields before becoming too specialized. *Affordable* is the key word. When a liberal-arts education is not only priced out of the reach of most middle-income families but also appears to be a frill in a job-hungry society where there is no public assistance for either job finding or translation of a general education into a specific entry credential, than we encourage single-skilled people unable to function on the kinds of cross-disciplinary teams that produce innovation—and less adaptable when circumstances change. Thus, the potential for a corporate Renaissance would be enhanced by public—and really, federal—financing of higher education, particularly in the liberal arts.

Clearly we will always require a large number of specialists, particularly technically trained personnel skilled in the newest technologies. But if their education is balanced by a general education giving them a broader view and an ability to make intellectual and interpersonal connections with people in other fields, then the potential innovative capacity of the organizations that employ them is expanded. Some of those who become general managers in the most innovative high-technology firms have minimal technical competence but are well educated in an integrative discipline—including lawyers or personnel experts I met who had risen to head divisions in engineering-based companies. Purely technical experts are often unable to put all the pieces together to manage a business in a demanding, rapidly changing environment; Renaissance people are required.

If we were to have a corporate Renaissance, the organization itself would be the arena in which its great achievements would take place: new products, markets, policies, structures, methods, and philosophies. The excitement of change, the drama of invention captures the imagination in a way that routine, everyday work in a defined job does not. Being part of a team designing a new program for the company can give people a heightened sense of importance and involvement, an experience of creation that punctuates the rest of their ongoing work experience. Changing a part of an organization, inventing its shape can be fun, can be uplifting. And thus, some of the more deadening aspects of work in segmented systems could be alleviated by the opportunity to move beyond or outside of the job to innovate.

Of course, the organization itself can be the arena for innovation only if corporate leaders are focused on their own operations as the realm for investment, rather than seeking financial gains by manipulating assets—merging, acquiring, and divesting bundles of capacity rather than putting resources into increasing or redirecting that capacity itself.

As the recent Bendix debacle has made clear, attempts at mergers and acquisitions that serve no productive purposes are made possible in part by the ability of companies to write off certain of the costs involved against their taxes—in essence, a public subsidy of such activity. But it would be more clearly in the public interest to encourage companies like Bendix to reinvest their profits (or gains from the sale of assets) in the development of their own businesses, as Edgar Bronfman, chairman of Seagram's and himself a player in a large takeover battle with Du Pont, suggested in a column in *The New York Times*. To the extent that the marriage metaphor applies to a merger—whether it is a "shotgun romance" or a "courtship"—we can also see that our present system encourages companies to increase the "divorce" rate by "trading in spouses" rather than working on improving the quality of existing marriages. Under these circumstances, less attention is paid to internal innovation and fewer resources are made available to invest in it. But internal investment is what creates the climate for the innovations allowing companies to stay ahead in a changing environment.

In a corporate Renaissance, in short, companies would be more like "families" making long-term commitments to the development, health, and prosperity of each of their members, and looking to all of them for productive new ideas.

The potential exists for an American corporate Renaissance, with its implied return to greatness. Because recent economic conditions have been so unfavorable for American business, leaders should be motivated to search for new solutions—and to engage their entire work force in the search. I argue that innovation is the key. Individuals can make a difference, but they need the tools and the opportunity to use them. They need to work in settings where they are valued and supported, their intelligence given a chance to blossom. They need to have the power to be able to take the initiative to innovate.

Whether the promise of this corporate Renaissance is fulfilled depends on how fully corporate leaders understand this need and decide to act on it. It depends on whether we can come to embrace change, to see it as an opportunity, and thus to stimulate the people in our organizations to take action to master it.

As a nation, we can no longer afford to do otherwise.

QUESTIONS FOR CRITICAL ANALYSIS

1. Kanter advocates "human resource" programs as a determining factor in corporate success. What does she mean? How would such programs affect the viability of the company?

2. What does Kanter mean by the phrase "corporate entrepreneur"? Can you translate this concept to your campus? What would "campus entrepreneurs" do?
3. How do companies "take on their shape" from their industry and history? What does this imply about the future?
4. What is "parallel organization"? How would it work in a practical sense?
5. Discuss the ways Kanter uses the renaissance analogy. Why does she refer to the Renaissance? What connections does she make with corporate America? What other connections could you make?

QUESTIONS FOR STRUCTURAL ANALYSIS

1. What are the implications of the Janeway quote which prefaces the essay? How does the reference to Rip Van Winkle work in the introduction? Are these good devices to introduce the subject? Why, or why not?
2. Examine the third paragraph closely and notice the conditional words and phrases: "if," "potential entrepreneurs," "could be." What is the affect of these words? What tone do they set?
3. Kanter uses many examples from business and industry to support her points. What kind of information does she provide the reader? Does she give you enough for you to understand why the company is a useful example? Evaluate the examples according to your response to them.
4. Kanter organizes this essay into three major sections. Summarize each section and discuss how they work together to develop her ideas.
5. At which point in the essay does Kanter switch to give advice explicitly? What does this switch indicate about who she believes her audience is? What response does she expect from her reader?
6. The conclusion includes a wrap-up, a warning, and a call to action. Is it an appropriate conclusion for the essay? What are its strengths?

*M*ANAGING *B*ETTER

SHELDON WEINIG

Sheldon Weinig (1928–), chairman of the Materials Research Corporation, presented this paper at a symposium on the state of the U.S. economy in 1986 to celebrate the fortieth anniversary of the Joint Economic Committee of the U.S. Congress. Among other things, Weinig argues that if American business and industry are to increase productivity, they must invest in people as well as in machines.

Before you begin reading: *What do engineers do? What images come into your mind when you think about engineering? Think about these questions and then, in your reading notebook, write a paragraph describing why you think engineers are important to America's economic future.*

◆

IT IS QUITE OBVIOUS THAT IF WE ARE TO RETAIN ANY SEMblance of our international competitiveness, we must increase productivity in the United States. Our record to date is quite dismal and this, of course, was clearly evidenced by the 1.5 percent annualized decrease in productivity posted during the fourth calendar quarter of 1985.

We speak of productivity as the key to future prosperity. I am afraid that is too optimistic. Before prosperity, we had best consider sustaining some semblance of competitiveness in the international marketplace. Much has been discussed about the impact of the cost of capital (US cost of capital is threefold that of the Japanese), the level of corporate taxation (considerably higher for growth companies as compared to "smokestack industries"), and various tax incentives on productivity in the US (with productivity lagging, the Government desires to withdraw the investment incentives of the 1981 tax-cut law).

I don't mean to minimize the impact of financial factors on productivity. But of one thing I am certain, without committed employees in general and specifically committed engineers, there cannot be any significant increase in productivity.

It is much too easy to forget the human dimension in the productivity equation as we become more and more computer and automation oriented in our thinking. Computerization and automation are the results of human effort, and in turn their ongoing successful operation in the flexible manufacturing environment required for the future is also highly people-dependent.

The human dimension is a somewhat different vantage point than the cosmic view of macro-economics. It is not as easy to formulate a quantitative analysis of the people effect on productivity. Capital cost, accelerated depreciation, investment tax credits and R&D tax credits lend themselves to a myriad of calculations and predictive equations of their single and collective effects on US industry; however, I am not so sure the relationship to productivity is clearly definable. All, of course, are important and definitely have some effect, but none is as critical as the human dimension. It probably cannot be understood until you view the problem from the "enterprise level," or perhaps even lower at the "trench level," of doing business.

The task of developing committed employees, never easy, may be even more difficult in the future than it has been in the past. For example, managing human resources in the future will present entirely different challenges for corporations and the old methods will be, for the most part, anachronistic. The traditional workforce of yesterday, whose main focus was salary and salary-equivalent benefits, who found strength as part of a collective group that rarely *intellectually* challenged management, has been replaced by a non-docile, individualist, provocative and creative body of mixed gender, mixed language, and mixed work objectives. Even to think of applying the quick fix remedy of emulating Japanese management techniques is nonsense.

We are not a homogeneous people similar to the Japanese, and our culture is in many instances in direct opposition to many of their business practices. The heterogeneity of the US population is not a second-order effect, it is primary to our thinking and behavioral patterns. It must be an important aspect of our strategic planning of human resource management.

I recently asked a vice president of a major US semiconductor manfacturer with operating plants in both the US and Japan why the device (chip) yields in their Japanese facility was nearly 20 percent greater than in their US plants. He explained that the most critical factor in semiconductor yields is the quantity of particulate (dirt) that falls onto the surface of the silicon wafer. Each falling particulate can effectively destroy a chip. Particulate comes from the normal and continuous shedding of human skin, cosmetics worn by the operators, lung particulate from smoking and about every other source imaginable. Cleanliness and care are primary to running a semiconductor business.

In Japan, he explained, the company's workforce consists entirely of Japanese women and management has been able to train this homogeneous, dedicated employee group not to wear makeup, not to smoke for at least one hour before entering the clean room, to be fastidious about personal cleanliness and even to take fewer tea and toilet breaks because entry to and exit from the clean room exacerbates the particulate problem.

In contrast, he said, his US workforce consisted of a polyglot mixture of whites, blacks, hispanics, orientals, etc. "Can you imagine asking this heterogeneous group of American workers not to smoke for one hour before entering the clean room, not to wear makeup for women (no beards or mustaches for men), and to take fewer coffee or toilet breaks?" That the difference is only 20 percent is surprising. This doesn't mean that we have to give up manufacturing semiconductors in the US; it means our approach to human management must be vastly different.

Secondly, corporate America must rid itself of the illusion that technical superiority is an American birthright. In the 1950s and 1960s, US technology was so advanced that is was possible for US industry to ship almost anything without the necessity of troubling themselves with anything as mundane as product reliability or even operability. (I sometimes think that some process equipment shipped by my company to customers like Texas Instruments worked only on Thursday afternoons, during which time TI produced silicon wafers with semiconductor yields of 10 to 14 percent; and yet both TI and MRC, producer and supplier, grew rapidly and profitably during that era.)

The US as a country in that time frame truly had world dominance in technology. We perceived that technological leadership position as an absolute—we truly believed that our high-tech creativity could not be challenged, let alone equalled. Not only is this no longer valid, but Americans now understand that it *can* be invented there ("there" for the most part meaning Pan-Pacific countries like Japan and Korea). Perhaps the greatest danger to our society is that many Americans no longer believe that *it can be invented here*.

Is there a viable solution, or at least course of action, for this country if we aren't to witness the total disintegration of our technological and manufacturing capabilities. Are we really all going to end up as griddle men at local McDonalds? Are service industries going to be the only available source of employment for American youth? I would like to think not, and yet I must admit that this country's plans, actions and results to date have not been overly effective.

I believe that the key to any improvement in our technological and manufacturing position is strongly dependent upon the human dimension in industry and, more specifically, highly dependent upon the contributions of the engineering profession. If we don't improve the attitude, effectiveness and number of our engineers, then I do not believe that we can avoid industrial catastrophe in this country.

The United States requires a large number of high quality, committed engineers. Without them, there is no possibility of altering the downward spiral of our technological position or manufacturing base. Engineering skills are fundamental to a turnaround.

Shocking as it may seem, if I were beginning a new technological enterprise today, my play would be as follows:

Innovate in the United States
engineer in Japan
produce in Korea
sell like hell all over the world.

(Please note where I would do the engineering.)

Let us examine some aspects of the engineering problem in the United States. First, let us deal with the numbers. Seven percent of college graduates in the US are engineering majors, whereas in Germany and Japan the total is approximately 40 percent. These numbers, although depressing, do not accurately reflect how really bad it is. For example, in Japan nearly 100 percent of graduating engineers go on to practice their profession. In the US, five years after graduation approximately 35 to 40 percent of the engineers are no longer practicing their profession. The five-year sticking ratio for the profession is about 0.6 (perhaps the worst sticking ratio for any profession).

The disillusionment of practicing engineering is manifested in many ways. For example, engineers are the single largest group of candidates pursuing MBA degrees. This course of study doesn't enhance the possibility of their continuing in real engineering positions. Thousands of engineers choose to go into sales because they perceive the monetary rewards as practicing engineers to be insufficient for their financial ambitions. Others go into medicine, law, anything, so they don't have to pursue an engineering career. Further, the relatively low salaries paid to engineers as compared to other professions make one question whether superior students are being attracted to the engineering schools.

And yet, despite the obvious shortage of qualified engineers in the US, thousands of engineers were *laid off* in 1985 when the electronics and computer industries experienced one of their periodic economic downturns. This country is the only free world nation that uses layoffs as a corrective method of countering the vagaries of the economic business cycle.

The real question then is how do we improve the plight of the engineers so that we can attract more and better students and then keep them motivated to remain engineers. It is obvious that employment security is an absolute necessity for American industry, especially technology firms and especially for the hard core of engineering and technical talent.

Dr. Eric Block, president of the National Science Foundation and formerly vice president of IBM Corporation, noted that the productivity revolution which should result from the greater use of computer applications and robots should ultimately enrich all of our lives. Scientists, engineers, technicians and production workers will all benefit from the rapid changes occurring because of the computer revolution. Production workers, instead of operating machines, will control their operations and the factory will be process rather than product driven.

In productivity jargon, it means that the factory will be flexible and that rapid changeover to permit different products to be manufactured could be made in the shortest possible time. This, however, requires far better educated employees than we have ever had in the United States. It means that industry must make significant investments in employees to train and educate them so that they will be able to be productive in this new environment. Dr. Block's conclusion was that "*universal continuing employment could well be the result of this type of productivity revolution.*"

This is not a surprising conclusion for a former employee of IBM, where employment security has been practiced for decades. My company, Materials Research Corporation, has also been practicing employment security for 25 years, and there are a scattering of other companies, such as Hewlett-Packard and Eli Lilly, who have pursued this enlightened policy. However, let us not believe that this practice is acclaimed by all. The investment community, for example, whom we depend upon for the capital required to sustain and grow the business is extremely critical of this policy of continuing employment. This was succinctly addressed in a January 9, 1986, *Fortune* Magazine article titled "Most Admired Companies." After significant business analysis of the most admired companies and their financial results, the author notes,"Once again, profits provided the shortest road to admiration."

Personally, I believe that employment security is a fundamental requisite to developing the commitment required by all employees, but particularly by engineers who are absolutely critical to the improvement of productivity in this country. However, employment security is only one part of the overall fabric of human asset management. For example, as Dr. Block clearly noted, companies are required to make more significant investments in the education of their employees and, hence, when employment security is provided by a corporation, it is necessary to have an enlightened educational program as well.

MRC's educational program is quite simple. "You pass, we pay." Our employees can take whatever courses they desire without any relationship to degree matriculation or job improvement. Again, I can assure you that this program has not met with acclaim by the investment community. They ask why stockholders should pay tuition for an engineer to study English literature. Well, frankly, there is no easy answer. But it is interesting that companies can provide gyms and support baseball and bowling teams without any need to justify their activities. Our educational program allows exercise for the brain which I believe is of value to the company equal to or greater than well-toned muscles and trim waists. It is not a case of either/or.

There is another aspect of management which I believe must be changed. Usually when economic conditions turn down due to cyclicality of an industry, everyone freezes wages. In other words, given the choice of management by stick or carrot, in tough times we throw away the carrot and use the stick. This is backwards. What we require is to continue wage increases which are performance based and where "fully satisfactory" is zero wage increase. But those who excel, be it in good times or bad times, let us continue to reward generously.

Finally, employees must participate in the fruits of their labor and the company's successes. Whether this is accomplished by means of profit sharing, stock options, stock purchase plans, any other or all of the above, it is an absolute and necessary part of involving employees in the company's activities. It is of critical importance in gaining their total commitment to the success of the enterprise.

Let us not ignore management's role in this new scenario. Warren Bennis,[1] a professor at UCLA, wrote a book called *Leaders* in which he notes that when we talk about business we refer to good or bad managers, whereas when we speak of government we refer to leaders. Conversely, I think American business needs leaders and government needs managers. (If all of the MBAs we produce in the United States were to go directly into government, American business would be markedly improved; I can't be certain what the impact would be on government.)

The only legitimate reason for a manager to exist, whatever the level, is to create, cause change for the better, or innovate new ideas, according to Rosabeth Moss Kanter.[2] We must throw away the concept that there is a limit to the number of people managers can have directly reporting to them. Superb leaders can lead vast numbers of people providing they don't try to make the decisions for all of their people. Push decision-making down. We need leaders in business who are prepared to dream, create, motivate, train, and have the courage to run their organizations in a counterculture manner when necessary. Quarterly results, short-term project planning, layoffs and other kneejerk reactions to business downturns are anachronistic and will accelerate the total destruction of our technology and industrial position.

Another problem of US industry that permeates the entire organization is the "we/they" syndrome. *They* refers to all the things wrong in a corporation. The servicemen visiting a customer: "*They* certainly shipped you a piece of garbage." The production person: "*They* screwed up this time in engineering." And so on. Examples abound all around us in every phase of our lives.

We is taking responsibility for ourselves as well as our organization. The serviceman: "*We* have never had this type of problem, but don't worry, *we* will resolve it to your satisfaction."

How do we get this type of commitment from our employees and especially from our engineering staff? There is no single nostrum. It is the careful administration of all of the above. An environment must be created in which the employee feels important, in which employment security is a fact of life, in which participation in decision-making and profits is well understood and, most importantly, where there is a leader to convey the substance of dreams and point the way. It is an organization in which *We* matters and *They* refers only to the competition. *We* makes profits, *They* don't!

Some pundit defined commitment as "high productivity, low turnover, and a better chance of avoiding corporate death at the hands of the Japanese." I have no argument with that definition.

NOTES

1. Warren G. Bennis and Burt Nanus, *Leaders: The Strategies of Taking Charge* (Harper & Row, New York, 1985).

2. Rosabeth Moss Kanter: *The Change Masters—Innovation & Entrepreneurship in the American Corporation* (Simon & Schuster, New York, 1983).

QUESTIONS FOR CRITICAL ANALYSIS

1. What are the financial facts that affect productivity? Why does Weinig think the human dimension is even more important? Do you agree?
2. Early in the essay Weinig compares the traditional U.S. work force to the present work force and Japanese semiconductor employees to American employees. Based on these comparisons, what characteristics seem to be present in the American work force? How can these characteristics be both beneficial and problematic for a company?
3. According to Weinig, what attitude in American business has to change before we can succeed? Why do we have this attitude? Knowing how difficult it is to change attitudes, what proposals would you make to begin this change?
4. What roles do engineers play in industry? How does American business and industry treat its engineers? Why are engineers critical to our future?
5. Weinig describes five areas that must be changed if America wants to increase its productivity. What are they? What changes does he propose? What effects do you think would occur if Weinig were successful in securing these changes?
6. Weinig claims that he will benefit if his engineers further their education, even if the classes they take have nothing specific to do with engineering. He gives an example of taking a class in English literature. Look back at Caroline Bird's essay, "The Liberal Arts Religion" (Part II), and discuss what her response would be to Weinig's views. Which author do you think is right? Why?

QUESTIONS FOR STRUCTURAL ANALYSIS

1. How does the opening statement set the tone and theme of the essay? What was your reaction to this statement? Is it an effective way to begin? Why, or why not?
2. How do Weinig's language and word choice identify him as coming from the business world? List words, phrases, and specialized usage.
3. Explain the implications of the four-line "play" on page 674. Why did Weinig set it off from the text as poetry?
4. Weinig has written this essay in the first person. What makes this especially effective? Point out sentences or sections in the essay that benefit from first-person point of view.
5. In his conclusion, Weinig refers to managers and their emerging role. How well does the conclusion fit with the rest of the essay? What response do you think Weinig's audience had to his paper?

*T*HE *P*AYOFF FROM *E*XPERT *S*YSTEMS

BETH ENSLOW

Beth Enslow (1965–), works as assistant editor for Across the Board, *a monthly publication of the Conference Board directed to senior management of the Fortune 500 companies, government officials, and academic leaders. "The Payoff from Expert Systems," published in* Across the Board, *both defines what expert systems are and what they do and describes how the use of expert systems can benefit a company or organization.*

Before you begin reading: *What does the term "expert systems" imply? Have you heard it before? Write a definition of expert systems in your reading notebook. Below the definition list examples of things you might consider to be expert systems.*

◆

FOR YEARS MANAGERS HAVE STRUGGLED TO IMPROVE white-collar performance, with little success. Throughout the world, productivity gains in so-called nontouch work have been near zero.

Some companies are now reporting dramatic progress through use of "expert systems." Once considered a lab researcher's fantasy—a dream of recreating higher brain structures—these systems today have a wide variety of more down-to-earth applications, and a potentially large commercial market. In some manufacturing companies, as well as a number of firms in the service and public sectors, the payback from expert systems has been tremendous.

Jerry R. Junkins, chief executive of Texas Instruments, Inc., explains why his company is looking beyond quality production: "Not too long ago, the ability to manufacture defect-free products consistently and at a low cost was viewed as the pinnacle of quality achievement. Today it is a minimum requirement for staying in business." To stay competitive, TI is building expert systems to improve its white-collar productivity. One of TI's many expert systems is a capital-proposal package that guides managers through the bureaucratic forms for requisitioning goods, making the process 20 times faster. TI expects the system to reduce cost overruns and preparation expenses by an average of $2 million a year.

Other companies report similar results: American Express Company estimates that expert systems increase the efficiency of its credit authorizers by between 45 percent to 67 percent. E.I. du Pont de Nemours & Company estimates a return on investment in expert systems through 1987 of 1,500 percent and an aggregate savings of $10 million. Digital Equipment Corporation believes it is saving $70 million a year from the 10 major expert systems it uses. One of those systems now makes it possible for sales people who are not systems engineers to design computer networks for DEC customers.

For three decades, artificial-intelligence scientists have struggled to build a computer system that would mimic human thought patterns and improve human productivity. Expert systems are the first commercial fruits of their labors. The systems are created by programming the knowledge of human experts and the logical steps those experts follow to solve a problem using a series of if-then rules. For example: "If payment of American Express card is six months past due, then deny credit." The if-then rules enable expert systems to reason and infer, rather than merely crunch numbers or store data. The systems can tell users not only what is the best solution to a problem but why it's the best. They give less-experienced employees an alternative to wading through a 5,000-page technical manual for the answer to an air-conditioning problem or tracking down the one retired engineer who knows how to prevent slag drift in a phosphorous furnace.

A recent book, *The Rise of the Expert Company* (Times Books), celebrates the advances that expert systems have made in the 1980s. Written by Edward Feigenbaum of Stanford University, widely regarded as the father of expert systems, along with Pamela McCorduck and H. Penny Nii, the book highlights the work of dozens of junior engineers, middle managers, and CEOs and shows how they have championed the use of expert systems in their companies.

For instance, Ken Lindsay and Bob Joy are two young engineers working for Northrop Corporation who attended a computer conference where they were given a "toy" expert-systems program that plays a kind of computerized "Twenty Questions"—guessing which zoo animal one is thinking of by asking such questions as, "Is it a mammal? Yes. Is it carnivorous? Yes. Is it striped or spotted? Spotted. Is it a leopard?" Lindsay and Joy decided, on their own, to adapt it into a program that plans the manufacturing of fighter-plane parts. Using an Apple personal computer, they secretly labored after work and on weekends to rewrite the toy program. (Their program consists of rules such as, "IF the edges of a sheet metal part are irregular, and the minimum internal radius is greater than .156 inch, and the length is between 90 and 140 inches, and the width is between 2 and 45 inches, THEN rout this part using the Marwin router.") Once they converted the program to plan airplane parts, they put the Apple on a dolly and dragged it around Northrop to drum up corporate support. Their tale, like all of the stories presented in the book, has a happy ending. A vice president of research took up their cause and today Northrop reports that Lindsay and Joy's system reduces the time spent planning a manufacturing process from several days to four and a quarter hours and allows a trainee with only a few weeks' practice to behave like a master planner with a decade of experience.

As with most technical advancements, the success of expert systems rests on gaining the users' support. Predictably, the Feigenbaum book reveals that engineers and scientists have embraced expert systems, while salesmen and accountants have required a bit of arm twisting. Ironically, the authors of the book found that the stiffest resistance to expert systems came from MIS departments. "In company after company we were told of the struggles between the expert-systems champions . . . and the powerful corporate service bureaucracy known as Mangement Information Systems, the dreaded MIS." MIS, it seems, suffers from a worldwide case of the not-invented-here syndrome. MIS has the ability to undermine an expert system by failing to provide computers that have fast enough processing speeds. Studies show that if the time between a user asking a question and the computer responding to it is too long, the user will become impatient and won't take advantage of the system—even if it improves his performance.

Feigenbaum and his co-authors also provide a bit of commentary on how a company can develop its own systems. Disappointingly, the insights are mainly on ways to weasel money out of top management and exploit the old-boy network to garner people's support. Problems are breezed over throughout most of the book. In a section on DEC, for instance, the authors conclude that its "history with expert systems isn't a tale of nonstop success. Some areas, such as planning and scheduling, haven't noticeably yielded to expert-system treatment, though prototypes were designed and built." However, it is never explained why there were difficulties; details are only provided for successes.

The literature on failures is generally scarce, but what is available provides useful guidelines for developing systems that will work. *Institutional Investor* noted last July that the first failures in financial expert systems were caused by lack of support from upper management—including one for interest-rate swaps by what was then Lehman Brothers, a loan analyzer built by Mellon Bank, and an underwriter evaluator developed by St. Paul Companies. Later failures, the article claims, were caused by too much support from middle management and not enough guidance from above, leading to costly duplication of efforts and ugly turf battles.

Senior management must continue to be involved after the system has been developed and put into use. Some systems have faltered in the field because management hasn't insured sufficient maintenance. Maintenance simply means entering new information into the system, whether it be new regulations or a better way to solve a problem. A system that is not maintained will soon be outdated and fall into disuse. Maintenance, however, may not be cheap: DEC spends $2.5 million a year on updating its expert systems and employs 15 people to do the work.

We've all used automatic teller machines and other computer systems that answer our questions. So what is so special about expert systems? The key lies in their flexiblity. Compared with structured programs created by languages such as Pascal and C, expert systems are relatively easy to adapt from one situation to another (remember the zoo-animal-turned-fighter-plane system) and are much easier to update. Because the technology is not as complex to use as many had expected, a lot of companies are turning to it to improve their performance. One analyst estimated in *High Technology Business* that half of the *Fortune*-500 companies are now investing in the development and maintenance of expert systems.

Some of the systems are quite simple and have been designed on PCs by experts with no programming experience using inexpensive commercial software packages called shells. A shell is somewhat analogous to a spreadsheet in that it prompts the user to "fill in" knowledge. The 1st-Class software shell, produced by First Class Expert Systems of Wayland, Massachusetts, sells for just $495—a far cry from the $100,000 systems marketed just a few years ago. In the past three years, the firm has sold 3,500 copies.

Du Pont is one company that has taken full advantage of low-cost, user-friendly shells: By the end of 1987 it had put 1,500 employees through its two-day expert-systems course. Students learn to use 1st-Class and Insight (another inexpensive commercial software package) as well as Du Pont's own shell, Tool Kit. Du Pont's grass-roots approach has met with much success. By mid-1988, it had more than 200 expert systems in routine use, with 600 under development or in field tests. A typical system requires one man-month of effort to build and yields $100,000 in savings per year, says Ed Mahler, director of Du Pont's artificial-intelligence program.

The popularity of low-budget systems has forced artificial-intelligence companies to change their marketing strategies. They have had to accept the idea that expert systems are simply an advanced form of software—and that most companies will only pay for their services if the systems can be used on the personal, mini, or mainframe machines that the companies already own. Many of the original artificial-intelligence companies are now millions of dollars in the red because they marketed systems that required esoteric programming languages and expensive, specialized computers, which couldn't "read" corporate data bases. Today the leaders in the field, such as First Class, are selling inexpensive, compatible software that novices can program in everyday English.

Yet some companies remain convinced that purchasing large, customized systems that require highly trained programmers is the way to go. Robert Flast, vice president of transaction services at American Express Travel-Related Services, argues in the Feigenbaum book that if expert systems are going to be useful to a firm, it's best to develop those of great impact and value first. To design its expert system, which sorts through as many as 13 data bases and makes recommendations to authorizers as to whether or not to grant customer credit, American Express contracted out to Inference Corporation of Los Angeles. After more than a year of development, American Express is estatic about the results and anticipates a return on investment of $27 million. Flast, according to the book, feels that the greatest opportunity for expert systems lies in improving customer service while reducing losses from bad decisions on whether or not to grant credit—usually antagonistic goals, since giving more service usually costs more.

The debate between "cheap and dirty" shells and "dear and spotless" customized programming will linger. A few prescripts, though, may be drawn. If the system is expected to make better judgments than the user and perhaps do some of his work, a customized program such as American Express's is most likely necessary. By contrast, if the system is designed to advise the user and let him make the ultimate decisions, a commercial shell is probably sufficient.

Most experts warn against tackling far-reaching projects that promise flashy results. A customized program not only costs 10 times as much as a shell, on average, and takes 10 times as long to develop but also can dampen employee enthusiasm for expert systems if it doesn't live up to expectations. Customized systems will have to offer extraordinary increases in productivity to justify their higher costs and greater risks.

It may also be foolish to develop too limited a system. A recent British book by Michael L. Barrett and Anabel C. Beerel, *Expert Systems in Business*, claims that while the Du Pont method of letting experts build their own systems has the advantages of low cost and quick development, it has the drawback of producing systems that are suitable only for the experts who designed them. "At Du Pont," according to Barrett and Beerel, "the great majority of the live systems are only used by one person." To get the most out of the technology, managers should promote the development of systems that will improve the performance of a number of people—perhaps by insuring that amateur developers are helped by experienced programmers.

Once a firm invests in a shell or customized program, it is likely that it will have to address workers' fears that their jobs will be replaced by these computers. In *The Rise of the Expert Company*, the authors credibly argue that most systems capture knowledge that will be lost as human experts retire or die. They also point out that it is often most efficient to automate the mundane part of an expert's job, leaving him time to concentrate on the remaining "difficult" problems. In the Feigenbaum book, Dr. Robert Fallat, who helped develop a diagnostic system for lung diseases, explains a view common among users: "If the computer can handle the routine 80 to 90 percent of the cases, that's okay. It frees me to work on the other 10 to 20 percent, which are the really interesting medical cases." Bruce Johnson, a partner at Arthur Andersen & Company, is also cited as believing that these fears are mostly unfounded. "Three-quarters of the Arthur Andersen expert systems have been new value, new products, and new services, as opposed to mere cost reduction. If cost savings is the only goal, it's too limiting. Manpower saved through expert systems isn't nearly as important as faster response, improved quality of service, and competitive differentiation."

Though many companies are investing in expert systems to help their employees perform better, not to replace them, workers remain skeptical. The Feigenbaum book quietly mentions that IBM's manufacturing system for making computer printers is a success because it has reduced the number of workers on the production line by 10 percent. And, in *Expert Systems in Business*, American Express's system for helping salesmen design computer systems is said to have permitted the team of experts who check the sales force's work to remain at a constant size of about 12 people. Without the expert system, the book says, it has been estimated that 100 experts would be required to cope with the current workload.

A company that reduces manpower by relying on expert systems may be hurt in the long run. Expert systems can impose uniformity on its users, stifling imagination and conceptualization. An overreliance on expert systems for making business decisions could produce a generation of managers who have little faith in their own intuition or expertise.

The future also holds the threat of liability suits. Who is liable if the expert system fails? Some expert systems may fail due to their design, while others may fail because they are improperly used. In either case, third parties—workers, consumers, community residents—may be harmed as a result. Possible lawsuit targets include the user, the programmer, the supplier of the shell, and even the expert whose knowledge was captured. There have already been failures in expert systems used in medical diagnosis and radiation treatment (allegedly because of their design defects) that caused severe injuries and deaths. Systems used in air transport have also allegedly failed.

Regulation and legal precedents on expert systems are just beginning to emerge. This past September, the Food and Drug Administration announced that software "intended to be used without competent human intervention" is subject to FDA requirements. It also warned that it will keep tabs on medical uses of expert systems for possible future regulation. Courts, according to Christopher Gill in an article for *High Technology Law Journal*, must soon decide whether an expert system is a product or a service. "Classification as a product," Gill writes, "means that the developer, manufacturer, and seller may all be subject to strict liability." Strict liability means they may be liable without the need for the victim to prove the defendant's wrongdoing. If expert systems are classified as a service, an injured plaintiff would most likely have to establish negligence.

A number of other issues must also be decided by the courts, including whether a human expert has a right to royalties for a system that contains his knowledge. One ongoing lawsuit involves a client who provided the expertise for a system as part of his job. He has since lost his job and is suing the company for royalties on the system he created. Another headache for companies involves the type of hold-harmless agreement they must provide if they choose to market their systems. These disclaimers, which deny responsibility if the software fails to work as promised, often carry little weight in the courtroom—one reason is that most buyers never sign the license-agreement cards. To protect themselves from lawsuits, companies may have to provide warnings about hazards posed by their products. An additional debate, yet to be settled by the courts, is the meaning of informed consent in doctor-patient relationships involving expert systems. Can a patient give a machine the right to make decisions about his treatment?

Meanwhile, companies are moving cautiously. According to an article in the October 1988 issue of *High Technology Business*, one company that was planning to sell a medical expert system "sank a couple of man-years [of development time] into it and, when they looked at the cost for liability insurance, they said 'no way.'" Ironically, some law firms are using expert systems to decide when it is profitable for clients to file suit. A smart manager will reduce the risks of using expert systems by insuring there are adequate contracts with the expert whose knowledge is to be immortalized, devising systems that recommend action without acting on their own, and obtaining liability insurance.

Finally, expert systems pose a security problem. Are the standard methods for data protection sufficient for protecting a company's proprietary expertise? Given the outbreak of computer viruses that have infected Pentagon, university, and corporate mainframes, it is clear that computer sytems are vulnerable. When it comes to expert systems built on PCs, the odds of computer espionage skyrocket because a corporate spy can take a floppy disk and quickly copy information. Companies developing systems for financial- or business-management purposes in the hopes of gaining a competitive edge are especially concerned about this. Unilever P.L.C., for example, was touted in 1984 as being the bellwether of British users. In 1987, however, every one of its expert systems was being kept completely confidential.

Expert systems are practical means of increasing white-collar productivity and improving customer service. But problems of scope and liability remain. Dorothy Leonard-Barton and John J. Sviokla, assistant professors at the Harvard Business School, wrote in a recent *Harvard Business Review* article that "realization of the potential of this evolving combination of human and machine knowledge hinges as much on management as on the technology itself." They claim that the projects that succeed are usually driven by either the preeminent expert in a field or a business manager. "That person, being the best judge of the tradeoffs that often must be made during development, should have the last word on the content and process of the actual expert system."

QUESTIONS FOR CRITICAL ANALYSIS

1. What are "expert systems"? How does Enslow define the term? Restate the definition in your own words.
2. Why are MIS managers the most reluctant to accept expert systems programs? How

do they sabotage the system? Why does Enslow say such an attitude and behavior are ironic? Do you agree with her? Why, or why not?

3. Discuss the failures Enslow presents in light of Kanter's organizational recommendations. Would a participatory management model help to avert the problems? Why or why not?
4. What are the disadvantages of expert systems in a company? Can you think of others Enslow doesn't mention?
5. How would expert systems improve some of the processes of college life? Imagine you could streamline a campus function that now frustrates you, and describe the expert system program you would design.

QUESTIONS FOR STRUCTURAL ANALYSIS

1. After reading the entire essay, characterize the reader Enslow envisions. What clues do you have indicating her expectations?
2. Describe the different ways Enslow uses examples from different companies. For example, compare her early descriptions of Texas Instruments, American Express, and E. I. du Pont de Nemours with the description of Northrop Corporation. How are these examples effective?
3. Why does Enslow spend so much time discussing the Feigenbaum book? How does the description enhance the essay? How does it detract from the essay?
4. Enslow often prefaces her remarks about the Feigenbaum book with an adverb that directs the reader's response. Point out sentences where this occurs. Is this an effective technique? Why, or why not? How did you respond to it?
5. In the course of her essay, Enslow refers to several articles and books. If you were interested in learning more about expert systems, how would you use her references as sources?

CREATING A WORLD-CLASS TEAM

LESTER THUROW

Lester Thurow (1938–), dean of the School of Management at Massachusetts Institute of Technology, describes himself as an "economics educator." In addition to teaching and administrative activities, Thurow provides informed commentary on public policy issues and the state of the economics profession for the general public through writing and public speaking. He was a contributing editor of Newsweek, *frequently writes for national newspapers and magazines, and often appears on televised public affairs programs. Two of his recent books,* The Zero-Sum Society *(1980) and* The Zero-Sum Solution *(1985), provided readers with an analysis of the American economy and its future. "Creating a World-Class Team" was presented at the same symposium on the U.S. economy at which Weinig delivered his paper, "Managing Better."*

Before you begin reading: *Many of us have grown up assuming that the United States ranked first internationally: the best in manufacturing and production, best in research and development, best educated, and most knowledgeable citizenry. Think about this assumption carefully. In your reading notebook, write what you think is America's place on the world scene. Whenever possible, support your ideas with illustrations and examples.*

◆

SUSTAINED ECONOMIC GROWTH

WITH THE ADVENT OF KEYNESIAN ECONOMICS, MACROeconomics came to be identified with demand management. The reasons for that identification are not hard to find. In depressions or recessions the economic gains to be made from returning to full employment dwarf all other possible economic gains in magnitude. The Great Depression was clearly a demand management problem that required 100 percent of the policymakers' attention. The same perspective legitimately dominated economic thinking in the first two decades after World War II. Frequent recessions (five in number) were the main enemy of economic growth. Productivity was above trend, growing between 3 and 4 percent per year, and the United States enjoyed across-the-board technological leadership.

In the future, however, it will be important not to identify macroeconomics exclusively with demand management. Macroeconomics will, like binoculars, require both a supply and a demand focus.

THE DEMAND FOCUS

The demand focus will be as important in the future as it was in the past since it is just as impossible now as it was 40 years ago to have a satisfactory growth performance with frequent recessions. But it is important to note that the nature of the anti-recessionary problem has changed. Thirty years ago recessions occurred accidentally and it was the job of the policymaker to prevent those accidents from happening.

The problem of accidental recessions, however, has been cured. There have been no accidental recessions in the US economy since that of 1960–61. Each and every recession since then has been deliberately created to stop inflation. Some of these recessions have occurred later, lasted longer, or been more severe than desired, but none of the last four has been an accident. They have all been deliberately generated by the Federal Reserve Board or the administration in power.

As a result the nature of the anti-recession problem has fundamentally changed. The key to full employment without recessions is not to be found in demand management but in some alternative to negative demand management—be it a share economy, a social contract, or something else—for curing inflation. To make demand management work requires changes in the microeconomic structure of the economy. With the current income setting arrangements, demand management is not a device for achieving full employment, but a device for creating unemployment. If macroeconomics is to accomplish what it is supposed to accomplish, it needs different income setting arrangements.

With inflation more or less under control and commodity prices falling inflation is not today's problem, but changes in the microeconomic structure of the economy to make demand management work should be today's problem, for the appropriate time for changing the microeconomic parameters of the wage setting system is when inflation is not a problem. Once inflation has again become a problem it will be too late to make the necessary changes.

There is another respect in which the demand management problem has changed. In a very real sense it is the industrial world's supply of money and the industrial world's tax and expenditure policies and not just the American pieces of that total that matter for the American economy. Today it is not just Americans sitting at the demand management controls of the American economy. When demand management is needed it is going to have to be coordinated with the policies of Germany and Japan if it is to be successful.

This can be clearly seen by thinking about the deficit reduction problem in the United States. If the United States were to cut expenditures or raise taxes to cure its $200 billion deficit without expansionary policies being simultaneously adopted in Germany and Japan, the result would be a massive world-wide recession. Since the world's industrial economies are not now operating at full employment, if $200 billion of American demand were to be subtracted from the system, then $200 billion of extra demand would have to be added to the system somewhere else. Thus even American deficits cannot be reduced without foreign cooperation. Americans now live in a world where they are merely part of a larger world economy; a world where they control less than they used to control.

THE SUPPLY FOCUS

The past 15 years have proved that supply does not take care of itself. No one can be satisfied with the economy's *per capita* growth rate (1.9 percent) or its productivity growth rate (1.5 percent).[1] Such growth rates are unacceptable relative to America's past, relative to the performance of the rest of the industrial world, and more importantly relative to the rate at which Americans would like to see their own standards of living grow.

While there are many places where private markets can be liberated to improve performance, a supply focus is not a synonym for *laissez-faire* or lower taxes. In economy theory one can show that *laissez-faire* economies have some desirable properties (they optimally distribute private goods relatively to the initial distribution of income), but a high rate of growth is not one of them. This is most clearly seen in one of the weak points of the US economy—its low rate of investment and savings.

Given the institutions of the American economy (tax deductibility for consumer and mortgage interest, no low or down payments, long periods for repayment) it may be rational for the average American to take advantage of those institutions and make generous use of consumer and mortgage credit. But if each and every American does so, the net result is a very low aggregate rate of savings. Government at the very least has a responsibility to set the parameters within which people maximize their private utility to yield aggregate results that are consistent with a good long-run economic performance. Free market economies can be organized with or without generous provisions for consumer credit and will have very different performance characteristics depending upon how they are organized. In the end free market economics depend upon the social organization that goes into them.

To accelerate economic growth America needs to make economic growth one of its policy goals. Full employment and low inflation are most often cited as economic goals but it is important to understand that they are only means to an end. The real goal is a high rate of growth in *per capita* income. While American policy makers talk about economic growth, they have not traditionally set growth targets as they have set unemployment or inflation targets. They should start to do so. To set a target is to make something important, but more importantly it is to set a standard of success and failure relative to which the policymakers can and will be judged.

America's growth target should be set relative to the performances of the rest of the industrial world. Basically the United States should have a standard of living that grows in pace with that in the rest of the world. This means that if other leading industrial countries have productivity growth rates in the 3 to 4 percent range the United States should aim for a similar result. Given this goal one can then ask what must be done to achieve it.

POLICIES FOR ECONOMIC GROWTH

Growth policies can operate at several levels, but the appropriate place to start is with the quantity and quality of the inputs (capital, labor, technology) going into the economy. In each area the aim should be inputs as good as those going into the economies of the best of our industrial competitors. Everywhere Americans should aim for world-class inputs.

THE QUANTITY OF CAPITAL

Unfortunately America does not now have an economy marked by world-class inputs. American investment in plant and equipment is roughly half that going into the Japanese economy and two-thirds that going into the economies of Europe. America should aim to bring investment up to the levels of these competitors. An interim target should be set for bringing investment up to European levels, and once this is achieved the target should be raised to the level that will make the United States competitive with Japan if Japanese investment is still above that in the United States.

In theory, with a world capital market, it is not necessary to have a world-class level of savings to have a world-class level of investment. One simply borrows from the rest of the world what is necessary to make the necessary investments. In fact it does not make sense from a national or a world perspective for the United States to be borrowing much of its capital from the rest of the world. Ultimately interest payments on those foreign debts become a drag on the US economy and the world's surplus capital should more appropriately be invested in the developing world and not in the United States.

This means that higher investment rates will in fact require higher savings rates within the United States. In addition to shifting the federal government from being a net dissaver to being a saver, higher savings rates will require changes in tax laws (eliminating the tax deductibility of interest payments) and limitations on consumer and mortgage credit to raise initial down payments and to shorten repayment periods. The American political system seems to be in the process of proving that such changes cannot be sold in the guise of tax reform. It also seems to be proving that it cannot raise taxes as a part of federal deficit reduction.

Whether such changes can be sold as necessary for economic growth remains to be seen. If they cannot, the United States is unlikely to enjoy a world-class rate of growth investing much less than the rest of the industrial world.

THE QUALITY OF THE WORK FORCE

Ultimately the quality and skills of the workforce are a country's only real comparative advantage. As the inventor of mass public education America for many years had the best educated and most skilled work force. But all of the current evidence indicates that the United States now has a work force that does not meet world-class standards when it comes to education and skills.

Eight percent of American youths 14 to 21 years of age test out as functionally illiterate (i.e. they cannot read and write at the fifth grade level).[2] Using slightly tougher definitions of functional illiteracy, as much as 20 percent of the American work force may be functionally illiterate. In contrast less than 1 percent of the Japanese labor force is functionally illiterate.

When 19 different achievement tests were administered to students in different countries, Americans never ranked first or second, and if comparisons are limited to other developed nations only, the US ranked at the bottom seven out of 19 times. Mean scores placed America in the bottom half of the rank-order distribution 13 times and in the top half only six times.[3] In an international study of mathematics ability for eighth and twelfth graders, the eighth graders ranked in the bottom tenth internationally and the twelfth graders were 'markedly lower' than the international average in all seven of the areas tested.[4]

Those are unacceptable results that must be altered. Education may be a state responsibility, but no national government can for long tolerate an education system that is not generating a competitive work force.

If one looks for the reasons for a poor American performance, one factor stands out. The United States has a much shorter school day and school year than most of the rest of the industrial world. Students go to school 240 days in Japan and 220 in Sweden. In contrast, American students are in school only 180 days. Americans cannot learn in 180 days what it takes the rest of the world 220 to 240 days to learn.

To lengthen the school year, half of federal educational aid should be conditioned on a longer school year. The other half should be conditioned on a school's achievement test scores relative to what one would have expected from the historical norms for schools with students of the same socioeconomic background. If one does well on performance measures relative to schools with similar student inputs one gets more federal aid than if one does poorly relative to similar schools.

If the federal government can set standards for interstate highways if a state wants federal highway money, it can set standards for educational inputs and outputs if a state wants federal education money. When it comes to that famous bottom line a well educated work force is much more important to national economic success than a good highway system.

If one looks at the US education system there is a major gap. No training system exists for the training of the non-college bound. Germany fills this gap with an elaborate system of publicly financed but privately run apprenticeship training and private firms provide such training in Japan. America has no general system of publicly financed training for the non-college bound and because of high labor force turnover rates, private firms find that it is not in their immediate self-interest to pay for the extensive training of workers who are unlikely to remain on their payrolls.

Such a gap is both inefficient (the economy has a perpetual shortage of skilled non-college workers) and unfair (the average American college student gets a public subsidy of $12,000 over the life of his college career). It is a gap that must be closed. Individual training accounts are one possible answer, but some answer must be adopted if the US is to grow rapidly in the future. In the past the United States could count on immigration (principally from Germany and Austria) to provide skilled blue collar workers but now that real standards of living have essentially reached parity in northern Europe that source of supply has essentially ended.

MAINTAINING TECHNOLOGICAL PARITY

In the last few decades Americans have relied on superior technology to offset other handicaps. America may not have had the best labor force or the newest capital, but it had the best technology and many goods were only to be had from American sources. But that era is now gone. The rest of the world has caught up with the United States technologically and few if any goods are only to be had from US sources. While it is impossible for the United States to go back to the effortless technological superiority that it had in the 1950s (it was a product of the human and physical destruction of World War II), it is important that the United States maintain civilian technological parity.

While the United States is not yet generally behind technologically, it is clear that there is a technological problem. Process technology is a clear American weakness. In too many leading industries American firms are operating with inferior processes. Foreign firms could pay the same wages and still sell below American costs. Expenditures on civilian R&D as a fraction of the GNP are now below those in Japan, Germany, and France.[5] Both Japan and Germany graduate about 40 percent of their college students in science and technology while less than 10 percent of American students graduate with engineering or science degrees.[6] In addition 40 percent of America's scientific personnel is involved in defense work.[7]

It is interesting to note that in the decade of the man-on-the-moon effort, the United States thought that it was necessary to have programs for augmenting the supply of scientific manpower so that the demands of the space effort did not cripple domestic industries. Yet in the 1980s with a much bigger build-up underway in the defense department no similar efforts are being made to increase the supplies of scientific manpower.

In reality America will need a similar intensification of scientific effort in the 1980s if it is to enjoy a competitive rate of growth. This intensification of effort is not going to occur automatically. In a closed economy a shortage of engineers would lead to higher wages for engineers and in the long run a larger supply of engineers. Given the high costs of scientific education, however, even in a closed economy it should be emphasized that the long run might be very long and that for this reason the man-on-the-moon effort did not rely on automatic market mechanisms to cure potential shortages of scientific personnel.

In an open economy a shortage of engineers need not lead to more engineers even in the long run. Those industries that are engineering intensive simply move to those countries that have an adequate supply of engineers. If one looks at the industries that are now moving abroad (machine tools, electronics) it is perhaps not an accident that these are precisely those industries that are intensive users of technical personnel.

TAXES AND HIGH QUALITY INPUTS

In maintaining technological, labor force and capital parity, the main problems are not those of what must be done or how should it be done, but in politically deciding that something must be done if the United States is to enjoy a competitive rate of growth. "Cut taxes" or "do nothing" are the current winners when it comes to public policy prescriptions.

At the moment the federal budget deficit is usually advanced as the main reason why it is impossible for the United States to undertake any new federal expenditure programs. Yet both a skilled labor force and technological parity are realistically going to require some new expenditure programs. Perhaps it is well to point out that with Japan having just passed the United States it is now true that all of the major developed nations pay a larger fraction of their GNP in taxes than the United States. The United States is not an over-taxed society. It is in fact an under-taxed society.

To be a nation with the world's lowest industrial tax rate is not a desirable goal if achieving that goal means an economy that cannot generate a competitive rate of growth. At some point Americans will have to face the fact that higher taxes will be necessary to have a competitive economy.

If the Federal government is to shift from being a net dissaver to being a net saver (and it must if savings rates are to increase), higher taxes will be necessary. If the United States is to have a labor force with skills second to none, higher taxes will be necessary at some level of government to pay for a better education system. If the American economy is to maintain its technological base, it is going to have to pay higher taxes since research and development expenditures are everywhere paid for by government. The externalities are simply too great to rely on private markets to generate adequate research and development efforts.

If higher taxes are politically impossible, then it is impossible for the United States to have a competitive growth rate for it cannot grow at competitive rates investing less, employing a less skilled labor force, and working with inferior technology.

Implicitly Americans are now assuming that if they are willing to play a free market game they will automatically be winners of that game. Yet no such outcome is guaranteed. There will be winners but they need not be American. Economic growth requires social organization. Those economies with rapid rates of growth of productivity are those that pay attention to good social organization.

THE GAME PLAN

The winners in economics as well as in sports are those who play with the best inputs, but what about the game plan—America's economic strategy for success? In the past America has not relied solely on its private firms to guarantee economic success. America's first great process invention, interchangeable parts, was financed with money from the War Department. The railroads were financed with grants and loans from the government. The steel industry developed behind trade barriers that kept cheap British steel out of America during the railroad building era. America's advantage in agricultural productivity can be traced to government programs such as its agricultural colleges, its extension service, its reclamation projects, its electrification programs and a plethora of financial institutions that made it possible for farmers to mechanize. The civilian aviation industry is a by-product of defense spending. Historically the American government has often intervened at strategic points to improve economic performance.

If the managers of any large American company operated without a strategic plan, they would be considered derelict in their duties. Yet because strategic thinking has been equated with economic planning in the socialist sense American policy makers publicly maintain that the American economy does not need a strategy *vis-à-vis* its international competitors. Yet if one looks at America's principal economic competitors—Germany, Japan—they each undertake some form of strategic planning. Outside observers argue as to how much of their success can be traced to their strategic planning and how much can be traced to other factors, but it is interesting to note that both think that such strategic thinking is useful.

In the past these strategies have most often been implemented with government investment banking or with government allocation of scarce foreign exchange, but in the present foreign strategies seem to be operating primarily at the level of research and development. Just as the American government has picked SDI as a target area for defense research so have foreign governments picked various civilian industries (electronics, new materials, biotechnology) as target areas for industrial research.

If one wants to look at the impact of such foreign policies one need only look at the current plight of the American semiconductor industry. Starting first with a governmentally financed research effort to leapfrog American technology and develop large (64K RAM and up) chips but continuing with a designated and limited set of producers, quasi-protected home markets and production loans that did not have to pay interest or principal until and unless profits were earned, Japan has succeeded in capturing more than 90 percent of the market for 256K RAM chips and may have prevented any American firms from attempting to build the megachip (100K RAM). Yet semiconductor chips are the building blocks for the rest of electronics. It is difficult to believe that an industry can ultimately be competitive when it cannot competitively build its own basic ingredients. Consumer electronics has been captured by foreign producers and the same trend is now visible in the rapidly diminishing competitiveness of American industrial electronics products.

Germany has announced similar efforts in the new materials industry (powdered metals, metal ceramics, pressed graphites, etc.) that is now emerging. It is too early to say whether they will be as successful in materials as the Japanese have been in semiconductor chips, but no one should discount their effort.

If one looks at America's mounting trade deficit in research-and-development-intensive products, one has to be a little concerned whether the United States is going to be able to maintain its traditional position in leading edge new industries. Current trends are not running in the American direction.

Japanese strategic planning is coordinated by a government agency (MITI) while German strategic planning is coordinated by the large private investment banks, but in both countries government and industry meet to formulate a strategy to increase economic growth and to maximize international competitiveness. America need not organize itself as either Germany or Japan is organized, but it needs some forum for doing what is being done abroad.

Americans often think that private American firms will do whatever strategic planning is necessary for the American economy to be successful and that, as a result, government has no role to play. Private firms simply will not do what is necessary. In a very real sense there are no private American firms. There are firms legally headquartered in America but they can locate their research and development, office or production facilities anywhere in the world. *Per se* they have no direct company interest in the success or failure of the US economy. They have a direct interest only in their own success or failure. Often it is cheaper for an American-based company simply to move production or engineering abroad than it is for it to make its American operations competitive. Yet foreign production is not a solution to American growth problems even if it is a solution to the competitive problems of American-based companies. If economic strategies are necessary for the United States to be successful in world markets they are going to have to be developed with the impetus of government leadership or they will not be developed.

While government has to be an organization catalyst for strategic planning, the plans have to be developed and implemented with the cooperation of private industry and labor. Only they know what must be known to chart the correct directions of movement. Once plans are formulated only they can implement. But to bring the interested parties together in a serious way some locus of decision-making authority must exist. Historically government investment banking has played this role. A key missing ingredient has often been capital, and industry automatically takes a potential source of funds seriously. Bankers, government or private, can demand information before making loans.

Since such a government banking vehicle raises political hackles and may in any case not be the currently appropriate vehicle for strategic planning, let me suggest that American strategic planning should take place in a government funding institution for industrial research. The federal government should set up a research and development institution for industry similar to the National Science Foundation that now exists for basic (mostly university based) research and development. Just for the sake of a title let me call the agency the National Industrial Research Foundation or NIRF.

This institution should be separate from the NSF since stimulating industrial research is fundamentally different from paying for basic research and development. In all cases firms would be expected to play a leading role in formulating the target areas for research, always be expected to contribute part of the funds and help organize cooperative efforts with other firms, and have priority rights to the products and processes that were developed. Since the agency must have an interest in process research (making old products cheaper) and since process research can only be developed and tested in the context of actual production the agency will be interested in a level of research and development that is now far outside of the scope or expertise of the NSF. With government funds involved, the government would also insist that technologies developed in cooperation with the agency could only be used in the United States for some period of time, say 5 years. Government would also expect to earn its share of the profits on products and processes that were successful.

Government money is not a grant but a contingent investment that will be repaid with a share of the profits if the investment is successful. In many ways NIRF would be doing for civilian industry what the Defense Department now does for defense industries.

Of necessity an industrial research agenda can only be formulated in the context of information on a more general set of economic parameters. As a result the need to formulate an industrial research strategy would automatically lead to discussions on more general economic strategies.

CONCLUSION

To maximize the macroeconomic parameter of economic growth requires changes in the microeconomic structure of the American economy on both the demand and supply sides of the equation. Frequent recessions can only be avoided if alternative means of fighting inflation are developed and if the principal industrial governments can coordinate their demand management policies, be they fiscal or monetary.

On the supply side of the equation the general quantity and quality of the fundamental inputs going into the economy have to be of national concern. Local school districts are not going to solve the aggregate problem of creating a world-class labor force. Since each district's contribution to that result is vanishingly small and each district can imagine itself hiring skilled personnel from elsewhere in the economy, every local district has an incentive to under-invest in education. Yet if each district does so the end result is an American disaster. Similarly each individual finds it rational to take full advantage of the current generous provisions for consumer and mortgage lending and each company finds it rational to cut back on general research and development expenditures. Yet if each does what it is individually rational to do the general result is social irrationality and an economy that does not perform as it should perform.

In economics, social organization matters and government has to take responsibility for insuring that America's social organization is second to none. If it is to do its thing free enterprise needs the right operating context. Without that context it can only fail.

NOTES

1. Council of Economic Advisers, *Economic Report of the President, 1985*, pp. 234 and 278; Council of Economic Advisers, *Economic Indicators*, 1985 (Nov.), pp. 2 and 16.
2. Gene Maeroff, 'Task force reports 8 percent of city youths are illiterate', *New York Times*, April 7, 1982.

3. Barbara Lerner, 'American Education: How are we doing?', *Public Interest*, 69 (1982), Fall, 64.
4. Edward B. Fiske, 'American students score average or below in international math exams', *New York Times*, Sept. 23, 1984, p. 30.
5. National Science Foundation, *National Patterns of Science and Technological Resources, 1982*, p. 33, IP no. 12.
6. National Science Board, *Science Indicators, 1982*, 1983, p. 22.
7. Charles L. Schultze, 'Economic effects of the defense budget', *Brookings Bulletin*, (1982) Fall.

QUESTIONS FOR CRITICAL ANALYSIS

1. What is a recession? How did you react to the information that all recessions since 1961 have been created by the Federal Reserve Board? (What is the Federal Reserve Board?)
2. According to Thurow, how has the demand focus changed? What has caused the changes?
3. Discuss the economic, political and social implications of Thurow's statement: "Americans now live in a world where they are merely part of a larger world economy; a world where they control less than they need to control."
4. What policy recommendation does Thurow make for accelerating growth rates in the American economy? Would such a recommendation work? Why or why not?
5. Thurow states that "40 percent of America's scientific personnel is involved in defense work." What effect does that have on the whole economy? Discuss the implications of this, referring to Krauthammer's argument for maintaining a large military arsenal.
6. Thurow specifies several roles the federal government should assume in "creating a world-class team." List them and next to each one, discuss the pros and cons of increasing federal involvement.

QUESTIONS FOR STRUCTURAL ANALYSIS

1. Headings and subheadings provide an outline for the reader. Why are they present? How easy would the essay be to read without them?
2. Examine the second paragraph closely. Make a list of things Thurow assumes his reader knows about his subject. Look up events and terms you don't know.
3. Thurow's prose style can sometimes be difficult to understand. Read paragraphs 6 and 16 carefully, and then explain what they mean in your own words.
4. Look carefully at the way Thurow argues for increased taxes. What reasons does he provide? How does he present them? How would someone opposed to raising taxes respond to each point?
5. Thurow concludes with comments on social organizations and illustrates his remarks by describing the behavior of local school districts. Restate the conclusion. How does it relate to the entire essay?

*B*USINESS FOR THE *T*WENTY-FIRST *C*ENTURY

TOPICS FOR WRITING ESSAYS

Many of the questions following each essay can serve as appropriate writing suggestions. Some of the topics listed below expand the prereading exercises, but they can be used without completing that step first.

1. Kanter is optimistic about the future of American business as long as it begins to invest in people. Reread Kanter's essay and make sure you understand what she means by this, and then apply these ideas to the management of a place where you have worked. How do your experiences compare with Kanter's proposed management style? Write a report to your former employer suggesting ways he or she could enhance the business by employing Kanter's ideas.
2. Weinig writes of his concern about the American worker's attitudes, preparation for the job, and effectiveness on the job. He believes that unless we can change all three, American business will not be able to compete in the world market. Colleges and universities could play a significant role in developing the type of employees Weinig envisions for successful companies. Evaluate the current courses and opportunities for business majors on your campus, and write a paper to the dean of the business or engineering school suggesting changes that would result in better-prepared workers.
3. Both Weinig and Thurow discuss the critical need to improve American education. Compare their comments with those you encountered in the section "How to Improve the Schools." Write a paper, to be sent to senior executives in local businesses, discussing why the business community must be concerned about education (from elementary school through graduate school).

RESEARCH POSSIBILITIES

1. Kanter calls Minneapolis the capital city of the progressive ideas she presents in her essay. Find out about Minneapolis: the corporate climate, education opportunities, arts, and architecture. What is the community's attitude toward innovations, citizen involvement, social responsibility, and so forth. Why (and how) is this community a model for the rest of the nation? Use Minneapolis as an example for a proposal you write to your mayor and city council proposing local change.
2. What is the relationship between the "participatory management" Kanter describes, Weinig's better management practices, Enslow's expert systems programmers, and Thurow's world-class team? How do these ideas differ with the traditional style of American management? Are these ideas influenced by "Japanese-style" management? Write a paper describing the management style of the future, providing reasons that explain why it is necessary for American business to change the way it manages people. Write your paper to a management professor who believes the old style management is still the best.

PART SEVEN

*H*OW TO *W*RITE FROM *S*OURCES

How to Write from Sources

When you learn to write about what you do not yet know, you develop useful skills. Writing from sources doesn't always mean that you write from outside your personal experience, but it does mean that you enlarge your personal experience to include something new.

In the process of research you have the joy of developing your ideas about a subject. In writing about your research you share your perspectives with others. While understanding that "truth" is too big for anyone to grasp completely, you have decided that a subject is worth exploring and that you have done your best to understand it. In doing this, and in expressing a point of view about it in writing, you take another important step to intellectual maturity and independence.

Research serves as the underpinnings of many of the essays in this reader. Some authors *interviewed* people personally involved in the events described or experts in the subjects. For example, Studs Terkel's "Evelyn Fraser" is the transcript of an interview with a woman who served in the Women's Army Corps during the Second World War; six survivors of the atomic blast on Hiroshima provided John Hersey with stories of their experiences; Dennis Bernstein and Connie Blitt integrated first-hand accounts of people working and living under the threat of chemical disaster with interviews by officials from the Nuclear Regulatory Commission; A. G. Mojtabai includes conversations she had with Amarillo citizens living in the shadow of a nuclear weapons plant.

Other writers developed their essays with material from *written sources*, sometimes using the researched information as a starting point from which to generate their ideas, as James Thurber does in "Courtship Through the Ages," and at other times using the information to support arguments and points of view. Tom Goldstein, for example, includes examples of how journalists deliberately deceive others in order to write a good story, and Jonathan Kozol blends statistical data with anecdotes to show the impact of adult illiteracy on the nation.

As you write your own essays from sources, consider how these writers prepared themselves: What information do they include that comes from outside themselves? What evidence is there of an effort to educate themselves about a subject? How do they present the information and words of others in their essays?

Choose a Research Topic

Finding a suitable topic for writing from sources is not different from finding a topic for an essay you could sit down and write without research. To get you started, we have included research possibilities in each Writing Suggestions section. Here are some questions to ask when you begin to consider these and other topics:

1. Is there something you want to learn about right now? For example, if you need to find out what are the current prospects and requirements for a particular career, why not use this occasion to do the research? Many college students face decisions about majors. Why not write on a topic in a field you are considering? If you end up enjoying your research on the Civil Rights Act of 1964, maybe history is a good major for you. A writing-from-sources project offers you the chance to test your interests.
2. Is there a subject about which you want to become knowledgeable? Perhaps you have been reading everything you can get your hands on about the explosion of the Challenger, or about the race to develop the superconductor. Since you have already demonstrated an interest and have, in fact, begun to educate yourself on the topic, why not pursue it further?
3. Is there something you'd like to develop a more thoughtful opinion about? Perhaps you are unsettled in your ideas about abortion, biotechnology, the death penalty, euthanasia, U.S. involvement in Central America, or some other important controversy. When you conduct research on a topic, you educate yourself, and you can write a more convincing argument to persuade others of your views.
4. Is there something new you'd like to explore just for the fun of it? Maybe you've wondered lately about what it would be like to go mountaineering in Nepal, or how the St. Louis Arch was built, or what influences foreign investors exert on American policy. Why not use this opportunity to find out?

As with any writing topic, it is important to listen to yourself. If your interest wanes quickly, look for another topic. Writing an essay from sources is usually a big project; look for something that will sustain your interest.

Be careful, also, not to take on more than you can handle. When you select a general topic like those listed above, quickly decide why you want to write on the topic: what do you want your reader to learn from reading your paper? What action do you want your reader to take as a result of hearing your argument?

Then focus your thoughts, identify a point of view and generate a narrow thesis that you have the time and other resources to investigate. Don't try to write an essay on a topic that could easily be the subject of a book.

Focus Your Investigation

When you begin your research, your reading is likely to be for the purpose of self-education and without much focus. If you are trying to find out about child abuse, for instance, you will start reading general sources that contain much repetitive material. Taking extensive notes at this time would be time-consuming and unnecessary until you develop a clear focus for your research. An easy way to begin your research is to write a specific question you want to explore about your topic; for example: Is child abuse passed from one generation to another, or are single-parent children more likely to be abused than two-parent children? When you have narrowed your topic, you are ready to begin your research.

Find Your Sources

If you are uncertain at first about whether you will be able to investigate the topic of your choice within the time available, do some initial exploring.

Every topic is different and requires different resources. Some topics involve only library research; others involve none. Your instructor may ask you to select a topic partly on the basis of giving you a certain kind of research and writing experience. If experience in library research is an important component of your writing course, select a topic that requires library time.

As you begin your research, you may discover that you need to change the focus of your study based on the availability of information. For example, your plan to do first-hand research on a nearby nuclear power plant may be thwarted when its administrators do not allow students to visit the facility. Or, the synthesized protein you're interested in investigating in the library is so new that little has yet been published in the journals. Be prepared for the unexpected!

BOOKS For many topics, the catalog of the library's books—accessible through a computer terminal, subject-author-title cards, or subject-author-title books—is the best place to start your self-education project. Some titles alone may tell you which books will help you; others will need close scrutiny before you can determine their usefulness. Notice the publication dates of all books you examine. (The date will appear in the catalog citation or you can find it on the reverse of the title page). For an historical topic, it can be very illuminating to read sources close to the event you are investigating. In general, however, new books will incorporate the information in previous ones. Check the bibliographies and "books cited" lists that often appear at the end of books for titles of other sources that could be useful. You will soon be able to identify the "classics" or the influential books as you notice how often—and in what context—they are referred to by other experts.

In your preliminary book search, try for some variety too—a sampling across the political spectrum, if the topic is political, a variety of viewpoints, a combination of academic and popular writing on your chosen subject. If you are able to find several promising books on your subject, spend time actively reading them.

PERIODICALS Once you have some basic background—or if your topic is so new no books on it have been published yet—you can begin to look at more recent print sources in the form of magazines and journals. The periodical indexes in the library's reference section provide the means to look up articles according to topic. While the *Reader's Guide to Periodical Literature* covers popular periodicals, sources such as the *Humanities Index, Applied Science and Technology Index, Business Periodicals Index,* and *Education Index* (among others) index scholarly journals and make specialized information accessible.

How can you identify articles and essays that are suitable for your research? First of all, recognize that you are going to need to check many more sources than you will end up using for your paper. In other words, don't think that by consulting two or three books you are conducting research. Secondly, use discretion in selecting magazines and journals as sources. Newsstand magazines such as *People, TV Guide, Time, Newsweek,* and others are not usually good sources for college-level research. You want to read provocative, thoughtful analyses and examinations of your topic. Finally, just as with the books you consult, use the footnotes and bibliographies in the articles as leads for additional sources to check.

Be sure to make complete notes when you list articles from magazines and journals. The volume, date, and page numbers identify the specific issue of the periodical you need and they will make it easier to discover whether it is available in your library. When you have listed the magazine and journal articles you want to look at, you may need to refer to the library's periodical catalog to find out if the library has the volume of the magazine you need in its permanent collection.

ABSTRACTS AND BIBLIOGRAPHIES Other reference section resources include abstracts and specialized bibliographies. Abstracts, such as *Psychological Abstracts, Physics Abstracts, Historical Abstracts,* and others, provide short summaries of published articles in the field and can save you time determining their usefulness.

Bibliographies are lists of writings, and specialized bibliographies include lists of publications in a specific field or on a specific topic. The *MLA International Bibliography of Books and Articles in the Modern Languages and Literature*, for example, is a yearly publication listing articles, books, and monographs devoted to modern languages and literature; George Sarton's *A Guide to the History of Science* includes information on journals, institutes, societies, museums, and international congresses in the sciences; the *International Bibliography of Political Science* lists articles and books published on government theory and practice in many countries and many languages. There are bibliographies devoted to authors, works, and very narrow fields of interest, and you may find many of them in your library's reference section.

GOVERNMENT DOCUMENTS The United States government, one of the largest publishers in the world, publishes pamphlets and books—often the result of extensive research and often providing authoritative information—on almost every subject. The *Monthly Catalog of United States Government Publications* provides the most comprehensive list of publications; the *Index to Publications of the United States Congress* lists and abstracts most of the hearings, reports, committee prints, and House and Senate documents, with the exception of the *Congressional Record*, which carries its own index. *Statistical Abstracts of the United States* covers industrial, business, social, educational, financial, and other statistical information.

NEWSPAPERS For even more up-to-date information, consult *Facts on File* and *Newsbank*, which select stories from a variety of newspapers. *The New York Times, The (London) Times, The Wall Street Journal,* and *The Christian Science Monitor* have separate indexes, as do other local newspapers.

DATABASES A developing resource for writing from sources is the various electronic databases accessible through Dow Jones and other computer services. *The National Newspaper Index* and *Magazine Index* are not yet as comprehensive as the print indexes, but they are useful nonetheless. You can type a topic into a database service and the computer will respond with a list of sources. While this obviously saves you time and legwork, these services include only a fraction of the available material and should serve as a good starting place but not as your only source of information.

OTHER SOURCES Other important print sources are encyclopedias and dictionaries, both general and specialized. You're probably already familiar with the *Encyclopedia Britannica*, but there's also the *International Dictionary of the Social Sciences, The McGraw-Hill Encyclopedia of Science and Technology*, and others.

Someone looking for information about the American singer Billie Holiday, for instance, would do well to start with entries about her life in *The Dictionary of American Biography, Notable American Women,* and *Grove's Dictionary of Music and Musicians.*

Also, don't overlook such "armchair" reference books as the *Oxford Companion to American Literature* or the *Oxford Classical Dictionary.*

Take Notes from Print Sources

Two traditional methods of note-taking involve using notecards or notebooks. Notecards (3 × 5 or 4 × 6 index cards) are easy to handle and easy to rearrange. With one item of information or one quotation on each card, you can quickly put them in order for writing your paper. Write on the top of each card a few words indicating where you think the note will fit in your outline, and be sure to write down the source and the page number somewhere on the card. Keep a separate set of bibliography cards which list the complete publication information[1] for each source, and you'll save yourself a lot of tedious copying.

Some people prefer using notebooks, keeping a separate section for the bibliography. If you use a notebook, you may want to write notes on only one side of the page so that when you get ready to write your paper, it's easier to find the information you need.

With the advent of laptop computers, many people prefer to type their notes directly into their computer. As with the notebook, make sure not to separate your notes from their source. Use headings liberally so you can easily identify the topics.

Whichever system you use, be meticulous about copying quotations and noting your sources. Your note-taking system should make it easy for you to tell what you are quoting directly from the source, what you are paraphrasing in your own words, what is a summary of the information, and what is your original thinking. Accuracy is essential. You need to be able to give appropriate credit to your sources and to enable others to locate each passage you cite.

Interview Experts

Personal interviews are a rich resource for writing. Although journalists and professional writers get a great deal of their information from interviews, few students consider how essential this type of research can be. Consider, for instance, writing a research paper about women in law enforcement. While print

[1]Samples of complete publication information appear in the section, "Listing Sources at the End of the Essay," at the conclusion of this chapter. Follow the samples carefully. Ask your instructor for more information as needed or consult a reference manual.

sources will be useful resources on this subject, your investigation would be greatly enriched by talking to women in law enforcement and to those officials who supervised the entry of women into the field.

People new to interviewing are often surprised by how willing others are to discuss what they know with someone seeking information.

BEFORE THE INTERVIEW The first step in a successful interview is to make a satisfactory contact by telephone. Call the person and explain the purpose of your visit: Tell him or her briefly about your investigation, along with the particular information or perspective you are seeking through your interview. If the person is unable to see you, ask for the name of someone else who could supply similar information.

Always prepare for an interview. Ideally, before you interview an expert, you will have completed the reading part of your research. (Be aware that you will waste the interview if you arrive ignorant about the subject because you won't know which questions to ask nor how this particular person might help you.) Write out questions you want to make sure to ask. Include questions on your research, to give you another perspective on your sources.

AT THE INTERVIEW Take a notebook and more than one pen or pencil to the interview. If you plan to take along a tape recorder, make sure that it works and that you have additional tapes. Do not, however, tape record any interview without first obtaining permission to do so. Making a tape without the subject's knowledge is unethical and possibly illegal.

Dress neatly. If you arrive early to the interview, you'll be more calm and can spend a few moments reviewing your list of questions. Before you begin the interview, be sure to thank the person for his or her time.

Even if you are recording the interview, you should take notes. As with print sources, make sure your notes distinguish between what is a direct quotation and what is not. If you are confused by anything said, ask for clarification. Listening well is a different skill from reading well. Try to relax so that you don't leap in with another question immediately, but allow the person time to develop a response. If you disagree with some statements, do not enter into an argument with the subject. You are there to listen, to observe and to think, not to present your own views. Save those for your essay!

After you have answers to all your questions, see what the person has to tell you that you didn't think to ask. For example, you could say, "Is there anything we haven't discussed that you think is important for me to know or think about?" At this point—usually quite spontaneously, if you just get out of the way—the person may give you the most interesting insights of the interview.

Before concluding an interview, ask the person for names of other people to interview. Be sure to leave your phone number in case he or she remembers something else important, and ask if you can call back to check a fact or quotation. Most of the time, you leave an interview with fresh information and ideas about your subject.

AFTER THE INTERVIEW Even though you thank the person for the interview at its conclusion, you should send a brief letter expressing your appreciation again for his or her time. If you have followed up any suggestions made during the interview, include a specific reference in your letter.

Think About Your Subject

As you read and talk to people, as one source leads to another, you should think carefully about your subject. Ask the same questions of your sources (books, articles, or people) that you do any text:

1. What claims does the source make?
2. What evidence—facts, examples, cases, statistics, and so on—does the source use to support the claims?
3. Do I believe the source? Why, or why not?
4. Do I agree with the source? Why, or why not?
5. What basic assumptions or knowledge underlie the source's claims, and where do they fit in?
6. What is the relationship of this source to other sources about the subject?
7. What is the source's point of view? Does the source have a vested interest in the subject? How does that affect the information?
8. What is my point of view? How does that coincide with the information?
9. What information from this source could I use to support the thesis of my essay?
10. What do I consider outdated or false or otherwise not useful for my purposes?

Over time you will evaluate some sources as more valuable, or more believable, than others. It is important, as always, to be aware of your interpretation of the material.

You will reach a point when your research will seem repetitive: You have heard it all, or at least it seems very familiar. What has happened is that you are becoming knowledgeable on the subject. Ideally, you can take time to pause and consider your subject thoughtfully. Seek out other people to talk to, if that method helps you, or keep a journal of your thoughts, if that is your inclination.

Write an Essay from Sources

Writing a research essay follows the same process as writing shorter, more personal, essays. You have learned about a subject and focused your investigation on a narrower topic. You have thought about the subject and broadened your knowledge. Still, writing an essay based on research can be daunting because you are writing a long paper, incorporating sources into the text, and you probably have a great deal of complex material to analyze and organize.

What can be more daunting, however, is a lack of confidence to speak knowledgeably about the subject, a natural fear for a beginner. Now you, like professional writers, are writing an essay about an important subject and asking other people to accept your interpretation. Some beginners respond to this fear by being timid—avoiding a strong thesis and making the paper a string of quotations from sources. Resist this temptation.

As with every paper you write, develop a clear and forceful thesis, focused on both your topic and your attitude or position toward the topic. Make a detailed list or outline of each major point you want to make, being sure to include the supporting evidence: facts, statistics, illustrations, quotations, and so forth, that will make your discussion convincing.

As you write the essay, you use what you learned from your sources the same way you use supporting ideas in any essay. Keep a balance between your thoughts and the evidence you provide to back them up. Remember that you can't include everything you read or heard, so choose your information and quotations carefully. In general, paraphrase—put the ideas in your own words—rather than quote unless the language in the quotation is particularly persuasive.

INCORPORATE SOURCES Always introduce your source. You can think of yourself as an attorney putting a witness on the stand to speak on behalf of your case. You need to present your source as someone to be taken seriously, and you need to place your source in context. For example,

1. According to Harold Smith, M.D., a research psychiatrist working with the National Institute of Health, . . .
2. A study conducted by a special commission of the City of New York investigating white-collar crime in 1987 reached the following conclusions: . . .
3. As Sarah Jones, prosecuting attorney for the case, explained . . .
4. "It was the worst mishandling of agricultural loans I had ever seen," said state banking examiner Katharine Saxby after a week's investigation of Farm Federal.

5. On the other hand, not everyone agrees with Professor Green about the forecasting technique. Professor Ellen Black of Stanford's economic department said, . . .

By providing a clear introduction to the information or quotation from your source, you connect it to your essay as a whole, using the source to develop and authenticate your ideas.

DOCUMENT SOURCES WITHIN THE ESSAY Your readers must be able to distinguish between what information, ideas, and language are yours and what are someone else's. They must feel assured that you researched your subject carefully and that they can find the same information by consulting your sources. By documenting your paper, you give credit to those who studied the subject before you.

Plagiarism—presenting another person's work as your own, intentionally or not—is a serious academic offense because it is dishonest and denies your reader knowledge of other publications on the subject. Sometimes thoughtlessness or carelessness results in the appearance of plagiarism when there has been no malicious intent. The rule to remember is: Whatever is neither yours nor in the public domain requires a footnote. When in doubt, footnote.

Sometimes students fear that the paper will have hundreds of footnotes and won't have any unfootnoted material. If this is true about your paper, then you have not processed the material thoroughly enough; you are hiding behind sources instead of reaching your own conclusions. The research essay is primarily your thoughts, with sources used only to support and supplement your points. Footnotes, then, should appear in the middles of paragraphs, not at the beginnings and ends where the ideas are.

With rare exceptions a footnote is a specific page reference, telling the reader exactly where you found a particular passage that you have quoted or paraphrased. However, information that you did not generate yourself, unless it is widely known and widely accepted knowledge, needs a footnote. Everyone agrees, for instance, that Columbus came to the New World in 1492, and you don't need to footnote that information. If you have discovered an historian's theory that the date should really be 1491 or 1493, you need to document your discovery with a footnote.

When you begin educating yourself about a subject, you seldom know what is widely known and accepted information. Because of your uncertainty, be sure to include specific references to sources and page numbers while you are taking notes. Early in your research, however, you will begin to recognize what is new and "proprietary" and what is established and needs no footnote. Again, if you are in doubt, include the footnote.

Sometimes you will want to use an "omnibus footnote." In a paper on child abuse, for instance, you might state in your essay that this behavior is passed down through generations and usually continues until someone gets treatment. Fifty years ago that idea would have been original, needing a footnote. Many research studies have since been conducted that support this idea, and some important theories have developed as a result. In an omnibus footnote, you would say:

[1]For a review of the relevant literature, see . . .

and then you would list the authors, titles, and publication information. In this way, you not only give credit to your sources but you also direct your reader to important background information.

METHODS OF DOCUMENTATION If your instructor provides you with a specific documentation system, follow the model examples slavishly—every space, period, and comma in place. Make sure you copy page numbers accurately, include the correct dates and volume numbers, and have the correct spelling for authors' names and titles.

If your instructor does not require a specific method, you will discover many reference books to provide you with models: the *MLA Handbook for Writers of Research Papers*, Third Edition (1988), the *Publication Manual of the American Psychological Association*, Third Edition (1983), *The Chicago Manual of Style*, Thirteenth Edition (1982), and others.

There are two basic methods for documenting your sources: (1) including the author and page number within the essay, and (2) numbering each citation within the essay and listing the citations in numerical order following the essay. Below are examples of each method, using the Modern Language Association (MLA) style:

1. Citing the author and page reference in parenthesis within the essay and listing all cited sources alphabetically at the end of the essay:

   The citation in the essay:

   CRITERIA One book by author cited in essay; author's name not included in text

   ```
   Bertrand Russell wrote that "all the noonday brightness
   of human genius [is] destined to extinction in the vast
   death of the solar system . . ." (Bush 188).
   ```

   CRITERIA Two books by author cited in essay; author's name not included in text

Bertrand Russell wrote that "all the noonday brightness of human genius [is] destined to extinction in the vast death of the solar system . . ." (Bush, Science 188).

CRITERIA Two books by author cited in essay; author's name appears in text

Bush quoted Bertrand Russell who wrote that "all the noonday brightness of human genius [is] destined to extinction in the vast death of the solar system . . ." to illustrate an extreme view of man's futility (Science 188).

CRITERIA One book by author cited in essay; author's name appears in text

Bush quoted Bertrand Russell who wrote that "all the noonday brightness of human genius [is] destined to extinction in the vast death of the solar system . . ." to illustrate an extreme view of man's futility (188).

The citation after the essay:

Bush, Vannevar. Science Is Not Enough. NY: Morrow, 1967.

2. Using a superscript number within the essay and listing all the citations in numerical order after your essay:

Bush quoted Bertrand Russell who wrote that "all the noonday brightness of human genius [is] destined to extinction in the vast death of the solar system . . ." to illustrate an extreme man's futility.[1]

The citation after the essay:

[1]Vannevar Bush, Science Is Not Enough (NY: Morrow, 1967), 188.

LIST SOURCES AT THE END OF THE ESSAY List your sources at the end of the essay so that the reader can refer easily to material you located. Include all your sources (books, articles, interviews, and so forth) in the same master list, and alphabetize your list by authors' last name. The documentation examples below follow MLA style.

Books

Book by a single author

Rigden, John S. Rabi: Scientist and Citizen. New York: Basic, 1987.

Book by two or more authors

Applebaum, Judith, and Nancy Evans. How to Get Happily Published. New York: NAL, 1982.

Levine, Marsha, and Roberta Trachtman, eds. American Business and the Public School: Case Studies of Corporate Involvement in Public Education. New York: Teachers' College P, 1988.

Book by a corporate author

Committee for Economic Development. Public-Private Partnership: An Opportunity for Urban Communities. New York: CED, 1982.

Anonymous author

Writer's Market: 1988. New York: Writer's Digest, 1987.

Translation

Flaubert, Gustave. Madame Bovary. Trans. Lowell Blair. New York: Bantam, 1987.

Work in an anthology

Barnes, Julian. "The Follies of Writer Workshops." The Best American Essays 1986. Ed. Elizabeth Hardwick. New York: Ticknor, 1986. 1-8.

Sacks, Oliver. "The Disembodied Lady." In his The Man Who Mistook His Wife for a Hat and Other Clinical Tales. New York: Harper, 1987. 43-54.

Articles

Article from a journal with continuous pagination

Barzun, Jacques. "Look It Up! Check It Out!" American Scholar 55 (1986): 495–509.

Article from a journal that pages each issue separately

Goodman, William B. "Thinking About Readers." Daedalus 112.1 (1983): 65–84.

Article from a newspaper

Broyard, Anatole. "The Price of Reading Is Eternal Vigilance." New York Times Book Review 10 April 1988: 11–12.

Interviews

Published interview

Márquez, Gabriel García. "The Best Years of His Life: An Interview with Gabriel Garcia Marquez." With Marlise Simons. New York Times Book Review 10 April 1988: 48.

Personal interview

Nemerov, Howard. Personal interview. 18 Nov. 1986.

PART EIGHT

How to Write Argument and Persuasion

*H*OW TO *W*RITE *A*RGUMENT AND *P*ERSUASION

Arguing opinions and persuading others are verbal skills you began to learn as a child, partly from observing how people got others to see things their way and partly from experimentation. In advertisements, political debate, speeches, talk shows, books, articles, court decisions, and sales pitches, people present their cases and hope to gain acceptance for their views. This chapter will help you write more effective argument and persuasion.

You write argument and persuasion when you have reached a conclusion about a subject and you want to show others why you think you're right and convince them to accept your position. Persuasive writing draws heavily on skills you have been developing in this writing class, especially the skills of critical reading and research. The first step in developing a sound argument is to analyze the topic and develop your thesis. The next two steps may be less familiar: (1) you must make sure your argument contains adequate evidence and does not suffer from logical fallacies, and (2) you must consider how best to persuade your audience.

ANALYZE A TOPIC FOR ARGUMENT

As with any research, you must choose a suitable topic and begin by educating yourself about that topic. Skills you have already learned apply here: What topic do you feel strongly enough about that you want to convince other people of your views? What kind of information is available on the subject, including local sources and people to interview? Can you do a good job treating this topic in the time you have to research and write the essay?

An argument is essentially making a claim or stating a conclusion based on evidence provided by other statements. In conducting your research, be sure to expose yourself to a range of opinion about your subject. The success of your argument is in direct proportion to your informed thought on the subject. Take notes on your reading and select facts, statistics and quotations for later use. You are making a case, preparing to bring your witnesses to the stand. If you understand only your own perspective on an argument, you don't understand very much. It's when you understand the subject as a whole that you will know what issues are central, what questions of evidence are critical, and how an effective argument might be made.

Make an Argument

Once you have completed your reading and research, write the claim, or argument, you want to make at the top of a page. Next write a list for each side of the argument: What does each side hope to prove? What evidence can each side provide to support its claim? Go through both lists carefully and try to find the weaknesses in each argument. When you write your essay, you will not use the list attacking your own arguments, but knowing the opposition will help you make a stronger, more "attack-proof" case.

Most arguments have these essential elements: the proposition, supporting evidence, credibility and a refutation of opposing views.

The proposition states the claim you are trying to make. Usually your proposition will do one of the following: (1) state a fact: "A third of the nation cannot read these words" (Jonathan Kozol); (2) express an attitude: "The 'best' colleges are the liberal arts schools which are the most 'academic': they don't teach students anything useful in particular" (Caroline Bird); or (3) make a recommendation: "It is quite obvious that if we are to retain any semblance of our international competitiveness, we must increase productivity in the United States" (Sheldon Weinig).

In the body of the paper, you support each point of your argument with persuasive evidence, statistics, case studies, quotations or testimony from experts.

Before your readers can be convinced of your point of view, they must believe that your supporting evidence is credible. If you cite unreliable sources or provide only anecdotal evidence, your readers may dismiss your claims or challenge your views.

Make sure your evidence is up to date and dependable. Where do the statistics come from? Reliable sources for statistical data include government agencies, national polling organizations, and research associations. Are the experts you want to quote credible? Pay attention to the credentials of people you want to cite: the surgeon general's recommendations for combatting the AIDS virus are probably better-informed than those of a television talk-show host. Notice the way the opinions of these experts are treated by others writing on the subject, and talk with professors working in the field who can guide you to the best sources.

As you know, few arguments have only two sides and you may find it effective to acknowledge opposing views and show why they are insufficient. In presenting your case—which may be moderate, radical, or highly original—you want to help your readers understand why you believe as you do and persuade them of the rightness of your view.

Use your conclusion to reassert your claim and remind the reader of the main points in your case. You may want to include a special example, case, or testimony for dramatic use in the conclusion. Be careful that any evidence you bring into the conclusion supports your main point.

An effective argument depends on drama as well as facts, so you need to spend time discovering the best order for presenting your case. Keep your tone and views consistent throughout the essay; your conclusions should be no less and no more bold than the evidence you present.

Analyze the Evidence

We reach conclusions about a subject by two kinds of reasoning: induction and deduction. Simply stated, induction means that you draw conclusions from the evidence. Before you can decide whether or not you agree with the claim of an argument, you must test the evidence used to support that claim: Is the evidence reliable? Is it representative? Is it sufficient?

Deduction, the opposite of induction, means that you begin with a statement (called the "major premise") such as: "All dogs have fleas." Then you follow a series of logical steps to reach the conclusion: "Rusty has fleas." In formal argument, these steps are stated in a syllogism, a series of three statements: major premise, minor premise, and conclusion.

Major premise: All dogs have fleas.
Minor premise: Rusty is a dog.
Conclusion: Therefore, Rusty has fleas.

Do all dogs have fleas? No, indeed—so this syllogism has failed the first requirement of deductive reasoning: The major premise from which the conclusion is derived must be sound. Whether or not all dogs have fleas is a matter to be researched, and the evidence from that research must be reliable, representative, and sufficient. In other words, the major premise must be a valid piece of *induction* before you can reach a valid conclusion *deductively.*

To create an effective deductive argument, each step must follow the proper syllogistic form:

Major premise: A = B
Minor premise: C = A
Conclusion: Therefore C = B

It is important to note that syllogisms in proper form are called valid instead of true. The syllogism presents a way to deal reasonably with ideas and avoid error. From a true major premise, a true syllogism is the inevitable result. However, the major premise, which is inductively derived, has no equivalent test of its validity and its truth may, even in the face of facts, receive varying interpretations. For example, consider the following syllogism:

Major premise: Killing a person is wrong.
Minor premise: Capital punishment is killing a person.
Conclusion: Therefore, capital punishment is wrong.

Many people may argue with the major premise, believing that killing a person is not wrong under all circumstances. A valid syllogism is not a guarantee of truth.

While you are writing early drafts of your argument, express your conclusions in syllogistic form to reveal the strengths and weaknesses of your position. Make syllogisms of opposing arguments as well to strengthen your refutation of opposing views. Use syllogisms to help you develop your ideas, but not to present them in the essay. Few writers set their argument in true syllogistic form.

Avoid Logical Fallacies

Even the best writers slip up sometimes and include evidence or make statements that do not support their conclusions logically. Be aware of these errors when you develop and write your own argument, and use them in analyzing the reasoning behind opposing views.

When you make an *argument* ad hominem *(against the man)*, you attack your opponent's personal characteristics rather than his or her arguments. Politicians sometimes find it to their advantage to discredit their opponents on personal and moral issues rather than to engage in policy debates. Some people think that focusing on Gary Hart's womanizing in the 1987–88 presidential primaries was engaging in "argument against the man"; others saw his behavior as an important index to his character.

An *argument* ad populem *(to the people)* is made when you incite the public by appealing to their emotions and prejudices rather than their intellect. Writers who manipulate their readers by using language designed to invoke an emotional response are unfairly gaining an advantage. Once readers recognize how they have been tricked into supporting an issue, they lose confidence and trust in that writer.

You use *argument by authority* when you rely on an authoritative source or person to make a point. "Because I say so" is an argument parents sometimes make, and how is a child to refute the authority behind that statement? Remember that arguments by authority are only as sound as their sources, and not every reader will accept the same sources as authority.

You *beg the question*, or engage in circular reasoning, when your major premise and the conclusion are essentially the same, and you don't really provide evidence to support the claim of your argument. You *ignore the question* when, instead of focusing on the subject, you address a related issue and deflect the argument from the original premise.

When you avoid committing yourself to a position, you are *equivocating*. By using vague, general, and often ambiguous language to confuse and mislead the reader, you can sound as if you support a conclusion when, in fact, you do not. Equivocating occurs because you haven't developed your argument thoughtfully enough, you don't have enough information, you don't want to take a stand on the issue, or you want to deceive the reader.

Analogies are often persuasive in an argument, but when the comparison is inexact (the two items are more different than similar) or when the comparison cannot be extended usefully, you are relying on a *false analogy*. For example, at a recent Super Bowl victory celebration, a spokesman compared American society to football, calling for "a new game plan." While the analogy seems interesting, you soon need to ask: Who are the opponents? Who is keeping score? What counts as a touchdown?

Write an Argumentative Essay

Once you have gathered and organized your evidence and identified the weaknesses of your opposition, you are ready to complete your essay. You need to organize your main points and their supporting evidence so that you can persuade your reader to understand your point of view and accept your conclusions. The following advice may help you write an effective argument:

1. Define your terms. Many times an argument about a complex issue can become derailed into an argument about definitions. If you want to argue that more high school students are functionally illiterate today than they were 40 years ago, you will need first to define what you mean by "functionally illiterate." How do you measure functional literacy? How was it measured in the past? Are you comparing the same thing, past and present?
2. Respect your readers. People usually don't pay attention to someone who talks down to them or preaches at them. Treat your readers as equals, intelligent people with thoughtful ideas on the subject.

3. Be thorough in your research. Know your topic well and present your best evidence. Avoid unfair techniques so your reader will have confidence in you and your views.
4. Select evidence carefully. Don't include repetitive or unnecessary facts. Bring in authoritative sources where they can do the most good, but don't count on your source to make your argument for you.
5. Use appropriate language. Remember that inflated language, innuendo, vitriolic attack, and emotion-laden sales pitches usually repel rather than persuade a reader.

As with all other writing, revise your essay carefully. Set your essay aside for at least a day before working on the final revision. Argument and persuasion frequently involves emotions you can better understand and manage when you allow some time to elapse between writing and rewriting. The final manuscript should be as forceful as you can make it.

Copyrights and Acknowledgments (continued from page iv)

Applebome, Peter, "Texas City Journal: Where a Chemical Leak Seems an Accepted Risk." From *The New York Times*, November 3, 1987. Copyright © 1987 by The New York Times Company. Reprinted by permission.

Baldwin, James, "Fifth Avenue, Uptown: A Letter from Harlem." From *Nobody Knows My Name* by James Baldwin. Copyright 1960 by James Baldwin. Reprinted by permission of Doubleday and Company, Inc.

Baldwin, James, "Mass Culture and the Creative Artist: Some Personal Notes." From *Daedalus*, "Mass Culture and Mass Media," vol. 89, Spring 1960. Reprinted by permission of *Daedalus*, Journal of the American Academy of Arts and Sciences, Boston, MA.

Beckmann, Max, "On My Painting." Permission granted by the executor of the Mathilde Beckmann estate.

Bernstein, Dennis and Connie Blitt, "Lethal Dose." From *The Progressive*, March 1986. Copyright © 1986, The Progressive, Inc. Reprinted by permission from *The Progressive*, Madison, WI 53703.

Berry, Wendell, "In Defense of Literacy." From *A Continuous Harmony*. Copyright © 1972 by Wendell Berry. Reprinted by permission of Harcourt Brace Jovanovich, Inc.

Bettelheim, Bruno and Karen Zelan, "Why Children Don't Like to Read," as it appeared in *Atlantic Monthly*, November 1981, from *On Learning to Read: The Child's Fascination with Meaning*. Copyright © 1981 by Bruno Bettelheim and Karen Zelan. Reprinted by permission of Alfred A. Knopf, Inc.

Bird, Caroline, "The Liberal Arts Religion." Reprinted by permission of Caroline Bird.

Bowen, Catherine Drinker, "We've Never Asked a Woman Before." From *The Atlantic Monthly*, March 1970. Copyright © 1970 by Catherine Drinker Bowen. Reprinted by permission of Harold Ober Associates Incorporated.

Boyer, Ernest, "Four Essential Goals." From *High School*. Copyright © 1983 by Carnegie Foundation for the Advancement of Teaching. Reprinted by permission of Harper & Row.

Bush, Vannevar, "The Search for Understanding." From *Science Is Not Enough*. Copyright © 1965, 1967 by Vannevar Bush. Reprinted by permission of William Morrow and Company.

Calandra, Alexander, "The Barometer Story: Angels on a Pin." From *Saturday Review*, December 21, 1968. Copyright © 1968 by *Saturday Review Magazine*. Reprinted by permission.

Calder, Alexander and William de Kooning, "What Abstract Art Means to Me." From *The Museum of Modern Art Bulletin*, Vol. XVIII, No. 3, Spring 1951. Reprinted with permission.

Caputo, Philip, "Epilogue." From *A Rumor of War*. Copyright © 1977 by Philip Caputo. Reprinted by permission of Henry Holt and Company, Inc.

Carson, Rachel L., "The Obligation to Endure." From *Silent Spring*. Copyright © 1962 by Rachel L. Carson. Reprinted by permission of Houghton Mifflin Company.

Cary, Joyce, "The Artist and the World." From *Art and Reality*, p. 107. Copyright © 1958 by Michael Cary, Arthur Lucius, David Alexander Ogilvie, Executors of the Estate of Joyce Cary. Reprinted by permission of Harper & Row, Publishers, Inc.

Chernin, Kim, "The Flesh and the Devil." From *The Obsession*, pp. 20–28. Copyright © 1981 by Kim Chernin. Reprinted by permission of Harper & Row, Publishers, Inc.

Clendenin, John L., "Weaving the Invisible Tapestry." Copyright © by BellSouth Corporation. Reprinted by permission.

Dell, Floyd, "We're Poor." From *Homecoming: An Autobiography*. Copyright © 1933 and renewed 1961 by Floyd Dell. Reprinted by permission of Henry Holt and Company, Inc.

Dillard, Annie, *An American Childhood*, pp. 101–9. Copyright © 1987 by Annie Dillard. Reprinted by permission of Harper & Row, Publishers, Inc.

Ehrlich, Gretel, "Wyoming: The Solace of Open Spaces," as first published in *The Atlantic Monthly*, May 1981. Copyright © 1981. Reprinted by permission.

Einstein, Albert, "Physics and Reality." From *Out of My Later Years*. Reprinted by permission.

Enslow, Beth, "The Payoff from Expert Systems." Reprinted by permission.

Erikson, Kai, "Of Accidental Judgments and Casual Slaughters," *The Nation*, August 1985. Copyright © 1985. Reprinted by permission of The Nation Company, Inc.

Feynman, Richard P., "The Value of Science." *Frontiers in Science: A Survey*, Edward Hutchings, Jr., ed. Copyright © 1958 by Basic Books, Inc. Reprinted by permission of the publisher.

Florman, Samuel C., "The Existential Engineer." From *The Existential Pleasures of Engineering*. Copyright © 1976 by Samuel C. Florman. Reprinted by permission of St. Martin's Press, Inc., New York.

Galbraith, John Kenneth, "The 1929 Parallel." *The Atlantic Monthly*, January 1987. Copyright © 1987. Reprinted by permission of the author.

Gass, William, "The Artist and Society." From *Fiction and the Figures of Life*, 1970. Copyright © 1970 by William Gass. Reprinted by permission of International Creative Management, Inc.

Goldstein, Tom, "Journalists Who Masquerade." From *The News at Any Cost*. Copyright © 1985 by Tom Goldstein. Reprinted by permission of Simon & Schuster, Inc.

Gregory, Dick and Robert Lipsyte, "Shame." From *Nigger: An Autobiography*. Copyright © 1964 by Dick Gregory Enterprises, Inc. Reprinted by permission of the publisher, E. P. Dutton, a division of NAL Penguin Inc.

Hardwick, Elizabeth, "The Heart of the Seasons." *House & Garden*. Reprinted by permission of Elizabeth Hardwick.

Hersey, John, excerpts from "A Noiseless Flash." From *Hiroshima*. Copyright © 1946, 1974 by John Hersey. Reprinted by permission of Alfred A. Knopf, Inc. Originally appeared in *The New Yorker*.

Himmelfarb, Gertrude, "Manners into Morals: What the Victorians Knew." From *The American Scholar*, Vol. 57:2, Spring 1988. Copyright © 1988 by Gertrude Himmelfarb. Reprinted by permission of the publisher.

Hughes, Langston, "My America." From *Journal of Educational Sociology*, February 1943. Copyright © 1943 by the Journal of Educational Sociology. Reprinted by permission of Harold Ober Associates Incorporated.

Hughes, Langston, "Salvation." From *The Big Sea*. Copyright © 1940. Copyright renewed 1968 by Arna Bontemps and George Houston Bass. Reprinted by permission of Hill and Wang, a division of Farrar, Straus and Giroux, Inc.

Jaspers, Karl, "Is Science Evil?" *Commentary*, 1950. Reprinted by permission.

Kanter, Rosabeth Moss, "Reawakening the Spirit of Enterprise: Toward an American Corporate Renaissance." From *The Changemasters*. Copyright © 1983 by Rosabeth Moss Kanter. Reprinted by permission of Simon & Schuster, Inc.

King, Martin Luther, Jr., "On Being a Good Neighbor." From *Strength to Love*. Copyright © 1963 by Martin Luther King, Jr. Reprinted by permission of Joan Daves.

King, Martin Luther, Jr., "Why We Can't Wait." From *Saturday Review*, May 30, 1964. Copyright © 1964 by *Saturday Review Magazine*. Reprinted by permission.

Kingston, Maxine Hong, "No Name Woman." From *The Woman Warrior*. Copyright © 1975, 1976 by Maxine Hong Kingston. Reprinted by permission of Alfred A. Knopf, Inc.

Kolderie, Ted, "Education That Works: The Right Role for Business." From the *Harvard Business Review*, September-October 1987. Copyright © 1987 by the President and Fellows of Harvard College; all rights reserved. Reprinted by permission of the *Harvard Business Review*.

Kozol, Jonathan, "A Third of the Nation Cannot Read These Words." From *Illiterate America*. Copyright © 1985 by Jonathan Kozol. Reprinted by permission of Doubleday and Company, Inc.

Kraus, Carolyn Wells, "Searching Out Creation's Secrets." From *Detroit Monthly Magazine*. Reprinted by permission of the author.

Simic, Charles, "Reading Philosophy at Night." From *Antaeus 59*. Copyright © 1987 by Charles Simic. Published by Antaeus/The Ecco Press in 1987. Reprinted by permission.

Sizer, Theodore R., "Better Schools." From *Horace's Compromise*. Copyright © 1984 by Theodore R. Sizer. Reprinted by permission of Houghton Mifflin Company.

Stangl, Juthica, "India: A Widow's Devastating Choice." From *Ms. Magazine*, September 1984. Reprinted by permission of Juthica Stangl.

Syfers, Judy, "I Want a Wife." From *Ms. Magazine*, 1972. Copyright © 1970 by Judy Syfers. Reprinted by permission.

Szarkowski, John, Introduction from *The Photographer's Eye*. Copyright © 1966. All rights reserved. Reprinted with permission of the Museum of Modern Art, New York.

Terkel, Studs, "Evelyn Fraser." From *"The Good War": An Oral History of World War Two*. Copyright © 1984 by Studs Terkel. Reprinted by permission of Pantheon Books, a Division of Random House, Inc.

Thomas, Lewis, "Ponds." From *The Medusa and the Snail*. Copyright © 1974, 1975, 1976, 1977, 1978, 1979 by Lewis Thomas. All rights reserved. Reprinted by permission of Viking Penguin, Inc.

Thurber, James, "Courtship Through the Ages." From *My World—and Welcome to It*. Copyright © 1942 by James Thurber. Copyright © 1970 by Helen Thurber and Rosemary A. Thurber. Published by Harcourt Brace Jovanovich, Inc. Reprinted by permission.

Thurow, Lester, "Creating a World-Class Team." From *The Changing American Economy*, David Obey and Paul Sarbance, eds. Published by Basil Blackwell, 1986. Reprinted by permission of the publisher.

Updike, John, "Going Barefoot." From *On the Vineyard* by Peter Simon. Reprinted by permission.

Walker, Alice, "The Civil Rights Movement: What Good Was It?" Copyright © 1967 by Alice Walker. Reprinted by permission of Harcourt Brace Jovanovich, Inc.

Weinig, Sheldon, "Managing Better." From *The Changing American Economy*, David Obey and Paul Sarbance, eds. Published by Basil Blackwell, 1986. Reprinted by permission of the publisher.

Welty, Eudora, "A Sweet Devouring." From *The Eye of the Story: Selected Essays and Reviews by Eudora Welty*. Copyright © 1957 by Eudora Welty. Reprinted by permission of Random House, Inc.

White, E. B., "The Ring of Time." From *Essays of E. B. White*, pp. 142–49. Copyright © 1956 by E. B. White. Reprinted by permission of Harper & Row, Publishers, Inc.

Wiesel, Elie, "To Be a Jew." From *A Jew Today*. Translated from the French by Marion Wiesel. Copyright © 1979 by Elirion Associates, Inc. Reprinted by permission of Random House, Inc.

Wilson, Mitchell, "On Being a Scientist." From *Atlantic*, September 1970. Reprinted by permission of Stella Adler Wilson.

Rhetorical Index

PERSONAL EXPRESSION AND NARRATION

DESCRIPTION AND EXPLANATION

ANALYSIS

ARGUMENT

Index

A 9
B 0
C 1
D 2
E 3
F 4
G 5
H 6
I 7
J 8

To Instructors and Students

In an effort to make future editions of *The Shape of This Century* a better textbook, we invite you to rate the essays. If you have suggestions for topics and/or essays you would like to see included in the reader, please include that information.

AUTHOR, ESSAY	Excellent	Good	Poor
Finding Out Who We Are			
Annie Dillard, "An American Childhood"	____	____	____
Eudora Welty, "A Sweet Devouring"	____	____	____
Langston Hughes, "Salvation"	____	____	____
Elie Wiesel, "To Be a Jew"	____	____	____
Floyd Dell, "We're Poor"	____	____	____
Dick Gregory, "Shame"	____	____	____
Learning Our Responsibilities			
Margaret Sanger, "My Fight for Birth Control"	____	____	____
Maxine Hong Kingston, "No Name Woman"	____	____	____
Juthica Stangl, "India: A Widow's Devastating Choice"	____	____	____
Martin Luther King, Jr., "On Being a Good Neighbor"	____	____	____
Living with Uncertainty			
Dennis Bernstein and Connie Blitt, "Lethal Dose"	____	____	____
Peter Applebome, "Where a Chemical Leak Seems an Accepted Risk"	____	____	____
A. G. Mojtabai, "After Long Silence"	____	____	____
Christopher Marquis, "When the Fires Go Out"	____	____	____
Demanding Civil Rights			
Langston Hughes, "My America"	____	____	____
James Baldwin, "Fifth Avenue, Uptown: A Letter from Harlem"	____	____	____
Martin Luther King, Jr., "Why We Can't Wait"	____	____	____
Alice Walker, "The Civil Rights Movement: What Good Was It?"	____	____	____

AUTHOR, ESSAY	Excellent	Good	Poor
Understanding Relationships Between the Sexes			
James Thurber, "Courtship Through the Ages"	____	____	____
Kim Chernin, "The Flesh and the Devil"	____	____	____
Judy Syfers, "I Want a Wife"	____	____	____
Michael Norman, "Standing His Ground"	____	____	____
Catherine Drinker Bowen, ". . . We've Never Asked a Woman Before"	____	____	____
Look at Nature			
Gretel Ehrlich, "Wyoming: The Solace of Open Spaces"	____	____	____
E. B. White, "The Ring of Time"	____	____	____
John Updike, "Going Barefoot"	____	____	____
Lewis Thomas, "Ponds"	____	____	____
Elizabeth Hardwick, "The Heart of the Seasons"	____	____	____
See the World Through Art			
John Szarkowski, "The Photographer's Eye"	____	____	____
Max Beckmann, "On My Painting"	____	____	____
Alexander Calder, "What Abstract Art Means to Me"	____	____	____
Willem de Kooning, "What Abstract Art Means to Me"	____	____	____
The Role of the Artist			
Joyce Cary, "The Artist and the World"	____	____	____
William Gass, "The Artist and Society"	____	____	____
James Baldwin, "Mass Culture and the Creative Artist"	____	____	____
Learning Through Books			
Charles Simic, "Reading Philosophy at Night"	____	____	____
Gertrude Himmelfarb, "Manners into Morals: What the Victorians Knew"	____	____	____
Kathleen Raine, "Premises and Poetry"	____	____	____
Caroline Bird, "The Liberal Arts Religion"	____	____	____

AUTHOR, ESSAY	Excellent	Good	Poor
Know About Our World			
Carl Sagan, "Can We Know the Universe? Reflections on a Grain of Salt"	____	____	____
Mitchell Wilson, "On Being a Scientist"	____	____	____
Vannevar Bush, "The Search for Understanding"	____	____	____
Harold Morowitz, "The Beauty of Mathematics"	____	____	____
Carolyn Kraus, "Searching Out Creation's Secrets"	____	____	____
Alexander Calandra, "The Barometer Story: Angels on a Pin"	____	____	____
The Meaning of Science			
Albert Einstein, "Physics and Reality"	____	____	____
Richard P. Feynman, "The Value of Science"	____	____	____
Howard Nemerov, "On the Resemblances Between Science and Religion"	____	____	____
Margaret Mead, "The Role of the Scientist in Society"	____	____	____
Is Science Evil?			
Karl Jaspers, "Is Science Evil?"	____	____	____
Samuel C. Florman, "The Existential Engineer"	____	____	____
Rachel Carson, "The Obligation to Endure"	____	____	____
The Threat of Peace			
Kai Erikson, "Of Accidental Judgments and Casual Slaughters"	____	____	____
I. I. Rabi, "Approaches to the Atomic Age"	____	____	____
Jonathan Schell, "A Republic of Insects and Grass"	____	____	____
Charles Krauthammer, "In Defense of Deterrence"	____	____	____
The Power of the News			
Lewis Lapham, "Gilding the News"	____	____	____
Robert MacNeil, "The Media and the Public Trust"	____	____	____
Tom Goldstein, "Journalists Who Masquerade"	____	____	____

AUTHOR, ESSAY	Excellent	Good	Poor
Michael Parenti, "The News Media and Class Control"	____	____	____
Reporting War			
Studs Terkel, "Evelyn Fraser"	____	____	____
John Hersey, "A Noiseless Flash"	____	____	____
William L. Laurence, "Atomic Bombing of Nagasaki Told by Flight Member"	____	____	____
Philip Caputo, "Epilogue to *A Rumor of War*"	____	____	____
The Problem of Illiteracy			
Jonathan Kozol, "A Third of the Nation Cannot Read These Words"	____	____	____
Bruno Bettelheim and Karen Zelan, "Why Children Don't Like to Read"	____	____	____
Nancy Larrick, "Illiteracy Starts Too Soon"	____	____	____
Wendell Berry, "In Defense of Literacy"	____	____	____
Can We Improve the Schools?			
Richard Mitchell, "The Columbus Gap"	____	____	____
Theodore R. Sizer, "Better Schools"	____	____	____
Myron Magnet, "How to Smarten Up the Schools"	____	____	____
John L. Clendenin, "Weaving the Invisible Tapestry"	____	____	____
Ted Kolderie, "Education That Works: The Right Role for Business"	____	____	____
Ernest L. Boyer, "Four Essential Goals"	____	____	____
The Business of Business			
John Kenneth Galbraith, "The 1929 Parallel"	____	____	____
Robert Boyden Lamb, "The Battlefield Medics"	____	____	____
Walt W. Rostow, "Danger and Opportunity"	____	____	____
Felix Rohatyn, "Commitment"	____	____	____
Business for the Twenty-first Century			
Rosabeth Moss Kanter, "Reawakening the Spirit of Enterprise: Toward an American Corporate Renaissance"	____	____	____

AUTHOR, ESSAY	Excellent	Good	Poor
Sheldon Weinig, "Managing Better"	____	____	____
Beth Enslow, "The Payoff from Expert Systems"	____	____	____
Lester Thurow, "Creating a World-Class Team"	____	____	____

Topics I'd like to see included in a reader:

Essays I'd like to read:

Name ______________________________

Mailing address ______________________________

School ______________________________

School location (city, state) ______________________________

Course title ______________________________

Send your responses to:

English Editor
College Department
Harcourt Brace Jovanovich, Inc.
1250 Sixth Avenue
San Diego, CA 92101